BRITISH GENERALS IN BLAIR'S WARS

D1465088

Generals may talk, but rarely write self-critically: this collection of essays is a remarkable exception. Jonathan Bailey – himself an exceptional soldier–scholar – along with Hew Strachan and Richard Iron have assembled an extraordinary array of senior officers (and one or two civilians) who reflect on Britain's last decade of war. The resulting essays are often excoriating – of politicians, but also of the military institutions from which these soldiers have sprung. A British audience will find the generals' self-examination sobering, even disturbing; Americans will take away insights into our most important ally; students of military affairs more generally will wish to ponder carefully these reflections on generalship in the twenty-first century.

Eliot A. Cohen, Johns Hopkins School of Advanced International Studies, USA

This excellent book contains a revealing collection of papers, written by senior officers and officials charged with the command and direction of British forces in the last decade. They record the efforts and decisions made within circumstances of: controversial and ambivalent political direction, uncertain popular support, scarce resource, unsatisfied planning assumptions and unrealisable expectations; complicated by the nature of coalition operations. This book is recommended to all who wish to understand the atrophy of Britain's strategic faculties.

General Sir Rupert Smith, KCB DSO OBE QGM

This collection must be almost unique in military history. Seldom if ever have senior military commanders discussed so frankly the difficulties they have faced in translating the strategic demands made by their political masters into operational realities. The problems posed by their enemies were minor compared with those presented by corrupt local auxiliaries, remote bureaucratic masters, and civilian colleagues pursuing their own agendas. Our political leaders should study it very carefully before they ever make such demands on our armed forces again.

Sir Michael Howard, formerly Regius Professor of Modern History,
University of Oxford, UK

How military forces adapt to changes in the international environment and the tasks it sets for them is a significant factor in whether wars are won or lost. In this long-overdue book, a number of prominent British practitioners and thinkers on war take a hard-eyed look at how well Britain has adapted to the wars of the past decade. The answers are not always pleasant, but capturing and learning them now is a blood debt owed to those who have fought so fiercely in Iraq and Afghanistan.

John Nagl, Center for a New American Security, USA

Military Strategy and Operational Art

Edited by Professor Howard M. Hensel, Air War College, USA

The Ashgate Series on Military Strategy and Operational Art analyzes and assesses the synergistic interrelationship between joint and combined military operations, national military strategy, grand strategy, and national political objectives in peacetime, as well as during periods of armed conflict. In doing so, the series highlights how various patterns of civil–military relations, as well as styles of political and military leadership influence the outcome of armed conflicts. In addition, the series highlights both the advantages and challenges associated with the joint and combined use of military forces involved in humanitarian relief, nation building, and peacekeeping operations, as well as across the spectrum of conflict extending from limited conflicts fought for limited political objectives to total war fought for unlimited objectives. Finally, the series highlights the complexity and challenges associated with insurgency and counter-insurgency operations, as well as conventional operations and operations involving the possible use of weapons of mass destruction.

Also in this series:

Confrontation, Strategy and War Termination
Britain's Conflict with Indonesia
Christopher Tuck
ISBN 978 1 4094 4630 9

Joining the Fray
Outside Military Intervention in Civil Wars
Zachary C. Shirkey
ISBN 978 1 4094 2892 3

Blair's Successful War
British Military Intervention in Sierra Leone
Andrew M. Dorman
ISBN 978 0 7546 7299 9

Russian Civil-Military Relations
Robert Brannon
ISBN 978 0 7546 7591 4

Managing Civil-Military Cooperation
Edited by Sebastiaan J.H. Rietjens and Myriame T.I.B. Bollen
ISBN 978 0 7546 7281 4

Securing the State
Reforming the National Security Decisionmaking Process at the Civil-Military Nexus
Christopher P. Gibson
ISBN 978 0 7546 7290 6

British Generals in Blair's Wars

Edited by

JONATHAN BAILEY, RICHARD IRON, HEW STRACHAN
University of Oxford, UK

ASHGATE

Published by
Ashgate Publishing Limited
Wey Court East
Union Road
Farnham
Surrey, GU9 7PT
England

Ashgate Publishing Company
110 Cherry Street
Suite 3-1
Burlington, VT 05401-4405
USA

www.ashgate.com

British Library Cataloguing in Publication Data
A catalogue record for this book is available from the British Library.

The Library of Congress has cataloged the printed edition as follows:
Bailey, J. B. A. (Jonathan B. A.)
  British generals in Blair's wars / by Jonathan Bailey, Richard Iron, and Hew Strachan.
    p. cm. -- (Military strategy and operational art)
  Includes bibliographical references and index.
  ISBN 978-1-4094-3735-2 (hbk) -- ISBN 978-1-4094-3736-9 (pbk) -- ISBN 978-1-4094-3737-6 (ebook)
1. Iraq War, 2003---Participation, British. 2. Afghan War, 2001---Participation, British. 3. Great Britain--Military policy. 4. Generals--Great Britain. 5.
Operational art (Military science)--Case studies. 6. Great Britain--History, Military--21st century. I. Iron, Richard. II. Strachan, Hew. III. Title.
  DS79.765.G7L44 2011
  355.0092'241--dc23

2011031892

ISBN 9781409437352 (hbk)
ISBN 9781409437369 (pbk)
ISBN 9781409437376 (ebk – PDF)
ISBN 9781472401571 (ebk – ePUB)

Printed in the United Kingdom by Henry Ling Limited,
at the Dorset Press, Dorchester, DT1 1HD

Contents

List of Figures and Maps   *ix*
Notes on Contributors   *xi*
Preface   *xvii*

Introduction   1

PART I SETTING THE SCENE

1   The Political Context:
     Why We Went to War and the Mismatch of Ends, Ways and Means   5
     Jonathan Bailey

2   The Northern Ireland Campaign: The Challenges of Command   27
     Alistair Irwin

3   Command of Kosovo Force 1999   41
     Mike Jackson

4   Sierra Leone 2000: Pregnant with Lessons   55
     David Richards

PART II HARD LESSONS

5   Rebuilding Iraq 2003: Humanitarian Assistance and Reconstruction   69
     Tim Cross

6   Southern Iraq 2003–2004: Multi-National Command   79
     Andrew Stewart

7   Great Expectations: Broadening the Military Role to Include Nation Building 89
     Barney White-Spunner

8   Iraq 2004: The View from Baghdad   97
     Andrew Graham

9   Modern Campaigning: From a Practitioner's Perspective   109
     John McColl

10   The British Army and Thinking About the Operational Level   119
      John Kiszely

11   Twenty-first-Century Operational Leadership:
      Sierra Leone, Baghdad and Northern Ireland   131
      Nick Parker

PART III IRAQ 2006–2009: SUCCESS OF A SORT

12   On Generals and Generalship   143
      Graeme Lamb

13   'Best Effort': Operation Sinbad and the Iraq Campaign   157
      Justin Maciejewski

14   Basra 2007: The Requirements of a Modern Major General   175
      Jonathan Shaw

15   Campaigning and Generalship: Iraq 2008   181
      Bill Rollo

16   Basra 2008: Operation Charge of the Knights   187
      Richard Iron

17   The Psychological Impact of Operations in Iraq:
      What Has it Been, and What Can We Expect in the Future?   201
      Simon Wessely

PART IV IMPROVING IN AFGHANISTAN

18   Multinational Command in Afghanistan – 2006: NATO at the Cross-Roads   217
      Chris Brown

19   Southern Afghanistan 2006–2008:
      The Challenges to a Comprehensive Approach to Counter-Insurgency   225
      Nick Pounds

20   NATO Operations in Afghanistan 2008–2009: A Theatre-Level View   237
      Jon Riley

21   Helmand 2007–2008: Behavioural Conflict – From General to Strategic Corporal   249
      Andrew Mackay

22   Campaigning: An Air Force Perspective   265
      Iain McNicoll

PART V WHAT HAVE WE LEARNT?

23 The Political-Military Relationship on Operations   273
    Desmond Bowen

24 Too Busy to Learn:
    Personal Observations on British Campaigns in Iraq and Afghanistan   281
    Alexander Alderson

25 Adapt or Fail: The Challenge for the Armed Forces After Blair's Wars   297
    Paul Newton

26 British Generals in Blair's Wars: Conclusion   327
    Hew Strachan

List of References   *347*
Glossary   *359*
Index   *373*

List of Figures and Maps

Figures

17.1 Study design   203
17.2 Changing rates of PTSD on homecoming, US versus UK data   210

Maps

5.1   Iraq – ethnic and sectarian divisions   67

12.1 Iraq – deployment of multinational divisions   141

13.1 Basra Province and City   155

18.1 Afghanistan – ISAF regional command structure in 2011   215

19.1 Helmand Province   223

Notes on Contributors

Colonel (Retired) Alexander Alderson OBE, PhD
Alexander Alderson retired from the British Army in 2012 after 29 years as an Infantry officer. A graduate of the Army Staff College, Camberley, he commanded 1st Battalion The Highlanders. He was the colonel responsible for the Army's operational lessons and its tactical doctrine (2004–2007), and for General David Petraeus's Chief of Campaigns Plans in Baghdad (2007–2008). He was a Defence Fellow at the University of Oxford (2008–2009), before setting up and directing the Army's Counterinsurgency Centre (2009–2012), for which he was appointed OBE. His final assignment was in the NATO Training Mission in Kabul as a special adviser to the Chief of the Afghan General Staff.

Major General (Retired) Jonathan Bailey CB, MBE, PhD
Jonathan Bailey retired from the British Army in 2005. His last appointment was Director General Development and Doctrine. He served in Northern Ireland; commanded Assembly Place Romeo in Rhodesia in 1979–1980; was Operations Officer, 4th Field Regiment Royal Artillery, during the Falklands War; and in 1999 was KFOR's Chief Liaison Officer to the Yugoslav General Staff and to the Kosovo Liberation Army. He has written books and articles on defence and strategic themes. Since 2005 he has worked in the defence industry, and led the seminar series on *Campaigning and Generalship* at the University of Oxford.

Desmond Bowen CB, CMG
Desmond Bowen was a career civil servant, working mainly in the MOD. He was much involved in policy for the engagement of the Armed Forces overseas, whether in operations or defence diplomacy, throughout his career from 1973 to 2008, which he concluded as the MOD's policy director. He also served in the Cabinet Office as deputy head of the overseas and defence secretariat from 2002 to 2004, and was director of the NATO Secretary-General's private office from 1999 to 2001. He was educated at Oxford and was a fellow at Harvard's Center for International Affairs.

Lieutenant General (Retired) Chris Brown CBE
A soldier for over 36 years, Chris Brown has seen operational service in eight theatres: Northern Ireland; the Falkland Islands; Western Sahara and Cyprus with the UN; Bosnia, Kosovo and Afghanistan with NATO; and Iraq as Deputy Commander of Coalition Forces and Senior British Military Representative. He has commanded at all levels from platoon to division, including 7th Parachute Regiment RHA and General Officer Commanding Northern Ireland. He recently led the MOD's analysis of lessons from the Iraq campaign. He was educated at University College Cardiff, where he read Law, and Peterhouse Cambridge, where he read International Relations.

Major General (Retired) Tim Cross CBE
Tim Cross joined the British Army in 1971. He commanded at every level, from a small bomb disposal team to a 30,000-strong division. He served in the 1991 Gulf War and later in Bosnia. In 1999 he led the NATO response to the humanitarian crisis in Macedonia, Albania and Kosovo. In

2002, he became Deputy in the US-led Office of Reconstruction and Humanitarian Affairs, later retitled the Coalition Provisional Authority. He commanded one of the UK Field Army's three divisions from 2004 to 2007. Now retired from the Army, he holds a number of directorships, trusteeships and visiting professorships. He also acts a defence adviser to a number of international companies.

Lieutenant General (Retired) Andrew Graham CB CBE
Andrew Graham was an infantry officer, commissioned into The Argyll and Sutherland Highlanders (Princess Louise's) in 1975. He commanded companies three times in the Argylls before taking command of the 1st Battalion in 1995. He has served in the Ministry of Defence on three occasions. After completing the Higher Command and Staff Course he commanded 3 Infantry Brigade in Northern Ireland (2000–2002) and was Deputy Commanding General Multi-National Corps – Iraq in the summer of 2004. After a two-star tour commanding the Army's Recruiting and Individual Training Division he took over as Director of the Defence Academy in 2008, and left the Army in 2011.

Colonel (Retired) Richard Iron CMG, OBE
Educated at Trinity Hall, Cambridge, Richard Iron has served in the Sultan of Oman's Armed Forces and completed several tours in Northern Ireland. He commanded 1st Battalion, The King's Own Royal Border Regiment in the Balkans. He was subsequently responsible for British and NATO land doctrine. He was a prosecution expert witness in the Sierra Leone War Crimes trials. He was chief mentor to the Iraqi commander in Basra from December 2007 to November 2008, including Operation Charge of the Knights. He left the Army in 2012 and is currently a visiting fellow at the University of Oxford.

Lieutenant General (Retired) Sir Alistair Irwin KCB, CBE
Alistair Irwin joined The Black Watch in 1970 after graduating from St Andrew's University (Political Economy). His military career took him to many parts of the world and very often to Northern Ireland. His last two appointments in the Army were General Officer Commanding Northern Ireland, and then Adjutant General, the Army Board member responsible for all personnel matters in the Army. Since leaving the Army in 2005 he has been closely involved in veterans' affairs in Scotland and serves as a Commissioner of the Commonwealth War Graves Commission. He lectures regularly on leadership, international relations and military affairs.

General (Retired) Sir Michael Jackson GCB, CBE, DSO
Mike Jackson was Chief of the General Staff from February 2003 to August 2006, after a career in the British Army spanning four decades. Previously, he was Commander in Chief Land Command, Commander Kosovo Force, Commander ACE Rapid Reaction Corps and Director General Development and Doctrine. He has seen considerable active service: he commanded a company and a brigade in Northern Ireland, a division in Bosnia, and a corps in Macedonia and Kosovo. He is now Senior Adviser at PA Consulting Group.

Lieutenant General (Retired) Sir John Kiszely KCB, MC
John Kiszely retired from the British Army in 2008 having commanded on operations at every level from platoon to division. His appointments included command of the 1st Battalion Scots Guards, Director of Studies at the Army Staff College, Deputy Commander of the NATO force in Bosnia (2001) and of Coalition Forces in Iraq (2004–2005), and Assistant Chief of the Defence Staff at the

Ministry of Defence. He is now a defence and security consultant and a Visiting Professor in War Studies at King's College London. He recently retired as President of the Royal British Legion.

Lieutenant General (Retired) Sir Graeme Lamb KBE, CMG, DSO

Graeme Lamb joined the British Army in 1971 and was commissioned into the Queen's Own Highlanders. He served in Northern Ireland, Bosnia, Africa, South America, Iraq (four times) and Afghanistan (twice). He has enjoyed operational command from second lieutenant to lieutenant general, and retired after 38 years of active service. He was credited by author Linda Robinson for convincing his US colleagues to adopt the principle of 'limited war'; a process requiring 'patience, subtlety, and a willingness to accept that Iraqis' own proclivities were going to drive much of the war's outcome', and so had substantial influence over the evolution of counter-insurgency in Iraq from 2006 onwards.

General (Retired) Sir John McColl KCB, CBE, DSO

John McColl was commissioned into 1st Battalion The Royal Anglian Regiment in 1973. He has commanded at every level, including a tank squadron, 1st Mechanised Brigade and 3rd (UK) Division. He commanded NATO's first International Security Assistance Force in Kabul. As a lieutenant general, he was Commandant of the Joint Services Command and Staff College and then Deputy Commander of the Multi-National Force in Iraq. On return, he was Commander Regional Forces and, from early 2005, the Prime Minister's Special Envoy to Afghanistan. He became Deputy Supreme Allied Commander Europe in October 2007 and left the Army in 2011.

Major General (Retired) Andrew Mackay CBE

Andrew Mackay joined The King's Own Scottish Borderers in 1982. He was deputy head of the NATO cell responsible for strategic planning for the Balkans. He served in the UN Mission in Kosovo where he led the Advisory Unit on Security and Justice; he subsequently assisted Lord Ashdown's preparation for the Office of the High Representative for Bosnia. He established Iraq's Civilian Police Assistance Training Team in 2004. He headed a Government team to assist the Lebanese Armed Forces during the 2006 conflict. As Commander 52 Infantry Brigade he led the Helmand Task Force (2007–2008). Subsequently, he commanded 2nd Division in Edinburgh. He left the Army in March 2010 and is now a director of a company working in Africa and the Middle East.

Air Marshal (Retired) Iain McNicoll CB, CBE

Until April 2010, Iain McNicoll was Deputy Commander-in-Chief Operations at Air Command, responsible for preparation and delivery of RAF front-line personnel and equipment for operations. Joining the RAF in 1975, he was a fast-jet pilot and weapons instructor, flying 4,363 hours, the majority on Tornado GR1/4. He took part in operations over Iraq in 1993–1994 and Kosovo in 1999. He commanded No. 17(F) Squadron from 1992 to 1995, RAF Brüggen in 1998–2000 and No. 2 Group from 2005 to 2007. His staff tours concentrated on Defence policy and strategy development. At senior levels, he was Director of Force Development in 2000–2002 and Director General Joint Doctrine and Concepts in 2002–2005.

Brigadier (Retired) Justin Maciejewski DSO, MBE

Justin Maciejewski is a history graduate from Selwyn College, Cambridge and was commissioned into the Royal Green Jackets in 1985. During his Army career he commanded from platoon to brigade levels, with operational experience in Northern Ireland, the Balkans and Iraq. As a

Divisional operations officer he was heavily involved in the build up to and the invasion of Iraq. He commanded 2nd Battalion The Rifles in Basra City during the height of the fighting between 2006 and 2007. His final appointment in the Army was as Director Combat, the first professional head of both the Royal Armoured Corps and Infantry.

Lieutenant General (Retired) Sir Paul Newton KBE, MPhil

Paul Newton spent 38 years in the Army. Educated at Sandhurst, Camberley, the University of Cambridge, the Higher Command and Staff Course, and the Royal College of Defence Studies, he completed eight tours in Northern Ireland, including battalion and brigade command, and two in Iraq – his last as military director of the insurgent outreach programme. His final two military appointments were Director Developments, Concepts and Doctrine and Commander Force Development and Training, charged with driving change in the Army. Appointed KBE in 2012, he is now Director of the Strategy and Security Institute at the University of Exeter. He also has a niche business, Paul Newton Strategic Consultancy, and is a Senior Associate Fellow at RUSI.

General (Retired) Sir Nicholas Parker KCB, CBE

Nick Parker was commissioned in 1973 and commanded 2nd Battalion The Royal Green Jackets from 1994 to 1995. He attended the Staff Course in 1986 and the Higher Command and Staff Course in 1996. He commanded 20th Armoured Brigade from 1997 to 1999 and 2nd Division (2002–2004). He was the Commandant of the Joint Staff College (2004–2005). Operational tours included commanding the UK Joint Task Force Sierra Leone in 2001 and Deputy Commanding General Multi-National Corps – Iraq (2005–2006). He took over as General Officer Commanding Northern Ireland in July 2006, was appointed UK Commander Regional Forces in August 2007, and was Deputy Commander ISAF in November 2009–2010. He was Commander-in-Chief Land Forces and was then commander of military security for the London Olympics.

Nick Pounds

Nick Pounds retired from the Royal Marines as a brigadier in 2005 after a 35-year career, which included active service in Northern Ireland, Dhofar, the Falklands campaign, Iraq and Afghanistan. After retirement, he gained a masters degree with distinction in Post War Recovery Studies from the University of York and worked briefly for an Afghan NGO, before becoming engaged with the UK Government's Stabilisation Unit, as one of its original Stabilisation Advisers. In this role he has spent several years engaged in Afghanistan, both running district offices and as an adviser for two ISAF Southern Region commanders.

General Sir David Richards GCB, CBE, DSO

David Richards was commissioned into the Royal Artillery in 1971. He commanded 3rd Regiment Royal Horse Artillery and 4th Armoured Brigade before becoming Chief Joint Force Operations, commanding the UK Contingent in East Timor in 1999, and twice commanding in Sierra Leone in 2000. As Commander of the Allied Command Europe Rapid Reaction Corps, he led the International Stabilisation and Assistance Force Afghanistan in 2006–2007. He is currently Chief of the Defence Staff, having previously been Commander-in-Chief UK Land Forces and Chief of the General Staff. Among other appointments, he is chairman of the Gurkha Welfare Trust, Admiral of the Army Sailing Association and patron of the Afghan Appeal Fund.

Lieutenant General (Retired) Jonathon Riley CB, DSO, PhD

Jonathon Riley joined the Royal Armouries as Director General and Master in 2009 after a long and distinguished career in the British Army. He served in Northern Ireland, the Balkans, Sierra Leone and Iraq. He was British military adviser to the United States Central Command and his final appointment was deputy commander of NATO forces in Afghanistan in 2008–2009. He is a keen historian and has published eight books; he is also chairman of the Royal Welch Fusiliers Museum and Archive Trust.

Lieutenant General (Retired) Sir William Rollo KCB, CBE

Bill Rollo joined the Blues and Royals in 1978. He commanded the Household Cavalry Regiment in Bosnia as part of UNPROFOR in 1994–1995, 4th Armoured Brigade in Macedonia and Kosovo in 1999, Multi-National Division (South-East) in Iraq in 2004, and was Deputy Commander Multi-National Force – Iraq in Baghdad in 2007–2008. He served as Adjutant General and set up the British Army's new Force Development and Training Command. He was most recently the Deputy Chief of Defence Staff (Personnel) in the Ministry of Defence.

Major General (Retired) Jonathan Shaw CBE

Jonathan Shaw joined the Parachute Regiment in 1981 after Oxford and a short stint in the City. He was a platoon commander in 3rd Battalion, The Parachute Regiment in the Falklands campaign and subsequently commanded a company and the 2nd Battalion in Northern Ireland, 12th Mechanised Brigade in Kosovo and Multi-National Division (South-East) in Iraq. His staff posts have majored on counter-terrorism. He is the Colonel Commandant of the Parachute Regiment and was recently Assistant Chief of Defence Staff (Global Issues) in the Ministry of Defence.

Major General (Retired) Andrew Stewart CB, CBE

Conceived in Iraq when his father was commanding the Iraq Levies, Andrew Stewart was commissioned into 13th/18th Royal Hussars. He commanded that regiment in 1991 before amalgamating it to form The Light Dragoons. He later commanded 7th Armoured Brigade, including an operational tour to Bosnia in 1997. Following appointments running operations in the Permanent Joint Headquarters and being responsible for overseas military assistance in the MOD, he commanded in Basra in December 1993 for seven months. His final appointment was in the MOD, running policy and defence diplomacy. He retired from the Army in 2007 and is currently Chief Executive of The Queen's Club in London.

Professor Sir Hew Strachan

Hew Strachan is Chichele Professor of the History of War, Fellow of All Souls College, Oxford and was Director of the Oxford Programme on the Changing Character of War. He was Professor of Modern History at the University of Glasgow prior to coming to Oxford in 2002. He is the author of several highly acclaimed books on military history, including *European Armies and the Conduct of War* (1983), *The Politics of the British Army* (1997) and *The First World War: Volume 1: To Arms* (2001). He sits on the Chief of Defence Staff's Strategic Advisory Panel, and is a member of the Commonwealth War Graves Commission.

Professor Sir Simon Wessely

Simon Wessely holds the chair of Psychological Medicine at King's College London. He directs the King's Centre for military health research and is civilian consultant adviser in psychiatry to the British Army. He has authored over 500 academic papers on many aspects of physical and mental health, but with a particular emphasis on the health of the Armed Forces. He is now Vice Dean of the Institute of Psychiatry, and is worried he is turning into a bureaucrat. Secretly he wishes he was an historian.

Lieutenant General (Retired) Sir Barney White-Spunner KCB, CBE

Barney White-Spunner joined The Blues and Royals in 1979 and most recently commanded the Field Army. Early appointments included Military Assistant to the Chief of Defence Staff and command of The Household Cavalry Regiment. He commanded 16 Air Assault Brigade, with operations in Macedonia in 2001 and Kabul in 2002. He was Chief of Staff of the UK's national contingent during the 2003 invasion of Iraq. As a major general he was Chief of Staff at Headquarters Land Command and commanded the 3rd Division. He commanded Multi-National Division (South-East) in Iraq in 2008. He retired in 2012 and is currently Executive Chairman of the Countryside Alliance.

Preface

British Generals in Blair's Wars could not have been produced without the help of many. Most particularly, we thank the senior officers and others who contributed chapters, including those still serving who were denied permission by the Ministry of Defence to publish their papers, the Secretary of State for Defence having banned serving officers and officials from writing publicly on matters that could be construed as politically controversial. This delayed by about one year the publication of *British Generals in Blair's Wars*, which the editors nevertheless believe still to be a timely and valuable contribution to serious debate about the role of strategy and Britain's armed forces in the twenty-first century.

We also thank the Leverhulme Trust for its support of the Changing Character of War Programme, and for meeting the costs associated with the Campaigning and Generalship seminars; the Warden and Fellows of All Souls College, Oxford, who hosted the seminar speakers; Dr Audrey Kurth Cronin and Dr Sibylle Scheipers, successive Directors of Studies of the Changing Character of War Programme; and Colonel David King, Dr Andrew Fairweather-Tall, Andrew Wasiliweski, Naomi King and Rosemary Mills, all of the Changing Character of War Programme.

Finally, we thank our publishers, Ashgate, for their tireless support and patience throughout the difficult birth of this book.

Introduction

There is no collective noun for generals as there is for a flock of sheep or pack of wolves. For generals are a varied and eclectic bunch: they defy simple categorisation, despite attempts to typecast them, or ascribe to them a singular fixed view. This book looks, through their eyes, at the campaigns of the British Army that followed the First Gulf War of 1991. All played leading roles in a momentous period of British history. It was a time when armies were struggling to revise their Cold War concepts and doctrines, and to find new and relevant ways to meet the demands placed on them by political leaders in what was seen as a 'New World Order'. As it turned out, the world is certainly ordered very differently, but history had ambushes in place for those who suggested that it might have ended.

It was political leaders who decided whether the UK should take military action, to what end, in what manner and with what resources. They were presumably confident that their campaigns in, for example, Kosovo, Sierra Leone, Iraq and Afghanistan, would achieve success, however defined, if only the military could perform some alchemy, applying educated violence moderated by other ingredients that allow success broader than mere military victory.

This book looks at campaigning and generalship, through the eyes of the British officers charged with both, over the decade or so of what some term *Blair's Wars*.[1] It offers the personal testimonies of senior officers delivered in a series of seminars at the University of Oxford, between 2005 and 2011, as part of the Leverhulme Programme on the Changing Character of War. The purpose of the seminars was to bring to bear the experiences of practitioners, direct from operations, and informed by their decades of military experience and education. These testimonies reflect their thoughts at the time they were delivered, and have not been revised with hindsight; they retain the immediacy of the moment. Each chapter bears the date it was presented at Oxford. Taken together, they offer an insight into how the thinking of this corps of officers developed, during a time of rapid change in how we consider and use military force, and against a backdrop of intense political controversy and popular unease.

Their testimonies are preceded by a description of the evolving strategic environment after the Cold War and the novel ideas that came to dominate Western strategic thinking, which led to the military operations that these officers were tasked to conduct. However, while observations on political leadership are a necessary precursor to any thoughts on campaigning and generalship in a democratic society, this is not primarily the story of the political leaders who sent the nation to war. Rather, it is about those officers who played key roles in the ensuing campaigns. The generals played their hand, they didn't deal it.

Although generals are neither a flock nor a pack, from their individual views we may learn something about the broader nature of campaigning and generalship: the dynamics of the relationships between politicians and their generals; between nations in a coalition, particularly between Britain and America; between commanders and the commanded; between Whitehall and those deployed; between our forces and the people amongst whom they operate; between generals and the media; and between generals and the law.

---

1 Kampfner 2004.

The stories told in this book reflect differing perspectives on modern conflict, and how British generals understood and confronted the professional and personal challenges they faced. Some are controversial; others disagree with each other. Each is the personal view of the individual author and does not necessarily represent the views of other generals or editors. However, they provide insights into modern conflict, in particular in Iraq and Afghanistan, and the nature of senior command, from which we hope others may be able to develop their own educated judgement about the art of war. Learning lessons from them may be a vanity too far.

PART I
Setting the Scene

The British Army that invaded and occupied Basra in 2003 was the child of many experiences. The chapters that follow in this section explore some of the experiences that shaped not just the Army but those selected to command it.

It was by no means inevitable that the British Army would be sent to fight in foreign lands that, at first sight, have very little to do with our national interest, or take a lead in international policing alongside the United States. That we did so in Iraq and Afghanistan is partly a result of previous experience, partly because of a renewed political interest in the doctrine of liberal interventionism and partly because of the personality of political leadership. In Chapter 1, Major General Jonathan Bailey explores these issues to establish the political context in which the remainder of this book is set. As he concludes, 'it was against this political background that a generation of senior British officers was sent off to achieve operational success … by politicians who had launched these campaigns for complex and controversial reasons'.

The 38-year campaign in Northern Ireland was one of the most significant influences on the British Army of the early twenty-first century, starting with the deployment of British troops to Belfast in August 1969, and formally ending in July 2007. It remains the British Army's longest campaign and has caused it more casualties than any other since the Korean War. Lieutenant General Sir Alistair Irwin is one of a small body of officers whose military career almost exactly mirrors the length of the Northern Ireland 'Troubles'. He served there at every level of command from second lieutenant to lieutenant general; there can be no better man to reflect on the challenges of command in Northern Ireland. He examines, in Chapter 2, why it was so difficult to establish a campaign plan, describes the difficulties of harnessing all aspects of Government to the fight, and provides a fascinating insight of senior leadership in a complex long-running campaign.

The primary challenge facing the British Army in the later 1990s was peacekeeping as experienced in the Balkans. Caused by the disintegration of post-communist Yugoslavia, the fighting eventually tested the United Nations and the international community's ability to respond, eventually prompting robust NATO action in both Bosnia and Kosovo. General Sir Michael Jackson commanded a division in Bosnia as part of IFOR (the Implementation Force) and then the corps that formed KFOR (the Kosovo Force) in 1999. It is of this latter experience that he writes in Chapter 3, examining in depth the events that resulted in the deployment of NATO forces into Kosovo. He writes of the need to rebuild a country shattered by war, and of the political tightrope he had to walk between Kosovars and Serbs. He also explains the truth behind the now famous confrontation with his American commander, General Wesley Clark.

Finally in this section, General Sir David Richards (currently the UK's Chief of Defence Staff) recounts his command of British forces in Sierra Leone in 2000, and how a comparatively small force was able to turn the tide in a country that had been ravaged by war for ten years and was rapidly disintegrating into total chaos. In a decade scarred by Iraq and Afghanistan, he concludes that:

it is too easy to surmise that overseas intervention will always be difficult and expensive; that we will always be resisted by a significant proportion of the local population; and that we will always struggle to adapt to local conditions and find a winning formula. Sierra Leone stands as an important example where overseas intervention was not only justified, it was also successful and, equally importantly, relatively inexpensive.

Chapter 1

The Political Context: Why We Went to War and the Mismatch of Ends, Ways and Means

Jonathan Bailey[1]

Clausewitz urged that 'The first, the supreme, the most far-reaching act of judgement that the statesman and commander have to make is to establish ... the kind of war upon which they are embarking.'[2] If a nation is to be prepared for conflict, its leaders should ensure they have understood the nature of the mission and the tasks it entails. That understanding should offer the best chance of achieving success, and marshalling the resources to deliver it. However, Clausewitz also described the frictions in military affairs that would make this simple formula difficult to execute.

Politicians provide constitutional authority for the conduct of campaigns, muster the popular support to make them domestically viable, assure their legal justification and secure sufficient international support to share risk and avoid disabling sanction. They provide the means, commensurate with the demands of a campaign, based on their understanding of its nature; and they will be heavily reliant on senior officers of the Armed Forces for professional advice in all of this.

The political decisions to launch the UK's campaigns of the last two decades were shaped by intellectual trends and shifting cultural assumptions. These also influenced how their nature was understood, and how they were conducted and resourced. Without considering these trends and cultural assumptions, it would be hard to gauge the thinking and experiences of those sent to command these campaigns, whose accounts and insights constitute the core of this book.

It was never the intention that the *Campaigning and Generalship* seminar series should dwell upon the origins and merits of strategic decision-making; but events since the start of the seminars in 2005, and the furore surrounding those events in public debate and various inquiries, means that these cannot be glossed over here. It is the ongoing strategic controversy, as much as the original strategic decisions, that has added significantly to the complexity of the environment in which commanders have had to operate, and which makes their experiences the more interesting for it.

Ideological Tides and the Evolution of British Policy

Defence Policy: Assumptions and Planning

In 1998, the UK's new Labour Government produced a Strategic Defence Review (SDR), which marked a significant break from the Cold War's focus on the European Central Front, and sought to

---

1   The views expressed in this chapter are those of the writer, who is solely responsible for them. They do not necessarily reflect the views of his present or past employers, who will not be responsible or liable for any inaccurate or incorrect statements, and to whom the opinions expressed should not be ascribed.

2   von Clausewitz 1832, 88.

address the UK's new global interests and challenges. It called for the creation of forces designed to gain rapid success on expeditionary operations, lengthy operations being regarded as undesirable. It was felt such limited operations would allow the UK to 'punch above its weight'. Otherwise, the UK would have had to fund and create capabilities of a very different and probably unaffordable kind. The danger lay in trying to 'punch above one's weight' against a formidable opponent in a bout that 'went the distance'. More complex and potentially longer operations were deemed less likely; and the strategic premises upon which actual capabilities were built were, to an extent, reverse-engineered to align with what was preferred and affordable – expeditions in which British forces would be 'first in, first out'.

The UK's Ministry of Defence (MOD) was given Defence Strategic Guidance (DSG) based on the SDR, and Defence Planning Assumptions (DPAs) were derived from this guidance. The DPAs explained the concepts, force structures, equipment and the overall capabilities required to meet those assumed tasks. Such tasks appeared in the Defence Planning Directory. Contingency planning was thus shaped by foreign policy objectives; but the formulation of foreign policy and much of its execution have often proved to have been the jealous preserve of the Prime Minister more than of the Foreign Secretary. Under a Prime Minister with a keen interest in foreign policy, less inhibited by departmental strategy, it was easy for foreign policy to move sharply in a different direction from that upon which the DSG and DPAs were premised.

Meanwhile, the British constitution was undergoing rapid modification with the decline of cabinet government and the concentration of defence and foreign affairs in the Office of the Prime Minister, a quasi 'White House'. The second dominant figure in shaping defence policy and military capability was arguably the Chancellor of the Exchequer, more so than the Defence Secretary, the latter having to persuade the Chancellor of the justification for all planned expenditure.[3]

The SDR of 1998 was not costed, and the strategic developments that were actually to transpire were apparently discounted. There had even been talk of a new 'ten-year rule'[4] which would have cut further the equipment judged necessary for 'high-intensity' conflict. What was not foreseen was an immediate need for a major re-equipping of the Army for high-intensity conflict of another prolonged sort.

Concurrently with designing military forces for rapid, decisive action and effects, an idea was growing with implications of another sort: Britain's foreign policy was to be an ethical one, supported by armed forces which thereby became 'a force for good', establishing an awkward *Gott mit uns* connection between their actions and moral rectitude.[5]

The emerging thinking in the West about ideas and values entailed not merely the possible need to overthrow hostile regimes, but also to ensure their societies be thoroughly reordered to neutralise potential future threats; and to comply with Western norms of democracy, open economies and

---

3   In Geoffrey Hoon's evidence to the Chilcot Inquiry on 19 January 2010, he explained how few of the Prime Minister's crucial meetings prior to the invasion of Iraq he had been invited to attend. In 2007, the role of the Defence Secretary was seen to decline further when the post was held by Desmond Browne, who combined the appointment with that of Secretary of State for Scotland, even as the MOD was put on a war footing.

4   The 'ten-year rule' was a guideline, first adopted in 1919, that the Armed Forces should base their estimates on the assumption that they would not be engaged in any great war over the next ten years. Defence spending was cut as a result.

5   A senior MOD official explained that this branding was legitimate because it was necessary to make the troops feel that they were taking part in morally worthy operations.

human rights. It seemed to some that national interest had become diminished in the formulation of foreign policy, replaced by the need to lead on grander global agendas.[6]

After the al-Qaeda attacks on the USA in 2001, a 'New Chapter' was added to the SDR, but there was no assessment of the realistic costs these new risks might entail. A new DSG was produced in 2005, and again in 2008, but neither was costed. The emphasis on 'values' that had grown in the late 1990s appeared to be validated by these emerging military threats, some of whose objects seemed, in their own words, to be the very destruction of Western values and way of life.

In the UK, a chasm thus grew between emerging foreign policy goals, the size and focus of the defence budget, and actual military planning; this had profound operational impacts after 2003. From 1990 to 2010, the UK's defence budget fell as a percentage of GDP, and although the Government of the day asserted it had continued to rise in later years in absolute terms, spending did not keep pace with defence cost inflation. Funding was also insufficient for the campaigns after 2003 as the Armed Forces were not configured or equipped for lengthy, intense campaigns of this type. The defence budget is intended only to prepare armed forces for operations, not to pay for those operations; and between 2004 and 2009 the Government provided about a further £5 billion to meet campaign costs. Whether this funding was adequate became a matter of heated debate, both at home and in theatre.

Political Decision-Making and the Personality of Mr Blair

The key factor in the decisions to launch the campaigns that form the major part of this study was the Prime Minister of the day. Much of the criticism of Mr Blair's decision to join the Coalition's invasion of Iraq in 2003 was based on his unusual personality and style of leadership.[7] Not all attributed Mr Blair's failings in this respect to malign calculation, for the more sincere and intense his expression, the more likely he is to be saying something that is not the case. And what makes it worse it that, as the former Lib-Dem leader Paddy Ashdown reflected (from bitter experience …): 'he always means it at the time'.[8] Lord Owen, a former Foreign Secretary, attributed Mr Blair's political failings to 'three characteristic symptoms of hubris: excessive self-confidence, restlessness and inattention to detail'.[9]

Mr Blair seems to have believed that all men of goodwill would share his views and values, rooted in those of the British middle classes to which he belonged. He had difficulty explaining the serious differences of others, except in terms of their 'extremism'. Today's apparent, but frequently denied, clash of civilisations is often portrayed in terms of culture, and rights versus denial of rights, whereas in the past it was often portrayed in terms of race, and civilisation versus barbarism. In a bold construction, Mr Blair denied that there was a clash 'between' civilisations, rather a clash 'about' civilisation.[10] This formula obviated any judgemental 'them' and 'us' dichotomy, for all are in fact 'we', presumably all belonging to a single civilisation. The issue, he claimed, is about 'progress' versus 'reaction'; all of 'us' being in favour of what 'we' term 'progress'.

'We', he said, 'is not the West. "We" are as much Muslim as Christian, or Jew or Hindu. "We" are those who … believe in openness to others, to democracy, liberty and human rights.' 'We'

---

6   The opinion of Sir Christopher Meyer, British Ambassador in Washington in 2003, reported in Lawson 2010, 14.

7   See descriptions in, for example: Parris 2003; Radford 2003; Johnson 2004; Sieghart 2006; Norman 2007, 49; Wheatcroft 2007; Dalrymple 2007; Owen 2008, 1–2.

8   Wheatcroft 2007, 36.

9   Owen 2008, 1.

10   Mr Blair speaking at Canary Wharf on 21 March 2006, reported in *Metro*, London, 22 March 2006, 4.

appears to be those who agree with Mr Blair, although perhaps the majority of mankind would not. His view of the world ignored the fundamental differences between the values of the cultures he cited and the modern Western constructs he would project onto all, conscripting 'them' as 'us'.[11] Categorising 'good' and 'evil', 'progress' and 'reaction' without pondering why others might think differently does not help understanding. This incomplete and Manichean lack of a broader, more complex cultural understanding can set traps in forming foreign policy and understanding the nature of campaigns launched in the pursuit of that policy.

Lord Owen noted the dramatic change in Mr Blair's position in the years before the invasion of Iraq. In 1998 Mr Blair maintained that, 'We are not working to bring down Saddam Hussein and his regime. It is not for us to say who should be President of Iraq, however much we might prefer to see a different government in Baghdad.' Three and a half years later, Mr Blair was unwilling to have a detailed discussion of the subject, '... Blair was a very different man from the one I had met over dinner three and a half years earlier'.[12] Lord Owen reported a conversation between a concerned senior official and Mr Blair in which the latter suggested, 'You are Neville Chamberlain, I am Winston Churchill and Saddam is Hitler.' Lord Owen concluded that '[i]t is difficult to conduct a serious dialogue with a leader thinking in this emotional and simplistic way'.[13] Dr Owen was concerned that 'Actor-politicians [Blair] tend to be especially narcissistic – which makes the hero role almost irresistible', and also that in 'his view of himself he thinks he is always good. Someone who believes he cannot act badly will also believe they cannot lie, so shading the truth can become a habit.'[14]

In October 2009, Cherie Blair told an audience at the Cheltenham Literature Festival that decisions such as that to invade Iraq '... are not black and white ... instead of being 80-20, many of them are actually more like 51-49. When taking those decisions, Tony is able to step back, absorb all the information and then choose.' She added: 'He is also very good at then convincing everybody else that it was a 70-30 decision all along. I think it [the Iraq war] was one of those 51-49 questions.'[15]

Many seem to have agreed with Cherie Blair, but were less certain that he was prepared to absorb, let alone ask for, 'all the information'. Sir Rodric Braithwaite, a former ambassador to Moscow and Chairman of the Joint Intelligence Committee, claimed that Mr Blair '... has manipulated public opinion, sent our soldiers into distant lands for ill-conceived purposes, misused the intelligence agencies to serve his ends and reduced the Foreign Office to a demoralized cipher because it keeps reminding him of inconvenient facts ... He prefers to construct "foreign policy" out of self-righteous soundbites ...'.[16]

---

11   By August 2006 Mr Blair had expanded his thesis: 'We must commit ourselves to a complete renaissance of our strategy to defeat those who threaten us.' He was referring to militant Islam, extremists who must be defeated, '... at the level of values'. Bennett and Charter 2006, 1. Presumably, these extremists cannot be 'we' but must be 'them'.

12   Owen 2008, 1.

13   Owen 2008, 1. A similar insight is offered by Jonathan Steele, who reports the experience of the Arabist George Joffe on 19 November 2002, invited to Downing Street to offer an expert view on Iraq under Saddam Hussein. He explained the complexity of Iraq and that 'don't imagine you'll be welcomed'. Mr Blair 'looked at me and said, "But the man's uniquely evil, isn't he?" I was a bit non-plussed. It didn't seem to be very relevant.' He found Mr Blair to be '... someone with a very shallow mind, who's not interested in issues other than the personalities of the top people, no interest in social forces, political trends ...'. Steele 2008.

14   Owen 2008, 2.

15   Brady 2009.

16   Braithwaite 2006.

Mr Blair's reference to God in the formulation of his foreign policy in an interview with Michael Parkinson, on ITV on 4 March 2006, was indicative that conviction had become an important factor in his foreign policy. John Burton, Mr Blair's constituency political agent, explained, 'It's very simple to explain the idea of Blair the Warrior. It was part of Tony's living out his faith.' 'He believed strongly at the time, that intervention in Kosovo, Sierra Leone – Iraq too – was all part of the Christian battle; good should triumph over evil, making lives better.'[17] Mr Blair himself spoke of wars of 'ideas and values'.[18] As he told the Labour Party Conference in 2004, 'I only know what I believe.' Matthew Parris thought it went even deeper than that. He asked, on the eve of the Iraq War, 'Have the rest of the Cabinet tumbled yet to the understanding that this may not be about Iraq at all, but about the Prime Minister? My guess is that those closest to Mr Blair must be beginning to wonder privately. It is time people pooled their doubts.'[19]

Critics of Mr Blair's policy on Iraq in 2002–2003 were most likely to come from his own party, and while he secured a mandate for action in the House of Commons, with the backing of the Opposition, he had arrived at that point having seemed at times to have ignored his own Cabinet. There was a cultural gulf between rigorous, closely argued and documented military staff planning, and ad hoc subjective intuition. In the past, such a gulf has often been bridged by collaborative working. In this case, it was not. The deliberate absence of the military staff from strategic summit meetings, such as Mr Blair's meeting with President Bush in Crawford, Texas, in April 2002, was the most damaging example of this defect in British policy. Its presence at that and other meetings might have constituted the sort of constraint Mr Blair might not have welcomed while determining policy.

Although policies were crafted largely by intuition, without audit by his own ministries, it does not mean Mr Blair's campaigns were necessarily mistaken, or that history will not validate his propositions about civilisations and the future of Islam. However, he does not appear to have thought through the consequences of his policies, committing the UK to prolonged conflicts intended to reorder other countries' underlying cultures. Perhaps it was merely an attractive foreign policy 'big idea' akin to the notion of 'Cool Britannia' at home. But it does appear there was an inner contradiction between his pride as a militant interventionist and his desire to be a popular peacemaker, not exposed by early triumphs in Sierra Leone and Kosovo, but increasingly at odds after 2003.

A New Doctrine of Humanitarian Interventionism

After the Cold War, a body of political opinion was forming in the UK, and elsewhere, related to the idea that the universal validity of human rights might necessitate military intervention. It was argued that the previous international consensus on the integrity of the sovereign state had become morally dubious. It was a broad international debate, but one which at times was led by Mr Blair himself.

Colonialism and imperialism have generally been anathema to those who currently seek to intervene around the world militarily, perhaps to change regimes, perhaps on humanitarian grounds and frequently to build nations. They have typically preferred to see themselves as coming from the various traditions which opposed the British imperial project, yet these pioneers of the new

---

17   Wynne-Jones 2009, 10.

18   Mr Blair speaking at Canary Wharf on 21 March 2006, reported in *Metro*, London, 22 March 2006, 4, and also in a speech in Plymouth on 12 January 2007.

19   Parris 2003. When Mr Blair said that Saddam's possession of WMD was 'beyond doubt' he was creating a coincidence, maybe unconsciously, between objective fact and his own belief.

interventionism are now regarded by some, rather to their surprise, as the neo-imperialist heirs of Gladstone, or even of Palmerston and Disraeli.

The idea that all people are of equal worth and are to be treated equally is an especially Western notion, and a relatively recent one. Human rights are claimed to have enduring moral imperatives, and a universalism for which the West recognises no frontiers. The frontiers of that morality are being extended ever further in the drive to fulfil some new Western 'soft' notion of Manifest Destiny, asserting values to be defended by some new 'Monroe Doctrine', tolerating little interference in its new empire of ideas. Yet in most of the world's cultures, people are deemed fundamentally unequal by race, caste, gender, social position, party membership or religion, creating potential causes for conflict with the West.

Because the West's own values of equality are deemed to be fundamental and held in common by all people, it may view any regime that does not defend them as oppressive. It is, however, possible that such regimes may represent the popular temper in some unfortunate way. It may well be that in some sense Saddam Hussein was a true reflection of Iraqi society, although many preferred to see him as a tyrant ruling over people of very different cultural assumptions and traditions from his own. Equally, when some countries hold democratic elections, the West is disappointed when anti-Western governments are placed in power, such as Hamas in Gaza.

Ideas about the primacy of individual rights over those of the state gained traction in the formulation of policy shortly after the end of the Cold War. In *An Agenda for Peace* of 1992, the then Secretary-General of the UN, Boutros Boutros-Ghali, wrote, 'The time of absolute and exclusive sovereignty has passed.'[20] The first expression of this new mood had already been seen in Operation SAFE HAVEN in 1991, to protect the Kurds in Northern Iraq. Humanitarian interventions have only been feasible once evidence has been available of outrageous behaviour, often when it is too late to stop it – in the words of the Universal Declaration of Human Rights, in situations which are 'a shock to the conscience of mankind'. Even so, military intervention was not readily embarked upon. In 1994, even the warnings of the UN commander on the ground in Rwanda were insufficient to galvanise the international community into action. It was not until the summer of 1995 that Major General Rupert Smith, the commander of UNPROFOR, could use NATO airpower to halt the onslaught of the Bosnian Serbs. The calls for a more robust approach became louder.

Informed by the searing experiences of massacres in Rwanda and at Srebrenica, and responding to public opinion demanding 'something must be done', a new doctrine emerged based on the precepts of human rights.[21] This was supported by a broad spectrum of interests including NGOs, human rights activists, legal experts and a willing media.

This doctrine was a reflection from a distant mirror. A.T. Mahan asserted the right of people to be governed under their own arrangements, but it should not be assumed that this meant oppressive regimes represented the interests of those they ruled. Regimes should therefore be overthrown in the interests of their people. 'There need be no tenderness in dealing with them as institutions.'[22] After all, 'force has been the instrument by which ideas have lifted the European world to the plane on which it now is, and it still supports our political systems, national and international, as well as our social organization.'[23]

---

20   United Nations 1992, section 1, paragraph 17.

21   Current opinion on military intervention is in keeping with the old measures of *jus ad bellum*: it should apply proportionality, do more good than harm, be successful and preserve the immunity of non-combatants.

22   Mahan 2003, 104.

23   Mahan 2003, 115.

In 1998, Kofi Annan, perhaps unwittingly, echoed Mahan: 'The (UN) Charter protects the sovereignty of peoples. It was never meant as a licence for governments to trample on Human Rights and human dignity. The fact that a conflict is "internal" does not give parties any right to disregard the most basic rules of human conduct …'.[24] The West's new 'civilising mission' thus set the rights of the individual above those of sovereign governments who might deny them those rights.

In 1999, at the UN General Assembly, Mr Annan called on states to accept the necessity for intervention wherever civilians are threatened by war and mass slaughter. He invoked the principle of 'rights beyond borders', and called for unity to ensure that massive and systematic violations of human rights should not be allowed to stand. He accepted intervention should always be the last resort, but asserted that not to act when confronted with crimes against humanity was to be complicit in them.

Many wondered how far this new direction, away from the primacy of the sovereign state, might go. Some saw in it justification for a broader agenda to reorder the world; others noted it was precisely to prevent such ambitions that the old principle of state sovereignty had been so tenaciously defended. Did any state have the right to intervene on its own judgement, given that consent of the UN was apparently no longer required? In practice, however, an ill-defined line had to be crossed and outrages committed, endured, debated and condemned before decisive counter-action could be taken.

Mr Blair's early inclinations had been against military action to remove oppressive regimes. For example, in 1982 Mr Blair opposed British military intervention in the Falkland Islands to free its British inhabitants from occupation by the Argentine military regime, asserting that the wishes of the people of the Islands should not be the primary consideration. On 27 May 1997, Mr Blair addressed international leaders in Paris, convinced that, 'Mine is the first generation able to contemplate the possibility that we may live our entire lives without going to war or sending our children to war.' Mr Blair did not foresee that his tenure as Prime Minister would be remembered primarily for the military operations he launched.

The principle of not overthrowing unpleasant regimes by force still seemed to be intact in Mr Blair's thinking in 1999. On 22 April 1999, at the Economic Club of Chicago, Mr Blair gave a speech on the 'Doctrine of the International Community'. He asserted the right to intervene to prevent ethnic cleansing, but also that '[o]ne state should not feel that it has the right to change the political system of another.'[25]

In Chicago, Mr Blair articulated five major preconditions for intervention. Are we sure of our case? Have we exhausted all diplomatic options? Are there military operations we can sensibly and prudently undertake? Are we prepared for the long term? Do we have national interests involved?[26] For the invasion of Iraq, criteria one and two were not met, criterion three was misunderstood, and four was not considered adequately because of a broad miscalculation about the nature of the undertaking.

In that speech, Mr Blair declared 'we are witnessing the beginnings of a new doctrine of international community … We are all internationalists now … We cannot turn our backs on

---

24   *Reflections on Intervention: 35th Ditchley Foundation Lecture* 1998.

25   Blair 1999.

26   It is thought that the intellectual content of this speech was crafted by Professor Sir Lawrence Freedman. Professor Freedman is reported to have been surprised when he heard and read Mr Blair's Chicago speech, which was based largely on a memo he had sent to Number 10. See Crick 2009. Professor Freedman became a member of the Chilcot Inquiry in 2009.

conflicts and violations of human rights within other countries, if we want still to be secure.'[27] Mr Blair had taken the language of the old Left. 'Internationalism' was no longer that of 'the Red Flag' or the 'International Brigade' of the Spanish Civil War. Rather, he made it synonymous with free global markets and human rights, outraging the Left whose lexicon he had colonised. 'Globalization is not just economic, it is also a political and security phenomenon.'[28]

The Foreign Office was dismayed by this formulation of policy 'on the hoof', often against its advice. 'Where does this end?' asked Sir John Kerr, the Permanent Secretary.[29] On 3 May 1999, Mr Blair and his wife Cherie visited Stankovic in Macedonia to see refugees from Kosovo. After some minutes in a refugee tent, Mr Blair emerged to pronounce, 'This is not a battle for NATO, this is not a battle for territory, this is a battle for humanity. It is a just cause.'[30] The attack on Yugoslavia in 1999 over the disputed Serbian province of Kosovo, strongly supported by Mr Blair, was apparently illegal in international law; but it seemed a compelling humanitarian imperative, it seemed to be effective, and there were few apparent negative repercussions from stepping across this legal boundary.[31] On 31 July 1999, in Pristina, Mr Blair proclaimed, 'We are succeeding in Kosovo because this was a moral cause ... we now have a chance to build a new internationalism based on values and the rule of law.' He hailed the embarkation 'on a new moral crusade'[32] – an incautious use of a term that would perhaps confirm others in the belief that his intent was malign to their own interests and values.

In a speech to the Global Ethics Foundation on 30 June 2000, at Tübingen University, Mr Blair spoke about values and community. 'I believe we will only succeed if we start to develop a doctrine of international community ... a community based on the equal worth of all, on the foundation of mutual rights and mutual responsibilities.' It sounded inspirational, but what if many, with radically different sets of values, did not agree with the rules of the community as approved by Mr Blair? Were the aspirations of al-Qaeda, and the millions in sympathy with it, really to be deemed 'of equal worth' to those of his own; and if not, what should be done? Were those of other views still part of the community, or some 'other' entity to be confronted if not named; but how could they be termed 'them', for they are also 'us' in his inclusive lexicon. It was this inner contradiction in his argument that would surface in 2006 in explaining why multiculturalism in the UK could not include cultural traditions at odds with those of the majority of the British people, and especially with his own perceptions of human rights.

The Canadian Government established the International Commission on Intervention and State Sovereignty, which in December 2001 produced a report called 'The Responsibility to Protect'. This concluded that when people are being harmed it is a sovereign government's responsibility to protect them; failure to do so surrenders that responsibility to the international community. The international community's responsibility is then to prevent, react and rebuild. Humanitarian intervention should be with the right intentions, a last resort, with proportional means and reasonable prospects of success. It recommended that it should probably be undertaken most appropriately by the UN, although the UN did not adopt the report.[33]

---

27   Kampfner 2004.
28   Blair 1999.
29   Kampfner 2004, 53.
30   Kampfner 2004, 54.
31   The Kosovo War is generally regarded as illegal in as much as it was a unilateral action not authorised by the United Nations Security Council. Many, however, deem it legitimate, albeit illegal, under emerging humanitarian law. For a sample of this debate, see Legault 2000, 63.
32   Kampfner 2004, 60.
33   See Sloboda and Abbott 2004.

Humanitarian necessity would not be the UK's justification for the invasion of Iraq in 2003, although pre-emption of Saddam Hussein's future outrages was subsequently alluded to, and his removal retrospectively justified the invasion in the eyes of many. The difficulties of pre-emptive humanitarian intervention have yet to be resolved, but remain a major challenge to the international system, rather like arresting someone deemed a potential criminal before a crime has been committed.

On 29 January 2002, President George Bush told Congress that the USA would not wait on events while dangers gathered from the 'Axis of Evil', signalling the use of pre-emption in US policy. 'If we wait for threats to fully materialise, we will have waited too long. We must take the battle to the enemy, disrupt his plans and confront the worst threats before they emerge.'[34] Paul Wolfowitz apparently claimed the US settled on Weapons of Mass Destruction (WMD) as the reason to invade Iraq because it was the one reason all could agree upon.[35] Certainly, it was the one cited by Mr Blair, who elaborated on the threat of WMD and their readiness for use by Saddam Hussein.

On 7 April 2002, speaking at the George Bush Senior Presidential Library, in College Station, Mr Blair struck an even more militant note, claiming, in his new view of international affairs, utilitarianism and utopianism combined: 'I advocate an enlightened self-interest that puts fighting for our values right at the heart of the policies to protect nations. Engagement in the world on the basis of these values, not isolationism from it, is the hard-headed pragmatism for the 21st Century.' The promotion of Western values was, '… not just right in itself but part of our long-term security and prosperity'. 'If necessary, the action should be military and again, if necessary and justified, it should involve regime change. I have been involved as British Prime Minister in three conflicts involving regime change.'

Mr Blair reflected on the USA's role in international affairs, and by implication the special relationship. 'American power affects the world fundamentally. It is there. It is real. It is never irrelevant. It can affect the world for good or bad. Stand aside or engage, it never fails to affect. You know that I want it engaged. Under President Bush, I am confident it will be and for good.' Clearly the USA was expected to champion and lead interventionism on this agenda. '[W]hen America is fighting for those values, then, however tough, we fight with her. No grandstanding, no offering of impractical advice from the comfort of the touchline …'. 'If the world makes the right choices now – at this time of destiny – we will get there. And Britain will be at America's side in doing it.'

Having urged the USA not to be isolationist, and pledged that Britain would stand with her, Mr Blair could not decline to do so in 2003. It seems likely that preserving the special relationship with the USA was the primary reason for Mr Blair's decision to join the USA in invading Iraq, an understandable pursuit of national interest; but this was realpolitik of a different character from his justifications based on WMD, or what seem to be his retrospective thoughts about the struggle within Islam.

Did this apparent underlying pragmatism benefit the UK's interests? In 2002, Mr Blair had compromised and seems to have allowed some of his political conditions for Britain's support for the Iraq invasion to be ignored. In return, as State Department analyst Kendall Myers put it, in a telling speech at Johns Hopkins University on 28 November 2006, '[i]t was a done deal from the beginning, it was a one-sided relationship that was entered into with open eyes … there was nothing. There was no payback, no sense of reciprocity.'[36] National interest may have been

---

34 Kampfner 2004, 173.
35 Kampfner 2004, 338.
36 Quoted in Baldwin and Webster 2006, 1.

involved in Mr Blair's decision in the sense of preserving and strengthening the UK–US alliance, but, in the event, there may have been unintended negative consequences for this relationship when US and UK approaches came to diverge in Iraq after 2006.

The new idealism had a religious hue. President G.W. Bush asserted in various speeches that freedom was God's gift to every individual, implying the USA acted as His agent in its 'forward strategy of freedom',[37] against an 'axis of evil'. This public association of religion with foreign policy had a Victorian ring to it, which had been absent from Western discourse for many decades. President Bush explained operations in Afghanistan in the same context in London in 2008: 'This isn't the American empire, the British empire or the Coalition empire. This is freedom's march. And freedom has had a way of taking hold in some places where people have never given freedom a chance.'[38]

The invasion and subsequent operations in Iraq in 2003 were a legal novelty. With the case for the imminent use of WMD lost, Mr Blair linked Coalition operations to the Global War on Terror, asserting in Sedgefield on 5 March 2004, '… we surely have a right to prevent the threat materializing …'.[39] This was a major departure from his Chicago speech of 1999, which did not provide grounds for preventive regime change, but was in accord with his remarks in Texas in 2002.

The legality of military intervention in Iraq is not a concern of this study, per se. However, the various reasons given for intervention, with the need to make a legal case for Cabinet and Parliamentary support, is relevant since the reasons given affected the type of preparations made, and created a mindset that dominated the early stages when a 'tipping moment' might have had a profound effect on the course and outcome of the campaign. Some commanders in the field felt that the issue of legality materially affected troops in the field. On 14 December 2007, Brigadier Andrew Mackay, commanding 52 Brigade in Helmand Province, contrasted his situation with his time in Iraq: '… sitting in Iraq you did not enjoy the British public's support. I think Iraq is mired in the whole legality issue – spin, dodgy dossiers, the way it turned out.'[40]

There has been much acrimonious debate about whether the British Attorney General, Lord Goldsmith, was always consistent in his opinion as to whether toppling Saddam Hussein would be legal or not. It was reported that a secret letter written by him in July 2002, six days after ministers were told that the USA and the UK were set upon ousting Saddam, made clear that war could not be justified solely on grounds of regime change, and that Britain could not rely on claims of self-defence to justify war since Iraq was no threat to the UK. 'Humanitarian intervention' was also ruled out as a justification. The leader of the Liberal Democrat Party, Nick Clegg, claimed that, in view of this letter, assertions that the Attorney General had indeed given the 'all clear' were a 'gross betrayal of all the institutions of the British state'.[41]

The reasons for invading Iraq remained mired in controversy and offered commanders in the field little clarity. Had British operations been undertaken to remove WMD from a country which might use them against its neighbours, against Western interests, or place them in the hands of al-Qaeda? Were they to pre-empt Iraq's use by al-Qaeda as a base at some future date, or to topple a human rights abuser? Were they to make Iraq a democratic society at the heart of the Arab world,

---

37   President Bush speaking at the Royal United Services Institute, London, 27 November 2003.
38   Speaking in an interview with Sky News on 15 June 2008.
39   Quoted in Sloboda and Abbott 2004.
40   Quoted in Edwards 2007.
41   Quoted in Shipman 2009, 4. This letter was eventually declassified and made available to the Chilcot Inquiry. Available at: http://www.iraqinquiry.org.uk/media/46499/Goldsmith-note-to-PM-30July2002.pdf [accessed: 31 May 2011].

as a bulwark against growing militant Islam, or as part of a broader global agenda to propagate Western 'values and ideas'? Or, were they intended primarily to maintain the strength of the UK's relationship with the USA?

Whatever the reason, a clear understanding of it would be essential to understanding the appropriate ways to achieve it, and the means that would be required. Worse than misunderstanding the objective would be to maintain it was one thing when in fact it was another. In the latter case, disconnections between misconstrued ends, ways and means would be even more likely.

The Global Vision Expands

Mr Blair's global vision to change the world for the better seemed to be shared by his Chancellor of the Exchequer, Gordon Brown, responsible for funding it. On 10 October 2006 at Chatham House in London, Mr Brown called for 'the modern equivalent of a Marshall Plan for Africa' and he announced another ambitious project: '... our "education for all children" initiative ... showing that globalisation is not just a cause of injustice and poverty but a force for justice on a global scale'. Mr Brown asserted that '... the values that respect the dignity of all individuals unite peaceful religions across the world ...'.

The problem with this construction is the implication that all who share a common view with the West are deemed moderates and true representatives of their religion; and all those whose faith has fundamentally different precepts from Western secular notions of democracy and human rights are by implication branded 'unpeaceful'.

Mr Brown insisted 'this is not a clash of civilisations nor of cultures'. Rather, he maintained 'on the one side stands all civilised societies', so awkwardly using two meanings of 'civilised' to deny that those who do not share the values of his own particular civilisation are fit to be categorised as civilisations. He understood the likely duration of the undertaking proposed: 'We should explicitly state that American values and European values are as one in counter posing to extremist ideology' and that all should work 'to win this generation-long struggle'. Here, in effect, was a prospectus for a long struggle against those of other beliefs who oppose the values of the West, represented especially by the intellectual traditions of the USA and Europe.

Mr Brown developed his own and Mr Blair's thesis to link his idealism and Britain's national interest in an even more surprising way. On 17 January 2007, he chose Bangalore, apparently without irony, to set out his agenda. He called for a 'new world order', built on British values and in Britain's interests. Britain's 'ethical foreign policy' had now merged with Western interests in the imperative to create a new world order. 'We can help build things and shape this new world order, and I want it to be shaped in a way that is good for Britain and for British values.'[42] This apparent call for a new world order based on British culture seemed to be at odds with the avowed multiculturalism of New Labour. This directness rivalled the pronouncements of Victorian imperialists such as Ruskin and Disraeli, although it was unlikely to have the same support or effect. Mr Brown had certainly not made budgetary provision over the previous decade for his varied and ambitious agenda. On 31 July 2007, he struck an even more militant tone with an unfortunate and incautious turn of phrase, when discussing current operations which were a 'generation-long battle' in which 'we can give no quarter'.[43] Perhaps his phrasing was an unconscious acknowledgement that his words should be taken as rhetoric, not a practical prospectus for action.

42   Quoted in Wilson 2007, 6.

43   Gordon Brown speaking at a press conference at Camp David, Maryland, on 30 July 2007.

In February 2008, the Foreign Secretary David Miliband expressed similarly forthright views, urging that Britain pursue a moral mission to spread democracy throughout the world. Supporting democratic government with the full range of diplomatic and military tools satisfied both a 'moral impulse' and Britain's national interest. He explicitly urged the Left to reclaim the position taken by the neo-conservative movement in the 1990s when 'the Left seemed conflicted between the desirability of the goal and its qualms about the use of military means ... the goal of spreading democracy should be a great progressive project ...'.[44] Ends and ways were thus described, but the means omitted.

The Home Front and the Front Line

This debate about values was as much about domestic as foreign policy, as the two became entwined and globalism met parochialism. This may explain New Labour's conviction that multiculturalism in Britain would pose no fundamental challenge to what were generally accepted to be British values, for surely these values were shared by all? Later, when experience had proven this not necessarily to be the case, Mr Blair would come out against the multiculturalism which he had earlier championed.

In 2000, the Commission on the Future of Multi-Ethnic Britain found that Britain should be recognised as a multicultural society, and that its history needed to be 'revised, rethought or jettisoned'. It asserted Britain to be a community of communities rather than a nation. The concept of multicultural Britain was ardently espoused by Mr Blair, who declared '... it's a good thing, not something to be frightened of'.[45]

In his speech of 10 October 2006, Mr Brown took a different position, speaking in the figurative language of cultural combat when noting the need to take on religious 'extremists', noting that in the UK civic organisations 'formed a front line in this cultural effort'. Multiculturalism in the UK would be challenged by a new plan to educate young people in 'the values and traditions of what it is to be British'. Mr Blair followed Mr Brown's direction shortly after, advocating a set of common values in one society that might be taken to imply a common culture of morals and essential manners.

The possible effects of campaigns in Iraq and Afghanistan had done much to bring about this change of view, even though Mr Blair insisted they had not damaged Britain's security, but were necessary for it. As Home Secretary, John Reid broke ranks with Mr Blair in asserting the wars in Iraq and Afghanistan could be 'a factor' in turning young Muslims into extremists. 'I do believe that foreign policy is sometimes a motivating factor in radicalization of young Muslims and the potential recruitment to terror.'[46]

On 8 December 2006, Mr Blair effectively declared the end of Britain's 30-year multicultural experiment, which he had championed since 1999, telling immigrants they had a 'duty' to integrate. Speaking paradoxically of British tolerance, '[c]onform to it, or don't come here ... the duty to integrate. That is what being British means.'[47]

The Chief of the General Staff, General Sir Richard Dannatt, voiced similar concerns about the scale of the cultural challenge facing the UK. It was reported he had warned in June 2007 of 'a generation of conflict' and of the dangers of a 'strident Islamist shadow'.[48] A paper written by

---

44   Barker 2008, 6.
45   Quoted in Johnston 2006b, 10.
46   Reported in Carlin 2006, 2.
47   Quoted in Johnston 2006a.
48   Evans 2007.

Professor Gwyn Prins and Lord Salisbury, based on a series of seminars with security officials and others, and published by the Royal United Services Institute in February 2008, was said to assert that in the face of Islamic terrorism, 'The United Kingdom presents itself as a target, as a fragmenting, post-Christian society, increasingly divided about interpretations of its history, about its national aims, its values, and in its political identity.'[49]

Following the attempted destruction of Detroit-bound Northwest Airlines Flight 253 on 25 December 2009, numerous security and political advisers in the USA condemned Britain's multicultural model, as compared with the USA's 'melting pot'. Daniel Pipes even called the UK '… a menace to the outside world. It's been a problem for years now';[50] yet it was over the most damaging years of this radicalisation that Mr Blair, believed by many to be the USA's best ally, was Prime Minister, supporting and leading multiculturalism.

After the attacks of 11 September 2001, it became clear that the 'home front' was also the 'front line'; and the concept of campaigns being 'amongst the people' might indeed also apply to the home front and to the people of the UK. Ideas about domestic multiculturalism were thus directly relevant to the campaigns in Iraq and Afghanistan, because concern about the reactions of Britain's minority communities became a common feature of the debate about the purpose, justification and consequences of those campaigns.

The views of minorities have also been a cause for caution in how campaigns are conducted, how the campaign narrative is offered to the public, and the style of 'war leadership' the Government feels able to project. Just as the 'home front' had come to have a second meaning, so too the comprehensive approach had become even more encompassing; and the front line and the home front were linked in a way that gave new meaning to globalisation.

Rationalisation of Motives Post-2003

It is unclear whether Mr Blair believed his campaign in Iraq of 2003 to be a part of a cultural struggle over the future of Islam, or whether he came to rationalise or conclude this in the light of events after 2003, having not understood what he was originally embarking upon.

On 21 March 2006, Mr Blair made a speech in London about operations in Iraq and Afghanistan.[51] He was keen to distance himself from being labelled a de facto 'neo-con', claiming that there was a fault line between 'progressives' such as himself and 'conservatives'. He maintained the defeat of global terrorism would be assisted by the victory of democracy in Iraq and Afghanistan. Mr Blair noted that in over 30 countries terrorists were plotting action: 'Its roots are not superficial, therefore, they are deep, embedded in the culture of many nations and capable of eruption at any time'; and yet at other times Mr Blair maintained that terror was the work merely of extremists who do not represent the true character of their religions and cultures, which are all part of a single global community, for he held that there is no clash of cultures, only struggle with the extremists who do not truly represent other civilisations and cultures. He attributed problems in Iraq to too speedy de-Ba'athification, the murder of UN staff, failure to establish security and thus reconstruction, growth of creeping criminality and the opposition's adoption of sectarianism as a tactic. His own and the international coalition's lack of provision to pre-empt or deal with such setbacks remained unexplained.

---

49   Prins and Salisbury 2008, 23.
50   Harnden 2010.
51   Available at http://www.guardian.co.uk/politics/2006/mar/21/iraq.iraq1 [accessed 3 March 2013].

In his speech, Mr Blair claimed the ongoing campaigns were essentially about modernity, and his premise was that others must accept it. 'It is a battle of values and progress, and therefore it is one we must win.' This was in many ways a traditional British imperial agenda; but in this case imperial resources were wanting; and it had been material, as much as psychological, exhaustion that had brought Britain's imperial project to a close 40 years earlier.

Mr Blair's rationales came under closer scrutiny, and he had increasingly to defend his decisions. In an interview on *Al-Jazeera* TV, on 17 November 2006, Mr Blair incautiously agreed with Sir David Frost that the invasion of Iraq had been a 'disaster'. He quickly withdrew the remark, but the damage had been done. He was not helped by his Industry Minister who, apparently believing she was speaking off the record, was reported as calling Mr Blair's policy 'moral imperialism'.[52]

The intent of operations in Afghanistan also lacked a compelling clarity. Was the intent to destroy al-Qaeda and to prevent its future use of that country as a base to attack the UK? Was it to eradicate the opium industry, which at one time was cited as the greater security threat to the UK home-base? Or was it to transform Afghanistan into a society espousing Western values? This damaging ambiguity was highlighted by Sir Malcolm Rifkind, Secretary of State for Defence 1992–1995, who urged the British Government to be more honest with the British people: 'When British soldiers first went to Helmand, the government suggested that these troops would be acting in support of the civil power, rather than fighting in a war. There remains an ambiguity as to our objectives and to what can be achieved by military means alone.'[53]

Lieutenant Colonel Stuart Tootal, Commanding Officer of 3rd Battalion The Parachute Regiment in Afghanistan in 2006, whose battalion fired 479,236 small-arms rounds in six months, noted that, 'We confused ourselves – and the public – that this was a peace support mission, but that presupposes parties signing up to a peace deal. The Taliban had signed up to nothing. This was counter-insurgency.'[54] On 20 November 2006, on a visit to Kabul, Mr Blair's ideological perspective appeared undimmed. He told the troops their mission against the Taliban was a test of the determination of the civilised world to defeat an 'evil ideology',[55] ignoring other complex motives why various Afghan opponents might fight an international force.

In a lecture in Plymouth on 12 January 2007, Mr Blair described the threat to the West from Islam, which was 'akin to revolutionary Communism in its early and most militant phase. It is global. It has a narrative about the world and Islam's place within it that has a reach into most Islamic societies and countries.' He expanded this theme in a BBC TV interview with Fern Britton in December 2009. Referring to his decision to join in the invasion of Iraq, Mr Blair revealed more of his thinking about the true nature of the struggle he believed himself to be championing: 'I happen to think that there is a major struggle going on all over the world, really, which is about Islam and what is happening with Islam ... (and this has a) ... long way to go.' His opponents came increasingly to sound like 'them'.

The validity of his assertion about Islam may have merit, and it may prove to be the crucial strategic insight of the times; but this was not explained to the British public in 2003 to enlist their support for the invasion of Iraq. If it was indeed Mr Blair's judgement from the outset, no serious provision seems to have been made to develop the ways and means that would be necessary to prevail in the prolonged campaigns that would be a consequence of this insight.

---

52   Quoted in Jones 2006.
53   Rifkind 2008.
54   Lamb 2008.
55   Reported in Helm 2006.

Given the agendas of multiculturalism in the UK at the time, his own party might well have rejected any such argument.

Ironically, despite this growing emphasis by Mr Blair on the moral justification for his military decisions, their purpose was discussed less in terms of 'ideas and values' by those left to conduct campaigns after the departures of President Bush and Mr Blair. On 1 December 2009 at West Point, President Obama announced his new plan for the campaign in Afghanistan and his intent to 'dismantle, disrupt and defeat' al-Qaeda; but he also noted that America did not have the budget or willpower for an 'open-ended commitment'.[56] This marked a significant change of direction and ambition. There was no focus on a 'long war', the term adopted in the USA by 2005 to accommodate the realities of counter-insurgency (COIN) operations in Iraq. President Obama made no reference to the establishing of democracy, women's rights, economic growth or the eradication of the narcotics trade. He seemed keen to shape an expectation that this was to be a campaign of military utility, not a campaign of 'ideas and values'. The 'Obama Doctrine' was formalised in his *National Security Strategy* of May 2010.

President Obama's presentation was at odds with the view of some of his allies as to why they were fighting in Afghanistan. On 2 April 2009, President Karzai announced draconian restrictions on women's rights, outraging many who saw the military mission in Afghanistan as primarily about 'ideas and values'. Stephen Harper, the Canadian Prime Minister, said he was offended by the law and would lobby to have it repealed: 'This is antithetical to our mission in Afghanistan.'[57] Mike Gapes, the chairman of the British Parliament's Foreign Affairs Select Committee said, 'We did not go into Afghanistan to remove the Taleban only to have Taleban-style policies re-implemented by the Government.'[58]

By 2010, the dominant campaign perspective seemed to have become not so much cultural transformation and the 'generational' nature of the conflict in Afghanistan, but rather the imperatives of the American and British electoral cycles. The stated intent was to start withdrawing American forces from 2011 and for British troops to have been withdrawn by 2015.

An epilogue to Mr Blair's rationale for the wars in Iraq and Afghanistan was provided by the Chilcot Inquiry of 2009–2010, and in interviews given to coincide with it. Speaking to Fern Britton on BBC 1 in December 2009, Mr Blair said he would have favoured going to war with Iraq in 2003 to depose Saddam Hussein, even if he had known that Iraq had no WMD: 'I would still have thought it right to remove him.'[59] This was supported by previous interviews; on 25 March 2007 he had asserted he would not apologise for the invasion of Iraq because 'I don't believe it was wrong to get rid of Saddam.'[60] The Britton interview suggested confusion about his rationale for war, for he explained he would then have had to use different arguments to justify toppling Saddam Hussein. Yet in 1999 he had said that it was wrong to intervene to change the political system of another country. Thus, even if he had believed there to have been WMD, this justification appears not to have been the prime motive for the invasion of Iraq, rather the factor of WMD seems to have been merely a tool to further some objective which itself could not be stated openly. Mr Blair later asserted to the Chilcot Inquiry that his words had been misunderstood.

Mr Blair's BBC interview threw light on his thinking about why regime change in Iraq was necessary, and illuminates his confusion about the nature of the undertakings which continued to dog the Iraq and Afghanistan campaigns. He cast these in broad historical and ideological terms,

---

56 Quoted in Spillius and Farmer 2009.
57 Quoted in Philp, Coghlan and Jagger 2009.
58 Philp, Coghlan and Jagger 2009.
59 Quoted in Gledhill and Brown 2009.
60 Quoted in Brown 2007.

as he had done in January 2007, linked to immediate military utility, but with the two unreconciled in terms of military requirements and their resourcing. The need to topple Saddam was justified by Mr Blair in terms of military security in the region and as a necessary episode in a struggle about the evolution of Islam, a rationale not explained to Parliament in 2003. He had neither rearmed the nation nor built a national capability to deal with such a broad and complex challenge. Did this cultural perspective about the future of Islam grow only after launching the campaigns in Iraq and Afghanistan; or was it genuinely the unspoken motivation in his mind in the approach to war in 2002–2003?

This BBC interview sparked strong reactions from some who had been close to Mr Blair. Sir Ken Macdonald, the Director of Public Prosecutions from 2003 to 2008, accused Mr Blair of an 'alarming subterfuge' with George Bush, 'misleading and cajoling the British people into a war they did not want'. Accusing him of sycophancy to those in power, Mr Macdonald charged that '... he couldn't resist the stage or the glamour that it gave him'.[61] 'Mr Blair's mantra that he did what he thought was right was a "narcissist's defence" because self-belief was no answer to misjudgement and no answer to death.'[62]

Resourcing Campaigns

As a result of the SDR of 1998, the Labour Government reconfigured the Armed Forces for short operations not long before it would launch them on enduring and demanding ones, based in part on the new doctrine of humanitarian interventionism espoused by Mr Blair. The Ministry of Defence was forced to cut its structure to match the slender resources which the Government made available. Specific cuts in capability are often said by politicians to be enacted on the advice of the Ministry of Defence, but this does not absolve politicians from their responsibility to fund defence to meet the objectives they set.

Mr Blair launched the UK on a 'blitzkrieg of benevolence', but little provision was made to develop actual capabilities for the prolonged and complex operations in which the military would play merely a part. If the intent of such an operation is to change the lives of others, their thinking, culture and practices, by force, in some permanent way, that process will involve more than mere military force. Success will depend upon the manner in which force is applied in conjunction with other broader dynamics; and is likely to take a long time. Cultural change is generally not amenable to blitzkrieg, for the ways of others are not readily reshaped to a common and 'correct' view, congruent with the ideas of the conqueror. At root, nation-building requires changing of culture, and that is the hardest objective to achieve and the most bitterly resisted.

The plan to invade Iraq in 2003 did not entail a thorough comprehensive approach, encompassing all Government departments, probably because the Prime Minister feared losing the compliance of his Cabinet colleagues if he had told them they had a crucial role in the campaign. Lord Boyce, the Chief of the Defence Staff in early 2003, told the Chilcot Inquiry that planning for the invasion had been hampered by the Defence Secretary, Geoff Hoon, restricting it to a few people.[63] It seemed to have been hoped that early military success would set in train a sequence of beneficial outcomes in political, social, economic and cultural life in Iraq which would be substantially self-sustaining. In due course, the Armed Forces developed their thinking and the practice of COIN and nation-

---

61   Macdonald 2009; and Webster 2009.
62   Macdonald 2009.
63   Macdonald 2009.

building; but without the other elements of nation-building and reconstruction, the security they provided would not of itself deliver campaign success.

Misunderstanding the nature of the campaigns lay at the heart of the problem, exacerbated by absence of the structures and resources needed for operations of that kind. A further problem was the scale and coincidence of the two campaigns, both embarked upon by choice rather than by necessity. In the spring of 2004, the British Government decided to send a large British force to Afghanistan in 2006; the troops and resources becoming available due to assumed reductions in Iraq and Northern Ireland. It was felt success in Afghanistan would come more readily – 'the good war' – than it had in Iraq, which had come to seem 'the bad war'. There now seemed to be an opportunity to secure a military success after disappointments in Iraq.

However, the UK failed to ensure NATO allies were willing to contribute substantial forces to combat operations in Afghanistan to complement those of the British. Those which did have troops in Afghanistan had very diverse views about the nature of that mission, and how it would be conducted. Aware of the dangers, British commanders asked for certain troop levels, and when these were not available were directed to proceed anyway.

In the event, wishful assumptions about the ability to reduce forces in Iraq proved to be flawed, and attempts to reduce force levels at a time when the US was committed to its 'Surge' created a fundamental divergence in policy between coalition partners. There were insufficient British troops to 'clear, hold and build'. Many have blamed this strategic overstretch for what some have described as the British failure in Basra, and the accompanying damage to Britain's military reputation in American eyes. Others saw the scaling back of British operations in Basra as necessary if the Iraqi Government was to accept responsibility for the city.

The demands of two medium-scale, enduring operations in Iraq and Afghanistan, each requiring a brigade rotating through theatres every six months, called for a field army of ten brigades, but only eight were available. As a result, two new light brigades had to be created at short notice. It also became clear that so-called 'light brigades' would have to be equipped very differently from previous light brigades. They required the latest heavily-protected armoured vehicles to achieve the protected mobility that had proven essential in both theatres. Even so, the number of troops deployed to Helmand Province proved insufficient, only reaching an adequate number in 2010 with the deployment of a substantial American force.

John Hutton, Secretary of State for Defence in 2008–2009, also acknowledged the difficulty of sustaining simultaneous campaigns in Iraq and Afghanistan: 'We do not have sufficient resources to be able to sustain that over the long term. The question is whether or not this country has the resources and the political will to commit the capabilities that will be needed.'[64] This view was reinforced by the DSG of the time, but had been discounted when launching the campaigns in question, perhaps because the consequences of doing so were not comprehended.

Responsibility for strategic decisions and their resource implications was clearly a political one, and much criticism was levelled at politicians by senior officers speaking at the Chilcot Inquiry and other fora. However, the former soldier Adam Holloway MP, a member of the Defence Select Committee, laid the blame for poor planning for the campaigns in Iraq and Afghanistan more widely on a failure in civil–military relations, including military leadership:

> Labour suborned the Armed Forces from the very top, creating a system that enforces what is politically convenient, not what is militarily right … Our political leaders became so caught up in fabricating reasons to invade and occupy Iraq that they never stopped to set a clear and achievable

---

64   Brown 2010b.

goal for Britain's involvement ... It was not just politicians who were incapable of setting clear objectives in Iraq. Our leaders of the MOD, the Chiefs of Staff and senior Civil Servants, men who were selected for their clarity of thought, became caught up in the opaque, politicised confusion that was driving our involvement ... They failed to provide the Government with hard facts and choices to confront it with the strategic implications of under-resourcing the Army ... Our soldiers were expected to give their lives ... but at the very top shrank from committing "career suicide" by standing up to politicians and telling them the uncomfortable truth ... A "good news only" culture has begun to emerge within the military – the culture of politically aware advice.[65]

Criticism in the press of named serving officers and civil servants is rare, but on 9 and 10 June 2010 *The Times* ran a series of articles based on interviews with over 30 senior officials. These accused politicians of sloppy planning for the UK's expanded role in Afghanistan in 2006, but more painfully they accused senior officers of failing to give unwelcome military advice to their political masters, or even of being over-eager for action when resources were bound to be inadequate for the task.[66] An unnamed source is reported as saying that, '... it was a neat solution in 2004. They got a lot of kudos for taking on Afghanistan, but then they went into institutional denial about what they'd entered into.'[67]

Shortage of resources turned from being a military grievance to a domestic political threat. Attempts were made to recover from this, but they did not succeed. In 2006 Mr Blair asserted that, 'If the commanders on the ground want more equipment, armoured vehicles for example, more helicopters, that will be provided. Whatever package they want, we will do.'[68] This promise could not, however, be made good given the long lead-times to acquire equipment, let alone train the personnel who would man and maintain it.

For example, in November 2006 the press reported that the Commander of 12 Brigade, Brigadier John Lorimer, had taken the Prime Minister at his word and requested a shopping list of armour for his brigade's deployment to Afghanistan in 2007. 'The denial of John Lorimer's operational requirements shows how empty Mr Blair's words were ... his requests were rejected out of hand.'[69] The MOD swiftly issued a statement on the brigadier's behalf with careful phrasing to say of his requests for assets that he was '... perfectly happy that those are being considered in the normal way'.[70] The MOD stressed that no decisions had been made about the force package for 2007.

The press took up the grievance over equipment and linked it to the price being paid in casualties. The press also highlighted the difference between compensation paid to military casualties and those less seriously injured in civilian clerical employment. The state of military housing, hardly 'homes for heroes', also attracted adverse comment. The Director of the Royal British Legion maintained that, 'the nation has failed to live up to its commitments under the (Military) Covenant'.[71] *The Independent on Sunday* launched a campaign supported by over 40 military officials to pressure the Government to keep its side of 'The Military Covenant' which it was accused of betraying. Such popular movements were without precedent. The Government was unpleasantly surprised to find itself subject to stiff criticism by the Oxfordshire coroners holding inquests into the deaths of

---

65   Holloway 2009. Much of Holloway's criticism of the conduct of operations in Iraq, such as the rescue of kidnapped SAS soldiers in Basra in 2005, focused on 'politically motivated decisions' taken in London.

66   Haynes, Lloyd, Kiley and Coghlan 2010.

67   Haynes, Lloyd, Kiley and Coghlan 2010.

68   Leake 2006.

69   Leake 2006.

70   Leake 2006.

71   Quoted in: Daily Telegraph editorial 2007.

soldiers being repatriated at RAF Brize Norton and RAF Lyneham.[72] Even the lengthy delays in holding inquests attracted criticism. The Armed Forces came increasingly to be seen as victims of politicians.

Many who had held senior positions in Whitehall agreed that long-term failure to resource defence lay at the heart of the problem. Sir Kevin Tebbit, Permanent Secretary at the MOD in 2003, told the Chilcot Inquiry on 3 December 2009 that defence had been under-funded, given the demands that were placed upon it: 'The problem was a basic one – the defence budget was too small.'[73] Speaking at King's College London on 15 September 2009, the Secretary of State for Defence, Bob Ainsworth, called for a national debate about Britain's role in the world and how much it was prepared to spend on defence.[74] Such a call had not been made in 2001, 2003 or 2006, the years in which key decisions and deployments had been made.

At the Chilcot Inquiry on 19 January 2010, the former Secretary of State for Defence, Geoff Hoon, accused Mr Brown of personally vetoing spending on essential helicopters in 2004.[75] This was a serious charge, for these helicopters could have been in service by 2007, by when many commanders claimed that their absence was handicapping their operations and leading to unnecessary casualties, and by when Mr Blair claimed that the forces could have anything they needed.[76]

He also claimed Mr Blair had delayed equipment orders by refusing to allow active war preparations in case they jeopardised diplomatic efforts to secure a United Nations resolution, and as a result some equipment failed to reach troops in time.[77] However, when Mr Blair was questioned at the Chilcot Inquiry on 29 January 2010, he maintained the Armed Forces had not lacked necessary equipment for the invasion of Iraq in 2003. Evidence given on 1 February 2010 by Air Chief Marshal Sir Jock Stirrup, the Chief of Defence Staff, seemed to be at odds with this perception.

It may be that Mr Blair genuinely believed that British forces had sufficient for their task in Iraq. If so, it is likely this resulted from his lack of understanding of what the task would entail, or unwillingness to acknowledge its scale. Major General Tim Cross, who would be Jay Garner's deputy in the Office of Reconstruction and Humanitarian Assistance in Iraq in 2003, recalled telling Mr Blair, 'We want to be jolly careful that we don't start this war until we know how we are going to finish it. And I, for one, am far from clear on how we are going to do that.' Of Mr Blair, he noted that, 'He didn't seem to have the instinct for or understand the scope and complexity of what was going to be needed in the aftermath of the invasion. I don't think he understood what the possible consequences could be.'[78]

Major General Cross noted that, across Whitehall,

---

72   The case of Captain James Phillippson, killed in action in Afghanistan on 11 June 2006, probably drew the strongest condemnation. One coroner accused the Secretary of State for Defence of 'massive insensitivity', and called for a review of the Government's Defence spending. Reported in Harding 2008a.

73   Quoted in Higginson 2009.

74   Quoted in Kirkup 2009.

75   Oliver 2010; and Brown 2010a. Mr Brown denied culpability, under questioning by the House of Commons Liaison Committee, on 2 February 2010, saying that the choice of what to cut in 2004, when the Defence budget was actually rising, was a decision for the MOD.

76   A similar high-profile connection between under-funding and casualties arose with the Nimrod MR2 crash in Afghanistan in September 2006, which cost 14 lives and resulted in severe censure of many individuals and departments of the MOD.

77   Brown 2010a.

78   Kingstone 2007.

there was no clearly accepted end-state, no consensus on what we wanted to achieve; nor was there a coherent and joined up pan-governmental "campaign plan". It was apparent that Whitehall had got itself locked into the US way of thinking, not realizing just how little America understood of the issues. When we got to Iraq and things started to go wrong there was just this stunned silence. There was no reserve to fill the vacuum, no ability to rethink the issues.

His first briefing to the then Chief of the General Staff, General Sir Mike Jackson, visiting Baghdad, was titled 'Snatching Defeat from the Jaws of Victory'.[79]

It may have been an assumption that if there was a need for a major reconstruction effort, the USA would make it, and that any British contribution would not be decisive and so could be skimped. As it turned out, early American misunderstandings about the requirement may have been even more wayward. Jonathan Powell, Mr Blair's Chief of Staff during his premiership, concluded, 'We probably hadn't thought through the magnitude of what we were taking on in Iraq. This is something that will take many decades to sort itself out … I don't think any of us had thought through the much bigger question of what we are dealing with.'[80]

On 25 January 2010, Gordon Brown is reported to have said, 'I think the mistake in the war was not to do the reconstruction and plan it in the way that was necessary so that Iraq could recover quickly after Saddam fell.'[81] As Chancellor of the Exchequer at the time, Mr Brown was responsible for funding military operations and reconstruction, and he presumably made this remark as a self-criticism. Richard Kemp, a former Army officer seconded to the Cabinet Office shortly after the invasion, considered Mr Brown's assertions that the UK had not been prepared to provide an army of occupation and that the problems of post-conflict Iraq could not have been foreseen as '… a lazy assumption … His statement is the strongest case I have heard for politicians to study military history.'[82]

Some maintained that ongoing underfunding of operations was a critical failure. Much of the controversy focused on whether troops had died in poorly armoured 'Snatch' Land Rover vehicles, used for want of a better alternative. Mr Brown was criticised, not only for his assertions that campaign funding was sufficient, but also for his implied condemnation of commanders in the field for choosing to put troops at risk in those vulnerable vehicles. When Mr Brown appeared before the Chilcot Inquiry on 5 March 2010, he robustly defended his decision to impose new controls on defence spending in 2003 as a measure to control broader Government spending. He also claimed, 'At every point we were asked to provide money and the resources for the new equipment or for improving equipment, we made that money available.'[83] His argument, couched in careful phrasing, brought widespread criticism from a swathe of former military commanders[84] who pointed out that the problem was long-term systemic underfunding, not any single refusal of a specific request.

---

79   Kingstone 2007.
80   Webster 2010.
81   Brown 2010b.
82   Kemp 2010.
83   Brown 2010a. Not every request for additional resources from theatre reached a political decision-maker. The Treasury rules for the procurement of Urgent Operational Requirements meant that if items requested had utility beyond the immediate theatre of operations, they might be denied during the staffing process.
84   Lord Boyce, the Chief of the Defence Staff prior to the invasion of Iraq in 2003 said of Mr Brown, 'He's dissembling, he's being disingenuous.' Reported in Brown 2010c.

Mr Brown also claimed on 5 March that, '... the defence budget was rising every year. Every spending review – 2002, 2004, 2007 – involved a rise in real terms.'[85] He made similar assertions in the House of Commons on 10 March, and to the BBC on 11 March. However, on 17 March he had to recant in the House of Commons, admitting, 'I do accept that in one or two years, defence expenditure did not rise in real terms.'[86] In fact, in four years during Labour's period of Government between 1997 and 2009, the UK's defence budget fell in real terms.[87] Meanwhile, between 2000 and 2010 the British Government's spending doubled in absolute terms; and while public-sector employment burgeoned, the size of the Armed Forces fell.[88]

On 8 March 2010, the MOD's senior Civil Servant, Sir Bill Jeffrey, told the Chilcot Inquiry that small annual increases in the defence budget did not meet the rising costs of operations and equipment: '... in successive years, I and ministers, we have had to think hard about what we could cut', resulting in a significant financial problem that 'persists to this day'.[89]

Arguably, it was Mr Blair's failure to gather the wholehearted, open-eyed support of the British people for campaigns whose purpose and costs had been made clear that posed a major risk to their success. Maybe he thought he could rely on his powers of persuasion when times got tough. Unfortunately, in this case the penalties for any failure would not be merely lost votes, untimely Cabinet reshuffles or scuffed reputations.

Were Mr Blair's policies triumphs of statesman-like and historic perception, necessarily couched in the language of compassion and political correctness to try to make them palatable to his own party and the electorate, but as hard-headed in their own way as Palmerston's? Or, will history not be kind to what it may see as a politician of personal convictions who failed to align strategic ends, ways and means. This is a judgement probably best left for several decades.

It was against this political background that a generation of senior British officers was sent off to achieve operational success, however that was defined, on behalf of the nation, by politicians who had launched these campaigns for complex and controversial reasons. The following chapters contain the thoughts of many of those officers about the 'hand' they were dealt, and how they played it.

---

85 Kirkup 2010b.
86 Kirkup 2010b.
87 Kirkup 2010b.
88 For details, see http://www.ukpublicspending.co.uk/classic [accessed 3 March 2013].
89 Kirkup 2010a.

Chapter 2

The Northern Ireland Campaign:
The Challenges of Command

Alistair Irwin – 1 November 2006

This chapter focuses on the planning and conduct of operations in Northern Ireland, a campaign that will have lasted 38 years by the time it is officially declared to be at an end next year.[1] I think that it must be the longest continuous, uninterrupted, campaign ever conducted by British Armed Forces, and if not, it must certainly be the one most shrouded in perplexity. In this attempt to lift the shrouds, it is possible, in the first place, that I may not succeed and that, in the second, at least some of what I focus on here may sound uncomfortably like criticism of my elders and betters.

Campaign planning, or rather the lack of it, has to be considered, as does the exercise of high command in the particular circumstances faced in the Province.

Starting with the former, at no stage from start to finish was there anything that recognisably had the features of a campaign plan. I confess that I went through a stage of believing that this was a fatal and incompetent omission. Now I begin to believe that the circumstances were such that it was never possible to have one.

In 2001 I said these words to the officers on the Joint Services Command and Staff Course:

> This is no ordinary campaign, the Northern Ireland campaign. The conditions that constitute the military end state will have to be made possible to a large extent by political developments. It is highly unlikely that we shall be able to reach the military end state without the politics first having been substantially, if not completely, settled.

> The campaign plan (if you can call it that) is therefore simply stated. It is for the police and armed forces to act as if they were a rock in stormy seas: constant, dependable, always there, unmoveable by the crash of waves upon them. On the steadiness of that rock will depend the successful outcome of the political negotiations.

> So there are no lines of operation applying military force through time and space, passing through decisive points on the path to the centre of gravity. There is no sequence of operational events taking us from today to the end state. Although this is not a view that is shared by Sinn Fein/IRA, the speed and course of that journey will be a natural consequence of, and not a pre-cursor to, political progress. It is a curious inversion of the state of affairs that you would expect to find when you are engaged in a proper war.

Although I hesitate to explore this idea in depth, what I described as a proper war ought to follow this sort of pattern: a breakdown of political and diplomatic consent followed by conflict until a military conclusion is reached; politics and diplomacy then resume. This is a description which

---

1 Operation Banner, the code name for the British Army's operation, finally ended on 31 July 2007.

I think Clausewitz would recognise. And yet the following, admittedly selective, quote from his *On War* seems to echo much more closely what we have faced in Northern Ireland, rather than a 'proper war':

> We maintain that war is simply a continuation of political intercourse, with the addition of other means. We want to make it clear that war in itself does not suspend political intercourse. The main lines along which military events progress and to which they are restricted are political lines that continue throughout the war.[2]

This sounds almost exactly like the Northern Ireland affair, although Clausewitz would have assumed I think that the war had to be won before politics could resume prime position. As my words of 2001 suggest, the Northern Ireland experience, and perhaps therefore all counter-insurgency campaigns, turn that notion on its head; it was only the politics that could produce the peace in Northern Ireland, not military action.

At any rate, if I was right in what I said, the idea of a campaign plan seems to be a bit *de trop*. To start at the beginning would, in the Irish context, be to consider from when the peoples of Britain started visiting, interfering with, and taking over the affairs of the emerald isle, but I take as my starting point 1969 when the first troops deployed in support of the police, at which point *The Times* quoted the MOD as saying that they did not expect the troops to be on the streets for more than three weeks. I think that this is very telling because it highlights three important points.

First, despite all the signs that were so obvious in retrospect, the need for military involvement came out of the blue. The apparently simple nature of the problem, a breakdown of law and order in the face of overwhelming public dissent and sectarian violence, required an instantaneous, unplanned response designed simply to re-establish calm and the authority of government and police.

Second, the circumstances suggested that the authorities themselves assumed that law and order would soon be restored. And therefore, third, there was no need to regard the situation from a military point of view in anything other than the very short term. Get the troops on to the ground, restore calm, return the troops to barracks and normal life would be resumed. There was no need for a campaign plan because there was going to be no campaign. I understate the complexity of the appreciation that must have been carried out but that seems to have been the burden of the conclusion.

So what then? If you start with a misappreciation of the situation, without any idea that it will develop into anything other than what you can see at the time, at what point do the scales drop from the eyes? At what point do you begin to take a long view? (Do you hear echoes of Iraq and Afghanistan here?) Those questions, so easy to ask in retrospect, would not have occurred so readily to those in charge 38 years ago. I suppose that the moment when the stones and petrol bombs were displaced by bombs and bullets was the moment when thoughts of a long campaign, and therefore the need for a plan, might have intruded into the consciousness of the commanders and staff at Headquarters Northern Ireland. But even that moment was ill-defined because the transition to extreme violence was neither abrupt nor exclusive.

So even if there had been no other factors involved, it is perhaps not altogether surprising that long-term military campaign plans were not laid at the outset. But there *were* other factors involved and it was these that in my view, and with the benefit of hindsight, suggest that the

---

2   von Clausewitz 1832, 605.

formulation of a campaign plan was *never* going to be either possible or plausible, not even some way down the track.

The first was that there was no recognisable strategic goal either at the beginning or later on. Consider the clarity, if awesome in magnitude, of the tasks laid successively upon Eisenhower. I paraphrase of course, but in essence: gain a foothold in Europe, liberate France and the Low Countries, get into Germany and force their unconditional surrender, without upsetting the Russians (or de Gaulle or Montgomery!) too much. However daunting the task, there can have been no doubt in his mind about what was expected of him by the political leadership of the Allies.

Contrast this with the rather more imprecise requirement to restore law and order in Northern Ireland, a requirement made more problematic when, much, much later, the Major Government made it clear that the British had no selfish interest in forcing Northern Ireland to remain part of the United Kingdom; if the majority wanted to stay, that was fine, but it was equally fine if the vote was to join the Irish Republic. Whether this would have been the case if oil had suddenly been found off the north coast of Antrim is not entirely clear!

The purpose of a campaign plan is to set out how a strategic goal is to be achieved through military action. Although it abbreviates the argument somewhat, I define the strategic goal as a political goal. The politicians state what is in their mind, usually with plenty of restrictions and caveats; and the military then articulates the forces required and the sequence of operational-level actions or events that will lead to victory, or at least the satisfaction of the strategic goal. The tactical commanders then set about delivering the required success in each of these sequential events.

So if the strategic goal for Northern Ireland was as nebulous as I have suggested it was, it is not easy to see how anyone could have articulated a sequence of actions designed to achieve it. It is a bit like descending into the London underground system and trying to work out which combination of tube lines to take when you do not know where you want to end up.

The military mission was correspondingly imprecise. It went through several iterations over the years, iterations of refinement rather than fundamental change. The final version, which I worked to in my time as General Officer Commanding (GOC), was this:

> The mission of the Armed Forces in Northern Ireland is to support the Police in the defeat of terrorism and in the maintenance of public order in order to assist Her Majesty's Government's objective of returning to normality.

Could the *defeat of terrorism* and *the maintenance of public order* or the *return to normality* be seen as a strategic goal? At first, the *defeat of terrorism*, or at least the sufficient suppression of terrorism, was seen as an end in itself; later, it was seen as a necessary prerequisite to allowing the politicians to regain control of the agenda and to solve the crisis politically and democratically. So there was no doubting its importance as an aim *en route* to the restoration of normality. But was it going to be achieved by having a fancy campaign plan? I am going to leave that question hanging because the answer rather depends on the argument that follows.

If the lack of a recognisable strategic goal was the first impediment to classic campaign planning, the second was that, as I have already hinted, the nature of the problem kept changing. So too did governments; so too did the internal political dynamics inside the Province. The nature of the enemy also changed. Sometimes it was exclusively the republicans in their many chameleon-like guises; sometimes it was the equally diverse loyalist side; sometimes it was both.

It all began on the back of the largely Catholic demand for civil rights; then for the IRA it became a question of protecting the Catholic population from the assaults of the loyalists and, as it was claimed, the partisan police, B Specials and the Army. And then it was a fight for independence mixed with increasing doses of inter-sectarian and anti-British hatred.

Towards the end it was more a question of dealing with maverick and ultimately wholly pointless acts of violence. And as if all that were not enough, the smuggling of fuel and cigarettes and the trade in drugs gradually introduced gangsterism of Chicago proportions onto the scene, so that by the end it was impossible to know whether we were dealing with terrorists earning a little on the side or common criminals who didn't mind killing someone when business was a little slack. A campaign plan might have itself been hard pressed to keep up with each spin of the terrorist wheel.

The third impediment to classic campaign planning was the fact that Northern Ireland was a developed part of the United Kingdom in the late twentieth century. To put it bluntly, this precluded taking the sort of long-term military and political actions that were used, for example, in Malaya and elsewhere in the empire in earlier decades. We could not have removed people from their homes; we could not have imposed free fire zones; we could not have conducted that classic ink-spotting technique that had worked so well in colonial days, although perhaps not so well now in Afghanistan.

These sorts of activities are exactly the sorts of activities that could be classified as a sequence of operational steps so characteristic of, indeed indispensable to, the construction and pursuit of a campaign plan. You could argue that something akin to these operational steps was in fact in evidence in Northern Ireland. I think, for example, of the plans: to establish secure bases in the heart of terrorist territory; to generate local defence forces (who paraded for the last time before the Queen only three weeks ago[3]); to penetrate the terrorist organisations covertly; and to conduct operations in such a way as to encourage the police to dispense with military support. These could possibly be said to be, if articulated appropriately, the basis for a campaign plan worthy of the name. But it would not be enough I think, and in any event my own experience as a company, battalion and indeed brigade commander suggests to me that those sorts of decisions and aims were set in the context of the short term and never the long term.

Here is another diversion to explain what I mean. When I commanded my battalion in South Armagh, all movement down there was either on foot or by helicopter. Very occasionally we would use civilian vehicles under cover of darkness but it was just too dangerous to use military vehicles at any time except as part of major pre-planned base construction operations. This irritated me; that Her Majesty's Armed Forces could not drive the roads of South Armagh because of the threat of terrorist activity was monstrous. So I devised a scheme to get military vehicles back on the roads. It involved a lot of very careful preparation and vigilance but on two separate occasions for a few days at a time we went everywhere in vehicles; we temporarily grounded the helicopters for everything except emergencies. I remember saying in my post-tour report that this would amount to no more than pointless bravado unless subsequent battalions, under the long-term direction of brigade headquarters, gradually extended the scope and duration of these vehicle-only operations. I was disappointed, but not surprised, to discover when I went back as GOC 15 years later that, in terms of tactical transport in South Armagh, no progress of any kind had been made.

Another and much more substantial example concerns the famous watchtowers dotted round South Armagh. The idea for them had surfaced when I was down there as a battalion commanding officer. I had overseen the early engineer operations to determine how feasible it would be to erect these things. They represented an attempt to make it more difficult for the IRA to mount attacks by

---

3   The last three 'home service' battalions of the Royal Irish Regiment were declared non-operational in October 2006 and formally disbanded in July 2007. The Royal Irish Regiment home service battalions were the successors to the Ulster Defence Regiment formed in 1970.

keeping their territory in general, and individual suspects in particular, under constant and obvious surveillance. As an idea it had obvious tactical attractions but I am not aware of any consideration of the long-term problems that would follow on from their construction. For structural and defence reasons they had to be substantial edifices, blots on the landscape, a constant source of irritation to the inhabitants. When I returned as GOC I considered the watchtowers to be my most troubling assets, both militarily and politically. I will return to this point later.

I now turn to a fourth factor that inhibited any attempts to formulate a campaign plan. It is the fourth but it is easily the most important. For a campaign to be successful there needs to be clarity of purpose. There needs also to be unity of command. In Northern Ireland, however closely we all worked together, there was always a triumvirate plus one at the command table: the politicians, the police and the Army, plus the security services. That is a simple description. The complex and more accurate description would be to include the multiplicity of other people and organisations who all thought they had a role to play in the direction of Northern Irish affairs, not the least of whom were the Americans and the Irish.

But let's stick with the simple model. Each of the three plus one at the top table had a perfectly proper but specific attitude to the handling of the problem. Each played its part to the best of its ability but the coordination was never what it should have been, especially between those responsible for the Government's efforts to revitalise the politics, the economy and the infrastructure of the Province, and those responsible for waging the war against the terrorist. That, as we all recognise, is a false distinction, because a counter-terrorist campaign is about forging all these things together into a cohesive whole.

In 1994 (that is to say a quarter of a century after the start of it all), the Northern Ireland Office produced a document called *Alignment Between the Security Forces and Civil Government*. The document referred to 'the Government's holistic strategy for defeating terrorism' and reinforced the idea with these words:

> It is therefore axiomatic that the policies or actions of the security forces and the agencies of civil government should complement and reinforce each other to the maximum extent possible.

Curiously, it is reported in today's media that, in referring to the struggles against international terrorism, the Home Secretary, Dr John Reid, said:

> The struggle has, of course, to be conducted at the level of trade, aid, diplomacy, finance and politics, which addresses the underlying drivers of impoverishment or perceptions of injustice.[4]

So the right words are being said now, as they were 12 years ago in Northern Ireland. However, despite the encouraging sentiments, not once did I ever attend, or hear of, a meeting which included representatives of all those who might collectively have been said to be responsible for the countering of terrorism.

Perhaps because of that it is possible to make my point with two examples. I vividly remember the atrocious standards of housing in many parts of Belfast in those early days; they alone were enough to give people a genuine sense of grievance, leave alone the unemployment and discrimination. The Government very properly embarked on a major building programme both to replace unfit housing and to provide houses for people from one community or another who had been forced out of their homes in a process that would have been called ethnic cleansing if the

---

4   ITN 2006.

phrase had been in use then. But no one in the housing world saw fit to ask the police or the Army about the layout of the new estates. So all too often they were laid out in such a way that there was only one way in and out, making it very easy for patrols to be spotted and avoided or, worse, for patrols to be ambushed. Many of them became perfect havens for terrorist activity. This was not coherent.

The other example concerns the Housing Executive, which was responsible for allocating and maintaining state-owned housing. It was a good operation and its maintenance was carried out by an in-house team of plumbers, glaziers and so on. Then, in the early 1990s, the decision was taken to dispense with the in-house maintenance; it was judged to be cheaper to put the work out to contract. Whether or not this was a good idea administratively is neither here nor there. The point is that this gave the IRA an opportunity. Without going into the details, they were able to set up a scheme that allowed them to get to the scene of a repair before the contractors. They were able to fix a broken window and decline payment in return for 'cooperation' when the need arose. A little consultation about this might have avoided handing this nice advantage to the terrorist.

So the various strands marched forward, but not always hand in hand. Could this have been solved by appointing a supremo? Yes, but it would not have been possible in the UK, or any Western democracy for that matter. Why? The police, servants of the law and the people, are not constitutionally amenable to the orders of politicians. So a politician or political appointee could not be the supremo.

Because this was all treated as a matter of law and order, the police were in charge; the Army was in support. So the supremo could not be a soldier either; much less an official from the security services.

So why not make the Chief Constable the supremo? Obviously the politicians in their turn were not going to do what *he* told *them* to do. And even without that insurmountable problem to overcome, it seems to me quite unlikely that the police could ever have been the source for a well-crafted long-term campaign plan.

I do not mean this rudely or with any sense of criticism. It is simply a reflection of what it is that the police do. They deter crime and they react when a crime is committed. The deterrence element obviously involves a bit of forward planning; the gathering of criminal intelligence and crime prevention initiatives are all part of trying to keep a step ahead of the criminal. But the essence of their work is catching the criminal *in flagrante*, or catching him after his crime has been committed. The idea of long-term campaign planning is not relevant to their work.

I am not of course implying that the police do not think ahead when it comes to matters such as procuring equipment, or laying down their network of police stations, or crime prevention procedures and so on. But that is not the same thing as campaign planning.

I might clinch the point by summarising, perhaps unfairly, what was stated as being the Chief Constable's strategy in the early 1990s:

1. to reduce the incidence of terrorism;
2. to enhance the relationship between the police and all sections of the community by increasing public confidence and support;
3. to reduce the incidence and enhance the detection of non-terrorist crime;
4. to reduce the incidence of road traffic accidents;
5. to maintain public order;
6. to progress the support priorities of the force in order to enhance our operational effectiveness.

This is not a strategy in the way we would recognise one.

So for all these reasons, the Northern Ireland operation lacked from start to finish anything that might reasonably have been called a campaign plan. And I think that I have persuaded myself, at any rate, that that was inevitable; and it may not even have been a mistake. What certainly *was* a mistake was the absence until very late on of any document that could have earned the accolade of being described as a high-level directive.

Here I may be in danger of conceit, but the point I have to make is worth the risk. I am an early graduate of the Higher Command and Staff Course (HCSC) established under the direction of the great Field Marshal Bagnall to raise the game of senior officers in all three Services when it came to the conduct of high-level operations. Late onto the scene though it was, it was, and no doubt remains, a remarkable course which has unquestionably shaped the conduct and outcome of British campaigns from the First Gulf War to the present day.

Having been a student on the third course I then spent two happy and educationally exceptional years running the course. So when I then proceeded, full of operational and doctrinal verve, to take command of 39 Infantry Brigade in Belfast, I was determined to put into practice what I had been learning and teaching for the last two years.

I had no sooner sat down behind my desk than I asked the chief of staff to produce my orders, by which I meant the orders that I had from the GOC. He looked rather startled and departed at speed. Much later he shamefacedly returned literally blowing dust off a document called the Northern Ireland Operations Order.

It was definitely a pre-HCSC document for it instructed me and the other brigade commanders to do specific tasks, down to providing four men and an NCO to guard the entrance to the British Telecom exchange building in the heart of Belfast. There was no hint of the context or of the effects that we were supposed to be achieving. In the written document there was no way of knowing whether, for example, we should be conciliatory or uncompromising in our activities, much less what was the ultimate aim.

In the same vein, I inherited a set of brigade orders for the units under my command that were themselves a mere list of tasks, despite my predecessor in command having been a graduate of course No. 2. This is not the place to go into the detail of the directive that I produced, but for the first time there was a written document that made it perfectly clear why we were doing the work, what effect we were trying to achieve, and in what frame of mind we should do our business.

In due course the Headquarters produced something similar and from then until the end of the campaign each successive GOC produced, in one form or another, a directive that actually and genuinely influenced the way that everyone down to individual members of foot patrols carried out their duties.

The appearance of these directives was an important element in the process of lifting the eyes from the day-to-day tactical issues and taking a longer view more consistent with the concept, if not the reality, of a campaign plan. It was, of course, a move in the right direction, but did little to remove the curious fact that the British Army's longest ever continuous campaign has been conducted without a plan!

And here I revert to a question that I left hanging earlier. Was a fancy campaign plan necessary to achieving the aim? Obviously not, because the aim has been achieved, all bar a few more decibels of political shouting. Could it have been achieved better and quicker with a campaign plan? Who knows, but I think that if the whole effort had been better coordinated from the early days we might just have got there a bit sooner.

And where is *there*? This is how I articulated *there*, or the end state in other words, back in 2001:

The following three conditions constitute the military end state:

- The Police no longer routinely require military support.
- Our own protective security measures are broadly equivalent to those in force elsewhere in the United Kingdom.
- Northern Ireland ceases to be an independent command and is absorbed in all respects into LAND Command.[5]

This is not very exciting or punchy and it certainly does not set the blood flowing in eager anticipation but it is the reality. And it is consistent with, but much more limited than, the *political* end state (although no-one in the Northern Ireland Office is likely to call it that). The *political* end state is the establishment of a climate in Northern Ireland in which: peaceful political development can prosper; terrorism has been isolated and eradicated; and all the security, political, economic, cultural and social measures as anticipated in the spirit of the Belfast (or Good Friday) Agreement[6] have been brought into effect.

So even if we had no plan we at least knew eventually where we were trying to go.

In offering some reflections on the exercise of higher command in the particular circumstances of the campaign in Northern Ireland, I am certain that there are aspects that are applicable elsewhere but I do not claim to articulate a blueprint for command in all campaigns, whether counter-terrorist or not.

I suppose that the first thing that strikes me as I look back on my time as GOC is that the whole experience was a remarkable blur of dealing with prime ministers and private soldiers, of politics and soldiering, of ceremony and eating for Britain, of the management of a top-level budget and steadying the troops in the midst of some of the most vicious rioting ever seen in the Province, of dealing with the firemen's strike and foot and mouth in the context of a continuing counter-terrorist operation, of helicopter flights to the scenes of incidents and trips in RAF executive jets to London for consultations, of directing covert operations and inspecting driver training in the North Irish Horse, a Territorial Army squadron entirely unconnected with the operation but nevertheless under command.

Shortly after I took over as GOC I wrote a long appreciation and statement of intent for my commanders. It included these words:

As GOC my first operational responsibility is to focus on the political/civil power/military interface, providing advice upwards (to NIO and MOD) and sideways (to the Chief Constable and Security Services). It is here that I expect to devote the largest slice of my personal effort.

Non-operationally I shall be devoting further significant time to my duties as a Top Level Budget holder and member of the Executive Committee of the Army Board.

---

5   LAND Command is the peacetime headquarters of the British Army, based in Wilton outside Salisbury during this period.

6   The Belfast Agreement was signed on 10 April 1998 between the British and Irish governments and was endorsed by Northern Ireland's political parties. It established the Northern Ireland Assembly and played a major part in political development in Northern Ireland.

As to my style of command, this is not a theatre that requires the urgent decisiveness of a Slim or a Guderian (although one hopes that this will be forthcoming should it be required). Instead we have the opportunity at the operational level to consult and debate. I expect all of you to contribute freely and originally to a process which will conclude (please note) with direction and clear orders from me that will certainly *not* be the subject of further debate!

As for you, the brigade and force troop commanders, on your shoulders rests the detailed responsibility for the conduct of tactical operations within your areas based on the several orders and directives that you receive from me. You are not to hesitate to ask for advice or a second opinion when you want them and I shall not hesitate to offer both when I think you need them! Although I shall tend to leave matters of detail to you, I shall not hesitate to enquire about minutiae, and to issue orders as a consequence, when something catches my eye.

Aspects of some of these things will resurface in the pages that follow, but I think that this gives a flavour of what might be called a command style suitable to counter-terrorism.

The next and very significant reflection is that although, like the Biblical centurion, I was completely in charge of all those Navy, Army and Air Force personnel under my authority, I was not completely in charge of what they and I could actually do operationally. I was not free to give orders, deploy troops or conduct operations as I might have done if I had been a genuinely independent commander. There were three things that very particularly constrained my independence of action.

In 1977, police primacy was reintroduced in Northern Ireland. Until then the Army had run counter-terrorist and civil disorder operations with the police in support. By 1977, the police were judged to be more than ready to resume their full responsibilities. This was in any case necessary and logical since it was a matter of Government policy that acts of terrorism and their perpetrators should be treated under criminal law, as opposed to the laws of war or indeed martial law.

So police primacy was reintroduced and this had the interesting effect of pushing the Army into a supporting role. Army officers are selected, and subsequently promoted, on the basis, amongst other things, of their willingness, indeed ambition, to take charge of things. Without question, one of the most difficult things to do for us commanders at all levels was to come to terms with the reality that we, in effect, could do nothing in operational terms without it being agreed by our police counterparts. In fact, most of us were very good at dealing with this strange requirement, but up and down the chain of command there were more than enough examples over the years of tension, and sometimes outright warfare, between police and Army commanders unable or unwilling to work with the situation in which they found themselves. Deferring to another authority has the potential to present problems for go-ahead soldiers who expect to be in charge, but it is a measure of the organisational and human sophistication of the whole enterprise that both parties to this extraordinary, perhaps unique, partnership became entirely comfortable working within its spirit.

As GOC I was quite clear that it was my duty to have a trouble-free relationship with the Chief Constable, partly because in that way our work would be done better together, and partly because I had no doubt that if *we* were seen to be getting on together the chances were that everyone else would get on as well. I suppose there was something akin to dealing with coalitions in other environments.

In fact I was extremely lucky for I had the legendary Ronnie Flanagan as my opposite number for most of my time in command; we had known each other for years and we had no difficulty in working together. But even we had our disagreements and I would like to give a flavour of one of them, simply to illustrate further the sort of things that a GOC had to concern himself with.

It is no secret that the Army ran undercover operations throughout the campaign. They were ever more closely tied in with the Special Branch, and indeed in the latter years the Special Branch ran the show. There is no doubt in my mind that without these operations a great many more terrorist atrocities would have been committed.

By the time I arrived on the scene it was clear that for many reasons there was a growing anxiety about these covert military operations on political and presentational grounds. The Chief Constable wanted the operations to cease; so did I, actually. But we differed about when. No commander can do anything sensible without intelligence; I was happy for our activities to cease if the intelligence they provided could be guaranteed from other sources, the police and security services. The moment I had the guarantee was the moment I would start to wind up the operations. In point of fact, for various good reasons, that guarantee was never forthcoming in my time and so the operations continued. I realise that some of that may all seem a little Delphic but it provides the flavour of the sort of 'coalition' negotiation that the GOC had to engage in.

The second inhibition of my freedom of action was the role of the politician, and this of course chimes exactly with the experience of any high-level commander in any theatre. In Northern Ireland, the interaction between military commander and political master was very intimate, not least of all because we both lived on the job. It was as if, in Iraq for example, the Secretary of State for Defence or, even worse, the Prime Minister, were permanently resident in Basra. It is of course the politician's job to worry about the political consequences of one action or another. Senior commanders, though, are not exercising their duties properly if they too do not understand and take into some account the political consequences of their actions. But in Northern Ireland this phenomenon was supercharged because hardly anything that happened in a military sense was immune from the probability of it being manipulated politically in one way or another.

There were places, for instance, where we knew weapons were cached, but these were places that under no circumstances could have been searched without handing the opposition a propaganda gift. There were military bases that no longer satisfied a military need but which we could not vacate because the howls of protest from one section of the community would have lost us more politically than we would have gained militarily. And so on. The net result was that I probably found myself informing the Secretary of State of things that were being planned far more than I might have done under more remote circumstances.

And the third inhibition was the law. Do not misunderstand me – I am not suggesting that this was a bad or unfortunate thing; nor am I suggesting, I hope, that it was only the law that prevented me and others from doing things we would otherwise have done without a second thought. And, of course, all commanders everywhere operate in a legal framework, whether it is domestic or international law or the Geneva Convention. So I am saying nothing startling here. But a campaign of this kind, in our country, imposed, I think, far more restrictions on the freedom of military action than would be applicable elsewhere. The net result was, quite simply, terrorists walking free who might otherwise not have been. And this must have had the effect of prolonging the whole affair. Or did it?

I would now like to outline a typical day in the life of a GOC in Northern Ireland. It is not of course exactly typical because I have constructed this day by conflating into it a number of activities that did not necessarily all materialise simultaneously. The day begins with a staff briefing on what has happened in the last 24 hours and of what they expect to happen in the next 24 hours, both administratively and operationally. In my time this was usually routine stuff, but it served to focus the mind before the day's work.

Then to Stormont for one of the regular Security Policy Meetings, chaired by the Secretary of State. These usually happened once a month. Here we would agree the intelligence picture and inform Ministers of our joint police and Army plans for dealing with the marching season or whatever else was the issue of the day. You would have thought that this would have all been high-level, 'grown up' sort of talk, but sometimes details intruded. I remember, for example, fielding a question about some work we were doing on one of the towers in south Armagh. We were, in fact, installing a new and very powerful surveillance gadget at a time when any enhancement to the towers was bound to stir up trouble. I had given orders that work could only proceed if it was not noticed by the terrorists and that, if it were (as I suspected it would be), we would say that it was nothing more sinister than a temporary water tank while repairs were carried out on the main system. Needless to say, despite all precautions this new work was indeed spotted and immediate protests were made by Sinn Fein. Hence the ministerial enquiry. And why this high-level interest in something so very tactical? Precisely, of course, because of the political implications of practically everything that we did, even down to the actions of every private soldier on patrol.

The meeting over, I have a quiet moment or two with the Director and Coordinator of Intelligence (in fact a misnomer, not quite in the same league as the Holy Roman Emperor, but a misnomer nonetheless). These were opportunities to hear more of what lay behind the assessments produced at the meeting itself. One of the frustrations of command in Northern Ireland was that there were several different sources of information and intelligence, and even in the latter years it could never have been said that information flowed freely and completely between all the different agencies. So it was a constant duty to chat up everyone in the hope of getting as much background as possible.

This done, I climb into my helicopter, known throughout the theatre as Gazelle 1; it meant that it was impossible to sneak up on anyone for a surprise and perhaps unwelcome visit! Usually these trips were to battalion locations round the Province, but often they were to the scene of some incident or other.

During the course of my military education, spread over many years, one of the much-argued topics was to do with the proper place on the battlefield for a senior commander. In modern warfare the dilemma was whether to be well forward at the point of crisis, Rommel-style, or to be in the headquarters where all the communications were. This dilemma did not apply in Northern Ireland (nor perhaps in any counter-terrorist campaign) because the nature of operations was such that once the incident had occurred the manner of dealing with it was more or less routine; there were set tactics and procedures which were familiar to everyone. There wasn't much that a commander could contribute by remaining in his headquarters, except staying mercifully out of the way.

But actually what he *could* contribute was comradely interest. On this mythical day in question I fly in marginal weather to a remote and very wet part of Tyrone where a large mortar has been intercepted on its way to a target. The circumstances demand that great care is taken in defusing the device; the site has to be staked out for more than three days. It seems only right to go out and see how the men are getting on. But unlike some other senior officers that I have come across before, I do not pay much attention to the tactics; that is their affair and they know their business. I am deliberately more interested in the humanity of it.

Unlike these men I am able to head for home when I like, and so back to the office for a planning session on the towers. The towers consisted of a chain of fortified observation posts chiefly round south Armagh but also in Belfast and Londonderry. They no doubt served a purpose when they were built, but they eventually became a political and military millstone. Politically they provided the republican axis with a wonderful propaganda tool with which to beat the British. The towers were undoubtedly intimidating and dominating; they were always shown to visiting republican sympathizers and TV crews who then meekly contributed to the propaganda effect. On the other side of the political divide, the towers were seen as powerful symbols of the Government's resolve to protect the unionist minorities in the deep green areas. So any mention of their removal drew instant high-level political complaint.

Politically there was no easy solution. And militarily they presented me with my biggest worry. In the first place they did something that goes against the grain for a force that is capable of manoeuvring: they tied quite large numbers of troops to fixed positions; the terrorist knew exactly where they were. That was bad tactics and bad use of manpower.

But more importantly they were quite vulnerable to attack, and indeed they were often assaulted by large crowds of people armed with every sort of weapon short of firearms. On at least two occasions the small garrisons came close to being overrun. That was bad enough, but there was an interesting twist.

As we began the slow process of removing these towers one by one (it took over five years to do the job in the end), I started to wonder what we would do if one of the towers was destroyed by a mortar attack. It was quite feasible. If that had in fact happened we would have been in a fix because here we were taking the towers down, but in my view we could not possibly leave it at that. We would have had to reoccupy and rebuild, otherwise we would have been accused of being driven off by the terrorists. Would we have been allowed politically to rebuild? Fortunately we never had to answer the question and the purpose of this planning session was to do everything we could to reduce the risk of having to do so to the minimum.

There is a little coda to this tale. At one stage I had become so exasperated by the assaults on the towers that I said to the Secretary of State that, if the republicans thought that they would get us to take the towers down more quickly by attacking them, they were very mistaken. I suggested to him that when he next spoke to Gerry Adams he should make that point. It is probably no more than a coincidence, but shortly afterwards the attacks ceased.

Towers settled, I turn my attention to budgets, quarterly returns to the MOD with forecasts of outturns and other highly military matters, the sort of things that really attracted us into the Army in the first place! The planned working day ends with the hearing of a grievance brought by a civil servant against another; if I were to retell the story it would not be believed.

And then, just as I set off for home, a drink and a bath, the hotline from London flashes red. They want to take most of my helicopters away because apparently they are needed in the Balkans and Afghanistan. This was the start of a protracted struggle whose greatest interest for me was that this was a small piece of military *strategy* at work. The Armed Forces had a fixed number of helicopters. There were worldwide demands that exceeded those numbers. It was my job to argue my case; it was the job of the fellows in the Balkans and elsewhere to argue theirs. And it was the job of those in London to make a military strategic decision. It was interesting to be involved in this albeit small beer example of decision-making at the military strategic level.

My fanciful day comes to an end. When, next year, the campaign is officially declared to be over, we might ask the question: who won? Yet this is the wrong question, and is probably not a legitimate question for *any* counter-terrorism campaign.

For no one wins in an affair of this kind. Nearly 3,700 people, 3,665 to be precise, died as a result of the Troubles. This figure includes 709 soldiers and 303 policemen. It is worth just noting, perhaps, that the worst single year for Army deaths was 1972, when 134 men were lost in action, a figure not yet reached after four years of Iraq and Afghanistan combined.

It is highly questionable whether it was necessary that all these people should die to achieve the undoubted improvements to the social, economic and political scene in the Province. The Province remains part of the United Kingdom; extreme counter-state violence has disappeared from the agenda. But that is merely returning things to what they should have been all the time, and does not in my view qualify for the word victory, in the same way that it can be applied to VE Day at the end of the Second World War.

Perhaps if anything or anyone has won it is the human spirit, it is the rule of law, it is the determination to ensure that violent minorities who do not have the spirit of democracy sufficiently within them to accept the wishes of the majority are held at bay. If any sort of victory has been achieved it is the victory of an ordered society over anarchy and chaos. Although individuals won many a George Cross and other prestigious gallantry awards, this victory was not the stuff of battle honours and tales of great sweeping battles, nor is it the basis for renown amongst the pantheon of generalship. But at least it is duty done.

Chapter 3
Command of Kosovo Force 1999

Mike Jackson – 8 February 2006

In 1992 a young American academic, Francis Fukuyama, earnestly pronounced 'The End of History', prophesying the inexorable spread of Western liberal democracy throughout the world.[1] Even those who judged this theory naïve had not predicted the eruption of primitive ethnic struggle within Europe itself. It rapidly became clear that the Cold War had contained ancient tensions, not destroyed them. Well might one Balkan specialist entitle his book *The Rebirth of History*.[2]

In early 1997 I found myself commanding the Allied Command Europe Rapid Reaction Corps, or ARRC, in Reindahlen, Germany. Its headquarters is under operational command of the Supreme Allied Commander, Europe (SACEUR), and I therefore reported directly to General Wesley 'Wes' Clark. In May 1998, at SACEUR's annual conference, Clark told his key subordinates: 'things are beginning to hot up in Kosovo, NATO may have to intervene.'

For years, informed observers had warned of a potential bloodbath in Kosovo. This was where the breakup of Yugoslavia would reach its climax. Serbs believe Kosovo is the homeland of their nation. In 1389 they had fought the Ottomans at the battle of Kosovo Polje, suffering a heroic defeat that looms large in national mythology. Serbs see themselves as Christians in the front line of the millennium-long struggle with Islam. Kosovo was part of the Ottoman Empire for more than 500 years, before being reconquered by Serbia in the early twentieth century. At the end of the First World War, Kosovo became part of the new kingdom of Yugoslavia. Under Tito's post-war Communist rule, it became a province of Serbia, but nevertheless Kosovo enjoyed a degree of autonomy and ethnic tensions were kept in check.

Kosovo is also important to the Albanians. The proportion of ethnic Albanians in Kosovo had increased steadily for many decades, and by the late 1990s had reached almost 90 per cent. Yet despite the demographic predominance of Albanian Kosovars, most official positions were taken by Serbs, who dominated the security forces in particular. Kosovo was ruled as if it were a Serb colony. Ethnic Albanians in Kosovo have both a different language and religion from the Serbs.

When Milošević became President in 1989, he began stripping Kosovo of its autonomy. The result was to stimulate a movement for Kosovan independence. For some years in the 1990s, Albanian Kosovars maintained their own parallel administrative structures under the benign leadership of Ibrahim Rugova, advocating non-violent resistance. But not all were content with this approach; in the mid-1990s the Kosovo Liberation Army (KLA) was formed, and in 1997–1998 began a guerrilla campaign against Serb security forces.

The KLA received support from Albania itself and from ethnic Albanians abroad, particularly in the USA, and by the summer of 1998 claimed to have 30,000 men under arms. Clashes between the KLA and the Serb security forces intensified that autumn. A pattern began of KLA attacks and heavy-handed Serb reprisals. Ethnic Albanians fled the security forces; by autumn, there were estimated to be several hundred thousand internal refugees living in the woods, and the prospect

---

1   Fukuyama 1989.
2   Glenny 1990.

of a humanitarian disaster loomed. Richard Holbrooke warned Milošević against repression in Kosovo and allowed himself to be photographed alongside KLA fighters, indicating US support for the KLA. On 23 September the UN adopted Security Council Resolution 1199 calling for a ceasefire and dialogue between the warring parties. It also called for a withdrawal of Serb security forces used for repression, particularly the Serb Army, still then known as the Vojska Jugoslavije (VJ), and the Serb special police (MUP).

Back in Rheindahlen, we tracked these developments closely as the odds began to shorten on an ARRC deployment to Kosovo. We carried out a series of planning exercises, from which emerged a clear concept of the ideal composition and structure of a peace implementation force. We decided, prior to entry into Kosovo, that our in-theatre headquarters should be sited near the Macedonian capital Skopje, only about ten miles from the Kosovo border. Our line of communication would be from the Greek port of Thessaloniki, about 150 miles to the south, connected by a good road and a railway line. There were political difficulties, in that there was tension between Greece and Macedonia – not least over the name 'Macedonia' – but this was the only sensible supply route. The alternative through Albania, although shorter, was less attractive because of inadequate ports and a poor road network.

In October, Holbrooke visited Milošević, and came back with a deal – oral, not committed to paper. Faced with the threat of NATO air strikes, Milošević offered concessions, and allowed a 2,000-strong force of unarmed observers into Kosovo, known as the Kosovo Verification Mission (KVM). We had little faith this deal would outlast the winter. We sent in a reconnaissance party, disguised as members of KVM, who provided us with intelligence reports, both political and military.

In fact there was never a complete ceasefire, and fighting intensified towards the end of the year. NATO deployed 1,800 troops to Kumanovo in northern Macedonia, ready to extract the KVM from Kosovo at short notice if they seemed threatened.

In mid-January 1999, reports of a massacre of some 45 ethnic Albanians by Serb security forces in the Kosovo village of Račak evoked memories of Srebrenica and prompted calls for NATO intervention. Talks between Serbs and Kosovar Albanians, organised by the so-called 'Contact Group' of France, Germany, Italy, Russia, the UK and the United States, took place at Rambouillet, near Paris. The proposed agreement provided for an independent military implementation force under NATO auspices to compel compliance.

By then I had visited Macedonia several times. The plan was for the ARRC to integrate the various scattered forces there under a single unified NATO command known as KFOR (Kosovo Force). KFOR's outline mission at this stage was to provide stability in Kosovo following a political settlement, prevent any further outbreak of fighting, and ensure the return of all refugees once the Serbs had withdrawn.

By mid-March 1999, Headquarters ARRC was established at the Gazela Shoe Factory in Skopje, and was in the process of coordinating the various national contingents already in Macedonia. At this stage there was still a hope of a diplomatic solution, even though Serb negotiators at Rambouillet had refused to sign the agreement. Meanwhile, Serbian security forces in Kosovo increased their attacks.

The crisis was seen as a test of Europe's ability to deal with problems 'in its own backyard'. It threatened the stability of several western European governments, whose ruling parties were deeply divided on the issue. For them, the decision to take military action against Serbia was a tough one, but Milošević's unacceptable actions left them with no alternative. Grim stories of ethnic cleansing emerged from Kosovo in a steady stream. The KVM was ordered to withdraw because of the worsening security situation. Western politicians began to use the term 'genocide' to describe what was happening there.

On 24 March, NATO air strikes began. Bombing dragged on for 78 days, and during this period we in the ARRC were in a supporting role, almost spectators. At first we had only a few thousand troops scattered across northern Macedonia, but later the force grew into five multinational brigades led respectively by France, Germany, Italy, the UK and the USA. As COMKFOR, my immediate superior officer was US Navy Admiral Jim Ellis, NATO's Commander in Chief for Southern Europe, who in turn reported directly to SACEUR. In practice, Wes Clark often bypassed Jim Ellis and dealt directly with me, which was frustrating for both of us.

SACEUR was under a lot of pressure. I observed Clark each morning on the video conference (VTC) held twice daily among all NATO centres involved in the Balkan operation. He seemed tired already, not helped by having to work Washington as well as European hours. We knew Wes was having trouble with his superiors at the Pentagon, many of whom saw little reason for America to become involved in Kosovo. President Clinton's administration had shown itself extremely reluctant to commit ground troops against the Serbs. But this seemed to make Wes all the more determined. At first he argued that bombing would bring the Serbs to heel. 'I know Milošević', he would say, time after time. It was a peculiarity of the Kosovo War that all the main protagonists had met beforehand.

My old friend General Rupert Smith was by now Clark's deputy. He and I spoke at least once a day. Rupert was a moderating influence on Wes, as Jeremy Mackenzie had been before him.

The last of the Red Cross personnel to leave Kosovo painted a grim picture of a breakdown in law and order, with rape, executions and looting taking place on the streets of Priština. As the fighting worsened, the prospect of a humanitarian disaster loomed once more. Hundreds of thousands of displaced persons or those fearing for their safety were making their way west and south to the mountainous border regions, hoping to cross into Albania or Macedonia. Others were loaded on trains by the Serb security forces and shunted to the Macedonian border, where they had to cross on foot. At the height of the crisis, it was estimated that 750,000 people, approximately one-third of the entire population, had fled Kosovo. The refugees came in waves, sometimes 5,000 or more in a day, completely overwhelming the small number of personnel from the UN High Commission for Refugees on hand to provide them with food or shelter. Refugee assistance was not, of course, part of KFOR's mission. But we had to respond – both on humanitarian grounds and to deny Milošević his political goal: the fall of the Macedonian Government.

KFOR did most of the spadework, literally and metaphorically, of establishing refugee camps, and we ran them until UNHCR and the various NGOs got their act together. The lion's share of the administrative support for the refugee crisis was taken by the British 101 Logistic Brigade under the inspired leadership of Brigadier Tim Cross. Some of the relief professionals took exception to the military being involved in the humanitarian effort, but this was a case of needs must.

The Macedonian Government allowed the refugees across the border reluctantly, fearing the effect of adding to their own significant Albanian minority. Like us, they recognised ethnic cleansing was Milošević's tactic to destabilise their Government. The huge numbers of refugees formed a substantial addition to Macedonia's Albanian population, already around 30 per cent of the total. At the beginning of the refugee crisis the Macedonians had denied them entry, confining them to the no-man's land between the two countries where they squatted on the ground, exhausted. Under pressure from international opinion, the Macedonian Government relented and allowed the refugees in, restricting them to camps near the border.

My planning team started looking at options for a forced entry into Kosovo if all other options failed. This had to be done discreetly, as it was politically extremely sensitive. For one thing, NATO rules did not permit us to start formal planning without prior authorisation of the North Atlantic Council. For another, the Macedonian Government would not countenance their territory being used as a base for an invasion; at least, not publicly. A ground offensive was anyway a daunting prospect, given the formidable size of the Serb Army and the challenging terrain. We reckoned we would need at least three corps of 50,000 each. Even with those numbers, and complete command of the air, it would still be difficult. There were only a few routes into Kosovo, all easily blocked. And there was little political support for a ground war. When Clark began to argue for a ground offensive against the Serbs, he found himself cold-shouldered in Washington and denied access to the President.

There was a great deal to be done while we waited for the bombing campaign to force Milošević to concede, not least the complex task of coordinating the disparate national forces into one effective fighting formation. We also steadily built up strength as new units and supplies arrived by road, rail or air. We needed to keep our plans under constant review to take account of rapidly changing circumstances. The refugee relief effort complicated all of this. I had to work hard to keep the Macedonians on side. There were also problems with the Greeks: over 90 per cent of the population opposed bombing another Orthodox country, and once bombing began there was a succession of demonstrations and other difficulties. We relied on the Greek port of Thessaloniki for our line of communication, and I had a number of meetings with concerned Greek officials worried that public unrest would affect our logistics.

By now, NATO's objectives had simplified to sound-bites: Serbs out, NATO in, refugees back. NATO's strategy, as championed by Clark, had been to bomb the Serbs into backing down. But this was taking a long time to work. Bombing continued for more than two months with little sign that the Serbs were about to capitulate. Overall, NATO aircraft flew more than 38,000 combat missions with surprisingly little effect on Serb military capability, as we discovered when we eventually occupied Kosovo: there were hardly any burned-out tank hulks. There was also, rightly, much sensitivity about 'collateral damage'. Pilots often found their targets changed after they had taken off on a mission.

Inevitably, there were mistakes. Early in May, NATO aircraft attacked and largely destroyed a Kosovar refugee convoy, mistaking it for a convoy of Serb military vehicles and killing the very people it set out to protect. Then NATO in error bombed the Chinese Embassy in Belgrade, prompting a diplomatic uproar.

But there was a sense that the end-game might be in sight. Britain, ever on the front foot, decided to make the necessary arrangements to reinforce its existing contingent, then still largely based on 4 Armoured Brigade. In the event, Headquarters 3 Division under Major General Richard Dannatt with 5 Airborne Brigade deployed as reinforcements.

Late in May, Viktor Chernomyrdin, President Yeltsin's special envoy to Serbia, issued a stark warning to the West: 'The world has never in this decade been so close to the brink of nuclear war. I appeal to NATO leaders to show the courage to suspend the air raids … it is impossible to talk with bombs falling.' Unless bombing stopped soon, he warned, he would advise Russia's President to suspend Russian participation in the negotiating process, put an end to all military/technical agreements with the West, delay ratification of the SALT II arms reduction agreement and use Russia's veto to block any UN Security Council Resolution on Yugoslavia.

This was a chilling statement, but there was an element of bluster in it. The Russians felt protective towards their fellow Slavs and extremely sensitive about NATO's attack on a former Communist country. Nevertheless, they recognised the need to end the fighting in Kosovo. On behalf of the G8 group of industrialised nations, they pressured the Serbs to compromise.

On 2 June Milošević received Chernomyrdin and Finland's President Ahtisaari in Belgrade. Later that day Milošević announced he would withdraw all military and paramilitary forces from Kosovo, a decision ratified the following day by the Serb Parliament. Even today, it's still unclear why Milošević backed down, but one can surmise: the bombing campaign, now including strategic targets in Serbia, was at last really hurting Milošević and his coterie; NATO had not splintered under the political strains of going to war against his country; the threat of an eventual ground attack was known to him; Russia had made it clear he would be on his own; and on 27 May he had been indicted by the International Criminal Tribunal for the former Yugoslavia (ICTY) at The Hague for crimes against humanity in Kosovo.

The agreement provided for an international security force 'with substantial NATO participation under unified command and control'. This implied a unified NATO chain of command, under the political direction of the North Atlantic Council. Talks were taking place in Moscow about the involvement of Russian forces. In Bosnia, a Russian brigade was deployed as part of IFOR/SFOR within the American Sector. This was the model we were keen to adopt in Kosovo, but it was by no means certain that the Russians would go along with it.

Much debate followed about the wording of the so-called Military Technical Agreement (MTA) to determine the arrangements between withdrawing Serb security forces and the incoming KFOR. Our first meeting with Serbs was on 5 June, to finalise the details. Brigadier Jonathan Bailey was dispatched to the border to set up a meeting with Serb representatives the following morning at the Café Europa, a small, run-down establishment 500 yards inside the Macedonian border.

The demeanour of the Serb delegation was resigned. They were obviously depressed. I was determined not to show any hint of triumphalism on our part. The atmosphere was workmanlike and professional. One sensed the Serbs didn't really understand why we were there. As one said to me, 'you are an honourable officer, a general from Britain, a fine country, our allies in two world wars. Of course we in the Serb Army will treat you with honour. But Albania is not a proper country. The Albanians are not a proper people. There is no requirement to treat them with honour.'

On our side of the table I had my own small team: Mike Venables, an MOD civil servant who was my political adviser; US Air Force three-star general Robert H. Fogelsong, representing US national interests; Admiral Kaskeala, a Finn who had accompanied President Ahtisaari to Belgrade; and my Military Assistant, James Everard.

The Serbian delegation had spent the night driving down from Belgrade and didn't have the latest version of the MTA. So we had to go through it again, line by line. It was slow, ponderous work. The Serbs were insisting on a UN Security Council Resolution. It soon became clear the delegation was not empowered to negotiate significant changes to the MTA without authority from Belgrade.

This set the tone for the next five days of exhausting and frustrating negotiation. One meeting broke up after only 14 minutes. The Serbs had a number of concerns. I had some sympathy with them. Once they withdrew their security forces, the Serb minority in Kosovo would be unprotected. After all that had happened in Kosovo in the past year or so, one could well imagine Albanian reprisals on Serbs remaining there.

It was very difficult to negotiate when amended drafts of the MTA kept arriving in short order. I was aware that there was a lot of talking going on, but it seemed to me all that should have been done before I was asked to start negotiating with the Serbs. But we knew what we were trying to achieve. The aim was to choreograph several different sequenced events: first, the text of a Security Council Resolution had to be approved by the G8; then the MTA had to be agreed and signed; then a verifiable withdrawal had to be agreed which would bring an end to the bombing; then the Security Council Resolution had to be ratified – only then would KFOR go into Kosovo. The MTA provided for phased Serb withdrawal from three designated zones of Kosovo, ending in complete withdrawal 11 days from signature. The concept was that we would enter the zones in phases as Serb forces withdrew.

At last, at 21.07 on Wednesday, 9 June 1999, we signed the agreement. We had been negotiating for more than a hundred hours.

Our daily routine at KFOR Headquarters began with a morning update at 08.00 hours, when 25 to 30 members of the command team would gather in the conference room in the Shoe Factory. The morning update on Friday, 11 June was good-humoured. We were all tired, but there was a feeling that at last all the ducks were lined up. The bombing campaign had been suspended and we had the authority of UN Security Council Resolution 1244, passed the previous evening. H-Hour was set for 05.00 hours the following day, Saturday, 12 June. I planned to spend the day visiting each of the six brigades that would be moving into Kosovo at dawn the next morning. I didn't know then all these plans were going to be overtaken by events.

The morning update was followed by the morning VTC. Talks taking place in Moscow between the Russians and the Americans were not going well. There was still no agreement about the command and control or the deployment area of any Russian contingent to KFOR. SACEUR was particularly concerned by reports that a Russian column in Bosnia was on the move.

At 10.34 we received confirmation that a Russian column of approximately 30 armoured vehicles had crossed the River Drina into Serbia, presumably headed for Kosovo. Interestingly, the Russian vehicles had 'KFOR' painted on their sides, indicating they were coming to take part in the peacekeeping mission as authorised by UN Security Council Resolution. But SHAPE's assessment was the Russians would try to secure the airfield at Priština, Kosovo's only airport, before delivering more troops by air from Russia. It looked like the Russians might be pre-empting us, establishing themselves on the ground prior to a possible partition of Kosovo. The column was expected at Priština by 15.00 hours. Clark phoned and gave me a warning order to secure the airfield before the Russians arrived.

I didn't like this idea one bit. This was only a warning order, to plan and prepare, and could not be executed without a confirmatory order. But if confirmed, it meant sending helicopter-borne troops into Serb-held territory where they could easily be isolated. We had already looked at a similar option – as part of KFOR's main force advance into Kosovo – but concluded it was too risky.

By going into Kosovo ahead of time we would be breaching our newly signed agreement with the Serbs, providing them with a pretext not to withdraw and perhaps to fight. Though our bombing campaign had damaged the Serbs' capability, their armed forces remained formidable, with well over 300 tanks in Kosovo alone. At the time, KFOR was comparatively small, only about 15,000 men in six brigades with 40-odd tanks. The airfield was only 35 miles or so from the border, but intelligence revealed the bridges and tunnels on the road through the narrow Kačanik defile into Kosovo had been prepared for demolition. If any were blocked or blown, we would have been in real difficulty. So even if we didn't have to fight our way in, it might be days or even weeks before we could relieve our soldiers at Priština overland. Moreover, there would be a serious risk of confrontation when the Russians arrived. They had played a key part in persuading the Serbs to withdraw from Kosovo, and we needed their continued participation to make the agreement stick.

Despite misgivings, I instructed my staff to prepare a plan to secure the airport with at least one battalion of heliborne troops. It was now 11.45. Our assessment was that a decision to launch the airfield operation needed to be taken by 14.00 hours at the latest, given the Russian convoy's estimated time of arrival of 15.00 hours.

At 13.15 hours I received a written order from Clark 'to move and occupy Priština Airfield'. But it contained a constraint. No move was to take place before Clark had approved a 'back-brief' of the operational plan. To 'use the long screwdriver' was characteristic of Clark, and in general I didn't much like this. To have your boss looking over your shoulder when you were already under pressure was asking for trouble. But in this instance it gave me another chance to make the case against the operation.

At 13.30 I received an intelligence re-assessment of the Russians' progress. The new estimate was that the column would not reach Priština until 18.00 hours. There seemed, moreover, to be no hard evidence that any military planes had left Russian airspace. These two pieces of information bought us a little more time. I telephoned Rupert Smith and ran through the logic behind my very grave reservations.

There was another potential problem with this order: the operation fell outside the terms of the UN Security Council Resolution, and so the commander of each national force was entitled to consult his superiors back home, and if the response was negative, he could decline to participate. Sure enough, ten minutes later the French played their 'red card'. Paris had conducted a risk assessment and decided to pull out. Earlier we had also contacted the American Brigade. They offered six Apache attack helicopters to support the operation, but no ground troops. 1 Para – now lined up in a cornfield close to the border on 15 minutes notice to go – was on its own. I suspected Richard Dannatt was holding the British national red card in his pocket, but as KFOR commander it would be a cop-out for me to rely on this. Since my judgement was so strongly against this operation I should be prepared to oppose it, even if it meant putting my own career on the line.

Clark called a video conference for 15.00 hours. This was obviously the decision point. I asked Richard Dannatt to attend. As we assembled in the conference room before the video camera, I was ready to resign. For the first time in almost 40 years in the Army I had been given an order I could not in principle accept. In a few minutes my career could be over. But Clark had a surprise in store. 'We are not now going to execute this option', he announced as the conference began. 'We will now wait to see if Yeltsin has lied to the President.' Clearly, there had been some communication between the two leaders and I didn't to have to resign.

We were back to Plan A: entry into Kosovo at first light the next morning.

At 05.05 Sky TV showed the first Chinooks flying 5 Airborne Brigade forward across the border into Kosovo. As the morning progressed, reports came in that the advance was going smoothly, though minefields and difficult terrain were delaying the French. We had expected to come under fire from scattered Serb units opposed to the order to pull back, but it seemed that there was very little resistance. I had to restrain 5 Airborne Brigade from confiscating weapons, which was not allowed by the terms of our agreement with the Serbs. Later in the day we received reports that Serb police and militia were coming under attack from the Kosovo Liberation Army. I tried to relay a message to the KLA leadership to get them to stop.

I emerged from updating Clark at the morning video conference to find a Russian colonel in full dress uniform, peaked cap and all, waiting for me. I was introduced to Colonel Gromov, the local military attaché in Skopje. He handed me a letter from the Russian Ministry of Defence, informing me the 'leading element of the Russian KFOR contingent' now controlled the airfield at Priština. This was confirmation that the Russian column in Priština wasn't just a rogue element of soldiers doing their own thing. They were part of 'the Russian KFOR contingent'. The letter was addressed to me by name as 'Commander, KFOR'. It seemed a significant acknowledgement. The Russians were saying they were willing to be part of what we were doing.

If Clark was thinking in these terms, he didn't show it. He wanted me to do all we could to prevent the Russians from 'creating facts on the ground'. He urged me to increase the tempo. He was planning to fly down to Skopje himself early the next morning. I re-jigged our plans, ordering 5 Airborne Brigade to push on towards the airport as quickly as possible. By mid-afternoon they had got there and Adrian Freer, the brigade commander, had established contact with the Russian commanding officer, who turned out to be a two-star general, a mark of the importance of this relatively small column in Russian eyes.

By 18.30 hours we had secured the 10-mile-long defile into Kosovo, and the leading British elements were closing on Priština itself. I flew to Priština Airport that evening to give a short press conference and to make contact with the Russians, to establish some kind of relationship. There I met General Viktor Zavarzin. My first impression was of a burly man who seemed slightly nervous. I greeted him in my rather rusty Russian, even though I had an interpreter with me. He was a bit frosty at first and pretty hard going, but I had a flask of whisky in my map pocket and relations warmed after that.

Clark was still obsessed by the threat of Russian troops invading the Serb enclaves, particularly in the north, and establishing de facto partition of Kosovo. To prevent this, he wanted the runway blocked by KFOR helicopters. He was convinced they intended to reinforce their troops at the airport. I failed to see the logic in this. We already controlled the airspace, so the Russians would have to run the NATO gauntlet if they wanted to fly in. Putting helicopters on the runway would simply confuse the situation, and provoke the Russians. Again I stressed that confrontation was not the answer. Russian support had been crucial in delivering the deal with the Serbs. They were major players and should have been treated as such. To have alienated them would have been counter-productive in both the short and long term.

Either Wes wasn't listening, or he wasn't convinced. It seemed he had agreed a common position with the NATO Secretary General, Javier Solana. Clark ordered me to block the runway one way or another. I don't mind admitting I was furious.

We had a serious discussion in private where I laid out my grave misgivings. Clark called Charles Guthrie, the Chief of Defence Staff in London, who fortunately supported me, as did Clark's boss, Hugh Shelton, the Chairman of the Joint Chiefs of Staff in Washington. However, Clark still insisted on giving me a direct order as SACEUR, and that if I didn't accept it I would have to resign, despite the risk of a confrontation with the Russians.

I suggested armoured vehicles would be better suited to blocking runways than helicopters, in the almost certain knowledge that the UK would decline such a provocative move. Clark agreed that vehicles would be preferable. I went out to pass the order for 4 Armoured Brigade to place a combat team on short notice to move to the airfield, knowing it would be referred for national approval, which was not forthcoming: London played the red card.

Clark seemed to feel somehow that this was my doing, although I had deliberately not spoken to Richard Dannatt to avoid any accusation of collusion. There was nothing more to be said.

The crisis was over. We had avoided an unnecessary and potentially dangerous confrontation with the Russians, but my relationship with my superior officer had suffered. I had come to the brink of refusing a direct order, though in the event it had not quite come to that. And Clark himself had been damaged. Two months later it was announced that he would be replaced as Supreme Allied Commander, earlier than expected.

Operation 'Joint Guardian' proceeded according to plan. Within a few days, KFOR units had penetrated all of Kosovo. Whenever a KFOR vehicle drove through a village, children ran out waving and cheering. It was obvious most inhabitants saw us as deliverers. The atmosphere was euphoric.

I flew around the brigades in the first few days, meeting commanders and dealing with their immediate problems. From the air you could see plumes of smoke curling up from burning buildings: Albanian Kosovars were indulging in typical Balkan behaviour, burning the houses of enemies. The Serbs fulfilled their obligations under the MTA, withdrawing their security forces on schedule and in good order. Before long we began to discover grisly evidence of their activity: sites of mass graves scattered across the country. Jonathan Bailey was my liaison man at the Serb Army headquarters in Priština; he witnessed scenes of frantic activity as files were hurled out of the windows to be burned in the incinerator. On their last night they drank the place dry. Despite difficult circumstances, Jonathan forged a good relationship with the Serbs, and he continued to liaise with them after they'd left Kosovo. Once a week he would go over the border into Serbia to discuss issues arising over a Balkan lunch.

Many Serb officials – administrators, judges, prison warders, utility workers, teachers and doctors – quit Kosovo when the security forces left, presenting KFOR with the task of filling the vacuum. The Serbs remaining in Kosovo were fearful of revenge attacks by ethnic Albanians. Plenty of scores were settled in those first few days. There was widespread looting, burning of abandoned houses, grenade attacks, beatings and shootings. In the worst such incident, we found the bodies of 14 Serb farmers lying in fields about 12 miles south of Priština. It was one of our core tasks to try to retain as many Serbs as possible; if too many left, the Western ideal of ethnic balance would appear to be hollow. Their security was at the heart of this.

Within a week, we moved our main headquarters up from Skopje to Priština, in a film studio on a ridge overlooking the city. At night you could see many fires burning in the city below and in the surrounding countryside. The building was a modern office block which we referred to as the Film Factory, with a cavernous studio below which quickly became known as the Bat Cave.

It was crucial to get the infrastructure working as soon as possible. If you don't get the water supply working quickly, you get problems with hygiene and disease, and since many of the Serb doctors had left with their Army compatriots we couldn't afford this. But without electricity the pumps couldn't operate. Many Serb technicians and engineers had disappeared when the security forces withdrew. And without a working telephone exchange it would be more difficult for Kosovo to get itself back on its feet. So we set our Army signallers to sort out the telephone exchange, put Army medics into the hospitals and allotted Army engineers to reconstruction projects – just to keep as much as possible functioning until the UN civil administration was ready to shoulder the burden. I sent an engineer squadron up to the old power station outside Priština to see if there was anything they could do. After that we had intermittent power. Later on, the Central Electricity Generating Board sent out two very capable engineers who soon had the power station running as well as – probably better than – it had ever done.

The Territorial Army railway gang came into their own, getting the train line south to Skopje running by D+14. Once it was working again it took a lot of traffic off the road. The line continued all the way down to the port of Thessaloniki, so from that moment on we could bring in supplies and vehicles by rail.

The refugee crisis solved itself, melting away like spring snow in a thaw. When D-Day arrived, most of the people in the camps in Albania and Macedonia just got up and went home, many on foot. It was an amazing sight, tens of thousands of people at any one time streaming back into Kosovo. There was one hell of a traffic jam on the road coming up from Macedonia, as our convoys of military and UN vehicles struggled to pass the slow-moving masses. But within a few days it was clear. The refugee problem was over.

Before KFOR moved into Kosovo, a negotiating mechanism had been set up with the KLA. We hoped to conclude an agreement before we went in, but that didn't happen. So we didn't have rules telling us how to deal with the KLA on entry, as we had in our dealings with the Serb armed forces. NATO had not forced the Serbs out in order to leave Kosovo in the hands of 'warlords' – though if

KFOR was going to restrain the KLA, clashes were almost unavoidable. The issue became more and more pressing as each day passed. Serb withdrawal resulted in a dangerous vacuum. Armed KLA fighters emerged, unrestricted by any Serb security presence. Many seemed to imagine they were now free to lord it over the population. Despite our best efforts, different KFOR brigades took different national lines with the KLA. The British wanted the KLA fighters disarmed; the Germans and the Dutch, on the other hand, were much cosier with them. These differences in attitude mirrored contrasting views of the KLA within NATO: some regarded them as not much better than terrorists, others saw them as freedom fighters.

The concluding phase of NATO's negotiations with the KLA took place in their field headquarters in the hills, some 25 miles west of Priština. Lieutenant General John Reith represented NATO, with the help of Jamie Rubin, Clinton's State Department spokesman. Negotiations continued until D+8, the last day of the 11 given by the MTA for the Serbs to withdraw. Eventually the KLA agreed to sign an Undertaking, renouncing the use of force and acknowledging KFOR's sole authority under UNSCR 1244.

This was an important moment in the transformation of the KLA into what would become a legitimate organisation. The terms of the Undertaking committed the KLA to a timetable for their disbandment as a military force, commencing on its signature. Monday, 21 June became 'K-Day' in our diaries, with a programme dating from then onwards. Within seven days (K+7) the KLA agreed to establish secure weapons sites, to be registered and verified by KFOR, to clear minefields and booby traps, to vacate any fighting positions, and to move to assembly areas as agreed with me as COMKFOR. Thereafter, only personnel authorised by COMKFOR would be allowed to bear arms outside these assembly areas: I restricted this concession to senior officers of the KLA with their close protection personnel (not exceeding three), carrying side arms only. By K+30 the retention of any rifles would be subject to my authorisation, and all personnel not of local origin would be withdrawn. And so on, up to K+90 (19 September), when KFOR would assume full control of the weapons storage sites. By then the KLA were to have completed their processes of demilitarisation and would cease wearing either military uniforms or KLA insignia.

In the weeks that followed, I flew around the country meeting KLA regional commanders and endured yet more elaborate Balkan lunches. It seemed to me important to make contact with the lower levels of the KLA as well as the leaders, to get everyone involved in the process of demilitarisation. Meanwhile, I began to develop a good working relationship with Agim Çeku, the KLA military commander. We had a Joint Implementation Committee (JIC) which met regularly to monitor the progress of demilitarisation. At these meetings I would tell Çeku what he should do: we're not satisfied with this, you must do that.

The first Special Representative of the UN Secretary-General (SRSG) was Brazilian Sergio de Mello, later killed by a suicide bomb in Iraq. Sergio and his small UN team were in Priština almost as soon as KFOR were there; he immediately began building up UNMIK, the UN 'international civil presence' set up under UNSCR 1244 to work alongside the 'international security presence', which was of course KFOR. He was a great man, a true internationalist, and he saw the civil administration off to a flying start. But his appointment was only temporary, until a more permanent candidate was in place. Just before he left, he instituted the Kosovo Transitional Council, which was an attempt to bring together leaders of the various factions in Kosovo under his chairmanship. UNMIK's role was to provide an interim administration until such time as it should be replaced by a locally elected government.

There were no police; but there was also no system of justice, because the judiciary, prison warders and so on had all been Serbs, and almost all had chosen to leave. Under UNSCR 1244, KFOR had responsibility for maintaining a 'secure environment', so in effect we were the police

– at least until the UN police had built up their strength. To stem the tide of killings, a system of justice was needed. Sergio de Mello empanelled a number of judges, both Serbian and Kosovar Albanian. Initially the judges were given the power only to hold a prisoner, not actually to sentence him; that came later. There were no rules for this situation: Sergio and I had to make them up as we went along.

There was much political activity among the Albanian Kosovar activists, both KLA and others, attempting to establish a 'government', which contravened the terms of UNSCR 1244. With hindsight, one can see that the KLA Undertaking should have included a prohibition on political activity by its members.

As K+90 approached, our focus was increasingly on the transformation of the KLA into a legitimate organisation. The pressure increased as the deadline drew nearer. The major issues of demilitarisation had been agreed, but the emotional issues remained unresolved. The KLA accepted their weapons should be held in KFOR-controlled storage sites, but only reluctantly: for many of their members, possession of these was a symbol of virility.

Richard Holbrooke rightly commented that in this final negotiation we were caught on the horns of a dilemma: we had to persuade the KLA to change, but if we pushed them too hard they might go underground again. It would be a horrible irony if we found ourselves in the same position as the Serbs, fighting a counter-insurgency campaign against a national resistance movement. Inevitably there was going to have to be an element of compromise on both sides. Holbrooke told Hashim Thaçi that 'the degree of international support' for Kosovo depended on its commitment to democracy, and that democracy was the way to independence. Thaçi didn't seem to understand. It was not just the organisation that had to change, but its leaders. I negotiated with Çeku, observing his difficult and often painful metamorphosis from a guerrilla commander into a national leader.

The KLA's insignia may seem a small point, but the symbolism was potent. The KLA had worn on their uniform the red and gold insignia of the double-headed Albanian eagle. Such an emblem was unacceptable to the international community, suggesting as it did an aspiration for a Greater Albania, incorporating Kosovo. Moreover, it would have been intolerable to the sizeable Serb minority remaining in Kosovo. Çeku took the point intellectually, but he would have to sell any changes to his commanders, and it would be hard to overcome their emotional attachment to the double-headed eagle. This was the symbol under which they had fought; to abandon it would be insulting to the memory of those who had been killed. But I told Çeku that the eagle would have to go all the same. Even if I had agreed to it, NATO would have vetoed the proposal.

Çeku accepted it was politically impossible for Kosovo to have its own army in the immediate future, and that the transformed and demilitarised KLA would have to be called something different. The name of the new organisation proved to be one of the most difficult issues to resolve.

As the eleventh hour arrived, the negotiations became extremely tense. K+90 passed, still without agreement. I reminded the KLA that the Undertaking had expired, and that officially they no longer existed as a legal organisation. If there was no agreement by midnight on the following day, and their members continued to carry weapons or wear uniforms with the old KLA insignia, they would be deemed to be non-compliant and would face arrest.

Wes Clark flew in to add weight to the negotiation. He was in his element, working the room confidently, telling stories about his experiences in Vietnam which had the KLA commanders hanging on his every word. Afterwards he made a rousing, virulently anti-Serb speech that would have had our diplomats reeling if they could have heard what he was saying. It became clear that the differences between the two sides had narrowed. We resolved the issue of the insignia, agreeing an outline of the shape of Kosovo itself. Our new Canadian political adviser, Wendy Gilmore, came up with a wording on one of the remaining issues, access to weapons, which satisfied everybody. Finally we settled on the name Kosovo Protection Corps for the reformed KLA.

Two days later there was a football match between a KFOR XI – including a young Russian soldier – and Priština FC. Our team lost 4–0, but the crowd applauded both teams enthusiastically none the less. I returned to the Film Factory to find Çeku dressed as I had never seen him before, in smart civilian clothes.

Çeku became Prime Minister of Kosovo, before being replaced by Thaçi. I have met him several times since, and when he came to England recently we had lunch together. He is proud of the fact that Kosovo still has a significant Serb population, and that one of his personal staff is a Serb. I saw him grow in stature from 'freedom fighter' to statesman, renouncing violence and embracing democracy. It was a fine thing to watch.

Many commentators had predicted genocide in Kosovo. Bad things happened there, but we'd largely put a stop to them, and set Kosovo on a road to a better future. We reckoned it had been a job well done.

Some Reflections

We have come a long way since the Kosovo operation. British forces have also undertaken successful operations in Sierra Leone and East Timor, and today are fighting in Iraq and Afghanistan. Yet it is hard to imagine that the British Government would have entered into those wars so easily if we had not achieved palpable success in both Bosnia and Kosovo, demonstrating that armed force, in the right circumstances, can be used to halt mass abuse of human rights. These two Balkan operations were also examples of Western nations exercising a moral right to intervene in another state's affairs in the interest of human rights – under the developing doctrine of the responsibility to protect.

UNSCR 1244 was manna from heaven for me. Although bombing Kosovo and Serbia may have been of arguable legality, there was no question that KFOR's occupation of Kosovo was underwritten in international law and supported by the international community. This legitimacy gave immense weight to KFOR's authority and gave us great power in our negotiations with both sides – in particular, the KLA who were struggling to gain international recognition.

This was a NATO operation, conducted by NATO units and headquarters. The command structure was well established with a clear chain of command. This was no coalition organisation with an ad hoc headquarters put together at short notice. Headquarters ARRC is a standing headquarters with a well-trained and integrated international staff. We all knew each other beforehand and understood each other's strengths and weaknesses. At times of stress, such as the debate over Priština Airport, we could trust each other in the headquarters without fear of national agendas intruding.

Once the MTA was signed and the Serbs had left, our greatest challenge was transforming the KLA from a guerrilla army into something that could not pose an internal threat. We had to use fine judgement to permit them dignity and give them enough to think they had a future, lest we drive them back into the hills or, even worse, they disintegrate into multiple armed Albanian nationalist groups, each of which could have threatened Kosovo's fragile peace. As it was, we were able to bring the KLA to accept their role as a democratically accountable institution without driving them back to insurgency or fragmentation.

It was critical to get the country working again, which was why I was surprised by the failure to address infrastructure issues promptly in Iraq in 2003. Our hard-won experience should have impressed upon governments that if people's lives don't quickly improve, they rapidly become disenchanted. It's difficult enough to build a civil society in a country devastated by war; without the basics of life, it's near impossible. Gilbert Greenall's[3] rule of thumb of the first hundred days being crucial remains very pertinent. I think it was Donald Rumsfeld who said, 'We don't do nation-building.' To my mind, this is both nonsensical and operationally detrimental, because overall success depends on reconstruction. In Iraq, the Americans had the naïve idea that people would be so happy to be liberated that nothing else mattered; and democracy would flourish overnight. It's a very ideological approach, and one which is intellectually bankrupt. This difference in doctrine between us and the Americans would be a recurrent difficulty in the years ahead. Military force should never be used for its own sake, but always to achieve a political objective. The generic political objective of any intervention should be to bring about those circumstances in which the country becomes at peace with itself and its neighbours; stable, with a representative government accepted by at least a respectable majority of its citizens; and the prospect of a better future for all.

---

3   I got to know Dr Gilbert Greenall well as the head of the DfID team during the earlier Bosnia operation.

Chapter 4

Sierra Leone 2000: Pregnant with Lessons

David Richards – 18 January 2006

The British academic and strategist Richard Connaughton has described the conflict in Sierra Leone as one that is 'pregnant with lessons'.[1] There are compelling reasons for believing he may be right. Whether one is examining the reasons why Sierra Leone descended into the abyss it did in the 1990s, the role of the Economic Community of West African States (ECOWAS) and its armed monitoring group (ECOMOG) in nearly bringing order to the country on three occasions, the UN's initial inability to stabilise the country, the role of the British, or the persistent failure of the international community to build on an improving security environment, there is certainly no shortage of relevant topics to study and from which to learn.

At a time when our operation in Iraq is proving difficult and expensive, it is too easy to surmise that overseas intervention will always be difficult and expensive; that we will always be resisted by a significant proportion of the local population; and that we will always struggle to adapt to local conditions and find a winning formula. Sierra Leone stands as an important example where overseas intervention was not only justified, it was also successful and, equally important, relatively inexpensive. Yes, we need to learn the lessons from Iraq; but in doing so we must not forget those learnt in Sierra Leone.

Background

Sierra Leone's civil war began in March 1991 when a small armed group known as the Revolutionary United Front (RUF), accompanied by Liberian fighters and Burkinabe mercenaries, entered south-eastern Sierra Leone from Liberia. Their stated aim was to overthrow President Momoh's corrupt Government, and they claimed that their larger goal was a radical, pan-African revolution based upon the Libyan Gaddafi model. Foday Sankoh and other leading figures in the RUF were heavily dependent on Charles Taylor of Liberia. They had all met in the mid-1980s while undergoing guerrilla training in Libya and Burkina Faso. Taylor launched his own attack on Liberia in 1989 but was thwarted in large part by ECOMOG, the West African intervention force, led by Nigeria, sent to Liberia. Taylor's support for the RUF was reputedly motivated by a desire to punish the Government of Sierra Leone for its participation in ECOMOG. More importantly, he aimed to prevent Sierra Leone from being used as a base by his Liberian opponents, the United Liberation Movement for Democracy (ULIMO), as well as to acquire diamonds and other plunder to finance his own campaign and subsequent regime.

The next nine years of civil war in Sierra Leone consisted of immensely complex and fluid forming and reforming of alliances among the different parties striving to control the spoils of the state. While it is not necessary in this chapter to track all the twists and turns of these years, the

---

1   Discussion between the author and Richard Connaughton, Freetown, Sierra Leone, 28 October 2000.

broad outline is needed in order to understand how the international community in general, and the British in particular, came to the aid of President Kabbah in May 2000.

On 29 April 1992, a group of young Sierra Leone Army (SLA) officers, disillusioned with his Government, overthrew President Momoh in a military coup. However, the new National Provisional Ruling Council (NPRC) administration, consisting of 18 military officers and four civilians headed by Captain Valentine Strasser, soon adopted a style reminiscent of its predecessors. It also suffered a series of military defeats at the hands of the RUF. Despite military government and the expansion of the SLA from 3,000 to over 13,000, the RUF advanced to within a few kilometres of Freetown, the country's capital. Moreover, it became increasingly apparent that the SLA often avoided fighting the RUF. Some army and rebel commanders even reached informal understandings not to confront one another. Both sides lived off the countryside, murdering, plundering, looting and abusing the civilian population. Militarily, neither side was able consistently to achieve an advantage.

Valentine Strasser was ousted in January 1996 in a bloodless coup led by Brigadier-General Bio. Bio undertook to permit the elections scheduled for February 1996 to go ahead. The oldest political party in Sierra Leone, the Sierra Leone People's Party (SLPP), won 36.1 per cent of the legislature vote. Its presidential candidate, Ahmed Tejan Kabbah, a UN development worker[2] and veteran politician, won 59.49 per cent of the presidential votes in a run-off second round election in March. This election and these figures are important because, along with the evidence of the infringement of fundamental human rights (through torture, mutilation and the recruitment of child soldiers), it underpinned the international case supporting Kabbah rather than any of the other factions competing against him.

At the end of 1996 a peace agreement was made between Kabbah and Sankoh, but in name only. Kabbah was doubtful of the loyalty of the SLA and used irregular Kamajor 'hunters' and mercenaries from the South African company Executive Outcomes[3] to wage bush war against the RUF, in which good progress was made for the first time. The Kamajor could match the RUF in knowledge of the forest tracks and so block their supply routes. However, in May 1997 frustration in the armed forces resulted in another coup, led by Major Johnny-Paul Koroma. Kabbah was forced to flee to Guinea and the Armed Forces Revolutionary Council (AFRC), with Koroma at its head, entered into a power-sharing arrangement with the RUF.

There was widespread international condemnation of the coup. The United Nations mandated ECOMOG to intervene in order to restore Kabbah. The Nigerians, who provided the greatest part of ECOMOG, launched a fierce attack on Freetown in September 1997. In October, the AFRC/RUF Government conceded. At Conakry a deal was struck which would give immunity to Koroma, a 'role' for Sankoh and a six-month period of transition to restore the Kabbah Government. But the Conakry agreement did not hold. ECOMOG continued to fight Koroma's regime until it was overthrown in February 1998. Kabbah was restored in March that year.

However, the violence continued intermittently and with growing intensity. In January 1999 the AFRC/RUF invaded Freetown and only narrowly failed to secure the city, killing and mutilating thousands in the process. A counter-attack by a combination of ECOMOG, loyal SLA and Sierra Leonean irregulars, including the Kamajor, known collectively as the Civil Defence Forces (CDF), pushed the AFRC/RUF back into the countryside before the fighting subsided into months of indecisive stalemate. There were allegations of atrocities committed on all sides. Britain provided material assistance to the pro-Kabbah forces who, assisted by considerable international pressure,

---

2   Kabbah had worked for the UN for 22 years before returning to Sierra Leone in 1992.

3   These were the mercenaries who had restored Kabbah to power – a result which could not be deplored with conviction.

were able to force the RUF to negotiations that ended in the Lomé agreement of 7 July. At Lomé, the RUF dropped their demand for the removal of ECOMOG forces, which made way for an agreement to permit power-sharing. The terms gave the insurgents four key Government posts and effective control over the country's mineral wealth. Also, significantly, there was to be a total amnesty for the RUF and the death sentence imposed on Sankoh was lifted.

Before being too critical of the Government and international community's role in the Lomé Agreement, it should be emphasised just how low the country had fallen in the early part of 1999. The functions of state had practically collapsed, with ministries in confusion and officials lacking any direction. The Ministry of Defence staff, for example, comprised three officials. Most businesses and Government offices had been looted and vandalised during January's AFRC/ RUF attack. There were no water, electricity or any other public services operating in Freetown. Large numbers of armed military, paramilitary, ex-SLA, civilians and CDF roamed the city, occupying buildings, manning checkpoints throughout the town and extorting money from the populace to permit passage. The Sierra Leone Police Force (SLP) was totally ineffective, untrusted and seemingly corrupt at every level. There was no communication to towns outside Freetown other than via radio and satellite telephone, and no safe road access to the interior. To quote *The Economist*:

> Sierra Leone manifests all the continent's worst characteristics. It is an extreme, but not untypical example of a state with all the epiphenomena and none of the institutions of government. It is unusual only in its brutality: rape, cannibalism and amputation have been common, with children often among the victims.[4]

The life expectancy of the population was only 49 years. That population was desperate for peace and, albeit cautiously and with a scepticism born of previous failure, was prepared to give Sankoh a chance.

United Nations Involvement

The international community welcomed the Lomé Agreement, because at least it appeared to have stopped the fighting – an assumption that soon proved wrong; but the amnesty was heavily criticised and seen as a major victory for the RUF. On 3 October 1999, Sankoh and Koromâ returned to Freetown and held a joint press conference with President Kabbah. They apologised for the atrocities carried out during the eight years of the civil war and promised to strive for a speedy implementation of the Lomé Agreement. On 22 October the Security Council unanimously adopted Resolution 1270 to establish a 6,000-member peacekeeping force to be known as the UN Mission in Sierra Leone (UNAMSIL), with a six-month mandate to oversee the implementation of Lomé. In December, the International Monetary Fund (IMF) approved 15.56 million SDRs (Special Drawing Rights) for post-conflict reconstruction. The wider international community at last appeared to be paying serious attention to Sierra Leone.

Following the Security Council resolution, the process of putting together the force elements for UNAMSIL began. In February 2000, as it became apparent that there would be a security vacuum with the phasing out of ECOMOG, the Security Council voted to increase the force from 6,000

---

4   Economist editorial 2000.

to 11,000. But UNAMSIL forces[5] encountered difficulty as soon as they entered Sierra Leone; the RUF prevented Indian and Ghanaian elements from deploying to the eastern Bendu region. Furthermore, UNAMSIL, despite a Chapter VII mandate, interpreted its brief in a traditional UN peacekeeping manner, as one of neutrality between the parties. This seriously impeded the development of close relations with the democratically elected Kabbah Government it had been sent to help, and ensured little cooperation between the latter's army and the UN.

Matters did not improve for UNAMSIL. On the very day that ECOMOG officially transferred its duties to the international force, the RUF attacked Kenyan UN soldiers. On 4 May 2000, 208 Zambians who had been sent to relieve the Kenyans were taken hostage and their 13 armoured personnel carriers (APCs) were captured. On 6 May, 226 Zambians surrendered to the RUF, bringing the total number of hostages now held by them to over 500. The same day, the Secretary-General of the UN requested that the United Kingdom and other countries act to improve the situation. On 6 May the RUF, using the captured APCs, began to advance on Freetown. Lunsar, on the approach road, fell to them and on 7 May the RUF were only 40 km from the capital.

The UN mandate for UNAMSIL and Kofi Annan's urgent request must be seen in the context of acute and general recollection of the international community's failure to act in Rwanda. The UN report on general failures over the crisis, including those committed by its own organs, was widely praised for its candour. Annan in particular was applauded for ordering the enquiry since his own role at the time was subject to criticism. One of the decisions following the Rwandan crisis had been to establish a high-readiness brigade known as the Multinational Stand-by High Readiness Brigade for United Nations Operations (SHIRBRIG), but SHIRBRIG was not to be seen in Sierra Leone. Richard Connaughton cites a letter which he received from the military adviser to the United Nations Department of Peacekeeping Operations, Lieutenant-General Giulio Fraticelli, which explained that SHIRBRIG at that time was only available to Chapter VI (embargo and sanction) operations, and that the Sierra Leone mandate was under Chapter VII (enforcement).[6] Since Chapter VI peacekeeping is initiated after due diplomatic process and with the consent of the parties involved, it arguably covers the precise circumstance when there is no requirement for rapid reaction.

The British Intervention

The UN appeared powerless to stop the RUF and indeed started to evacuate their civilian staff from the country. The Government and UNAMSIL seemed, and indeed believed themselves to be, on the verge of collapse. Into this deteriorating situation, on 5 May 2000 I was ordered to lead a British military team to assess the situation and to recommend whether or not to respond to Annan's request. I advised in favour of intervention to conduct a non-combatant evacuation operation, but using the whole Spearhead Battlegroup with significant helicopter support: in my judgment, such a force was necessary given the geography, the strength of the approaching RUF force and the UN's inability to stop it.

Within 36 hours, a sizeable British military force, that at its height grew to 5,000 people, started to arrive. It became clear to me that such a force could achieve much more than an evacuation operation if we were able to stiffen the resolve of the better UN contingents and turn the loyal

---

5   Contributors of Force Troops were: Bangladesh, Ghana, Guinea, India, Jordan, Kenya, Nigeria and Zambia.

6   Connaughton 2001.

rump of the SLA and the Kamajors into an effective fighting force. So we secured Lungi Airport and much of the Freetown Peninsula, including the site of UNAMSIL's HQ. With their vital ground secured for them, UNAMSIL was given a chance to regroup and reorganise.[7] Although dysfunctional for weeks, UNAMSIL was accorded an opportunity to which, under great pressure from UN HQ in New York, they started to respond. Their evacuation was curtailed and confidence slowly started to return.

What UNAMSIL could not, and would not, do was push the RUF back from their positions close to Freetown. To do this we, the British, coordinated and sustained the efforts of a disparate grouping of Sierra Leoneans, largely CDF and ex-SLA, who remained loyal to their president. Guided at every level by British officers and NCOs, over the next few weeks they succeeded in securing much of the inland road route between Freetown and Lungi, relieving the military and political pressure on Freetown and its beleaguered Government. The British themselves fought few battles directly, although when we did, our overwhelming firepower left no room for doubt in the minds of the RUF rank and file in particular. The RUF started to splinter into different factions, and Taylor began to lose his grip. This, at first ad hoc, twin-track operation by the British, giving support to the UN on the one hand and assistance to the Government of Sierra Leone on the other, soon became official strategy. To give it further effect, the UK deployed additional forces including a sizeable amphibious force.[8] The result was total psychological ascendancy over the RUF that bought the Government and the UN the time they needed to reassert themselves. And perhaps more important, in a different psychological sense, was the impact of the UK's role on the mood of the people. They at last felt the glimmerings of genuine hope for the future, a feeling reinforced when many RUF leaders were detained, including, on 17 May, Foday Sankoh himself, taken into custody while trying to escape from Freetown.

By mid-June 2000 the security situation stabilised sufficiently to allow the British operation to be terminated, although we agreed to provide additional military support in the form of financial and training assistance to the new SLA, now renamed the Republic of Sierra Leone Armed Forces (RSLAF). Suspicion of the UK's motives dissipated with the departure of the main force. A German journalist, who had arrived sceptical of the British a few weeks earlier, caught the prevailing mood in Sierra Leone well:

> Intervention in the fate of Sierra Leone has also awakened suspicion of re-colonization. That may be. But this kind of intervention does have a certain charm – especially as the locals have given the Whites such a hearty reception whilst they fear their own soldiers and regard the Blue Helmets as useless. The withdrawal of the main British contingent has allayed any suspicion of over-presumptuousness – and makes the operation appear all the more justified.[9]

---

7   By chance, Bernard Miyet, the head of the UN's Department of Peace Keeping Operations, was in Freetown when the British arrived. There is no doubt that his presence and pragmatism eased the way for what potentially could have been a very difficult relationship between the UN and UK forces. 'The arrival of the British is good for us', said a UN spokesman, despite initial problems.

8   HMS *Illustrious* arrived off Freetown on 11 May and the HMS *Ocean* Group on 14 May.

9   Tkalec 2000.

Sequel

For a while, the security situation continued to improve as UNAMSIL finally began to deploy troops outside Freetown. But it soon became clear that they had neither the will nor the capability to push home their advantage. Nor, at that stage, was the fledgling RSLAF in a position to do better.

In early October 2000, the situation was deteriorating again. UNAMSIL, far from gaining strength and authority, appeared to be in danger of moving backwards, especially when India announced the withdrawal of its contingent. The RUF remained in control of over half the country and were strengthening their grip on some key areas, including the diamond-producing regions needed to finance their operations. They showed no sign of returning to negotiations, and were beginning to expand their operations into Guinea. Charles Taylor continued actively to support them and seemed impervious to ill-coordinated attempts by the international community to bring him into line. The UK's efforts with the RSLAF were beginning to bear fruit but lacked a powerful coordinating headquarters to bring coherence to the work and to develop a plan to defeat the RUF, harnessing and informing other work at the strategic level.

So I was sent back to the country with the same team that had succeeded in May, this time explicitly charged with development of a coherent plan that would ensure the RUF's defeat while devising a long-term solution that would ensure stability into the future. The work, combined with some bold initiatives by UNAMSIL's civilian and new military leadership, forced the RUF to sign a ceasefire agreement at Abuja on 10 November. The RUF's new leader, Issa Sessay, publicly conceded that the British commitment to Sierra Leone, and the opportunity it had provided the UN, was the distinguishing factor in their decision to seek a peaceful outcome. They had succumbed to the British aim of 'persuading the RUF of the inevitability of defeat'.[10] Although too much time was taken exploiting the agreement, this was a conspicuous success for the UN, the Sierra Leonean Government and the UK. It signalled the end of the conflict and an opportunity to start bringing a real improvement to the lives of the long-suffering people of the country.

That process is still in train. Despite the security framework provided by the UN and the British-trained RSLAF and the police, the country's situation remains fragile. Although the country benefits from sizeable natural resources and a relatively well-educated populace committed to democracy, inward investment is too low to stimulate self-sustaining economic growth. The UK has so far failed to turn the RSLAF into a force confidently able to secure the country's borders. Five years on, in order to prevent the country slipping back, the UN mandate has had to be extended, albeit on a reduced scale. Standards of governance are only slowly improving and corruption is still endemic. The jury on Sierra Leone is still out. Huge and continuing international expenditure on UNAMSIL and, by West African standards, on international aid has not yet succeeded in placing it on a secure long-term footing. Why not?

Lessons

Many lessons may be drawn from this account, ranging from the essentially military through to broad issues of international behaviour and competence. My purpose is not to examine the military per se, although there is clearly a huge overlap with other areas. For those who do want to focus on

---

10   My direction to the force commanders, and specifically those officers with responsibility for the campaign's information operation – Freetown, 10 October 2000.

this aspect, Richard Connaughton[11] and Professor Gwyn Prins of London University[12] both offer penetrating and highly readable analyses. How the UN's approach to peacekeeping might improve further is a fertile theme that they both exploit well.

Here, I want to look at the broader issue of how the international community might better go about assisting deeply failed states such as Sierra Leone. My thesis is that, in essence, the international community is guilty of too much talk and not enough coherent and timely pre-emptive action. There is no shortage of analysis, but implementation is something in which we are far less expert. Why are things moving so slowly in Sierra Leone and in many other countries whose populations deserve better? To find the answer requires a stern examination of how, firstly, to produce a coherent multi-dimensional plan tailored to the long-term needs of a particular country and, secondly, how to implement that plan energetically and coherently to ensure success. This absence of coherence has been a key failing in Sierra Leone and other failed or failing states.

But, before proceeding to offer solutions, what immediate lessons can be gleaned from Sierra Leone's experience?

First of all, the right security environment (and thus 'the military') is as much a *sine qua non* for success in Africa as it is in any other region of the world. Conflict resolution may just be the start. If there is not enough money spent on a country's army and police, and this means investment in the round, not simply on equipment, then that army will soon bite the hand that inadequately feeds it.

Secondly, and self-evidently, a good military creating a secure environment will not alone solve a country's problems. It is fundamental to progress, but it must be part of a much broader effort across a range of interdependent dimensions – political, diplomatic, legal, economic, industrial, humanitarian, as well as military. Whilst this is well understood, too often the actors in these different areas work narrowly within their own discipline, even parochially; blind to the requirement to ensure their work remains coherent with the overall effort. This need for much greater intra-government and agency coherence is critical to future success.

Thirdly, when solutions are eventually agreed they are applied far too slowly. In the military, the concept of tempo – acting relatively quicker than one's opponent – is recognised as vital to success. When one fails to achieve this, the initiative is lost and the enemy will surely win. In Sierra Leone it became clear too often that well-intentioned solutions were being overtaken by events. Applied too late, they would become irrelevant, often aggravating the new problem.

Fourthly, bureaucratic inertia and incompetence are endemic and positively inimical to progress. Worse, it is clear that sometimes those responsible for solving problems deliberately take longer than they might because the problem they are charged with solving is their working life, income and even *raison d'être*. This is a recurring criticism of many UN workers.

Lastly, NGOs are often less effective than they should be because they suffer from the same institutional rivalry and bureaucratic inefficiency as government agencies. They too pull in too many directions, undermining each other and failing to see the big picture.

Whilst these broad observations apply to many states at all stages of development, in Sierra Leone they are especially applicable. For example, in 2000, there was massive international investment by West African standards, but all focused on the slow implementation of an unimaginative security plan that was very poorly integrated with the wider political, diplomatic, legal, economic and other issues, without which any military success would be, at best, transient. Furthermore, there was open and almost anarchical inter-agency rivalry, coupled with the absence of a coherent, multi-dimensional plan. Too often, organisations that should have been acting in

---

11 Connaughton 2001.
12 Prins 2002.

concert were, often unwittingly, undermining each other. All this resulted in a bewildering lack of urgency and of tempo.

But such was the severity of the situation that for once a single actor, in this case the UK, could impose solutions on all the others involved. The Sierra Leonean Government, UN and the few NGOs that continued to function needed British help too much and were in no position to argue. The results were the flowering benefits of coherent multi-dimensional action based on a widely understood and firmly directed plan. President Tejan Kabbah, certainly charitably but with some justification, described the British Army as 'the architects of Sierra Leone's salvation'. Indeed, it is he who first encouraged me to expose the approach taken in Sierra Leone more widely.

Two issues are key. How, firstly, does one devise a recovery plan from scratch that ensures coherence over time across all dimensions? And secondly, how does one ensure the plan is implemented efficiently, remaining adaptable and responsive in the process? Here, the military has something to offer civilian colleagues. When confronted by novel operational or strategic problems, military commanders employ a rigorously logical and deductive analytical tool to produce a coherent plan. By necessity, in recent years it has become highly sophisticated. The result of the analysis in Sierra Leone was a plan in which a number of interdependent lines of development (political, humanitarian, economic, financial and reconstruction) were actively pursued, through a number of necessary way points or 'decisive points', to a defined end-state. Success in achieving these points ensures continuing coherence across and through the life of the plan. They are also useful indicators of the pace and depth of progress.

But how does one ensure that something so complex remains relevant to developments as they occur and is implemented with the necessary tempo? The key is devolving responsibility to talented, empowered people who understand the big picture, work to clear intent and are authorised, indeed required, to use their initiative and energy to ensure that what they are doing meets their narrow objectives and yet remains compatible with a clearly understood overall plan.

But should we expect a country to do all this for itself? Many think not. On a visit to Guinea in 1999, the Finance Minister showed me yet another sophisticated and highly technical blueprint for recovery he had received. 'I hardly understand it', he said, 'and certainly my team does not. What am I meant to do with it?' One possible solution is to develop a concept of 'embedded support', where a team of highly motivated practical people with proven track records (bankers, industrialists, diplomats, civil servants, doctors and soldiers), drawn from both inside and outside the country, is put together to work with and alongside the host government's departments and agencies over a period long enough to teach and train indigenous successors. Donors would agree to devolve responsibility for helping the country to this single team working throughout the government. Crucially, this demonstration of long-term and coherent commitment by the international community, and the high quality of the implementation team, would serve as a vital confidence-building catalyst to inward commercial and industrial investment.

An intellectually rigorous analytical and planning tool, accompanied by the dynamism and leadership of an embedded support team throughout the implementation phase, has considerable potential to accelerate progress when applied to the most undeveloped states in Africa. The era of muddled aims, inertia, confusion and contradictory action could be a thing of the past. And it must be emphasised that external assistance of this type and 'African-based solutions' are not inimical to each other; indeed, the opposite is true. This is to do with teamwork, playing to people's strengths and, most importantly, the laying of long-term foundations. It offers the real promise of inducing external investment and sustainable growth. The era of fine analyses but inadequate practical help must come to an end. It is time for the practitioners to join the team. The international community's watchwords, and its judge, must become implementation and delivery. To paraphrase Winston

Churchill, a little 'less jaw-jaw' and a little 'more war-war' is required if the failed or failing state is to recover in a time frame that will satisfy its people and our consciences.

PART II
Hard Lessons

Although it was obvious to most that 9/11 was an event of historic proportions, few in the British Army could have envisaged that it would presage the most difficult decade it had experienced since the 1940s. The chapters that follow in this section describe the experiences of those, mostly in Iraq, who were asked to play a leading role as the British Army struggled to learn hard lessons.

After months of planning, with dubious legal basis, faulty intelligence on weapons of mass destruction and inadequate planning for what was going to happen afterwards, American and British forces invaded Iraq in 2003. The success of the invasion exceeded all expectations, but very quickly Coalition forces became bogged down in an inadequately planned occupation. There is no better person to describe the failings of the Coalition occupation in Chapter 5 than Major General Tim Cross, the British deputy initially to General Jay Garner of the Office of Reconstruction and Humanitarian Assistance and then to Paul Bremer of the Coalition Provisional Authority. He explains the politics in both Washington DC and London that lay behind failings in Iraq and how the Coalition's strategic errors helped to sow the seeds of the Sunni insurgency.

While the Americans in Baghdad faced both a Sunni insurgency and inter-ethnic strife, British forces in Basra were initially welcomed as liberators by the majority Shia population. But all that was about to change. Major General Andrew Stewart was the British commander in the south of Iraq in late 2003 and early 2004. He describes in Chapter 6 how, when he arrived, British soldiers were playing football with Iraqis in the streets, but with the launching of the Shia uprising in April 2004, British forces became involved in some of the most difficult fighting since Korea. He also explains how and why the first cracks started to appear in the US–UK alliance, with Mr Paul Bremer and the Coalition Provisional Authority demanding a much more robust military approach to deal with the Shia uprising than the British thought wise. Andrew Stewart's tour ended with the formation of the Interim Iraqi Government, returning authority to the Iraqis at the end of June 2004.

It was easy to forget, in those difficult early days in Iraq, that we were simultaneously conducting an operation in Afghanistan, albeit at a much smaller scale than after 2006. The NATO International Security and Assistance Force (ISAF) was set up in Kabul in 2002, after the initial successful operation to remove the Taliban from power in late 2001 after 9/11. Lieutenant General Sir Barney White-Spunner was then a brigade commander, charged with forming an international brigade in Kabul. He describes in Chapter 7 the lack of real understanding of the Afghan problem, and how the West's inability to address the serious economic problems of the country and well-being of its people sowed the seeds of later problems. Barney White-Spunner's thesis is that armies should expect to do nation-building as a matter of course and, if we wait for civilian agencies to arrive, often it will be too late. He also describes an earlier, successful operation to disarm Albanian rebels in Macedonia in 2001. This was in many respects a textbook example of the successful use of British forces and military leadership in an intervention operation, akin to the more widely known Sierra Leone operation.

The next three chapters are written by officers who were all deputies to US commanders in Baghdad in 2004 and 2005. Lieutenant General Andrew Graham deployed in March 2004, initially as deputy to the overall US commander. Shortly after he arrived, the Coalition split their Baghdad headquarters: Multi-National Forces Iraq (MNF-I) was in overall command, setting the strategy for the campaign and dealing with the Iraqi Government and others; Multi-National Corps Iraq (MNC-I) was based at Baghdad airport and ran operations across Iraq. Andrew Graham then became the British deputy in MNC-I. In Chapter 8, he describes the range of players in Iraq as they were perceived in 2004, how the campaign was designed at that time, and an early understanding that the battle for perceptions was all important.

General Sir John McColl was at the centre of events in both Afghanistan and Iraq. In 2002, as a divisional commander, he was the first commander of ISAF in Kabul. In 2004 he was the British deputy in Iraq to the US commander of MNF-I, General Ricardo Sanchez. He was the senior British officer in Iraq during Major General Andrew Stewart's tenure in Basra, described in Chapter 6, and he gives an interesting insight into US politics and their view of the British performance in Basra at the time. In Chapter 9, entitled 'Modern Campaigning', he explains the highly complex context within which modern commanders have to operate.

Lieutenant General Sir John Kiszely succeeded John McColl in Baghdad from October 2004 to April 2005. In Chapter 10 he examines the evolution of the operational art and how British understanding evolved throughout the twentieth century. One of the most important results of the British military intellectual development he describes was the formation of the Higher Command and Staff Course in 1989, which became the most influential educational experience for most, if not all, subsequent British commanders in Iraq and Afghanistan. John Kiszely reflects on the impact of this education on his own experience in Baghdad.

In Chapter 11, General Sir Nick Parker takes a similarly wide view, reflecting on personal experiences of command in Sierra Leone in 2001, deputy command of MNC-I in 2005–2006, and then command in Northern Ireland in 2006 and 2007, the final year of the British military campaign there. He concludes by examining the qualities needed of a commander in the twenty-first century – pragmatism, persistence, a collective approach and clarity.

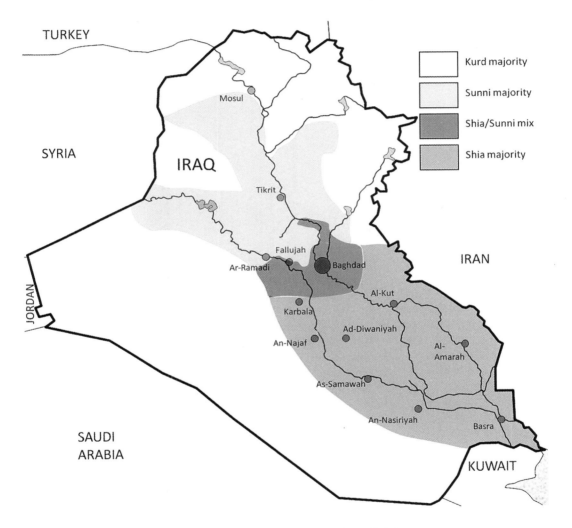

Map 5.1 Iraq – ethnic and sectarian divisions

Chapter 5

Rebuilding Iraq 2003:
Humanitarian Assistance and Reconstruction

Tim Cross – 23 November 2005

In October 2002, having attended the Royal College of Defence Studies in London for a year where we had addressed the political–military strategic level of war, I was stood up to be the two-star Joint Force Logistic Component Commander and Commander British Forces in Turkey. The intent was to establish, alongside the US Forces in their European Command, an 800 km line of communication from the eastern Mediterranean, through Turkey to an area around Silopi, as part of the Northern Option for the invasion of Iraq. Should events dictate, the British 1st Armoured Division would then move down that line of communication in order to move into northern Iraq and then, together with the US Army's 4th Infantry Division, seize the northern oilfields.

This appointment took me, along with the Joint Task Force Commander and the other component commanders, to Tampa in Florida and the US Central Command headquarters, to take part in the various coalition planning conferences and 'rock drills'. Several things struck me over those initial weeks.

First, the political debate was clearly confused. The situation in the UN, the intent of Turkey – would they or would they not let us pass through – and the uncertainty of Saddam Hussein's response to US/UK pressure kept us all guessing. Secondly, as the Logistic Component Commander I certainly tried to think through the immediate implications of the proposed operations. Not just the military logistic implications, but the issues of refugees, humanitarian support and immediate reconstruction; as the Logistic Component Commander, at least some of these problems were sure to come my way. But that said, and thirdly, I gave no immediate thought to longer-term reconstruction, physical or political, of Iraq. Nor, perhaps, as an operational-level military commander, should I have done. But, importantly, I got no sense of anyone else doing so, either here in the UK or in the US. Indeed, I saw no evidence of a clear strategic-level end-state for what we were about – the omens were not good.

In Tampa, General Franks and his staff at Central Command were keen to go. They were, and indeed are, an impressive headquarters. They had been incredibly busy for the previous 18 months, particularly since 11 September 2001. They had planned and then executed operations in Afghanistan, and had been planning options for Iraq for some time.

They were tired – 18-hour days over many months – but they had a good, robust military plan. They held the usual planning 'rock drills' and it was pretty clear to me anyway that the military Phases I–III[1] would not fail. However, there were a number of worrying factors apparent even then. General Franks was due to hand over in the summer of 2003, and he wanted to crack on: future hero, victory parades and book sales reminiscent of General Schwarzkopf and 1991 beckoned. There also was a strong sense that the military was leading the charge. Diplomacy was being left

---

1 The phases for the invasion of Iraq followed a standard pattern: Phase I – Preparation; Phase II – Shape the Battlespace; Phase III – Decisive Offensive Operations; Phase IV – Post-Hostilities.

behind. Given half a chance, General Franks would have begun operations by the turn of 2002–2003. Finally, there was scant evidence of any serious Phase IV planning. These were war-fighters, and any attempts to introduce Phase IV reconstruction planners (of which there were a few, led by a one-star engineer) into the inner circle were rebuffed.

By Christmas, the UK was pretty convinced that Turkey was not going to play ball. I for one was pleased when the decision was made to pull plugs on the Northern Option and go for the southern approach, via Kuwait. We probably could have made the north work, but logistically life would have been tough, and sticking to some of the proposed timelines would have been extremely demanding.

So, with some regrets but overall relief, I handed over the logistic lead to a one-star-led HQ, and I returned to my day job. But barely two weeks later I was asked to go to Washington. Working to Deputy Chief of Defence Staff (Commitments),[2] I was initially to act as a liaison officer to a new organisation being established in Washington.

On 20 January 2003, the President had signed Presidential Directive No. 24 which authorised the creation of an Office of Post-War Planning (OPWP). Whilst this was undoubtedly a good move, it was, to put it mildly, a bit late; compare this with the detailed planning for the reconstruction of Germany, which began months before D-Day in 1944 with a team several hundreds, if not thousands, strong.

I am unclear as to how the decision came about, but it was clear that Rumsfeld had seized control of the team. A core member of the neo-conservative clique, along with Wolfowitz and Doug Feith, and, I sense, led by Cheney rather than Bush himself, Rumsfeld set up the OPWP right in the heart of the Pentagon itself. I arrived in the very early stages, under instruction to discover if this was genuinely a pan-Washington bureau, with authority to drive the overall planning effort, or simply a sideshow. I arrived to find Jay Garner and a small team setting up in about half-a-dozen offices. Jay was a man I immediately warmed to. A retired US Army three-star general, he had met Rumsfeld in 2000 when, as I understand it, the company that he had established was doing some work on the space programme. Rumsfeld clearly liked and remembered him. Perhaps more importantly, Jay had commanded what we called Operation Haven, the deployment in northern Iraq to bring relief to internally displaced Kurds in the mountains after the 1991 Gulf War. We had put a good part of the Commando Brigade under his command, which had worked well. Jay had responded immediately to the call from Rumsfeld and, at very little notice, had given up leading his company, effectively becoming a civil servant, at a substantial material cost. He then did exactly what I had done when I was told to form the two-star headquarters for Turkey; he rang his mates and comrades. He quickly gathered a crop of retired one-, two- and three-star generals and, via contacts in the Pentagon, got a hold of some young blood to support them. I brought with me just my military assistant, a Royal Navy lieutenant commander called Louis Notley, and we settled in.

I had a number of contacts in Washington. Some in the UN were as a result of my earlier work with various agencies, but crucially I knew the then boss of the United Nations Development Programme: Mark Malloch-Brown, now Chief of Staff to the UN Secretary-General. Mark is actually a relative, but more importantly a long-standing family friend; he and his wife and family then lived in Georgetown and I was to spend just about every weekend with them. Through Clare Short – whom I had got to know well as a result of the operations in Macedonia, Albania and Kosovo and who had come to dinner just before I deployed to discuss how events were unfurling

---

2   This was the three-star military officer who led planning and implementation of military strategy in the Ministry of Defence.

– I received introductions into USAID, including an opportunity to meet with Nastios, the head of the agency. I also had links to the Embassy and to other parts of the Pentagon via military contacts.

The early days were inevitably a bit of a blur but we quickly got stuck in, and several issues emerged by mid to late February, that is, within two to three weeks. First, I began to really grasp the enormous effect of 11 September on the psyche of the Washington Beltway. I had understood it intellectually, but now I began to understand it emotionally. Secondly, pan-Beltway there had been and was a great deal of serious thought going on about Iraq. But it was not being brought together anywhere else. Garner was it. Having confirmed that fact with the UK, I was reinforced, but only with two mid-level Foreign and Commonwealth Office (FCO) people, albeit very capable, and with support from the British Embassy in Washington. I did have contact with a DfID official who was based in New York, but Claire would not allow him to work with us full time because of her well-known concerns. This was unhelpful, but I have to say that the man himself was not particularly dynamic anyway.

By putting the OPWP deep in the Pentagon, Rumsfeld alienated the rest of the Beltway Bandits. It took me quite a while to secure the necessary pass so that I could enter and move around unescorted, but civilians, even US Government officials, were reluctant either to come into the Pentagon or couldn't get in anyway. There were a few, but very few, non-military folk who joined the team, of which more later.

By spending my weekends with Mark, I met a very wide range of UN and US officials, and I was able to build up a picture of the inevitably varied views and opinions. Apart from anything else, through these contacts I was struck by the deep animosities between the various Washington departments. It was clear, for example, that many in the State Department deeply resented the Department of Defense (DOD) and Rumsfeld, almost to the point of wishing strategic failure.

We held various meetings and study periods, including a rock drill on 20–22 February, from which it became clear that there was no clear plan; there was a huge disparity and diversity of views and opinions, but there seemed to be virtually no political direction as to what post-war Iraq was to look like. No declared end-state; no campaign plan.

Garner was being pulled any number of ways, and found himself in an almost impossible position. At one point we managed to find someone who had clearly given much thought to post-war Iraq. Jay brought him into the team, only to be told a week or so later that he had to 'let him go'; this direction came either from or via Rumsfeld, maybe from Cheney himself, and was almost certainly because the man concerned, Tom Warwick, was not a neo-conservative and worked for the State Department. Put simply, he was not 'one of the team'; even though he was clearly a man with clear views and great knowledge. The clear message was that Jay was not at liberty to build a genuinely pan-Beltway team and that he was subject to veto – if people's views did not reinforce the neo-con paradigm, then they were not allowed to interfere.

Whilst Jay had indeed been given the task of post-war planning, he certainly had no authority over anyone working elsewhere across the Beltway; and crucially there were significant gaps in his team. No media plan was being developed; indeed there was no embedded professional media staff; no political advisors in the widest sense; no one focused on the WMD issue; no one from the Treasury, Health or Education. And as far as those departments who did provide people, it was clear from people like Nastios that they were on attachment; the majority would report back to State or USAID for their direction. They were not truly under Jay's command.

It was not certain at this stage if Jay and the team would actually deploy. What became clear was that he was becoming fed up with Washington, and his personal solution was to get out and deploy to Kuwait where he believed he would find greater freedom to operate. At this stage I was still a Liaison Officer, but Jay and I were at least beginning to get to know one another. My sense was that this move away was a mistake. Hard though it was, this office had to be genuinely pan-Beltway or it was nothing, and I told Jay that I believed he shouldn't leave Washington until we had a properly constructed team; if he didn't get one, we shouldn't go anywhere.

The situation is perhaps best summed up using the telephone directory from these Washington days; at its starkest it shows:

- A command team of Jay Garner and a deputy, chief of staff and three outer office staff.
- An immediate support team of four people in a sort of think tank, his 'brain trust' who took on so-called special initiatives; three in the legal team; and one in Public Affairs – a mid-West newspaper Naval Reservist.
- A humanitarian coordinator, George Ward, who had a deputy and just six slots in the telephone directory, but four were still vacant.
- A reconstruction coordinator, Lew Lucke, a deputy and 30, nine of whom were focused on getting the oil business up and running; four of his slots were vacant.
- A civil administrative coordinator, Mike Mobbs, his deputy plus ten; six of these posts were still vacant.
- Three Regional Teams, two led by retired one-stars; the third, focused on Baghdad, was to be led by a lady from the State Department called Barbara Bodine, who joined us in early March. These regional teams were to be capable of getting out onto the ground, to act as Jay's eyes and ears and to coordinate the overall effort. Each, at this stage, was barely a handful strong.
- Supporting the whole structure was a retired three-star, Jerry Bates, who was to coordinate the communications and life-support infrastructure. His team, according to the telephone list, was to be 85 strong, but as we prepared to leave Washington some 63 of those slots were vacant.

In all there were 165 line serials on the directory, 77 were vacant; this for the office that was going to be responsible for the initial humanitarian support and reconstruction of Iraq and, in theory anyway, was to be the focus for longer-term reconstruction planning. It was all woefully thin.

Throughout February–March 2003 I worked from early morning until late evening trying to wrap my mind around how this was all coming together; I then retreated to the Embassy to construct a summary of what was happening to send back to the UK, before flopping into bed for a few hours in a flat we had rented in Arlington. Initially I tried to be positive and suspected that there was a lot I hadn't yet seen; there must be more than this! Pretty quickly I began to realise there wasn't. To be fair, back in the UK things weren't much better. Whitehall finally formed the Iraq Planning Unit, but not until mid to late February and then with only a very small team; embedded within the FCO (quite rightly), they too were quickly overwhelmed and suffered like Jay from the chaos, lack of coherent planning and chorus of competing voices.

I returned to the UK on a couple of occasions, mainly to brief the Iraq Planning Unit and the Chiefs of Staff. Looking back, I wonder if I was as blunt as I needed to be about where we were. I am told I was, but I wonder if that is really true.

As we prepared to leave Washington we were joined by an Australian liaison officer, a Major General Ford. If I had it tough he was in an impossible position, trying to fathom everything out as everyone was focused on personal administration and the move to Kuwait. I spent as much time as I could with him and briefed the Australian Embassy staff.

One final Washington cameo: at a lunch with Rumsfeld and about a dozen others in early March 2003, I was asked for my opinion on how things were going. I responded that I had two principal concerns. First, troop levels. I reminded them that in Northern Ireland in the 1970s we had up to 23,000 troops deployed to deal with security. In Kosovo in 2000 the International Force was around 60,000 strong for a province the size of a couple of UK counties. For a country the size of Iraq the coalition had about 150,000, and I knew the explicit desire was that within six months the US would reduce to around 50,000. This to me was ambitious, to put it mildly. Secondly, we needed to broaden Jay's team and internationalise the post-war rebuilding of Iraq. I understood the political difficulties but, if we were to build democracy and rebuild the physical infrastructure, then we needed a much stronger team, the international community, and we needed the UN and its expertise in a wide range of areas.

This did not go down well – my views were not welcomed! To be fair to Jay he did actually go up to New York and meet with the Deputy Secretary-General, and even offered to have a UN liaison officer. The meeting was not easy, with Louise Frechette and her team constantly reminding Jay, and indirectly me as the UK's man, that we would be legally accountable for Iraq once the fighting was over. They recognised the offer of a liaison officer but could not accept it. Whilst there we met with Jeremy Greenstock and John Negroponte, amongst others, but it was a short visit, up and down in a day, and I reluctantly came to the conclusion that it was not a really serious attempt to engage; the UN was seen virtually unanimously as a side issue.

I should add that at this stage the UK Ambassador's post in Washington was empty. The Deputy Head of Mission was excellent and could not have been more helpful to me personally, but it did seem incredible that the principal appointment was not filled – although with all the rumpus over Christopher Meyer's book,[3] maybe the Prime Minister thought it was better that way.

We finally left Washington in early to mid-March. I deployed via the UK, briefing various people and having a couple of days at home on the way. In Kuwait, we were established in a hotel complex by the sea, south of Kuwait City, and very comfortable it was too. As we deployed, the name changed from the OPWP to the Office for Reconstruction and Humanitarian Assistance (ORHA), not an insignificant change and one that we didn't fully exploit, as it turned out. During the weeks before the war started, finished and our move up into Iraq there was the inevitable chaos and whirl of events unfurling.

Washington politics continued to be enormously frustrating. Numbers began to increase, but slowly; the names of people to head up and to be a part of the various Ministry teams constantly changed as first the State Department and then the DOD vetoed one name or another. In order to deploy, the civilians had to attend some military-style training at one or other of the military bases in the US, so if the DOD didn't like a State Department nominated person, they simply ensured they couldn't get trained, and hence were not able to deploy.

Another important dimension emerged alongside this. Back in Washington we had seen a number of exiled Iraqis who occasionally came in to brief Jay; their role was not apparent to me at the time but here in Kuwait it became obvious that they were pretty vocal and Jay spent a fair bit of time meeting or avoiding any number of Iraqis, all of whom lobbied for one thing or another. Taken together this whole business made it very difficult for Jay to build his Ministry teams, and every attempt to construct a plan for an Interim Iraq Authority (IIA) was frustrated. The lead for this 'future of Iraq' work stayed very firmly in Washington, where Chalabi's influence was obviously strong, with Jay kept out of the loop.[4]

---

3   Meyer 2005.
4   Ahmed Chalabi was a member of the Iraqi opposition in exile, and was an important figure in Washington DC prior to the invasion, lobbying the US Government.

The Chief of Staff, Jerry Bates, began to gather his support team; many serving US military, but strengthened by private and contracted personnel, including a Gurkha guard force, many of whom had served in the British Army, and a bunch of South Africans, who were Jay's personal guard. We also had some heavy discussions about how well armed everyone should be: nearly every American wanted to be fully 'tooled up'. I was dead against the idea; not quite a lone voice but nearly so.

I now spent increasing amounts of time meeting with and briefing just about every Embassy in Kuwait. Jay had made it clear that he wanted me to be his 'Coalition' Deputy; notwithstanding the fact that the UK had still not confirmed publicly that we had anyone in Jay's team, and that I kept being told by Whitehall not to commit the UK to anything. I was still a liaison officer with a very small team, and I was not receiving any clear direction. Nonetheless, I accepted that Jay needed my full support and I tried to provide it. I agreed that I would be his 'International' Deputy, and that I would take the lead on our interface with the outside world. I therefore actively set about meeting with all those other nationals who approached us. Many of the State Department people asked to work with me on the attaché briefings, which I welcomed; and with their support we did manage to draw in several other national representatives. We also met with many of the UN, IO and NGO representatives in Kuwait, attempting again to strengthen our links and keep them aware of our plans.

My UK team was strengthened a little, but it was only a couple of weeks before our move into Baghdad that my appointment as the Deputy to Garner was formally approved and announced. This happened when the Foreign Secretary, Jack Straw, visited, spending quite a while with us. I briefed him, he met Jay and some of the team, and then we had a longer session at the Embassy over dinner. I presented him with what I termed the 'must', 'should', 'could' paper: essentially a list of skill sets that I felt were needed if we, the UK, were going to play a full part in the post-war business, and if we wanted to ensure influence with the US. These skill sets covered everything from health, education and treasury experts to senior diplomatic and, in particular, media teams – both to deal with the outside world and to work internally as our mouthpiece to the Iraqi people. The list was well received, but I sensed even then that Jack Straw was still hopeful that there would not be a war; there was certainly no quick response to my requests.

The dialogue with DfID continued to frustrate. I had several telephone conversations with Clare Short. Although she felt unable formally to support the team, we did have DfID representation, but it was nowhere near what we needed. Considering the expected scale of human suffering, internally displaced people and civilian casualties, this was more than a little disappointing.

We did establish reasonably strong links with the Military Land Component Headquarters, and we began to conduct some joint planning. But Jay had no authority over the US military and I felt that he was reluctant to force the issue over who would work for whom. My view was clear: he would be the 'Viceroy' of Iraq, and the military must work for him once he arrived in Iraq. The timing of that arrival was quite a bone of contention. The military campaign was expected to be fairly short and sharp, and as it turned out it was. My view was that Jay should wait until the military combat phases (I–III) were fairly obviously over, and then he should fly in, in a civilian plane, and be presented as the 'Viceroy': a sort of Templer figure. He would then be clearly seen as separate from the military, with authority over them. This view was not shared by the US military, nor really by Jay, and it was one of the few times I publicly spoke out against him.

Linked to this were our attempts to work with the UK 1st Armoured Division. Jay wanted to establish an ORHA office in or around Basra as soon as events allowed, and he wanted it to be UK-led, initially by me. Whitehall refused to countenance the idea, frightened that this would lead to the UK having to bear the brunt of reconstruction costs in the south and south-west. I was given clear direction *not* to agree to this: just about the only direction I received!

The tension between the US ex-military and military team members and the civilians grew. At the highest level there was a serious breakdown, and I found myself acting as a bridge-builder on numerous occasions. The retired one-, two- and three-stars would spend a lot of time together, often in the evening sitting around a pool drinking whisky and smoking cigars. The civilians, particularly Barbara Bodine who was to lead the Baghdad team, found it very hard to break into this 'club'. Tears literally flowed with frustration; and there were some serious rows: Bodine was eventually to leave Baghdad in frustration and anger.

One other important cameo of my time in Kuwait was my various telephone conversations with Alastair Campbell, Director of Communications and Strategy for Prime Minister Blair, my visit to No. 10 and our collective attempts to strengthen and professionalise the media team. I found Alistair actually very helpful, and he did provide, at the eleventh hour, a useful and pretty capable media team effectively from No. 10. I briefed him there, and had a time with the Prime Minister, trying to put across the reality of post-war planning, or lack of it. I was pretty blunt, arguing that we should not start the war until we were clear what we wanted from it and how we would deal with the aftermath. This lack of clarity was, of course, to prove to be a crucial failure.

As the war began the atmosphere within ORHA changed noticeably. Amongst the retired senior military there was an air of excitement and anticipation. For many this was a chance to return to 'operations', which I somewhat reluctantly put down to a failure to realise that what we were about was not military operations but humanitarian support and reconstruction; it also rather reflected the Presidential encouragement to Jay when he had an audience at the White House back in Washington to 'kick ass'; not exactly a recognition of what was required. Amongst the non-military the atmosphere was different. The senior amongst them realised that we were far from ready to get anywhere near what was going to be required of us, and for all of them there was an understandable air of uncertainty and trepidation – especially when the odd missile sailed past our headquarters and explosions rocked Kuwait.

Fulfilling my worst fears, we finally left Kuwait to fly into Baghdad in the dead of night in the back of a military Hercules C-130 aircraft. There were barely a dozen of us, with a media pack of around the same size. It was a chaotic start; we spent the first few hours in one of Saddam's old palaces near Baghdad airport and then had a frantic day visiting a power station and a hospital in the city. We then moved north to visit the Kurdish area. Here, the response was quite different from what we had experienced in Baghdad city. We were literally welcomed as conquering heroes, with streets full of people; we visited a number of places over about two to three days and met with both Massoud Barzani and Jalal Talabani, the leaders of the two main Kurdish political parties. Jay was in his element. He remembered them all, and their wives and children, even though he had not seen them for some 12 years. He was personally hugely popular. I was very pleasantly surprised by what we saw; the Kurds had survived reasonably well under the umbrella of the Northern No-Fly Zone; their schools, hospitals and parliament were all easily the best I would see in the whole of Iraq.

We then returned to Baghdad and set up the headquarters in what became, and still is, the Palace in the Green Zone. From there we travelled around and about, visiting the south and attending a myriad of meetings and press conferences. What we found is best summed up as: fear; long years of neglect; very high expectations of the Coalition; but at the same time a strong desire for the US military to leave.

From a day-to-day survival point of view, life was far from easy. The so-called Palace was very grand but there was no running water, electricity, sanitation or air conditioning, and the food was pretty basic: mostly cold military rations and bottled water. The main party of the headquarters came up by road from Kuwait and eventually there was some hot food, but the contracted support was not good. Life support, communications, vehicles and so on failed on a regular basis; indeed, in order to talk to anyone one had to stand out in the heat with a satellite phone – which didn't work indoors – hoping that the person you wanted to speak to was doing the same. The non-military staff immediately began to struggle; simply existing in those conditions was not easy for anyone not used to being away from home.

Garner's lack of authority now became brutally exposed. The Ministry teams fanned out and each reported back initially quite positively: most found Iraqis prepared to work with us, buildings standing and files available, many having been secured at the homes of various officials. But as the security situation began to deteriorate the US military commanders refused to provide sufficient escort vehicles, and yet stopped anyone moving around without an escort; meetings were disrupted and, most crucially, the Ministry buildings began to be targeted and burnt and looted. Garner repeatedly asked for crucial key points to be guarded, but his pleas met with little response.

Linked to this, the contractual support from the USAID reconstruction effort failed to materialise. There were little money or resources to work with, and a vacuum of inactivity was created.

Jay also initiated a series of meetings with the key Iraqi players – essentially the London Seven[5] plus the Iraqi leadership who had not gone into exile. He worked hard to encourage them to work together in order to form an Interim Iraq Authority, which Jay wanted up and running by the summer. Jay realised that we couldn't possibly run the country – we had nowhere near enough people to do that – and we had to enable them to do it themselves. But his efforts were undermined and he received little support from Washington.

As the security situation worsened the US military response was poor and fragmented. There were not enough troops to tie Baghdad down, never mind the rest of the country, and those troops that were there only managed to inflame things – their posture was aggressive and they only succeeded in alienating Iraqis who, whilst they were not pleased to see US troops in Baghdad, were relatively pleased elsewhere and were largely prepared to work to improve things.

The good news was that there was no humanitarian crisis, no initial reconstruction crisis. The war had indeed been hugely successful: no chemical weapons had been used, no burning oilfields, no mass movement of people and no immediate need for massive aid. There was a serious window of opportunity here, but it closed quickly. The high expectations were not met, the media were their usual self and the atmosphere changed for the worse within two to three weeks. We did fly up to Qatar to meet with John Abizaid and others, attempting to influence things, but all to little avail.

For me personally the UK was even less helpful. To be fair, communications were difficult, but I was given little support: I still had no idea what our UK strategic intent was; there was no response to my 'must-should-could' paper. If it had not been for my personal contacts within the UK military I would have had no vehicle, no protection and no communications. When General Mike Jackson, now Chief of General Staff, visited, I briefed him as bluntly as I could. Luckily I knew him well, but my briefing entitled 'Snatching Defeat from the Jaws of Victory' did not go down well. By then I did have a senior FCO man alongside me: John Sawes, previously our man in Cairo, had just arrived and was bringing in an FCO team. It was then that the US announced their decision to remove Garner and bring in Bremer. This was in my view very badly handled. Jay was effectively hung out to dry by Rumsfeld and the US Administration in general. He was pilloried in the US press and treated disgracefully. There is no bigger critic of Jay than I in some regards, but he was given an impossible task with no resources or support. He operated at the operational military level, in some respects because he had to, but he should never have allowed himself to be forced

---

5   A group of Iraq exiles led by Ahmed Chalabi.

there; as I alluded to earlier, he should never have actually left Washington. But he did, and when he left Baghdad there was genuine sadness and much anger.

Bremer arrived in early June. I flew up to Qatar to meet him and briefed him on the flight back. He could have been presented to the world in a number of ways; his arrival certainly established a fully civilian authority, and that was good: Bremer was effectively the Viceroy, the Civilian Provisional Authority, hence the CPA, and he was indeed empowered by Washington. He immediately summoned the senior US military commander and ordered him to move his headquarters to collocate, and made it clear that he expected full cooperation. More resources, particularly people, began to arrive and there was a genuine air of expectancy. Until he dropped his bombshells. Against all UK advice, from myself and, I think, John Sawes, Bremer announced:

- First, we were to demobilise the Iraqi Army.
- Second, we were to de-Ba'athify the Ministries and all other Iraqi Government structures.
- Third, he would be slowing down the political process – there would be no Interim Iraqi Authority.

These were serious errors of judgement, and they were not his, or not just his. He clearly came armed with these decisions from Washington; the result was that the CPA would now have to run the country, and it was self-evident to anyone with a modicum of a sense of history that they would fail.

For me, the last couple of weeks were framed by the arrival of Sergio de Mello and the UN team. I knew some of them and spent quite a lot of time briefing and visiting, including trying to prepare Sergio for Bremer, who had reluctantly accepted that he had to establish a personal relationship with Sergio, but who was not prepared to allow the UN any freedom of action. This, together with trying to convince Bremer to establish an International Council, were my last rolls of the dice. I left in late June, frankly dog tired and glad to be away.

So, what does all this tell me? Leaving aside the mass of tactical level detail, I am in no doubt that we do need to have a fairly radical shake-up, both in the military but also pan-Government. We need much better coordination across Whitehall, a comprehensive approach to dealing with the complex emergencies of the twenty-first century. I conclude that we need to transform the architecture of Government. I liken it to the journey that we in Defence have been on for the last 50 or so years, the move from a separate War Office, Admiralty and Air Ministry to a Ministry of Defence and finally – and painfully slowly – to a Permanent Joint Headquarters (PJHQ) and now a reasonably joined-up approach to joint and combined operations. We need now to see how we can better bind together the workings of MOD, DfID and FCO in a similar way, creating in my view the equivalent of the PJHQ for pan-Whitehall strategic campaign planning, in order better to deliver the Prime Ministerial and Cabinet intent as we grapple with issues like Africa, global warming, world poverty and the implementation of, for example, the UN Millennium Development Goals, as well as our responses to conflict around the globe. And we need to see this alongside the other major players such as trade, the Church and the media.

Within the military itself we need to recognise that the enemy are no longer all the people of a particular nation or group – all Frenchmen at the turn of the nineteenth century, the Russians in the mid-1850s, the Boers at the turn of the twentieth century, the Germans for most of the first half of the twentieth century and the Communists in the second half. In today's world the enemy lies within the people; the people are the vital ground, and the aim is not physical occupation of the enemy's territory but occupation of people's minds with the concepts of democracy and freedom. In this sense Fukuyama[6] is right: a free, democratic world is what we are aiming for, but rather than a Huntington[7] clash of civilisations along the way we must strive to isolate the enemy and his ideology. In one sense there is nothing new here, but our military structures and operating procedures, our equipment programmes and conceptual thinking need to reflect twenty-first-century realities, not 1950s Malaya, still less the industrialised warfare that has dominated our thinking for around 200 years. The military are an enabler; we serve others, providing the secure environment to enable stabilisation and development, and in so doing we need to understand better the overall effects of our actions – tactical, operational and particularly strategic – within the construct of the complex emergency.

Finally, we need to develop our thinking on the moral imperatives. British military doctrine recognises three components of fighting power: the physical component – the equipment and our ability to sustain it; the conceptual component – our understanding of warfare, our ability to fight with that equipment to best effect; and the moral component – our leadership, our ability to get people to fight and our ability to turn into reality force with compassion, complying with the spirit as well as the law of armed conflict, the Geneva Convention and so forth.

We need to think through the applicability of the idea of a just war in the twenty-first century – the impact of the so-called War on Terror; the musings of Prime Minister Blair in Chicago back in 1999, and elsewhere, particularly on the moral imperative or duty to intervene in the affairs of other states when they commit genocide or conduct ethnic cleansing; and on what Henry Shue,[8] amongst others, has called 'Conditional Sovereignty'.

---

6   Francis Fukuyama (b. 1952), best known for his 1992 book *The End of History and the Last Man*.
7   Samuel P. Huntington (1927–2008), who in 1993 wrote *Clash of Civilizations*.
8   Professor Henry Shue is an American political scientist at the University of Oxford who has written widely on war and justice.

Chapter 6

Southern Iraq 2003–2004: Multi-National Command

Andrew Stewart – 9 November 2005

I arrived in Basra in December 2003. I had been closely involved in the strategic mess we are now in, as I was part of the British strategic planning team for the invasion of Iraq. The UK military was brought in reasonably early and the Government played a straight line with the Americans, saying we are not going to play this game with you without certain conditions being met. One of the key elements was that we believed we needed a green light on five things before it was a sensible thing to go to war. First, it was important it needed to be legitimate, which is why the UK wanted to gain UN support for an invasion. Second was that without legitimacy we would not get the support of the British people; I think this is coming home to roost now: we certainly had popular support at the time of the invasion but we started to lose that support as a result of the fifth requirement which I will cover later. The third requirement was that the operational plan should work, and we were entirely confident it would. The operational plan actually was estimated to take Baghdad in 120 days, so we did rather better than the plan, in those terms. The fourth requirement was discernible progress on the Middle East peace process; this was never really a possibility. And the fifth requirement was that the post-conflict reconstruction plan had to be prepared and that we should not cross the start line until it was ready. We did not meet this requirement; my personal belief is that we were driven by the local politics of the timing of the US election. We therefore went a year earlier than we actually probably needed to. The additional year may have brought us greater legitimacy; it certainly would, I think, have given more time for post-conflict reconstruction planning.

So having been part of the planning team for hostilities, and then being in the Ministry of Defence crisis management organisation during the conflict itself, I deployed eight months after hostilities had been declared closed, as commander of the newly formed MND(SE) – Multi-National Division South East – taking over from the 3rd UK Division. My headquarters was not a headquarters at all in the sense we understand it, where we train and exercise together, but a newly arrived mix of officers from the UK and other nations who contributed forces.

When we arrived there was very little hostility in south-east Iraq. The biggest difficulty was essential services, and that life for the Iraqi in Basra and the entire south-east was rather worse than it had been before the war in terms of electricity, sewage and other services. On the other hand, we were still seen as liberators, identified as having removed Saddam from a part of Iraq that produced 60 per cent of its wealth and received 5 per cent in return.

If you fly from Basra to Baghdad, preferably at tree-top level, both to avoid the anti-aircraft missiles and to get a good view, you see as you go north how the infrastructure improves, how much richer everything is. The 1950s technology in south-east Iraq was totally broken, and still is. It was a complete mis-assessment by the strategic planners, of which I was one: we simply did not know what a mess that place was in, and I would say that it will be 15 to 20 years before it reaches a level that would be considered reasonable by most standards, even in the Middle East. This meant we were still seen as liberators, but also as members of a coalition whose leading partner had put men on the moon but could not give people electricity.

So when I arrived, the security 'line of operation' was not my greatest concern and was not my main effort. My predecessor's greatest concern, in August and September when the temperature was 50°C with 90 per cent humidity, was the rioting caused by lack of electricity. Bear in mind that demand for electricity was probably doubling every month. When I walked round the souk in February, I asked a shopkeeper how many washing machines he sold every week. He told me he sold 19 every day. The trouble was there just was not enough electricity generating capacity to run these, let alone the huge expansion in the number of air conditioners – and so the demand on this broken infrastructure was going to be difficult.

We had a small insurgency going on, maybe two or three teams of Sunni who were attacking Coalition forces. But we did have, three weeks before I arrived, a vehicle-borne suicide bomb in Nasiriyah, which killed 19 Italian Carabinieri. When you consider that Mr Berlusconi had backed the war probably against the wishes of much of his population, losing 19 people placed him in a very difficult position. I was told that the commander of the Italian brigade in Multi-National Division South East, in Nasiriyah, received two telephone calls a week personally from Mr Berlusconi. Whether or not he did, he was under considerable political pressure not to lose another soldier, because if he did Berlusconi's premiership would be under severe threat. So some of the national commanders had considerable demands from their national headquarters before they were able to deal with the demands I made of them as their multinational commander.

Initially I was due to finish my tour on 30 June 2004, which was, I thought, a thoroughly sensible date as that was the day Mr Bremer's Coalition Provisional Authority (CPA) would hand over to the Iraqi transitional Government, returning sovereignty to the Iraqis. So for my tour I was in the position effectively of being the sheikh of sheikhs in the south-east: I was the one who could wield coercive force. I had most of the weapons, and until 30 June, in military terms at least, I was the boss. It was logical I should leave then so that my successor could take on a new role, effectively operating to Iraqi instructions. In my mind it was important we demonstrated very clearly to the Iraqi people that from 30 June we were no longer an occupying force. In the event, I stayed on for an extra three weeks because we came to the view that it was probably better if I saw the transition through. So, on arrival I found myself in a position where there was not much hostility, some of the multinational elements were under a certain amount of pressure, and the end game for me was to hand over sovereignty and demonstrate we were no longer occupying forces.

Mr Bremer, as head of the CPA, was effectively in charge of Iraq. I had working alongside me CPA South, run by Sir Hilary Synott and later Patrick Nixon, both from the Foreign Office. Sir Hilary had just finished as High Commissioner in Islamabad. I commanded one of five divisions under command of General Sanchez, Commander V US Corps, which had participated in the original invasion; V Corps had already been there eight months by the time I arrived and remained until the following April. It faced a significantly different problem from those of us in the Shia south. Whereas we were welcomed as liberators, in the Sunni north this was not at all the case; the insurgency, about which Andrew Graham writes in Chapter 8, was in progress when I arrived, with some support from external terrorists.

General Sanchez and the Americans were very focused on dealing with the Sunni insurgency. My initial interview with General Sanchez was simple: it lasted 30 minutes. I flew up to Baghdad on Day Two; he effectively asked me whether I could deliver the four provinces in southern Iraq. He gave me very clear direction: to ensure those four provinces remained reasonably peaceful; he did not want to have to divert any reserves or resources to the area. He gave me clear directive command and let me get on with it, something the Americans are not well known for, and I respected him for doing so.

Actually, because the main problem in my area was not security but governance and economy, I ended up working mostly for Mr Bremer, through the CPA South. Everything, therefore, depended upon everybody but my soldiers. It depended on money, disbursing that money, getting NGOs there to start helping, getting the infrastructure rebuilt and giving Iraqis jobs. The difficulty was that all money in Iraq was centralised, so it could be dispersed in a fair manner in the areas where it was most needed.

This caused us immense difficulties, because money was most needed where things were worst: in terms of infrastructure, it was worst where we were. But in terms of the insurgency, things were worst in Anbar Province and the Sunni triangle. It was here that the CPA wanted to spend money to buy consent and demonstrate we were there to help Iraqis. I spent much time trying to explain the military maxim of reinforcing success not failure; we should have spent money where we were welcomed and had the support of the people, rather than trying to buy consent where it was unlikely that we would ever get that support except over the very long term. I think this really brings into highlight the whole failure to understand what Iraq was like before we crossed the start line, and a failure to recognise what the Sunni reaction would be.

So I spent most of my time dealing with economy and governance; security was dealt with by my field commanders, at lieutenant colonel or battalion level. The brigade commanders and I spent most of our time resolving local governance problems, identifying and sometimes appointing provincial representatives. We argued strongly for local elections very early on. We believed the way to empower the Iraqis was to give them the choice, to force them into having to make decisions on whether to spend $100,000, say, on a hospital, or a school, or sewage, or water, and so become accountable to their citizens. I am utterly convinced that if we had been permitted to do that in the south, at least, we would now be a long way ahead of where we are today; early elections would have been hugely helpful. Another major stumbling block for us was twenty-first-century propriety rules. We are not allowed to spend money unless, when we do a project, we advertise it on the internet, obtain three bids and then choose the best value for money, usually the cheapest. That company probably already has six jobs going and cannot do it for two months, but you are not allowed to choose someone else. And that is because we apply twenty-first-century Western propriety to something that does not need it. We were hostages to Western ways of thinking. Of course if we had got Iraqis to do it, 30 per cent might have gone into the pockets of individuals, but Iraqis would have got jobs, they would have felt they were helping their own country, and it would have improved the situation dramatically.

So far I have not really mentioned the Iraqis; I will come to them shortly. But first I will go quickly through the seven months of the campaign to give a flavour of it, and then finish with a few specific lessons about multinationality.

When I arrived at the end of 2003, we were playing football with children in the streets. Everywhere we walked we were welcomed and cheered; I could walk through the souk, admittedly with my close protection team, and buy things – although the only thing I might want to buy were pistachios. The dates were good, but I was given those by the imams, so I did not have to buy them. The situation is not like that now. I am not saying we cannot get back to it, and my view fluctuated even while I was there, from glass half full to half empty. By the time I left, I was definitely a half-full man. I went away for two weeks' holiday, when I deliberately avoided newspapers and television. When I returned I spent a week catching up, and was depressed since everything seemed so much worse than it had before. Actually it was not that bad, but the way it was reported had definitely changed. Right now, I am just on the upward swerve again, towards optimism; it all depends on the elections.

I was responsible for the four southernmost provinces of Iraq: Basra, Dhi Qar, Maysan and al-Muthanna. One size definitely does not fit all. First, I was in the Shia heartland. The Americans were not: they had the Kurdish area and they had the Sunni area. Just to my north, Multi-National Division Centre was a mishmash of 23 nations commanded by a Polish two-star. It was utterly incoherent, and none of it their fault. The Brits, in our inimitable fashion, established our multinational division very early on, and identified the partners we wanted alongside us, leaving the others for the Poles. The language used in Multi-National Division Centre was English, but not a single nation in the division spoke English as its mother tongue; you can see how difficult it must have been for the Polish general. And what is more, they also had Najaf in their area, the home of Ayatollah Sistani, the Shia Marja: its history gives it religious primacy over Qom in many Shia eyes, and it became an absolute hotbed during 2004.

But even within the Shia heartland one size did not fit all. Much of Maysan is made up of the marshes, on the Iranian border. If you were an Iraqi from Maysan, your principal enemy was the Iranians. They were Persians; they had fought against you over your area for eight years; you had lost one and a half million people. The Iranians, what is more, were not secular. The Marja in Qom saw politics and religion as inextricably intertwined, whereas Ayatollah Sistani in Najaf viewed it entirely differently. For him, Islam had to be a part of the constitution and of culture, but it should not be the political lead. So those in Maysan did not trust the Iranians at all, but there were a lot of Iranians there, and after 1991 many from Maysan had taken refuge in Iran from Saddam. Since the 2003 invasion, and indeed throughout the 1990s, much of the insurgency that took place in Maysan was conducted from Iran by Iraqis who came from that province.

In al-Muthanna province, on the other hand, people viewed their number one enemy as not the Iranians but the Saudis, whom they thought to be Salafis and Wahhabists dedicated to the destruction of the Shia religion. The governor of al-Muthanna was conscripted into the Army in 1981, fought against the Iranians on the Basra front, but deserted to Iran in 1982. He reappeared fighting against Saddam Hussein in Sulaymaniyah and Salah ad-Din provinces in 1986. He was gassed by Saddam at Halabja. He then went back to Iran. He reappeared in al-Muthanna in 1997 as the head of the Badr Corps, and by 2001 was leading the insurgency against Saddam in both al-Muthanna and al-Qadisiyah provinces. In al-Muthanna he was seen as a patriot; in Maysan he would probably have been executed because he had deserted to Iran, even though he fought against Saddam. We never really understood these intricacies, only starting to learn when we got there.

Funnily enough, what is *not* that relevant is the Iraqi ethnic or confessional breakdown. Sunni, Christian or Kurd, they are all Iraqis and proud of it; it was in understanding them and their political chemistry that we failed. They are all Arabs, wheeler-dealers, merchants and masters of the half truth, but immensely proud.

When I first arrived I asked many people whom they would vote for if there were elections, because I wanted to see who had the greatest influence on them. I asked, 'Would you vote for your imam, if he stood for election?', to which they said, 'He will not stand. Politics and religion do not mix here. This is a secular state. He will not stand for election.' Let me say here, the imams were the best people I met in Iraq; better than the NGOs, Brits or Iraqis. They were good people because they cared for their flock and were determined their people should be looked after, and if we had given them the reconstruction money, I think life would have been a lot easier. Then I said, 'In that case, would you vote for your sheikh?' And they said, 'Why do I need to vote for my sheikh? If my brother gets run over by you, the sheikh is going to make sure you pay me blood money, or compensation, isn't he?' Which we do if we kill somebody accidentally, because we are taking away the livelihood of that family, or an element of it, and it is part of the culture. So the sheikh was effectively the welfare system for the Iraqis within the tribe. Therefore people were not going to vote for him because he had to look after them anyway. The lesson I learned from that was to tell the sheikh that if we were shot at and in response killed someone from his tribe, then we would not pay the blood money; which meant the sheikh had to pay it himself. So I discovered we had significant leverage over a highly influential group of people. They were very useful in helping stop what later became resistance to our occupation from Moqtada al-Sadr's Jaysh al-Mahdi. Then I said, 'In which case, I suppose you will vote for the political parties', to which they replied, 'What are political parties? They are nothing but pressure groups, they don't have any idea, they are here to get power for themselves.' 'So who would you vote for?' 'We'd vote for the local teacher, or we'd vote for the man who's been exiled in Bahrain for the last ten years, made a million, came back, and proved he can do something.' In other words they would vote for the technocrats. I believe if we had had a bottom-up election right at the beginning, we could have had a fairly decent technocratic government. If we had trusted them and given them the development money, some would of course have gone into their pockets, but we would be a lot further ahead than we are now.

Everybody involved in Iraq had a different agenda: the interim Government, run by Allawi then, the contributing nations, the UN out on a limb (I arrived just after the attack on the UN in Baghdad). In an age when every operation is multinational, when the media reports what they see when they see it, with a slant, it is practically impossible for a government to get a single message across. This is the great difficulty for information operations, and especially strategic communications. I personally looked at the audiences for my messages: soldiers' families; the people of Britain; the Iraqis in Basra; the Iraqis in al-Amarah, different from Basra; the Gulf States; the Syrians; and the Iranians. Each audience was different and needed different messages. If someone from one audience listened to a message for another audience, you gave a mixed message.

As a commander I had to decide which audience was most important, where the message had to be completely unambiguous: I decided it was the Iraqi, not UK, audiences. Local papers tell the truth, national papers report what they wish, probably with a political slant. I embedded Al-Jazeera, not the BBC, into my division, since I believed what they reported would be good because my soldiers were doing good. If they reported British soldiers going through a souk in Basra, that was good news; if they did not report it, nothing was lost. If it had been the BBC, they would have reported someone picking up an apple and eating it, which the stall holders told us to do, as soldiers stealing apples from the Iraqis. In these circumstances you had to prioritise your time and effort.

In Multi-National Division South East, the British brigade had four manoeuvre units, three infantry battalions and an armoured regiment, with an artillery regiment, an engineer regiment, and logistic units. It looked after Maysan and al-Basra provinces under the command of the British brigadier. It also had a Danish battalion under command. Dhi Qar province had an Italian brigade consisting of the Carabinieri battalion and a mechanised infantry battalion. In al-Muthanna I had a strong Dutch battlegroup of about 1,200 men with the addition of 500 Japanese, about which more later. There were also many other smaller detachments: the Italians had a Romanian battalion under command; there were 130 Portuguese and 100 Czech military police; a Norwegian engineer squadron which was later reduced; five Australian staff officers; the Danish battalion included a 60-man Lithuanian platoon. About 15–20 per cent of my force were military policemen, because training the Iraqi security forces was one of my most important tasks, as making them effective was our exit strategy, and the police were the most broken and needed the most rebuilding.

All the commanders in the multinational division spoke almost perfect English. I gave all my orders in English; all the staff work in the headquarters was in English. Every country was represented in my headquarters, and most contributed well. The Czechs in particular were simply outstanding and had no constraints from their capital.

This was the first deployment for the Japanese since the Second World War. They came with $1.8 billion, which was really important, about 80 engineers to spend it, and another 500 soldiers to protect those engineers. Back in Japan Prime Minister Koizumi was in a very sensitive position as he had made the highly controversial decision to deploy the force. When the advance party of 25 people arrived, 130 Japanese journalists accompanied them. Their rules of engagement were different, as were everybody's. But complaining about rules of engagement and national constraints is like complaining about the weather – there is nothing you can do about it, you just have to take it into account. The Japanese were there on a humanitarian mission, to spend that money; their rules of engagement did not allow them to fire except in absolute self-defence. If, for example, they were in a joint patrol with us and we were attacked, they could not fire back and help to protect us. In theatre this was not really a problem because we all understood. The Japanese are still there in al-Muthanna, which needs development more than security, with a British battalion to provide force protection. So if we were looking to get out of Iraq, we could easily withdraw one battalion today; but it is necessary politically to keep the Japanese and their money there. This means the operational plan should ensure that none of them gets badly injured, since they would probably be withdrawn and our mission in Iraq harmed.

I mentioned earlier the external threat. I think there are fewer than 1,000 external insurgents in Iraq today, and certainly not that many when I was there. My own view is that as soon as we go, the Iraqis will sort them out in their own way. The head of al-Qaeda in Iraq, Abu Musab al-Zarqawi, is not liked even by the Sunnis. They use him because it helps their insurgency, but he has killed so many Iraqis that I think he will not last long when we go. Al-Qaeda are responsible, of course, for many of the worst atrocities in Iraq.

On 14 April 2004 we had four vehicle-borne IED suicide bombs against police stations in Basra, which resulted in the deaths of 76 people, and about 450 injured. When we rushed to help, the immediate response was, 'go away, we don't need you and, in any case, you did it'. Now, why did we do it, in their eyes? At the time of the incident there was a Puma helicopter flying over Basra. The explosive used in the IEDs was old ammunition, including rockets, and there were rocket tails in the debris from the explosion. The Iraqis' logical conclusion, from Al-Jazeera showing Israeli helicopters killing Palestinians with rockets, was that we had done it. My response, with my brigade and battalion commanders, was to spend two and a half hours speaking to Iraqis to put the message right, and to get the governor of Basra to say it was not us on local television. We also persuaded the imams to say in Friday prayers that it was the work of outsiders, and pressed them not to retaliate against the tiny Sunni minority in Basra. That is what life is like for a modern general on these sorts of operations. You do not spend a lot of time fighting or moving manoeuvre units around; instead you spend time calculating the consequences of your actions and working out how you can alleviate them. It was al-Qaeda who exploded the Nasiriyah bomb against the Carabinieri, and a suicide bomb in Basra more recently. I do not see them as a long-term problem for Iraq; they may be a problem elsewhere, but not in Iraq.

There was some Sunni resistance to our occupation in the south, despite the vast majority Shia population. There were about six cells when I arrived in December; but we did a lot of lift operations over Christmas and brought it down to two. I was happy with that level; if we had over-reacted, then it would have turned more of the population against us. We almost got to an acceptable level of Sunni violence: one bomb a week. Of course it was totally different in the north, where there was a Sunni insurgency in the Sunni area. They have a political intent, not so much to regain power, but to gain a fair share of power, which I think they are going to get, which is why I am a glass 'half-full' man.

In the south we were mainly concerned about the Shia and their politics, in particular the Shia militias such as Jaysh al-Mahdi who are loyal to Moqtada al-Sadr, who I contend will be running Iraq in about 15 years time. Currently an immature fiery cleric, he is the son of an important ayatollah, a nationalist who believes in Iraq for the Iraqis and wants occupation forces out. He supports elections, since he knows the Shia will win. He does not want Sharia law, but would like far more Islam in the constitution than currently. He was supremely badly handled when he started speaking out, and at the end of March 2004 his newspaper was closed down in Baghdad. It was a newspaper which had a readership of about 30,000 in a population of millions. On 2 April his chief spokesman, who spoke on Al-Jazeera occasionally, was arrested. The result was that on Friday, 7 April, throughout the whole of the Shia south, all the town centres were taken over by Jaysh al-Mahdi. For example, in Nasiriyah they encamped on the bridges, stopped all movement, and set up road blocks in the centre of town. In Basra it was different: they attacked British forces about 70 times in an hour and a half, with shooting and bombings. In al-Amarah it was considerably worse, and I will come back to that. The attacks were the result of the Coalition command in Baghdad not thinking through the political situation in the round and thus causing a second front to be opened up; so we had to deal with not just Sunni but also Shia insurgents attacking Coalition forces.

My initial response was, again, to get on the telephone and meet the main decision-makers to try to change things, but it became immediately clear that Jaysh al-Mahdi intimidated the sheikhs and others, and that we would probably need to defeat them. Maybe we did not need to defeat them militarily, but we would certainly have to dissuade them from fighting, probably by removing their causes for complaint. This happened through April and May 2004. This was a period when there was much speculation in the media about the different approaches of British forces in the south and American forces in Najaf. The Spanish withdrew; the Ukrainians evacuated Kut; and the Polish-led division, with troops not designed to fight, was almost overwhelmed by the Shia uprising. On the other hand, we had troops with us ready to fight, but we decided the best way was to persuade local people not to support the Moqtada militia, so we set about it in a different way.

The result was that I was charged with not killing enough people. The CPA asked for my removal, because Mr Bremer's strategy was one of strong coercion: we must defeat Moqtada al-Sadr militarily, and here was a chicken-livered Brit, down in the south-east, who was trying to get the locals to resolve the problem themselves, and who was trying to kill as few people as possible. Bremer's coercion elsewhere helped me in the south, because I could go to al-Amarah and tell them if they wanted me to turn their town into Faluja, I could do so, as I was the sheikh of sheikhs, but surely that is not what they really wanted. So in the end the town leaders persuaded the militia to give up what they were trying to do, but not before the 1st Battalion The Princess of Wales's Royal Regiment earned one Victoria Cross, three Distinguished Service Orders, seven Military Crosses, and something like 15 Mentions in Despatches. It is no exaggeration to say it was the most concerted assault on a British battalion since Korea. I could, but shall not, speak at length about the courage and restraint of British soldiers under fire; how they interpreted their rules of engagement to ensure they used the minimum force necessary; and by so doing turned the populace of al-Amarah from being against us to being for us. So it was the people of al-Amarah who put an end to the fighting, rather than us.

In the urban areas the population was pretty disenchanted by now: 90 per cent of males between 16 and 45 were unemployed. Not only were they not getting essential services, but because of the Sadrist uprising the NGOs were not coming in to improve the situation. So this was another point of leverage we had with the locals: we could say, look; if you want water in your village, you will have to stop fighting because the NGOs are not going to come in and do it. This is a tactic we used in Maysan province to quite good effect.

In doctrine, we are taught to work out what we have to achieve, why we have to achieve it, and what we have to do to achieve it. In Iraq, there is not much the military has to do. The principal problem is adequate law and order, which is primarily a police problem. Here we got it wrong, as we used UK civil police to train the Iraqi police, mostly at the sort of psychological/cultural level, although we used British soldiers for much of the basic training. But British civil police should not be expected to go into an area like that: one of the four Basra suicide bombs was targeted against the police academy, which had 30 multinational civilian police in it, including ten British police, and they were hugely lucky. So we need to find a better way of training indigenous police, perhaps using a Carabinieri or gendarmerie model.

Basra should be a wealthy city. It sits on a sea of oil and has Iraq's only port. Historically it is a merchant town. But it was actually very poor because of the state of the infrastructure and lack of employment. It is no good if the NGOs, who can do reconstruction and create employment, cannot get in because of the security situation. Security, the economy and governance are all part of the same thing: it is too simplistic to say we cannot rebuild a country until there is security, since you cannot get security with a dissatisfied and disenchanted population. So you have to do it as a whole, simultaneously. We know all this, but we did not actually do anything about it, although we are now, at last.

I mentioned my mission earlier. It was:

> MND(SE) will conduct security and stabilisation operations within boundaries in order to create the conditions for the transfer of civil authority and control to the Iraqis.

So our end-state was transfer of civil authority and control. I had to create a whole series of effects – such as to defeat terrorism, ensure force protection, maximise Iraqi control, reduce criminality to an acceptable level, maintain and improve consent, neutralise non-compliant forces and so on. Actually to defeat terrorism was my bottom priority; force protection was very high, since we could not afford to lose people like the Japanese. Reduce criminality meant training the police and improving essential services. Maximise Iraqi control was very important – I received a letter from General Sir John Akehurst, who commanded in the Oman during the Dhofar War, and he told me to get the Iraqis to do as much as they could. I took him to heart; the Iraqis would fall into a dependency culture if we did everything for them, and so we had to make them assume responsibility.

Another effect I had to achieve was to *neutralise the militia*, and I think overall we failed: it was one of the hardest jobs to work out how to deal with them. The consent of the population, or at least the majority of the population in each of our four provinces, was my centre of gravity. If I lost that, my soldiers, the NGOs and the CPA could not move matters forward. For every Iraqi we killed, we knew we would have four more fighting us, because that is the way of life there. Therefore, it was logical that we should use the minimum necessary force.

On the morning of the Shia uprising on Friday, 7 April, when I woke to hear what had happened, I received widely differing reports. Of course, it was all bad news. I flew round the area to obtain a personal assessment by talking to the commanders, and then returned to headquarters to work out what to do next. My Chief of Staff was back in the UK training the next brigade due to come out. It was training to train the Iraqi security forces, but in the event it had to take over under fire in al-Amarah. On his third day in theatre, the commanding officer of the battalion got lost in the middle of al-Amarah, had his Land Rover destroyed by an RPG7, and had to take cover with his close protection team behind a wall. Twenty-seven RPG7s later, the wall was about two feet high before anybody could get there to extract him. By the fourth day this battalion was traumatised, and I seriously considered having to change it over because it had not been trained for what it was having to do. I felt that to be my fault, but in retrospect I suppose it was the right decision at the time, even if it had proven to be wrong. We had not thought through the 'what-ifs'. But within two weeks the battalion had become a hardened, professional, determined group of people, who spent over 12 weeks of their six-month tour under constant fire. It was a quite outstanding performance, and a tribute to the fact that the Army trains to fight, and is able to fall back on everything that has been learnt in the past; and because they were a regiment, and they were very much a family, The Princess of Wales's Regiment fought as a family; on top of that, when necessary the restraint they showed was equally magnificent. Our soldiers are fantastic; that nation is lucky to have them; I was lucky to command them.

Winning hearts and minds is all important; you do that by restraint, not by killing people if you can avoid it. And our soldiers did not kill people if they could avoid it. They would walk down streets with people with RPG7s at their feet, and because they were not threatening life, they could not fire at them. The moment anyone picked up an RPG7 they could engage, and they did. They conducted a dismounted infantry company attack with bayonets fixed, with a troop of tanks, against a position of 30 insurgents dug in on a road, with another enemy position of 30 with fire support about 400 metres to the right. They put in a company group attack. When the insurgent fire support group started to run away, the tanks stopped firing, because they were no longer a threat to life. They knew they would have to fight them again later, but they recognised they had to use minimum necessary force. To do this shows real discipline, and the result was that they changed the mindsets of the people in Maysan province who saw that they were trying to keep loss of life to a minimum.

I want to finish by making a few points about multinationality. It is a political necessity, but in some ways a military nonsense. Yet it is also a military requirement: apart from the USA, there are no armed forces in the world that have all the capabilities needed to wage modern warfare; and we could not have succeeded in the south-east without everybody else. There is a real need for cultural empathy in multinational operations. As a commander you have to understand the people you are commanding, and the position they are in. You need to cultivate your partners of choice; there are some who think the same way as we do. Obviously, there are Commonwealth countries that have the same doctrine and approach as us; they are easiest to work with, but you also need to understand those who do not think the same way and have different constraints, and you have to base your operational plan upon that. Language is a problem; I was immensely lucky to speak some Spanish so I could engage with the Italians, which was hugely helpful, as the Italians were in the most difficult position because of their national constraints, and getting them to do what I wanted was quite difficult.

Coalition partners need to have a common understanding. We were a junior partner to the US; they value the warrior ethos and see us as having it too. They found it difficult when I did not employ that ethos to the same extent that they did. On the other hand, other nations do not emphasise the warrior ethos as much. You might think I would say that about the Italians. After the Shia uprising they were politically not allowed to do anything in Nasiriyah for about six days. I asked, pleaded, tried coercion; every single method I could think of to persuade them to do something. Eventually I did it through shaming, by saying I would do it with my troops. This was politically unacceptable and they then got rid of the militia on the bridges very quickly, very clinically, and the Italian soldiers were simply brilliant. After that the morale of that brigade rose immensely.

As I said earlier, complaining about national constraints is like complaining about the weather; you just need to live with it. When I was commanding a brigade in Bosnia I had a Canadian battlegroup under command, which was not allowed out of the Canadian area of operations. I needed to impose martial law in Banja Luka overnight; I needed three battlegroups to do it, and I wanted to use English-speaking troops, which meant one British, one Dutch and one Canadian. Neither the Dutch nor the Canadians were allowed out of their areas and Banja Luka was in the British area, so I ended up cobbling together a battalion under Czech command. You have to be flexible and understand these constraints, and I should never have tried to persuade the Dutch and Canadians to go against the political constraints placed upon them. In multinational operations the commander must have a reserve and that reserve must be from his own nation. Unless you have an independent manoeuvre unit that is unconstrained and whose rules of engagement you control, then you will not attain the rapidity of reaction and the freedom of manoeuvre you need on operations.

You need to know your partners' strengths and weaknesses, and use them. The Italian Carabinieri are brilliant at being Carabinieri, and are good at training Iraqi police in how to be hard-nosed policemen. So we should have used them for that rather than for security operations.

The free release of intelligence is absolutely essential if it impacts on force protection, even if it puts a source at risk. You cannot afford to lose a coalition partner because it has found out it has lost life because you withheld information.

Good electronic communications are important, but face-to-face communication is far more effective. I never managed to speak to General Sanchez by radio or telephone in the seven months I was there because secure communications were so difficult: we were on the American system and the bottom priority. Instead, I flew to Baghdad for regular face-to-face meetings, and it was much better than speaking by phone. When you give an order, it is much better to look the Dane, Italian, Dutchman or Japanese in the eye; they understand it so much better.

To give you a feel for how I spent my time, I would get briefed on what had happened overnight at 0830; at 0900 I would be in a helicopter or a vehicle visiting, negotiating or listening, and I would get back at 1730. I did that six days a week; but not when an Ipswich Town match was being shown on Sky television because I would watch that. I spent 15 per cent of my time with UK forces, who provided 50 per cent of the command; I spent 20 per cent with people like NGOs and the civilian authorities; 25 per cent with the Iraqis, whom I was dealing with; and 40 per cent of my time with other nations, and it took that much effort to be able to understand them, and for them to understand me.

Chapter 7

Great Expectations: Broadening the Military Role to Include Nation Building

Barney White-Spunner – 22 November 2006

Whilst a number of interventions over the past decade have been successful – Bosnia, Sierra Leone and Macedonia to name three – several have not fully met expectations, both ours and those on whose behalf we are intervening. Although the nature of the intervention has changed dramatically since 1989, governments, although realising this, have found it a difficult truth to react to. My contention is that governments (of all countries prepared to intervene and from all parties) intervene without fully realising what they are trying to do, and that the armed forces are forced to compensate for this but can only do so with difficulty. I will illustrate my point by drawing on two examples. First, a successful intervention: the NATO operation in Macedonia in 2001; second, an operation which, whilst not actually failing, could have started succeeding rather sooner: the establishment of the International Assistance Force in Kabul in 2002. I had the privilege to command on both. I will not focus on Iraq, although inevitably I will draw on examples from there as I was Chief of Staff with the joint US/UK headquarters that ran the initial intervention. I will then develop some conclusions, which can be summarised by saying that it is probably our Armed Services that need to adapt.

I believe our failure to meet expectation is because we, both government and forces, have not thought out what we are trying to do. We have not understood the significant change in the scope of military operations since the fall of the Berlin Wall, and whilst Fukuyama[1] was lampooned, probably correctly, for calling that period the 'End of History', I maintain that it certainly marked a significant change in history.

In the Army, we now accept, and in fact embrace, the concept of a three-block war. This theory states that modern conflicts require forces to deal simultaneously with three different types of operation all in different city 'blocks'; block one is war-fighting, block two is peace enforcement and block three is economic and social reconstruction. Armies love categorising conflicts, usually once they are over, but this is one categorization that can be helpfully predictive. However, whilst we are quite good, if a bit under equipped, at the first block, and reasonably experienced at the second, we have not yet properly addressed the third block, which undermines our success in the other two, for it is this third block that is the enduring and decisive phase.

We have also drifted into a mistaken mindset in Western armies, a malaise caught from our politicians, of interpreting our missions from our own perspective and interests rather than from our host nations or the populations whom we are trying to help; those whom in a previous generation we would have referred to as 'the enemy', only conflicts today are not so simple.

We make two big mistakes. First, we do not take enough trouble to understand fully the countries or populations with whom we will be living. This was particularly true in Iraq, but also in Afghanistan. It is partly a feature of having to do too much with too little too often, but it is also

---

1   Francis Fukuyama (b. 1952), best known for his 1992 book *The End of History and the Last Man*.

because we have caught the disease of 'quickness' that politicians so love but which would have been such an anathema to our forebears in India or Africa. I sometimes think wistfully of the days when officers had to speak a native language to qualify for Staff College. This means that we do not appreciate the very great expectations of people like the Pashtuns or the Arabian Shia tribes of southern Iraq. We deploy, obsessed with our own short-term objectives, and fail to see what our deployments mean for those who have so often been eagerly awaiting our arrival. This attitude was expedient when armies intervened for selfish reasons, but now they do not.

Secondly, and more significantly, even if we do fully appreciate just what people expect of us, we are not organised or equipped to deal with them. The British Government, like that of the majority of Western democracies, turns in the first instance when there is a problem abroad to its Armed Forces. There are several reasons for this. First, Armed Forces are easy. They are arranged in organised teams and equipped to move relatively quickly; they are usually, certainly in the UK if not in the rest of NATO, more or less deployable; and they quickly make a visible public impact. Secondly, they can deal with the often chaotic security situation, which usually necessitated intervention in the first place. But this automatic reversion to Armed Forces exposes a lack of objective analysis. Why are we intervening? The ostensible reasons for intervention are very laudable. We do not, on the whole, now intervene because we want to annex territory, or to assist our European allies who might be threatened with annexation themselves, or even, if we go right back, to make people change religion. Instead, we tend to intervene mostly for reasons which, whilst not entirely selfless, do possess at least a modicum of altruism. We intervene now because we want countries to be stable and peaceful, with flourishing economies, and not to cause us any trouble, whether that be economic instability or terrorism. I would argue that this is a significant change since the drawdown from Empire and the Cold War, and one that, although acknowledged, is not actually recognised.

If your aim is therefore to intervene to restore stability, with all the political, economic and administrative activity that implies, then your force, in the widest sense, has to be equipped and financed to do that. This is what we are missing. We send Armed Forces to execute each block of our three-block war, and then wonder why we are unable to deliver even a small degree of normality. Our Whitehall machinery is still arranged as it was prior to 1914, with only a few small differences. Organisations like NATO, with its Byzantine bureaucracy, find the concept of reconstruction difficult to reconcile outside Europe, an important distinction to which I will return, whilst the European Union, with its 'Three Pillars',[2] and which could potentially emerge as the organisation which is able to deploy forces able to deal with all three blocks, has not matured far enough to do so and still lacks the confidence both of its member states and of its own ability to act.

If we fail to address this serious structural imbalance, then Western governments will not risk using armies for intervention. The political damage will be too great for them and they will find it easier to allow countries like Afghanistan to fester. The world, and our lives, will become more dangerous and gradually our global system will wither. Maybe armies should now accept it is no use complaining they are left on their own to deliver not only security but reconstruction, and accept that other government organisations are simply not interested in that aspect of wider government policy, seeing their remit as more the general alleviation of world poverty. I will come back to answer that at the end. It would be a major change in the concept of the use of military force, but then maybe the interpretation of what is military has changed without us realising it.

---

2   Between 1993 and 2009, the European Union legally consisted of three pillars: the European Communities pillar that dealt with economic, social and environmental policies; the Common Foreign and Security Policy pillar; and the Police and Judicial Cooperation in Criminal Matters pillar.

I am now going to look briefly at the events in Macedonia, or FYROM,[3] in 2001 and then contrast them with Afghanistan later the same year. In examining these two case studies I hope to make the point that the resolution of such conflicts is only possible if that third block is dealt with as effectively as the first two, and if the population believe in their economic and political future. I will also describe the operations themselves, as they are of intrinsic military interest, and I will also make some related points about the general conduct of operations along the way.

In the summer of 2001 I led the NATO Task Force which deployed to Macedonia to oversee the surrender of weapons and consequent disbandment of the Albanian National Liberation Army (NLA). This was led by Ali Ahmeti, a most remarkable man. He was an unlikely rebel chief. He is a short, slightly built man, with a pale face, beaky nose and huge eyes, which he would fix on me directly and unfalteringly as we negotiated. Physically he resembled a baby owl, but I rapidly came to appreciate that he had the wisdom of a much older one. He had originally been a philosophy student at Priština University, and taken part in the protests against the Serb administration in the late 1970s. Between 1981 and 1983 he was one of the main leaders of the Kosovo Albanian Student Movement, for which he was beaten and imprisoned by the Serb Police. In 1986 he gained political asylum in Switzerland, where he continued to be active in the Albanian movements in the Balkans. He also, he told me, developed a firm respect for a society that fostered ethnic tolerance and used the diversity of its population to achieve stability and commercial success. He became determined to introduce a similar system to his native Macedonia, where he believed that the Albanian minority, which comprise around 30 per cent of the population, did not enjoy the same privileges and opportunities as the Slav majority. They were denied employment in the public service, their language was not recognised and they had less access to higher education. Ali Achmeti returned to Macedonia and started to develop the NLA, which fought an insurgency campaign against the Macedonian Government from February 2000.

By May 2001 he had achieved international intervention, in the form of a European team to negotiate a ceasefire and try to establish the basis of a settlement. These negotiations resulted in an agreement being signed in early August 2001 between the Macedonian Government and the Albanian parties at Lake Ohrid. This required the Macedonian Government to withdraw its forces partially from the crisis areas and to enact a package of constitutional reforms, in return for which the NLA would hand over their weapons voluntarily to a NATO force and subsequently disband.

The weapon handover would be in three phases, arranged to coincide with the staged progress of the Ohrid reforms through the Macedonian Parliament, but with the whole process being complete within 30 days. The brigade which I had the honour to command, 16th Air Assault Brigade, was offered by the British Government to be the framework brigade for the NATO force that was subsequently assembled to oversee weapon collection and the NLA disbandment. NATO called this 'Operation Essential Harvest', which was at least a seasonal and partly descriptive name, and generally preferable to some of the more emotive titles under which other recent NATO operations have laboured. We had been warned this operation might be a possibility two months before, and conducted some limited planning and reconnaissance, but it was not until August 2001 that it became clear that we would actually deploy. Typically, the call came as we were one week into our summer leave, but we managed to get the headquarters into the Macedonian capital, Skopje, within three days, charged initially to judge whether the parties really were serious and whether NATO should risk deploying the full brigade force to start weapon collection.

---

3   NATO uses the name Former Yugoslav Republic of Macedonia (FYROM), apart from Turkey which recognises Macedonia by its constitutional name.

Our view was that the NLA at least were serious, and during our first meeting with Ali Ahmeti we discussed the number of weapons that his brigades would hand in. The North Atlantic Council eventually decided to authorise deployment on 22 August, but the Parliamentary timetable meant that the first third of the NLA's weapons had to be handed in by 29 August. We therefore had to get adequate forces into theatre to achieve this within six days.

The Brigade was growing rapidly and by this stage we numbered some 15 different nations. We took our full brigade headquarters and signal squadron, and our own logistic and medical regiments, together with one of our infantry battalions (2nd Battalion The Parachute Regiment, which took a Dutch mechanised company under command), a composite engineer regiment and the tactical control groups from our Gunner regiment, 7th Parachute Regiment, Royal Horse Artillery. They worked together with our Pathfinder Platoon, and G Squadron of the Special Air Service under a Special Forces Task Group to form what we called 'Harvest Liaison Teams'. We also took three other battalions: a French one, with two German and one Spanish companies under command, an Italian one with a Turkish company, and a Greek one. Our helicopters were supplied by the USA, the Explosive Ordnance Disposal (EOD) role by the Norwegian Navy and the Portuguese, as well as by our own Royal Engineers. The Canadians and our own Household Cavalry Regiment provided the recce, the Belgians our transport company, and our headquarters protection was provided by an extremely professional Czech parachute company. Lastly, the weapon destruction task was done with great enthusiasm by a mobile Hungarian team from a company which specialised in destroying ex-Warsaw Pact tanks after the end of the Cold War. This was to prove fortunate, as the NLA handed over two T55s to us in less than pristine condition. This posed something of a problem in that they had to be started, made roadworthy, moved out from a fairly inaccessible valley and then destroyed. The French Foreign Legion dealt with the first part of the problem, having no less than five trained T55 drivers in their ranks, and our Hungarians boasted that they could reduce a T55 to a pile of scrap in hours. In the event they accomplished it in something under ten! This was multinationality taken slightly too far, and, although just about workable on a straightforward operation, would have been hard to work had things gone less successfully.

It was also far too large a force, arousing Macedonian suspicions that we were more of an invasion force, and shows the folly of putting together force packages in the glorious isolation of London or Brussels.

Our plan for weapon collection was developed in the knowledge that the Macedonian Government was suspicious that NATO would become trapped by the NLA into occupying some sort of buffer zone, thereby effectively dividing their country, and making it impossible for NATO to leave, hence their suspicion at the number of troops – four battalions, whereas realistically the job could have been done by one. They were doubtful that the weapon collection could be accomplished within 30 days, and the most sceptical believed that the operation was some sort of NATO/Albanian plot to create a greater Albania, an option aired regularly by the paranoid Macedonian Slav media. Consequently we avoided giving each battlegroup a geographical area of responsibility, concentrating them instead around Skopje, with the Greeks running the weapons staging site.

We used the 'Harvest Liaison Teams' to work out the fine detail locally, and only deployed troops forward into the so-called crisis areas to mount a specific operation. These usually lasted about three days, and were conducted mostly using helicopters, given the remoteness of some of the sites and our desire to minimise NATO presence. The Liaison Teams numbered about 100, and it was they who lived in the forward areas. Each team consisted of four people, and within that team they built up parallel links with both the NLA and the Macedonian security forces, so that there was rapid and effective communication between the factions. This helped enormously, not only in arranging weapon collection but also in policing ceasefire violations, a task that was strictly outside our remit but without which we would have been unable to do any collection at all. The first week was a bit hectic, but we used what troops we had in theatre to collect the first third of weapons on time. This was not an entirely straightforward affair, as we had first to ensure that the Macedonian security forces had observed their part of the agreement and had withdrawn from the specified areas.

Whereas the Macedonian Army were generally compliant, the police were less so and many of their more extreme members were opposed to any agreement with the NLA. These groups called themselves after various animals, and we had to deal with Scorpions, Lions, Tigers and Wolves. Many of the members of this menagerie were paramilitaries and not under any effective control. They would try to start firefights with the NLA just as we were about to commence weapon collection, a tactic they quickly abandoned having tried it on with the Foreign Legion! The NLA stuck fairly rigidly to the agreements we made, and the predetermined number of weapons was always handed in, or on some occasions exceeded. They were grouped in five brigades, each responsible for a geographical area with a majority Albanian population. Numbers varied, from about 500 in the area of Kumanovo, to about 150 in the small Raduša valley. We estimated that 80 per cent of the NLA were ethnic Albanian Macedonians, with only a small number of Albanians from Kosovo or the Presseve Valley in their ranks. Some brigades pre-collected their weapons, and the quartermaster handed them over in bulk, whereas in other areas they staged a disbandment parade, marching up to the sites in good order (or relatively good order) with their heavy weapons and ammunition being carried by pack animals in wicker panniers. We never, incidentally, saw a NLA horse or mule in poor condition, even though forage was in short supply.

The second weapon collection phase proceeded relatively smoothly. The details were negotiated at long lunches with Ahmeti, and his chief of staff, General Ostreni, and the NLA chain of command worked effectively, so that Ahmeti's decisions were passed rapidly down to the local commanders. It was, however, more difficult to persuade them to proceed with the final third as political progress in the Macedonian Parliament was not keeping up with the agreed Ohrid timetable. We began to believe that the Government had never really believed that the NLA would disarm, and consequently had given little thought as to how to persuade the hard line Slav MPs to back the unpopular Ohrid Agreement. The NLA, on the other hand, always realised the importance of maintaining international support and were very conscious of their media image. It is impossible to condone their tactics overall, as these were overtly terrorist at times, but they did have a well-calculated strategy which was successful and which allowed them to achieve a considerable amount in a very short period. Consequently, they realised that to maintain international support they had to be seen to be honouring their part of the agreement, and Ahmeti eventually agreed to hand over the final third on time.

The Brigade completed the weapons collections by 26 September 2001, with the overall total exceeding the agreed figure by nearly 600. We began to recover on 27 September, in keeping with our agreement with the Macedonian Government, with Brigade Headquarters leaving on 4 October. We left the Harvest Liaison Teams in place for a further week to complete a thorough handover to the much smaller German-led monitor protection force which took over from us. Its mission was to provide support for the OSCE and EU monitors. This mission was originally called 'Task Force Amber Fox' by NATO, but this was rapidly changed to just 'Task Force Fox' when it was pointed out in the media that Amber Fox was the name of an American gay rights lobby group. The Macedonian Parliament finally passed the final phase of the Ohrid reforms in mid-November, and the omens for the future look relatively positive, with elections due in the New Year.

Although our mission was strictly limited to weapon collection, our deployment achieved a dynamic of its own. By the time we left after nearly seven weeks, there was an effective ceasefire, the Macedonian Army had largely withdrawn to barracks, the NLA had disbanded, nearly 40,000 refugees had returned home, the schools had opened, and farmers were working their fields in the Albanian areas for the first time in nine months. So let me return to my point. Why did it work? Why was Macedonia able to avoid civil war and the tragedy that befell Bosnia? There are several reasons. First, NATO, for once, under the energetic leadership of George Robertson, acted early. They followed up a political initiative with military force and were content for the deployed military commander (that is, me) to deal with the top of the Macedonian Government, reinforced, when necessary, with heavyweight political intervention.

Secondly, but much more importantly, it worked because Ahmeti had planned it in detail. His strategy was aimed at NATO deploying. Why? Because he knew that with NATO would come the development and enfranchisement he so passionately wanted. NATO succeeded in Macedonia, and achieved stability, only because with it came potential membership of the Europe Union and the promise of a standard of living which most Albanians only dreamed of and which the Macedonian Serbs were not prepared to risk losing. In 2002 Ahmeti founded a new political party, the Democratic Union for Integration, which, in September that year, won the elections amongst the Albanian parties, and Ahmeti became a Deputy in the Macedonian Parliament, and a coalition partner with a Government that had once charged him with terrorism. Macedonia has now gone beyond the NATO Partnership for Peace Programme and overtaken its Balkan neighbours, joining the Membership Action Plan; it may become a full member in 2008 or 2009 and, however much one might question the validity of NATO as an organisation today, it certainly remains something of a security gold standard in Eastern Europe. But we succeeded because we were seen as the means to a better way of life and economic opportunity; we should never forget that.

Whilst we were in Macedonia, the attacks of 11 September 2001 happened and within two months of my return I found myself, and my Brigade Recce Team, standing in the muddy wasteland of what had once been the British Embassy garden in Kabul.

Pause to consider the position in Afghanistan in late 2001. The Taliban were in the process of falling, Karzai was trying to form a government and the Bonn talks were attempting to establish who would be in it. There was almost universal acclamation at the ousting of the Taliban, particularly in Afghanistan, and huge support for Karzai's fledgling Government abroad. Within two months, US $3 billion had been pledged in reconstruction aid, of which more, or more accurately a lot less, later. Yet Karzai's position was far from firm. The country still saw itself, like Macedonia, as a loose federation of separate entities, the predominant Pashtuns, the Tadjiks and the Hazara, the perpetual hewers of wood and drawers of water, as Levi accurately and sympathetically termed them. The Government was dominated by what we called the 'Panjshir Trio', being Qanooni, as Minister of the Interior, Fahim Khan as Defence Minister and Abdullah with the foreign portfolio. In the background, ever present, were the spirits behind the preceding civil war, men like Hekmatyar Gulbudin, in exile but still influential, and Sayef. We did not understand the complexities of the tribal and family allegiances, nor the huge impact of narcotics, not only on peoples' livelihood but also on politics. Drugs were the only viable Afghan export in 2001, worth $600 million to farmers, $1–2.5 billion as they left Afghanistan, but $8.4 billion on Western streets.

Put yourself, therefore, for a moment, in the position of an average Afghan in 2001. You live in one of the poorest countries in the world. Your population of around 20 million live on something less than $100 per annum, and 80 per cent of you are employed in agriculture. And remember that only 12 per cent of your land is arable; 40 per cent is mountain and 2 per cent forest. The remainder is effectively desert. The recent very serious drought, which was at its worst in 1999 to 2001, meant that your land went from being self-sufficient in the 1970s to being heavily dependent on the World Food Programme to feed itself. You have lived through 20 years of war, both foreign invasion and civil war. Your cities, especially Kabul, have been destroyed and your irrigation systems in your villages haphazardly smashed by the Taliban. Your children can only find work abroad and your daughters have missed out on a generation's worth of education. You actually look back with some nostalgia to the Russian occupation when at least women had some equality. You will all be familiar with some of the excellent modern Afghan literature that tells the story of this time, in books such as *The Kite Runner*.[4]

Yet everything is not that bleak to you, because now the West owes you a very big favour. You have not only defeated the Soviet Empire, and caused the downfall of Communism worldwide, or so you think, but now it is your people, both Tadjik and Pashtun, who have defeated Bin Laden and al-Qaeda, and who have, with your American and British allies, started the decline of the Islamic terrorist you hate because it besmirches your religion. And now it is time for your reward. Now your allies send in troops. You have expected this as the security situation remains bad and you know that there are remnants of the Taliban to be defeated. You are not sure who all these foreign troops are, as there seems to be a multitude of different nations policing your streets. In fact at first you think they could be Russians again as they all seem to arrive in Russian aircraft. But whoever they are they do bring security, and refugees start returning, your children who have been working in Pakistan, and you know that soon these extraordinarily powerful nations will have the electricity on, the water flowing, the goods in the shops. And you wait … and you wait … and you wait.

And this was what we found so difficult. Between December 2001 and January 2002 we assembled a brigade in Kabul; 17 nations this time, even more difficult than the 15 in Macedonia. Security was fairly easily re-established, but only in the Kabul area. In fact, most of the trouble was with criminal gangs or warlords whom no one dared face up to, rather than the Taliban. We found some problems with communications, there being no newspapers, very limited television and no radios. The most effective method of explaining what we were trying to do was through the Mullahs. One of the most encouraging aspects of that period was how warmly we were welcomed by the clerics, who were ashamed at the manner in which the Taliban had besmirched Islam. Every Thursday the Chief Mullah in Kabul would gather his suffragans, both Sunni and Shia, and I would be invited for tea and to explain myself, so that our doings could be explained at Friday prayers.

But the real problem, even in those early days, was that no one would grip reconstruction. Armies of officials arrived, and study after study was commissioned, but after six months I recall talking to one village headman who said that he was delighted to see me. I belonged, he said, to a very powerful nation, one who could fly invisible aircraft which could kill a man at the press of a button, so I would very soon be able to accomplish the simple task of installing a village pump.

Why were we in this position? First, the new Afghan Government had no overall strategy for engaging the West in reconstructing Afghanistan. They found themselves dealing with conflicting groups of officials from UN, force contributors and NATO. The Government functioned insufficiently well to run redevelopment itself, since there was still considerable factionalism and corruption, and was unable to force one foreign agency to take a lead. Secondly, the international reconstruction money promised early in 2002 failed to materialise. This was partly because the international community did not have the mechanisms to spend it, and was reluctant to trust the military to do so. This was mistaken, as it was we who had first-hand knowledge of what was required. Thirdly, though, we lacked planning and organisation. We went into Afghanistan absolutely clear that we had to 'pump prime' the economy and to start redevelopment, but with

---

4   Husseini 2004.

no plan as to how to do so. And did we repeat the same mistake in Iraq a year later? There was, in Afghanistan and Iraq, no European dream on offer. So what has happened? Effectively we have to start again. There has been a failure of analysis, and that is because our system has no one body who sees it as their responsibility to do that analysis.

So what can we conclude from these two examples? To me this means that we have to re-address *why* we intervene and then establish the means to deliver our policy. Macedonia worked because we delivered Europe – with all that meant. If we are to intervene outside we need to appreciate that the UN cannot deliver the same. Armies must continue to deliver blocks one and two; it is what we are for, and the need for that capability will continue for decades, probably centuries. We have therefore to be equipped and organised to be successful at war-fighting and peace enforcement, and that means we need people and equipment. Yet increasingly we are coming to realise that there is little point in achieving success in blocks one and two if you fail in block three.

At this stage I should emphasise that I am not downplaying the difficulties of reconstruction. I am talking about starting it – not implementing Marshall Plans. I am talking about pump priming, engaging local resources, and relying on our old economic friend, the 'accelerator', and local initiative to take effect. But this requires organisation. I find it odd that we have highly developed security structures but trust the critical area of aid to an unaudited group of voluntary organisations. Maybe, therefore, the time has now come to change. Armies must accept that the task of defence has changed since 1989. They must not only destroy but also rebuild. And why not extend the expertise developed for wielding spears into expertise for manufacturing ploughshares? Because, to continue the Micah analogy, if a man cannot sit at peace under his vine, then he may well pick up his spear again.

The challenge is economic. Armies can only just afford to prepare themselves for success on blocks one and two. There are no spare resources. But then if governments are serious in their strategic intentions, they will realise that a small redistribution of money will achieve a lot. Personally, I see reconstruction as now being an integral part of defence. Without it, armies are unusable and Western foreign policy must become isolationist. My own solution is to use the Territorial Army.

There is nothing difficult here. What needs doing is really quite simple. The resources, the goodwill and the machinery are there – what is lacking is any initiative to bring them together. *The March of Folly*, Barbara Tuchman's wonderful book,[5] takes up examples of governments knowingly pursuing policies that must ultimately lead to them suffering serious damage or even being defeated – but despite all the powers at their disposal, they are unable to react. I think we are in that position now.

---

5   Tuchman 1984.

Chapter 8

Iraq 2004: The View from Baghdad

Andrew Graham – 26 October 2005

I deployed in late March 2004 as a major general, to be the Senior British Military Representative in Iraq and the UK's Deputy Commanding General in the Headquarters of Combined Joint Task Force 7 (CJTF-7), commanded by Lieutenant General Rick Sanchez. Within a fortnight a more senior, three-star British Senior Representative[1] had been deployed and my appointment was to shift to become one of the two,[2] and later one of the three,[3] deputies to the Commander of Multi-National Corps – Iraq (MNC-I). I venture that history will consider 2004 to have been a catalytic year, not only for the US-led Coalition attempting to help Iraq reach a state of 'normality' (a definition for 'normality' was certainly needed here), but also for the longer-term future of the country as a forward-looking, singular, stable, not vengeful, and independent, prosperous state.

Omens

Anyone reading the omens in March and April 2004, one short year after the successful breakthrough and stunning advance to Baghdad, the defeat of the Iraqi Armed Forces and the toppling of the regime, might have had reason to be gloomy.

The decisions to disband the Iraq Army and to bar former members of the Ba'ath party from Government, administrative or professional office had deprived the country of two essential prerequisites for stabilisation – governance and security. The impact was starting to be felt in terms both of leaving a vacuum that the collective efforts of the Coalition were unable to fill and of fuelling a sense of resentment in a significant proportion of the population for whom the loss of livelihood and prestige was now a pressing concern.

During the Shia festival of Arba'aeen in February, huge car bombs had infiltrated Coalition security, killing a large number of worshippers and injuring many more. This was an ominous sign of a militant Sunni backlash against what was seen as the threat of an emerging Shia powerbase.

The President of the Iraq Governing Council (IGC) was assassinated by a car bomb in Baghdad less than three months before governing authority was to be passed to the Iraqi Interim Government.

The arrest of Moqtada al-Sadr's advisor, Yacoubi, in Najaf, and the closure of the al-Hawza newspaper in late March, sparked a Shia backlash manifested by very fierce fighting first in Sadr City – home to one million disenfranchised, militant, unemployed Shia, displaced from the south by Saddam Hussein. The fighting and unrest resonated across the south of the country, including in the holy cities of Najaf and Karbala, and in the major towns of the southern provinces including al-Kut, al-Amarah, Na'asariyah and Basra.

---

1   Lieutenant General (now General Sir) John McColl; see Chapter 9.
2   One Canadian and one British.
3   One Canadian, one British and one Italian.

The almost obsessive drive to hold elections as a way of demonstrating progress towards some sort of democratic ideal held sway, yet the bombing of the UN headquarters in the autumn of 2003 meant that there was only a skeleton UN presence in the country to provide the electoral process with the stamp of legitimacy.

The revelations about the mistreatment of the internees in Abu Ghrayb prison had broken with the inevitable and very damaging impact on the perceptions that Iraqis and the broader Arab and Muslim world held about the Coalition.

The investment and development effort that was expected to be at least restoring and, better still, improving services (sewage, water, electricity, trash and so on) and starting to upgrade the country's oil refining and pipeline infrastructure had not yet materialised for a variety of security, contractual and capacity reasons.

Still to come were the barbaric and very public murders of four Blackwater employees in Fallujah in March, and the subsequent takeover of that town by Iraqi extremists offering safe haven to foreign fighters, including Abu Musa al-Zarqawi, whose ruthless use of the media to transmit atrocity as an instrument of terror and whose declared hatred of the Shia threatened civil war.

Coalition Command Arrangements

The combination of these and other events and factors was certainly enough to stretch the capacity of a civilian-led, military-enabled coalition effort whose structure and Command, Control, Communication and Coordination arrangements were still in transition. After the truncated involvement of ORHA, the responsibility for running the country lay with the Coalition Provisional Authority led by Paul Bremer III, with a network of provincial teams dispersed to provincial capitals and working alongside, but normally not collocated with, the Coalition military. By March 2004 the Coalition Provisional Authority's eyes were on the imminent handover of governing responsibility to the Iraqi Interim Government in July 2004, so an understandable 'end-of-season' atmosphere prevailed.

On the military side, command and control clarified incrementally in the first quarter of the year with the arrival of the US Army's Headquarters III Corps (and two of its subordinate divisions) to replace Headquarters V Corps and form the framework for Coalition military headquarters. III Corps was a 'swept-up' headquarters whose preparation had included conducting a mission rehearsal exercise to defeat the invasion of South Korea by North Korea. It was a very sensible decision therefore to optimise command and control arrangements in April–May 2004 by splitting CJTF-7; to create a permanent Headquarters Multi-National Forces – Iraq (MNF-I), at four-star level, to focus at the political/operational level, including directing the work to establish, train and organise the embryonic Iraqi police and security apparatus (army, police, border guards); and to use III Corps as a subordinate Headquarters Multi-National Corps – Iraq, at three-star level, to plan and conduct corps-level operations at the higher tactical level. From a British perspective, establishing British deputies to both US four- and three-star levels of command improved the UK's capacity to influence, engage, monitor and contribute. This was essential, since the UK's responsibility as a Joint Occupying Power did not lapse until the transition to Iraqi authority and the Iraqi Interim Government on 28 June 2004.

In my view the command arrangements were good enough to provide for the parochial and short-term requirements for running the Coalition, but were not yet sufficiently ordered nor sufficiently capable, comprehensive and relevant to deal with the situation in which the Coalition found itself. The task at hand was significant; to provide stability for a country turned over by war, whose people were dissatisfied with the internal situation and unsure of the direction of travel through elections towards an unpredictable political, institutional, security, economic and development outcome. From a military perspective the campaign planning, and many of the design and execution arrangements, were uncertain.

For example, did US Central Command have responsibility for planning and conducting the military campaign? If not, then did the Commander CJTF-7? And if he did, then were the neighbouring countries of Iran, Turkey, Syria, Kuwait, Jordan and Saudi Arabia as well as the northern waters of the Arabian Gulf within his Area of Interest, even if not within the Joint Area of Operations?

Arrangements to implement the concept of a single civil-military plan enabled by civil-military authority and responsibility at subordinate levels were at best opaque and at worst non-existent. That included inside the Green Zone, where Commander CJTF-7 did not coexist closely with Paul Bremer, preferring, for span of command reasons as much as anything, I believe, to focus on the significant range of tactical issues being faced by the six very diverse Major Subordinate Commands (MSCs), the divisional-level areas which comprised the Coalition's military deployment in Iraq.

The Iraqi Theatre

While the stage upon which CJTF-7 was acting was limited to the national boundaries of Iraq, and the terrestrial ones at that, the Iraq theatre of operations was, or should have been, considerably broader. There were many influences on the activity taking place within Iraq's borders, summarised in the following paragraphs.

Then, as now, the Iraqi nation was not homogeneous. The demographics are well known (see Map 5.1): a Shia majority living predominantly in the south or in Sadr City; a very significant Sunni minority living for the most part in Baghdad and the centre, centre-west and north of the country; the Kurdish centres of population in the Kurdish Autonomous Region in the north-east of the country.

Iranian influence on, and support for, Shia parties such as the Badr and SCIRI factions, and the religious influence of Iranian ayatollahs on the Iraqi Shia, were pervasive, potentially destabilising and oblivious to frontiers.

Jordan and Syria provided safe havens for former Ba'athists whose financial influence and authority stretched back into Iraq. Extremist recruits crossed the western and south-western borders to join the organisations fighting in and around Baghdad, Ramadi and Fallujah. This was exacerbated by tribal and ethnic boundaries that crossed international frontiers, exemplified by the Kurds living in Turkey, Iraq and Iran – one ethnic nation, three countries.

In command and control terms, the handling of all matters external to Iraq were US Central Command's responsibility – yet Turkey was in US European Command's area of responsibility, not Central Command's.

Iraq's oil was drilled north of the capital Baghdad and transported by a fragile, vulnerable pipeline system some 400 miles south for export through the two offshore loading platforms off the mouth of the Shatt al-Arab river.

The choice of Balad, 60 miles north of Baghdad, to be the logistic hub for US forces was excellent, in a perfect world. The fact that two of the three principal overland logistic routes required convoys to either circumnavigate Baghdad or pass through the Fallujah–Ramadi corridor was to prove a significant vulnerability.

Situation – The Players

'Enemy Forces'

The stresses and strains on the country from dissident insurrectionist, insurgent groupings and criminals in 2004 were encapsulated in an assessment Venn diagram put together by the J2 briefers at the time. In no particular order of size, potential for violence or disruption, scale of threat or effectiveness, the actors who fell most naturally into the 'enemy forces' category (at least from a Coalition Force viewpoint, since they were either shooting at us, threatening violence to the people we were trying to protect, or disrupting our and the Iraqi Interim Government's activity, and local life, trade and society) could be loosely placed into five groups.

The *Former Regime Elements'* goals were to remove the Coalition, return Saddam Hussein to power, and to restore Ba'athist rule. In simple terms they represented those for whom defeat had meant a loss of power, wealth and position and who wished to turn back the clock. The leading light at the time, Izzat Ibrahim al-Duri (Number 6 in the 'Pack of Cards'[4]), had formed the National Council of Iraq in the summer of 2003 and was still at large in the summer of 2004.

The *Sunni Arab Rejectionists* represented the moderate Sunni community, whose perceptions of having seen their rights removed and powers abased were reinforced by a fear of what they perceived to be the threat of a rising tide of Shia hegemonic supremacy. Their numbers were swelled by Sunnis whose resentment at lost jobs, limited opportunities and promises of improvement not having materialised, manifested itself in the taking up of arms on an opportunity basis. After the capture of Saddam Hussein, the shared and linking objective of the rejectionists and Former Regime Elements was the removal of the Coalition. Thus, both could appeal to Iraqi nationalist and to co-religionist fervour.

Unconnected to these groupings, but wrapped into the 'dissident' or 'insurgent' mix because they shared the aim of throwing out the Coalition or, at least, making life as difficult as possible for the Coalition and the emerging Iraqi Government in order to consolidate their negotiating, power-broking, position, were the *Shia Extremists* – the militant wing of the Shia. In 2004 the violence was led by Moqtada al-Sadr, son and grandson of populist, dissident figures, whose father and brothers had been murdered by the Ba'athist regime. The lack of promised betterment was tinder to his populist brand of nationalist, anti-Coalition rhetoric, and by March 2004 he was emerging as something of a talisman for the young, unemployed, disaffected, disenfranchised, ill-educated urban Shia, with a particularly receptive audience in Sadr City, east Baghdad. It is too simplistic to say that Moqtada represented the noisy, irreverent, militant, less doctrinal Shiism against the quietist tradition exemplified by Grand Ayatollah Ali al-Sistani. Nonetheless, the violence that raged across the south in early April 2004, and again in August 2004, which included the occupation of the Imam Ali Mosque in Najaf and forced the redeployment of three US battalions from Baghdad and Mosul, was sufficiently destabilising for it to be suggested that Gulf War Three was imminent – and only half jokingly!

The number of *Foreign Islamic Extremists* increased in 2003, driven by the lure of jihad against what they saw as occupying forces, with Fallujah providing a particular focus for attention. The spring and summer of 2004 saw the emergence of a particular brand of extremism advocated and practised by Abu Musab al-Zarqawi, a Jordanian operating in and around Fallujah, whose message was that the invasion was an affront to Islam which must be avenged by the waging of jihad.

---

4   In 2003 the US Army produced a pack of cards showing the 55 most-wanted members of Saddam Hussein's Government.

These people operated at the extreme limits of the spectrum of violence – large, complex IEDs, ambushes, suicide bombings, kidnaps and public assassinations – and close to the extreme limits of the tolerance of the local population for their activities. It was ominous that al-Zarqawi considered Shia to be apostates and would not shy from taking action that would split the country irrevocably on doctrinal lines. Ominous too that the concept of jihad, which is an essentially offensive idea about spreading the message of the Prophet through military means, was morphing to give the concept of 'defensive' or 'lesser' jihad credibility.

The mix was completed by an eclectic range of criminals, facilitators and *Iraqi Islamic extremists* – loosely defined as those who espoused the Wahhabi and Salafist traditions. These were outnumbered by, and therefore suspicious of, the foreigners; they were very aware that you sup with those particular devils with a very long spoon, but happy enough to be allies when goals coincide, and shared the belief that rule by non-Muslims was 'a blasphemous inversion of God's dispensation'. Instability encourages criminality, and where the salary for an insurgent exceeds the salary to be made by legitimate means, then some will take up arms who might not have done if other opportunities existed; but other opportunities were scarce.

'Friendly Forces'

The 'friendly forces' category was clearer, and included the cross-party Iraqi Governing Council established under the Coalition Provisional Authority, which provided the Presidency on a monthly rotational basis and laid a veneer of legitimacy as the country moved towards the transition for governing authority planned for 30 June – 1 July 2004. Over the summer the Governing Council morphed into the Iraqi Interim Government.

The Iraqi Interim Government and its ministers presided over ministries that were ministries in name only, since they lacked a civil service, coordinating machinery or a means of deriving policy and giving direction, and with pay and funding hanging by a thread. The concept of partnership in Government was to develop through 2004, and especially once Dr Allawi was Prime Minister from 28 June, working on a tripartite basis with the US Ambassador John Negroponte and the Commander MNF-I, General George Casey. The tripartite relationship's cohesion depended on a free exchange of advice, on partnership and on a commitment to engagement to see things through. There was a clear understanding that UN involvement to lead the move towards elections and give necessary legitimacy was essential, but the UN could not become so important that it made itself a target that could be attacked again and forced to withdraw, thus rendering the whole enterprise illegal or at least hamstrung.

The 18 provinces each had a Governor and governing council able to operate virtually autonomously, given that the Coalition military provided the only effective means of exercising command and control or of communicating reliably in the country.

The transformation from HQ CJTF-7 to MNF-I, with two subordinate three-star commands – MNC-I, and the Multi-National Stabilisation and Transition Command Iraq (MNSTC-I) – was a significant moment for the campaign, marking as it did the shift from an invading posture to that of stabilisation and support. MNC-I was charged with executing the military activity to support the MNF-I campaign plan (see below), particularly along the security line of operation, but helping where it could in governance, communications and the economy. MNSTC-I was charged with recruiting, training and equipping the Iraqi Security Forces (ISF) – Government ministries, the police, Army, Navy and National Guard – effectively from a standing start.

MNC-I consisted of six major subordinate commands, essentially multinational divisions under one-/two-star command, with a seventh added in the late summer of 2004 as the Republic of

Korea sent a force to operate in Iraq, on the strict understanding that it would neither undertake offensive operations nor should be deployed in an area of threat, since its mission was to support development.

Mission(s)

Initially, the theme of the missions given to CJTF subordinate formations was offensive: 'to conduct offensive operations in order to ...'. That theme changed over the summer as recognition that in the situation in which Coalition forces found themselves, namely operating in support of a sovereign Government, however impotent, 'being offensive' was just one operational or tactical technique among many. The strategic context within which such missions were framed could be explained as having four stages:

Phase 1 – *Liberation*, achieved by June 2003, leading to:

Phase 2 – *Occupation*, where the CPA, advised by the IGC and with the security muscle provided by the Coalition forces, governed the country. The transition to:

Phase 3 – *Partnership* occurred on 28 June 2004, when the IGC (becoming the Iraqi Interim Government) governed the country, 'advised' by the Coalition diplomatic missions, MNF-I and the UN. The elections planned (and held) in January 2005 were to be a significant milestone, along with the development of capable Iraqi Security Forces, ministries and state institutions, on the road to:

Phase 4 – *Self-Reliance*. The timeline for the transition from Partnership to Self-Reliance was indeterminate – described in August 2004 as 'after January 2006'. Self-Reliance was characterised by there being an elected Government, effective governance, and effective, capable ISF sustained by what were euphemistically termed 'continued diplomatic relations'. The absence of a strategic economic or development strand is noticeable, and was remarked upon by the military at the time.

I do not recall a CJTF-7 campaign plan, but I may have missed it. General George Casey's arrival to command the newly constituted MNF-I stimulated a flurry of work. The resulting plan, with its four lines of operation – Security, Governance, Economic Development, Communication – driving towards a clear strategic end-state,[5] and with clear indicators of 'what success looks like',[6] seemed a pragmatic and realistic model of its kind, at least for the time and circumstances (always providing that the resources and the necessary civil support and activity materialised). Significantly, General Casey accepted that the final outcome for Iraq could not be precisely determined. It would fall within an 'arc of acceptability' that might look strange to Western eyes but was acceptable, especially 'if it works for, and suits, the Iraqis'.

---

5   End-state: Iraq at peace with its neighbours, with a representative Government that respects the rights of all Iraqis, and security forces sufficient to maintain domestic order and to deny safe haven to terrorists.

6   Indicators of success include: a legitimate and functioning Iraqi Government; changed image of the Coalition; insurgents and terrorists neutralised; basic needs met; etc.

The operational concept for the Force was to secure the borders, secure Baghdad, neutralise the insurgency in the 'Sunni Triangle' and sustain support by the Shia and the Kurds. The main effort was the neutralisation of the insurgency in the Sunni Triangle, but the importance of sustaining the support of the Shia and Kurdish populations was recognised. Particular emphasis was put on activity in the south, where the majority of oil installations were sited, and through which our principal line of logistic communication ran. The concept presupposed a relationship between the political/governance, development and security lines of activity, underpinned by a strong communications line.

Observations

The discussion of the situation, mission and concept of operations above relates to the situation at hand in 2004, evolving as it was. In seeking to establish some relevant conclusions from my experience it is not useful to try to pick a snapshot moment upon which to focus, but better to offer some key observations and lessons identified as events unfolded through the summer.

Coalitions

Coalitions are a fact of military life. Political leaders like to draw in other nations to support an enterprise and to give it body, legitimacy and balance. Iraq in 2004 exemplified both the benefits, primarily in terms of political buy-in and burden-sharing, and the challenges of creating an effective coalition force and then getting it to work. My notes show that on one particular day there were 163,930 military members of the Coalition from 30 countries (not including Iraq) in Iraq. Contingents varied in size from 139,524 (USA) to nine (Norway), and the posture of each contingent, and particularly the extent to which it would or not participate in offensive operations, depended on the national mandate.

Time spent in understanding the nuances and peculiarities of coalitions is time very well spent. Commanders need to consider how best to construct them to be effective (or at least to minimise their potential to be ineffective), and to spend time getting to know the members of the coalition and their strengths and limitations. You should never have to ask a question, make a demand or give an order to which the answer will either be 'no' or a 'yes' that is so qualified that it is a licence to consent and evade in order to save face. The key must be to have sufficient knowledge of national mandates, constraints and freedoms under which the military are operating.

Of the six Major Subordinate Commands, two were not framed around a US division or USMC equivalent. Multi-National Division (Centre South) – MND(CS) – offers an interesting example of the challenges faced by contributing nations working to a dominant framework nation. The division was headquartered on the historic site of Babylon, commanded by a two-star Polish general, and consisted of between 15 and 17 national contingents for the majority of whom English was not the second language of choice. The division's area of operations covered four provinces and included: the cities of al-Najaf and Karbala with their mosques and shrines sacred to the Shia; the volatile (as it was to prove) town of al-Kut on the Tigris; a northern boundary that fringed the southern suburbs of Baghdad; the main supply routes from Kuwait which ran through its centre; a mix of Sunni and Shia in the northern and western areas, particularly those closest to, but across the Euphrates from, Ramadi and Fallujah. Exactly how, or indeed why, the strategic importance of the four provinces had been underestimated in the initial lay down of forces was not clear to me. The fact that the UK's ambition after the invasion seemed limited in scope to occupying ground that was convenient rather than important may have had something to do with it, or the potential volatility of the Shia population may have been underestimated.

On two occasions in 2004, al-Kut exploded into violence as part of the reaction to public disorder in Sadr City, al-Najaf and Karbala. On the first occasion (April 2004), the CPA centre was nearly overrun, but the in-place Ukrainian force was prohibited from taking action other than self-defence and so was powerless to intervene without ignoring the national red card. US forces were forced to redeploy from the west to restore order. On the second occasion, in August 2004, the Iraqi Governor came under threat from the mob but no local Coalition response could be generated. A Stryker battalion had to be deployed from Mosul to restore the situation; this was an extraordinary example of operational agility involving a more than 350 km road move, a helicopter airlift of spares and stores to enable and support the redeployment, and excellent battle procedure and staff work that saw the battalion operating on completely new ground within 48 hours of the initial warning order.

On 11 March 2004, Madrid was struck by bombs detonated on packed trains. Within three weeks the Spanish Government had fallen, a new Government promising the withdrawal of the Spanish contingent had been elected, and the Spanish contingent had been effectively confined to barracks with only the most limited self-protection roles allowed. Nothing could have prepared the Coalition commanders for that eventuality, especially since the Spanish themselves had been amongst the more forward-leaning of contingents in MND(CS).

In early April 2004 the violence in Sadr City and across the south prompted the US to consider relaxing their rules of engagement to allow pre-emptive offensive action in a situation where the principle of 'hostile force' applied. This relaxation was fine in theory, except that the divisional areas of operation where such a relaxation might have been relevant lay under the command of nations who either would not or could not amend their rules of engagement accordingly. In coalition operations the commander's ability to influence such things as rules of engagement is significantly curtailed; however dominant one member may be, and however frustrating it may be, the force simply will not dance to one tune in areas where national prerogative applies.

Also, some coalition members join for specific political or economic, rather than military, purposes, and their objectives have to be accommodated within the operational framework. In 2004, Japan's contingent was deployed into al-Muthanna Province on the south-west of the country to a very strongly protected, entirely self-sufficient base with a mission to provide humanitarian (primarily potable water) and medical support to the local population. By mid-2004 the Republic of Korea's contingent had also been offered and accepted; this time to be deployed to an area where the chance of attack was minimal but where it could provide humanitarian, engineering, educational, economic and other support to the local population. To meet these requirements eyes turned to the Kurdish Autonomous Region, with security assured by the local peshmerga in return for promised investment.

Perhaps eclectic coalitions incorporating all the instruments of power are the way of the future; there are certainly lessons to be learnt from Iraq in 2004. However, political expediency has to be balanced against hard reality in theatre since not everyone can be deployed to the places where freedom from attack is assured and the requirement not to conduct military tasks beyond those needed for self-protection is guaranteed.

Transitional Government

Iraq in 2004 offers an example of a transition in Government without the benefit of an election. The military practicalities of effecting such a transition, or at least of trying to demonstrate on the ground that something has occurred, were exemplified by the approach of 1st US Cavalry Division in Baghdad. The commanding general had made it clear to his division that he saw the population of Baghdad, and particularly those he termed as fence-sitters, to be 'vital ground'. His division attacked the problem of securing that vital ground with the unique military tool of SWET operations (sewage, water, electricity, trash), underpinned by military tasks designed to create the security bubble within which those operations could take place, ideally using the labour of the population and thus creating jobs and building a sense of participation, engagement and ownership. In the run-up to the 28 June transfer of power, the Division increased its efforts to ensure that as many Iraqi police and soldiers as possible would be available and prepared to patrol in selected areas of Baghdad, to brief the incoming mayor and his people on their SWET efforts and to highlight where the earliest wins for Iraqi national and city Government action lay. Despite the criticism from some in the military chain of command that the plans were not kinetic enough, the people of Baghdad who were prepared to notice would have seen that the emphasis, shade and character of activity in Baghdad had shifted, with 1st Cavalry Division attempting to be 'in support of' rather than 'supported by'.

Deputies

The use to which the US Army puts deputies is instructive; we have something to learn. Each division has two deputy commanders – one for manoeuvre and one for support; every divisional commander in Iraq in 2004 had been a Deputy Commanding General of a division; MNC-I had three deputies – one (Canadian) embedded as part of Headquarters III Corps and two from other nations (UK and Italy). In the words of Lieutenant General Tom Metz Commanding MNC-I: 'if there were 48 hours in a day then the Commanding General would be everywhere; but there aren't and he can't, so deputies fill the spaces where he would wish to put emphasis but cannot'. With the Corps commanding 13 separate brigades (including intelligence, military police, aviation and transport) outside the divisional structure, and with cross-Corps responsibilities in addition to the six Major Subordinate Commands, and with the scale of logistic support effort required to sustain the Coalition and additional tasks of clearing, re-storing and securing ammunition compounds, preparing to receive and employ Iraqi forces, civil-military tasks, support to developing ministries, there was plenty of work for deputies to do. And this was quite apart from getting involved with the day-to-day planning for operations and getting around the theatre as the Commander's eyes, ears and directed telescope, and as a sounding board for the divisional commanders.

Private Security Companies and Contractors

Private Security Companies and contractors are establishing themselves as another fact of life in any military operation. They fill gaps in capability, release troops for more military tasks and take up the slack for the routine security and protection tasks. On the other hand they are expensive, they present numerous command, control, communications and coordination problems and, while not part of the coalition machine, are judged as such by the local population. The abduction and slaughter of the Blackwater operatives in the environs of Fallujah stimulated an uprising that was to become a focal point for extremist propaganda and presence, and to generate a subsequent Coalition military operation to eliminate a terrorist safe-haven that was to last more than seven months and consume vast amounts of blood, treasure and local goodwill.

More recent incidents have highlighted the extent to which the activities of private security companies can damage local perceptions. On the other hand, 2004 saw the imaginative initiative by the Aegis Group to establish a commercially run intelligence, communications and protection capability to sit alongside the military and facilitate the safe passage of civilian convoys and the achievement of development tasks.

Doctrine

In 2003 the then Major, and Dr, John Nagl was commanding a company in Ramadi. Addressing the XVIII Corps mission rehearsal exercise in November 2004, General Casey endorsed Nagl's book[7] to the audience. His evaluation of the way in which the British and American armies tackled insurgency compares and contrasts history, techniques, principles and approaches. His crucial deduction that 'you should use your mass and technological edge to protect the vital ground, and that is the people, over which the struggle is being waged', resonates today, especially when the dual meaning of the word 'over' is considered.[8]

Logistics

On 9 April 2004 the logistic update to the morning's Battlefield Update and Assessment contained the immortal words: 'it's raining bridges ... Ayakoko may have coined the phrase "just in time logistics" but Ayakoko wasn't in Iraq, today' as the bridges carrying the routes around Baghdad were targeted by large IEDs. What seemed like the world's supply of military bridging and of Mabey & Johnson bridges would be required to ensure the sustainment of the force.

For a force requiring hundreds of thousands of gallons of fuel each day to keep its engines running the impact of those attacks, particularly when the location of the main logistic hub at Balad north of Baghdad was considered, could have been operationally crucial. Jomini's words that 'Logistics define the operational limits of the campaign ... sustainment on a contested battlefield requires establishing and organising lines of supply and the successful arrival of convoys',[9] hold as true today as in the 1840s.

Not All Weapons Shoot

Money is not traditionally seen as a command resource, but the scale of the Commander's Emergency Response Program (CERP) funding available to the MSC commanders (some $12 million each month until September 2004) was a substantial tool in the armoury. The standard arguments over the enduring value of quick-impact projects took place. At a time when the large-scale projects – that would have improved the supply of electricity to those households with electric cabling and extended its provision to those households without it; removed the sewage from front gardens and streets; upgraded oil infrastructure and refining capability; and provided employment opportunities – all seemed stalled by bureaucratic wrangling or thwarted by the uncertain security situation, then the short-term advantages seemed clear.

---

7   Nagl 2002.
8   That is, 'over' as in 'a dog fighting over a bone', and 'over' as in 'above or on top of, i.e. amongst'.
9   Jomini 1838.

Command and Control

In the spring of 2004, Headquarters CJTF-7 morphed into Headquarters MNF-I, and then separated into the two headquarters of MNF-I and MNC-I. Headquarters MNC-I was configured around Headquarters III Corps. The lesson to be drawn from these evolutions is that it is a command responsibility to look at the situation with which you are faced and to configure the headquarters and staff accordingly. The creation of MNSTC-I, to replace the arrangements in place under the CPA, and to concentrate the responsibility, authority and accountability for developing the ISF, including ministries, is an excellent example of taking appropriate command and control action to achieve an effect; separating the Force and Corps functions is another good example; embedding Iraqi Liaison Officers into the headquarters is another.

On the other hand, it is an altogether more difficult thing to change the internal workings of a headquarters to ensure things that really make a difference – training, munitions clearance, engineering, civil and economic projects, strategic communications and money – are given due priority. But it must be done if stabilisation, with its implicit nod to the principles and techniques of counter-insurgency and its requirement to use military capability to support and enable civil effect, is to be done successfully. Question 4 of mission analysis[10] applies for headquarters as much as for any other activity; commanders must constantly ask themselves whether the situation has changed and whether the configuration of the headquarters needs to adapt to reflect the demands of, and to be successful in, the changed situation. The deployment and constructive behaviour and advice of a JFCOM mentor team, led by retired General Luck to look at the headquarters and the tasks being done, was instructive.

A Final Comment

It was a privilege to act as the Deputy Commanding General of MNC-I and to command the Corps for two weeks in the absence of the Corps Commander on leave. The August violence in al-Najaf and Karbala culminating in the occupation of the Imam Ali Mosque by the Jaysh al-Mahdi Army, and the deployment of three battalions into the south from Baghdad and Mosul, showed the agility and capability of the US Army and USMC to respond rapidly and effectively to an entirely changed set of circumstances.

I learned in the six months that you may have the capability to win any and every kinetic fight that you get into, and you may have the intelligence capability to have a clearer view of the situation than any other player in the game, but if you lose the perception battle then you stand in grave danger of not succeeding at all. The danger of overwhelming firepower and intelligence capability is that they lend themselves to action that is pre-emptive and offensive; as Templer said: 'the shooting side of the business is only 25 per cent of the trouble, the other 75 per cent lies in getting the people of the country behind us.'

The MNF-I so-called Drumbeat was an initiative to get good news out and try to influence the fence-sitters to get behind the Government. The source of that good news lay not in the successful conduct of combat operations but in the restoration or improvement of services, encouraging economic pluralism, promoting good governance, and training and employing effective ISF.

---

10   Question 4: Has the situation changed; if it has does my mission change; and even if my mission does not change does my plan need to change to accommodate that change of circumstances?

The summer of 2004 saw two outbursts of violence that affected the three million Shia in Sadr City and the entire south of the country, and the emergence of the Fallujah situation as a crucial issue to be resolved. Over the summer the number of attacks on Coalition and Iraqi Security Forces rocketed. At times it seemed as though the emphasis of Coalition effort had been sidetracked by the so-called Shia insurgency. Yet these were the very people who, at least at the time of the invasion, were expected to hold the keys to Iraq's future success as a nation. At the operational level it was a distraction, serious enough at the time, but a distraction nonetheless from the prime effort of dealing with the developing Sunni insurgency focused around al-Anbar Province, Fallujah, and north and west of Baghdad.

Arguably, the fact that the Shia were so inclined to resort to violence behind a maverick leader with a compelling voice was proof of failure of post-invasion planning. Doctrine suggests that campaigns have a shaping, a decisive and a sustaining element to them. Considering the invasion and defeat of the Iraqi Armed Forces and the overthrow of the regime to be the decisive operation threw the planners off track; the decisive operation was always going to be managing the aftermath of invasion. The importance of using the doctrinal framework correctly and of making the first decision a good one (since every decision is only as good as the one made immediately before it) cannot be underestimated.

The summer of 2004 was to be the time when the euphoria of liberation for some of the population was wearing off, while resentment at having lost so much was galvanising another significant element of the population to hostility and violence. At the same time, the summer of 2004 saw the transition to an Iraqi Government, at least in name, changes to the Coalition organisation and structure (MNF-I, MNC-I, MNSTC-I) that were to stand the test of time, and the development of a campaign plan whose themes – security, governance, economic development, communications – drove towards a clear strategic end-state[11] and with clear indicators of 'what success looks like'.[12] All these brought some rigour and sense of direction to the business at hand.

---

11   See note 5.
12   See note 6.

Chapter 9

Modern Campaigning:
From a Practitioner's Perspective

John McColl – 24 May 2006

The former Secretary of State John Reid said in a speech in February 2006 at King's College London that 'the job of soldiering has never been harder than it is today'. I suspect veterans of the Somme or Normandy might disagree. But what he meant is that it has become increasingly complex.

In considering some of the complexities of modern campaigning from a practitioner's perspective, I focus on practicalities not philosophy, based primarily upon my experiences in Afghanistan and Iraq, and offer a personal perspective on the context of operations, the implications of inter-agency operations, the constraints, including those on our command doctrine, and the impact of being a junior partner in coalition warfare.

National, International and Political Context

Once the decision to undertake an operation has been taken the military need to generate the force. In the run up to a deployment, particularly a rapid deployment such as Afghanistan or Sierra Leone, many pressures are brought to bear: political, diplomatic, legal, financial and intelligence to name just a few. So whilst you as the commander may think that generating and deploying your force must be the most important, high-profile thing going on in the world, others will not. The requirements of the force can almost become an irritation – given a lack of available forces; given the contradiction between Services designed for expeditionary war fighting, small and high technology, and the reality of enduring, low technology, peace support operations. Who's going to pay for UORs, and when? How can we sustain the force? How do we deal with media dissent? How do we pull together an alliance?

The result is that others, the main decision-makers, will be distracted, their views skewed, responding to recommendations reflecting the immediate pressure upon them: 'the political reality'. 'Simple soldier, my dear boy, you really don't understand.'

So a commander needs to be sensitive to the wider political context, when to bend and when to stick, but not to be shy about insisting upon a particular issue, be it force composition, numbers, rules of engagement and equipment, because as the military commander on the ground your perspective will have clarity and immediacy. No one else will have focused upon delivery and effect with the same priority. Whilst 'political reality' is important, politicians want success as *the* most important requirement and are relying upon the commander to deliver it. They rely on you to fight your corner. If you are having difficulty, put your judgement in writing and invite others to take responsibility for overriding you. But don't do it too often.

Theatre Context

We are generally sent to a country to support a government. In the cases of Iraq and Afghanistan the term 'government' is a loose one. They are factional, fragmented and complex. In order to support the strategic objectives laid down in international agreements, Bonn, Dayton and the like, we need to develop levers to make things happen. I emphasise three points.

The first is *uncertainty*. The mission, measurement of progress and *modus operandi* in the 1970s–1980s were clear. The rules of the game, success or failure, were tangible; for example, in Northern Ireland orders were specific, almost prescriptive, and success was judged in terms of arrests, finds and sightings. In today's environment we have moved from certainty to uncertainty. A study conducted by the Human Resources body at Farnborough into the Balkans in the mid-1990s found that the most difficult thing for commanders at all levels was that they had moved from an environment where decisions were, if not SOP, then subject to detailed guidance, to one where judgement is needed on the basis of limited direction with hazy parameters; and success is hard to define. The role of commanders has moved from mission execution to mission interpretation and often mission definition. This is particularly so at the political-military level, where the commander will be subject to national and multinational direction, one sometimes conflicting with the other. A good example of this is the current UK, US and NATO positions on narcotics in Afghanistan. The US has invested a huge amount of money in counter-narcotic activities, setting up command structures, interdiction and eradication forces, alternative livelihoods and infrastructure. There is a pressing demand from Washington to see tangible progress in the form of reduced hectares under cultivation and tonnage produced. The security forces, but the UK and NATO in particular, do not want to see widespread eradication before alternative livelihoods are in place, since eradication in isolation will drive Afghans into the arms of the Taliban, thereby fuelling the insurgency. Alternative livelihoods will take years to introduce and therefore early results are unlikely. In the meantime, it is likely that soldiers will be photographed patrolling through poppy fields without taking any action, with inevitable presentational problems.

The policy agreed between Washington, London and Kabul is that there will be a balanced strategy of interdiction of traffickers, alternative livelihoods and eradication. The result of mutually exclusive objectives is a bland policy document liable to radically different interpretation. And right now in Afghanistan we have just this taking place: the US intent on eradication; the UK with forces arriving in Helmand very keen to avoid it.

Those on the ground are handed the problem; in this case a UK officer, David Richards, commanding the ISAF mission, using judgement to deliver the intent. Unsatisfactory, but also reality.

The second key point is *personality*. You don't need to be an eminent historian to understand the impact of personality upon history, but it is a, perhaps the, key element of command. People and leaders shape nations. We need to understand the strengths and weaknesses of individuals and their interrelationships. Developing relationships takes time. When I am asked by my children: 'What did you do in Afghanistan, Daddy?', I reply: 'I drank tea and ate kebabs.'

Drinking tea with, listening to and understanding local leaders is a critical operational activity for a commander. Your conscience may be eased by sharing the danger and discomfort by being on patrol with your soldiers – it's debatable whether this adds or subtracts from the sum of military capability – but it is only a small part of your job. A critical element is forging relationships that deliver leverage, at the operational and strategic level.

The third point is *delivery*. Words are not enough, nor is security on its own. The newly emerging governments we are sent to support need to deliver across the full spectrum of political, social, economic and security sectors. They need to demonstrate that life will be improved under the new regime. And, as perhaps one of the few effective, capable organisations in theatre, the force needs to be able to help and the commander needs to have the freedom to intervene.

An example is the Afghan Hajj, in the early spring of 2002. The Hajj from Afghanistan relies upon charter flights to get the pilgrims to Mecca. Immediately before it was due to start it was established there were no aircraft, the funds were missing, and shortly after that the Minister was assassinated. President Karzai summoned the Cabinet, the US Ambassador and myself as ISAF Comd and simply explained that the Taliban had enabled the Hajj when they were in Government; it was inconceivable that the new Government, with the support of the most powerful countries in the world, could fail to do likewise – so fix! As a consequence, favours were called in from Muslim countries and the UK took a risk on the air bridge and used RAF air transport to move pilgrims to the Middle East. The effect in terms of numbers was limited; the effect in terms of our relationship with the Afghan Government and the Islamic conservative critics of the Coalition was significant.

What has this to do with security? Not much directly. What has it to do with empowering the Government (which is the political intent)? Everything. There is a need to understand that the military is deployed to provide security but to do much more as well: empowering the fledgling Government as part of the national and international effort is also a central task.

Our politicians are often criticised for being conservative, meddling and weak. My experience is that they are actually, once committed, quite bold. They clearly understand the need for empowerment, the requirement to operate beyond the operational envelope. But we need beware the enemy within. It is the officers and officials in between that create the tension, limiting the freedom of those on the ground in response to apparently legitimate concerns over overstretch and resources. But the rule must be that the man on the ground gets the freedom and resources to do the job as he defines it, unless there is a very good reason why not.

Other Actors

We are vulnerable in many of today's operations because, unlike in a war-fighting scenario, we do not have success or failure in our own hands. Within the context of the kind of operation in which we are now routinely included, mid-intensity conflict and peace support operations, this 'warfare of our age', it is the role of the security line of operations (which of course includes the judicial system, prisons, police and security sector reform, so we are therefore not even in control of that single line of operation) to hold the ring. Hold the ring whilst the other lines of operation, such as governance, economics, social development and counter-narcotics, take effect. These are the instruments of strategic success. It is they that solve the problem; security deals with the symptoms, the other lines of operation deal with the cause. But these lines of operation are subject to the independent actions of various actors, such as NGOs, the UN and the EU. I do not cover them in detail, but will focus on national coordination. Within nations there are departmental frictions. I will use as an example Omah's village. Omah was an ex-jihadi leader who lived in a village outside Kabul. He was, we thought, responsible for organising attacks against Coalition, particularly British, troops. We wanted to cut the ground from underneath him by building schools and clinics in the area. A fairly obvious tactic, the logic was compelling. But DfID would not agree, because their mandate is to relieve poverty, and the need elsewhere in Afghanistan was greater. It didn't happen; so, if it is difficult to coordinate on coherent objectives within a single nation, how much more difficult in a country like Afghanistan with 19 nations in the Coalition, numerous bilateral engagements outside the Coalition and 1,600 NGOs registered with the Ministry of Planning, as well as the main actor that is the Government of Afghanistan? This coordination poses a huge challenge. And of course it can and does go wrong. So what?

Well, the so what is that commanders need to understand these levers of effect, and even if we don't control them, know how to influence them. Of course read the lessons of Montgomery and Slim, but we also need to understand the way in which these new campaigns are fought and effect is *concentrated* in the fullest sense. There are ten principles of war, of which 'concentration of force' is generally considered to be the most important. These principles were, of course, identified within the context of war-fighting. Concentration of force remains the key principle, but achieving it includes focusing politics, economics, security and information, and of course we don't control all of them. We need to understand the FCO, DfID, security agencies; furthermore, we need to understand the UN, EU and others. How can we leverage from them and for them? What control mechanisms can we set up in theatre and in the UK? What is reasonable and unreasonable? For commanders today, inter-agency relationships, which used to be the province of the Ministry of Defence, are now a tactical issue. These skills are just as important as artillery target indication, forward air control and movement plans in war-fighting, and more likely to be used. There are some hopeful signs of more joined-up government currently in play in the context of our current deployment for Afghanistan; such as the Reid Group,[1] the cross-Whitehall campaign plan, the Strategic Delivery Unit in Kabul, a one-star in Kandahar at national level. Internationally, the Afghan Compact is an attempt at an integrated plan across all the lines of development. You might think this more an international political issue rather than a theatre one, and of course there is that aspect. However, I have deliberately mentioned it under the theatre context because it is coordinated delivery, not coordinated policy, which counts. We tend to focus on the latter, and not the former.

Political-Military Relationships

It is important, also, to have the right political-military relationship. Without this, it is difficult to bring any kind of coherence to a campaign.

In 2004 in Iraq, the relationship between General Ricardo Sanchez and Ambassador Paul Bremer was always difficult for reasons of circumstance (specifically, the lack of post-war planning in Washington) and also of personality. Ever-present in the atmosphere was Secretary of Defense Rumsfeld, the neo-con agenda, and the close control exercised from Washington DC. An example of this lack of communication occurred in early April. Washington took the unusual step of issuing a démarche to the British Government over the way in which the British-run Multi-National Division (South-East) was dealing with disruptive Shia elements in Basra. They wanted a harder line than Major General Andrew Stewart, the British General Officer Commanding in Basra, was prepared to direct.[2] That in itself is surprising, but what is more surprising is that when Generals Abizaid and Sanchez (the US military commanders) were shown the démarche and asked for their view, they knew nothing about it. The démarche had gone from Bremer to Washington to London without the military commanders being consulted. Indeed they, the military leadership, seemed to be content with the British approach. As a consequence of the frictions in political-military relationships the full implications of ideologically driven decisions were not fully thrashed out on occasions. Specifically, two key strategic decisions: the disbandment of the army and the de-Ba'athification

---

1   The Reid Group was a cross-Government group formed in 2006 to assess high-level lessons from Iraq. It was chaired by the Secretary of State for Defence.

2   See Andrew Stewart's description of this incident in Chapter 6.

policy, which at a stroke marginalised Sunnis, created mass unemployment amongst the military class, and humiliated the proud Muslim male; the basis for the scale of insurgency that now exists.

At a tactical level, the decisions to enter Sunni Fallujah by force following the murder and burning of the Blackwater drivers in March[3] (overriding the military advice of the MEF Commander General Conway) and then the arrest of one of Moqtada al-Sadr's lieutenants in the Shia Jaysh al-Mahdi and the closing down of his newspaper, effectively opening up a simultaneous second front, were again products of this lack of communication. Both were political decisions taken without a dialogue to allow full understanding of the security implications.

The transfer of sovereignty on 28 June 2004 brought in a new team, the passing of responsibility from Defense to State, and also a new player: the Iraqi Interim Government (IIG). The dialogue improved dramatically between the political, that is the Embassy and IIG, and Multi-National Forces (MNF). This was partly the result of personality but was also structural. At the end of June 2004, the Coalition force headquarters split to form Multi-National Force – Iraq (MNF-I), focused upon strategic issues, and Multi-National Corps – Iraq (MNC-I), focused at the operational and tactical levels. The clarity of responsibility has been important, and generally speaking it is helpful to split the political-military-strategic from the operational and tactical levels. Both are full-time jobs. This improvement in the political-military dialogue has been reflected in the campaign direction.

The underlying point is that involving politicians in military business, and soldiers in politics and diplomacy, generally produces a better answer. 'Get out of my lane!' was a cry often heard in the Bremer–Sanchez era. 'Tell the military commander what you want to achieve then leave it to him to decide how.' I do not subscribe to that approach. That might work in a war-fighting environment where the military line of operation is more discrete and less reliant upon politics and economics for tactical and operational success – it is not the answer in peace support operations where the interrelationship between lines of operation is less sequential and completely integrated. But there is a difference between involvement, influence and, at the extreme, interference. I would suggest that in the examples I have given, Defense under Rumsfeld and Bremer got it wrong, State under Colin Powell and John Negroponte got it right. As Clausewitz said:

> When people talk, as they often do, about harmful political influence on the management of war, they are not really saying what they mean. Their quarrel should be with the policy itself, not its influence. If the policy is right – that is, successful – any intentional effect it has on the conduct of war can only be to the good.[4]

The rule of thumb must be integration, not separation. I agree to a degree with Elliot Cohen in his book *Supreme Command*.[5] Politicians should be encouraged to be fully involved in the preparation of a campaign – they should ask questions, probe and demand justifications; they should be involved in campaign design; they should be involved in measuring success. Tactics and the equipment used should be justified by the military.

But it works both ways. Given that the military are hostages to the other lines of operation, politics and economics, in delivering success, and indeed in looking after the safety of their

---

3   On 31 March 2004, Iraqi insurgents attacked a convoy operated by the Blackwater private security company. Four US nationals were killed.

4   von Clausewitz 1832, book 8, chapter 6.

5   Cohen 2002.

soldiers, commanders have a right to interrogate, question, probe and recommend tactics along the other lines of operation.

Cohen has a short passage entitled 'The Unequal Dialogue'. What is needed is an open dialogue which allows common understanding by policy makers and practitioners of all disciplines. We are some way from that position nationally, and further away internationally.

So how do we bring any kind of order to this chaotic environment of competing interests? You will notice I haven't really mentioned a procedure that helps produce order out of chaos: campaign planning. It forces you to write down what you want to happen. It imparts intent coherently. It is also a process which integrates the lines of operation, if used properly. It uses an internationally agreed and defined language, so we all understand what we mean when we use terms such as centre of gravity, decisive points and lines of operation.

The production of such a plan is a useful way of binding in international partners and other government departments. I mentioned the Afghan cross-Whitehall campaign plan earlier. NGOs and the UN, of course, are a different matter and different arrangements are necessary. For example, the Afghan Compact signed in London in January 2006 between the Afghans and the international community charts the way forward for the following years; all other plans need to be in step with this capture document. And there *will* be a large number of plans. For example, in Afghanistan at present there are:

- the Afghan Compact
- the Afghan National Development Strategy
- the Afghan Drugs Control Strategy
- the NATO plan for ISAF
- the US plan for Operation Enduring Freedom
- the UK plan (+19 other nations)
- UN agencies, each with their own plans with autonomy

So a campaign plan is not a panacea, but it is a help. The danger with the process is that it can become a goal in itself; agreement is often hard-fought and painful. Arriving at an agreed campaign plan can be exhausting, but of course the final plan is irrelevant unless it leads to delivery!

Manoeuvrist Approach and Mission Command

The operational environments in the theatres I have described are unpredictable and volatile. It is therefore perhaps surprising that the Army has been as successful as it has been since the Falklands. We have achieved this through conducting operations in a way which empowers individuals and encourages initiative and reasonable risk taking. Since 1990 we have embraced the Manoeuvrist Approach and Mission Command as our doctrine and given substance to it. We have been able to do so, in a way that few armies have, but that freedom is at risk from three main sources:

The first is *technology*. We now have the ability to communicate from Prime Minister to private. Politicians and senior commanders need to think about their role, where it starts and where it finishes. The temptation is to do the job that you did last or before that; presumably you were quite good at it, otherwise you would not have been promoted. It may also be more interesting, but separation brings clarity and objectivity. Technology is a threat and a temptation that needs to be resisted and controlled.

The second risk is from *multinationality*. There are 29 countries in the Coalition in Iraq and 19 in ISAF. The early days of peace support operations when conflict is still bubbling are the critical ones. Multinationality creates frictions, and in the early days a single lead nation may be needed to provide command and control and a spine of capability. In the early days of ISAF, under 3rd (UK) Division and 16th Air Assault Brigade, there was a suggestion to change the headquarters to reflect a 60:40 UK-international split, offered as we crossed the line of departure, attempting to project a force of more than 5,000 personnel by air half way across the world and to establish a relationship with the Afghan Government. It was suggested, because more nations wanted to join the alliance than could be accommodated, that we should deploy without a UK battalion. Can you imagine the position of a commander who in a volatile situation has no troops of his own in harm's way? Or has no troops of his own nation to turn to when things get difficult without worrying about red cards and vetoes? Extraordinary and unworkable. The point is that multinationality has become almost a good thing in its own right; well, it may be for burden-sharing and risk-sharing but not for military capability. A pragmatic compromise must be struck between political and military requirements. In this case, multinationality was not fully implemented until after the force was established. And when national forces are assigned they need to have roles appropriate to their rules of engagement, equipment and competence. The commander on the ground and key staff should have a role in determining the level of multinationality. The political imperative of multinationality is a reality we will have to live with, but the requirement for success is a higher priority. We should rely on the commander's judgement; and he needs to make himself heard – the advisors will be invisible when it goes wrong.

The third risk comes from the *media*. Of the three, this is the most powerful. You will hear media presenters tell you that they are committed to obtaining an objective assessment of the news. Rubbish. Consider the BBC house in Kabul, where I was being interviewed by a young reporter whose assessment of the situation in Afghanistan was balanced and objective. But the message from the editor in London was 'that's not what I want – go and get me some news', that is, sensational, dramatic and attention grabbing. The media in general are, I regret, after air time, column inches and, ultimately, audience figures.

Against this background you have soldiers, each the master of his or her own destiny, interpreting the intent individually and perhaps through a couple of languages, capable of independent action and speech. Every missed step is captured, magnified and transmitted around the world. It is enough to make the blood of any commander run cold.

The language of strategic direction and command can quickly become one of accountability and control, not empowerment and support. We are in danger of becoming over-controlled and risk-averse. The objective becomes to get into theatre and out again without getting it wrong, rather than using initiative to move things on, secure in the knowledge that you will be supported. Some allies already have this mindset.

An example was in 2000 in Sierra Leone, when a patrol from the Royal Irish, out and about making the peace in the way that the British Army does, in line with their commander's intent, took a wrong turn, and were captured by a gang known as the West Side Boys. With their lives in danger, PJHQ authorised the technically adept and very successful Operation Barras, a Special Forces raid to rescue them. Despite the success of the operation, a trooper was tragically killed, and in the follow-up, the question was asked, 'should the original patrol commander be held to account for the incident, and disciplined accordingly', that is, court-martialled? CGS represented the view that around the world young men and women were straining every nerve and sinew to go the extra mile, taking risks to make a difference; and the country and the politicians basked in the reflected glory of their success. If we wished to retain that level of success, he observed that we needed to protect the freedom of action of our soldiers and to support them. Thankfully these arguments carried the day, but we need to be on our guard against encroachment upon them.

Junior Partner Warfare and the US Army

Working embedded within MNF Headquarters in Iraq confirmed some of my earlier preconceived ideas about the US Army: some hugely impressive officers; industrial-scale activity; lack of inclination to pass on bad news; a complex staff-led command system that is thorough but process driven; amazing information technology that at times impedes the flow of information rather than speeds it up; but also some new impressions.

The first is their generosity. They are extraordinarily open to involvement and access, but there is no special relationship. Our influence as a junior partner depends upon what we do. Here our apparent lack of commitment and reluctance to commit reserves to support influence costs us dear.

For example, in Iraq we deployed the Black Watch to Camp Dogwood in October 2004, when the US were focusing operations upon Fallujah and needed to draw forces from less-threatened areas, such as MND(SE). It was a sensible, clear military requirement. A number of similar earlier requests had been turned down, but eventually this one was supported, but with significant media fallout. It is a constant frustration of deployed senior commanders that they are required to deliver influence but without the necessary commitment to justify it. The reluctance to provide tangible support is often understandable political caution, but is more often based on the availability of our forces, since that depends on their size and shape.

The second new impression is about honesty and disagreements. During the Fallujah operation in the summer of 2004 there was no falling out with US commanders. They recognised my right to express a view, but I recognised their right to command as they saw fit given the overwhelming weight of their contribution: 2,456 US fatalities in Iraq to date compared to 111 UK fatalities; 17,869 US casualties – the UK number is hard to define, but the MOD claims 230.

People are the critical element. It is the quality of our people that make our Services what they are. If we are to attract and keep the people that produce the performance that we expect from our Services, we need to value them and make them feel valued. My contacts with the US Army have revealed many things, but a lasting impression for me from my trips with the Advanced Course at the Staff College and subsequently embedded within a US Army Headquarters was the pride of all those that served, from US private to US general. It was more than the patriotism that is part and parcel of US life. The US serviceman feels valued because he is invested in, as are his healthcare, base facilities, accommodation and quarters. We should challenge British Defence to bring reality to its claim that people are our highest priority after operations. They are not, they should be, and it is a challenge for commanders at all levels in the Army.

Now this will be difficult for the lot of other ranks, but even more difficult for officers. Don't feel embarrassed to argue for conditions of service that make this an attractive life for our officer corps, because it is in my view the quality of our officers above all else that makes the British Forces what they are. Others quote different reasons for our successes. Some cite the Warrant Officers' and Sergeants' Mess, some cite tradition – the Regimental system, some might even cite equipment; but I disagree. It is the officers that make the difference. To quote Dennis Healey when he was Secretary of State for Defence:

> The best of my … military advisors had an intellectual ability and breadth of experience I have never found surpassed, and the average were above average in the comparable walks of life.

That was true in 1964, and our young officers are better now than they were then.

I am told that analysts of Vietnam casualty statistics deem that no Harvard graduates were killed whilst serving in the Army. Had the British Army been involved in such a conflict the number of brightest and best from the finest universities would have been significant. Military service continues to attract extraordinary quality in the UK: university officer training corps are 180 per cent recruited. We need the quality more than ever to cope with the complexity of modern conflict.

The elements of conflicts that we are involved in are generally not new: insurgency, global war on terror, failed state reconstruction, civil war, drugs, organised crime, disarmament, demobilisation and reintegration, security sector reform, dramatic technical innovation and extensive multinationality and multi-agency involvement.

All these elements face us now, but the number of different elements that compound together in each conflict is, I suggest, unpredictable, the whole magnified by a persuasive, intrusive and unsympathetic media – that's the complexity of modern campaigning.

Chapter 10

The British Army and Thinking About the Operational Level[1]

John Kiszely – 12 October 2005

The operational level is one of the four levels of war or conflict identified in British Defence Doctrine: grand-strategic, military-strategic, operational and tactical. Sometimes referred to as the theatre level, the operational level is that 'at which campaigns and major operations are planned, conducted and sustained to accomplish strategic objectives within theatres or areas of operations'.[2] The skilful orchestration of military resources and activities for this purpose is called operational art. The operational level is the vital link between tactics and strategy. As the Soviet theorist Aleksandr Svechin neatly put it, 'tactics make the steps from which operational leaps are assembled; strategy points out the path'.[3] Without consideration of the operational level, it is easy to see the achievement of strategic success as merely the sum of tactical victories, and but a small step from there to believing that every successful battle fought leads to strategic success. But, in the words of Bernard Brodie, 'war is a question not of winning battles, but of winning campaigns'.[4]

Yet the British military only incorporated this 'vital link' into its doctrine in the 1980s, over half a century after the militaries of some other nations, notably the Soviet Union, did so. Why was this? What was the impact? And what do we have to learn from the experience? This chapter sets out to answer these questions.

The intuitive application of what we now call operational art can be seen in the method of many commanders in history – perhaps most notably Napoleon – but identification and articulation of a level between the strategic and the tactical can be traced back in Prussia to Moltke the Elder, and in Russia to the General Staff Academy in the early years of the twentieth century, with subsequent development by former Civil War leaders who were also military thinkers, such as Tukhachevskii and Triandafillov, and their contemporaries. A level between the tactical and strategic had also been identified by Baron Jomini, writing in the 1830s: a level he termed grand tactics. Jomini was much admired and quoted by many British military writers, such as E.B. Hamley, so that Jomini's concept of grand tactics was well known to the military establishment; for example at the Staff College where Hamley was the commandant from 1870 to 1878. An instructor there at the end of the nineteenth century was the military historian Colonel G.F.R. Henderson, who developed his own ideas of grand tactics which he defined as the higher art of generalship: 'those stratagems, manoeuvres and devices by which victories are won'.[5] But the greatest development of thinking in Britain about this level resulted from the work of J.F.C. Fuller. He, too, used the term grand tactics, which, in his 1926 book *The Foundations of the Science of War*, he described as 'the plan

---

1   An article based on the first part of this chapter appeared in *RUSI Journal* in December 2006 (vol. 151, no. 6) entitled 'Thinking about Counterinsurgency'.

2   *British Military Doctrine* 2001; and *UK Glossary of Joint and Multinational Terms and Definitions*.

3   Quoted in Glantz 1991, 23.

4   Quoted in Gooch 1990, 2.

5   Holden Reid 1996, 67 and 70.

of the war or campaign ... [which] secures military action by converging all means of waging war towards gaining a decision'.[6] He subsequently defined grand tactics as 'the organization and distribution of the fighting forces themselves in order to accomplish the grand strategic plan, or idea',[7] which is a long way from Jomini's rather prosaic concept[8] and comes close indeed to our definition of the operational level today. But Fuller's understanding of this level, although partly shared by B.H. Liddell Hart, was not developed further by other British military thinkers into the practical functions that would give it substance and thus define operational art.[9] This was a significant factor in the absence of operational art in the mainstream of British military doctrine for over half a century.[10]

There were a number of reasons for this. First, despite the title of Fuller's book referred to earlier, there was, within the British military, little tradition of the study of war as a science. In part, this was due to an anti-intellectual ethos in the British Army. Officers were expected to indulge in gentlemanly outdoor pursuits such as hunting and sports; those who chose to read were in danger of being stigmatised as 'bookish'[11] or, worse, 'clever'. There was little appetite for theory, and a general mistrust of doctrine as an unwelcome constraint on a commander's initiative and freedom of action. Even at the Staff College, although there was reference to what was called 'the science of war' – Henderson published a book under this title – as Jay Luvaas has pointed out, 'the method they used was historical rather than scientific'.[12] Fuller certainly brought a scientific approach to the Staff College during his time as chief instructor there from 1923 to 1925, and with it an encouragement of innovative thinking and an emphasis on military education – 'how to think' rather than 'what to think' – but the momentum for these changes was lost with his departure. The unscientific approach of the military was a favourite theme not only of Fuller but also of Liddell Hart, who wrote

> The soldier has never been taught to approach his problem in a scientific spirit. His early training is directed, above all, to the cultivation of loyalties ... The attitude of uncritical loyalty may be essential toward the winning of the war, but it is a fatally blind attitude in which to prepare for a war ... [what is needed is] a change of thought towards criticism and independence of thought.[13]

A related reason was the general lack of encouragement for those serving members of the Armed Forces who were also military thinkers to get into print, although not all of the most senior officers went as far as Lord Cavan, Chief of the Imperial General Staff from 1922 to 1926, who 'considered it improper for serving officers to publish books on military subjects'.[14] Additionally, Fuller and Liddell Hart's abrasive and dogmatic style, and bitterly critical tone, did little to endear them to

---

6   Fuller 1926, 107–8.
7   Holden Reid 1996, 65; see also Chapter 5, 'Fuller and the Operational Level'.
8   'Grand tactics is the art of posting troops upon the battle field according to the accidents of the ground, of bringing them into action, and the art of fighting upon the ground, in contradistinction to planning upon a map.' Jomini 1838, 69. According to Holden Reid 1996, 66, Jomini's influence on Fuller was 'negligible'.
9   For examples of such functions, see Glantz 1991, 10–11.
10   Contrary to the views of some. For example, Bellamy 1990, 60.
11   Luvaas 1965, 275.
12   Luvaas 1965, 351.
13   Winton 1988, 127.
14   Winton 1988, 30.

the military establishment[15] or to attract establishment support for the development of their ideas – which, of course, says as much about the military establishment at the time as it does about Fuller and Liddell Hart. In any case, the main subjects for contemporary military debate did not concern abstract concepts such as levels of warfare, but the practical and emotive issues of mechanisation, the demands of Imperial Defence and restructuring in a time of financial stringency.

These factors were reinforced as Britain approached and entered the Second World War. The main challenges facing the military were those of the rapid expansion, training and equipping of the Armed Forces, with the doctrinal focus at teaching establishments, such as the Staff College, remaining where it had always been: at the tactical level. This did not preclude consideration of strategy, but the very compartmentalisation of warfare into strategy and tactics served to obscure the level that lay between and linked them. Additionally, between the wars the British Army had been busily involved in 'real soldiering': imperial policing, that resulted in expertise in irregular warfare, but allowed little time, and gave little cause for, developing skills in, or thinking about, large-scale operations. Nor was the eve of war the best time to be contemplating radical changes in doctrinal approaches, particularly in the circumstances of a rapidly expanding Army where the overriding training principle had to be simplicity. Furthermore, the ability of the Army to manoeuvre was greatly constrained by the small amount of mechanisation and armour. True, the proportion of the Army that was mechanised was higher than in any other European army, but by the same token the British Army was small. Moreover, British doctrinal perception of the battlefield was relatively linear and shallow; although exploitation of breakthrough was considered, deep operations – a main expression of operational art – featured little, if at all. For the British military tended to think in terms of achieving success by pushing back the enemy front line, thereby gaining ground. By contrast, the German goal was not ground-oriented, but enemy-oriented: annihilation (*Vernichtung*), enabled by manoeuvre – a goal requiring creative thinking, even if in practice this rarely rose above the tactical level. Of even greater contrast was the Soviet goal: operational-level, catastrophic shock (*udar*) to the enemy system – the result of operational art. Finally, there was also the command style of the British grand-strategic leader, Churchill. Churchill played a very direct role not only in the formulation and implementation of strategy, but also in tactical direction, at least in those theatres in which he, personally, was particularly interested.[16] Here he saw little requirement for his tactical commanders to do anything other than fight and win the battles that he, Churchill, had directed – and to do so quickly, whether or not they believed themselves to be ready. In these circumstances, freedom of action at theatre level would not have seemed to him to be either necessary or desirable. Tactical successes would lead inexorably to strategic success – as it happens, a view shared by Hitler. A level between the tactical and the strategic was superfluous.

What is more surprising, perhaps, is that such a level did not feature in British military doctrine for almost 40 years after the war.[17] An important factor here is the triangular and symbiotic relationship between the operational level, the manoeuvre/attrition balance in approaches to warfare, and command style. Freedom of action at the operational level allows for the expression of operational art, a major medium for which is manoeuvre, both physical and mental (or psychological), in the sense of mentally out-manoeuvring your opponent. An attritional approach focuses on the defeat of the enemy by destruction of its forces; a manoeuvrist approach, however, sees the enemy's forces as but one part of its 'system', and looks for the most cost-effective means of defeating that system,

---

15   For example, Field Marshal Montgomery-Massingberd (CIGS 1933–36) who had 'an obsession with loyalty'. Reported in Harris 2002, 231.

16   An example of a theatre which became of lesser personal interest for Churchill, exemplified by his lack of tactical meddling, was Burma.

17   See Kiszely 1997.

which may or may not involve the destruction of its forces. The manoeuvrist approach steers you towards fighting only when to do so is necessary for achievement of your campaign goals. Successful manoeuvre, however, requires a command system which is not based on command by detailed orders, but on one which allows opportunities to be exploited faster than the enemy can react.[18] During the Second World War, with exceptions – notably, Slim's campaign in Burma – neither manoeuvre (whether physical or mental) nor command by anything other than detailed orders were strong suits for the British Army. Indeed, the British Army's success was perceived by many to have been due to the adherence of commanders such as Montgomery to the principles of largely static, attritional battles and a tight, centralised command system. Montgomery's predecessors in the Western Desert were perceived as having dabbled with manoeuvre and a slack command chain – in retrospect, due to a superficial understanding of some very immature concepts originating from Fuller and Liddell Hart – a potentially disastrous situation redeemed, it was perceived, only by a return to the 'teed-up', 'tidy', tightly controlled battlefield advocated by Montgomery.[19] And, in Montgomery's defence, it is fair to say that he identified the strengths of the British Army in this matter, and played to them. He may also have drawn the conclusion that where he deviated from this, for example in trying his hand at deep operations at Arnhem, abject failure had resulted. Furthermore, it was significant that the new Chief of the Imperial General Staff, appointed in 1946, was Montgomery himself; his influence over the mythology of the war, the lessons-learnt process, the subsequent development of doctrine and the appointment of his acolytes was immense: effects that greatly outlived his tenure of office. The doctrine of the British Army thus remained focused at the tactical level (how to fight battles), attritional in approach and with a centralised, tight command system.

There was a further, increasingly significant factor which focused attention away from the operational level. The British Army's primary post-war role was as a garrison in Germany – the British Army of the Rhine (BAOR) – facing the threat of an invasion by Soviet-led forces of the Warsaw Pact. The strategy was one of 'Forward Defence'. NATO nations were to deploy to the eastern boundaries of West Germany and fight shoulder-to-shoulder, with those governments which possessed nuclear weapons resorting to them if NATO's conventional forces were overwhelmed. The tactics were to hold ground; it was largely a positional battle of attrition. As a platoon commander in what was called the Main Defensive Position, the role of my battalion was to die gloriously. The operational level played little or no part in forward defence. Such was the emphasis in the Army as a whole on BAOR that the Army not only trained primarily, at times it seemed almost exclusively, for BAOR operations – how to fight at the tactical level – but also equipped itself largely for this single role. It chose its tanks and armoured vehicles not primarily for their ability to manoeuvre, but on the basis of their perceived performance in a largely static, defensive slogging match. The more it did so, the less capable it became of manoeuvring even if it had wanted to. And for an army that saw its greatest strength as its regimental system, it has to be said that many of its members, including very senior ones, felt comfortable focusing on the minutiae of the tactical level and commanding formations (up to, and including army group) as if they were large regiments. Lastly, winners in war tend to become victims of their own success; victory does not so much provoke change as appear to excuse it.

It might have been expected that research or interest in academia might have led to wider examination of this subject, particularly with the advent of war studies departments in universities.

---

18   The Soviet and German armies solved this in different ways: the German Army through *Auftragstaktik* (mission command), the Soviet Army through the application of drills at a high level.

19   Montgomery 1942, 8–14.

But for at least two decades after the war, their attention was primarily on more obviously 'relevant' issues, such as strategy in the nuclear age, or on softer issues such as the Armed Forces and society. That does not, of course, mean to say that the subject of the operational level was being ignored in this country. There were a number of individuals who were studying Soviet military doctrine at British universities, notably John Erickson at Edinburgh, and a group of academics at the Royal Military Academy, Sandhurst. In 1971 this group, with Chris Donnelly, was formalised into the Government-sponsored Soviet Studies Research Centre using open-source material, of which there was a surprisingly large amount.[20] Increasingly authoritative articles appeared, such as that in 1971 on the Soviet *desant* capability[21] and in 1975 on the Soviet concept of operations.[22] Focus on the threat to NATO's central front posed by Soviet Operational (level) Manoeuvre Groups raised awareness of the operational level itself.

This coincided with post-Vietnam doctrinal reappraisals in the United States. Following the publication of the US Army's new doctrine in 1976,[23] some civilian commentators, notably William Lind, published articles highly critical of the perceived limitations of the doctrine: its emphasis on firepower and attrition at the expense of manoeuvre; its 'industrial approach' to warfare which relied on materiel superiority; the narrow focus at the tactical level; the lack of emphasis on creativity and originality. The ensuing debate was highly influential in the production of a revised doctrine, one which acknowledged the existence and importance of the operational level. It is not the purpose of this chapter to examine that evolution, apart from noting a number of significant features. The debate, at times heated, included participation from both the civilian and military communities – academics, journalists and politicians as well as retired and serving officers – and took place not only in professional journals but also in public newspapers and magazines. Serving members of the Armed Forces were not discouraged from participating, or at least were not deterred from doing so, and significant contributions came from the military-academic community. Schools of thought emerged which advanced the level of understanding; the debate moved forward. The leader of the Army's Training and Doctrine Command, General Donn Starry, played a prominent role in steering this debate, and in adopting a systemic resolution to it. The result was a new doctrine in 1982, entitled 'Air Land Battle' which centred on the operational level,[24] and the establishment of an operational-level course, the School for Advanced Military Studies (SAMS) at Fort Leavenworth.[25]

This evolution was undoubtedly influenced by the Soviet Studies Research Centre in the United Kingdom. Shimon Naveh, in his authoritative study, *In Pursuit of Military Excellence*, assesses that the Centre

> ... exercised great impact on the perception of Soviet operational theory held by the American school of reformers. Being far ahead of their American colleagues in the study of Soviet deep operations, the British analysts managed to illuminate essential issues ... and managed to translate the abstract principles of the Deep Operations theory into operational scenarios understood by the military planner.[26]

---

20   See, for example, Savkin 1972.

21   Donnelly 1971.

22   Donnelly and Vigor 1975.

23   Field Manual 100-5. *Active Defence*, 1976.

24   'The operational level of war uses available military resources to attain strategic goals within a theater of war.' It was not, however, until the 1986 version that the concept of operational art was recognised, 'a perceptional breakthrough'. Naveh 1997, 12.

25   For fuller accounts of this evolution, see Naveh 1997; Clarke 1984; and Romjue 1984.

26   Naveh 1997, 273–4.

But this lead in research and analysis was not readily translated into doctrinal change in the British military. This was partly due to the fact that the Centre was independent of and separate from the official doctrinal department, but also because doctrinal development in the British Army at the time was sluggish, and there was no active senior patron to drive through change. Moreover, participation in even semi-public debate on any subject that could possibly, by the widest stretch of the imagination, be construed as contentious was greatly discouraged by the Ministry of Defence, and this extended to publication of books and articles. Among the unintended consequences of this was a stifling of the dialectical debate which could have resulted, and thus of the advancement of military science.

There was, however, one contemporary British theorist who had not only recognised the operational level for what it was, but developed the mechanics of operational art. Richard Simpkin, a retired brigadier, had made a lifetime study of Soviet military theory and applied the mind of a polymath to the future of warfare. His book, *Race to the Swift: Thoughts on Warfare in the Twenty-First Century*, published in 1985,[27] a major work of military philosophy, gave substance to operational art by articulating key operational concepts – such as centre of gravity, simultaneity, tempo and manoeuvre – and by entwining the operational level with the manoeuvrist approach and a decentralised command system. Simpkin was highly influential with like-minded theorists, mostly international, but less than he deserved to be in British military circles. Like Fuller, he was not helped by his sometimes abstruse prose, nor by the fact that he was a self-styled heretic who enjoyed baiting the military establishment. Simpkin's view that '[t]he peacetime military establishment of most advanced countries enjoys an unrivalled and largely deserved reputation for blinkered thinking'[28] was all the more irritating for being uncomfortably close to the truth. He was, therefore, an outsider, and not an influential patron for doctrinal change.

Such patronage, however, was not far off. As Commander of the 1st British Corps in Germany in 1981–1983, Lieutenant General Sir Nigel Bagnall had been openly critical not only of the lack of manoeuvre and of the centralised command system inherent in the Central Front doctrine, but also what he saw as over-literal interpretation of the strategy of Forward Defence itself. Not only was Bagnall a friend of Simpkin and aware of the doctrinal debate in the United States, but he had also established a close professional and personal relationship with a number of senior German officers, serving and retired, who shared his interest in conceptual and doctrinal development.[29] As Commander of NATO's Northern Army Group 1983–1985, he advocated a focus on the operational level and instituted a General Deployment Plan based on manoeuvre at army group level, rather than one based on a series of corps battles, fought largely in isolation. When he became Chief of the General Staff in 1985 he personally instituted an Army-wide doctrine, centring on the need for manoeuvre and for decentralised command and control, and established at the Army Staff College at Camberley in 1988 an equivalent to the SAMS course – the Higher Command and Staff Course (HCSC) – which focused at the operational level. The British doctrine establishment had no operational-level expertise, so what was taught on HCSC was internally produced at the Staff College, drawing heavily on US establishments, notably SAMS, and influenced by authors such as William Lind and Robert Leonhard in the US,[30] as well as by Simpkin. Also in 1988, the Staff College adopted what became known as the Manoeuvrist Approach to operations – one that aims to shatter the enemy's cohesion and will to fight, rather than eroding its forces and materiel

---

27 Simpkin 1985. See also Simpkin 1987.
28 Simpkin 1985, 166.
29 For example, Gen von Senger und Etterln, Commander of NATO's Central Region, scholar and author.
30 Lind 1985. Leonhard 1991.

– and a decentralised command ethos, Mission Command, which was the antithesis of command by detailed orders. From that time, HCSC graduates, officers (from all three Services) trained in operational art, were to be found in operational-level appointments in the equivalent ranks of colonel and brigadier. Importantly, with their participation on the HCSC, all three Services had 'bought into' the concept of the operational level, and by 1995 all three had incorporated it into their doctrine,[31] although it was not until the publication of a joint British Defence Doctrine in 1996, and the establishment of a Permanent Joint Headquarters in the same year and of the Joint Services Command and Staff College a year later, that significant numbers of middle-ranking officers were trained in, and practising, operational art. It could therefore be said that operational art had become institutionalised in the British Armed Forces.[32] The coincidence around 1990 of the recognition of the operational level with the demise of the Warsaw Pact caused some to question the relevance of operational art in a perceived age of smaller-scale operations. This misses the point, but helps to illuminate it: operational art is defined not by scale, but by an activity: the linking of military-strategic objectives with tactical level actions. Certainly, the greater the complexity of the campaign, the greater the demands on operational art; and a facet of these new operations is their complexity. Such operations also tend to highlight the shifting overlap that always exists in practice between the various levels, the constantly evolving nature of operational art, and the fact that the operational level is not tied to a particular level of command or even to location. The operational level is determined by where operational art is practised: in the past, it has most often been carried out 'in-theatre', but it need not be, and is not always so. In the United Kingdom, for example, it is most often carried out at the Permanent Joint Headquarters outside London. This proximity might tempt policy-makers and strategists to bypass the operational level, a temptation they would be wise to resist.

How, then, did the evolution of operational-level thinking impact on the conduct of major operations since the late 1980s? In the time available this cannot be a full examination,[33] but I offer some personal observations by way of illustration, and will devote a disproportionate amount of time to ongoing operations in Iraq since I have recent personal experience of it. But to establish some context, I shall start with the major operations earlier in the 1980s, starting with Northern Ireland.

In Northern Ireland, Army officers with an understanding of, and training in, the operational level arrived there from 1989, some 20 years after the British Army was sent to assist the police after the escalating violence at the end of the 1960s. The impact of these HCSC graduates in campaign direction in Northern Ireland was not only in applying the operational-level tools of the trade, but also in the application of those concepts associated with the operational level – the manoeuvrist approach and mission command, particularly the former. Previously, commanders typically focused on achieving strategic objectives by tactical level actions. Success was normally measured in attritional terms: a monthly report which focused on the number of terrorists killed or captured, the number of own forces killed or wounded, the number of weapons and the amount of ammunition and explosives seized. Success in the Province as a whole, and for units within it, was therefore determined in attritional terms: how many terrorists could a unit kill or capture in a six-month tour? How much ammunition or explosive could it find? What HCSC graduates brought to the process was the seeking of answers to some different and fundamental questions, such as: what

---

31 Army Doctrine Publication *Operations* 1989; *Air Power Doctrine (AP 3000)* 1991; *British Maritime Doctrine (BR 1806)* 1995.

32 This evolution is well covered in Mader 2004.

33 For this see Griffin 2005.

was the desired end-state; what were their opponents' centres of gravity; what were the decisive points which led to it; and how could ends, ways and means best be linked? This, in turn, led to a rather different approach. For example, if the terrorists' centre of gravity was the support of the population, then the decisive points which were to unlock it were those actions that resulted in erosion of that support. The aim was to out-manoeuvre the terrorists, not primarily to destroy them. Offensive operations such as search operations (or, to the population, 'raids') needed to be seen in this context. The success of a unit's six-month tour was nothing to do with how many terrorists its soldiers had killed and captured, or how much ammunition and explosives they had found, and everything to do with whether at the end of the tour the support of the local community for the terrorist had decreased, and by how much.

The 1982 Falklands Conflict (war was never declared), in which I served as a company commander, preceded any British military recognition of the operational level, and although it was a large and complex logistic challenge it was, logistics apart, a relatively small-scale and simple campaign. This in part mitigated the absence of clear joint doctrine, of which there was none above the tactical level. In effect, the Joint Commander, Admiral Fieldhouse at Northwood, was the operational-level commander; it was he who orchestrated the military resources to achieve the military-strategic objectives set by the Chief of Defence Staff (CDS). The senior deployed officer, Vice Admiral Woodward, although sometimes referred to as Task Force Commander, was in effect no more than *primus inter pares* among the tactical-level commanders.[34] That this lack of clarity did not have more deleterious effects is largely due to the outstanding quality of some of the key personalities involved, notably Fieldhouse and the CDS at the time, Admiral of the Fleet Sir Terence Lewin. The subsequent lessons learnt exercise identified a number of measures such as a joint headquarters, and more joint doctrine and training. But the fact that the conduct of the campaign had resulted in unqualified victory resulted in more fundamental questions not being asked, and was used as justification of the status quo by those, mostly vested interests, opposed to change in structures and responsibilities.

By the time of the 1991 Gulf War, six years after the production of the US Army's new FM 100-5 doctrine, and nine years after the first SAMS course, understanding of the operational level in the United States had come a long way and SAMS graduates were prominent in the US campaign-planning team. British involvement in such planning was small but significant. A British HCSC graduate was allowed by the United States theatre commander to be part of his campaign planning team, and played an active role in it. This highlights the problems of the junior partners in a coalition – how to influence events – particularly since at the time the American planners were described by one witness as '… pathologically secretive about their plans: they habitually classified documents "Noforn" (not to be shown to foreigners), and at least once tore down maps from the walls when a British officer entered the room unexpectedly.'[35] Undoubtedly, the British military's shared understanding of the operational level was an important factor in the US wishing participation in this influential group, but the leverage exerted is harder to measure. Since there were comparatively few differences of approach or areas of contention, there was probably a limited requirement to exert leverage. The British operational-level commander was nominally the officer designated by the Chief of Defence Staff as Joint Theatre Commander, Air Chief Marshal Hine, initially operating from his headquarters in England, but then deployed to Saudi Arabia. But as junior partner in a coalition, his role was largely that of National Contingent Commander (NCC).

---

34   Band 2005, 32.
35   de la Billière 1992.

Within a year of that Gulf War came British military involvement in post-Tito Bosnia, with the deployment of a battlegroup with the United Nations Protection Force, expanded to a brigade group the following year. The UK also provided a three-star commander, firstly Lieutenant General Sir Michael Rose, subsequently Lieutenant General Sir Rupert Smith, although not as theatre commander. The regrettable absence of any effective plan linking tactical action to strategic objectives in Bosnia was clear at the time as well as in retrospect, and reflects among other things the paucity of senior military advice at the UN, particularly military advice in campaign planning. Lieutenant General Rose perceived the requirement, and commissioned the Army Staff College, Camberley to help him formulate a campaign plan. This may have been useful as a mind-clearing exercise for him, but it was never an official plan, and there was little appetite among some of his senior staff to countenance it.[36] Lieutenant General Smith also had a clear idea of the necessary link between the strategic and tactical levels and, in his words, '... spent a lot of time trying to explain to a range of senior figures in the UN and in various capital cities that ... keeping 20,000 lightly armed troops in the midst of the warring parties was strategically unsustainable and tactically inept'.[37] In retrospect it is easy to see the benefits that would have been brought by clarity of thought in linking tactical actions to strategic outcomes and vice versa. When NATO's Intervention Force took over from the UN in late 1994, with a US theatre commander and headquarters, it brought with it an operational-level focus, in no small measure the product of graduates of the SAMS course and HCSC. For the NATO operation in Kosovo in 1999, structures were less clear, not least because '... a bombing campaign anticipated to last a week stretched over seventy-eight days'[38] and, as so often happens, military action preceded formulation of a campaign plan. The UK MOD then produced its own plan and was closely involved with the US and others in the formulation of the overall plan. The military activity in Kosovo was in essence an operation rather than a campaign. The theatre of operations was not restricted to Kosovo, but was the Balkans as a whole – a parallel operation was ongoing in Macedonia. The commander in Kosovo was therefore not acting at the operational level, but at the tactical level. It is also worth noting in this campaign the compression and overlap of the levels of conflict, increased by modern communications. Thus, the campaign was largely planned and directed by the military-strategic level commander, SACEUR, based in Belgium. In practice, delineation of activity at each level is seldom clear, is almost always overlapped to a greater or lesser extent, with levels mutually dependent. In the UK, although in theory the operational level resided with whomever was chosen as Joint Commander, the establishment of a Permanent Joint Headquarters and a three-star Chief of Joint Operations meant it would be exceptional for anyone else to be selected as Joint Commander. Thus, in practice, the military-strategic and operational levels are both to be found in London – one in Whitehall, the other at Northwood – the close geographic proximity and natural overlap between the levels causing, at times, some blurring of perceived responsibilities.

Finally, the current ongoing campaign in Iraq. Here I will focus on the period of my own deployment from October 2004 to April 2005 in Baghdad as Deputy Commanding General of the Coalition force and Senior British Military Representative Iraq, and offer a few personal observations. The Coalition force, Multi-National Force – Iraq (MNF-I) was commanded by a US four-star general, General George Casey, with a British three-star deputy, and a headquarters in the International ('Green') Zone in the middle of Baghdad. Identification of the operational level is complicated by the fact that the Iraq commander formally reports to and through the Commander

---

36   Rose 1998, 24.
37   Smith 2005, 4.
38   Smith 2005, 5.

Central Command based in Florida, but General Casey was the theatre commander for Iraq, and in practice reported on most matters direct to the Pentagon in Washington. Subordinate to HQ MNF-I was a Multi-National Corps commanded by an American three-star general from a headquarters close to Baghdad airport.

General Casey's job, therefore, was in directing military resources to achieve military-strategic objectives; objectives given to him from Washington via Commander Central Command based in Florida, and after consultation with Coalition partners. One of the first tasks which General Casey set when he and his HQ arrived in July 2004 was formulation of a campaign plan. In the HQ were a number of British staff officers ranging from major to brigadier, all carefully selected, and placed in key and potentially influential posts. It was to one of these officers that General Casey's chief of staff turned to write the campaign plan. There are aspects of the plan which could be said to reflect British influence, including the selection of the centre of gravity of the insurgents (or 'Anti-Iraqi Forces') as the support of the Iraqi people, and the importance of out-manoeuvring the insurgents by depriving them of popular support. The plan, as it should be, was subjected to continual review and amended when deemed necessary. Although there were members of the planning staff responsible for this, it was most useful for me to be reasonably familiar with the operational level, to be able to think conceptually about what we were doing, apply theory in the campaign review process in a complex campaign, and above all, to be asking the right questions.

A large part of the art of command at the operational level lies in thinking at the right level which, compared with the tactical level, means 'thinking big'. In Iraq, the structure of the force into the force headquarters and a corps headquarters greatly assisted in focusing the force commander's attention at the operational level, rather than involving himself with the minutiae of tactical detail. A large part of this operational-level role was liaising with the Iraqi Transitional Government: a daily business both for General Casey and me, him with the Prime Minister, at that time Ayad Allawi, and me with the Deputy Prime Minister and the Ministers of Defence and of the Interior. A further interface for both of us was our embassies, and both General Casey and I enjoyed close relationships with our respective ambassadors and their staffs. A further important task at this level was working closely with the national contingent commanders of the 30 or so nations represented in the Coalition, going out to visit them and team-building. Time had also to be spent with the media, of which there was a large contingent in Baghdad, and a proportion of each week (or, for General Casey, almost each day) devoted to reporting back to capitals by VTC. It can therefore be seen that command at the operational level involves, to a large degree, activities not perhaps normally seen as core military functions or, put another way, it involves a lot of non-military roles and requires different competencies.

Amongst the most important is the understanding of the political context, and having a good feel for the political mood in capitals, not just one's own, but those of all coalition members. It is certainly a help here to have worked at both the military-strategic and grand-strategic levels, and to be able to anticipate the needs of those levels in theatre, and have an awareness of sensitivities. This was particularly important during the three election campaigns that occurred during my tour of duty: US, Iraqi and UK. It is important also to understand the inherent conflicting demands of campaign planners and politicians. The logical starting point for the campaign planner is the desired end-state, working back to the first step to be taken. For the politician, the starting point is more often the first step – what can be done now – with subsequent actions depending on how the plot unfolds. What is important is to avoid railing at the other party's apparent illogicality, and reconcile these approaches through dialogue. Not the least of the military planner's duties is to preserve to the maximum the politician's freedom of action. But as well as an understanding of the military-strategic level, I found it invaluable to have considerable experience of the tactical level in the relevant environment, the land environment, in similar operations. This drew me to conclude that since the main function of the operational level is to provide the vital link between the military-strategic and the tactical levels, an essential competency of the operational level commander should be to have a deep understanding not just of one of those two, but of both.

Among the more military roles at the operational level was the key activity of helping the Iraqis build up their security forces, both army and police, to allow them to take the lead in the security of their own country. This became the top-priority activity for all Coalition forces after the January elections, and is an ongoing process. The task has involved simultaneously setting up from scratch a new Ministry of Defence, recruiting and training the soldiers and police, providing their logistics, building their barracks, equipping the force and procuring all its new equipment for it, while at the same time running a counter-insurgency campaign and providing security for the Iraqi population: a huge challenge. The determination of the Iraqis in the face of a vicious campaign of terror has been, and continues to be, remarkable. In helping the leaders of the new Iraqi Army, a policy of pairing was introduced where most Coalition commanders at every level paired off with their Iraqi opposite number to provide help and mentoring support. My opposite number was the Iraqi Vice Chief of the Defence Staff equivalent, an Air Force general whom I greatly liked and admired, making the time we spent together a welcome pleasure.

Command at the operational level is also a rather different business than at the tactical. At the operational level command is joint and multinational, and more often than not, multi-agency as well. It is therefore much more about diplomacy and gentle persuasion than giving orders. Although other nations' contingents are theoretically under command, the theoretical nature of this is likely to become apparent if they receive an unwelcome order. This is likely to be referred through the national contingent commander to capitals and to take an inordinate amount of time to extract a reply, often not in time for participation in the planned operation. Most contingents will also have limitations on their use placed on them by their governments. It is surprising, though, what can be achieved by good personal relationships, trust, and prior discussion and consultation. This is also true of non-governmental organisations, some of which will be vital to the success of operations, particularly in the reconstruction phase, but which may have no desire whatsoever to cooperate, or be seen to cooperate, with the military. This calls for a rather different command style from the days of, say, Montgomery. Just how far would an unreconstructed Montgomery get in today's Army? Not far, I suggest.

As an example of a Deputy Commander's role at the operational level, I gave considerable encouragement to a potential change, already identified by General Casey, of bringing together all the lines of operation – such as diplomatic, intelligence, military and economic – in each commander's area of responsibility, under the hand of that commander. Some commanders saw themselves as responsible only for the military line of operation, with the responsibility for the others within their area being that of the functional specialist in Baghdad. This changed so that an important specified task for commanders was to bind together all lines of operation within their area, and ensure unity of effort among and within them. Although nothing to do with my input, it was encouraging to see that when the new corps arrived towards the end of my tour, this had become part of their doctrine.

Finally, an observation about the preparation needed for an appointment at the operational level. At this level preparation is more about education than training. The challenges are so diverse, uncertain, unpredictable and complex that training needs to be largely a matter of education, developing minds to cope with this environment, and to be creative within it. In my view and experience, a study of history, and a continuous study at that, is of huge benefit in seeing events and issues in context and perspective. For the operational-level commander, therefore, the necessary preparation is largely a question of self-education.

A number of conclusions offer themselves from this brief study: first, those concerning the consequences of the absence of the operational level from British military doctrine. The resulting doctrinal focus on the tactical level led, for better or for worse, to a focus on the conduct of battles. It contributed to a single-Service rather than joint-Service focus, to an attritional tendency in the attrition/manoeuvre balance, to a pedagogic approach of 'what to think' rather than 'how to think', and to an emphasis on the personal qualities perceived by the military to be important at the tactical level, such as obedience, loyalty, conformity and discipline, often at the expense of qualities more valuable at the operational level, such as intellect, independent-mindedness, scepticism and creativity.[39] It led some people towards the false logic that every tactical victory would lead to strategic success, and that, therefore, every opportunity to destroy the enemy should automatically be taken – what today might be termed 'the kinetic solution'. And it led to a tendency for senior officers to be thinking small when they should have been thinking big.

Lastly, there are some conclusions that the British military might draw about itself: in particular, the difficulty of conceptual and doctrinal development in an instinctively conservative and hierarchical organisation. For, as Sir Michael Howard has pointed out,

> The disciplined acceptance of traditional values and traditional solutions is the natural product of the military environment, and the problem of combining this attitude with the scientist's scepticism and agnosticism lies at the root of military education and military training at every level.[40]

Those at the top of such hierarchies need to be tolerant of heretics and of criticism, and need actively to stimulate and encourage participation in professional debate, if they are not to be seen to be disapproving of it, and thereby stifling it. There is an important role to be played in such debate from outside the Armed Services and the Ministry of Defence, and it behoves the military to ensure that it communicates externally to a sufficient degree to allow such a contribution to be well informed. Finally, the slow evolution of operational art in the United Kingdom would undoubtedly have been accelerated had the British military as an institution been more receptive to the idea of progress through military science, as opposed to reliance on an essentially empirical approach. There is certainly indication of change in this respect over the past couple of decades – change linked, in part, to the study of the operational level itself – and a change which, with the establishment of the Defence Academy and its academic partnerships, should now be institutionalised. But we should nevertheless be aware of our heritage of reliance on the purely empirical approach, and beware of its return, particularly in an era when, for members of the Armed Forces, the evolving nature of conflict has seldom made greater calls on military education, but the time available for it has never seemed to be less.

---

39   As Shimon Naveh has noted, for the Russians: 'The principal quality required from the operational director was defined as *tvorchestro* (creativity).' Naveh 1997, 186.

40   Howard 1974.

Chapter 11

Twenty-First-Century Operational Leadership: Sierra Leone, Baghdad and Northern Ireland

Nick Parker – 26 November 2008

Personal experience is something one rather takes for granted. I have been incredibly fortunate in that the last 10 years of my career have enabled me to serve in the Balkans, Sierra Leone, Iraq and Northern Ireland, and the preparation of this chapter has made me think hard about my own practical campaigning skill and experience, or lack of it, and what might be relevant to others.

The operational level of conflict is something that I have grown to know well. I find the levels of conflict a particularly useful framework; they help to bring some structure to the modern campaign, but they are not universally understood – or maybe they are interpreted differently. I was taught about the levels of war at the Higher Command and Staff Course in 1996; at the time my interpretation was far closer to the Higher Tactical level in a high intensity conflict. I remember serving in Banja Luka in the late 1990s and being struck by the complexity of the command structure then. The Multi-National Division I was serving in had different relationships with PJHQ, SFOR in Sarajevo, and the senior national representatives from the troop-contributing nations. There seemed to be at least four chains of command because there was also a US link, and one to the so-called 'Host Nations'. I do not remember comparing this reality to the levels of conflict at the time, but it was confusing and I know that different perspectives were crashing together in a rather haphazard way. I now recognise that this was the first evidence I experienced of the complexity of coalition command and control which has repeated itself in every operation that I have been involved in since.

Leadership has changed dramatically during my career, particularly at more senior levels. My experience during the Cold War was of a clearly defined military environment where decision-making took place in a unilateral context, consequences were limited and success seemed to be defined as winning or losing; or more truthfully not losing too badly. I have learnt over the past 10 years that the leadership challenge is so much more complex than just 'taking the hill'. We also have to operate in an environment where there is an endless mass of processes with an input rather than an output focus – as an aside I was relieved to see that the Government's reaction to the current economic challenge was to throw out those parts of the rule book that they didn't fancy: this should be a glimpse of what will happen when we next go to war. Today, on operations, conventional military hierarchies are also much less in evidence. Multinational and multi-agency operations break up neat command relationships and simply giving an order is not good enough.

I have set myself the task in this chapter of considering operational leadership in the twenty-first century; and it is this part of my title that establishes my context. It may be rather presumptuous, but I am assuming that the command and control challenges we will face in the future are likely to be more like those that I have faced in the latter part of my career than those faced by our predecessors in the 1980s.

In the following three vignettes, I examine strategic context and how this related to command at the operational level, and I attempt to draw these observations together by proposing some qualities which I believe to be important for operational leaders who are to succeed in the contemporary operating environment.

Sierra Leone

In 2001 Sierra Leone was on the brink of a lasting ceasefire. The rebel Revolutionary United Front was exhausted, if still tactically belligerent. They were contained by a very large and rather ponderous UN force which, because of a restrictive mandate, were reluctant to do anything. Their great advantage was that, unlike the Sierra Leone Armed Forces, they were dispersed across most of the country. West African political pressure, particularly from Nigeria, was mounting; there had been a number of unsuccessful attempts to broker a ceasefire and there were indications that there was an excellent prospect of progress if pressure could be maintained. But the UN approach was conciliatory. From a military perspective the force was not particularly convincing, the Indian contingent which hitherto had been the backbone of the force had left and the Pakistanis who had agreed to replace them were slow to generate force and had not yet reached critical mass.

The British were in a rather strange position – we had intervened almost by accident: an operation designed to evacuate UK nationals had had considerably greater impact. Without realising it we had acted as a very active deterrent to rebel advances on Freetown, and some months later the operation to release hostages from our training mission who had been captured by the West Side Boys (not part of the Revolutionary United Front) had reinforced the perception that we meant business. Our colonial links had resulted in the Government of Sierra Leone asking us to train and equip their Armed Forces, which meant a military advisor to the President and the Chief of Defence Staff, senior staff in every key part of the Headquarters, and training advisers in brigades and battalions. So we found ourselves exerting considerable influence at every level. With a national reserve earmarked 'over the horizon' if things went wrong, we were providing the country's military backbone both physically and conceptually: this was a classic example of exercising influence with very limited committed force.

Our position was very different from the 17,000-strong UN Force who, operating under direction from New York, with a Nigerian Special Representative of the Secretary-General and a Kenyan Force Commander, saw the British contribution as part of the problem they were facing. They were intensely irritated by our parallel structure and the degree of influence we were exerting over the Government of Sierra Leone without committing ourselves to support the UN, other than by a rather patronising agreement to use our 'over the horizon' reserve if they got into difficulty. They saw us as irresponsible and reckless; we complained about the lack of leadership in the UN force and were pressing for a swift military conclusion. This was in part because the FCO objective was to hold free and fair elections across as much of the country as possible before the current president's mandate ran out in 2002. And we were training the Army that had in many people's view caused the problems in the first place. Ironically the UK had put some key staff into the UN Force Headquarters – the COS and a handful of lieutenant colonels – to make it more effective. There was real tension in New York: comments attributed to the UK about the capability and rules of engagement of the UN Mission in Sierra Leone (UNAMSIL) had caused considerable offence, and was having some more general impact on relations between London and the UN.

So as the British Joint Task Force Commander and the President's military advisor I found myself in a bizarre position. On the one hand I had almost total operational control over the Sierra Leone Armed Forces (this was not necessarily the case at the lowest tactical level: I am not certain how well we were able to control the behaviour of Sierra Leone soldiers, who were quite capable of behaving very badly). We were therefore in a position to develop aggressive operations that would provide a credible stick to balance the negotiation carrot, something the UN force continually failed to do. But on the other hand, from the UN perspective we were seen as aggravating the situation: having refused to put our troops into Blue Berets, we were now trying to drive the operation. The strategic direction coming from London was that they wanted us to get on with it, but they didn't want to upset UN HQ in New York, so no overt aggression and do everything we could to help, short of any action: a case of having your cake and eating it.

From a UK perspective this was a national rather than a coalition operation. There were some Commonwealth contributions, but these were not particularly significant. At the strategic level London had to manage the relationship with New York, very much Foreign Office business, but there were no other significant international players. The FCO was also the lead department for the 'road map' that led to a successful election. This was in effect the strategic campaign plan. DfID was committed to a successful outcome, reinforcing evidence that we were a 'Force for Good' in Africa; Claire Short was absolutely committed to the Millennium Goals and here we were helping to restore the economy of the poorest country in the world. The MOD was slightly less enthusiastic: for them this was yet another unplanned commitment when the main effort was in the Balkans. When the Macedonia operation kicked off in August their attention was distracted, and after 9/11 they were almost entirely diverted.

So how did this relate to me at the operational or theatre level? In my dealings back to London the outcomes were most keenly recognised in the FCO. I worked very closely with the High Commissioner and, although it was not specifically stated, he was in UK terms the operational commander. DfID, with a committed minister in London, wanted security to enable development aid to flow and were generally supportive, but did not have a properly empowered representative in-country with authority to support decisions made by the High Commissioner and myself. So some of their operational-level decisions had to be made at Cabinet level in London, and this made our lives difficult. The MOD chain of command was very clunky: I had to pass things through Permanent Joint Headquarters in Northwood, always very supportive, but when they entered the Ministry of Defence they seemed to get bogged down. In practice it was most efficient to use the FCO as the main chain of command. In this way it was possible to manipulate strategic decision-making, since it was far more likely that things would reach Cabinet level quickly. The outcomes were also usually positive, giving us plenty of leeway to develop sensible operational level plans.

My links to the President meant that I was able to influence theatre activity at the very highest level, in effect attempting to synchronise UN negotiations with plans to push Sierra Leone Armed Forces further into rebel-held territory. We had to take care not to go too far, but two operations, one which restored Government control to the border with Guinea in the North and allowed Presidents Kabbah and Conte to meet symbolically at the customs post, demonstrated that if the rebels did not concede they would eventually be beaten. The UN Special Representative Ambassador Adeniji was a brilliant negotiator; he understood the West African mind and I am absolutely certain he was able to do things that would have been way beyond us. But he wanted success, and he would have made many more concessions had we not been acting as the counter balance. President Kabbah was also encouraged on at least two occasions to speak directly to President Obesanjo of Nigeria to get him to exert influence on the negotiations on our behalf. This introduced a critical regional dimension which it was difficult for London to see – indeed I was amazed at the lack of communication between London and our diplomats in Nigeria who would have been well placed to exert influence on the situation. At no stage during this process did I feel that the UN recognised the synergy of our respective positions. But the ceasefire came through and we were able to start a Military Reintegration Programme.

I learnt many lessons as a result of this experience but I would like to flag up two. First, perspectives at the various levels in the chain of command were very different – even in a single national context. The operational level provided the greatest clarity and was where most of the interests came together. Secondly, key players needed empowered representatives in-country to enable properly considered and synchronised decision-making.

Baghdad

My second example is taken from Iraq in 2005. I finished being the Deputy Commanding General of the Multi-National Corps in Baghdad in early 2006 on the day that the Golden Mosque was blown up in Samarra. During my time working in a US Corps HQ for a US Airborne three-star general, I witnessed a referendum, an election, the slow rise in capability of the Iraqi Army and the extraordinary level of commitment demonstrated by the US military. This was another very different and illuminating experience.

I learnt that the US Army is probably more different from us than the French. I had to work hard to be understood and to understand; often in apparently violent agreement, the Corps Commander and I would draw completely different conclusions from our conversations, and as his subordinate from a nation that was providing only around five per cent of the force it was up to me to make the running.

The operational-level plan – owned by General George Casey and supported by US Ambassador Zalmay Khalilzad – was relatively simple: restore democracy, transfer the responsibility for security to Iraqis, and concurrently make everyone feel better through reconstruction. I do not intend to discuss its merits, rather to make a number of observations about the conduct of the campaign.

Starting again at the strategic level, the British, and particularly the MOD, seemed to me to fail to give sufficient priority to the Coalition's operational-level plan. There was plenty of strategic linkage between London and Washington, but how influential this was is debatable. There was certainly a great deal of effort put into it; there were close links between PJHQ and CENTCOM in Tampa but there was remarkably little interest in what we were doing in Baghdad. We put talented staff officers into the MNF-I planning hub. But it appeared to me that the British military focus jumped through the theatre/operational level and concentrated directly on what was going on in the Multi-National Division in Basra: Baghdad was a distraction. This did not particularly worry the US Corps Commander: his view was that provided the British were prepared to accept the tactical risk within their divisional boundary he would manage (rather than command) the operation. There was significant resistance by the British to 'interference': on a number of occasions we were told that US offers of assistance were unnecessary. This is of course the reality of coalition operations: the Czechs were doing exactly the same in MND Centre, although they were more prepared to have US support. It meant that the strategic perspective in London was focused on Basra, and there was a tendency to ignore the operational perspective. This had a direct impact on coherence – the training of the Iraqi Army and police was not consistent, the application of development money was uneven and Iraqi political relationships were distorted, with the British tending to deal with the Basrawi administration on its own without concurrently allowing levers to be pulled in Baghdad. Indeed, I remember taking an urgent call one night asking me to get the Iraqi interior minister to intervene with the Governor in Basra, but the links didn't exist and there was little understanding in Baghdad about what the British were doing. I also sense that there was a more short-term approach in the south; this may be unfair, but I am in no doubt that greater emphasis on the Coalition campaign plan would have mitigated against the 'six-month tour' tendency.

My second observation from Iraq concerns the role of the operational commander. I watched General Casey impose his will on an organisation that was extraordinarily resistant to change. In the summer of 2005 there was an urgent need to make the western Euphrates valley secure through the province of Anbar, so Sunnis could vote in the referendum and the election. This required a series of carefully timed clearance operations up the valley, followed by an in-place force to retain control. The US Marine Corps MEF was very reluctant to conduct the operation: they felt their forces were stretched already and there was no spare capacity. So as the orders started to emerge I was surprised to experience the phenomenon of 'non-concurrence'. The Marines simply said they would not do the operation. To make them comply a US Army brigade combat team had to be found from elsewhere, but the process of identifying this force provoked further non-concurrence from the US Army Divisions. To make it happen, General Casey simply kept on pushing. I watched what seemed to be tactical fiddling by a senior commander, but in truth what he was doing was constantly aggravating the system until what he wanted happened. In the end he waited for the Corps Commander to go on R&R and then turned on the hapless deputy and told him to do it! I was quite taken aback when I flew into the MEF to give the Commanding General orders when he told me to get out in very colourful language. In the end we persuaded them to do it, but it was a hell of an effort. So what? Even in a single national context, making things happen in a framework operation takes a massive amount of effort from the senior commanders. Add the coalition perspective to this and it gets worse. So while the manoeuvre gods may say that coalition operations by their very nature must be simple to plan and to execute, do not underestimate the levels of will power that are needed to make them happen.

Finally from Iraq, an observation on the Iraqi Army, who, it must be said, were certainly different from the rest of us; not only were they still pretty poorly trained but they also had a completely different military culture from ours, most significantly in the way that they exercised command. The mobile phone seemed to connect the Prime Minister with the leading section, making things happen in some unexpected ways. But they were the future and we had to work with them. There was a real reluctance within the Coalition to take them seriously. One particular area sticks in my mind. They had been repeatedly telling us that there was a route that was dangerous: the President's convoy had been attacked on its way to Kurdistan. We thought they were over-egging it and didn't take their advice seriously. In the end we planned the first Iraqi-led operation into the area they were so concerned about, and it turned out that there was a large enemy force that conducted a number of vicious attacks and caused us to shift significant Coalition support into the area. They did know what they were talking about, but they went about their business in such a different way from the Coalition that it was difficult to ensure they were taken seriously and properly integrated into our operations.

So the main conclusions to be drawn from Iraq centre on the criticality of the operational level in bringing continuity to a campaign; the complexity of coalitions and the impact this has on command and control; and the role of the indigenous host nation in meeting the enduring security challenge.

Northern Ireland

My third set of reflections is drawn from the year I spent as General Officer Commanding Northern Ireland. I left on 31 July 2007, the final year of Operation Banner and the conclusion of a 38-year operation. I don't think many would challenge the assertion that this was a successful campaign – although I have to say the lessons habitually drawn from it deserve some careful examination.

The British putting their berets on in Basra, our natural understanding of counter-insurgency, the corporals' war: all these have some truth but are not as significant as some would wish to make out. I would like to continue with my theme of looking at strategic, operational and tactical levels. Northern Ireland's strategic context was peculiar, dominated by domestic political issues with an increasingly important international dimension from both the Republic and the United States; but viewed from below it was relatively straightforward. Increasingly answering to a single point of command – the Prime Minister – and with complete backing for almost any request for resources, this campaign was almost unique.

At the operational level the Secretary of State for Northern Ireland was clearly responsible for all lines of activity and, over time, we built sophisticated mechanisms to ensure coherence. Critically this was a truly multi-agency operation: from the moment the Army recognised they were working in support of the police, the emphasis for ensuring security was properly balanced. In our final year I witnessed a cultural reluctance from both the police and the Army to let go. The former were concerned that they would not receive the protection they required if things turned bad, and they also had become used to having a cheap source of manpower available when overtime got tight. As for the Army, there was real reluctance to take risks and an attitude that the police would not be able to cope without them – not surprising after 38 years, but requiring firm direction to keep on track. As an aside, the campaign did not stop with the end of the Army operation. Multi-agency activity continues today to ensure security; it is just that the police are completely in the lead. I also believe that campaign-planning concepts will continue to help with analysis, planning and direction, but they do not come naturally to other agencies who tend to see them as the Army over-engineering solutions.

Looking for a moment at the tactical level, there are interesting parallels with both Sierra Leone and Iraq. The raising of in-place forces, with local knowledge, that took the burden off the regular troops was both sensible as an economy of force mission and in part to transfer security responsibility to the indigenous population. Northern Ireland's sectarian challenges meant this was never going to be a permanent solution and the trick in the last years of the campaign was to reintegrate the locally recruited Royal Irish Home Service back into their communities without upsetting the security balance. It took some time and considerable resource, but it worked. It is also worth noting the significant amount of effort invested in development; Belfast changed dramatically over the course of 15 years and this not just on the back of the enormous economic growth in Ireland in the 1990s and early 2000s. The British Government has put a huge amount of resource into all communities in the North; when I left, unemployment was low, the property market had gone berserk and the voting public across all communities was far more interested in personal prosperity than in sectarian differences. This may not have endured, but at the time it represented success in a key line of operation in the Northern Ireland Campaign plan.

So from Northern Ireland I conclude that operational coherence is critical, and that police primacy is a visible reminder that crude military security is only a small part of the solution – this is the multi-agency or comprehensive approach lesson.

Conclusion

In conclusion, I am convinced that an understanding of the operational level of conflict is critical to the effective prosecution of contemporary operations. Svechin's definition – tactics form the steps from which operational leaps are assembled; strategy points out the path – is absolutely right, but it is only part of the answer.[1] The strategic path is confused and tactical steps are often taken in a very distinct national context. Today, the operational level is almost certainly the same as the theatre. It is the point at which multinational, multi-agency and regional interests have to be brought together and fused into a campaign plan that shapes and connects the various tactical level activities. This is at the heart of the challenge that faces the modern military commander at the operational level. So what are the qualities we are looking for?

The operational commander must be *pragmatic*, not weak, but there is a tendency to aim for 100 per cent solutions which will not work in a complex multinational, multi-agency environment. Such a comment can light a fire in the eyes of Cold War commanders, with cries of 'if they don't do what they are told then sack them'. Oh so wrong! What we have learnt is that influence applied sensibly to set the conditions for success is critical. I am not suggesting that we should not stand up for what is right, indeed there will be a need to do just that, but there is a constant requirement for diplomacy that works to ensure the best possible conditions for whatever it is that we are trying to achieve. Increasingly, the person who can persuade and cajole, who can use influence to best effect is the one who really makes a difference at this level. Inflexibility can be very unhelpful and the best often remains the enemy of the good.

There is a need for *persistence*. There are two aspects to this. First, willpower has to be applied to force ideas through. I don't want to overstate it but my conclusion is that this is a remarkably physical activity – not because you are wandering around beating people up – but because constant engagement can be exhausting over time. If you want to make things happen you may also have to push through the layers either laterally (say into other Government Departments) or beneath you – sometimes referred to as the long screwdriver. Convincing people of your ideas, when not all will believe that what you are proposing is right, takes up a great deal of effort. Very often it's difficult to see the true strategic perspective and there will be quite aggressive resistance to new ideas because they are either not understood or not invented here. Persistence, coupled with a degree of self-belief, will be necessary to get things to happen as you wish. There is a flip side to this: you must be prepared to listen to the contrary view carefully and to have the courage to change or adapt what you are doing in the light of experience. Indeed, this can often improve the central idea and can be very positive. This is, of course, a very personal thing and I would not wish to overstate it; we have all encountered subordinates who can be intransigent: at some point there will still be a need to give orders.

Take a *collective approach*. The simple approach to leadership applied by a commander of a battalion or ship does not work in the complex operational environment. At more junior levels we are taught that the 'Chinese Parliament' or 'Kitchen Cabinet', using collective decision-making, is a bad thing because it undermines the place of the leader and adds too much choice to decision-making. I am clear that the complexities confronting the operational leader dictate the requirement to empower those around you, and to build a team that can cover the complexity – much in the manner of a Board of Directors. You have to delegate responsibility for areas of the business to others so their energy and ideas can be used to best effect. Decision-making needs careful but free-flowing debate; you have to hear and understand the nuances and must create the conditions that allow ideas to flourish, be developed and then included in the solution. There is, of course, a time when the decision has to be made, and this must rest at a point of command. But the best operational leaders will have prepared the ground sufficiently well to get what they require.

---

1   Alexander Andreyevich Svechin (1878–1938) was a Russian and Soviet military officer and theorist whose most famous work was *Strategiya*.

Strive for *clarity*. I have already indicated that operational leadership is conducted in a complex environment and this often generates convoluted plans. But no matter how complex the plan, it has to be put into effect, and success will often depend on people, far away from the decision-making, understanding what is required and the context in which it has to be done. For this reason clarity and simplicity are virtues. There is no substitute for time spent by the senior leadership defining what they want and describing the context in which it is to be done.

PART III
Iraq 2006–2009: Success of a Sort

On 30 April 2009, British operations ended in Iraq as 20th Armoured Brigade lowered the British flag in Basra for the last time. The then Chief of Defence Staff, Air Chief Marshal Sir Jock (now Lord) Stirrup, said:

> Whatever debate continues about the lead up to the invasion in 2003, whatever coalition mistakes were made along the way, we can be clear on one thing: the UK Armed Forces have made an outstanding contribution to the transition of Iraq from dictatorship and regional pariah to burgeoning democracy and constructive partner.[1]

The chapters in this section are the personal accounts of those in the UK Armed Forces charged with leading that outstanding contribution to Iraq's transition, often in the most difficult circumstances.

Lieutenant General Sir Graeme Lamb served four times in Iraq, most recently in 2006 and 2007, as the deputy commander to General Petraeus in Baghdad during the time of the Anbar Awakening and the beginning of the American Surge in the north. One of Britain's most experienced soldiers, he describes in Chapter 12 what it is to be a general and presents a candid appraisal of the state of British generalship today. It makes sober reading.

While Graeme Lamb was in Baghdad, the then Lieutenant Colonel Justin Maciejewski was commanding his battalion in Basra on Operation Sinbad, Britain's last (and arguably first) real attempt to control the growing Shia insurgency in the south. Operation Sinbad was conceived and commanded by General Sir Richard Shirreff, currently NATO's Deputy Supreme Allied Commander Europe. Unfortunately he was refused permission by the MOD to write about Sinbad in this book; but Brigadier Justin Maciejewski describes in Chapter 13 the exceptionally difficult task the Operation faced, given limited political and physical support from both Baghdad and London, and explains honestly why the operation was doomed to fail, but was still necessary to conduct. He is well placed to write about Basra, having being divisional operations officer for the 2003 invasion, commanded a battalion during Operation Sinbad, and been divisional chief of staff after Operation Charge of the Knights. He can therefore put the story of Basra into context, having been there at beginning, middle and end.

After the failure of Operation Sinbad, Major General Jonathan Shaw, the next British division commander in southern Iraq, was given the political direction to find a way out of Iraq for the British, but with honour. Chapter 14 is his description of how in 2007 he reappraised the nature of the problem facing the British, concluding the problem was basically self-limiting and that it could never be solved while the British were in Basra. Jonathan Shaw describes how he negotiated a deal with a militia commander to permit British forces to withdraw peacefully out of Basra City back to the airport some five miles outside.

---

1   Hughes 2009.

Meanwhile, in Baghdad, Lieutenant General Sir William Rollo had replaced Graeme Lamb as the deputy commander to General Petraeus. In Chapter 15 he uses this experience, and many others, to analyse the factors that have to be considered by modern leaders working in a coalition in a complex counter-insurgency.

In March 2008 the Iraqi Security Forces launched Operation Charge of the Knights to rid Basra of the Shia militia – principally Jaysh al-Mahdi. By this time the accommodation between the British and the militia had effectively broken down, and since the British withdrawal the militia had imposed their law in the City. Acting Brigadier Richard Iron was the British mentor to the senior Iraqi commander, and describes in Chapter 16 how he helped develop the Iraqi plan, assisted the Iraqi battle for Basra, and how the Iraqis imposed the peace afterwards. He also, with the benefit of hindsight, analyses some of the mistakes made during the campaign.

For the past 15 years, a team at the King's Centre for Military Health Research at King's College London has been examining the mental health of the UK's Armed Forces, including the impact of war. Professor Sir Simon Wessely leads this team, and has written in Chapter 17 of the results of their analysis into the effects of the Iraq War. His principal conclusion is 'that the mental health of the UK Armed Forces has by and large survived Operation Telic' (the British name for the operation in Iraq), although, not surprisingly, there was a higher impact on those in combat roles than in non-combat roles.

Map 12.1 Iraq – deployment of multinational divisions

Chapter 12

On Generals and Generalship

Graeme Lamb – 30 April 2008

A far better soldier than I once said 'True riches cannot be bought – one cannot buy the experience of brave deeds or the friendship of companions to whom one is bound forever by ordeals suffered in common – true friendship itself is an emerald simply beyond price.'[1] How often do you hear such words spoken today? For me, I am deafened by their silence.

I do not hear people speaking of courage as a worthy test of men or women; of purpose as a true path for life; of selfless commitment of Duty, Service, Sacrifice; and I would suggest that Britain is the poorer for it. What I see around me are the cold and timid souls of little people all too often unable and unfit for the rigours of a full life: safely complacent, safely non-committal, safely at home, much like the young lord who 'but for the vile guns would have been a valiant soldier'. So very many people are simply consumed in the certainty of their right to happiness and wish to drag others down to their miserable level of ordinariness. George Bernard Shaw saw this pursuit to mediocrity. 'This is the true joy of life', he said, 'being used for a purpose recognized by you as a mighty one. Being a force of nature, instead of a feverish, selfish little clod of ailments and grievances, complaining that the world will not devote itself to making you happy.'[2] We seem to be unable to see or make sense of our lives, certainly in such abstract terms as courage, honour and integrity, and increasingly measure ourselves against the false gods of image, material value and self interest.

> Go as a Pilgrim and seek out danger
> Far from the comfort and well lit avenues of life.
> Pit your soul against the unknown,
> And seek stimulation in the company of the brave.
> Experience cold and hunger, heat and thirst,
> And survive to see another challenge and another dawn.
> Only then will you be at peace with yourself
> And able to know – and say
> 'I looked down on the farthest side of the mountain
> And, fulfilled and understanding all,
> Am truly content that I lived a full life and one of my own choice.'[3]

So said Hassan on his journey to Samarkand – his vision captures for me the spirit of a worthy life: one beset by extremes; of danger and discomfort, hunger and thirst; and those challenges faced together in fearless company; a life of peace because you earned it, survival in spite of it; and choice; for I believe that it is what we choose to do with our lives that both defines and separates us.

---

1 Attributed to Lieutenant Colonel Paddy Mayne DSO and three bars, soldier, solicitor, Irish rugby international, polar explorer and founder member of the Special Air Service.

2 Shaw 1934.

3 Flecker 1922.

If you listen to the siren voices of the faceless critics, those sitting safely beyond the lions' reach, those not fit for the arena who claim with such conviction that we are not good enough, it will be so. For me, I am not inclined to listen to those who would hail me a donkey when they are quite evidently just a horse's arse.

My reputation I fear far exceeds me, so please accept my apologies before I take a shot at generals, generalship, campaigning and a view on Iraq. I did glance at the list of the other contributors, of whom I have served with most. The majority I would rate as fair, a few I would gladly join and assault hell's gate, and some I wouldn't follow to the latrine.

For I am drawn from the dragon's seed: more of a Cadmus type of general, foul-mouthed, silently intolerant and dangerously indifferent. I get the leadership and motivation stuff but am more inclined, and it is not against my better judgement, to manipulate people to do that they would not otherwise do and gladly. I use with cold-hearted deliberation emotion, passion, hatred, anger, commitment and any other of these powerful instincts to get people to get the job done. I really do not give a damn to those who think badly of me. They are entitled to their view and I take or discard their criticism as it is given; I draw from my own experience for this judgement, for life has had me walk with kings and clerics, struck me dumb by the stupidity and as often the brilliance of simple men and women, all of whom count with me but none too much, and I have had occasion to see the best in people but all too often just the worst. I am not, I think, ambitious, and recognise that it is on the shoulders of others that we in charge triumph. So people are either with me or against me; most fall into the latter category but lack the balls to say so – hardly unsurprising for moral courage is in my book a far more testing medium than the physical courage required to run down a man and kill him; and for that all that is required of you is strength and the brutal application of will power.

So how did I make general? Thirty-six years of soldiering; four wars and more operations than are good for any man; and an awful lot of luck. Today, I find myself still leading but just a little, using an awful lot of my hard-earned and now rapidly vanishing credits with young warriors who remember me but only just; fighting a lot less but increasingly challenging the institutional ordinariness of my kind; complacency is simply a sin. I have been taught to disassemble complex problems and re-assemble solutions. I operate best when left alone and can work with the minimum of guidance and the maximum delegation. I object to casual participation by others, both in uniform and out, having a go at this tough old bone that life has thrown me – soldiering, that is, and I will go to my grave having barely scratched the surface of understanding what a general does but having tried, and if nothing more lived a respectably full life that was of my own choice.

The view of General Joe Stilwell – American of Second World War Burma fame, affectionately known as 'Vinegar Joe' – on generals and generalship is worth a glance:

> The average general envies the buck private, when things go wrong, the private can blame the general, but the general can only blame himself. The private carries the woes of one man; the general carries the woes of all. He is conscious always of the responsibility on his shoulder, of the relatives of the men entrusted to him, and of their feelings. He must act so he can face those fathers and mothers without shame or remorse. How can he do this? By constant care, by meticulous thought and preparation, by worry, by insistence on high standards in everything, by reward and punishment, by impartiality, by example of calm and confidence, it all adds up to character.[4]

And then he asked himself a simple question: 'if a man has enough character to be a good commander, does he ever doubt himself? He should not. In my case I doubt myself. Therefore, I am

---

4   Stilwell 1949.

in all probability not a good commander.' His final reflection tells you more about his humility and character than it does his ability as a commander. So, an American perspective – being a general is all about character.

It is said that 'Fortune Favours the Brave'. Kurt Meyer, or 'Panzer' Meyer as he was better known, commanded an SS Division in Normandy, having fought through Poland, Czechoslovakia, Greece and on the Eastern Front; now you might question his political credentials but you could not challenge him as a field commander, battle leader or combat general. It was said of Meyer by his chief of staff not that fortune favoured the brave but, and far more insightful, 'Fortune Favours the Competent'. I am inclined towards the view that it is competence not bravery that matters – and if you recall Vinegar Joe Stilwell's reflections on why he could face those fathers and mothers without shame or remorse, it was down to high standards, constant care and meticulous thought and preparation. And, while you need character to carry a message, you need competence to craft it, having thought through what is intended, having considered the likely outcomes. Leadership is an obligation not a mark of a caste. Leadership is based on respect, on proven competence, and only that. When you ask men to die or endure great hardship they have the right to know the purpose that demands that sacrifice. It is for their leadership, those who decide their fate, general or leader, to bespeak confidence; calmness; optimism. So for a German, being a practical sort of fellow, it is competence that captures their mark of generalship.

But for us Anglo-Saxon types: 'When the blast of war blows in our ears, imitate the actions of the tiger, stiffen the sinews, summon up thy blood, disguise fair nature as an ill favoured rage.'[5] Shakespeare our playwright gets it. It's all about communication. So generals and generalship, I might suggest, is just about the three 'C's: character, competence and communication. Character gets people to do that they would not do and gladly; communication gets their soul, their passion and their commitment; and competence gets them through.

So do we select our generals on such criteria? Don't be daft, of course we don't. We pull them up through patronage, misplaced loyalty, self-promotion and a host of other rather tawdry reasons and, occasionally, on ability; but it is not always the brightest and the best that are selected for high office. In our defence, I do sense we are rather better than most industries which promote leaders who shaft the company and walk away with a ridiculously fat termination bonus, drawn up, not on performance, but on the litany of lies that is the modern curriculum vitae which seduced the shareholders into selecting the moron in the first place. I am constantly disappointed by my fellow human beings – selfish self-interest has for the moment replaced selfless commitment. Maybe the next ice age, the upcoming food wars, extremists or a climate catastrophe, will reverse the trend. But for the time being I'm just disappointed; hence my opening shot across my fellow officers' bows and why you now might reflect on my reasoning to be disinclined to cross the floor for some, and why others I would greet like long lost brothers. So how can two so very different classes of general officers share the same work space?

Well, the world for us is made up of two extremes: war and peace, which are unsurprisingly very different activities; activities that draw out and expose for better or worse two quite different characters. In peace the measure of one's business success is to be found in compromise, consensus, what the market will bear, management, the gains associated with clever debate, personal ambition (which should be made of sterner stuff but seldom is) and, oh, so clever arguments crafted to support a master's voice, selected arguments that are seductively eloquent, compelling arguments that brief well, constructed by wordsmiths whose object is simply to win the case, much like the legal profession at any cost – and, if you succeed and win the proposition for your leader,

---

5   William Shakespeare, *Henry V*, III.

then it is onward and upward, limitless promotion. So in peace it is superficiality, spin, image, short-termism, not substance, that more often than not will do nicely. We tend to do better in war and when operationally busy. I find the convergence of reality and accountability tends to expose officers and NCOs with 'Bottom' as the Edwardians would have it. The arena is not the place for comedians, clowns or the incompetent; it brutally determines those fit for operational service and those not; mistakes and errors can be counted and costed, and failure is measured and accredited to generals who make poor decisions; for you can run as a general officer but you cannot hide once deployed. In operational decisions, real lives, complexity and uncertainty, success and failure (those two impostors) are one and the same; these are the measures that test a general's character, his courage and his will.

And willpower is for the general the rock on which the tempest of uncertainty must break. Napoleon Bonaparte captured this conflict of will, this brutal confrontation with self – the test of character, when he talked of the three o'clock in the morning courage that commanders must face and always alone; where doubt, fear of failure and the burden of responsibility question their reasoning and challenge their sanity. For in uncertainty, at the boundaries of chaos, there is no shortage of roads to choose from; and equally there is absolutely no certainty as to which are the right and the wrong ones; and to compound this dilemma you will be damned if you don't and damned if you do.

Now you might just begin to realise why people like me try to stand for what might be, by holding onto the best of what has been.

The general has to act with honour and hope and generosity, no matter what you have drawn. You may not always have a choice on how you die, but it is my view that you can and you should try to pass the days between as a good man. Integrity, honesty and, for some, faith are all stoic values, reliable, dependable values proven in the furnace of chaos: these are the old-fashioned ideals that underpin military character – duty, service, sacrifice. Ernst Jünger, who fought in the Great War, probably the epitome of the German Storm Trooper, wrote in his classic *The Storm of Steel*: 'However cleverly people may talk or write, there is nothing to set against self-sacrifice that is not pale, insipid and miserable.'[6] Self-sacrifice, personal or career, is what the soldier knows and the official knows not. Play-acting and bravado works right up to the point when your signaller gets whacked and lady luck turns her back on you. The unexpected torches meticulous preparation and perfectly presented plans, turning them into little more than burnt ash, with the result that careers melt under the harsh glare of public and career humiliation; and it is against this maelstrom that competent commanders struggle to hold their people and the endeavour together. But if you cannot communicate, get your message and your will across to those in front of you and in the fight, to those alongside you and to those behind you supporting, then best-laid plans are for nought and disaster will surely follow. If your general is short-changed in these skills, if it is too hot in his operational kitchen, if he is consumed by self-doubt, then recognising that his time has passed or he has been found out, he should accept his lot, his limitations and depart; few do.

So maybe generals are an over-estimated bunch; too few I would judge are of the right stuff, but maybe I am already a dead or dying breed carrying a standard that is so 'yesterday': horribly outdated, overdrawn and the last of a lineage of old men rabbiting on and simply stuck on stupid. Or maybe that is what we are, cocksure, bloody-minded, brutally indifferent, fit for the arena, a throwback, but like the legions of Rome ready to defend your and my rights whatever the cost; attempting to stand for something and all the while challenged by the enemy in front and today increasingly by those behind: unworldly, wishful sorts; little people who somehow think that I

---

6   Jünger 2004.

am or wish to be in any way like them. For, as George Orwell reminded us, for a nation to sleep soundly in their beds takes rough men to bring violence to those that would harm you – and military service has taught me that there is no shortage of those that intend to harm us or those that would dictate to you and me how we should live our lives and by whose rules. The chilling statement of al-Qaeda leader in Iraq, al-Zarqawi, that we should obey or he would slaughter us, makes my point rather nicely. So maybe having people who are prepared to stand for something beyond self in an imperfect world matters; then again, maybe it doesn't.

So what do we actually do? Well we operate in a Hobbesian world; no arts; no letters; no society; and, worst of all, continual fear and danger of violent death; and the life of man 'solitary, poor, nasty, brutish, and short'. Africa, the Balkans, the Middle East and South America offer all of the above, and no shortage of violent and short. But just to add to our woes, returning to this world tour is the anarchist, the terrorist, the angry man or woman carrying a very large chip but no remorse. And he or she is for the time being every bit the match of those potentially larger, more organised, armed forces that we have historically found ourselves confronting.

Sir Percy Blakeney, described as an eighteenth-century dilettante, was to his friends a brainless English fop, but in working alone against those that sought to find him Sir Percy captures rather nicely the complexity of the emerging challenges I think we face today: 'we seek him here, we seek him there, those Frenchies seek him everywhere, is he in heaven – is he in hell, that damned elusive Pimpernel.'[7]

Today's global militant opportunists are, I sense, no less accommodating than Sir Percy, and we are little better than Chauvelin in finding them. They are elusive chameleons, increasingly non-state players, who have been brought up on an educated diet of hatred and intolerance. They feed upon the decency of our societies and, when it suits them, hide within its freedoms. They are manipulators of a growing disaffected and angry youth, they are well networked, well funded, media savvy, and target and terrorise by choice non-combatants – our civilian populations; they are a modern-day scourge, a formidable adversary, but an enemy that without any doubt I believe we as nations and an international community can defeat. The larger, more complex threat of Islamic militancy is significantly more problematic, but again I contend that this can be dealt with successfully so long as we are prepared to bring our nations' considerable energies to bear on the problem; an approach which would see a symmetric response to an asymmetric attack, applying our strength against weakness. My contention is not that we cannot deal with such emerging threats, but that our inability to craft a compelling response is increasingly the problem.

As that rather dull but nevertheless compelling Prussian General told us:

War is a wonderful trinity, of:

- The original violence of its elements, hatred and animosity, fruits of blind instinct;
- The play of probabilities and chance, which make it a free activity of the soul;
- And the subordinate nature of a political instrument.

That the first of these three concerns more the people, the second, more the General and his Army; and the third, more the Government.[8]

---

7   Orczy 1903.
8   von Clausewitz 1832. Book 1, Chapter 1.

And while obviously I am no expert in Carl Phillip Gottfried von Clausewitz's work, I have always recognised the underlying message in his writings: that the people and our politicians are the majority stakeholders in this business of ours; a business which in this new millennium, if I am not mistaken, is becoming increasingly more transparent and complex; and what we face are simply 'wicked problems'.

These are problems our own population and the broader international community do not have an instinctive feel for, and even less for what we in the Armed Forces do and how we do it. This is hardly surprising since the majority have never had reason or cause to fight for our and others' freedoms – a call answered today by small volunteer forces. Our own population's comprehension of what we do, why we train, even a question as fundamental as why we exist, is not well understood. A recent book aimed at the business community, titled *The Business General*, captures this concern rather nicely:

> For one thing, most people have very little first-hand knowledge of how the Armed Forces operate and the impressions they have … are often formed by exposure to war films and the stereotypical lampoonery of some television programmes. The average person has no real idea about what warfare really entails, beyond the narrow snapshots that television, newspapers and magazines provide. This is perhaps a mark of a relatively peaceful world. The real complexity, the risks, the scale and the human challenge of modern military operations, from warfighting to peacekeeping and nation building, remain screened from civilian life.
>
> Usually military and civilian life proceed alongside each other in a state of more or less blissful ignorance, until fate and history force them to collude – such as now in the conflicts in Iraq, Afghanistan, the Middle East and Africa …[9]

which are the wicked problems I referred to.

And these complex problems that challenge us on some foreign field are beamed directly to our stakeholders' plasma screens and rushed into our morning papers by the modern media business: aggressive and competing 24/7 TV news channels, broadsheet opinions which reflect a clear editorial and commercial slant, and occasionally the opposition's own information/terror campaign which can be surfed on an open internet. Our stakeholders are provided with a comfortable view, one with which they can sympathise, empathise or criticise, but increasingly one that borders on a snapshot and passing sound-bite of the actual facts of an unfolding event. Richard Holmes, the late but much respected military historian in the United Kingdom, captured my concern rather better when he said 'We watch "observational documentaries" and believe ourselves better informed.'[10]

The effect of this habitually raw and often sensational exposure is to have taken our Prussian General's individual concerns on warfare, that of the people, the Armed Forces and the politician, and squeezed them through a single multidisciplined prism with the result that there are no longer three separate parties but one general view presented to all three groups simultaneously. And of which only those deployed into the theatre of operations are, to quote Theodore Roosevelt, 'doing the rough work of a workaday world'. Our stakeholders, distant from the operation, are bombarded with images of slaughter and desperate grief; they are offered seemingly random uncertainty and the unfairness of war and conflict; and are confused and angered by the opaque layers of complex politics that surround it. My point is not to query their right to know what we do on their behalf,

---

9   Tom and Barrons 2006.
10   Holmes 2006.

both good and bad, but to question their competence to constantly stand in judgement on our every action while we in turn desperately attempt, and in good faith, against collapsing timelines, to bring a semblance of order to the wicked problem. This modern-day inquisition has already begun. It fundamentally challenges our way of warfare and our ability to prosecute these complex conflicts and campaigns. Most military forces operate under the broadly established tenets of mission command but – if you torque the problem – bring it home and into our living rooms and then fuel a recurring theme of constant failure when there has been no ridiculously quick and easy success, then this continuous negativity begins to crack the will of the people and, in turn, the will of our political parties. So the first casualty in this battle is mission command; its battlefield replacement an unscripted doctrine of mission control, the implications of which to the military are not insignificant.

Furthermore, if war and conflict are, as history and current operations indicate, a battle of wills, then no matter how strong the will of the military is, it will be the will of our stakeholders that truly matters, for it underwrites our authority to deploy and prosecute these difficult operations. But if the public or political backbenchers lose their will in the endeavour, no amount of clever technology, new equipment or restructuring of our organisation will make a jot of difference. We need to recognise that information operations are not just about the enemy; the confidence and support of our stakeholders are absolutely central to the prosecution of expeditionary operations. This is no mean challenge, for if we have not set the conditions for our use, or blindly assume their infinite confidence, beware; for if we lose them, we potentially lose all. 'And that's the way it is' – just ask American broadcaster Walter Cronkite.

So this is the twenty-first-century context we find ourselves operating in, both at home and abroad. But how do we actually close with these wicked threats? Well, we campaign – at least campaigning is believed to be one of our so-called competences. Actually I think today we do it rather badly; our predecessors, the likes of Marlborough and Wellington, from what I have read, did rather better.

Why? Because I believe we have increasingly allowed the science of war and management of modern business practices to dominate our thinking. It has set us on our current course towards a fixed framework of campaigning, and as a result we are increasingly guilty of oversimplifying a most complicated form of warfare. We have allowed process zealots, many in uniform, to present a seductive campaign lexicon: a framework which suggests certain success but only if slavishly followed; this science skews reality. We have been convinced by our own cleverness, arrogance and self-belief that, if you apply sufficient calculus to a problem, then 'world peace' ensues. When you attempt to compute people, anger, retribution, retaliation, religion, bloody-mindedness, bloody indifference, and throw in the architects of chaos, the disciples of Machiavellian principles, the opportunists, the criminals and corrupt, then there are not, nor ever will be, enough Cray Computers, great-grandsons of Deep Blue, to solve the campaign riddle.

That is not to suggest that campaigns cannot be won; you can set the conditions for success, and progress can be made towards that better peace which Captain Sir Basil Liddell Hart suggested as the object of war. It is my opinion that as the problem you face expands, and conflict amongst the people does just that, then you must correspondingly push forward to those on the front line the delegated authority that is needed to solve it. So widen the parameters; give those deployed the authority and the forces – be they economic, military, governance, whatever – to deal with an exploding and uncertain situation. It is about supporting not examining them. Asymmetry, to return to an earlier theme, is best defeated through a symmetric solution. Our failure is so often in our inability to apply this symmetric response by corralling the responsible departments of state under the banner of unity of effort; it is all about doing stuff. Fine words do not feed hungry nations, strong statements do not deter the wicked, your word should be your bond and we should be judged in this world by our actions. I sense we seldom do that, and we most certainly do not hold to account our ministers of state and their individual departments where they fall short of the commitment made.

Modern campaign management suffers from over-control, the simple lack of genuine delegated authority, and the petty in-fighting that plagues the departments of state that make up a modern democracy. This institutional inertia is compounded, as Sir Winston Churchill pointed out, by 'committees taking the sum of their fears', stern-faced officials sat around banks of monitors, mountains of information, summoning experts, consultants all immersed in their own limited understanding, yet comforted by their superior self-belief or cleverness following, like von Schlieffen's heirs, a technically perfect plan. The complexities, the subtleties, the realities, the fleeting opportunities, 'kingfishers flashing across the pond', are not lost on those in the front line engaged in the campaign where the art of war reigns supreme, but are constantly challenged by those distant from the fight who are consumed by the science of it. And while instinct and the art of war will find no end of sceptics, you might remind yourself that, based on science, Germany probably should have won the Great War; my history may be a little thin but as I recall that is not how it worked out.

Campaigning is not rocket science, but if war is too important to be left to the military then campaigning is too. So where are the others? Are the Foreign Office, DfID, the Home Office engaged? Hardly – interfering, sniping perhaps, with a few brave souls committed and little more: they should do better. For Clausewitz captured the relationship in his infamous line that, if war is nothing but a continuation of politics with the admixture of other means, then it is to politics it must return: different place, different circumstances, but still politics. In this light the importance of the others in our campaign is self-evident; their omission self-defeating; for sure as hell even we cannot make a chicken salad with chicken shit.

So I have attempted to cover rather badly what I think a general is, what he is supposed to do, in this case campaigning, and finally what he actually does. So now I turn to Iraq. I returned there in the summer of 2006 for my fourth tour of duty, supposedly for six months and stayed for nearly 11. It was a sporting time – all to lose, all to play for. It was an ugly situation, following the attack on the Golden Dome,[11] but more importantly a collapsing time line – US Presidential elections in late 2008, and the end of the UNSCR authorities in the spring of 2009, and a simple mathematical problem: too few Iraqi troops, army and police to stem the flow of violence and not enough time to train more. But on the up-side, the passage of time had shifted attitudes and allowed for an elected government, while the passing of time brought with it the possibility of a wind of change.

The adjustment by the Coalition and the Iraqis to the campaign in 2006 was not a case of desperation or sense of failure but an example of learning on the job while besieged with setbacks and an uncertain course, set by 'events, dear boy, events', as Harold Macmillan so rightly pointed out half a century ago; and all the while against a political and media public drumbeat of a lost cause. Wars and conflict, especially those amongst the people, are often much like this; a deadly game of chess in which your opponent has a vote, his moves are difficult to predict, and causality (the effects of your own decisions) present a shifting canvas of advantage, disadvantage, lost and seized opportunities, and there is no going back. In an interview in 2006, I referred to Iraq not as

---

11   On 22 February 2006 one of Shia Islam's leading shrines, the Golden Dome in Samarra, was very badly damaged by a bomb attack. This led to a surge in inter-sectarian violence between Shia and Sunni populations.

a simple chess game but likened it to a three-dimensional contest, played in a dark room, while someone was shooting at you. I think in truth I underestimated the game.

Solutions, especially those which involve people, passion and power, seldom lie in simple sequential thinking where you have to solve each problem before going on to the next. Complex operations are quite the opposite: they require anticipation, risk, a steady nerve, open-mindedness and the will to succeed. Solutions require the full ambit of capability and that capability applied concurrently: force, the threat of force, politics, economics, and applied socially and tribally – all those manoeuvres Sir Winston Churchill alluded to other than sheer slaughter to make progress. President John Kennedy said 'civility is not a sign of weakness and sincerity is always subject to proof'. We were at that stage in this campaign which required both civility and proof, a stage that recognised Iraq as a sovereign state in need of help in all quarters, for it was only the state that could, with the help of the Coalition, transition and fight its way towards a new national identity, shaking off considerable domestic differences while gaining the self-confidence to contest regional interference, be that from Iran, Syria or Saudi Arabia, in order to re-establish itself as a regional power. A sovereign nation that was comfortable with itself, its neighbours and fit for its future; and that future is not ours. This was the course we set upon: a change in force-ratio through the surge; a change in tactical deployments, leading the Iraq forces in the fight by Coalition example; a change in approach, embracing reconciliation.

In my discussions in Iraq with all sorts, I was struck by a common thread, a recognition by politician, insurgent, militia, religious cleric, tribal sheikh, whomever, of what constituted the major threats as they saw them, the real threats to Iraq. Their take, three years on from the invasion, was that, for the insurgents and some militias, we were *not* a force of occupation. Now that doesn't sound like much – but do not underestimate the importance when a significant proportion of the enemy you are fighting tells you the underlying reasons for armed resistance no longer apply. The Quran is fairly clear on the issue of occupation: it is to be resisted, as that force historically will threaten your faith and your way of life. It took three years, and you could not have done it sooner with the armies we had. It took three years for the Coalition to demonstrate, through its actions while under fire, that it was not a force that threatens the Iraqi faith or way of life. And it took three years for the insurgents to come to the stark realisation that what did threaten their faith was not the Coalition, but al-Qaeda, as their, not our, actions had demonstrated only too graphically that they intended to dictate to their fellow Muslims exactly how they wanted them to live their lives and practise their faith. The second threat that emerged was crime and corruption on a national scale; it too was eventually seen for what it was, Iraqis and other Muslims stealing the wealth of their nation, not the Coalition. We assessed in the autumn of 2006 that Baji oil refinery, north of Baghdad, was losing around $1.3 billion of refined product a year. By the time I left the US Multi-National Division (North) under Randy Mixon, the Iraq Government, the Iraqi oil industry and the local governors had turned this around to where refined product was increasingly available to provincial governors and the people. Corruption still takes place, but not on the same scale. The third leg of this common threat was the remnants of an ugly and bitter regime which remained arrogantly assured that Iraq was theirs to use and abuse. These Saddamists, not Ba'athists, were never far from the surface but, over time, as their coffers began to dry up and they moved no further forward towards re-living their dream of regaining power, they increasingly began to hedge their investments for themselves and for a rainy day. This fall in available cash from corruption and Saddamist financiers had a direct and corresponding effect on the insurgency. For it is probably true that, if you have enough loose dollars and the right circumstances, you can simply buy an insurgency; and much of what we fought was just that. At a rough estimate we were coming across around 30,000 improvised explosive devices (IEDs) a year. If these were being built and deployed under an ideological banner, I would have been the first to accept that my likely departure from Baghdad would have been from the roof of the American Embassy – shades of Saigon and 1973. The reality was that the vast number of these 30,000 IEDs was just part of a lethal business; the local Iraqi who had no love of the Coalition was presented with the opportunity to make money where no other opportunities lay.

The final threat was one and the same, just called by a different name: for the Sunni it was the hand of Persia; for the Shia it was those with a foreign agenda – either way it was the cold hand of influence and the even colder grip of interference from Iran. The sophistication of the Iranian interest in Iraq and the time and trouble they invested are not to be underestimated. Not all their actions were belligerent but some most certainly were. In the early stages of the new Government this attack on the sovereignty of Iraq was not obvious to its political leadership who, as Shia, were inclined to give their neighbours the benefit of the doubt. Over time, multiple insights from both the Coalition and their own intelligence showed beyond doubt to the Government the true nature of the Qods force and IRGC operations inside Iraq. Both the Coalition and Iraq are today more conscious of Iran's interference and see more clearly that her objectives remain unchanged – a desire to have a weak and compliant Iraq. So ideological al-Qaeda, corruption, Saddamists and Iran were seen as the major threats to stability by all sides in Iraq; of these, the corrupt, the Saddamists and the Iranians are ultimately reconcilable … the ideological are not, and that is where the fight lies; not, as many believe, in the violence of the sectarian divide.

I believe it was Emperor Napoleon, when asked what he craved most, answered 'time'. Iraq is an interesting study in this context for I have often observed *time compression* following significant events and campaign changes, rather than a *time delay*. Our experience and expectation from Northern Ireland and the Balkans is always the latter: everything goes into a time delay. The now famous photograph of Doctor Ian Paisley and Gerry Adams sitting opposite each other under the same roof and with a common agenda took some 35 years to deliver. In Iraq I saw a photograph of Sheikh Sittar's brother, one of the early architects of the so called 'awakening', of a Sunni tribal Sheikh in the company of two of Sadr City's Shia tribal leaders under the same roof and with a common agenda; the difference is that this accommodation under far harsher circumstances of death and distrust took not 35 years but just under three and a half. The Arab is able to make accommodations that we would find difficult, he sees opportunities as God's will and therefore God's guidance. The result is the speed at which change and accommodation can be made. As an example, the destruction of the Golden Mosque in February 2006 spurred violent inter-sectarian conflict and a new level of ruthlessness. A little over a year later al-Qaeda destroyed the last two remaining minarets at the same mosque. By normal criteria, what happened a year before would occur again, with interest. What actually happened was an immediate call for calm from the political authorities of all three camps, Shia, Sunni and Kurd, from the Coalition, the provincial governors, many of the tribes, and even from the insurgents. The result? Nothing happened. In one calendar year this nation had watched what it could do to itself and elected not to go back.

Iraq, I believe, is only too conscious of its own failings, its bloody past and present. It is struggling to move forward but at its pace and in a direction it believes is right for its future. It is not democracy per se, not democracy as we would recognise, but something more akin to a progressive Islamic nation. I believe it has a clear shot at this title albeit with a small 'P' progressive, a largish 'I' Islamic and a fragile but nevertheless clear 'N' Nation. Iraq has too many ugly neighbours to be reckless with its federated interests, and those interests are significant certainly in a financial sense, for from what I saw they are potentially richer than Croesus. They have an educated population, water in the two great rivers Tigris and Euphrates, an ability to trade north, south, east and west, a water port, and plenty of oil, gas and phosphates. Furthermore, it is the land of Ali Baba, so they know how to trade and were part of a global village dealing in transcontinental financial transactions and goods while we in Scotland wore blue woad and little else; and this all a long time before Wall Street and the City of London; they know how to do this stuff.

I started with a quote from George Bernard Shaw on the world and happiness. I finish with another, attributed to him, this time on the world and reasonable people.

> The world is formed by unreasonable men. A reasonable man looks at the world and sees how he can fit in with it. An unreasonable man looks at the world and sees how he can change it to fit in with him.

Generals are just reasonable men who, if asked, will continue gladly to contest unreasonable behaviour.

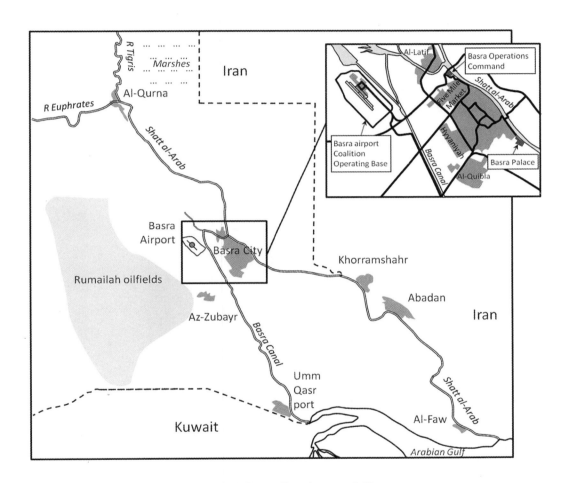

Map 13.1 Basra Province and City

Chapter 13

'Best Effort': Operation Sinbad and the Iraq Campaign

Justin Maciejewski

The Strategic Context

The majority of commentators on the British campaign in south-east Iraq view it as a series of almost disconnected initiatives and events. They point to a lack of British continuity of application and approach, and overwhelmingly they regard the campaign as a failure. Having been involved with Operation Telic in various staff and command appointments over six years from 2003 to 2009, I believe its story has not been adequately told. It was a campaign that had a consistent approach and a clear pattern, but these were defined primarily by the British and Iraqi political context, and the US view of Basra as an economy of effort mission, rather than by the various British military commanders charged with its conduct.

Operation Sinbad was a six-month operation, between October 2006 to May 2007, that sought to achieve the conditions needed for handover of Basra to Iraqi control. Previously, I had been the Operations Officer of 1st (United Kingdom) Armoured Division during the invasion in 2003. I then commanded a battlegroup in Basra City during the height of the fighting during Operation Sinbad. I returned to Iraq the following year as Chief of Staff of Multinational Division (South East) – MND(SE) – during the Iraqi-led Operation Charge of the Knights, planning the conclusion of British operations in Iraq. I also commanded the brigade that provided the troops responsible for the final draw down of the British presence in Iraq in 2009. I thus view Operation Sinbad, not as an isolated or failed attempt to have a decisive effect in Basra, but rather as a key and necessary waypoint in what was a difficult and hard-fought campaign, conducted within a context of extremely challenging and often irreconcilable constraints. There were three primary constraints, established in 2003 and maintained throughout the campaign with a high degree of continuity. The first and overriding factor shaping the British campaign in Iraq was that its purpose had nothing to do with Iraq. It was instead about the British political and institutional obsession with British–US security relations: if the US was going to invade Iraq, the British would be there alongside them; everything else was just military detail. Second, this approach, particularly to a war of dubious wisdom and legality, led to the Iraq war being controversial from the outset. This created the conditions where Iraq was perceived as a political threat rather than as an opportunity, resulting in the UK Government seeking to minimise political, military and financial exposure to the campaign. Third, there was also a political desire to differentiate British from the US, and to shroud its involvement under the cloak of legitimacy provided by the international community.

These three grand strategic factors meant that, from the outset, the British campaign in Iraq was designed to do just enough to underpin the credibility of the political and military relationship with the US, whilst minimising the domestic political consequences of financial and tactical over-exposure to events on the ground. From a British political viewpoint, the priorities for Operation Telic after the invasion were damage limitation and economy of effort. It was this geostrategic equation that established the scale of military resources available in theatre, not the requirements of the campaign itself. Operation Sinbad was a big idea that attempted to challenge the British economy of effort mindset, and concentrate the necessary resources on what was actually needed in Basra, rather than what was just sufficient to ensure survival of the UK/US security relationship.

In Whitehall, Iraq was viewed as Tony Blair's and, perhaps, the Ministry of Defence's war rather than a national war. As a result, the Iraq campaign never really received the attention or institutional support of Whitehall; ministers did not want to get involved. It became the responsibility of a stream of short-lived Secretaries of State who seemed to go from MOD straight to the political graveyard, or 'promotion' to less toxic portfolios. Throughout the campaign, the Treasury, the Foreign and Commonwealth Office and the Department for International Development attempted to limit their involvement to the minimum. Operation Sinbad was conceived to galvanise, mobilise and bring coherence to UK cross-government and coalition efforts to bring stability to Basra. Major General Richard Shirreff, the Divisional Commander in Basra, wanted Sinbad to be an exemplar of the new British cross-government doctrine for stability operations known as the Comprehensive Approach. This was not achieved because, however well conceived and compelling the theory of the Comprehensive Approach was, it did not have significant bureaucratic traction across Whitehall.

From the outset, senior American military commanders understood the conditional nature of the British involvement. For this reason, during the invasion, the British division was assigned a subsidiary task so that, if the British decided at the last minute not to participate, the operation could still go ahead. The operational task of capturing Basra was given to the 1st (United Kingdom) Armoured Division because it was seen as an economy of effort objective, which would soon become a rear area task as US armoured forces advanced north. Basra was about oil and liberating the Shia, not destroying Saddam Hussein's regime. The British desire for an ethical war and the American neo-conservative strategic objective of creating a democratic, pro-American Iraq overlapped in south-east Iraq, but not beyond. In the secret US Internal Look exercises in 2001 and 2002 that practised the invasion of Iraq, the British were always averse to the notion of regime change as an objective. This changed in late 2002, but there was still a bureaucratic desire to be on the periphery of such a legally dubious endeavour. Basra was where this unease could be minimised and, as a result, it defined Britain's strategic ambition. It allowed the British Government discernibly to differentiate its purpose from that of the United States. Critically, the US was content for this as they did not anticipate problems emerging from Basra: it was perceived as a backwater and represented a good 'fit' for the British contingent and its conditionality.

Therefore, from the outset the boundary between MND(SE) and the rest of Iraq was more than a tactical boundary: it was a political boundary which both the American corps headquarters and the British divisional headquarters were reluctant to cross. This was because the boundary represented a threshold of commitment between US forces and those European allies for whom commitment to Iraq was transactional and strictly limited. The US-led force was happy to accept these distinct thresholds in commitment in 2003 as south-east Iraq was seen as the soft rear area. In May that year, Lieutenant General Conway, Commander of 1st Marine Expeditionary Force (1 MEF), came to Basra to say thank you for the British contribution to the invasion. I recall the unease amongst the British staff when he thanked us for looking after the Marines' rear area. Compared to Baghdad and Anbar in the summer of 2003, Basra was quiet. 1 MEF's chief of staff, observing the concentration of Europeans in south-east Iraq as Multi-National Division (South East) began to form, commented that it was better not to use 'America's finest fighting knife to spread peanut butter'. He added that Europeans were 'fine peacekeepers'. It is instructive that prominent amongst the specified tasks assigned to MND(SE) by the US headquarters were the security of the Tigris bridge in Nasiriyah and of the main supply route to Baghdad, Route Tampa.

From the outset, US commanders viewed Basra as an economy of effort mission, principally to secure lines of communication. Brigadier Everard described this mindset well when, in 2006, he told newly arrived battlegroup commanders that 'as far as the US are concerned Basra is to Baghdad what Plymouth is to London, don't forget this'. This mindset perpetuated throughout the campaign, ensuring that Basra was only ever regarded as a distraction, apart from a fleeting interest during Operation Charge of the Knights in 2008.

The most significant impact on the British campaign of this US mindset was the low priority afforded to development of the Iraqi Security Forces in southern Iraq. This had dramatic consequences on Operation Sinbad. There has been much debate on the British approach to the mentoring and advising of Iraqi troops and police in Basra, but this misses the key point that most high quality Iraqi officers were sent to Baghdad and Anbar, with Basra being the repository for the lowest quality leaders. The same was true for equipment; the 10th (Iraqi Army) Division in Basra was still in civilian pick-up trucks with no radios when Operation Sinbad was launched. The force densities were also low compared to the rest of Iraq, with only two depleted Iraqi battalions being available during Sinbad. US Force commanders consistently treated south-east Iraq as a backwater and the lowest priority for deployment of Iraqi Security Forces as they developed.

The first challenge to this US Baghdad-centric view of the campaign was in the build up to Operation Sinbad, but the mindset was not broken until 2008 during the Iraqi-led Operation Charge of the Knights. It suited both sides until 2008 to view southern Iraq as distinct: the British and its eight European partners, most prominently the Italians, Dutch and the Danes, achieved a slight political air gap between themselves and the US; and US commanders were able to focus on the theatre main effort in central and, later, northern Iraq.

This gulf between southern and the rest of Iraq was crossed only once before Operation Charge of the Knights, when in 2004 The Black Watch were deployed north to assist the US reinforce Fallujah. The subsequent casualties, political effort and fallout in Britain led both the US and the UK to decide that, in the words of one American staff officer, 'the juice was not worth the squeeze'. The deduction drawn by both sides was that it was preferable to operate strictly within existing national tactical boundaries. By 2006 this boundary between MND(SE) and the rest of the force was more like an international border than a tactical divisional boundary. So the unstated agreement was that the US would not ask the British to deploy outside Basra, but in return they expected the British to resource Basra adequately. Operation Sinbad challenged this state of affairs: it was conceived to be part of a corps strategy to conduct decisive operations in urban areas, before handing over to the Iraqi Security Forces under the so called Provincial Iraqi Control or PIC process. Despite this, in the end, it had to be conducted largely with whatever the British could amass in Basra.

These conditions or constraints may in themselves have been manageable if the British had been able to rely on local power brokers, such as the Iraqi Security Forces and the government machinery left over from the previous regime. Several gatherings were held in Basra Airport immediately after the liberation of Basra involving prominent local powerbrokers; university chancellors, hospital administrators and local government officials who were all still in their posts waiting to receive instructions. The army was ready to return to work; much of the police force had already returned to work; and provincial technocrats and lawyers were re-establishing order and local governance. This early momentum was completely destroyed by Paul Bremer, now in charge of the Coalition Provisional Authority, who barred Ba'ath Party members from holding office. I will never forget the atmosphere in the divisional headquarters in Basra when this order was received: people stared into space as they tried to work out what to do next with no one to talk to! There was a sense of utter despondency and disbelief. The legacy of this catastrophic removal of the bourgeoisie from positions of power rendered the small British force in Basra unable to work through trained and capable Iraqi intermediaries. The economy of effort approach to Basra, combined with the political vacuum, made for a dangerous blend which ultimately Operation Sinbad was designed to tackle.

It was into this vacuum that Iran, through its proxies later known as the 'Special Groups' or 'Secret Cells', gained a foothold in Basra between 2003 and 2006. There was a fierce debate within the divisional headquarters, in early summer 2003, on the return of exiles from Iran and, in particular, Moqtada al-Sadr and his followers. The view from London was that their return was an encouraging sign of normal politics returning. The creation of the Iranian-backed Jaysh al-Mahdi by Moqtada al-Sadr, and the growth of its militia into the security and political vacuum in Basra, resulted in large parts of Basra being controlled by militias when Operation Sinbad was launched in October 2006. The challenge to the power of Jaysh al-Mahdi and its associated death squads was inevitably going to necessitate violence; by 2006 there was no other way.

It was in trying to fill the vacuum created by Bremer that six Royal Military Policemen rebuilding a new police force were killed in June 2003 in Majar al-Kabir, a small town in Maysan Province. This had a profound psychological affect on the entire British force and in London. This one event, more than any other, set the trajectory for the subsequent British approach to the training of Iraqi Security Forces. For Whitehall, it emphasised the importance of minimising British exposure and getting out of Iraq as soon as it could, without breaking the strategic relationship with the US. The institutional response in London to Majar al-Kebir was the belief that force protection should be achieved by limiting exposure of small groups of British advisers to their Iraqi police and army counterparts: there would be no embedding; the Iraqis were to be trained at arm's length. The later British policy not to embed advisers with the Iraqi Army and police in Basra was almost certainly born out of this early shock in 2003.

On the day Baghdad was liberated in April 2003, I was called to the Joint Force Headquarters in Qatar to discuss the drawdown from a division of three brigades to one of a single brigade. The Army Land Forces Headquarters at Wilton, outside Salisbury, knew that it could not sustain a force of more than 9,000 over a protracted campaign. A new force structure was designed, and the drawdown began in May with the withdrawal of two brigades. The timetable was driven not by the situation in Iraq, but by the institutional needs of the Army and the political desire to limit British involvement. During these meetings, scant regard was given to what was needed in Basra: force levels were set and then applied to the tactical problem, rather than the tactical problem defining the level of forces required. So, in May 2003, a system was instituted of six-monthly staff-led force level reviews, driven by organisational rather than campaign factors. This approach plagued the campaign from beginning to end. Operation Sinbad challenged this approach by putting the needs of the campaign ahead of the timetable for force reductions set by the Permanent Joint Headquarters (PJHQ) at Northwood, but successive commanders were unable to break this topsy-turvy paradigm for running campaigns. Ultimately this led to Operation Sinbad being a 'big idea' delivered by a small force.

Since, from the earliest days, force levels were not designed to resource a successful campaign plan, everything that took place between 2003 and 2006 was about managing events on the ground as pragmatically as possible while achieving mandated incremental force reductions. Violence ebbed and flowed; efforts were made to train and equip the emerging Iraqi Security Forces; but the low priority afforded to Basra by Baghdad and London meant that, at best, British forces in Basra were mere observers of the gradual transfer of power from the vestiges of the pre-2003 establishment to Iranian-backed militias. Throughout this period violence was kept at a tolerable level, except during the Shia uprising of 2004, particularly when compared to the rest of Iraq. Initially, it was in the interests of both the British and the newly emerging Shia militias to keep

Basra broadly quiet, until summer 2005 when the Iranians decided to escalate the conflict by using their proxies to attack the British and force their humiliating withdrawal from Iraq.

The Special Groups were trained and equipped by the Quds Force of the Iranian Revolutionary Guard Corps, with training of IED, rocket and sniper teams all taking place in Iran. The Special Groups targeted British troops with large numbers of deadly Iranian-made Explosively Formed Projectile (EFP) IEDs. It was during this protracted IED offensive against the British that the yawning gap between the reality of Iranian-backed Shia militia activity and the conditions needed for a credible British exit became obvious. The abduction of a number of SAS soldiers in Basra by militia in police uniforms in summer 2005, and their incarceration in the Jameat Police Station, revealed the full penetration of militia influence in Basra; by 2005 even the police seemed to be working for the Iranians.

It was the iconic photograph of a British soldier clambering out of a burning Warrior armoured vehicle that was etched in the mind of (the then) Major General Richard Shirreff when he conducted his reconnaissance of Basra in May 2006, ahead of taking over as General Officer Commanding (GOC) of MND(SE) in August. It was clear to him that, if the British Army was to emerge from Iraq with its reputation and credibility intact, something had to be done about the Iranian-backed militias in Basra. General Shirreff was emphatic: he stated he was 'under no illusion about the enemy; he is ingenious, capable and determined to inflict a humiliating defeat on us'. He was determined to do something about this and achieve 'above all ... militias subordinated to the rule of law'. Whitehall wanted an exit strategy; General Shirreff wanted a winning strategy. He stated very clearly to PJHQ that incremental withdrawal without decisive action would amount to defeat and humiliation for the British Army.

It was clear to General Shirreff that declared 'ends', available 'means' and existing 'ways' had been on diverging paths since 2003, and that this divergence could no longer be managed without a very public defeat in Basra, which he was not prepared to tolerate. As well as the reputation of the British Army, he also had to consider three other imperatives: the stability of Basra; the credibility of the British Army in the eyes of the US; and London's political desire to end quickly the most unpopular campaign since Suez. An adequate outcome would suffice but, in his words, 'standing still amounted to defeat'.

Unlike many of his predecessors, who assessed that limited means necessitated an essentially defensive approach, he believed that the British Army in Basra could have, and more importantly should seek to have, a decisive effect to create the conditions for a credible British handover to the Iraqis. He barely disguised his view that many of those involved in the higher management of the campaign in London were defeatists. He expressed particular frustration with the leadership of PJHQ and the MOD staff who seemed more obsessed with force levels than designing a winning plan for Basra; his relationship with General Sir Nick Houghton, the Chief of Joint Operations in Northwood, seemed particularly tense. General Shirreff was determined that, during his tour, the British would regain the initiative in south-east Iraq and take the offensive against those Iranian-backed militias who were in the ascendancy in Basra. To achieve this he would need to persuade the new Iraqi Government of the need for action, gain US support and resources from Baghdad, and win the backing and necessary resources from London. This was a tall order. He set about it with zeal and energy before assuming command in Basra in July 2006.

His conviction that something decisive had to be done in Basra was born out of his first reconnaissance to Iraq in April 2006. In discussions with Brigadier James Everard, the newly arrived brigade commander, it became obvious that the situation was deteriorating fast in Basra. It was clear that Iranian-backed Special Groups were determined to force a humiliating British withdrawal from Basra. There was a steady increase in both IED attacks against vulnerable Snatch

Land Rovers and rocket attacks on British bases. James Everard believed that more needed to be done by MND(SE) to tackle the issue of the Iranian-backed militia head on. He thought that Major General John Cooper, commanding MND(SE) in Basra, was too hesitant to take the offensive against the Death Squads in Basra. General Cooper almost certainly assessed, not unreasonably, that he lacked the resources to go head-to-head with Jaysh al-Mahdi. General Shirreff's trip to Iraq also included a stopover in Baghdad where he gained the perspectives of the US force commander, General George W. Casey, and the US corps commander General Pete Chiarelli. They left him in no doubt that they were losing confidence in British commitment to the mission in south-east Iraq. General Casey said rather tellingly that it seemed that the British approach in Basra 'was all about you and not about the mission'.

Planning for Operations Salamanca and Sinbad

When he returned from Iraq, General Shirreff initiated planning under his Chief of Staff, Colonel James Cowan, who had commanded the Black Watch under American command in 2004. He wanted a comprehensive plan comprising offensive military action against the Special Groups, alongside a broader Iraqi-led framework security operation, and a significant economic regeneration and development plan to provide jobs quickly for the many unemployed young males in Basra, many of whom were becoming involved in militia violence. The plan that emerged became known as Operation Salamanca, named after the pivotal battle of the Peninsular Campaign where Wellington turned the tide against the French. All the commanding officers and key staff of 19th Light Brigade, who would provide the bulk of the troops for Operation Salamanca, came to Bulford for a study week on Iraq and were briefed on the overall concept of operations. Basra would be cleared and secured district by district applying the new multi-agency doctrine known as the Comprehensive Approach.

The message General Shirreff gave his brigade and battalion commanders could not have been clearer, as were my notes: 'The time has come to take the offensive against the enemy and challenge the defeatists who seem to pervade Whitehall and much of Northwood. The British Army was not going to lose its name in Iraq.' He told commanding officers to ensure that their battalions were infused with the required offensive spirit before they arrived in Iraq, as the reputation of the British Army would be determined largely by what happened over the next year. We were to focus on low-level tactical skills to include combined arms integration and the use of tanks. All those in the hall that sunny May day in Bulford were inspired by what they heard. It was refreshing to approach an operational tour with a sense that we were not merely going to manage events, but actually go onto the offensive and set the tactical agenda to deliver conditions that resembled mission success. There was, I recall, also a degree of scepticism amongst some Iraq veterans about whether this success could be delivered.

General Shirreff's determination to do something decisive in Basra caused great alarm in senior levels of PJHQ. There, they were walking a tightrope between the political demands of London, the needs of commanders in Basra, the expectations of the USA and the growing British commitment in Afghanistan. A decision had been taken in late 2005 to commit a significant force to Helmand in Southern Afghanistan. There was a strong sense at the time, amongst those preparing for Iraq in the summer of 2006, that our commitment to Afghanistan was being driven by those generals who thought that Afghanistan was merely a way out of Basra; it was a political antidote to the deeply unpopular mission in Iraq. We regarded them as epitomising the defeatist tendency that pervaded PJHQ and London, and that investing in a seemingly popular war in Afghanistan, in order to escape an unpopular one in Iraq, was not a winning strategy. From a grand strategic point of view, few could see how a medium-sized province in southern Afghanistan could be more important to Britain than oil-rich southern Iraq.

The British build up in Afghanistan concurrent with Operation Sinbad during 2006 illustrates the divergence between General Shirreff and the MOD: General Shirreff sought a credible outcome in Basra to create the conditions for an orderly British exit from Iraq; the MOD appeared to want an exit under any circumstances. This divergence of approach created a war on two fronts for an Army designed to sustain only one brigade-level campaign. In the battle for resources, Helmand would take priority over Iraq in the medium term with a build-up in Helmand planned for 2007. This meant that any decisive divisional-level operation in Basra would have to take place between October 2006, when the large and augmented 19th Light Brigade arrived in Iraq, and May 2007, when the much smaller 1st Mechanised Brigade was due to take over. So, the resources available and the timing of what later became Operation Sinbad were defined by the build-up of forces in Afghanistan and the planned drawdown of forces in Basra, to no more than 4,500 by late 2007. The prospect of two bloody and protracted brigade-level simultaneous operations in Iraq and Afghanistan did not appeal to senior leadership in PJHQ or MOD. When Lieutenant General Houghton saw Major General Shirreff following his reconnaissance to Iraq, he warned him bluntly that he did not wish to see 'any unnecessary displays of military testosterone' on the streets of Basra. He did not want General Shirreff to write cheques that the British Army would be unable to cash.

Lieutenant General Houghton was, however, prepared to support the idea of a concerted effort to create the conditions for Provincial Iraqi Control in Basra, but those serving in Basra during Sinbad believed that, for PJHQ and the MOD, operations in Basra during late 2006 and mid 2007 were more about creating a credible *narrative* for exit rather than creating credible results, during the ensuing operation it was known by officers in Basra that Operation Sinbad was referred to by General Houghton as Operation Spinbad. General Shirreff tellingly wrote to PJHQ, following his May reconnaissance to Iraq, that he was not 'convinced that we have correctly identified the strategic Main Effort and resourced it appropriately to potentially avoid disastrous failure in Iraq'. He wrote that if the British wanted to avoid defeat in Basra they would have to 'clout' and not 'dribble' in terms of resources.

For General Shirreff, what started as Operation Salamanca, and went on to become Operation Sinbad, was not about the strategic narrative, but about creating conditions on the ground that were good enough for the British Army to hand over to the Iraqi Security Forces with its credibility, reputation and, crucially, its institutional offensive spirit intact. To achieve this, he determined to concentrate his forces in Basra and amass additional resources from wherever he could. Basra and Operation Salamanca/later Sinbad would be his main effort. His start point in this battle for resources was to view MND(SE) not as a separate fiefdom but as an integral part of a US-led Multinational Corps (Iraq) campaign. He wrote to Lieutenant General Chiarelli, shortly after arriving in July, saying that he viewed Operation Sinbad as part of a 'coherent Corps-level operation if we are to maximise effect'. He was perhaps the first GOC of MND(SE) genuinely to view his position as a tactical subordinate to his US Corps Commander as more important than his subordination to the UK national headquarters in Northwood.

As a subordinate divisional commander, in August 2006 he asked his US corps headquarters for reinforcements; in doing this he challenged the mindset that south-east Iraq was distinct from the rest of the country. This approach put General Shirreff on a collision course with those who viewed the reinforcement of MND(SE) by US troops as tantamount to British failure. The offer of a US infantry battalion was, bizarrely, turned down on instructions from PJHQ but, through persistence, General Shirreff did get some US National Guard attack helicopters (Task Force Palomino), and some US Desert Hawk Unmanned Aerial Vehicle (UAV) teams to provide a much needed surveillance capability; the British capability in both these areas was dedicated to Afghanistan. He also secured nearly $80 million of US tax payers' money to spend on small but highly visible urban regeneration projects in Basra. This limited flexing of US corps assets across the divisional boundary in preparation for Operation Sinbad broke the taboo of US involvement in Basra. Arguably, this use of US assets in Basra in 2006 and 2007 set the conditions for a much larger US reinforcement of Basra in 2008 during Charge of the Knights.

General Shirreff was also determined to increase the British resources available for his decisive operation. This he managed to achieve, but only for a limited period. PJHQ agreed to reinforce 19th Light Brigade, the formation charged with delivering Operation Sinbad, with a second armoured infantry battalion in the form of 1st Battalion, The Staffordshire Regiment, and with the majority of the Theatre Reserve Battalion from Cyprus. These units were made available for the period October 2006 to April 2007. The use of these battalions illustrates how overstretched the British Army was at this time: the Staffords had only come out of Iraq in November 2005, and the theatre reserve battalions were both split between Iraq and Afghanistan. In total, these modest reinforcements amounted to about 1,000 additional troops for Operation Sinbad.

If General Shirreff was partially successful in gaining additional military resources to mount his decisive operation in Basra, he was wholly unsuccessful in mobilising the Foreign and Commonwealth Office and the Department for International Development. The most that was achieved was the pulling together of existing efforts into the 'Better Basra Plan', to be launched prior to Operation Sinbad and driven by the newly established Provincial Reconstruction Team – initially based in Basra Palace until the rocket attacks were deemed an unacceptable health and safety risk. Little in the way of additional resources was made available to support Operation Sinbad directly. The formation of the Southern Iraq Steering Group, jointly chaired by the British Consul General, Ms Ros Marsden, and GOC MND(SE), did help bring greater coherence to civilian and military efforts in southern Iraq. But both DfID and the FCO had already decided to withdraw their presence from Basra Palace in the city before Operation Sinbad was launched. The civilian contractor-operated police training effort was already being scaled back, and the Provincial Reconstruction Team had withdrawn to Kuwait on health and safety grounds a full month before the commencement of the operation. For the historical record, very few British soldiers serving in Basra during this time had anything other than thinly veiled contempt for the paltry efforts of these two departments of state, given the scale of the challenge of Basra. It certainly did not feel like all of Government was pulling together towards the same strategic goal with the same vigour. In the end about $10 million of additional British money was spent in support of Operation Sinbad compared to nearly $80 million by US. This was both an embarrassment and a profound frustration for British soldiers serving in south-east Iraq. It seemed that British blood came cheaper than British treasure.

The fourth way in which GOC MND(SE) concentrated resources was to extract the British battlegroup from Camp Abu Naji outside al-Amarah, the capital of Maysan Province. This unit was a 'tethered goat': to resupply it took a fortnightly brigade-level operation involving the entire divisional reserve battlegroup and over 200 logistic vehicles over three days; sustaining its presence in al-Amarah consumed the equivalent of one and a half logistic regiments of effort. Any British operation in al-Amarah led to a protracted running battle in the streets, followed by rocket attacks on the British camp of Abu Naji. Here, General Shirreff decided to cut his losses. Although he was clear that Maysan Province was not ready for Iraqi control, little would be gained by retaining a British foothold on the outskirts of al-Amarah. Instead he would redeploy a smaller light cavalry regiment to the border with Iran to interdict lethal Iranian shipments across the border. He redeployed this regiment from the western province of al-Muthana which was left to the Australian Task Force, already in what was known as 'Operation Overwatch' posture. This cavalry mission in Maysan was to be an entirely mobile presence, negating the indirect fire threat that had been a daily feature in Camp Abu Naji. General Shirreff decided to dedicate a regiment to this task to demonstrate that he clearly understood his responsibility to guard the south-east flank of the US Corps. It was another example of the changing mindset of MND(SE) from being a separate tactical fiefdom to being an integral part of the Multinational Corps. He supplied this light cavalry battlegroup largely by air and thereby freed up further troops to focus on Basra.

The fifth area in which MND(SE) sought to amass the resources necessary for Operation Sinbad was that of the Iraqi Army and police. These had been particularly neglected since 2003 and, by 2006, the difference in capability between the Iraqi Security Forces in Basra, compared with in central Iraq, was stark. The US-controlled Multi National Security Transformation Command (Iraq) – MNSTC(I) – treated Basra as its lowest priority. Brigadier Everard, Commander 20th Armoured Brigade, commented in September 2006 that every time 'any commander of any promise emerges, the US or the Government of Iraq promote him to a post in Baghdad'. The absence of any significant investment in barracks infrastructure meant that soldiers and policemen lived at home in Basra, and were susceptible to militia intimidation. The weakness of the Iraqi Army in Southern Iraq was highlighted by the mutiny of the 2nd Battalion of the 4th Brigade of the 10th Division when ordered to Baghdad in September 2006. There was only one brigade of the 10th (Iraqi Army) Division in Basra, comprising two undermanned battalions, each of which was required to provide a company to reinforce Baghdad. There was also a notably good divisional military police company and an effective operations company, both of which became highly respected during Sinbad. This meant that the Iraqi Army could do little more than guard their own bases: in a city of over 1.5 million people there were only four Iraqi Army companies available for routine security operations. This was enough to conduct a security operation in a single neighbourhood for a few days, but no more. Even during Operation Sinbad, 10th (Iraqi Army) Division was still expected to provide one company per battalion to reinforce Baghdad. Furthermore, PJHQ refused MND(SE)'s request to be allowed to attach advisers to the Iraqi Army. The combination of a dearth of Iraqi troops, and the British arms-length approach to support them, was the Achilles heel of the forces being massed for Operation Sinbad.

The impact of the British decision not to embed advisers with the Iraqi Security Forces was exposed in Baghdad where the 10th (IA) Division companies performed badly in Baghdad compared to other US-mentored companies. Despite every effort, MND(SE) was unable to change the priority afforded to the Iraqi Army in Basra by MNSTC(I). However, some progress was made in the equipment made available to the Iraqi brigade commander, Brigadier Aqeel, who was eventually given new armoured command vehicles and surplus US Army armoured HMMWVs for Operation Sinbad. It was also agreed from March 2007 that British mentors would accompany Iraqi detachments as they rotated north to Baghdad to enhance their training.

In the police, the absence of mentors had over time allowed the Special Groups to infiltrate and, in some neighbourhoods, control the police. Infrequent visits by the health and safety obsessed Foreign and Commonwealth Office-contracted police advisors failed to compete with the more persistent and insidious influence of the Iranian-backed militia. By the middle of 2006, many British troops regarded the police as synonymous with the enemy, since they were invariably seen in the vicinity of attacks against patrols. The nexus of the so-called 'corrupt' or infiltrated police was the Jameat police station, in the Hyyaniyah district of Basra, which had been the scene of the kidnapping of the SAS patrol the previous year. General Shirreff was determined that he would deal with this symbol of militia infiltration unambiguously during Operation Sinbad.

To deal decisively with the Iranian-backed Special Groups and militia infiltration of the Basra police would need the support of the new, predominantly Shia, government in Baghdad led by Nouri al-Maliki, formed in April 2006. Prime Minister Maliki's strong rhetoric on law and order in early May indicated that he was determined to deal with lawlessness in Basra. He launched a new Basra Security Plan on 31 May 2006 which had four key objectives: the restoration of public confidence; dealing with corruption in the police force; tackling armed militias; and restoring the rule of law. He declared a state of emergency in Basra on 2 June 2006. On 24 July, he established a Basra Security Committee, chaired by General Hamadi. This committee bypassed the Governor of Basra, Mohammed al-Waeli, who was a political opponent of Maliki. General Hamadi and the Chief of Police, General Ibrahim, were charged with the implementation of the Basra security plan. This seemed a promising start in terms of command and control for a comprehensive security operation in Basra. Sadly, General Hamadi was ineffective and General Ibrahim appeared to have links with some of the militia. Safa al-Safi, the Prime Minister's representative on the committee, believed that a deal could be made with the Jaysh al-Mahdi. In addition, the state of near civil war in Baghdad and central Iraq prevented any reinforcements to Basra. Operation Sinbad would have to make do with whatever Iraqi Security Forces were already in place, led by a weak and equivocal Security Committee: there was to be no Iraqi surge of support to Basra in late 2006; the main focus was Baghdad. This was understandable given that, in August 2006, there were, per head of population, over four times more violent deaths in Baghdad than there were in Basra, with 1,536 killed in Baghdad against 87 in Basra.

The original concept for Operation Salamanca was briefed to the US corps and force headquarters in August 2006. It envisaged a two-strand operation, comprising so-called 'kinetic' and 'non-kinetic' activity, to deal with the militia and conduct urban renewal projects in health, education, sanitation and provision of utilities. Basra was to be divided into 16 neighbourhoods and each would be dealt with sequentially in a series of security 'pulse' operations, followed by a 'pause' where the initial surge of security force presence would be consolidated and backed up with urban renewal and job creation schemes. General Casey agreed the plan and supported it with financial and limited military resources, as described above. Gaining the support of the Government of Iraq was far more difficult; in many respects the operation's assertiveness provoked Iraqi sovereignty. The concept of the plan was first briefed to the Iraqi national security adviser al-Roubaie who rejected it on the advice of Safa al-Safi, the Iraqi Prime Minister's adviser on Basra.

The plan made Safa al-Safi, the Prime Minister's representative on the Basra Security Committee, very uneasy. Like many local power brokers in Basra, he had links with Sadrist groups who were in turn linked to those responsible for the killings in Basra. He believed that some sort of political accommodation with Moqtada al-Sadr was preferable to an intra-Shia battle for supremacy. He almost certainly spoke to both al-Roubaie and the Iraqi Prime Minister to ensure the original plan was rejected. As a result General Hamadi, the Iraqi Commander in Basra, was unsure of the political support for any decisive action in Basra. Maliki, like Safa al-Safi, was extremely concerned about the idea of the British conducting concerted attacks on the Jaysh al-Mahdi Secret Cells and other Shia militia groups. One suspects that the Iraqi Government believed that they, rather than the British, were best placed to make deals and fragment the Jaysh al-Mahdi through sharing the spoils of power rather than a head to head fight. Some of these groups were potential allies in an Iraq that seemed to be descending towards civil war, and pitched in a deadly battle against Sunni insurgent groups. He told General Casey that 'the political situation in Basra needs to be dealt with quietly, and that the security situation was not bad enough to warrant an operation that would upset the political balance'. He wanted to control both the timing and method of the reassertion of state control over Basra; he did not want the British to potentially disrupt his ability to build political alliances in Basra.

In 2006, when sectarian violence was spiralling out of control in central Iraq, Basra was still a relatively low priority, despite Prime Minister Maliki's earlier rhetoric on law and order; it had only 15 per cent of the violence seen in central provinces. Maliki was, instead, in favour of an operation that would begin the economic regeneration of Basra, supported by a modest series of joint Iraqi Army and Police security operations to bring order to the streets and tackle the worst excesses of the Special Groups. He often spoke of the importance of challenging the militias and corrupt policemen but he did not believe that the coalition were able to discern between those groups that needed to be attacked and those that could be reconciled. He did not want coalition raids against individual militia leaders with whom he may wish to deal in future. In a rare example of unanimity, the British Government,, and the Government of Iraq both agreed that operations in Basra should continue to be conducted on the basis of economy of effort.

General Casey briefed General Shirreff on the opposition of al-Roubaie and Maliki. He proposed that General Shirreff work with the Basra Security Committee to redesign the operation. This work took place between 16 and 23 September. The revised operation reversed the purpose to being one of urban regeneration enabled by security, it specifically excluded reference to precision strikes on the Special Groups. General Casey also warned General Shirreff not to underestimate 'Maliki's dislike and mistrust of the British'. The redesigned operation was briefed to al-Roubaie, Maliki and General Casey on 23 and 24 September. General Shirreff flew key members of the Bara Security Committee with him to Baghdad for the briefings. They flew to Baghdad in a Royal Flight Jet decorated with serene pictures of Balmoral, a juxtaposition probably lost on General Hamadi! In a series of briefings the revised plan was accepted and, in the final presentation to Maliki, his reaction was one of support for a robust approach to police corruption and the Special Groups in Basra. The redesign of operation Salamanca into Operation Sinbad was significant. It signalled the emergence of true Iraqi sovereignty. The operation had morphed from being a security operation with reconstruction in support, to a reconstruction operation enabled by security. The commander of the operation was to be General Hamadi rather than General Shirreff who was charged with tactical co-ordination. This represented an institutional acceptance by the British that, ultimately, delivering security to Basra would be an Iraqi rather than a British lead. In many respects, in terms of command and control, it served as a precursor to Operation Charge of the Knights in 2008, where the British Army were genuinely in support of an Iraqi-led operation.

Operation Sinbad was also distinct from the original proposal in two other ways. First, it was extended from three to nearly six months; this was largely a pragmatic response to the limited resources available, but it also resonated with the desire for a more gradual approach to addressing Basra's problems with urban renewal as the centrepiece of the operation. Second, 'kinetic' strike operations against the Special Groups in Basra would not be conducted as part of Operation Sinbad, but as distinct British operations on the grounds of force protection and under the auspices of existing UN mandates to detain individuals who threatened the security of Iraq. This was not briefed to Maliki in detail. Instead, General Casey presented to him the repackaged Operation Sinbad, portrayed as police and army security operation with urban reconstruction being the central theme. General Casey also visited Basra and spoke personally to General Hamadi, who had had a further bout of uncertainty. The operation was finally approved on 28 September 2006. In the words of General Shirreff, General Casey 'played a blinder on behalf of the British'. The British Ambassador Dominic Asquith had also been essential in building support on Baghdad. He added that British ministers had done 'absolutely nothing' to set the political conditions for Operation Sinbad.

The problematic birth of Operation Sinbad in 2006 illustrates that Maliki was beginning to assert the sovereignty of Iraq; this could be regarded as the beginnings of campaign success. General Shirreff reported back to Northwood that the run-up to Operation Sinbad showed that Maliki was not ready in 2006 to 'bite the bullet and enforce security in Basra'. Perhaps it should not have come as a surprise to the British that its own sense of timing was not synchronised with the Iraqis: the British were driven by thoughts of withdrawal; Maliki by longer-term political survival. The reputation of the British Army, and its desire to transition to operational 'overwatch' from Basra Air Station by mid-2007, drove the timing of Operation Sinbad rather than Iraqi politics. For Maliki, establishing law and order in Basra could only take place once his position was secure in Baghdad. This misalignment of objectives and timing between the emerging Iraqi Government and MND(SE) in Basra was perhaps the most significant impediment to the successful outcome of Operation Sinbad.

Executing Operation Sinbad

The Operation was launched on Saturday 28 October 2006 in the University District of northern Basra, a week later than envisaged. The operation was conducted district by district; sixteen in total with an average of 100,000 people in each, in a series of security and reconstruction 'pulses'. Each 'pulse' operation was mounted by a combined British and Iraqi Force of about 2,000, coordinated from the newly established joint Iraqi Provincial Joint Coordination Centre, established by a British battalion, at the Police Headquarters in central Basra, and commanded at the district level by a Tactical Command Centre set up in the District Police Station by one of the two British Basra city battlegroups, 1 Staffords and 1st Royal Green Jackets (later 2 Rifles). The Danish Battlegroup North of Basra also played a key role in delivering security 'pulses' North of Basra. These 'pulses' lasted three days and involved a security lock down of an area saturated by vehicle check points and joint Iraqi and British patrols. In parallel with the security operation, medical centres and schools were painted and refurbished, parks and public spaces cleared of rubbish, collapsed drainage ditches re-excavated and children's playgrounds and football pitches restored. Local community leaders, both local councillors and tribal leaders, were involved in deciding where the money should be spent. It is of note that even during a security 'pulse' the ratio of security forces to the population of 1:50 was below that judged as necessary for a security surge in the newly published US Counter-Insurgency doctrine.

Following each security 'pulse' there was a security 'pause'. This involved continued reconstruction projects and enhanced patrolling and police training. If the security 'pulse' was the phase in which an area was cleared and secured, then the 'pause' was the period of about a month when security consolidation and reconstruction took place. The resources dedicated to Operation Sinbad meant that there were few Iraqi and British troops to maintain a security presence beyond the initial 'pulse', so security was largely left to the police who were, at best, unreliable and, at worst, infiltrated by Jaysh al-Mahdi. Even if the police had been reliable and competent, the ratio of police to population was at best one law enforcer to every 250 citizens: wholly inadequate to maintain security in a lawless inner-city neighbourhood. To address this concern the main focus of the British patrols during the 'pause' period was police training and joint patrols with the police. The lack of reliable police to maintain adequate security once the initial surge of activity had taken place was the second greatest impediment to the success of Operation Sinbad behind the lack of Iraqi political support.

The operation was launched amidst considerable publicity, radio, television and posters. It generated a discernible sense of optimism and civic momentum. It was a 'big idea' and it appealed to the people of Basra who hoped that it signalled a new beginning. The logo, a dhow, and the name of the legendary sailor whom Iraqis claim set sail from Basra, seemed to resonate with the people as it sought to reconnect them with Basra's outward-looking, maritime and trading heritage. Local leaders spoke of re-establishing Basra as the major city of the North Arabian Gulf. This initial enthusiasm amongst military and civil leaders created the momentum for planning meetings and ensured the involvement of a wide variety of local power brokers, many of whom had long since stopped talking to the British Army. People were keen, above all, to ensure that their neighbourhood was not overlooked in the disbursement of reconstruction effort and US taxpayers' dollars. It underlined the importance of money as a 'weapon system' in complex stabilisation operations. Commanders on the ground lamented the absence of British money.

Wherever possible, reconstruction was carried out by the Iraqi divisional engineer company and, crucially, young men employed from the local area. Over 25,000 short-term jobs were created during Operation Sinbad. As the 10th (IA) Division's engineers and local workers cleared up areas around schools and medical centres, the British Army delivered what were known as 'schools in a box' and 'medical centres in a box'. These were delivered in ISO containers and consisted of flat-packed office furniture, stationary, IT and medical supplies to improve the quality of local public services. These were greeted with enthusiasm by local doctors and head teachers. Everywhere one drove, paving stones were being replaced by gangs of young men, and central reservations were being cleaned up and replanted. There was no doubt that Operation Sinbad caught the imagination of the Basrawis and was enthusiastically embraced by the Iraqi Army and many of the police. It was for this reason that Operation Sinbad was bitterly contested by Jaysh al-Mahdi Special Groups, as it challenged their growing power in Basra.

From the outset of the operation, British patrols were targeted with sniper fire during each security 'pulse'. On one such operation in November in the al-Quibla area of Basra, General Shirreff himself came under fire. The intent of the Special Groups, as articulated by many Iraqis and reiterated by General Shirreff, was to 'inflict a humiliating defeat on the British' in Basra. The Special Groups did not want to cause too many civilian casualties, so instead they targeted British patrols with IEDs on logistic resupply convoys, and during training visits to police stations following a Sinbad 'pulse'. Their attacks concentrated on the 'pause' phase, thus demonstrating that Iraqi and British security forces might secure an area for a short period, but they could not hold it for a prolonged period. Local leaders who had supported Sinbad were intimidated into disengagement shortly after the reconstruction projects were started. The Special Groups also began a concerted indirect fire campaign of Iranian-made rocket and mortar attacks on British bases. By mid-December, Basra Palace was the most rocketed location in Iraq; over 1,200 rockets and mortar bombs were fired at it between September 2006 and May 2007. Remarkably these attacks caused no British fatalities in Basra Palace, but there were many soldiers injured.

Jaysh al-Mahdi's response to Sinbad was a clear statement to the people of Basra that, despite the fleeting control they exerted over different neighbourhoods of Basra, British and the Iraqi Security Forces did not control the streets. Great efforts were made by Brigadier Aqeel, the Iraqi Army brigade commander, to mount counter-rocket patrols but with little effect. The two British battlegroups in the City had only sufficient resources to patrol those areas from where mortars could fire. The Iranian-made 107mm rocket's range of approximately ten kilometres made effective counter-rocket patrols unfeasible – the potential firing points covered too large an area. Battlegroups also had constantly to balance the indirect fire threat against the EFP threat: frequent counter-rocket patrols set patterns which the enemy could exploit with IEDs. The absence of anything other than very short range and short duration UAVs, and the withdrawal of US attack helicopters by December 2006, made counter-rocket efforts haphazard. On several occasions, however, a helicopter, equipped with a Broadsword camera, spotted rocket teams and tracked them to their safe house. An entire rocket team of six was captured by the Royal Green Jackets Battlegroup in Operation Phoenix in December 2006.

The full scale of Iranian involvement was revealed through intelligence material captured during this raid. Operation Phoenix became the generic name for counter-indirect fire operations and, as Operation Sinbad progressed, there was increasing success against rocket teams. The militia's patterns began to emerge and, using Royal Navy camera-equipped Sea King helicopters and direction-finding radar, from March 2007 MND(SE) struck back with artillery and precision airstrikes using 500 lb bombs dropped by US Navy carrier-based aircraft. However, despite all the effort and attrition on the militia rocket teams, rocket attacks escalated as did casualties, particularly civilian casualties around Coalition bases, made worse when less-experienced rocket teams were used.

Rocket attacks had a dramatic effect on the psychological state of the US and British Consulates based in Basra Palace. E-mails were sent back to capitals on a daily basis recording every attack on Basra Palace. They gave the impression that the British Army in Basra was inactive in dealing with the threat, rather than the truth that it had insufficient manpower and equipment. Simon MacDonald, the FCO Policy advisor, visited Basra Palace and asked pointedly whether British battlegroups in Basra could be more 'muscular' in their response to the rockets. The US Force Headquarters in Baghdad could not comprehend how the British in Basra allowed five attacks in a day. I recall being shown an e-mail from the State Department which asked 'what were the British doing about the rocket attacks in Basra or were they merely waltzing around Basra spending US taxpayers' dollars?' Under considerable pressure from the State Department, the US Corps Headquarters deployed radar detachments to Basra, and the MOD deployed close air defence systems from ships to shoot down rockets.

19th Light Brigade, commanded by Brigadier Tim Evans, responded to the attacks with a major offensive to capture or kill those involved with the Special Groups. This concerted and targeted campaign was conducted not as part of Operation Sinbad, but under United Nations Security Council Resolution (UNSCR) 1723, which authorised Coalition Forces to take 'all necessary measures to contribute to the maintenance of security and stability in Iraq', and the power to intern individuals that was included within the Annexes to UNSCR 1546 and subsequent resolutions. In total, nearly 50 night-time strike operations were conducted by British battlegroups; an average of three per week. Infantry companies became accomplished at conducting complex night-time operations that had hitherto been the preserve of special forces. The results were impressive: 198 detained and interned, of whom 68 were identified as leaders within the Special Groups. These night-time raids, and the associated explosive method of entry that was often used, were a symbol to people in Basra that the insidious power of the militia was not going unchallenged. It was during this period that many locals to referred to the British troops as the Lions of Basra: arresting known militia leaders was popular amongst the majority of the population; running gun-battles that followed ambushes of logistic patrols or police station visits were not.

By January 2007, over half of British patrols in Basra ended in an exchange of fire with the militia. There were on average four rocket attacks per day, many of which missed their intended targets and landed on residential buildings. The reality was that the combined strength of the Iraqi Security Forces in Basra and the British 19th Light Brigade was insufficient to dominate or hold the ground. The force ratios, despite the best efforts of the troops on the ground, were insufficient for the size of the task. Whenever the Special Groups and the British Army met on the streets, the superior training of the British soldier won the day. Over 340 armed militiamen were killed by the British and Iraqi Army between October 2006 and May 2007; many more were injured. This came at a significant price: 46 British soldiers were killed and 350 wounded; in addition there were significant losses amongst the Iraqi Security Forces. The collateral impact on the ordinary people of Basra was also considerable.

The escalation of violence on the streets of Basra made the locals and the Iraqi Security Forces question whether they would be better able to achieve security, or at least greater tranquillity, without the British attracting the attention of the Iranian-backed militia. Operation Sinbad had improved the confidence of the Iraqi Security Forces and the coordination between the police and the Iraqi Army. The last 'pulses' were conducted without British support and these attracted no militia attention; monitoring from the air and of radio communications showed that they were indeed working effectively. The idea was growing that perhaps there was an Iraqi solution to the problems of Basra, which did not have to involve British armoured vehicles and protracted gun-battles on the street.

It was for this reason that the Iraqis in Basra welcomed General Shirreff's proposal, in December, that Operation Sinbad should be followed by the gradual handover of all bases in Basra, known in British circles as Operation Zenith. The media narrative in the United Kingdom suggested that Basra was being abandoned. The feeling on the ground at the time was very different. The Iraqis felt that they had demonstrated their ability to conduct sophisticated security and reconstruction operations on Operation Sinbad, and the logical extension of this was to assume responsibility for the bases in Basra. They also believed that the British Army's presence, far from delivering security, was merely adding to the levels of violence in Basra. The significant attrition that had been achieved against the militia also led the Iraqi Army to believe that they had been sufficiently weakened and so would not threaten the Iraqi Army. The symbolic destruction of the Jameat Police Station, a nexus of militia activity, on 25 December 2006, did a great deal to encourage Basrawis, although the Iraqi Army was not prepared to publicly support the operation. General Shirreff, with the destruction of the Jameat and the disbandment of the notorious Serious Crimes Unit, synonymous with militia infiltration of the police, demonstrated to the Iraqis that there was an alternative to the insidious power of Iranian-sponsored armed militia. It was clear that for Basra to prosper a decisive act would be necessary to remove the militia. The problem was that the British brigade in Basra had insufficient combat power to achieve this and the Iraqis were not yet ready to do it for themselves.

Aftermath

When General Jonathan Shaw took over Command of MND(SE) in January 2007, he continued Operation Sinbad, but soon realised that it was insufficient in itself to bring order to Basra and break the power of the Special Groups. He judged that the only way to achieve stability in Basra was for the British Army to hand over and make it an Iraqi problem. He was confident that there would then be an Iraqi solution. Operation Sinbad morphed from being a decisive operation to being an operational phase in the planned handover from British to Iraqi Security Forces. It became the operation where we showed the Iraqis how such an operation should be designed, commanded and controlled. It defined the best effort of the British Army, within its limited resources, before handing over to the Iraqi Security Forces.

Having seen the escalation of violence in Basra during Operation Sinbad, the Iraqis were ready to take responsibility for security, believing that the militia would be reluctant to confront them, as they had shown during the closing stages of Operation Sinbad when they operated without the British. The Iraqi authorities wanted to assume Provincial Iraqi Control. They were given added confidence by the high levels of attrition that had been achieved against the Special Groups during the previous six months. The 'formal state', as General Shaw called it, was given a head start over the 'dark state' by the offensive action taken by the British since mid-2006.

Operation Sinbad therefore became the necessary narrative for the handover of bases to the Iraqi Army, which began in March 2007 in parallel with the final district 'pulses'. Operation Sinbad had become the necessary bridge into security transition. The respected and capable 10th (Iraqi Army) Division's military police company took over the Old State Building company location in central Basra in a high profile ceremony and banquet involving the Iraqi Navy Band, Governor Waeli, prominent Basrawi leaders and politicians, and a considerable media presence. The Union Flag was lowered and the Iraqi flag raised to great applause. It was done in an orderly and disciplined way. The barracks remained secure in the hands of the Iraqi Army with none of the looting that had taken place in al-Amarah in September 2006. This was followed by the orderly handover of the Shaibah logistic base on the outskirts of Basra, and the Shatt al-Arab Hotel in northern Basra in April 2007. Basra Palace was handed over in September 2007. These bases became, in the spring of 2008, the key locations from which five brigades of the Iraqi Army cleared and then secured Basra, driving the militia across the Shatt al-Arab into Iran during Operation Charge of the Knights. Operation Sinbad did not achieve its objectives, but it was nevertheless necessary in preparing and persuading the Iraqis that the rule of law in Basra was ultimately an Iraqi problem. Planning and delivering Operation Sinbad gave the Iraqi Security Forces the institutional confidence to mount a major security operation in Basra, once resources and political will were available, and it re-established effective communication and coordination between the army, police and civic leaders.

Operation Sinbad and its related series of offensive operations ultimately fell well short of its declared objectives to subjugate the militias to the rule of law and bring adequate stability to Basra. It could for this reason be judged a failure. The facts are clear: levels of violence against coalition bases and patrols continued to rise. By the end of the operation, Basra Palace was the most attacked location in Iraq. Forty-six British servicemen lost their lives, and freedom of movement for patrols in Basra was more constrained at the end of the operation than it was at the beginning. The Iraqi Army in Basra, although it had taken over and held all the British bases as part of Operation Zenith, did not have the mass or the inclination to take the fight to the militias. They were reluctant to take part in joint operations with the British battlegroup, and preferred to operate alone where they did not become the target of the Iranian-backed militia.

This stark assessment does not, however, paint a truly accurate picture: Operation Sinbad and the offensive against Jaysh al-Mahdi had changed the political and military balance in Basra. Many militia leaders were either killed or in detention. This challenged the perception of their invulnerability that had grown during the previous three years. The relationships built between the Iraqi Army, local leaders and elements of the police provided the foundations for the orderly handover of the remaining British bases in the city. In particular, tactical successes against Jaysh al-Mahdi gave the British a strong position from which to negotiate an orderly withdrawal from Basra Palace in September 2007, avoiding a retreat under fire. It showed the people of Basra that the real threat to their way of life came from the Iranian-backed militias, rather than a foreign occupier, and it was the catalyst for the re-emergence of the Iraqi state and its institutions as the predominant political force in Basra. By removing the British Army in an orderly way from the tactical equation in Basra, MND(SE) made the delivery of political stability an Iraqi problem.

The Operation Sinbad template created in 2006 was applied with great effect by the Iraqi Army and Police in Basra in the spring of 2008 during Operation Charge of the Knights, this time implemented by 15 Iraqi battalions, rather than two. The militia was driven from the streets and the density of check points prevented their return. The majority of their leadership fled across the border into Iran. There was some graffiti on the bridge over the Shatt al-Arab: a fleeing militia man had scrawled 'JAM will be back!' An Iraqi soldier had written next to it 'and when you come back we will be waiting for you!' This graffiti became a slide shown by General Petraeus to symbolise the new confidence of the Iraqi state and its army. It was in Basra that the Iraqi state decisively re-asserted itself in the spring of 2008 in Operation Charge of the Knights.

Operation Sinbad, although in many respects a tactical failure, played a key role in shaping the conditions for Iraqi success. The Special Groups had been weakened through attrition. Basrawis were made to realise that they had to confront Jaysh al-Mahdi themselves in order to build a better future. Operation Sinbad gave them a template of how they could do it. During Charge of the Knights, British and US troops, as part of a corps-level operation, genuinely enabled the Iraqis to achieve tactical success without being in the lead. All in all, it was not a pretty or linear progression to success, but in the end it was a success of sorts. The British Army was able to complete its mission in Iraq with its fighting spirit and tactical reputation preserved; the militia was eventually destroyed or driven out with British support; and the Iraqi Security Forces had secured Basra using techniques learnt during Operation Sinbad. Basra has remained calm since the last British troops left in 2009. In the words of one warrant officer, the British Army in Iraq 'won on penalties after extra time'. It was Operation Sinbad that bought the British Army in Iraq that vital extra time.

Chapter 14

Basra 2007: The Requirements of a Modern Major General

Jonathan Shaw – 12 November 2008

My experience as General Officer Commanding MND(SE) in Basra from January to August 2007 has enabled me to draw conclusions about the challenges facing a modern major general. While considering the situation I found myself in, the key decisions I took, by what logic, and informed by what training and education, I have been able to examine how those decisions have stood up with hindsight and to reflect upon observations about the political/military interface, coalition perspectives, the Comprehensive Approach, and the trends in our understanding of the nature of conflict.

I was born into a political family – my father was a Member of Parliament for over 30 years and is now in the House of Lords; I read Philosophy, Politics and Economics at Trinity College, Oxford and joined the Army by accident, on the rebound from accountancy, and, in the course of nearly 30 years in the Parachute Regiment and the wider Army, have been lucky enough to command on operations at every rank from lieutenant to major general bar only colonel – a rank which I spent mainly in COBR coping with fuel protests, foot and mouth disease, 9/11 and hostage crises. It was this wider experience of the theory and practice of government which I found invaluable in understanding the position I found myself in when arriving in Basra on 14 January 2007 to take over my most recent command.

For reasons of brevity and clarity, I will outline what was done and why, but I should admit that I am in part *ex post facto* rationalising, putting labels and lists to things that actually we as a team felt our way towards, taking one step at a time in the fog of reality in the hope that there was solid ground to tread on but aware the earth could consume us at any moment. I say 'we' because I was blessed with a strong team and we had three months to prepare before going. My Chief of Staff read History at Balliol College, Oxford; an SO2 read PPE at Hertford College, Oxford; the others were profoundly educated at the university of life. We took the chance to be educated on Iraq by the likes of Charles Tripp from SOAS and Mark Allen, whose book *Arabs*[1] I made compulsory reading. Our reliance on academics was I understand unusual; but it was on the strength of our theoretical understanding and our prior military experience that we based the speculative plans which we launched in Iraq and which, as I will assert, have proved so effective in achieving Iraqi and hence Coalition success in Basra.

I will begin with the nature of the coalition we found ourselves in. This was, and still is, characterised by weak political unity; countries took part for their own domestic reasons, with no NATO North Atlantic Council equivalent to cohere multi-national agendas; hence the strains on the military coalition. In this, Britain was no different from the rest of the Coalition, US included. The shift in US strategy from the drawdown recommended by the Iraq Survey Group to the surge inspired by the American Enterprise Institute was done with no apparent prior

---

1   Allen 2007.

consultation with the UK. This shift happened over Christmas 2006 after all our Whitehall briefs which had focused on transition and reductions in troop levels. I arrived with national orders to reduce our footprint, at a time when the US was increasing its. And on my first Friday, we had to brief the new US Secretary of Defense in front of General Casey, the Commander of the Multi-National Force in Iraq, on British plans. We recognised that we were working to three chains of command: politically, back to Whitehall; militarily to the US Corps and Multi-National Force; but ultimately to the Iraqi Government. Keeping those three constituents happy and harmonious filled a large part of our day throughout the tour but our presentation that day was perhaps the height of sophistry and nuance to cube what was very much a three-dimensional sphere. I shall consider conflicting national politics later.

National command and control is also worth considering. Professor Strachan has written at length about the failings of strategy amongst the Western governments, including UK, so there is no need for me to comment further, except to say that our national command and control reflects the very best and worst of cabinet government: it is stronger at being democratic than executive. The significance of this is that, as the senior deployed British commander in Basra – a tactical position which should have simply been executing orders – it fell to me to take on the responsibility for generating a strategic plan around which Coalition effort could cohere in my area of operations. My hope in so doing was to create a long-term campaign approach, and it proved to be one that I duly sold to my successor and which certainly continued until Operation Charge of the Knights and which, at its heart, continues to this day. The criteria I set myself were as follows:

- first, work within US tolerances and achieve UK mandated force levels by a certain time, conducting UK mandated tasks (my mission from PJHQ);
- secondly, promote the best interests of the Government of Iraq;
- thirdly, safeguard the British military and national reputation, in the eyes of a variety of audiences: in order, the British Army, the British Government and people, the US Army, the US Government and people, the Iraqi Government and people, the world of potential allies and adversaries. We talk a lot about information operations (IO) but that just illustrates the challenge of managing the messaging to, and judging the sensitivities of, each of those disparate audiences, in an era of instant transparency and communication.

In trying to create strategy from a tactical position, the task was to cohere policy, resources, reality on the ground, and time. I take it as a given in interventions that our time is limited. By contrast, in Northern Ireland we could look the opposition in the eye and match them on the strategic dimension of time. This key to strategic success was denied us in Iraq and is also denied us in Afghanistan. In a limited timeframe, it is vain folly to attempt to achieve cultural change to management consultant timelines. This meant we had to work with the culture as we found it, and aim at a solution that did not contain the Coalition in it.

Judging we were not part of the end-state for Iraq, we created a narrative, which focused on the potential for self-sustaining political success for Iraq. In retrospect, I can see our narrative methodology can be abstracted to four stages:

- first, understanding the political soil;
- secondly, estimating the tolerances of this political culture, the parameters of the art of the possible, leading to a preferred choice of self-sustaining polity;
- thirdly, identifying what the Coalition role was in helping Iraq reach this end-state;

- and finally (and only finally) understanding the role of the military in this fundamentally political context and in a fundamentally supporting role.

As a gross, but useful, simplification, I will focus on two key observations about the nature of the conflict we found ourselves in, observations that flowed directly from this Iraqi-focused narrative. First, the conflict we faced was qualitatively different from that faced by the Americans. The al-Qaeda-inspired violence in the central belt was essentially nihilistic in nature: escalation was open-ended, with total collapse an acceptable end-state for al-Qaeda. For the US, there was a population to protect and violence had to be controlled. My observation of the Shia south was that it was about gangsterism and absolutely not nihilistic. One fact, little reported on, is that there were almost no attacks on the oil infrastructure or the energy systems in the south. No one had any interest in the south not working; they just wanted to have as large a slice of the cake as possible. I judged Basra to be more like Palermo than Beirut. My judgement was, and is, that the inter-Shia power struggle was fundamentally self-limiting; hence I judged we could take risks with it. And 90 per cent of the violence was against us – there were no car bombs or suicide attacks to protect the population from. This was a hard sell because the favourite target for terrorist rocket fire was Basra Palace where the US Regional Engagement Office (their equivalent of the Consulate) was housed. Every attack report went direct to the US Department of State at Foggy Bottom and hence straight to President Bush and to the Force Commander. This distorted depiction of reality provided all the ammunition our critics in Washington could have wished for, leading to repeated inter-Coalition sniping that increased when Brown became Prime Minister with possibly a withdrawal agenda and, to judge from certain press utterances, a US attempt to shame the UK into staying – an ultimately successful IO campaign. But given that the conflict we were in was one of decisive influence not decisive kinetic strike, and remembering that Coalition cohesion was the Strategic Centre of Gravity of the Force, bad-mouthing an ally's performance does the opposition's job for them. The lack of a unified agreed Coalition IO campaign continues to be a crippling weakness to our global efforts in conflicts that are fundamentally about influence not kinetics.

The second observation about the Shia south is that, to quote Major General Jalil, the Basra police chief, 'the problem here is not training or equipment, it is loyalty'. As Mark Allen has observed, in Arab societies, the strongest loyalties are based on blood; institutional loyalty is the weakest. Whatever abstract appeals the Coalition might have offered in terms of democracy and development, they were powerless set against the blood loyalties of family, tribe, religion and ethnicity. The critical goal was to get Iraqi Security Forces (ISF) to be seen by the people as representing Iraqi nationalist aspirations, to which we could hand over. As long as we were seen as the occupiers, which we were, our association with the ISF tainted them in the eyes of the population and justified the actions of the terrorists as liberators. Whatever our addition to the ISF hard power (and this was and still is respected), our association with the ISF undermined their soft power, their nationalist credentials. And we got little support from Maliki's Government, which at this time contained within it representatives of precisely the factions attacking us in the south. Sensitivities about arresting Maliki's constituents put a limit on the Shia target set we could engage. So somehow we had to remove ourselves from the hierarchy of threats to the Basra Shias, a hierarchy that we judged to be, listed in order: a Sunni/Ba'athist revival, the Coalition, the Iranians, Baghdad. The fear of a Sunni revival (a shared Basrawi and Iranian fear) plus Iranian (especially the Iranian Revolutionary Guards Corps Quds Force[2]) economic interests in Basra,

---

2   The Quds Force is a section of the IRGC whose primary mission is to organise, train, equip and finance foreign Islamic revolutionary movements.

were key reasons why we judged Shia violence to be self-limiting. With a Sunni revival a distant risk, the Coalition was clearly the top threat. The challenge was to convince the population (and that particularly meant the terrorists) that the Iranians, not the Coalition, were the greatest threat to their aspirations. How to do this?

Before answering that question, it is worth laying to rest a picture that emerges from the press that there was a gulf between British and US approaches at this time. At the first Force conference I attended, in February 2007, with General Petraeus new in post, I surprised the audience by saying this was not our fight to win; it was for the Iraqis to win, and us to assist. In July 2008, Lieutenant Colonel (retired) John Nagl, a key adviser to General Petraeus, said 'foreign powers cannot win counter-insurgency campaigns, but they can enable and empower host nations to do so'.[3] Our approach and General Petraeus' were aligned. Admiral Fallon, COM CENTCOM, understood our situation and analysis exactly: 'I get it, Basra is just like New Jersey!' Generals Petraeus and Odierno were my commanders, accepted our depiction of Basra and gave their approval to everything we did. Indeed, at the same time as we were working the south, UK's Lieutenant General Graeme Lamb (Deputy Commanding General MNF-I) was convincing General Petraeus of the need to drive a wedge between the reconcilable and irreconcilable elements of the Sunni insurgency. Instinctively, both General Lamb and I had hit on the same methodology. The Anbar Awakening and what happened in the south followed the same logic, with equally beneficial results for Iraq and the mission.

So what did we do? We made two strategic decisions within weeks of arrival. First, we declared that this was a political problem, not a military one, that the FCO was in charge of the national effort on the Southern Iraq Steering Group (a group designed to cohere the UK comprehensive approach), and that what we needed was a political plan to support. Second, we recognised we had fooled ourselves by the J2 tidying up the battlefield with neat acronyms to describe what in reality were loose affiliations at best, generally for tactical and short-term local advantage, with little clear C2 as we understand it. Jaysh al-Mahdi (JAM) was a particularly large acronym bucket into which all kinds of badness were tossed (my suspicion is that 'Taliban' is an equally deceptive descriptor in Afghanistan). Hitherto, JAM had been targeted in order to kill them. Instead, I tasked the agencies to target JAM to understand them, and to find people in JAM to talk to. In retrospect, I can describe this as attempting to move UK policy in the south from an exclusive to an inclusive policy.

Students of the Northern Ireland campaign will recognise that these two strategic decisions were the two strategic shifts that Her Majesty's Government made with regard to that campaign – the shift to police primacy (a political approach) in 1976, and the shift from an exclusive to an inclusive approach through the 1990s leading to the Good Friday Agreement and Sinn Fein's inclusion in the political process. Whereas the Northern Ireland decisions were made by No. 10 and agreed in the Privy Council, these Iraqi decisions were made by the deployed tactical military commander.

We spent the next three months conducting the most intense and continuous strike operations since the invasion, leading to the death of the JAM leader Wissam Qadir at the end of 19 Brigade's tour in April 2007. Historians will have to judge the importance of this attrition to the deal that followed but, shortly after this, the first confidence-building ceasefire was negotiated with a JAM leader – which dropped rocket attacks on British bases to zero for three days. It is now a matter of public record that, as a result of this success, I found myself talking to the captive JAM leader Fartusi in our own detention centre and coming to the reconciliation whose effects persist to this day.

---

3   Nagl 2008.

The modalities of the reconciliation are worth spelling out, lest historians suggest this was a sell-out to save our skins. It did achieve this but that was not its motive. And it is worth pointing out here this was all cleared through Prime Minister Maliki's office and the Government of Iraq, regardless of what Maliki chooses to say now, as well as through the US command chain. The key point about Fartusi was that he was a rabid Iraqi nationalist. Not only did he hate us, but moreover he was fiercely anti-Iranian, and so respected by the hoods on the street that even the Iranian-backed Special Groups felt obliged not to work against his will. In conversation with him, it became clear to me that he and I wanted the same things for Basra – prosperity, self-rule, religious moderation, and education. 'So why are you attacking us?' 'Because you are the occupiers!' I assured him that, unlike the Iranians, we would leave when his Prime Minister told us to, that we had to leave with honour and could not be seen to be driven out, that we were killing his men because they were trying to kill us, and that he should cooperate with redevelopment instead of attacking it, and reap the political benefits that would accrue to him as the bringer of development and wealth to Basra. Confident we could work together, we could release his personnel as no longer being a threat to us. Thus reconciled, it was Fartusi's men who 'escorted' the troops to the Basra Air Station to prevent any attacks on them, whilst also milking it for their own publicity purposes.

Was this a success? I would argue it absolutely was. Most obviously, from a British point of view, it was a success for us. Indirect fire attacks dropped to minimal levels; we managed an orderly transfer of Basra Palace to the ISF and a relocation to the Basra Air Station without a shot being fired; British service casualties dropped from 41 in my seven months in command to one since. More significantly, but less well understood, it was a success for the ISF and hence for Iraq. That Maliki chooses to bad-mouth the reconciliation tells us more about his need for credibility as the dismisser of the occupiers; he turns on the UK now because he can; my expectation is that he will in due course turn on the US when he can. This should not surprise us: he has to do this to be seen as the strong representative of Iraqi nationalism. The benefit to his reputation is in danger of coming at the cost of our reputation, which is why the widest understanding of the so-called Accommodation is so vital for the UK's enduring reputation and credibility, and hence the success of the whole Iraqi enterprise.

None of this should obscure the benefits to the ISF of our relocation to the Basra Air Station, a relocation that was encouraged and supported by the head of Basra security, General Mohan. By removing ourselves from the streets of Basra, we left the Iranians as the greatest threat to the Basrawis and removed the 'liberator' justification for terrorism. Our relocation clarified the issue of what it was to be an Iraqi nationalist, and gave the ISF space to gain institutional loyalty. Operation Charge of the Knights was a military shambles, but proved to be a political triumph for Maliki. Crucially, what it demonstrated was the shift in political support within the population in favour of the organs of the Iraqi state and against the militia whose feuding and extremism, deprived of the liberator credibility, was revealed as self-seeking and working against what the locals wanted. In this new context, British Military Transition Teams[4] are welcomed on the streets as useful support to the ISF, in stark contrast to 2007 when their presence drew fire onto the ISF and undermined their nationalist credentials. It is this shift in the Basrawi population's attitude that shows the impact of the reconciliation as an influence operation. General Casey has said that the prize of conflict has changed. Whereas it used to be the destruction of the enemy force, now it is the will of the people. In a stability operation of influence such as this, I would suggest that the reconciliation was a good example of what 'manoeuvre' means.

---

4   Military Transition Teams (MiTTs) are mentoring and training teams embedded with the Iraqi Army, equivalent to OMLTs in Afghanistan.

Did we expect such a positive outcome in such a short time? No to both. The aim had been to create the conditions to allow Iraqis to reach their own power arrangements in Basra, something a foreign army is incapable of doing. Such a rapid and decisive shift in the population's attitudes and loyalties was at the extreme end of optimistic expectations. But such has also been the case with the Anbar Awakening and the rejection of al-Qaeda. Both these were based on the Iraqi rejection of foreign influence. The challenge now is to convert this into similar enthusiasm for Iraqi national unity.

Was Iraq an aberration or the shape of the future? I would support Rupert Smith in his assertion that we have witnessed a change in paradigm in the nature of conflict, and that therefore Casey's assertion should result in fundamental change to the way we organise ourselves for it. 9/11 saw us shift from a reactive to a pre-emptive posture; General Peter Chiarelli, one of the US's most successful commanders in Iraq, uses the term 'permanent engagement' to describe the preventative posture the US intends to adopt globally – preventing failed states, training indigenous force before rather than during or after conflict. For interventions since Blair's Chicago Doctrine have revealed the limitations of power as much as its possibilities, and asserted, to my mind, the requirement to work with the grain of the culture into which we intervene. Far from being the end of history, the collapse of the Berlin Wall appears to have been the high-water mark of capitalist liberal democracy as the global model for universal aspiration.

In this context, we can answer the three key drivers that face defence planners: current non-state actors and conflicts are *not* an aberration but the norm; state on state warfare *is* still a possibility; but it is likely to look remarkably *similar* to what we are seeing in current conflicts in Iraq and Afghanistan. This should give defence planners a clear aiming mark for investment and structures.

Whilst you may draw your own conclusions about the requirements of a modern major general on the basis of my experiences in Basra 2007, I will highlight here just a few that strike me as pertinent. I judge generals need to be:

- capable of strategic understanding, creativity and judgement;
- secure enough in personality to feel comfortable in chaos and directional dissonance, to have both the initiative to see what needs to be done and the courage to do it;
- an artist. Now I did take a piano along for relaxation in the evening, but that is not what I mean by an artist (and nor would you if you heard my playing). What I mean by 'artist' is someone widely *educated* in human sympathies by reading such as Virginia Woolf and her multiple narrative novels, more than deeply *trained* by reading the drill manual. The ability to understand and indeed anticipate where people are coming from is absolutely key to reading the 'influence' battlefield;
- characterised by humility rather than arrogance – the supporting role is absolutely not heroic, it is a permanent promotion of the indigenous leaders or other government departments;
- attracted by ideas, not to the exclusion of, but certainly prior to, action;
- and finally, they need to be a soldier, to direct and understand what's going on downwards and to be able to explain upwards.

This was not quite the CV required on the Inner German Border, I would suggest. And if Rupert Smith is right about his paradigm shift, then I suspect this altered list of requirements will become the norm for future major generals. And when the recession leads to resurgent nationalism à la 1930s, and tanks roll over the German Plains once more, you can seek me out and tell me I was wrong. Until then, I judge it is best to plan on a changed paradigm as a better planning yardstick for the future.

Chapter 15

Campaigning and Generalship: Iraq 2008

Bill Rollo – 27 May 2009

What are the challenges that modern campaigns pose for generalship, and British generalship in particular? I've tried to stand back from immediate issues – not least because I came back from Baghdad over a year ago and, I firmly believe, you lose currency as you step on the plane.

Introduction

What are generals for – and if you did not have them would you invent them? I've always liked Lloyd George's comment: 'a fully equipped Duke costs as much to keep up as two Dreadnoughts, and Dukes are just as great a terror, and they last longer'.[1]

Generalship ought to be about making plans and providing leadership in their execution, I think in that order, though Patton's maxim that no good decision was ever made in a swivel chair is always worth remembering. The book is admirably succinct, it tells you that you should establish ends, ways and means, give clear direction, and delegate appropriately; but whose ends? Do you control the ways and means? And are you in a position to give direction to the people who really matter, who might not be your own soldiers, indeed might not be soldiers at all, and if not what do you do about it?

I don't think today's problems are unique (even a cursory reading of our history will reveal that) but they do pose some significant challenges, perhaps particularly because of the relatively rapid tempo of change in the demands we are making on our leaders. I grew up thinking that generalship was about the moment you committed the reserve brigade or division, in the context of a massive Soviet attack and a war of national survival; which meant the only other decision a general had to make – whether to seek or avoid battle – had already been taken. Being a general looked pretty easy. After the Balkans, Iraq and Afghanistan, each very different, it looks more complex now.

I'd like to use that apparently simple framework, of ends, ways and means, to illustrate some of those complexities.

Ends

I'll start with ends, because the ends should, to any educated soldier, drive the remainder of the analysis. But I started by asking 'whose ends?' and it's worth pausing for a moment to think this one through.

Any British general – any general in a coalition operation – will receive at least two sets of orders. One from his national military command, reflecting his national political direction, and one from his alliance or coalition commander, which should reflect the political and military objectives

---

1 Lloyd George 1909.

agreed by the participating countries. In an ideal world these should be coincident. It is almost inevitable that they are not. Let me give a couple of examples.

At a strategic level countries may agree to participate in an operation for many reasons. If they are adjacent to the country concerned they may have a direct interest in its stability, for instance Italy in the Balkans. They may have a broader interest in maintaining international order in a region or even globally. They may wish to remove a perceived threat, as the US and its allies did in Iraq and Afghanistan. Or they may wish to participate because it is the price of membership in an organisation which in turn guarantees their own security, for instance the new members of NATO. Or any combination of the above.

It matters because this affects national expectations on the duration, scale and cost of a campaign. Ambitions vary. Country A may wish to effect fundamental political change and be prepared to stand the cost of doing so. Country B will be prepared to take part, but will wish to exit as soon as it decently can. Country A is prepared to take substantial casualties to achieve its aims. Country B emphatically is not, and will give instructions to its commanders which limit their freedom of action, for instance to undertake 'offensive operations' or to move outside an agreed area, either absolutely or without consultation; both limiting the freedom of action of the overall commander to organise his force to achieve the maximum military effect in a timely way. This may not matter in a relatively benign situation; its importance grows as a situation deteriorates.

It can get worse. All countries have their own politics, will have justified participation to their electorates in different ways, and will have their own narrative. When these get out of kilter with events on the ground, irrational decisions can result. A 'liberation' narrative can inhibit thinking through the legal reality of responsibility for maintaining order in an 'occupied' territory or, even more damagingly, in refusing to recognise a growing insurgency and the need to respond to it. A country which justified participation as peacekeeping may have difficulty in explaining to its electorate why armoured vehicles and attack helicopters are necessary to maintain their force's security. At the other end of an operation, countries which wish to exit will want to declare victory and leave, defining victory in their own terms; perfectly understandable given the different levels of ambition with which they commenced.

One might think that these are problems peculiar to coalition operations – to ad hoc groupings of the 'willing', and that in a long-standing alliance, such as NATO, with complex mechanisms to grind down national differences to a lowest common denominator and to agree objectives, they would be less. Well, they might be, if the lowest common denominator did not make the objectives so broad as to be meaningless, and if indeed the operation order arrived prior to the operation commencing rather than three months later as occurred in Kosovo; and if individual countries did not insist, in formal terms or otherwise, in putting national caveats on their force's participation. I point no fingers at anyone on this. Even in Kosovo, with a British officer commanding the NATO force, while the British combat brigade was relatively unconstrained, I retained national control of some supporting force elements and had to refer back to London to release them to NATO. In Iraq, moving out of our divisional area required permission from London. I was in command on the one occasion when we did so, deploying a battlegroup to the area south of Baghdad during the massive corps operation to retake Fallujah. It was the right thing to do, but it caused such political fallout in London that it was never repeated.

And so far, I have mentioned only the military elements of external participating nations. What of the politics in the country within which one is operating and to whose government one hopes to return the security file? In the Balkan operations we learned gradually to write international agreements of extreme precision to define the duties, freedoms and constraints of both the intervening force and the domestic government which could then be imposed, by force if necessary, with the sometimes reluctant acquiescence of the receiving government. In Iraq and Afghanistan, with domestic governments which were nascent or limited in their reach, the situation is significantly more complex. A UN resolution may provide very broad powers for an international force, but a domestic government which wishes to retain power has to offer something beyond blood, sweat and tears to its people. It has to be able to deliver security and promise future prosperity. It needs to deliver on its promises on jobs, health and education. It has to justify the way security is delivered, both by its own forces and by those intervening, and to say something about the duration of the campaign and the exit point of a foreign force. In a major stabilising or counter-insurgency operation it will also supply an increasing percentage of the force, in numbers if not effectiveness, and will expect an increasing say in how the force is used. The surge in Iraq was very largely Iraqi. Charge of the Knights in Basra reflected Maliki's political imperatives rather than the Coalition's military ones which were working to a different timescale.

So a wise general, regardless of the formalities of the agreements within which he is working, will forge close relationships with, and understand the difficulties of, the politician with whom he is working. Not always easy, particularly over issues such as so-called collateral damage (an issue in Afghanistan, but also highly emotive in Baghdad in my time) and when dealing with the enemy: witness the tensions which arose in Iraq over the 'Sons of Iraq' programme or in Afghanistan over talking to the Taliban. 'Why would I want a pet crocodile?' was the cry of the redoubtable Dr Bassima.[2]

The risks of all this are clear: divergent political objectives can result in incoherent behaviour within theatre which risk the success of the whole operation. So what? National operations today are a very low percentage of the whole. Even the US, with all its power, recognises that if there is one thing worse than operating with allies it is working without them.

I can't propose any magic bullets, but three things seem very clear. The first is that objectives, and the key freedoms and constraints, need to be agreed at national political levels if military commanders in theatre, whether supported or supporting, are not to be placed in impossible positions. There needs to be an effective process for this to occur in coalitions as well as alliances, and it needs to be one which provides for changing situations by regular and real consultation based on hard-nosed and honest assessments of the situation.

The second is the need to integrate resources effectively in theatre both by minimising formal limits on forces and by encouraging a joined-up approach. National fiefdoms may be effective in benign scenarios. They are dangerous in demanding ones. There is more on this under ways and means.

The third is the need to manage the politics of an evolving campaign, and therefore the media. This is absolutely not about spin. It is about substance and credibility. There has to be a credible plan to achieve success, with realistic timescales, and an understanding that the whole process is fraught with difficulty and that there will be good days and bad, good weeks and bad weeks. But, as Petraeus used to say, 'difficult is not impossible', and this applies to the political as much as the military aspects of a campaign. Petraeus put huge effort into explaining what he was doing to his own politicians and public: 60 per cent of Congress visited Iraq in the summer of 2007, and not only were given the Petraeus view but were sent out to Forward Operating Bases to talk to US and Iraqi soldiers and civilians. We, the British, need to be better about this.

---

2 Dr Bassima al-Saadi, secretary to the Iraqi Committee for National Reconciliation.

Ways

I do not think (but I may be wrong) there is much dispute today about the overarching approach towards a demanding stabilisation operation. There is, or should be, general acceptance that the provision of relatively high levels of security is a precondition for progress, but that this needs to be accompanied by commensurate improvements in governance and in economic conditions if it is to stick. The major differences in view seem to me to be far more about the relationship between ends and means (the resources required to fulfil the objectives set) than about ways (how those resources are used), but these are, or should be, shaped by ideas on ways. What do I mean?

If you accept that providing security to a population is essential to gaining and securing their support then you are accepting both a requirement for numbers and the time to train them, on the assumption that no Western army or coalition can or should alone employ the numbers required to provide security to a population in a high threat area in anything other than a very small country for a short period of time. You are also accepting the requirement to mentor and monitor, with the force requirements and force protection issues which go with this.

If you accept that security is about law as much as order then you need to consider police, judges, gaols and legal process as much as soldiers. I am not sure that we have taken this aspect of stabilisation seriously enough. Soldiers provide the framework within which policemen enforce the law. What then is the right mix of soldiers and policemen? Who trains them with what objectives? And within the police what are the responsibilities of the officers and the rank and file? What can they be in a society where literacy levels are very low? Are policemen best local? Or best from elsewhere in the country to lessen the risk of being at the point of corruption? Whatever the answer it will be different in each country and it will not be a straight Western model based on the office of constable.

If you accept that governance needs to improve, how is this best done? The answer should be both local and effective, but in Iraq we have encouraged devolution in a naturally highly centralised state and in Afghanistan we have sought to increase the power of the central state in a naturally decentralised country. At the risk of gross generalisation, flat countries are naturally more centralised than mountainous ones for pretty obvious reasons. Whatever the model, both local and central government needs to be effective. Again, I am not sure that we have done enough to record and study how limited resources are best used in a second or third world health, agriculture or education sector; not to impose but to encourage best practice.

Finally, if you accept that economic progress needs to match progress in security then you have, I think, to accept that money may be spent 'inefficiently' in the short term but that you should mitigate this by embedding short-term projects within longer-term ones.

So what?

A common understanding of what we are trying to achieve seems to me the most effective way of achieving the unity of effort required for anything like effective stabilisation operations. The military do this in staff colleges, but this is not solely or even largely a military problem.

Means

There seem to me to be three or four areas where the requirement for means is still not sufficiently understood. And I'll take as read the resources on which the media normally and not unfairly focus: helicopters and armoured vehicles.

The first is the requirement for *mass*. Historical analysis shows that in an intensive counter-insurgency campaign you need 20 to 25 security force personnel per 1,000 head of population; 25,000 for a million; 250,000 for 10 million; 500,000 for 20 million. Before you baulk, this is not necessary everywhere or forever, nor is the level of expertise required uniform. You just need to be better than the opposition. But the numbers do say a number of things. You cannot provide them from outside the country. You must provide an effective training organisation, together with the institutions – the C2 and personnel and logistic chains – to support it. You must invest in officers. You must invest in time. Rushing is not a recipe for success. Iraq holds many lessons here.

The second is for adequate *command and control*. This is not just about numbers but it is about organisation and clarity of responsibility. We overface tactical commanders equipped with small headquarters designed for a much smaller and different range of problems. This is as true for the theatre level as it is for a British brigade in Basra and Helmand. The same man should not be required to deal both with the tactical battle and with the politics and coalition management required of a theatre commander.

The third is the requirement for expertise in the *comprehensive approach*. We have too many projects and not enough programmes, too many programmes and not enough sector plans. We spend money disproportionately on security, and fail to train and resource the civil agents who will enable the progress in administration and economics which will sustain whatever security progress is made. I think less may be more here, but they need to be appropriately qualified and trained. And they really need to be local.

Last and most important is the requirement for *time* and *political will*, all of which links back to the objectives with which we started.

Summary

What does all this mean for my British general? I emphasise three things. He should demand, within the limits of democratic governance, that the orders he receives down the national chain are coincident with the orders he will receive from the coalition or alliance military chain within which he is working. He should recognise that he is working within a larger campaign within which his success or failure is but one element. But, thirdly, within that it is critically important that the ends, ways and means are in balance, and that the realities of what he can do are understood both nationally and within the theatre chain of command.

Chapter 16

Basra 2008: Operation Charge of the Knights

Richard Iron – 18 November 2008

Prelude: 1 December 2007 to 24 March 2008

By December 2007 the accommodation with Jaysh al-Mahdi in Basra had been in force for three months. From a British perspective things were going well: our forces were out of the city and were now mostly concentrated at the Contingency Operating Base (COB) at Basra Airport. Attacks against the COB had dropped to almost zero; and our convoy moves, mostly to the Iranian border and notified to the militia in advance, were similarly spared attack. Under the scheme agreed with Jaysh al-Mahdi, 70 or so Sadrist prisoners were being released in groups of two to five, each signing an oath of compliance that they would not again take up arms. Compared to levels of violence against British forces earlier in the year, before withdrawal from Basra Palace, this was a remarkable turnaround.

But the situation in Basra City was more difficult. Although Iraqi Security Forces under General Mohan al-Furayji had nominal control after we left, they were unable to challenge Jaysh al-Mahdi's rule of terror over much of Basra's population: the Iraqi Army was insufficiently strong and the police was thoroughly penetrated by the militias. Since we had lost many of our intelligence sources when we left the Basra Palace, we had much less understanding of the atmospherics in the city. So, when in December 2007 we received reports that 40 women had been raped and murdered in the city, the general assumption in the COB was an outbreak of immoral criminality, rather than the reality of Jaysh al-Mahdi exerting its power through terror by imposing extremist Islamicist law on women they deemed inappropriately dressed.

In early January 2008, some of General Mohan's troops found a lock-up in Basra filled with rockets and sophisticated IEDs, the weapons of choice for Jaysh al-Mahdi attacks on Coalition forces. The Iraqi Army confiscated them and arrested two people. Within two hours an Iraqi Army convoy was hijacked and two police stations were overrun by Jaysh al-Mahdi fighters. Almost immediately, Sheikh Harith, the head of the Office of the Martyr Sadr (OMS), the political wing of Jaysh al-Mahdi, phoned General Mohan to explain the people the Iraqi Army had arrested were good people and the weapons were for self defence … and if they could all be released then the convoy and the police stations would be freed. The Iraqi Security Forces were so weak in Basra at the time that Mohan felt he had no choice but to comply with these demands.

Through January and February 2008 the situation started to deteriorate. The last Jaysh al-Mahdi prisoner was released on 5 January; subsequently, attacks on the British base at the COB grew dramatically. For example, on 31 January there were four separate rocket attacks, one of which consisted of 23 rockets. Major General Graham Binns, the British divisional commander at the time, noted the attacks were becoming 'irritating'. Casualties were few, despite the number of attacks, since great effort had been expended on protection against rocket attacks, including encasing every serviceman's bed space in concrete, balloon-mounted surveillance of potential firing points, and radar-controlled Phalanx guns designed for ship defence to shoot down incoming missiles.

Such attacks on the British at the airport were expensive for Jaysh al-Mahdi. Although weapons were supplied from Iran, smuggling them across the border was a commercial activity that sustained Marsh Arab communities. So militia members had to buy from the weapons smugglers; a typical Iranian-made 107 mm rocket[1] cost about $400. A major attack on the COB would thus have cost in the region of $10,000 for the rockets alone.

One of the unfortunate and unforeseen consequences of the British accommodation with Jaysh al-Mahdi was that it permitted them unhindered access to cash for purchase of weapons, since they had effective control of Basra's commerce. Although corruption had probably always been present, it had been limited by the presence of Iraqi Government authority and balanced by competing organisations. So, for example, the main port at Umm Qasr had three police forces operating within it – the port police, the customs police and the local police – each limiting the corruption of the others. Jaysh al-Mahdi expended great effort to gain control of the port through intimidation, replacing all three police forces by one they manipulated. This permitted them to raise considerable sums; for example, each truck driver had to pay US$60 to get in and out of the port, raising up to US$30,000 per day for the militia. This cash was then available to support the Sadrist insurgency, not just in Basra but across southern Iraq and in Sadr City in Baghdad.

On 11 February, British journalist Richard Butler was kidnapped by militia members from the Sultan Hotel in downtown Basra despite, so he thought, having agreement to interview Jaysh al-Mahdi leaders. During subsequent negotiations for his release, it became clear that Jaysh al-Mahdi was in fact a myriad of insurgent groups: there was mainstream Jaysh al-Mahdi which was broadly moderate, and there were more extreme groups such as the Leagues of the Righteous and Lords of the Martyrs, which we described as 'special groups'. These were certainly Sadrist and contained many hard-line members of Jaysh al-Mahdi, but their loyalties seemed to be split between Moqtada and Iran. We dealt with mainstream Jaysh al-Mahdi, whom we characterised as the 'peace party', while the more radical elements were the 'war party'. We were convinced the peace party genuinely sought Butler's release, but in an illustration of where power within the militia truly lay, they were unable to secure his release from the war party. Butler was eventually rescued by force two months later by the Iraqi Army during Operation Charge of the Knights.

On 19 February, Mohan admitted for the first time that the situation with Jaysh al-Mahdi had become untenable and confrontation was inevitable. At least part of the motivation was the hardening political stance of Prime Minister Maliki. Previously he had depended on Jaysh al-Mahdi's support to keep his coalition in power, limiting Iraqi Government support for previous British attempts to confront the militia, especially before and during Operation Sinbad in 2006. But this time was to be different: Maliki's situation was much stronger; he was prepared to put his own political capital on the line in the forthcoming confrontation; and he pressured Mohan to action.

Mohan asked me to help develop the plan for the inevitable battle ahead. We already had a security plan for Basra, developed by my predecessor Andy Bristow, which bore many similarities to the security framework for Belfast in the 1970s–1980s, including a number of fixed vehicle check points around the city and plans for the development of a number of company and battalion bases to create a security force presence in militia urban heartlands. This became the basis for a concept whose principal aim was to create an impression of overwhelming Iraqi Government strength in the city, to the extent that no militia would wish to engage in a contest with it. We would build this impression of strength by increasing the number of bases and check points through the city; increasing the numbers of forces and improving their quality; and by increasing the quantity of heavy weapons available to the Iraqi Army. Although Mohan was under no illusions about the

---

1   The 107mm Haseb rocket is an Iranian version of the Chinese Type 63 107mm rocket.

use of armour in urban guerrilla warfare, tanks are a powerful symbol of authority that would reinforce his position of strength. Simultaneously, the plan required much greater control of the border with Iran through significant increase in Iraqi Army in the border area.

Only when we had built our strength would we confront the militias directly. We envisaged a period of several months of preparing the conditions for success, followed in the summer of 2008 by a six-week period for a weapons amnesty, and then a series of searches targeted at militia weapons caches starting in July or August 2008. Our intention was that the Iraqi Army should bear the burden of the operation. The police were considered to be thoroughly infiltrated by the militia and open to intimidation. The Army, however, was still respected as a national institution; once the militias had been defeated we thought we could then rebuild the police.

We stressed that offensive operations should be against all or any armed elements, and not specifically against Jaysh al-Mahdi. We hoped to exploit the divisions that had appeared in Jaysh al-Mahdi and reinforce what we categorised as the moderates. If we singled out the radical elements for attack, then it was likely the whole militia would unite against us (Arabic proverb: defend my brother, right or wrong). In this way, the proposed plan attempted to rebuild the accommodation with Jaysh al-Mahdi, busily unravelling as moderate elements of the militia were being sidelined by radicals.

Mohan and I knew we would need significant support to make the plan work: political, military and financial. Without it the Iraqi Army was just too weak to confront anybody. Support of this kind could only come from Baghdad, so Mohan asked me to engineer a meeting with General Petraeus so we could make our case. I was fortunately able to bypass the chain of command and make contact with Colonel Pete Mansoor, Petraeus's executive officer. I forwarded our one-page concept of operations and requested a meeting with the general.

David Petraeus acted with typical decisiveness. He organised a meeting in Baghdad with all interested parties – both Iraqi and Coalition – including Mowaffak al-Rubaie, the Iraqi National Security Adviser. So on 5 March 2008, Mohan and I found ourselves in one of Saddam's old banqueting suites in Baghdad, in front of an audience of senior Iraqi and Coalition officials, trying to persuade them to release the resources we needed for our Basra plan.

It was a bad-tempered meeting. The Iraqi officials tried to undermine Mohan's arguments, implying Basra wasn't that bad and the problem was simply Mohan's lack of grip. The Americans were not at all keen to divert resources to the south when they were planning a major offensive against al-Qaeda in Mosul. But Petraeus brought the meeting round and convened a joint Iraqi–Coalition committee that was to analyse what on our shopping list could be provided, and report back in two weeks.

The follow-on meeting was on Friday, 21 March 2008. The results of the committee (on which I served as Mohan's representative) were rather better than I expected. But it was all irrelevant. Prime Minister Maliki had already decided to intervene personally, flew to Basra on Monday, 24 March, and ordered Mohan to start the operation immediately.

Operation Charge of the Knights: 25 March to 7 May 2008

The operation started badly. Although Maliki had ordered two additional Iraqi infantry battalions to Basra, there were still insufficient troops to succeed against Jaysh al-Mahdi, who resisted the Iraqi Army's early operations to assume control of some of the smaller estates in Basra City. None of the preconditions that Mohan thought necessary for success was in place. One of the slides we had prepared for the 5 March meeting said that with the right conditions the confrontation would be short and quick; if we got the conditions wrong it would be a long and difficult fight; so it was to prove.

On Thursday 27 March, Jaysh al-Mahdi launched their main counterattack. Subsequently, Basra police chief General Jalil claimed they mounted 28 simultaneous dawn attacks against police and army posts in the City. Several fell, including a number of the partly built company and battalion bases in the City. It was the misfortune of the newly formed and trained 3rd Brigade of the 14th Division that it occupied the most recently built bases, closest to the Jaysh al-Mahdi heartlands of Hyyaniyah and al-Quibla, and therefore it had to face the greatest violence. The brigade effectively collapsed. It is difficult to estimate casualties, but Mohan thought about 1,200 men deserted that day.

The militia sustained a high level of attacks against the Iraqi Security Forces for several weeks. There was no shortage of militia weapons; when we eventually cleared their strongholds several weeks later there were still major stocks of rockets, IEDs and ammunition as yet unused. We also had reports of Jaysh al-Mahdi fighters coming to Basra from across southern Iraq to fight the Iraqi Security Forces. It is possible that they were able to field up to 5,000 armed fighters by the end of the first week of the operation.

News of the Iraqi Government's reverse in Basra spread across the global media almost immediately.[2] Maliki faced the possibility of a very high profile defeat in what was the first major Iraqi security initiative since the 2003 invasion. This could clearly not be allowed to happen, so the Iraqi Government flooded resources into the city. This included $100 million for development, and several Government ministries temporarily established themselves in Basra Palace.

More important in the short term was the redeployment of the headquarters of the 1st Iraqi Division, its 1st Brigade (the most combat experienced in the Iraqi Army), and several other elements of the division. Not only did they provide much needed stiffening for the Iraqi Army in Basra, they brought with them their USMC mentors and trainers – the so-called Military Transition Teams (MiTTs). These are teams of about 30–40 Coalition forces, embedded in an Iraqi division, brigade or battalion headquarters. Their main function is to maintain the professionalism of Iraqi units and assist in any way possible. The MiTT commander is the personal mentor to the Iraqi commander; most establish close and trusted relationships. Since they have access to Coalition secure communications and intelligence, MiTTs are also the conduit to provide Coalition airpower and surveillance to Iraqi forces.

The British decided relatively early (I think in 2005 or 2006) not to embed MiTTs in the Iraqi Army in Basra, although we were prepared to do so when Iraqi forces were temporarily detached to Baghdad. The argument against MiTTs at the time was that we could not guarantee their protection; since we were so short of troops we could not provide them dedicated support at the same time as running our own operations. In retrospect this was a poor decision: resourcing MiTTs should have been the *first* use of our troops, before our own operations. 14th Division in Basra was on its own in the first few days of Charge of the Knights, without access to Coalition airpower or surveillance. It is doubtful its 3rd Brigade would have collapsed if embedded MiTTs could have provided it with full access to Coalition firepower.

Concurrent with the arrival of 1st Iraqi Division was the establishment in Basra of the Coalition's Corps forward headquarters, under Major General George Flynn, together with a large number of Corps assets, including armed Predator drones, attack helicopters and considerable staff effort to assist in all aspects of operations in Basra. The Coalition could not allow Maliki to fail, so the

---

2   For example, Hilder 2008.

Corps' main effort was switched from Mosul to Basra, supporting it like any division on the main effort. It is unfortunate the media at the time chose to represent this as the Americans coming to save the Brits in Basra; they were American because the Corps Headquarters in Iraq was provided by the US 18th Airborne Corps. They provided invaluable assistance, but it was always a joint UK–US effort to support the Iraqis who actually did the fighting.

By the beginning of the second week of Operation Charge of the Knights the situation had stabilised sufficiently for the Iraqi Army to take the offensive once again. On Monday 31 March and Tuesday 1 April we had to persuade General Mohan not to use the reinforcing 1st Division in a direct attack on the Jaysh al-Mahdi stronghold in Hyyaniyah, but instead use them more circumspectly in a general operation to re-open the main arteries through the city and enable our own freedom of movement. We were concerned that, if the Iraqi Army's most experienced brigade was defeated in its first action, we would have few options left.

So the main Iraqi Security Force attack was launched on Wednesday 2 April. All available forces were involved, including a newly arrived National Police brigade, the remaining forces of 14th Division, and the trustworthy elements of the Basra Police. For the first time, we had access to plentiful Coalition airpower, with seemingly endless attack helicopters and armed Predators over Basra. The militia fought bravely but not intelligently: they defended in the open against Iraqi Security Force attacks to clear their road blocks. We found it easy to identify them with drones, and then destroy them one by one with Hellfire missiles. For example, in the al-Latif area of northern Basra, the militia attempted to block the northward movement of the National Police brigade by establishing road blocks and fighting positions around Qarmat Ali Bridge on the main north–south route into Basra. We quickly identified their headquarters and resupply centre in al-Latif school, and that they used a taxi to carry ammunition to their various defensive positions. We simply followed the taxi on the drone camera until we had identified all the positions, and then destroyed them with missiles.

By the end of the day, it was obvious to all who had won. The Iraqi Security Forces had captured all their objectives and the main routes were clear. Although Jaysh al-Mahdi still occupied their strongholds in the urban ghettoes, the initiative had swung dramatically to the Government forces. Late in the afternoon, we started to hear a rumour that Prime Minister Maliki intended to impose a seven-day ceasefire at midnight. I discussed this with Colonel 'Cas' Castellvi, the USMC chief mentor to the Iraqi commander of 1st Division; we agreed a ceasefire could be a disaster. Our view was that we had gained the military initiative and needed to sustain it: if we gave the militia time to reorganise into an urban guerrilla organisation, rather than fight in the open, it could potentially be a long and costly battle to clear their strongholds as we would find it difficult to use our firepower. But I lost my argument with Mohan. His position was that the Maliki had ordered it and who was he to question the Prime Minister.

As it turned out, the Prime Minister was absolutely right and I was absolutely wrong. The ceasefire eventually extended to 11 days, and it was a period of extensive information operations and political activity. Tribal and other leaders were brought to Basra Palace to swear allegiance to the Government of Iraq on television. On the way out, I saw they were each given a pink or light blue plastic suitcase which was so heavy they could hardly carry it, loaded with 'gifts'. In a reprise of our initial plan we ran a weapons amnesty, offering money for people to hand in their weapons. We found the most effective method was to offer the money to the sheikhs: they then used their influence to persuade people to give up their weapons to them in exchange for money.

It was a ceasefire in that neither Jaysh al-Mahdi nor Government forces launched ground attacks against each other's areas. But the militia continued rocket and mortar attacks unabated on our bases, especially Basra Palace and the Shatt al-Arab Hotels, both Iraqi bases, and on the British at the COB. In our turn, we continued to seek them out by air, and to destroy rocket and mortar teams as we found them.

One of the smaller but, for the British, more important results of the 2 April operation was the way it changed General Mohan's view on using Coalition forces in the city. He had previously agreed with the British position that it was our presence in the city that was the cause of much of the violence in earlier years, and was a strong supporter of the British move out of the city. 'Your presence' he said, 'confused the nationalism of the Iraqi Shia.' But two things surprised Mohan on 2 April. The first was the professionalism, at all levels, of the USMC-trained and mentored 1st Division, compared to the British-trained but not mentored 14th Division. The second was the sight of a USMC MiTT driving through the city centre in their armoured vehicles, being cheered by local Iraqis: at last someone was coming to help bring peace to the city. That evening he asked me to arrange for British MiTTs to embed into 14th Division in Basra, so they had support equivalent to 1st Division. In fact, Brigadier Julian Free, commander of 4th Mechanized Brigade, had already pre-empted the request, gained approval from the Ministry of Defence, and completely reconfigured his brigade to provide fully equipped and manned MiTTs. Within 36 hours British forces were back all over Basra, fully embedded into the Iraqi Army.

After the ceasefire ended on Saturday 12 April 2008 we relaunched operations by clearing al-Quibla, a large urban area in south-west Basra. Following the previous shaping operations, the clearance was easy. We went in overwhelming strength with two brigades supported by tanks. Troops announced their presence on vehicle-mounted loudspeakers, telling people to put their weapons outside their houses and then stay indoors. There were isolated instances of shooting, but nothing much. There was plenty of evidence of prepared defences, including many 'daisy-chains' of IEDs, but very few militia were prepared to fight. There were no serious Security Force casualties, and we were welcomed by the local population: there was a palpable sense of liberation from Jaysh al-Mahdi misrule which was replicated in every area we cleared.

As the operation progressed through the day, Iraqi bomb disposal teams cleared IEDs, generally with pliers since the bombs were simple, command-wire initiated, and not booby-trapped. Sophisticated American-supplied IED clearance equipment, including 'wheelbarrows', remained in the back of their HMMWVs. Weapons of all kinds – RPGs, IEDs, mortars, artillery shells, machine guns, Iranian-made 107mm and 122mm rockets – were collected from doorsteps and taken to central points in al-Quibla before removal to the Basra Operations Command. More militia weapons were found underground in hidden dumps, pointed out by local residents. Other residents pointed out militia members who were swiftly arrested and questioned. Iraqi Army engineers built strong points at predetermined spots in al-Quibla, mostly on road junctions. By the end of the day, the Iraqi Army was in complete control of al-Quibla. The nascent long-term security infrastructure of vehicle checkpoints and Security Force bases had already been established, occupied by a force that steadily reduced over the next few months from three battalions to one as confidence grew.

The next few weeks were the same. Each day, Mohan launched another clearance operation; most were relatively modest, nibbling away at small urban areas, but there were a number of major operations to clear the main urban estates such as the Hyyaniyah on 19 April and Khamsa Meel (Five Mile Market) on 25 April. The Hyyaniyah was the centre of Jaysh al-Mahdi support: a mass of close-built housing, established by Saddam for Marsh Arabs dispossessed by his draining the marshes. He deliberately broke up their tribal and social structure on relocation to undermine their resistance. The result of such social engineering was that there were no traditional structures to compete with the populist and popular message of the Sadrist movement.

The Coalition conducted intensive aerial surveillance in the days before the Hyyaniyah operation, and was able to provide a detailed map to Iraqi forces showing the locations of militia defences, including their IED daisy-chains. There had been heated discussion between Mohan and Major General Flynn on tactics. Mohan was keen to attack from multiple points to overwhelm any defence and create an immediate impression of great Iraqi Army strength. Flynn, on the other hand, wanted to tackle the area in a more systematic fashion, moving from north to south, to make it easier to define the forward line of our own troops at any stage, so air support was less likely to engage friendly forces. Flynn always won such arguments before the operation because he could threaten withdrawal of Coalition airpower; but Mohan countered on the day by changing the plan, taking advantage of a lack of resistance to seize the centre of the Hyyaniyah with his own close protection team and four T72 tanks well before the fighting brigades had reached it. There was resistance, but it was uncoordinated. Fighting positions didn't support each other and were easily dealt with individually. IED daisy-chains weren't covered by fire, and were simply isolated and cleared. At the time it felt as if the officers had fled and left the battle to the section commanders. We subsequently found this to be the case, most senior militia members going to Iran during the ceasefire period.

Prime Minister Maliki departed for Baghdad shortly after the success of 2 April. He left Minister of Defence Abdul Qadir al-Obeidi as Deputy Prime Minister with several other ministers, including Interior and Justice, all based at Basra Palace. Mohan as military commander remained at his headquarters at the Shatt al-Arab hotel, although he attended the daily evening meeting run by Abdul Qadir at Basra Palace. Abdul Qadir had plenipotentiary powers over all military and civilian aspects of the campaign reminiscent of Templer in Malaya. Although there was plenty of squabbling between individual Iraqi ministers and commanders, there was clear direction from the top and Abdul Qadir did a good job in ensuring unity both of command and effort throughout the operation.

More reinforcements arrived in April, in particular the 27th Iraqi Brigade – a Sunni brigade. Mohan tasked them with securing Hyyaniyah, and later al-Quibla as well. I was interested to see how they managed in such a strong Shia area, but there was surprisingly little tension between them and the population. Mohan's motivation was that they would be less likely to be corrupted or intimidated by remaining Shia militia elements, and he judged they were all Iraqi first and Shia or Sunni second.

The last area to be cleared in Basra was al-Latif, in north Basra, on 6 May. Again, there was no resistance, more weapons found, and more assistance from the local population. This marked the end of the offensive phase of Charge of the Knights, and although there continued to be clearance operations outside Basra City, in particular in al-Qurna to the north and in the marshes, we all felt the most dangerous, if not most difficult, job had been done. Mohan left Basra the following day, victorious, for a new job in Baghdad and was replaced by General Mohammed al-Huwaidi who had commanded 14th Division throughout the operation.

There has been some media speculation that the operation was planned jointly by the Iraqis and Americans, neither of whom informed the British. This is not true; it was Maliki's initiative alone and the US didn't know about it either. Petraeus only found out after the Friday 21 March meeting: immediately beforehand, al-Rubaie approached me and told me 'I have very good news for Basra; very good news for Monday.' He couldn't explain further, because he hadn't told 'the big boss' yet, gesturing to Petraeus on the other side of the table. He told him after dinner, on the terrace, where Petraeus tried to argue against it, but to no avail.

It is not possible to discern with certainty Maliki's motives for launching the operation early. Certainly the political landscape had changed to the extent that he no longer relied on Sadrist support. He had been pressuring Mohan since early November to take action to take control of Basra. I personally believe he misunderstood the situation in Basra, and had adopted the same position as the British: the problem was one of criminality not insurgency, akin to Palermo not Beirut. At the 5 March Baghdad meeting, his security adviser al-Rubaie questioned Mohan closely over his depiction of insurgency in Basra, telling him he thought he exaggerated the problem which was, at its root, criminal. At a National Security Meeting on Wednesday 19 March, al-Rubaie characterised the problems in Basra as being caused by four to five families only, a direct reference to the Palermo not Beirut analogy. Nothing could have been further from the truth: Jaysh al-Mahdi was an extremist movement that controlled Basra by force; its strength was in the poorest areas of Basra, and although Moqtada's own religious beliefs were not extreme, Sadrist militias used extremist religion to gain and maintain their control over the population of Basra through terror. Doubtless many joined the militia for power and wealth (it is noticeable how many fled when the going became tough during Charge of the Knights) but that is standard in any insurgency.

Consolidating Success: 8 May to End November 2008

The period following General Mohammed's assumption of the command of security in Basra was characterised by consolidation of control, although clearance operations continued in the rural areas to the north and in the al-Faw peninsula. Mohammed spent much time personally instructing his commanders and soldiers on the difference between what they were doing now – framework operations – and what they were doing before – offensive operations. It required a different attitude, protecting civilians and maintaining their support for the Security Forces, rather than chasing insurgents. He personally followed up civilian reports of abuse at checkpoints. He asked me to assist by running study days for the brigades on the differences in doctrine between 'clear' and 'hold and build' phases, in which I was ably assisted by my friend and counter-insurgency specialist Dr Daniel Marston, who was visiting at the time.

General Mohammed was in no doubt that, although the militias had been defeated during Charge of the Knights, the threat to Basra was not over. There was evidence of further training of Basrawi insurgents in Iran, as well as a steady flow of munitions across the Iranian border. It was clear to me that the new threat would not be like the last: it would not be an open insurgency with militias brazenly challenging Government control; instead it was much more likely, initially, to take the form of an urban terror network. The situation was rather similar to Northern Ireland post-Operation Motorman in 1972 and the ending of interment in 1975, which resulted in the Provisional IRA adopting an underground cellular structure. In Basra, we felt the threat would exist as long as Iran had an aggressive foreign policy towards Iraq.

We therefore proposed a long-term Iraqi counter-insurgency plan for the Basra Operations Command, which we described as a 20-year plan. It was designed to encompass what we were trying to do: secure Basra Province against insurgency so as to enable political and economic development to undermine support for anti-Government violence. We decided on three lines of operation:

- strengthen the security framework in Basra City to safeguard economic and political development;
- establish effective control of the border with Iran to limit the flow of insurgents, weapons and ideas;
- build an effective intelligence structure.

An important part of strengthening the security framework was the establishment of effective joint command of all security forces. This resulted in the British-led transformation of the Basra Operations Command from something akin to a medieval royal court to a modern, networked headquarters, with trained staff from all security services, including the police, border forces, Navy and Air Force. The British also led the information operations campaign to persuade insurgents who fled abroad not to come back, by publishing their photographs in the local media.

During the clear phase of Charge of the Knights a new Chief of Police was appointed: General Adil, a small punchy officer who made things happen. He had no interest in turning a blind eye to corruption or uncertain loyalty. At the beginning, he said 10 per cent of his force was absolutely committed and loyal whatever the circumstances; another 10 per cent was absolutely corrupt and disloyal; and the remaining 80 per cent would go with the prevailing current. Prior to Charge of the Knights, the prevailing current definitely flowed with Jaysh al-Mahdi. His concept was to reverse this by creating confidence that the law would be upheld. He did this by reorganising the entire police force in Basra Province, some 23,000 strong. He reduced to a minimum the individual detachments at the various police stations round the city and province, and organised the remaining manpower into battalions. He then twinned each new police battalion with a trusted and loyal Iraqi Army battalion; what he described as an older brother/younger brother relationship. The two battalions did nearly everything together, from manning checkpoints to conducting searches. It was remarkable how successful this simple solution was: whereas his predecessor Jalil had concentrated on getting rid of the corrupt 10 per cent and failed, due to militia influence in the Ministry of Interior responsible for manning, Adil managed to win over the 80 per cent and made the corrupt 10 per cent nearly irrelevant.

One of the greatest difficulties the Iraqi Army had in this period was understanding its position in law following Charge of the Knights. During the operation it was commonplace to arrest insurgents purely on intelligence information or suspicion without need for proof. They were interned, without trial. The Iraqis did this during the clear phase of the operation to take the heat out of the insurgency by removing insurgents from the streets. But afterwards, normal Iraqi law was re-established and there were strict time limits on how long Iraqi authorities could hold suspects without charging them. So the emphasis for the Security Forces had to switch from arresting on suspicion to gaining sufficient evidence to support prosecution. The Iraqi legal adviser and I spent many hours persuading Iraqi brigade commanders of their legal obligations, and how the situation had now changed after Charge of the Knights.

I was surprised by the quality of one legacy of British involvement in Iraq since 2003: a well-equipped Iraqi forensic laboratory with a competent staff fully trained by British specialists. The greatest difficulty we had, though, was in persuading both the Iraqi police and Army to preserve evidence at the scene of an incident, and call an Iraqi crime scene investigator. It is indicative of perhaps the dysfunctional approach of the British to the campaign in Basra: we spent great sums on establishing a twenty-first-century forensic capability but didn't train the Iraqi Army on how to exploit it to gain prosecutions under the law.

The border with Iran continued to be a problem. I had initially suggested to the Iraqis a physical barrier and had conducted surveys for how to construct it. Unfortunately the Iraqis had neither sufficient money to build the obstacle nor troops to man it. The British interest in the border was largely short term and parochial: what can we do, with our own troops, in the time available in each brigade's tour, rather than a long-term solution for the Iraqis to implement? Thus, by the summer of 2008 we were no further towards a long-term solution for the border than we had been six, 12 or 24 months previously.

Eventually the answer dawned on me when on leave in the south of France in August 2008. It is obvious in retrospect but the solution only came after nine months of my tour and when I was far away from the day-to-day business of counter-insurgency: the Marsh Arabs had neither religious nor ethnic reason to support Iranian meddling in Iraq; their motivation was mostly economic. As such, it should be possible to turn the Marsh Arabs as a community away from being conduits for Iran to being the primary defence against Iran. I was able to persuade General Mohammed that such an approach promised the best long-term option for control of the border, and he appointed the brigade commander whose area encompassed the border region to start an engagement with the Marsh Arabs.

So in September to November 2008 we ran a series of operations in the marshes. They were named after a quote from the 2nd Imam: he wished for a Jebel an-Naar (a mountain of fire) to appear on the Iranian border to keep the Persians at bay. The initial Jebel an-Naar operations were exploratory, to start overcoming the extreme suspicion of the Marsh Arabs towards Iraqi authority. These were people who for decades had been oppressed by the Iraqi Government, most recently by Saddam with his marsh draining and forced relocation programmes, and had no reason to trust the Iraqi Army. But they were also a community who had been starved of development: there were no medical centres, schools, mosques, electricity or clean water. So later operations, with great help from the US-led Multi-National Corps in Baghdad, brought medical, veterinary and other help to isolated communities, and eventually won their trust. In each case, operations were planned by embedded British officers at the Basra Operations Command, but wholly implemented by Iraqi forces, including the Iraqi Air Force who gave helicopter rides to Marsh Arab children for fun. The only disappointment was that we were unable to persuade the British command at the COB that this was an operation worth supporting, so assistance had to be provided directly by US forces from Baghdad.

Operation Jebel an-Naar was a model of how to do business in Iraq: Coalition know-how, organising capacity, and resources, but with a clear Iraqi lead to win over the Marsh Arabs. Admittedly we were very lucky in Basra: the Basra Operations Command had effective control over all Government Security Forces, a rare thing; General Mohammed was one of the most honest and open-minded generals in any army; and, despite everything that had gone on before, we British mentors were still greatly respected by our Iraqi peers and were therefore able to influence them effectively.

Conclusions

Whether or not we should have made the accommodation with Jaysh al-Mahdi in the summer of 2007 will doubtless continue to be a matter for debate. My own view is that we had little choice. By 2007 we had run out of strategic alternatives: the unpopularity of the war at home seemed to render impossible any other strategy requiring additional resources. Politically and strategically we had become de-linked from our ally the USA, and were both unable and unwilling to mirror their 2007 surge in Baghdad. Furthermore, there was not the necessary political support from the Iraqi Government to take action against Jaysh al-Mahdi; nor did we seem to have the political and strategic levers to gain that support. Ultimately, it was a strategic, not military, failing to be forced into a position where we had no choice but to adopt the course of action we did: otherwise we would have had to withdraw from Iraq under fire and taking casualties; a defeat obvious to all.

Nevertheless, the narrative that was developed to justify the decision to withdraw from the city contains a number of assertions that need to be examined.

The first assertion is that the insurgency was caused by what we might term 'reaction to the invader'. By late 2006 it had become accepted wisdom in the UK that it was us – the Coalition forces – who were the problem, rather than the militia. The evidence for this belief was in the statistics: 90 per cent of attacks were against us rather than Iraqi targets; so, the logic went, it's clear that if we weren't there then the problem would largely be over.

For example, in October 2006 the Chief of the General Staff, General Sir Richard Dannatt, said we should 'get ourselves out sometime soon because our presence exacerbates the security problems'.[3] It wasn't just the British: General Mohan, agreed our presence 'confused the nationalism of the Iraqi Shia'.[4] There was truth in both Richard Dannatt's and Mohan's insights. Our presence did provide a rallying cry for insurgents against us crusaders. But it wasn't just that simple. We also needed to view the problem through other lenses or from other viewpoints. If we had done this, we would have seen more clearly the contest for power between Shia militias and the democratically elected Government of Iraq; 90 per cent of attacks were against us because we were the only ones contesting control of the city on behalf of the Government. Once we left, we ceded not just British control, but the Government of Iraq's control too, whom we were supposed to be supporting. By looking at the problem through the single lens of the reaction to the invader, we lost sight of what we were really supposed to be doing: helping the legally constituted, democratically elected, Government of Iraq establish its legitimate authority in Basra.

One of the most important explanations for the British withdrawal from Basra City in 2007 was the characterisation of the problem as criminality rather than insurgency. The press was briefed that Basra was like Palermo, not Beirut, as if the problems were akin to feuding mafia families rather than a Hezbollah-style threat to Government.[5]

This narrative misinterprets the relationship between insurgency and criminality. In some way we thought of criminality as innocent, unconnected with insurgency; what in Northern Ireland we used to call 'decent honest crime'. For example, it was a common British view that smuggling helped to kick start the Basra economy and was therefore beneficial. For example, British naval commanders in Combined Task Force 158, an international naval task group responsible for security of the oil platforms in the North Arabian Gulf, told me they watched ships unloading stolen cars onto the al-Faw Peninsula for sale across Iraq. The Navy didn't do anything about it: it wasn't their job, and it was only smuggling; only crime. Once we left Basra City, the militia took control of the smuggling; so profits from smuggled cars went directly or indirectly to those who were trying to kill British and American servicemen.

Jaysh al-Mahdi was not a criminal enterprise whose principal aim was to make its leaders rich. It was an Islamicist insurgent group who used violence for political purposes, and enjoyed widespread loyalty and support from the mass of impoverished Shia living in urban ghettoes through the south of Iraq. It did, however, need large quantities of cash to support both its campaign of violence and its social services to the poor. As a result it indulged in widespread criminal activity, but this was not the aim of the organisation or its leaders, although some doubtless profited from the enterprise. Although it is impossible to be accurate, we estimated about 80 per cent of Jaysh al-Mahdi's total income came from Basra during the period of the accommodation.

There is a short postscript to the Palermo not Beirut narrative: when we started questioning captured Jaysh al-Mahdi insurgents during Charge of the Knights, one of the recurring themes was their training in Iran. Many of their trainers were Lebanese Hezbollah, returning experts to train

---

3   Mail editorial 2006.
4   Conversation with General Mohan in January 2008.
5   For example, Zavis 2007.

new insurgents under the aegis of the Revolutionary Guards. So not only was it not Palermo, it really *was* like Beirut.

We also failed to appreciate the depth of malign Iranian influence; or if we did we analysed it wrongly. As late as May 2008, the British Consul General in Basra described Iran's interest in Basra as entirely legitimate, likening it to the relationship between London and Paris. This was the wrong analogy. From what I saw, Iran's interest was entirely predatory: a better example would be the relationship between Berlin and Paris in 1940. The Iraqi Army's view on this was instructive: their formative experience as an Army was not 2003, or 1991; it was the eight year Iran–Iraq war in the 1980s. The vast majority of middle-ranking and senior officers harboured a visceral hatred of Iran. It doesn't matter whether they're Sunni or Shia: in their view, Iran was the principal threat to Iraq.

Although our intelligence throughout stressed the anti-Iranian credentials of Moqtada al-Sadr and his Jaysh al-Mahdi, the reality was that they were heavily dependent on Iran. It is inconceivable that Moqtada could run his organisation from Iran, train his insurgents in Iranian-run training camps, or provide them with Iranian-supplied weapons, without explicit support from Iranian Revolutionary Guards. The standard Iraqi officer view is that Iran's policy was to keep Iraq in a permanent state of weakness by maintaining a level of instability that would not cause it to implode but instead prevent it from growing in strength.

Iran supplied weapons continuously to Jaysh al-Mahdi from at least 2005 onwards. These were not small arms or explosives to make IEDs, with which Iraq was awash after the Saddamist era; instead they were primarily 107mm or 122mm rockets to attack Coalition bases, advanced anti-armour warheads to defeat our armoured vehicles, and sophisticated electronic circuitry to make up IED detection and firing mechanisms.

Finally, we also got it wrong by thinking we had to encourage Iraqi self-reliance. The British narrative went along the lines of:

- The Iraqi Army is now in charge, and we'll be soon gone.
- They need to learn to use their own systems and processes rather than relying on ours.
- If we keep on helping them, they'll never learn.

This narrative described the British concept of operations in Basra prior to Operation Charge of the Knights. It didn't matter what it said in the Divisional Operations Order about supporting the Iraqis; the reality was that by early 2008 they were effectively on their own. So, for example, the Iraqis were building strong-points, Belfast-style company bases, across the city. This was so Mohan could establish a security infrastructure and finally confront Jaysh al-Mahdi's control of the city. As in Belfast, the civil contractors were soon intimidated off site, leaving Iraqi Army engineers to complete the builds. They quickly ran out of resources, in particular Hesco bastions – the wire mesh frames which when filled with sand or rubble form the basis for defensive walls.

Mohan found he couldn't get more Hesco out of the labyrinthine Iraqi supply system, so he asked me to help. I knew we had 24 km of Hesco in our engineer resources yard, but I couldn't get the British to release any. The British answer was if we helped them now they'd never learn. Meanwhile, nearly every night Iraqi soldiers were being killed and injured guarding half-completed forts as Jaysh al-Mahdi tried to destroy them, fully understanding what these forts meant: if they were completed, the Iraqi Army would be able to wrest back control of the city from the militia. Not helping the Iraqi Army in their hour of need is not one of our proudest moments.

So much changed during Charge of the Knights; there was almost a complete reversal of our previous position. Not only did we provide them with Hesco bastions, Royal Engineers built them new strong-points. We created proper adviser teams, helped them to build joint operations centres, and worked with them out on the ground, sharing their dangers and discomforts. But I'm afraid not everything changed. There was still arrogance and hubris among the British. A sense of 'we're here to teach you so you'd better listen'. 'We understand; you don't.' When a senior Coalition officer, in front of all his staff, openly calls the Iraqi commander stupid, an idiot and worse, it gives permission for everyone else to disparage all Iraqis and their efforts.

It's all the more bewildering when you appreciate there was never any way we could fight a counter-insurgency in Basra *without* the Iraqi Army.

Basra is a city of about a million people. Were the British really trying to control that with three battalions, reducing down to one by the summer of 2007? Although originating in 1995 and updated in 2003, the Rand Corporation study into numbers needed for successful counter-insurgency is instructive:[6] you need about one security force per 50 of population. In Basra, we needed about 20,000 just to get the numbers to protect the population, not the 5,000 British troops or so we were prepared to deploy there. So we should have appreciated much earlier that the solution lay in combining British technology, training, firepower, logistics and advice with Iraqi manpower. Intellectually, we needed to view the operation in Basra as one which we fight jointly; not separately; not as us handing over to them; not as encouraging self-reliance; but as fighting it together, each contributing what we do best.

There was a British expression about the Iraqi Army, common in the divisional headquarters: 'they're our ticket out of here'. In some ways this is right. But it's also the wrong mindset. We build indigenous forces not so we can get out as quickly as we can, but so together we can actually win: combining their numbers and local acceptance with our capabilities. And once we've won, or have at least largely got the threat under control, we can then reduce our numbers. But it's a long-term project; it needs a long-term mindset, not the six-month viewpoint common on our operations.

Our model of forcing Iraqi self-reliance by not helping was completely wrong. We should have focused on winning the war.

---

6   Quinlivan 1995 and Quinlivan 2003. A more recent and arguably comprehensive study is Connable and Libicki 2010.

Chapter 17

The Psychological Impact of Operations in Iraq: What Has it Been, and What Can We Expect in the Future?

Simon Wessely[1] – 2 March 2010

Most of the contributions to this volume have concentrated on strategic, tactical and leadership issues around contemporary operations, including but not restricted to the UK deployment to Iraq (Operation Telic). However, in this contribution I wish to consider a different question. What, if anything, has been the psychological impact of those operations on those who served there? And what can we expect in the future?[2]

Why Did We Study the Impact of Operation Telic?

Many may be surprised to learn that, prior to Operation Telic, the UK Armed Forces had no robust mechanism by which they could measure the mental health of their personnel. Whilst the Defence Medical Services were able to collate the diagnoses of those who came forward to ask for help (see www.dasa.mod.uk), such data is unable to provide any insight into the health of the vast majority of personnel who do not come into contact with military health providers. The independent large-scale health surveillance programme, established and maintained by King's College London, to monitor the health impact of Operation Telic was thus a first for the UK Armed Forces. There were several reasons behind the decision to commission such a programme.

First and foremost was the legacy of the so called 'Gulf War Syndrome' saga. This chapter is not the place to provide a full account of the complex arguments about the ill-health effects associated with service in the Gulf in 1991.[3] We do, however, know that several years after that conflict a proportion, about one in five, of UK Service personnel who had taken part in Operation Granby began to report more symptoms of poor physical health than those who had not. The nature of this ill health remains obscure. We know that those who reported more symptoms were not more likely to experience any specific clear-cut outcomes, such as cancer, heart disease and so on, nor

1   The author gratefully acknowledges the assistance of Surgeon Commander Neil Greenberg, Royal Navy, in the first draft of this paper, and most of all the contribution of all the team at the King's Centre for Military Health Research and the Academic Centre for Defence Mental Health. It is a privilege to work with such a talented group of colleagues, especially when, as in this contribution, they let me take the credit for their endeavours.

2   I will include some selected references throughout the text. If readers wish to read the originals, all our papers can be found at http://www.kcl.ac.uk/kcmhr/pubdb. A good introduction is to be found at http://www.kcl.ac.uk/kcmhr/publications/10yearreport.pdf, although this does not cover most of our publications on Operations Telic and Herrick from 2006 onwards.

3   See Wessely 2006, 361, for a broad collection of review papers on the subject.

was their overall mortality increased. We also know that it was not due to clear-cut psychological injury, such as post-traumatic stress disorder (PTSD). However, in spite of considerable research into possible reasons for the ill-health effect, by our group and others, it has only been possible confidently to exclude possible causes, such as exposure to smoke pollution, depleted uranium and pesticides, rather than find one or more culprits. A question mark remained over the role played by other medical counter-measures, most particularly biological warfare vaccines, not least because of the gaps in medical record keeping.[4] Finally, no one knows when the increase in ill health observed not just in UK personnel, but also in Australia, Canada and most noticeably the USA, began. It may have been during the conflict, or perhaps some years later. We remain unsure if it reflected something that happened in the Gulf, or even before it. Or was it something that developed later as personnel returned, possibly influenced by media and cultural issues?

Whatever the possible causes of the Gulf War health effect, there is no doubt that the Gulf War Syndrome saga was a costly one. Many personnel undoubtedly felt sicker, and experienced a lower quality of life, as a result of the saga. It was costly in terms of war pensions, although our overall bill remains miniscule compared to that in the USA. And it was costly in terms of reputational damage to the MOD, who were, not unfairly, accused of being slow to react and unable to respond to the concerns expressed by personnel, families and the media.

Another important issue which focused the thoughts of senior MOD personnel, perhaps to a lesser extent, was the PTSD class action brought by ex-Service personnel against the MOD in 2001. Although it was successfully defended, this was achieved at a considerable cost (about £20 million). The case sensitised the MOD to the realisation that it was not sufficient to continue to simply provide high quality care for personnel injured or made sick in service. Thus both the Gulf War Syndrome experience and the PTSD case clarified that carrying out robust health surveillance was a necessity rather than a luxury. Without a pool of high quality data, the Armed Forces had been effectively at the mercy of those who might wish to speculate about longer-term health problems, including those that might develop after separation from service.

The result was the team at King's College London, which had been leading on research into the health effects of Operation Granby for some years, was asked to plan a large-scale epidemiological study of the possible effects of Operation Telic, to commence as soon as possible once the first stage of the operation was concluded, on the assumption that the campaign would effectively be a re-run of Operation Granby.

Why Do it That Way?

A few explanations are necessary at this point, given that many may not be familiar with the structure of medical research. Epidemiology is the study of illness in populations, rather than individuals – in this case the population under investigation is the UK Armed Forces. Epidemiologists study populations, rather than individuals, looking for overall trends in health, or for the risk factors which lead to people developing ill health when such factors might not be obvious from looking at individual sufferers. Lung cancer, for example, had been on the increase for many years, but it was

---

4   We are, however, more confident that the use of medical counter-measures, such as the anthrax vaccine before and during Operation Telic, has not been associated with either medium- or long-term side effects. This time we were able to use better data sources and also plan the appropriate studies from the start, instead of playing 'catch up' as happened after Granby. It is interesting, however, that concerns remain, largely because of the policy of making anthrax vaccine a 'special case', as opposed to including it within all the other routine vaccinations.

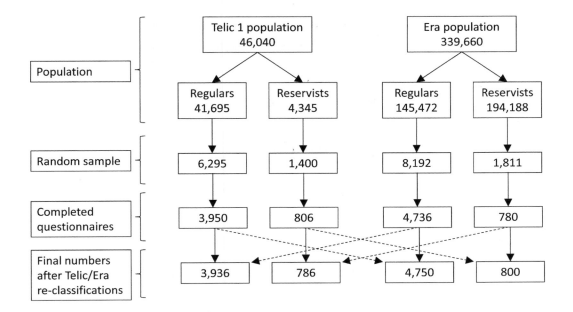

Figure 17.1 Study design

not until Doll and Hill carried out a survey of the smoking habits of British doctors, and then linked this to the development of lung cancer, that the links between the two became clear in 1956. Put another way, it is very hard for an individual doctor, or indeed an individual clinic, to spot trends in new conditions from seeing small numbers of patients suffering from them; epidemiologists look at large population samples in order to overcome this problem.

The situation might be different if everyone could be relied on to go and see a doctor when they were ill, even at an early stage. Then perhaps it might be possible to rely on medical records (provided one could get the appropriate approvals from the numerous bodies that regulate medical research; this is far from easy). However, many people do not seek help for symptoms they do not recognise, which they imagine will get better by themselves, or which they are embarrassed about. This is particularly important for possible mental health problems, which are frequently accompanied by stigma. Stigma may also occur for physical conditions, especially in the military where physical robustness is especially valued.

Overall, if you want to know what is going on in any group of people, then the best way is to carry out a large population-based study, looking not just at those who come to see the medical officers, but everyone, and ask about a large variety of conditions. It is also better if the people doing the asking are not the same as those who are taking decisions about your treatment, and hence your future. The independence of the research team avoids some of the natural reluctance to be open with those who ask questions for fear of what the consequences of your answers might be; this is another manifestation of stigma.

It was for those reasons that King's College London was commissioned by the MOD to carry out a forward-looking study of the physical and mental health of those who were about to take part in Operation Telic 1. We therefore decided to study a large random sample of all those who took part in Telic 1 (including all three Services, but excluding Special Forces for security reasons), and to compare them with another large randomly chosen sample of all those who were in the Armed Forces but did not take part in the invasion of Iraq. Since veterans' issues were high on the political agenda, we also decided that we would always include not just those still serving, but also Service leavers, and finally, because of the increasing use of reservists, including compulsory mobilisation for Telic 1, we decided to include both regulars and reservists (see Figure 17.1).

How Did We Do it?

Describing an epidemiological study is easy. Carrying it out is not. I will not bore the reader with the tedious details of the next two years – if anyone is interested please read the key papers. In summary, we designed a questionnaire which we hoped would ask the right questions. We were keen to know not just what people had experienced on deployment, but also about their upbringing, their relationships, their military experiences prior to deployment, and what their mental health and use of alcohol were at the time they completed the forms. Our main method of collecting data was by using the post and such was our persistence that we sent the questionnaires to everyone in our sample numerous times if they did not complete the forms on the first attempt. Additionally, the team visited over 50 different bases around the world, traced Service leavers using a variety of civilian data bases, phoned people at home in the evenings if we knew their numbers, and used every avenue we could to find people, especially after they had left the Services, and so persuade them to take part in the study.

It would be an understatement to say the job was not easy – epidemiologists know from bitter experience that the hardest group to persuade to cooperate in any medical research study are young men – and of course the UK Armed Forces are largely composed of young men, many of whom have far better things to do than to fill in questionnaires about their health and well-being. One has sympathy with them, because our team were not the only ones trying to get their cooperation, and because in the past they will have been approached by numerous researchers, and perhaps even filled in whatever questionnaire it was that was on offer that day, and never heard from the researchers again. We tried hard to avoid some of those errors – not least by informing all those who have taken part in the study what were the results, and how they have changed things, hopefully for the better. But it was, and still is, hard work.

Getting a good response rate from any study matters for two reasons: one important, one less important. First of all, it is vital that those who take part in the study are not different from those who do not, at least not in terms of the things you are studying. So in a health outcomes study such as ours, if those who respond are either sicker or alternatively less sick than those who do not, you are in trouble. This is called a response bias, and any form of bias makes it very difficult to interpret the results of the study, no matter how large it is. The second reason is that one loses what is called in the jargon 'power' – in other words the study becomes less efficient at detecting the outcomes in question.

As usual, we did not find everyone we needed, and we did not persuade everyone we found to take part. In fact the former was far and away the largest problem that we faced, especially for Service leavers; we were heartened by our base visits since although we only got about a third of those we were after to sit in the room with us, about 99 per cent of those whom we managed to talk to filled in the questionnaires without complaint. But the most important thing is that we are confident for various reasons, including comparing the age, gender, rank, medical downgrading and previous illnesses of those who did and did not complete the questionnaires, that the results of our study did not have a significant bias, and that the results are reliable, and can in another jargon word be 'generalised' to the rest of the Armed Forces.

What Did We Find?

First of all, our main conclusion is that to date (and in this case the date is end 2009), the mental health of the Armed Forces remains good.[5] In particular, and perhaps contrary to what the casual reader may have gleaned from the press, radio, TV and films, so far we have not been able to show any particular effect of Operation Telic on the mental health of regular forces.

That statement needs careful caveats. First, it emphatically does not mean that there has been no effect. PTSD, for example, affects somewhere between 2 and 4 per cent of those returning from Iraq. Given the numbers who have deployed there (in the region of 100,000 people, although some will have returned on numerous occasions) this means that there are likely to have been many thousands of cases of PTSD, related to serving in Iraq, to date. But this is no greater than the rate in those who have not served in Iraq. In other words, Iraq has not had any specific effect on mental health over and above the general rate in the UK Armed Forces.

Second, the above paragraph talked about regulars. The same is not true of reservists, who have experienced approximately a doubling of the rate of PTSD post Iraq. However, we need again to keep this in context – this means that the rate increased from about 3 per cent to about 6 per cent. Put another way, about 94 to 96 per cent of reservists who have served on Operation Telic do not have PTSD. And in other ways, most particularly alcohol, of which more later, deployed reservists do better than regulars.

Third, our data covers all three Services, and includes representative samples of every type of specialisation from marine engineering mechanic to explosive ordnance disposal technician. But those overall figures conceal some important subgroups, of which one is reservists. Another is those in specific combat roles, where there has been an increase in PTSD, although again not a substantial one (from 4 per cent to 6 per cent). But nevertheless, those who have served in combat roles have an increased likelihood of developing that disorder, which is perhaps not surprising. Likewise we have found that medics have slightly worse health than non-medics. We cannot fully explain this, but it might be related to the different tour patterns of medics, and also that they are more likely to go out as individual augmentees, and also of course are more likely to be reservists. It may also be related to the current work pattern of military medical staff who now mainly work in NHS settings rather than in military hospitals, which no longer exist.

Fourth, throughout our work we have consistently reported that PTSD is not the most significant mental health problem facing the UK Armed Forces, although it is the one that has attracted most attention. That honour belongs to alcohol misuse, followed closely by depression.

---

5   The two key references are Hotopf et al. 2006 and Fear et al. 2010. The former covers from the invasion of Iraq to 2005; the latter to the end of 2009, and also includes a random sample of those who had participated in Operation Herrick.

Alcohol

Alcohol misuse remains a significant problem in the British Armed Forces. It is easy to dismiss this by pointing out that alcohol is a problem in Britain in general, and amongst young males in particular. True, the Armed Forces largely recruits young men, but that alone cannot account for our findings. Overall, even when one adjusts for the levels of drinking in the same age and gender groups, both males and females in the Armed Forces are far more likely to be risky drinkers than their civilian counterparts.

There are several interesting aspects to this. First, it is not solely an 'Army thing'. In fact the Royal Navy and the Army have similar rates of problem drinking. Second, by and large, heavy use of alcohol is not explained by stress or, to put it more clearly, PTSD. In our latest study we have found that there is a significant increase in drinking, of the order of 20 per cent, in personnel when they return from deployment, an increase which persists for at least two years after homecoming, but that alone is not the explanation. On the other hand, deployment probably explains one further finding – that it is the social complications of alcohol as opposed to the medical that dominate. This may be because enforced abstinence as occurred in Telic and still continues in Herrick prevents the development of alcohol dependence, but sadly does not prevent the strong association that we find with domestic violence, other violence, accidents, trials by court martial, drink driving and other social consequences.

What are the risk factors for alcohol misuse? Some are similar to those in the general population. The single most powerful association is pre-service background – that is to say that personnel who have experienced troubled upbringings drink more often and in larger amounts – and as the Services do not recruit a random selection of the population this certainly explains some of the increase. Others are relevant to military life – we have now in our latest study found an impact of deployment, particularly in combat personnel. We also found an impact on drinking levels of tour length – albeit only when harmony guidelines have been violated.

Social factors associated with military life make alcohol misuse more likely. One of the main determinants of alcohol consumption in the general population is price and availability. Even though it is true that much of the excess of drinking goes on outside camp gates, the fact is that the cost of alcohol is subsidised in certain locations. And then there is culture. Few will doubt that alcohol plays an important role in the culture of the Armed Forces. And we are the first to admit, not being teetotallers ourselves, that there is a positive correlation between drinking and factors such as group cohesion and morale, as our own research has confirmed. But this comes at a cost.

Overall, what comes through our ten or more years of research is one clear and inescapable conclusion. Alcohol does more harm to the UK Armed Forces than PTSD. Also, in spite of very considerable sums of money having been spent on educating the Services about the evils of alcohol misuse through a variety of presentations, films and leaflets, military personnel are still heavy drinkers and if the military is to address this issue then more education is not likely to be the answer.

Why Reservists?

Our research on reservists is both interesting and perplexing.[6] For instance, in spite of us knowing that reservists are less likely than regulars to carry out higher risk combat duties, when questioned

---

6   See Browne et al. 2007 and Dandeker et al. 2010.

about what they have experienced in theatre they report more, rather than less, exposures to operational hazards such as indirect fire, encountering hostile locals and being shot at. This may be because reservists report lower levels of threat as traumatic compared with more experienced regular troops. However, our research also indicates that reservists, at least during the early parts of Operation Telic, did not feel as much a part of the 'military family' as regulars. It is indisputable that camaraderie and group cohesion are one of the fundamental influences that protect and maintain good mental health. Also, reservists who deploy tend to report less satisfactory relationships back at home. It might be therefore that when they return home they do not have as good support as regulars do, and it is certain that they report more difficulties with their employers in the post-deployment period.

There were numerous policy initiatives designed to address some of these issues as Telic continued. Unfortunately, although there is evidence from other sources that these have had a positive impact, we were disappointed to note in our latest 2009 study that these have not removed the differences in mental health outcomes between reservists and regulars, and that deployment continues to have a selective negative effect on the mental health of reservists, albeit not large.

In Theatre

So far we have been talking about data from our main study, covering the period 2003 to 2009. But we have also carried out different studies, some of them on entirely different samples, and some looking in more detail at subgroups within the main study. In 2009, towards the end of the main Telic operational effort, we deployed a small team to collect data in Iraq.[7] Although deployed Service personnel have traditionally traded their physical safety for the surety of not having to fill in surveys, we were able to survey some 600 personnel in Iraq both within the main base areas and in less austere locations. The results showed that on a 'mature' deployment the Service personnel's mental health was pretty much the same as it was back in garrison. The research also demonstrated the very powerful protective effects of good cohesion and good leadership; well-led and close-knit units had substantially better mental health even if they had been exposed to high-threat situations. The results also indicated that, as in garrison, stigma acted as a powerful deterrent to asking for help so that, even though about 10 per cent of the deployed force were interested in some additional support at the time they were surveyed, the majority of these were fearful of asking for it because of the potential career and reputational effects they perceived if they had done so. We carried out a second such study in Afghanistan in early 2010, with similar results. However, and perhaps not surprisingly, we did show a steady increase in symptoms associated with stress as the survey moved from the main bases (Kandahar, Bastion), via the forward operating bases to the patrol bases.

Decompression

One of the major trends to have emerged during the period of high operational tempo since 2003 has been the desire for the MOD to bring troops home in a methodical manner at the end of deployments. Whilst much is made of the apocryphal stories of the Royal Marines sailing home from the Falklands War and faring well whilst 5 Airborne Brigade flew home and created havoc in the local area – the story is unsubstantiated and in fact all troops sailed to Ascension Island before

---

7   See Mulligan et al. 2011.

anyone flew anywhere – the idea of troops having an operational pause before rejoining their loved ones has gained momentum. Our research into the perception of the usefulness of the 36 hours or so that formed units spend in Cyprus before returning home supports the idea of decompression to some degree. In spite of many troops being hesitant about the Cyprus stopover before they arrived, over 90 per cent thought it had been useful once they had completed the process. However, just because troops liked it, does not mean it will be beneficial to their mental health. Indeed, academic military psychiatry has worked hard to convince senior commanders that a stopover in Cyprus is highly unlikely to prevent PTSD, even if the troops enjoy it. It is also probable that decompression works best for formed units, most particularly in the Army, since satisfaction is less both for RAF and for individual augmentees.

Trauma Risk Management

Trauma Risk Management (TRiM) is a peer-delivered psychological support process that aims to ensure that personnel who develop psychological disorders, as a result of being exposed to traumatic events, are appropriately supported.[8] TRiM practitioners are volunteer non-medical personnel who have been trained in psychological risk assessment and provided with a basic understanding of trauma psychology. Although TRiM was developed within the Royal Marines, it was formally accepted as best practice by the Army in 2007 and shortly after by the Royal Air Force. TRiM itself aims to capitalise on the social cohesion available within military units. TRiM practitioners carry out structured risk assessments of those exposed to the events in order to identify whether individuals might benefit from additional social support. A further structured risk assessment is carried out after a month and personnel who continue to exhibit significant symptoms are referred on to formal mental health providers. Since practitioners are integral to military units, the TRiM process intends to reduce the stigma associated with military culture which may impede those who need help from accessing it.[9] It is worth noting that, unlike some other models of intervention, TRiM does not aim to be a treatment in itself; rather it aims to facilitate peer and unit support in the short term and, where necessary, to direct personnel towards formal sources of help.

TRiM differs from other post-trauma interventions because it is delivered by peers, as opposed to, for example, mental health professionals who used to deliver single session psychological debriefing, now known to be ineffective and perhaps even counter-productive. TRiM also is not about 'treating' people who are in fact simply showing normal emotional reactions, and avoids professionalising or medicalising distress.

King's College London have also carried out and overseen a number of studies which have looked at the TRiM process in order to ensure that its use is not associated with harm. The outcome of these studies has shown that TRiM training does indeed positively change the attitudes of those undergoing the training toward dealing with mental health problems and that, within military units, the use of TRiM is not associated with harm; indeed it appeared that its use had some organisational benefits.[10] It does not, however, prevent or treat PTSD – but it was never intended to.

---

8 Jones, Roberts and Greenberg 2003.
9 Hoge et al. 2004 and Langston, Greenberg and Gould 2007.
10 Greenberg et al. 2011.

How Does This Relate to What is Happening in the USA?

Overall, the pattern of ill health that we observe is different from that being reported from the USA. First, the absolute rates of disorders such as PTSD differ between the two armed forces, with the USA consistently reporting higher rates of all disorders, with the exception of alcohol. Second, US studies consistently report an overall negative effect of deployment to Iraq on mental health – as discussed above, we find that for reservists, not regulars. On the other hand, both the US and UK do report that those in a combat role, whether regulars or reservists, do have an increased risk of PTSD, although again the impact does differ.

There is no single explanation for these transatlantic differences. If we take our earlier studies, that covered the first three years of Operation Telic, there is little doubt, confirmed by our own and the US data, that UK Forces had lower casualty rates, and lower rates of exposure to combat, than the US. Given the compelling links between combat exposure and mental ill health, this clearly plays a part in the observed differences. In our later studies, when regrettably these differences became less, some of the differences in mental health outcomes also reduced. Second, there are several demographic differences between the structure of the two armed forces. At the start of the Iraq War, US personnel were younger, and had substantially less previous deployment experience. The US also uses approximately three times the number of reserve forces, who, as we and our US counterparts have shown, are more vulnerable to adverse mental health effects from deployment. Third, there are differences in tour length. Readers will know that, whereas the standard tour length in the UK Armed Forces is six months (at least for the Army and Royal Marines), the US in Iraq had a standard tour of one year, sometimes as long as 15 months. Increasing the duration of the tour after it had already started was also not uncommon in US Forces during part of Operation Iraqi Freedom. Our own data suggests that this practice has a particularly adverse effect on mental health.

So overall we do not find dramatic differences between the rates of psychiatric disorder in UK and US Service personnel, once one has taken into account key differences, most particularly combat exposure in the early stages of Operation Telic, and tour length. But there remains one further difference between the UK and the US. This concerns what happens to personnel with the passage of time. Many people who come back from operations can be expected to have some emotional reactions to what they have experienced. These are common, normal and should not be confused with psychiatric disorders such as PTSD. These do not require treatment, unless one calls the support of friends, family, chain of command and so on 'treatment', which we do not. Mostly these will go away as people readjust back to 'normal life'. In a relatively small number of cases these reactions will develop into formal psychiatric disorders. These may well require and benefit from treatment. Usually these will be apparent with a few weeks or months of return, although it often takes months and even years before personnel are either themselves willing, or alternatively persuaded by family or employers, to actually present for help. This delayed presentation is very common, but should not be confused with a genuine delay in the onset of mental disorder, as in delayed onset PTSD, which is actually relatively uncommon.

None of the above is controversial, and forms the basis of our standard public mental health approach to those who have experienced traumatic events, for example the victims of the 2005 July bombs on the London transport system.

But something different is being reported from the USA. A series of studies are documenting a steady increase in the rates of psychiatric disorder once people return from deployment. This is particularly striking in reservists. The increase in rates is not trivial, and influential think tanks such

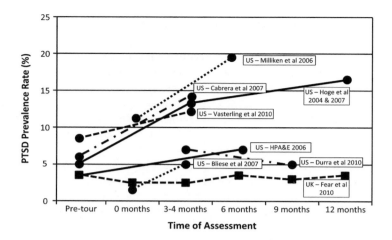

Figure 17.2 Changing rates of PTSD on homecoming, US versus UK data

as the Rand Corporation predict a final cost to the economy that may run into billions of dollars, if one bases this on previous experiences after the Vietnam and first Gulf Wars.

What about the UK? There have been numerous comments and predictions from various sources that we will also experience something similar to what has been observed in the USA. There are frequent references in the media, and from the Service charities and also senior figures within the Armed Forces, to a so called 'tidal wave' or 'bow wave' of mental health problems that will become apparent over time. But as Figure 17.2 shows, such prognostications may be premature. Our data shows only a small, albeit significant, increase in the rate of PTSD over time, with the data now extending for up to six years from the time last deployed.

So talk of bow or tidal waves seems as yet premature. However, it is important to make clear that the absolute number of military personnel requiring support and/or treatment is increasing. This is not because of an increase in the rate of mental disorders but as more and more of the UK Armed Forces deploy, the number of people needing help will inevitably increase. This should not be taken as evidence that the situation is getting worse, but it does mean that military mental health services, Service charities and the NHS must anticipate a steady increase in the number of serving and ex-Service personnel requiring support.

Conclusions

At the time of writing, it remains the case that the mental health of the UK Armed Forces has by and large survived Operation Telic. By that I mean that there is no evidence to support a significant decline in morale or well-being, or a significant increase in mental health problems such as, but not restricted to, post-traumatic stress disorder. Nevertheless, the campaign has highlighted certain problems that continue to need to be addressed. First, alcohol misuse remains at high levels, and whilst the primary determinants of this are not related to Telic, for the first time we have recently documented that deployment to either Telic or Herrick has resulted in still higher levels of alcohol morbidity, largely expressed in binge drinking and its social consequences. Second, whilst overall Operation Telic has yet to be associated with a particular adverse impact on the overall mental health of those who served there (compared with all other contemporaneous campaigns or deployments), it is the case that there has been an increase in mental health problems in certain subgroups – namely those in combat roles and those in the reserves.

What about the future? I am mindful of Tony Blair's possibly apocryphal comment to the effect that 'I don't make predictions, I never have and I never will'. Nevertheless, I can make some observations. First, many of those who have developed psychiatric injury as a result of their service in Iraq remain hidden. This is not because they have yet to develop problems, but because they have yet to admit to them, or at least have not yet taken the decision to come forward for help. Second, most of that group will probably already have left the Services and returned to civilian life. This is because those most vulnerable to post-service problems are those who have left the Services early, most often within the first four years. We know that early Service leavers are at greater risk of a wide range of social adversity – such as debt, alcohol and drug misuse, unemployment, homelessness, deliberate self harm and so on. This in turn poses a policy dilemma – at present the longer you serve, the greater the support and assistance you receive in terms of resettlement. Yet those who are most in need are most often to be found in the ranks of early Service leavers. Hence those who receive the most are those who perhaps deserve or who have earned the most, but paradoxically may not need the most. Third, whilst it is true that the military health services, the NHS and the Service charities can all expect, and indeed are already experiencing, an increased demand for their services, this reflects the increased absolute numbers of people who have served in either Iraq or Afghanistan, but does not mean that the true rate of disorders is increasing, and nor does it indicate any incipient failure of morale.

Finally, the Armed Forces have made significant strides in recognising not just the physical, but also the mental, costs of conflict. Numerous initiatives, ranging from pre- and post-deployment briefing, decompression, Battlemind,[11] TRiM and others, have been put into place or are being tested. It is too early to determine precisely what impact these will have, but, notwithstanding Tony Blair, I will make two predictions. First, none of these will eliminate the stigma of mental disorder, which remains the single greatest barrier impeding those who need help from seeking it. This is a problem wider than the Armed Forces, and indeed people may be surprised to learn that in a series of studies we have found no evidence that barriers to care and reluctance to seek treatment are any worse in serving and ex-serving military personnel than in the general population. These issues go well beyond the Armed Forces. I am unaware of any institution, profession or organisation that has solved this problem. Second, it is naive and utopian to believe that the risk of psychiatric injury can ever be banished from the profession of arms. Most people accept that the idea that a military operation, be it Operation Telic, Herrick or whatever follows, could ever be free of physical casualties is something devoutly to be wished for, but unlikely to be achieved. So it is also with psychiatric casualties.

---

11   Battlemind is a US initiative designed to assist personnel in the return from deployment. It is a very clever programme, that instead of pathologising or stigmatising behaviours and emotions, for example by saying that these are expressions of possible mental disorder requiring treatment, it does the opposite, by placing them in the context of the normal reactions, skills and mindsets that 'good soldiers' develop. Thus hyperarousal instead of being placed within the context of PTSD, is instead discussed as alertness, something all good 'warriors', as the US insists on calling them, need to possess. Likewise, confiding with your mates and buddies is an important part of mental resilience and cohesion, but will probably cause marital disputes if continued back home. It was developed by the innovative and impressive team at the Walter Reed Institute for Army Research, and shown to reduce psychological symptoms in a controlled clinical trial. We have carried out a randomised trial in UK personnel as they go through decompression in Cyprus, but our preliminary results have not been as impressive. Further details are at https://www.resilience.army.mil/.

In the meantime Operation Telic has shown that the military has little to be afraid of in acknowledging the reality of psychiatric casualties. Accepting this more sympathetically, as they are doing, poses no dangers to them, provided it is managed within the context of military culture (the goal of initiatives such as TRiM or Battlemind), and provided they also do not heed those voices who claim that stress can be avoided or prevented, as opposed to managed.[12] It is nonsense to believe that stress can ever be eliminated from a military organisation, and it is probably undesirable. The military deliberately stretch and test people because war is a stressful business – it always has been and it always will be. It is best to come prepared.

---

12   Wessely 2005.

PART IV
Improving in Afghanistan

The Afghanistan operation changed fundamentally for the British in 2006. Until then we had supported the ISAF Headquarters in Kabul, and provided a Provincial Reconstruction Team in the peaceful north of the country. Headquarters Allied Rapid Reaction Corps (ARRC) was the British commanded and supported corps headquarters that was nominated to provide the ISAF command during a critical time – expansion of the NATO mission to include not just reconstruction in the peaceful parts of Afghanistan, but also the counter-insurgency operation in the east and south, up to that point run by the US as a separate mission. As part of this expansion of NATO's remit, the UK offered to provide a task force into Helmand Province in the south of Afghanistan. The concept in 2006 was that additional forces could be provided for Helmand through anticipated withdrawals from Basra; as we saw in Part III, this was wishful thinking. The British operation in Helmand was to prove at least as difficult as Basra, and even more under-resourced.

Lieutenant General Chris Brown was Chief of Staff to General Sir David Richards, commander of the ARRC, for their ISAF mission. He describes in Chapter 18 the background to the expansion of NATO's responsibilities in Afghanistan, and the ARRC's initial intent as to how the operation should be conducted. It demonstrates that even in the earliest phases of the operation there was deep understanding of the need for civil development alongside security operations, although it was most difficult to achieve.

Nick Pounds is a member of the UK's Stabilisation Unit and has had a wealth of experience in southern Afghanistan. In Chapter 19 he describes the background to the development of the 'comprehensive approach', the integration of military and non-military activity, and explains some of the reasons why it has been so difficult to achieve in the counter-insurgency operation in Helmand.

In ISAF headquarters in Kabul, Lieutenant General Jon Riley was the deputy to the US commander in 2008 and early 2009. In Chapter 20 he conducts a wide-ranging analysis of the strategic and operational problems facing NATO in Afghanistan at that time, including the nature of our enemies, the problems associated with developing the capacity of the Afghan National Security Forces, the narcotics trade and the relationship between criminality and insurgency, the regional nature of the problem, and the difficulties of an alliance operation with varying levels of political commitment.

Major General Andrew Mackay commanded the Helmand Task Force in 2007–2008. He designed his counter-insurgency operation to focus more on the perceptions of the population than military operations per se, and subsequently analysed his experiences, including Operation Snakebite in 2008 to recapture Musa Kala, to develop his concept of Behavioural Conflict explained in Chapter 21.

The following chapter, by Iain McNicoll, gives an air perspective, illustrating that this seminar series was not just about generalship, but also about air marshalship. Although Iraq and Afghanistan are primarily land campaigns, not all campaigns can be assumed to follow this model, as Libya illustrates. McNicoll argues that even in a land-centric campaign, like Afghanistan, we should not ignore the air dimension, and that we could make much more of what airpower offers.

More recently, the United States Marine Corps has deployed an additional brigade into Helmand, as part of President Obama's Afghanistan surge. As a result, the British have been able to sustain high levels of forces in populated areas for the first time in the campaign. The jury is still out as to whether this will be enough to see success in the campaign before all British combat forces are withdrawn before the end of 2014.

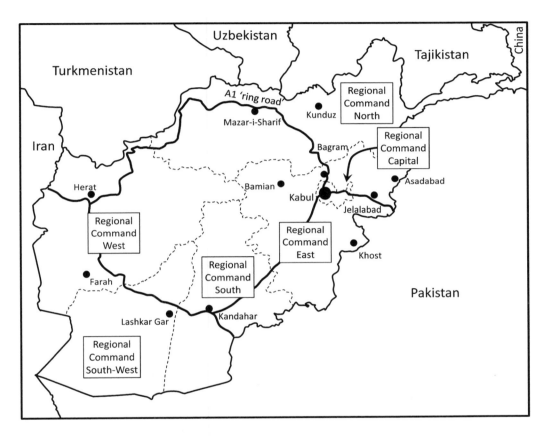

Map 18.1 Afghanistan – ISAF regional command structure in 2011

Chapter 18

Multinational Command in Afghanistan – 2006: NATO at the Cross-Roads

Chris Brown – 17 January 2007

Just over two years ago NATO was at a cross-roads. NATO nations had signed up to expansion of the ISAF mission throughout Afghanistan, but the tempo and impetus required to reach that goal, let alone convince the US that NATO was a worthy successor to Operation Enduring Freedom, were lacking. One contributing factor was the six-month turnover of NATO headquarters. The previous US Coalition commander, Lieutenant General Barno, had seen four different ISAF commanders and headquarters during his 22-month tenure. On average they spent two months getting established, two months being effective and two months winding down. Their understanding of the Afghan situation, particularly culture (where personal relationships are the key to establishing confidence) was a concern to Americans and Afghans alike. At this cross-roads one of the signposts read:

> An essentially European-focused Alliance, increasingly irrelevant in its traditional Article V Washington Treaty role, unable to nip terrorism in the bud wherever it occurred and therefore increasingly a political, rather than military, instrument, reliant on coalitions of the willing to deal with today's challenges.

It is also worth noting that at this time, mid 2004, the EU was becoming more confident in its ability to deal with security issues, even outside Europe. The other signpost read:

> European nations make NATO a relevant military alliance into the twenty-first century by their willingness to share the burden with the US.

Against this background the Italian and British Prime Ministers agreed an 18-month package to set off down the latter road with the specific aim of expanding NATO's ISAF mission throughout Afghanistan. The first nine months, led by the Italian National Rapid Deployment Corps as ISAF VIII, would set the conditions for the UK-led Allied Rapid Reaction Corps (ARRC) as ISAF IX to realise the goal.

The great advantage of an 18-month lead time was our ability to develop an understanding of the situation in Afghanistan; immersion not only in the military aspects but also in the other elements of the campaign, exemplified by the London Conference in early 2006[1] and the Afghan National Development Strategy. I had the privilege of being Chief of Staff of the ARRC for the two years before deployment and for the first five months of the tour.

---

1   The London Conference was co-chaired by Prime Minister Blair, President Karzai and UN Secretary-General Kofi Annan on 31 January and 1 February 2006; 66 states and 15 international organisations attended, agreeing the Afghanistan Compact which was a political agreement between the international community and the Government of Afghanistan.

When Headquarters ARRC arrived in Afghanistan in April 2006 under the command of the then Lieutenant General David Richards, now General Sir David Richards, the US was very much the majority shareholder in Afghan security. NATO ISAF numbered around 10,000, split roughly equally between Kabul (a multinational brigade, the ISAF Headquarters and its key airhead) and the northern half of the country, where the force was organised around Provincial Reconstruction Teams (PRT), designed to spread the Government of Afghanistan's influence throughout their respective regions. There was no significant ISAF combat capability outside Kabul. The US-led Coalition numbered around 30,000. Both Kabul and northern Afghanistan were relatively benign compared with the south. Therefore, although it might have looked as if NATO was looking after half of the problem, it was by far the easier half, as we already knew, but others were about to find out.

General Richards's intent was critical for the development of the campaign and guidance to the staff, and is reproduced in full below.

My guiding intent is, through our actions and a linked information operation firmly rooted in substance, to reinforce the people of Afghanistan's belief that long-term peace and growing economic prosperity from which everyone can benefit is possible if they continue to give their government, and its international partners, their support and encouragement.

ISAF, in partnership with the Government of Afghanistan (GOA) and the International Community, is to think and plan for the long-term future of Afghanistan, seizing short-term opportunities as they occur but always in a way that is in step with the long-term vision for the country. We are to focus on action that actively assists the GOA in nurturing and further developing the consent of the people to the GOA (our centre of gravity) and its international partners, not least NATO. Respect for the people of Afghanistan and their faith is to be central to all we do.

Within this framework, ISAF will:

a. In step with GOA's National Development Strategy, concentrate on those activities that will most clearly and quickly assist the GOA in its drive to establish the sustainable economic growth on which the future of the country depends. Some examples of this approach include:

(1) Helping ensure the security of mineral resources, border crossing points, and the transport network, water and power supplies.
(2) Supporting the GOA in the development and prosecution of its Counter Narcotics (CN) campaign.
(3) Assisting in the GOA's economic and human resource development strategy so as to enable Afghanistan to become increasingly self-sufficient.

b. Work to resolve conflict and reduce tension within Afghanistan, focusing on the holistic defeat of the residual insurgency threat to the country. Supporting and helping to train the Afghan National Security Forces (ANSF) to a standard that will enable them in time to assume full responsibility for the internal and external security of the country will be critical to success.

ISAF is to be prepared to respond positively to requests to help the GOA and International Agencies (IA) with its guidance, advice and coordinating skills as required, in order to assist actively in the achievement of these aims.

My Main Effort is to extend and deepen the areas in which the GOA and IAs/NGOs can safely operate in the interests of the people of Afghanistan, enabling the ANSF increasingly to take the lead in achieving this aim. In this way too I will seize the initiative against those who oppose the GOA through violent means, by using appropriate and well considered measures – including the robust use of force should it be necessary – at times and in places of my choosing thereby forcing them to respond to my design.

Note that the main effort was not the military line of operation. In essence it was to convince the Afghan population that it is better to play for President Karzai's team than for the Taliban.

How did we envisage the nine months of our mission? First, the command and control structure in ISAF needed to be changed both to prepare for the expansion and to give region commanders the authority necessary to command forces in their respective regions.

How did we structure the Headquarters? Despite the lesson learned by Coalition forces in both Iraq and Afghanistan that the operational and tactical levels should be commanded by separate headquarters, NATO directed that ISAF should carry out the functions in one headquarters. So General Richards established three deputy commanders, or DCOMs, all at two-star – one was DCOM Stability, and the other two were DCOM Security and DCOM Air. DCOM Security oversaw the running of the Coalition Joint Operations Centre, under a one-star director, which was directly responsible for the running of the tactical battle, while DCOM Stabilisation was responsible for the longer-term aspects of the campaign more normally associated with the theatre level.

The first test of ISAF IX's ability to deliver General Richards's concept of operations was an operation (Operation Turtle) to complement the Coalition Operation Mountain Thrust in the south. Until that point ISAF and Coalition operations had been planned and executed in isolation. Without a complementary ISAF operation in Farah Province, the enemy could not be fixed. Using the new ISAF command and control structure, reinforcing Region Command West with ISAF's only reserve (a Portuguese infantry company) and the Afghan National Army's 207 Corps, the largest ISAF operation outside Kabul was launched. But the key element, in line with Commander ISAF's intent, was not the military operation; it was the reconstruction and development – schools, hospitals, roads, water – which went in on the heels of the ISAF forces to show that the Government of Afghanistan could positively influence the lives of Afghans in far-flung provinces. And these economic enhancements continue long after the military forces have redeployed.

On 31 July 2006, NATO Stage 3 Expansion put ISAF in command of southern Afghanistan. NATO forces now numbered around 20,000, including a proper (Canadian-led) combat brigade in the south, thereby achieving broad parity with Coalition forces. Afghan National Army (ANA) and Afghan National Police (ANP) strengths also increased throughout this period. Note, however, that there were no ISAF forces based in Nimruz or Dai Kundi provinces. This is a disadvantageous aspect of NATO force generation, where nations accept responsibility for a defined geographical area. Unless nations are prepared to flex their forces, this results in both a force distribution which may not meet the requirements of the mission and a reduction in the ISAF Commander's ability to redeploy forces to meet the threat. NATO was now exposed to the greatest threat to Afghan security. Whereas the majority of Afghanistan is benign – good old-fashioned crime and tribal rivalries abound, but that's Afghanistan – the south is different: the further you go from Kabul, the less allegiance the population owes to the Government. Yes, they're all fiercely Afghan as long as it does not involve interference or taxation. In the five years since the Taliban had been ousted, the economy of force which the Coalition had allocated to the south had allowed the Taliban to return to provide an alternative security for many of the remote villages. In places like Helmand and Kandahar, British and Canadian forces were kicking rocks and finding unpleasant things underneath. Stage 3 expansion also created an artificial boundary between ISAF and the Coalition down the middle of southern Afghanistan. It made no sense to delay Stage 4 expansion into the east – indeed, we had argued strongly but to no avail that Stages 3 and 4 should take place simultaneously – but in the interim we had to ensure that the boundary was as seamless as possible.

In many ways what the Afghan National Development Strategy aimed to achieve was something no Afghan Government had ever achieved: influence over these far-flung provinces. General Richards, Commander ISAF, amplified his guidance at this stage; in particular the population needed to be given the *incentive, means, resolve* and *courage* to stand up to the Taliban. It had become clear to us over the preceding months that the Government needed to take control of the campaign demonstrably. In order to do that, they needed to be structured appropriately and be assisted.

One of General Richards's most important innovations was the Policy Action Group (PAG), a National Security Council or war cabinet, consisting of selected ministers and co-opted principals from the international community. It had a permanent secretariat with both ministry and international community representation. The PAG had four sub-groups whose work it directed and integrated: the Intelligence Group, the Security Operations Group, the Strategic Communications Group, and the Outreach Reconstruction and Development Group.

General Richards encouraged the President to set objectives for the PAG, of which Presidential Objective 7 was key:

> Identify strategically important geographic zones (initially in the south and east) where improvements in security and governance will create conditions conducive to more effective, noticeable development.

This led to the identification of Afghan Development Zones (ADZs), another of General Richards's important innovations, in which a higher level of security (with ANA and ANP to the fore), governance, and reconstruction and development would be undertaken to demonstrate the Government's ability.

In practical terms this meant selecting an area where the required effect could be achieved easily, building in many cases on existing PRTs and Government initiatives. This would act as a platform to expand the area. And this would happen in all provinces so that these areas would eventually link up. So in Helmand Province, for example, we selected for Phase 1 a limited area around Lashkar Gar, the regional capital, which in Phase 2 would expand north and south along the Helmand valley. This would gradually be expanded further in Phase 3 to join up with other ADZs in neighbouring provinces such as Kandahar.

It looked great on PowerPoint but, in order to achieve it, the Taliban had to be defeated in these ADZs. As a result, General Richards decided to launch Operation Medusa during the first two weeks of September 2006, NATO's first and only brigade attack at this time. About 500 Taliban had infiltrated an area to the west of Kandahar from which they could control movement on the ring road, the artery of all traffic and resupply in the area. Intelligence suggested that they intended to do the same to the east of Kandahar in order to isolate the city, control over which was a key Taliban objective.

NATO forces included a Canadian battlegroup, three ANA battalions, one US battalion, one Danish armoured recce company, a self-propelled Netherlands 155 mm artillery battery and UK elements, supported by the main effort of Coalition and NATO air power. Fighting was fierce and at close quarters. One night resupply of $1,200 \times 155$ mm artillery rounds was required (and achieved). Air-delivered ordnance during this period was more than 20 times the amount dropped during the invasion of Iraq. The operation drew in more enemy; estimates of enemy killed exceeded 1,000, but the key issue was that, by drawing resources away from other Taliban operations, it relieved pressure on UK forces in northern Helmand. A tactical defeat was inflicted on the enemy which sent a powerful message, not just to the Taliban leadership, but to the people of southern Afghanistan.

In Operation Medusa, however, the most important aspect was not the military operation. Reconstruction and development followed immediately in the wake of all ISAF operations. The imperative was to re-house the villagers who had been displaced by the Taliban, ideally before Ramadan and certainly before winter.

On 5 October 2006, NATO command and control over the whole of Afghanistan was achieved by Stage 4 expansion into the east of the country. US forces were under non-US command in a combat, as opposed to peacekeeping, mission for the first time since the Second World War. This was a big deal in Washington which had contributed to the delay imposed on Stage 4 transition. NATO forces now numbered around 27,000. Note that more than 10,000 forces remained under US command to deal with two missions which NATO had been unwilling to take on: high-end counter-terrorism and training the ANA.

One issue which emerged was that of red cards. There will always be caveats in any coalition or alliance. The key is early identification; if the red card is played only as the operation is about to commence, both the nation playing it and the NATO chain of command have failed.

The ANA and ANP are our ticket home. How we train them will determine the speed at which we can hand over to them as the majority shareholder. Willingness to take a greater role in this aspect, not just in Afghanistan but also in future missions of a similar nature, is a challenge for NATO.

What of NATO? Well it did, in my view, take the right route at the cross-roads. Under ISAF IX, NATO has become the majority shareholder in the security of Afghanistan. What I did not mention above was that the road is actually a dual carriageway and, although all nations went down the same route, some are in the fast lane while others are in the slow lane. The danger, therefore, is that we are faced with a two-tier NATO.

What of Afghanistan? It is fundamentally different from Iraq: the majority of the population is determined to work towards a peaceful, prosperous future and warmly welcomes the international community's assistance, not just in security, but along all lines of operation. However, the window of opportunity is not infinite: the greatest threat to destabilisation is the people's patience with their own Government.

Finally, this is not just about Afghanistan: it is a regional issue. Pakistan has over 80,000 troops deployed on the Afghan border in an effort to defeat insurgency on both sides of the frontier. Unless the insurgency is defeated in Pakistan as well as Afghanistan, the best we can achieve is some sort of inconclusive stalemate. Pakistan will need the West's assistance if we are jointly to resolve this issue.

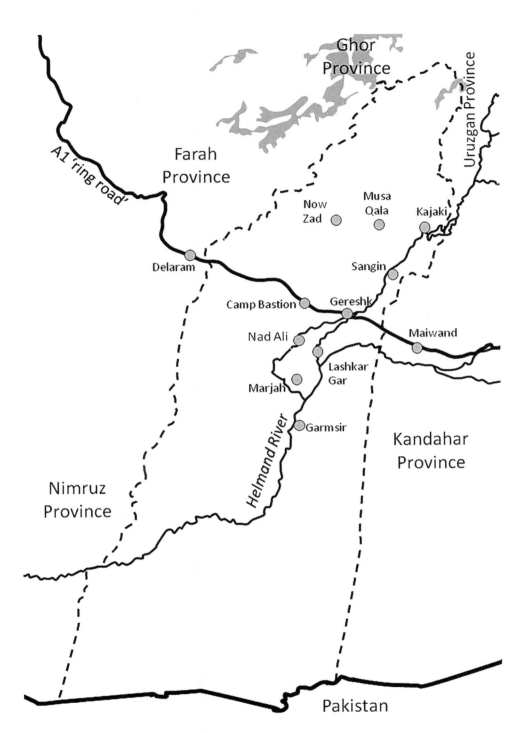

Map 19.1 Helmand Province

Southern Afghanistan 2006–2008: The Challenges to a Comprehensive Approach to Counter-Insurgency

Nick Pounds – 14 May 2008

It is an inconvenient truth for some that the Pashtun tribal conflicts and the criminal war economy, which were allowed to continue in the south after the highly successful ousting of the Taliban Regime in 2001, have been commandeered and transformed into an ideologically inspired insurgency, contesting control of some or all of the state, supported and encouraged to some degree by regional mischief makers. Whether they accept it or not,[1] ISAF and Coalition forces in the south are now engaged in a counter-insurgency campaign, which NATO has declared it will prosecute by means of a 'comprehensive approach'.[2] The question is whether this is an effective and pragmatic counter to the insurgency, which is essentially political in its goals, or a pious hope by contributing nations wishing to get away with a lesser commitment of resources to the campaign than conventional counter-insurgency doctrine would suggest are required.

I intend to look at the development and understanding of the comprehensive approach together with the notion of stabilisation, which features in ISAF doctrine and evolving UK thinking, touching also on how this relates to counter-insurgency, as practised by the dominant Coalition partner: the USA. I will then turn to the situation in southern Afghanistan and explain how theory is being applied in practice, examining the tensions it is creating within the alliance and the challenges posed for military commanders. Finally, I will outline how commanders have shaped their campaign plans to meet these challenges and offer a view on the current situation.

Understanding the Comprehensive Approach

This section will look at the evolution of thinking about employing a comprehensive approach to national and international crises and at the emerging concept of *stabilisation*, which the UK sees as the product of a comprehensive approach. I will then compare this to US thinking on counter-insurgency which, with a US military commander and a predominance of US resources, is shaping the ISAF military approach to the campaign in Afghanistan.

I am not sure where the term 'comprehensive approach' was first coined but it was formally articulated in a UK Joint Discussion Note, JDN 4/05 – published in January 2006. However, well before JDN 4/05, NATO had embraced the idea if not the term in its strategic direction to ISAF,[3] which set out governance and development as well as security lines of operation. The problem was that NATO did not, at the same time, establish the mechanisms to allow ISAF to coordinate

---

1   The Netherlands forces' mission is still declared to be development whilst the Canadian Government seeks to shift its focus back to development.

2   NATO 2008.

3   The NATO strategic direction was issued in an operational plan, OPLAN 10302, approved by NATO HQ on 14 April 2004.

effectively these lines of operation at the operational and tactical level which, at least as far as the UK was concerned, was the purpose of JDN 4/05. The term 'comprehensive approach' eventually entered the NATO lexicon at the Riga summit in November 2006, where it was stated:

> Experience in Afghanistan and Kosovo demonstrates that today's challenges require a comprehensive approach by the international community involving a wide spectrum of civil and military instruments, while fully respecting mandates and autonomy of decisions of all actors ...[4]

The summiteers stated that NATO had no requirement to develop alliance capabilities strictly for civilian purposes but tasked the Council in Permanent Session to bring forward proposals to improve NATO's crisis management instruments as well as practical cooperation at all levels, at the same time considering how NATO military and political planning procedures could be amended 'with a view to enhancing [the] civil-military interface'.

In truth, the comprehensive approach is little more than applying, at the operational or even tactical level, the grand strategic concept of using all instruments of state power in pursuit of strategic objectives. Of course this is not new to counter-insurgency doctrine, which has long emphasised the importance of political and economic as well as security lines of operation. So is there anything new or is the so-called comprehensive approach simply old wine in new bottles? In response, it has been argued that recent crises have led the military increasingly to engage with civilian organisations, both within their own government and in multinational multi-agency environments and, because different organisations often have different ideas of what the right solutions are, there is a need for inclusive processes and better tools in order to harness the efforts of all into a single coherent plan, seeking to ensure that all organisations play their part in an optimum approach. Furthermore, guidance is required for civilian leadership which, in such circumstances, has also to address the challenges of integrated planning and implementation in a difficult and challenging environment.[5]

JDN 4/05 asserts that Bosnia in 1991 first exposed the need for a firmer basis for understanding and cooperation of activity on the ground between the many governmental, non-governmental and international organisations which, by then, had become involved in 'complex modern crises involving, and occurring among, communities and populations'.[6] This was reinforced by subsequent operations but, as already stated, it was not until Kosovo in 1999 that NATO commanders acknowledged that arrangements were unsatisfactory and that the UK, for its part, made specific provision for military-civilian cooperation at the operational level, with the inclusion of other Government departments in the MOD's Crisis Management Organisation. This thinking was incorporated into military doctrine for Peace Support Operations which, in turn, laid the foundation for work fully to define a comprehensive approach that would promote 'collaborative processes, shared understanding and concerted action [which] is most required in the area of crisis prevention and resolution'.[7]

Of course, NATO's mills grind slowly and, at its 2008 summit in Bucharest, it was announced that work to develop a comprehensive approach is still underway. However, material that was released on this subject indicated that the focus of work is to improve the mechanisms for cooperation in the field between civilian and military entities within the Alliance as well as to develop more structured

---

4   NATO Press Release 2006.
5   SU 2007a.
6   JDN 4/05 2006, 1-1.
7   JDN 4/05 2006, 1-5.

relations with the United Nations and other international and non-governmental organisations. However, reflecting the tensions inherent in such activity, the need to respect the different mandates and the autonomy of decisions of all actors was emphasised and, furthermore:

> this is not to be understood as NATO's Comprehensive Approach, but as NATO's contribution to a comprehensive approach for the international community as a whole, which would need to be supported by all actors concerned.[8]

In practice, the support is not there and it is perhaps interesting to note that, in a recent visit to Kandahar, David Kilcullen[9] commented on the level of structural separation of military and other activity within NATO, which he compared unfavourably to that practised by the US, to which I shall return.

Nationally, the UK has progressed faster while still recognising that each individual department will want to conduct activity within its own area of responsibility, especially when it comes to the allocation of resources. JDN 4/05 calls for a mechanism to coordinate between competing priorities, to sequence actions and compensate for 'structural and institutional imperfections'[10] with the overriding consideration being to focus on the strategic aim. To achieve this there should be shared understanding through collaborative analysis and planning, and actors should think in terms of outcomes related to strategic objectives rather than the activities and processes so beloved by bureaucrats. This is, quite simply, a call for an effect-based approach, which was reflected also by NATO at Bucharest when announcing that 'work is ongoing to develop an effect based approach to operations in parallel with the broader framework provided by the comprehensive approach'.[11] Work by the UK Government's Stabilisation Unit[12] is seeking to provide an effect- or 'outcome'-based planning framework for stabilisation that could help to facilitate the collaborative principles set out in JDN 04/05.

Stabilisation is defined by the British Government as support to places faced with or emerging from violent conflict:

> it is not just support to counter-insurgency operations, peace keeping and peace enforcement, peace building or reconstruction and development, though there may be elements of all or some of these in a stabilisation process.[13]

At its heart, stabilisation is a political process, aiming to achieve a non-violent political settlement (or interim accommodation) but recognising that, ultimately,

---

8   NATO 2008, 340.

9   Dr David Kilcullen – retired Australian Army colonel seconded at the time as a COIN adviser to US Secretary of State Condoleezza Rice – visit to HQ RC (South) in March 2008.

10   JDN 4/05 2006, 1-8.

11   NATO 2008, 342.

12   The Stabilisation Unit was originally set up as the Post Conflict Reconstruction Unit (PCRU) at the end of 2004 in response to perceived weaknesses in UK cross-Government preparation and civilian response in Iraq and Afghanistan. A dedicated tri-departmental unit was seen as the best way of bringing together an understanding of stabilisation and the approaches of its three parent departments (DfID, FCO and MoD) in a way that would be seen as objective and sufficiently independent of the positions of any of its parent departments.

13   SU 2007b, 7.

only the state that can provide the functions that will bring about and sustain stability. Only the state has the legitimacy to assure security and services to its citizens, and to manage contests for power and control of resources; its ability to do this, and the perception of its legitimacy to do it, is the key to stability.[14]

However, in many cases, stabilisation requires external inputs, in order to compensate for the weakness of domestic institutions and political processes. Supporting political processes and helping the state fulfil its functions usually requires leadership from the diplomatic and development communities whilst, because stabilisation 'takes place in violent situations, it usually requires military input, particularly in protecting people and institutions, and in preventing violence by coercive means'. All of these inputs need to be mutually reinforcing and aiming at the same outcome. Stabilisation is, therefore, 'almost by definition, an integrated military and civilian endeavour'.

> Effective stabilisation depends on understanding what sequence and priority to accord to the vast range of potential tasks, in terms of their contribution to a political process that will bring about more stability. Signs of visible progress, or "quick wins", which give people a reason to have confidence in and support a political process and put their faith in the state, can often be an important factor in building momentum for positive change.[15]

Whilst military peace support operations are the platform on which stabilisation is mounted, the need to adopt a comprehensive approach that integrates the activity of military, development and diplomatic actors seems still not to be widely recognised.

> Successful stabilisation enables peace-building and reconstruction with a subsequent transition to more traditional development actors. Typical stabilisation activities include provision of security, promoting rule of law, delivery of basic services, and protection of human rights, in order to support the central theme of political outreach and settlement.[16]

In relation to this, JDN 4/05 stresses also the need for each actor to understand and accept the idea of acting in a supported or supporting role, depending on the main effort at any particular time, which is particularly important when dealing with protracted conflicts, such as that faced in Afghanistan, with the need for frequent reviews of the situation to judge how best these relationships should be set.

US thinking recognises that the 'success of any counter-insurgency campaign over the long run ultimately requires a combination of military, political, economic, and other efforts'[17] and also the need for a 'comprehensive strategy employing all instruments of national power'.[18] Whilst the US has established a unit to assist the 'inter-agency' process, unlike the UK, its doctrine appears to regard stabilisation as an element of counter-insurgency and, recognising that political and development space is contested by an insurgency, places greater emphasis not only on controlling levels of violence but also the need to eliminate insurgents or render them irrelevant. Furthermore, it is asserted that whilst

---

14   ISAF doctrine also emphasises that stability is rooted in the effectiveness and legitimacy of the state.
15   SU 2007b.
16   SU 2007b.
17   RAND 2006, xiv.
18   Field Manual 3-24 2006, 2-1.

[p]olitical, social, and economic programs are most commonly and appropriately associated with civilian organizations and expertise ... effective implementation of these programs is more important than who performs the tasks.[19]

The problem of 'non-permissive' environments, which are assessed as too dangerous for civilians to work in safely, is acknowledged by the UK Government as a major obstacle to implementing a comprehensive approach, an issue discussed in more detail below.

David Kilcullen, who has been influential in shaping the new US counter-insurgency doctrine, advocates a model for counter-insurgency based on security, economic and political pillars as a possible framework for an 'inter-agency' or comprehensive approach to counter-insurgency. He argues that it should be seen as a framework, not a template for campaign design, providing a basis for measuring progress and an aid to collaboration rather than an operational plan. Within his model, information is the basis for all other activities, arguing that perception is crucial in developing control and influence over population groups and that every action in counter-insurgency sends a message. The term information here includes intelligence collection, analysis and distribution as well as strategic communications. Kilcullen argues:

> security is *not* the basis for economic and political progress (as some commanders and political leaders argue). Nor does security depend on political and economic progress (as others assert). Rather, all three pillars must develop in parallel and stay in balance, while being firmly based in an effective information campaign.[20]

This section has demonstrated a degree of consensus on the need for a comprehensive approach to meeting the challenges posed by an insurgency. However, NATO thinking remains in the formative stage, whilst UK thinking and writing focuses on maintaining stability rather than creating it, noting the problems of civilian engagement in contested space. US doctrine, whilst sharing the same overarching goals, appears to be better focused for the guerrilla stage of an insurgency where political and physical space is contested. The next section looks at the complex conflict in Afghanistan and the challenges this has posed to the comprehensive approach that NATO aspires to employ.

The Situation in Afghanistan

The Coalition in Afghanistan has gradually found itself to be engaged in a complex social conflict with ideological, tribal and criminal dimensions, all underpinned by regional political positioning. This section seeks to outline how these factors have affected the transformation of conflict in the south, as well as to outline the structures and plans adopted by the international community to counter these developments and restore stability to the region. But first it is necessary briefly to describe the region.

Afghanistan is about three times the size of the UK and dominated by the Hindu Kush, which rises above 22,000 feet at its highest as it climbs through the Pamir Mountains into the Himalayas. These mountains isolate western provinces from the capital in Kabul and physically divide the ethnically mixed north from the predominantly Pashtun south of the country. I will be focusing

---

19   Field Manual 3-24 2006, 2-5.
20   Kilcullen 2006.

on the southern region as defined by NATO, which comprises six provinces: Nimruz, Helmand, Kandahar, Zabol, Uruzgan and the recently created Hazara province of Dai Kundi. The north and east are dominated by the Hindu Kush, whilst the south and west comprise largely infertile desert in the Dasht-i-Reg and the Sistan Basin. Two major rivers, the Helmand and the Argendab, track right across the region from the mountains in the north-east to the Sistan Basin in the south-west, with over 70 per cent of the region's population clustered along their flood plains, the main concentrations being around Kandahar city and the intersection of the two rivers, between Gereshk and Lashkar Gar. Zabol marks the rough division between the Ghilzai Pashtun in the east and the Durrani in the south, although many sub-tribal divisions, with their associated quarrels and disputes, exist within these major groupings. The most significant tension in the south is currently between the Popalzai, the Barakzai and the Alikozai, as they compete for power and patronage. There are also tensions between the Pashtun and the Hazara in Dai Kundi and Uruzgan, as well as with the Baloch, in the south of Kandahar, Helmand and Nimroz. The nomadic Kuchi, largely impoverished by years of war and drought, eke out a meagre existence across the region, many in refugee camps, with periodic disputes over grazing rights in their traditional pastures now settled by other groups. As a result, tribal and ethnic factionalism plays a major role in regional instability.

The political situation in southern Afghanistan is extremely fragile and Government control is weak in all six provinces. This is perhaps not surprising, given that the Government has never enjoyed strong influence beyond major population centres and there is no tradition of reliance on a central state or government. Even that which previously existed has been severely eroded by 30 years of social conflict, whilst high rates of illiteracy severely limit the human capacity available to fill the offices of Government. With secure areas largely confined to the major population centres, officials are unwilling or unable to venture far from their secure bases or, in more remote areas, are subject to intimidation and coercion by insurgents and other anti-Government elements. Furthermore, corruption is a way of life in Afghanistan, both in and out of Government. It is rampant at every level of Government from local to national and is a major impediment to stabilisation and state-building. In particular, the formal justice system is infested with corrupt judges and officials. Whilst the Afghan people lack a basic understanding of their own rights and of how the rule of law should apply in their everyday lives, they do understand that such corrupt systems fail to provide fair and reasonable resolution of their disputes and needs. Corruption undermines the principles of good governance and, to date, the central Government has failed to get it under control. The overwhelming and increasing reliance on poppy as the primary agricultural product and backbone of the local economy also undermines good governance, whilst fuelling crime, corruption and insurgency. Opium poppy is by far the most lucrative crop available and farmers are unwilling to abandon it for less profitable alternatives, preventing other, legitimate crops and businesses from becoming established. Between them, lack of capacity, security and corruption severely constrain attempts to establish good governance and hinder the delivery of services to the people which, in turn, detracts from the ability to win the support of the population against the insurgents.

There are some who argue that the insurgency was triggered by the arrival of significant Western military forces following the transition of responsibility for security in the south from the US-led Coalition to NATO. The truth is that the insurgency was quietly well underway but had no need to take military action, since there was little to challenge their growing activity and influence. Likewise, there was little to disturb the illicit activity of their criminal fellow travellers.

Intense fighting broke out in 2006 with the arrival of British, Canadian and Dutch forces into areas where the insurgency was already at a well advanced guerrilla stage, with many areas already run by a Taliban shadow administration. Buoyed by their perceived successes in 2006, the Taliban were estimated by intelligence staff to have fielded a force of around 8,000 fighters for their 2007 offensive. The overwhelming majority of this force was believed to be locally recruited and operating under local commanders, with less than 1,000 hard-core Islamist ideologues and foreign fighters. Against this, the Government could field an army 'corps' with around 7,000 reasonably well-trained and well-equipped troops organised into four brigades. NATO presence in the south is nominally 18,000[21] but around one third are national support elements and, once air, HQ and other supporting personnel are discounted, there are only some 7,000–8,000 ground manoeuvre forces available to commanders. These ground forces consist of four provincially focused task forces, and an under-strength British battlegroup, based in Kandahar, as a regional reserve. In addition, there are a number of NATO Special Forces units that report directly to the ISAF HQ in Kabul as well as a US Ranger battalion, entirely outside the NATO command chain, which operates across the region to a separate US agenda. Other military forces can be made available for specific operations but I will return to that later. There are no military forces, Afghan or international, based in Nimruz or Dai Kundi. In addition to the military, the Regional Police chief claims to have some 10,000 policemen stationed across all six provinces of the region but, in general, they are poorly trained and equipped and suffer from widespread corruption.

As well as the obvious lack of unity of command in this arrangement, the problem for the NATO regional commander is that force presence is set by the commitment of the contributing nations in each province, rather than by operational imperatives. Thus the largest force, a brigade contributed by the UK and Denmark, is engaged with the poppy barons of Helmand whilst the strategic centre of the insurgency in Kandahar has a single Canadian battlegroup. Zabol, through which runs the main insurgent line from Pakistan, boasts only an ill-equipped Romanian Battalion reinforced by a US Infantry company, and Uruzgan, another important supply and sanctuary area for the Taliban, has only a single Dutch Battalion supported by an Australian engineer company, both of whose declared mission is to support reconstruction rather than counter the insurgency. This situation has been ameliorated to some degree by judicious use of the small regional reserve and cooperation from the US Ranger battalion but it does not allow the commander to develop a coordinated regional approach to the campaign.

The governance and development elements of NATO's comprehensive approach are the responsibility of the Provincial Reconstruction Teams which have been established in Helmand, Kandahar, Uruzgan and Zabol, each one different in composition and fiercely independent, with national command and reporting chains that drive their activity, rather than the plans and orders of the NATO commanders, under whose operational command they are nominally assigned. In addition, PRTs are controversial among the wider international community. There is concern from aid organisations that the so called humanitarian space in which they like to operate becomes compromised by the development activity of PRTs. This is a long-standing debate, which I do not intend to address here except to note that humanitarian aid is a separate, albeit related, activity to development which, axiomatically, is partial towards the state and, by extension, to the regime which controls that state. More importantly, to my mind, the World Bank, among others, has recently criticised PRTs for undermining the very state that they are supposed to be assisting,[22] whilst, in his report to the UN Security Council, the Secretary-General stated a need to 'harmonise' PRT activities

---

21   ISAF 2008.
22   World Bank 2007.

with those of the Afghan Government.[23] This is unfortunate since, according to NATO direction in OPLAN 10302, the role of PRTs is 'to assist the Afghan Government to extend its authority across the country' and specifically to promote the policies of the central Government, stimulate security sector reform and support the process of reconstruction. NATO's direction allowed that different regional circumstances, as well as national capabilities and approaches would rule out a uniform approach, which has led to an extremely diverse range of organisation and activity. However, the World Bank noted that all PRTs to varying degrees 'provide a protective home for bilateral donor and other government agencies which undertake development programmes and initiatives in the provinces'.[24]

These are real impediments to the implementation of a comprehensive approach at the operational and regional level, representing a serious challenge to the NATO commanders who are charged with implementation of its strategy, and clearly do not match the rhetoric uttered at summits and in capitals. Whilst NATO speaks of a more systematic approach to consultation and cooperation at all levels, UK doctrine states that experience shows that in coalition operations an effective and timely response may be best served by recognising a 'lead framework entity',[25] such as NATO, the UN or a lead nation, and that the most likely scenarios for future stabilisation are ones that require working within coalitions where 'energies will need to be focused increasingly on developing the broader international architecture for integrated stabilisation operations'.[26] However, the UK, like other contributing nations, has appeared reluctant to surrender civilian authority to such entities. Whilst emphasising the importance of unity of command, US doctrine acknowledges that, in multinational and counter-insurgency operations, political considerations will most likely prevent this, stressing instead that achieving unity of effort, focusing on what needs to be done, should be the goal of command and support relationships.

> All organizations contributing to a counter-insurgency operation should strive, or be persuaded to strive, for maximum unity of effort. Informed, strong leadership forms the foundation for achieving it ... A clear understanding of the desired end state should infuse all efforts, regardless of the agencies or individuals charged with their execution.[27]

In the eastern region, where the force is predominantly US, this requirement has been met. In the south, with little Afghan Government presence, a weak UN office and lack of consensus between the contributing nations, it has not.

This section has shown that Afghanistan is not a homogeneous society. Rugged terrain, with a lack of good roads and transportation have prevented social adaptation and fostered self-reliant, locally and inwardly focused communities, leaving the country fragmented along ethnic, tribal and sub-tribal, linguistic and religious lines. The challenge of central Government is to overcome the inherent resistance to change of these centuries-old alignments. Unfortunately, weak government and lack of cohesion among the international community are failing to provide the comprehensive approach that is required to counter the insurgency that has been allowed to develop in the region. The final section will relate briefly how NATO military commanders have sought to overcome these challenges, the campaign plans they have developed, and the extent to which a comprehensive approach has or has not been achieved.

---

23   Moon, Ban Ki 2008.
24   World Bank 2007, 26.
25   JDN 4-05 2006, 1-11.
26   SU 2007b, 6.
27   Field Manual 3-24 2006, 2-13.

Campaign Plans

As the reader may imagine, in a NATO organisation there is a veritable blizzard of plans and political direction, from both Alliance and national headquarters, which commanders must take into account. However, ultimately it is the commander on the ground that must shape the campaign, faced with the situation and conditions described in the previous section.

General Sir David Richards was the first Commander of ISAF to take responsibility for the whole of Afghanistan, including the southern region, seeking to 'operationalise' the three NATO lines of operation: security, governance and development. Presumably aware that he lacked the force to immediately dominate the insurgency, he persuaded the Afghan Government to adopt the tried and tested 'ink spot' strategy to clear, hold and build in key population areas – the so called Afghan Development Zones (ADZs) – with a view to gradually expanding the influence of the Government in contested areas. To give this the necessary political leadership and promote unity of effort, Richards was instrumental in establishing a Cabinet-level crisis committee, known as the Policy Action Group, comprising key ministers as well as the principal military and political leaders of the international community. However, despite a promising start, the Afghan Government remained unable to deliver strong governance whilst contributing nations remained unable to agree regional priorities and UN authority remained weak.

Major General 'Jacko' Page took command in the south after a series of setbacks, the most significant being the loss of Musa Qaleh in Helmand to the Taliban and with a similar fate in prospect for Deh Rawod in Uruzgan. He found his forces largely fixed, trying to hold the existing ADZs, constantly 're-mowing the grass' as he described it, as the insurgents, in the absence of strong government and adequate policing, continued to re-infiltrate areas that had previously been cleared. Realising that, whilst governance was most important to campaign success in the long run, he could do little to influence it, except to provide the security that would allow governance and development to flourish, Page focused effort on developing the capability and coordinating activity with the ANSF, whilst allowing the Taliban to dash its forces against his bases. At the same time, he developed and began to use a small regional reserve, in conjunction with the US Rangers and Special Forces, to disrupt and degrade the insurgents in their stronghold areas. This design proved very successful with the Afghan National Army but lack of resources and effective mentoring, together with corrupt leadership, bedevilled police reform. As the campaign season wore on, it became clear that the insurgents were suffering huge attrition from their attacks on Coalition forces and, by the end of 2007, it was estimated that they had sustained something in the order of 50 per cent casualties. The effect began to show with increasing numbers of out-of-area and foreign fighters appearing in the region, as the Taliban struggled to recruit from the local tribes, who began to question the inevitability of Taliban victory and feared for their own power in relation to other tribes for a generation, if they lost too many of their fighting men. Meanwhile, a successful campaign of targeting the insurgent leadership by Special Forces started to impact on the tactical cohesion of insurgent forces, and the sophistication of their attacks visibly reduced. However, neither the Afghan Government nor the UN was exploiting this success to expand and improve the delivery of governance and economic development, whilst the agenda of the PRTs seemed to be set by the diplomatic and development agendas in Western capitals rather than the imperatives of southern Afghanistan. As attacks on Coalition bases fell off, pressure on insurgent sanctuaries was maintained into the winter and, most significantly, with the aid of the theatre reserve, a US airmobile battlegroup, Musa Qaleh was retaken.

Musa Qaleh is notable not only due to its totemic status for the Taliban but also because it represented the first truly comprehensive approach to counter-insurgency in the region and was the culmination of cooperative processes that the UK task force and civilian-led PRT had been developing through the previous few months. It was unique, in that it took as its end state the stabilisation objectives of the civilian leadership and incorporated all actors, civil and military, together with the UN and Afghan officials, in the planning process. Military activity was shaped not simply to drive out the Taliban but to best set conditions for rapid reconstruction, which meant minimising 'kinetic' activity and maximising the perception of Government leadership within the plan. The outcome is well known, and will not be covered here, but it provided an example and incentive for all actors in the region which the regional HQ has been able to exploit. This operation also saw the pragmatic adoption by the UK of the US principle that what is done is more important than who does it, with the formation of a military stabilisation team to start stabilisation activity in the non-permissive environment that initially existed.

With the insurgency largely pushed back to a subversion phase, relying on intimidation and terrorism for its effect, COMISAF, General Dan McNeill, declared that 'the Taliban are unable to bring down the Government, only the Government can now do that'.[28] With this in mind, the new regional Commander, General Marc Lessard, has sought to create greater momentum and cohesion in the governance and development lines of operation. On assuming command in February 2008, his priority was to engage with the civilian elements of PRTs and develop a new campaign plan that would balance the national agendas of the contributing nations with the direction he was receiving from COMISAF to take the fight to the Taliban and to compete for 'the ungoverned space'.[29] That plan was presented to contributing nations in Ottawa on 29 April 2008. At the time of writing, the outcome is unknown, but a previous meeting of foreign and defence ministers in Edinburgh had indicated a desire for partners in the south to agree objectives and develop a more cohesive and comprehensive campaign plan. At the same time, the lessons of Musa Qaleh were studied, and a planning guide for comprehensive stabilisation planning at the tactical level was produced and has now been used by both the Dutch and the Canadians to plan operations in Deh Rawod and Maiwand respectively.

This section has attempted briefly to trace the development of the campaign in the south. Bearing in mind that it began less than two years before this chapter was written, and that counter-insurgency requires a long-term view, it could be argued that, despite the shortcomings outlined here, there has been significant progress and success. The irony is that the reversion to subversion and terrorism by the Taliban has heightened the perception of insecurity among the civilian community, in particular the international community, many of whom have withdrawn from the area. This highlights one of the biggest shortcomings in the effort of the Government and the international community, the failure to develop a coherent and effective strategic communication strategy. In one of his key themes, Kilcullen argues that 'until an information base is developed, the other pillars of counter-insurgency cannot be effective'.[30]

---

28   General McNeill in conference call with regional commanders in December 2007.
29   General McNeill direction to General Marc Lessard in March 2008.
30   Kilcullen 2006, 5.

Conclusion

In summary, I have attempted to outline the development of thinking on the comprehensive approach both nationally by the UK and within NATO, and to compare that to US thinking on counter-insurgency, which shapes the direction given by COMISAF. I have argued that there is not yet consensus on the comprehensive approach within NATO, whilst US doctrine is more attuned than that of the UK to the idea of 'contested space', with greater emphasis on defeating rather than containing an insurgency. I have outlined the situation and conditions that pertain in southern Afghanistan and attempted to illustrate the shortfalls and challenges which exist, in particular the failure of the Coalition, so far, to develop a truly regional and comprehensive strategy for the employment of its resources. I have traced how military commanders have dealt with this and sought to achieve some convergence, if not integration, of effort by the Coalition partners, on the security line of operation, whilst seeking ways to extend this principle into development and governance. Finally, I have tried to illustrate, by way of the apparent success at Musa Qaleh, that whilst the comprehensive approach has not been well implemented in the past, there are signs and hope that it is being embraced and that it might represent more than the 'pious hope' with which this chapter was introduced. The challenge now for the Afghan Government and the international community is to consolidate recent success and to tackle rapidly the remaining shortcomings that threaten future stability, in particular strategic communications and the rampant corruption that continues to undermine the Government's legitimacy.

Chapter 20

NATO Operations in Afghanistan 2008–2009: A Theatre-Level View

Jon Riley – 29 April 2009

This chapter looks at the campaign in Afghanistan from the perspective of a NATO officer – the Deputy Commander of ISAF – outside the British national chain of command, and considers the enemy faced, the forces and techniques deployed, the development of Afghan forces, some words on the issues of counter-narcotics and civilian casualties, the role of Provincial Reconstruction Teams (PRTs) and the obstacles encountered other than insurgency.

Afghanistan sits astride the Hindu Kush mountains and its climate is continental: harsh winters well below freezing, with snow on the high ground for five months of the year. The summers are hot and dry with temperatures around 50 degrees Celsius, often with drought for many years in succession. The terrain varies from mountains up to 14,000 feet; deserts; river valleys and agricultural land where there is water; and a few large cities like Kabul, Herat, Kandahar, Masar-e-Sharif and Jellalabad. Eighty per cent of the people live on the land. The population is divided into Pashtuns, about 45 per cent; Turkic people such as the Uzbeks; Oriental Tajiks; Hazaras, the descendants of the Mongol invaders; Baluchis; and nomadic Kuchis. Afghanistan as a country cannot be said to have existed prior to 1919 and it has therefore little tradition of statehood. The Bonn constitution of 2001[1] imposed a centralised form of government on a country that has traditionally only tolerated the centre and, even now, the centre has little impact in remote districts. A strong unofficial state composed of tribes, clans and families, with all the traditional administration of government and justice that this implies, therefore underlies the official state. The glue that used to connect the two was the monarchy, but that is now gone. One of the challenges of modern Afghanistan is to reconcile these two systems of government.

What about the enemy? The Taliban (which means scholars) was formed in the refugee camps and madrassas in Pakistan, where thousands of young Afghan men, radicalised by Deobandi teachings and militarised by war during the Soviet occupation, came together under the flag of Islam to bring an end to the chaos that ruled their country. The Taliban movement consisted primarily of Pashtuns from the southern part of the country and had consolidated its power over the whole of Afghanistan by 1996.

After the Taliban were swept out of power following their involvement in the events of 11 September 2001, they spent several years regrouping in the Federally Administered Tribal Areas in Pakistan, and then re-infiltrating the Pashtun south and east. This neo-Taliban, re-formed by Mullah Omar on the structure of the original Taliban movement, forms the core of the insurgent movement. If the reader would like an insight into what sort of people they are, why their adherents fight and how badly they are brainwashed, I recommend the Canadian *Globe and Mail* newspapers

---

1   The 2001 Bonn Conference established the Afghan Constitution Commission which drafted the new constitution of Afghanistan that was adopted by the Loya Jirga on 4 January 2004.

series, 'Talking to the Taliban'.[2] It is an essentially rural insurgency fought by groups of fighters, either from Pakistan or locally recruited, under the direction of several organising groups or shuras. Its Pashtun basis makes it very hard for the current Government, which relies heavily on Pashtun support, even to utter the word 'insurgency' – especially when it will seek re-election this year.

In addition to the Taliban proper, the insurgency includes several former Mujahedeen groups such as the Haqqani Network, the Hezb-i-Islami Gulbuddin, or HiG, (led by Gulbuddin Hekmatyar), and the Lashkar-i-Taiba. The insurgency is also augmented by fighters from, among other places, Pakistan, Chechnya, Saudi Arabia, Libya and Uzbekistan.

Behind them lies al-Qaeda, which acts as a facilitation network for ideology, money, weapons, people and expertise through its contacts across the Islamic world. It provides, for example, groups of fighters and trainers with the technical expertise to construct roadside bombs – IEDs; it recruits, trains, indoctrinates and transports suicide bombers and their devices. It spreads the doctrines of hate through Wahhabbi teaching in the madrassas of Pakistan and elsewhere. By these means it works to spread the global jihad into Afghanistan.

In Afghanistan, the Taliban's aim is to re-establish its medieval style of rule and severe interpretation of Sharia law. To do this, their first goal is to force NATO and other international forces from Afghanistan; or if they cannot *force* us out, to *wait* us out. Without these forces, they know that the Government of Afghanistan is vulnerable. At the same time, therefore, they seek continually to undermine the Karzai Government. The weaker, more ineffective, and more corrupt the Government looks, the better the alternatives offered by the insurgents appear to the population.

The insurgency has without doubt grown hotter during the year prior to writing this chapter. There are three reasons for this. First, a change in insurgent tactics from a few, large engagements to many smaller ones; secondly, the insurgents' ability to operate from safe havens in Pakistan; and third, the bigger NATO, US and Afghan military footprint. Let me take these one at a time, beginning with the asymmetrical aspects. The insurgency, which began by trying to confront NATO and US forces head-on, in large-scale engagements, is now characterised by a proliferation of small groups, generally with defined areas of operation and highly mobile.

Having been unable to defeat US and NATO forces in head-to-head combat and with nothing to offer the population except a return to the highly unpopular Taliban rule of the late 1990s, the insurgency's military, administrative and information operations aim to dominate provinces without actually occupying territory: given our counter-insurgency doctrine and practice, this is a serious asymmetry. Through these activities the insurgents seek to exercise an all-pervading influence over local communities, paralyse government and undermine popular will and morale. Their methods include targeted assassination of Government officials and tribal elders, intimidation of local people and NGOs, extortion and taxation, closure of schools, the destruction of infrastructure, the effective use of all forms of communication media, a rapid dispensation of Sharia justice and the promotion of an alternative to a Government widely viewed as corrupt and ineffective. In military operations against ISAF, there has been a shift over the last year from fewer, large attacks to a much larger number of small and asymmetrical attacks using IEDs, indirect fire and complex ambush. However, where circumstances appear to offer the chance of an information victory, large attacks are still part of the insurgents' tactics.

The attack on French troops in Surowbi in August 2008 is a case in point. On 18 August, a French detachment of two platoons mounted in APCs, and partnered by an ANA (Afghan National Army) platoon and a team of US Special Forces, was conducting a surveillance mission in the Uzbeen and Tizvin valleys, 40 kilometres from Kabul city. This is a mountainous and remote area; the mission

---

2   Smith 2008.

had been going on since 15 August. Part of the patrol was engaged by at least 120 insurgents. Fire was returned and the troops in contact pushed through the contact area. Reinforcements were called and a further two platoons, located about ten kilometres away, moved up. Two armed helicopters were also on station. Close air support was provided and significant ordnance was dropped. The situation remained confused all through the night. By 0530 on 19 August it was clear that eight French soldiers had been killed and up to 20 French and ANA soldiers had been injured. The fighting had been close up and personal: many of the casualties had their throats cut. After the French withdrew, contact was maintained with the enemy by airborne surveillance as the insurgent group moved into two villages just over the Kabul River in Laghman Province. Follow-up Special Forces operations began at 0400 the following morning, involving Afghan Commando troops, US and Norwegian troops. Thirty-six insurgents were killed, and caches of weapons and IEDs seized.

However, these sorts of confrontation are now the exception not the norm: the Taliban's failed attempt to attack Lashkar Gar in strength in October 2008 was prominent in the media because it was an exceptional event.

By late October 2008 – the close of the Taliban's summer fighting season – Afghanistan had seen a 52 per cent increase in 'significant acts' reported by ISAF: almost all small events. IED attacks were up 51 per cent in the year to up to 1 October: 2,381 attacks compared with 1,576 for the same period in 2007, with 80 per cent of ISAF and Afghan Security Force casualties coming from IEDs – roadside bombs. Thus, the basis of the insurgents' hold over the population is the sense that they can appear anywhere, at any time, while the Government and its forces remain absent. It is emphatically not that they offer an alternative administration: their record is vulnerable to challenge on this and so they avoid it. Their claim that they offer security does not hold up either: Taliban rule may bring *order*, but individuals, especially women and non-Pashtuns, are far from *secure*.

During 2008, insurgents increased their presence on the roads. As ISAF and ANSF moved away from protecting roads, taking the fight to the Taliban in the rural districts, so the Taliban saw an opportunity and came back to the highways, mounting checkpoints, murdering officials, extorting tolls, controlling the narcotics smuggling and, where it suited them, destroying the physical infrastructure of roads, culverts and bridges. Every person stopped at an insurgent checkpoint tells ten others of his experiences, and fear spreads rapidly by word of mouth.

Many criminal groups either collaborate with the Taliban in this activity, or take advantage of the circumstances of insecurity. Even northern warlords, power-brokers and officials opposed ideologically to the Taliban will smuggle drugs one way over the border and weapons the other, taking their cut. Some people have described to me a system almost of franchise, where criminals are either paid or allowed by the Taliban to carry out robbery, smuggling and kidnapping in exchange for a share of the profits. For local people, whether their lives are being made intolerable by ideologically motivated Talibs or financially motivated criminals makes little difference: all they know is that their Government is not protecting them.

Despite this, detailed analysis over the past three years shows quite clearly that, although the levels of violence have intensified, the geography has not expanded. Around 80 per cent of violent activity takes place in only 15 per cent of the districts: the insurgency remains a Pashtun phenomenon.

Next, the safe haven in Pakistan. The various cease-fires and negotiations in the tribal areas of Pakistan have provided sanctuary for the insurgency to recuperate, train and operate with impunity. At the same time they are being bolstered by increasing numbers of foreign jihadists. As a result, insurgent activity rose significantly during 2008 in the north-east of the country as well as inside Pakistan itself. Worse still is the impunity with which insurgent leaders live and operate in

Pakistan: the whereabouts of, for example, the Haqqani brothers and Gulbuddin Hekmatyar, not to mention members of the Quetta Shura, is known to the Pakistani authorities who are either unable or unwilling to take action.

Next, the larger footprint of friendly forces. Our own operational tempo and reach has increased. ISAF and the ANA now operate in previous insurgent sanctuaries and along their infiltration routes. For example, in RC-East the ISAF force level has increased 20 per cent, not including the 10,000 or so troops under US national command (referred to as OEF, or Operation Enduring Freedom); and the strength of the Afghan 201st and 203rd Corps has risen by 65 per cent. Overall, the strength of ISAF has risen to 50,000 and the ANA field formations to more than 60,000. Helmand was certainly quiet until 5,000 British troops began stomping around the Taliban heartland there; before they started doing so, we had no presence and the Taliban and the drug barons did as they wanted – so it is, let us say, disingenuous to claim that we made the situation worse.

ISAF has contributions from 40 countries, of whom 17 countries, contributing half the total troops, will in theory take part in offensive operations. I say in theory because quite frequently there are *undeclared* caveats which become obvious through the behaviour of subordinates in response to orders that should be routine. There are also undeclared caveats on counter-narcotics and on Special Forces operations.

Then there is the matter of scale. Of these same 40 contributing countries, only nine (and not the same as will conduct offensive operations) have armies larger than ISAF. Most have no standing divisional or corps level of command. Even fewer have doctrinal understanding of combined operations, let alone complex counter-insurgency or counter-terrorism.

The tensions this brings are obvious: it hardens US determination to control offensive counter-terrorism, internment and air power. This, plus the part played by non-NATO member states, result in not only a coalition founded on an alliance, but a coalition within the alliance based on those who signed up for fighting counter-insurgency, rather than peacekeeping.

The bulk of our troops are deployed in Regional Commands East, which has nearly 20,000 mostly US troops under NATO command; and South, which has over 18,000 British, American, Canadian, Dutch, Australian and Romanian troops. Pure numbers are not as important, however, as capabilities: the ability to see the battlefield through high-tech modern surveillance; to deliver precision fires from the air or the ground; to manoeuvre troops rapidly by aircraft, helicopter or protected vehicles; to communicate securely over long distances and rough terrain; to synchronise conventional forces and Special Forces; to link support for governance, construction and an information campaign – all deliver an effect far greater than mere numbers suggest. Add to that the courage, tenacity and determination of our soldiers, marines and airmen which are undiminished from that shown by their fathers and grandfathers. Fighting modern jihadists is not a job for the faint hearted: the Chechen, Pakistani and other fighters we face simply refuse to surrender, and every fight is therefore a fight to the finish.

Regional Commands North, led by Germany, Capital, led by France, and West, led by Italy, account for the rest. Here our numbers of troops are smaller, and it is here that national caveats on employment severely restrict the employability of some contingents at the sharp end of the business. These are, however, the areas where development, rather than security, can lead but, even so, the Taliban will re-infiltrate where we are not present.

The role of military forces in counter-insurgency is to protect the population and separate the people from the insurgents so as to deny the insurgency its support or its ability to coerce. It is not just armed social work. With 50,000 troops, 60,000 Afghan soldiers and about the same number of lightly armed, semi-trained police, we are under-resourced to do this: Afghanistan is one-third as big again as Iraq, and Iraq has 600,000 Iraqi Security Forces and 150,000 Coalition troops; not to mention ten times the allocation of technical intelligence gathering assets; and the apparatus of a modern state, floating on a sea of oil! We are therefore forced to make choices about where we operate and ISAF does this through a sequence of shape-clear-hold-build. Areas are first cleared of insurgent forces by a combination of intelligence-led strike operations against key leaders and groups using air, conventional ground forces and Special Forces supported by information operations. Most of these operations are now Afghan led or are indeed wholly Afghan; ISAF-only operations are the exception. The selection of a target area likewise is Afghan led and is usually determined by the capacity to carry out the hold and build phases. Holding ground is the preserve of the Afghan police but, as I will discuss in a moment, their capacity to do this is thin. We therefore often have to use ISAF or ANA troops to do this and then, if we are obliged to remove them, the insurgents may return, requiring us to start the process again. Building involves the introduction of governance as well as infrastructure, which will be discussed below along with the subject of PRTs.

Let me offer an example from the British sector: the operation to capture Musa Qaleh in December 2007. The area was first invested in order to control movement in and out. A comprehensive surveillance network was established to identify insurgents and narcotics facilities. Tribal leaders were engaged through a turned Taliban leader, Mullah Salem, and offered rewards for working with us. A comprehensive information operation was launched. More than 100 hours of electronic warfare, including jamming, targeting and interception of insurgent communications, and broadcasts, were employed. After this had been given ten days to soak in, the district was cleared by Afghan Army troops supported by ISAF soldiers, helicopters, and air- and ground-delivered firepower. At least 300 insurgents were killed and the drug refining operation destroyed. A garrison of Afghan Army, police and British troops was installed along with a new district administration, backed up by short-term humanitarian aid, in order to hold the ground. Since then, the police force has been retrained and re-equipped, and the infrastructure repaired. There are still plenty of insurgents in the general area, but control has been retained by the Government.

But overall, with current ISAF and Afghan force levels, we are not able to protect the population to the degree we need. An additional US brigade arrived in December and has deployed into the provinces around Kabul; and we have received more French and Polish troops in the north-east. Special Forces operations have been targeted at some of the most dangerous groups and individuals. Throughout the winter, Operation Tolo will build on these short term measures to clear, hold and build in key areas. But security measures alone, unless supported by rapid improvements in local governance, will only abate the problem.

In the long term, we therefore look to transfer the lead for security to the Afghan National Army and Police. The force generation programme for the Army is well on track; but growing a professional army is not something one can achieve in a year or so; especially in a country ruined by war, where adult literacy rates average below 10 per cent, and where the most capable and educated people, who might provide the leadership and the administration, are either dead or in exile. Media whining about how slow we are to generate local security forces often overlooks this simple fact. It will be two to three years before the Afghan Army can begin to take the lead because it will take time to develop the Afghan Army's institutional capacity: its command and control, communications, officer and NCO corps, staff training, personnel and material management and so on. But where it has been in existence for several years, such as in the east and in the capital, we are close to the point where it can, in some areas, assume primacy.

ISAF's immediate role in the Afghanisation of security is through both embedded mentoring – Operational Mentoring and Liaison Teams (OMLTs) – *and* the partnering of units and formations, so that we can move to a situation over the next two years whereby Afghan forces take the lead in planning and executing security operations.

Once Afghan formations are able to take the lead, international forces, while maintaining their mentoring role, can switch their main effort away from combat towards supporting those areas where Afghan capabilities will take longer to develop: logistic sustainability; intelligence, surveillance and reconnaissance; precision fires – plus manoeuvre support and the provision of reaction forces. The first example of this process in action is the Afghans' assumption of security primacy in Kabul, beginning in August 2008.

In parallel, and once the force generation programme has been substantially completed by the US-led Combined Security Transition Command, NATO can take up a similar role to that undertaken in Iraq: developing the Afghan military institutions: the Ministry of Defence; the higher headquarters; the military schools and colleges; the logistic and personnel commands.

Such a progression of Afghanisation makes the point – important to the Afghans, the insurgents, the neighbouring countries and our own people – that ISAF is an *interim* force with a finite life, and with a mission that will evolve. An important signal might therefore be to change the 'I' in ISAF from 'International' to 'Interim'.

But in a normal society, it is not the army that leads on internal security – it is the police. The Afghan Army is also, therefore, an interim force in this regard. It is, however, not possible to hand over security responsibility to the police in most districts and municipalities of Afghanistan, since its level of development is far lower than that of the Army and its policemen are not able to face the firepower of the insurgents. Its development will take longer and the Army will have to hold the ring in the meantime. The current programme of police reform, called Focused District Development, is an important step, but without supporting developments in the justice sector it will remain a localised effect. I believe that, in time, the police will have to move away from local recruiting and basing, towards a national or at least regional solution, in order to break the links with tribal factionalism and corruption. ISAF's Provincial Reconstruction Teams or PRTs have a particular role to play here, not only by acting as coordinators and by providing a secure base for mentoring teams, but also by focusing efforts to develop the administrative and justice sectors at province and district level.

Despite all the difficulties, the insurgency is not delivering what its propaganda said it would. On current form, it will never beat us, NATO, on the battlefield, so long as the Alliance's will to keep us there holds. Despite media hysteria, security has greatly improved in Kabul, which has had only 35 security incidents in 2008. It is not Baghdad; it is not even Belfast when I was a young soldier! Our problem is not that the insurgency is strong, but that the state is weak. The insurgency sits inside the greater problem of nation building, and poisons it – because without security, development of essential services and basic governance cannot proceed: security is the most basic requirement for any government. It is bad enough that an absence of security hampers the development of governance and the rule of law – let alone socio-economic programmes – but in Afghanistan what little governance there is, is hampered further by weak leadership, a culture of dependency and blame, and entrenched, raging corruption. The World Bank now assesses that Afghanistan has slipped to 176 out of 180 in the league table of the world's most corrupt countries. State-sponsored theft, bribery and extortion are destroying the economy more effectively than the insurgency. Narcotics is the only part of the Afghan economy not being crippled by extortion dressed up as government regulation – it even benefits from our development assistance through the recycling of agricultural aid programmes. But what does corruption *mean* to people trying to make a living in Afghanistan? Let me give you some examples. If you are a businessman trying to bring a cargo of goods from Peshawar in Pakistan to Kabul, it means 47 different permits or passes for various stretches of the road, each of which may need eight or nine different signatures, each of which means a hefty bribe. If you are a traveller, it means getting stopped at a police checkpoint every ten miles, and paying a 'toll'. If you are the policeman levying such a toll, it means you probably have to do so to feed your family, because the district chief of police has stolen most of your $70-a-month salary. And his salary in turn has been stolen by the provincial chief, whose salary has been stolen by someone in Kabul, who is recouping the $200,000 or so that he laid out to buy his job in the first place. It may also mean that three out of the ten policemen who rob you are doing so to feed a heroin addiction which is costing $60 a day to service, in an economy where most families expect to live on $4 a day and where bread now costs three times what it did a year ago.

What about poppy? The UN Office on Drugs and Crime has recently reported that whilst poppy cultivation levels are down by 19 per cent in 2008, opium production has only reduced by 6 per cent due to higher yields. Ninety-three per cent of the world supply of opium is still grown in Afghanistan and 98 per cent of Afghan opium is grown in just seven provinces, mainly in the south. If Helmand were a country, it would be the world's largest producer of heroin. Moreover, those provinces now free of opium growing are not free of refining, trafficking, addiction or marijuana growing – and marijuana produces as much revenue as heroin.

We have an opportunity as well as a challenge: to change the behaviour of both farmers and bigger fish involved in trafficking and corruption. When you try to change behaviour, there are two levers: persuasion and coercion. Persuasion is principally directed towards the farmer – that is, it is *behind* the farm gate. It includes such things as the promotion of alternative livelihoods, access to good performance initiatives, better information and a more secure environment. It is Government of Afghanistan business, supported by the donors, and ISAF's involvement on the ground is led by the PRTs. This has become easier given that the price of wheat and rice has trebled this year, closing the gap between opium and licit crops; the gap is further closed when one takes into account the taxes the opium farmer must pay the Taliban, the high cost of his labour, and the need to buy off corrupt Government officials.

Coercion, which is where military force comes to play, is aimed both *behind* and *beyond* the farm gate – but chiefly beyond. It consists of eradication and interdiction. Eradication is led by the Government, and is a high-profile but thoroughly inefficient use of forces. Its only real value lies in demonstrating that those big growers who believe themselves untouchable can indeed be touched. Interdiction is far more effective, since it hits the refined product, while not alienating the small farmer. Seventy per cent of the profits lie beyond the farm gate: the farm gate price for raw opium last year was around $86 per kilo – nine times what wheat would bring. But that $86 had become $3,500 by the time it had been refined and left the borders of Afghanistan; and $35,000 by the time it hit the streets of London. Interdiction gives, therefore, a bigger return.

The interdiction of narcotics illustrates rather bleakly the current inability of the NATO Alliance to adapt to a changed world; and the way that human rights law, which protects individuals, can be used by lawyers to protect criminals and insurgents and so undermine the needs of collective security for states and peoples. Under NATO's Afghanistan Operational Plan (OPLAN) there is a requirement in law to prove the nexus between insurgency and narcotics. Reliable and recent intelligence must establish that a person is taking a direct role in military activities; our targeting nominations reflect this. Since international law prohibits military attacks on civilians and civilian objects even, where both might properly be described as criminal, forces assigned to ISAF cannot attack narco-traffickers and producers unless they are demonstrably insurgents. Similarly, we are obliged to prove significant participation in the insurgency. In practice, this means that the target's narco and insurgent activity is so intertwined that it is impossible to distinguish them. Thus direct action against individuals, facilities or items engaged with the narco trade *simply because it is narcotics* is inconsistent with the UN mandate, the SACEUR OPLAN, the Alliance-approved target sets and the Rules of Engagement. Merely changing the language of the OPLAN, as has been the approach so far, to allow direct action against narcos, will have no effect on the superior legal authorities that do not provide for it. Narcos per se are not on the approved target list, nor are they within the Rules of Engagement – they are in law civilians. Finally there are some nations, including the USA, that have domestic legal or policy constraints that do not allow military forces to engage in law enforcement, even when conducting coincident military operations overseas. If this is to be tackled, there will need to be a fundamental legal shift that describes narcotics as insurgent war materiel. Some progress has been made under the approach adopted by the 2006 Budapest Conference, which allows contributing nations to opt in to (rather than out of) counter-narcotics operations; and allows NATO forces to prosecute narcotics-related targets when requested to do so by Afghan authorities, using measures consistent with Afghan law. The extra-judicial killing of narcos, however, remains prohibited and the law of armed conflict still applies to the use of force.

The most effective thing ISAF can do is to synchronise security operations with those bodies whose mandate is strictly counter-narcotics: the US Drugs Enforcement Agency, our own Serious and Organised Crimes Agency, the Afghan Counter Narcotics Police, the Afghan Special Narcotics Force. What we can do by these means is to bring *less* risk to the lives of those who want to grow licit crops; but *more* risk into the lives of those who promote the trade: risk to their persons, their finances and their political aspirations. The biggest factor in combating the spread of narcotics, however, remains the unequivocal commitment of the Afghan Government to its own declared policy and its laws; without that, everything we do is only tinkering at the edges.

Continuing on the theme of areas in which ISAF supports other actors, I want to mention the role of ISAF's Provincial Reconstruction Teams. These are a mix of military personnel who carry out security duties or assist the development of Afghan Security Forces; and civilians who carry out development work paid for by individual governments. Because of this, there are wide disparities in their funding – from several hundred million dollars a year for some US PRTs, to less than $300,000 for the Lithuanians in Ghor in the Central Highlands. PRTs are therefore rather like those pot-luck parties, where everyone brings something to the buffet, but you never know quite what until they uncover the plate. The NATO mission statement for PRTs is therefore quite loose:

> PRTs will assist GIRoA to extend its authority, in order to facilitate the development of a stable and secure environment in the identified area of operations, and enable Security Sector Reform and reconstruction efforts.

ISAF is not a development agency; our job is to defeat the insurgents – but we do not aim simply to shoot our way out of the insurgency. PRTs support military action by helping to bring governance to remote and insecure districts in parallel with Afghan and ISAF military efforts to bring security; the two together provide *stability*. In turn, the PRTs must also support those efforts through targeted construction activities.

Governance, or rather its lack at national and local levels, is one of the greatest obstacles to progress in Afghanistan. I define governance as:

> The traditions and institutions by which authority in a country is exercised. This includes the process by which governments are selected, monitored and replaced; the capacity of the government effectively to formulate and implement sound policies; and the respect of citizens and the state.

The writ of President Karzai's Government is steadily eroded by its inability to deliver substantive and sustainable services to people. Good governance and enduring security provided by the legitimate institutions of state are critical to winning the battle to protect the population. Ultimately, good governance depends on the Afghans. At local level, PRTs can help develop governance through creation of administrative capacity, budgetary execution, fiscal controls, and law and order programmes to support the development of policing, courts and corrections.

Finally on the subject of PRTs, the vexed question of military involvement in development. Where stability is poor, the military can play a role in providing essential infrastructure or services. We should not fool ourselves that this is about winning consent or in itself bringing stability. Pursuing construction activities outside the construct of stability merely provides targets for the other side. Beyond that, construction activities can be used to further the development of governance and security. Beyond that again we enter the realms of development, which is a game for governments, business and professional agencies. The military are amateurs at this and must learn their place: when we plan a complex strike operation we do not call in a bunch of development geeks to do it for us; the converse is also true.

This is not to say that military operations do not take place to enable development. Operation Eagle's Summit took place in late August and early September 2008. It was an operation to move a $3.4 million, 220 ton, Chinese-made turbine from Kabul via Kandahar to the Kajaki Dam in northern Helmand. It was an interesting exercise in coordinating military forces with a development agency (USAID) and a private sector company. The shaping phase included key leader engagements and intelligence-led targeting of insurgent networks and commanders; the actual move involved British, Danish, US, Canadian and Afghan troops and police, supported by attack helicopters and aircraft, significant technical intelligence platforms, artillery and rocket systems. During the operation, nearly 500 Taliban were killed. Once the turbine is installed and the distribution network erected – which could take two years and cost $120 million – the dam will provide over 50 megawatts of electricity to Helmand and Kandahar bringing power to areas that have never had it before.

PRTs are also one of our weapons in the battle of strategic communications – connecting what we said we came to do with what we deliver; and, conversely, connecting what we have done with what we say. We have often been too slow with the truth, or silent, and far too defensive – in contrast to the opposition which is unconstrained by the need to tell the truth and makes skilful use of a wide variety of information media. We have improved, I believe, through a combination of better media operations, especially radio, which reaches more people in Afghanistan than any other medium: the development of the Government Media and Information Centre as the focus for all Afghan and international media issues has been a great step forward. We have also learned more about communicating our message through traditional tribal shuras, through the Ministry of Religious Affairs and its thousands of mullahs, through the NATO-owned media, and through the behaviour of our troops and of the Afghan Security Forces.

The issue of civilian casualties is perhaps the major strategic communications challenge. In spite of what the media would have you believe, there is no doubt that the vast majority of non-combatants are killed by the Taliban and other insurgent groups. It is not NATO troops setting off suicide bombs, or hanging boys for the possession of a dollar bill, or beheading village elders. Many claims are mischievous Taliban propaganda, or they are an attempt to get operations that are hurting them turned off, by leveraging tribal access to Karzai. Sometimes these claims are an attempt to get blood money in a society which regards this as a legitimate tactic: several Afghans have told me that there is an industry in this! Unlike the insurgency we do everything we can to avoid civilian casualties and to reduce them to a minimum when they are unavoidable. However, we do make mistakes. In the summer of 2008 I carried out a review of reporting, investigation and dealing methodology. As a result of this I realised that our figures, although subject to high quality investigation, were capturing only a part of the problem, and none of the wounded. I therefore directed new procedures to capture and deal with the issue. Moreover, both Generals McNeill and McKiernan have issued directives laying down clear rules for the control of fires and target identification in order to minimise the possibility of causing casualties. Now, when we receive claims of casualties, we move swiftly to investigate and either refute or accept responsibility; and then make amends through apologies, local engagement and payments.

I am often asked why we are in Afghanistan, and is the effort worth the pain? Through our sacrifices and the sacrifices of dedicated Afghans, there are some positive trends. Under the Taliban, Afghanistan had the highest child mortality rate in the world. That has been reduced by a quarter. Access to health care has gone from 8 per cent of the population to 65 per cent. More children, especially girls, go to school than at any time in Afghanistan's history: 3.8 million boys and 2.2 million girls. The road network and general infrastructure, although poor by our standards, is better than it has ever been; the white economy grew by 9 per cent last year; and the Taliban has been driven from many of its strongholds in the south and east. The Afghan Army is growing in size and competence. Afghanistan does have significant, if untapped, natural resources: hydro-electric power, a diverse agriculture, forestry, oil, coal, iron, copper, uranium and gems. It is, potentially, a rich country even without poppy.

Why we are there *is* also about drugs, but only partly, because most opium and marijuana produced in Afghanistan goes to Iran, Pakistan, China, Central Asia and Russia; little of it reaches Western Europe and the USA. But that is not the point. The point is that the money it produces buys weapons and fighters for the insurgency; and it fuels corruption, and corruption allows the Taliban to project a credible alternative to the Government and, in turn, undermines all that we do.

At the time of writing, in 2009, one senses that for many nations being in Afghanistan is as much about the institutional survival of NATO, their place as actors on the world stage, and bilateral relations with the US, as anything else. It could be argued that the US will judge whether continued investment in NATO is worthwhile, on the basis of performance. So if you believe that NATO must have a future, it has to be worth it.

Speaking as a NATO officer, if we are to achieve success then the effort needs more fighting troops and technical resources to buy what we do not have at present – time: time for the Afghan Security Forces to develop, time for governance to grow. If these troops are only to be Americans and British then the alliance risks being sidelined: the queue for the easy jobs is a long one.

But continuing in Afghanistan cannot be inspired by humanitarian motive – there are plenty of other deserving candidates for that – or institutional survival. There are more fundamental questions. First, to what extent are the developed countries of the world, faced with a massive financial crisis, prepared to invest in their own security against the spread of radical Islam, through intervention, to bring security, governance and development to areas that have none. The arguments are compelling but do we feel threatened enough and have patience enough to see it through? Secondly, is it right to spend our country's wealth and the lives of its young soldiers in such an intervention, without demanding a return from the receiving government? Are corruption, drug trading and abuse acceptable; or should we demand conditions?

What we do in Afghanistan – and Iraq – and how well we do it bears on the future viability of intervention by the West into failed or failing states. Intervention has worked in the past, it can be justified, and it can work: East Timor, Haiti, Sierra Leone, even Panama show this, even though it will never be perfect. One of the consequences of the Iraq intervention may be that the next generation will shy away from intervention in future, even when it is necessary and right, because they have seen the heat it has generated since 2001, and they want none of it. Afghanistan as a campaign sits at the cross-roads of this intervention argument: if it fails, or is even perceived not to have succeeded, it could reinforce an anti-interventionist sentiment that would take a decade to undo. If it is seen to succeed it could correct many of the objections generated by Iraq, and reinforce the belief that we in the West can succeed when we grip such problems. Those, especially in the international media, who demand a pull-out, or who seek to discredit our efforts, must answer one final question: 'what is it about al-Qaeda and the Taliban that is so admirable that you are determined to undermine our mission, eager to see them return, and anxious to welcome the consequences of what that would mean?'

Chapter 21

Helmand 2007–2008: Behavioural Conflict – From General to Strategic Corporal

Andrew Mackay – 9 June 2010

I believe success in war, or preventing war, depends on altering the behaviours of others; what I call 'behavioural conflict'. I use 52 Brigade's deployment to Helmand Province in 2007–2008 as this chapter's principal case study, examining the thought processes behind the decision to mount an influence-led operation that specifically sought to reduce hard kinetic engagement and place consent of the population at the centre of operational design. Indeed, success in battle demands as much of an understanding of social psychology, culture and economics as it does of military art and science.

We need to move influence from the periphery of a command's thinking to its epicentre. Counter-insurgency expert David Kilcullen explains:

> (W)e typically design physical operations first, then craft supporting information operations to explain our actions. This is the reverse of al-Qaida's approach. For all our professionalism, compared to the enemy's, our public information is an afterthought. In military terms, for al-Qaida the 'main effort' is information; for us, information is a "supporting effort".[1]

French COIN strategist David Galula is perhaps more succinct: 'If there was a field in which we were definitely and infinitely more stupid than our opponents, it was propaganda.'[2] Although the word 'propaganda' is contentious and linked to totalitarian regimes of the twentieth century, the comment shows that the challenges we face in 2010 are similar to those of the French military in the Algerian civil war over 50 years ago, that is, an adaptive and highly organised insurgency.

Communication can also engender passion. As Johnson-Cartee and Copeland note: 'facts inform; emotions inspire'.[3] In other words, emotions triggered by soft power can be extremely persuasive when applied in the right conditions and to the right audiences.

In current and future complex environments the British military must now urgently learn how properly and thoughtfully to apply influence. Contemporary conflict demands we are able to initiate behavioural change in combatants, in the populations from which they garner their support, and with those who exercise or seek power.

Perceptions are formed from a complex mix of sources; sometimes from first-hand experience, often not. They may be formed as a result of interaction within complex societal networks: family, tribe, ethnic group or religion. They may perhaps be formed as a result of interaction within an environment of bloggers or social network sites. Or, as we have learned from Afghanistan, they

---

1 Kilcullen 2007a.

2 Galula 1963 refers to the critical importance in a counter-insurgency of an effective information operations campaign.

3 Galula 1963.

may emanate from other stimuli – some centuries old, such as shuras, loya jirga, storytelling and codes of conduct such as Pashtunwali.[4]

Afghans are fundamentally pragmatists, an attitude forged through conflict, geography and sacred values. Few have any wish to return to the excesses of the pre-2001 Taliban government. Thus, the Afghan campaign, at its heart, is about stopping a deeply unpopular former government returning to power – for Afghan interests, for UK interests and for regional and global security interests. Indeed, the insurgency is unique in that it is probably the only one ever to be conducted by the previous government of the country. This should make the West's task conceptually easier since all that has to be done is to deny the Taliban popular support. Yet set against the reality of the environment it is hugely complex. In a land so scarred by conflict, nudging pragmatists in a specific direction by getting them to make better choices is easier said than done. Subsequently we have also learnt that our enemy also makes choices. For the ideologist, removing the 'infidel crusader from Muslim lands' may be the single goal of the conflict. Yet the Taliban are not all ideologues; dispossessed young men, drug barons and criminal elements are all in this mix and all make choices on a range of issues from repelling foreigners to poverty, to drugs or seeking power. In the grinding poverty and hopelessness of Afghanistan, people make any number of choices – pragmatism – if what is offered is better than what they have. Perception is a powerful and motivating aspect of making choices. What may appear to be irrational behaviour to an outsider may actually be entirely rational to an indigenous population. The subsequent consequences are obvious: our own perceptions can be profoundly wrong, which in turn can lead to poor decision-making.

52 Brigade in Afghanistan: A Case Study

52 Brigade was the fourth British brigade to deploy to Helmand. Each successive brigade had fought a differing campaign. 16 Air Assault Brigade's first tour, with limited resources, was highly kinetic. 3 Commando Brigade, because of force levels, went raiding and created manoeuvre outreach groups to disrupt and interdict. 12 Mechanised Brigade engaged in a more industrial scale of conflict which involved large clearances but without the force levels subsequently to hold and build in those areas. Each deployment had a significant effect upon the local population who were, inevitably, constrained in making appropriate choices through either lack of ISAF presence or fear of the Taliban returning. I therefore made an early decision in 52 Brigade's planning process to place the population at the forefront of operational design. 52 Brigade would *clear*, *hold* and *build* where it could and *disrupt*, *interdict* and *defeat* where it could not. Underpinning this would be a commitment to ensure a singular focus on influencing the population of Helmand so the brigade could gain and retain their consent.

One of the problems is appreciating the heterogeneous nature of the population; it covers 'good', 'bad' and just plain 'indifferent' attitudes, ethnic grouping, tribal grouping, educated, uneducated, wealthy, poor, literate, illiterate, religious moderates, religious zealots, government supporters, government enemies, et al.

It is, in essence, a conflict ecosystem where the actions of one actor have an impact on others, for good or for bad, and where each actor seeks some degree of advantage over other actors. The soldier, the diplomat and the aid worker are all actors in that system; one can impact positively and negatively on the other as much as on those they seek to influence. In counter-insurgency

---

4   A concept of living or philosophy for the Pashtun people. It is regarded as both an honour code and a non-written law for the people.

the commander has no choice but to place such ideas at the core of his thinking. To do otherwise would be to ignore the population who are the ultimate determinants in who wins a counter-insurgency campaign. Whilst placing the population at the centre of thinking is easy enough to say, we still have not developed the means by which that same population will be cajoled, persuaded, informed, reassured and convinced. The same also applies to the insurgent. Reconciliation, for instance, is only possible when the insurgent has decided it is the more pragmatic choice given prevailing circumstances. We should be in no doubt though that, if we do not shape the prevailing circumstances, the enemy most surely will. Influence operations are therefore at the very core of *shaping* but their role is too often relegated to the fringes of operational thinking.

In planning 52 Brigade's deployment, the Ministry of Defence's lack of corporate understanding of this challenge soon became an issue. Initial hopes that support could be sourced from the Directorate of Targeting and Information Operations (DTIO) were dashed when it became clear they saw themselves as providing generic strategic messaging, whereas what the Brigade needed was dynamic influence at the tactical level. Dr Dave Sloggett, a visiting researcher at the Defence Academy, was finally able to assist with the development of the Brigade's thinking, as were members of the Academy's small (now defunct) Advanced Research and Assessment Group, although both met with ardent resistance from DTIO who despite being able to offer no substantive support themselves were reluctant to see others working in their area. Sloggett identified very clearly why DTIO and cross-governmental products were of very little use at a tactical level:

> Any relatively simplistic analysis of the audiences that one is trying to reach in Iraq would quickly realise that it would not be right to have a simple set of messages for the Sunni and Shia communities. The same point applies in some areas of Afghanistan. Whilst there may well be some aspects of the messages to these community based audiences, which try to resonate with the communities as a whole, there will be elements that will also need to be highly localised. These must attempt to recognise specific local issues and grievances on the ground. Such ideas of balanced messages into communities at the regional and local level are clearly an element of a way forward. They must also be set in context with what one may refer to as strategic attempts to communicate to a much wider audience on the international stage as to the intent and objectives of the ongoing operations.[5]

Not only are Whitehall messages a diluted and distant memory by the time they reach tactical level, they may actually have no relevance at ground level anyway. This is not because they are unimportant (indeed they may be vital for domestic and Coalition audiences) but that they mean little to either a soldier or local during, for example, a patrol outside a forward operating base. The art therefore becomes how to ensure the message is tuned to local events and perceptions while retaining awareness of the higher-level context. This can only be achieved by striking a delicate balance between consistency and flexibility to fit local circumstances. So we could not allow a patrol in the Upper Gereshk Valley to say 'don't worry, we won't eradicate opium production because we don't want the insurgency to grow as a result', while another patrol in the Upper Sangin Valley says 'we are going to eradicate'. There has to be consistency whilst allowing for local variation. 52 Brigade referred to this as 'dynamic influence'. It involved delegating to the lowest levels the ability to apply influence and take account of local events, incidents and personalities. We created an influence organisational architecture at brigade, battalion and company level just as

---

5   Sloggett 2007.

we had for ISTAR[6] processes. Each compound, street, village, district or town contains a mass of ever-evolving contradictions, dichotomies, hopes and fears. Tapping into and turning this to our advantage is, by necessity, local in nature and cannot be achieved by generic messaging. An integral part of this is trust and we should empower our people, particularly strategic corporals and privates. My observation is that this empowerment, in any meaningful manner, is rarely forthcoming.

Influence operations have been described as: 'information operations plus targeted kinetic operations'.[7] This is too narrow a description which seems to endorse a raiding approach to counter-insurgency that cedes the initiative and battleground of perception to the enemy. As a consequence actions tend to reinforce rather than counter enemy propaganda. With the experience of 52 Brigade's deployment we believe a broader definition is required. The Ministry of Defence was unhelpfully stove-piped into information operations, psychological operations, media operations, consent-winning activities, profile and posture activities – all subsets of what I call influence. This may be a symptom of information operations concepts not having evolved as quickly as others. During the Cold War, responsibility for information operations could not be decentralised because the consequences of getting it wrong were so severe. But in counter-insurgency, decentralisation is absolutely essential. In their book, *The Starfish and the Spider*, Ori Brafman and Rod Beckstrom identify the requirement for hierarchy and central control to sit comfortably with autonomy and delegation.[8] More authority and responsibility has to be devolved to platoon and company commanders – they know the population, local life, its tempo and what influences it. They know how strong, or not, the insurgent may be in a specific area. They understand how a local population views its circumstances and can therefore empathise, or should at least try to, no matter how hard in reality. And taking responsibility for local influence includes living with the consequences. Brafman and Beckstrom identified the requirement for finding the 'decentralised sweet spot': the point along the centralised–decentralised continuum that was just about right. To achieve this, individuals at the sweet spot of decentralisation need to be enabled and given responsibility. For the Armed Forces to achieve this we need to formalise what is corporately understood by the term *influence*.

Academics and Theorists: Shaping Command Thinking

Before 52 Brigade's deployment we devoted a surprising amount of time to the study of key texts, not just counter-insurgency theory, but on the less well-known areas of behavioural psychology, economics and philosophy. These rarely feature on military staff courses but are the key to formalising influence within organisations and delegating it to as low a level as possible. 52 Brigade considered a number of conceptual ideas, much of which was later incorporated into the operational design. We sought to set aside conventional thinking (unlearn) and rethink the nature of the problems we would face. The starting point was to conceptualise what motivated people, and the first model we considered was *Homo Economicus* ('economic man').

Homo Economicus is a caricature of what, for some time, economists generally assumed people to be. It suggests that humans are rational and broadly self-interested. The model had proved influential in public policy because it suggested that influencing human behaviour was actually rather simple. To fight crime, for example, politicians need only make punishments tougher; when

---

6   Intelligence, Surveillance, Target Acquisition and Reconnaissance.
7   Kilcullen 2007b.
8   Brafman and Beckstrom 2008.

potential costs of crime outweigh potential benefits, criminals would calculate that the crime no longer advanced their interests and so would not commit it. As Mathew Taylor noted:

> For some time the model of Homo Economicus seemed to serve well enough: offer people choice and they will act in their own interest and in so doing will make the system work better for everyone. It is not a complete view of human action but it was a useful shortcut, and it had become the prevailing view of most policymakers in the US and Britain.[9]

Later, we recognised the shortcomings of the model:

> Over the past two decades, economists have been rediscovering human behaviour – real, irrational, confusing human behaviour, that is, rather than the predictable actions of the "economic man" who used to be pressed into service whenever modelling was to be done.[10]

But preparation needed to start somewhere, and in the absence of anything else it became a journey of discovery for 52 Brigade. This next led to the work of Daniel Kahneman and Amos Tversky, who wrote *Judgment Under Uncertainty: Heuristics and Biases*. This initiated a debate between economists, philosophers and psychologists and laid the foundation for the conceptual thinking that subsequently developed into behavioural economics. The critical issue was the acceptance of human fallibility in making judgements and decisions. Heuristics are nothing more than common-sense 'rules of thumb' or intuitive judgements to arrive at a choice or decision. Kahneman and Tversky made the point:

> that people rely on a limited number of heuristic principles which reduce the complex tasks of assessing probabilities and predicting values to simpler judgmental operations. In general these heuristics are quite useful, but sometimes they lead to severe and systematic errors.[11]

In other words, heuristics lead to bias and bias can be exploited in the manner in which choices are framed or presented. For example, consider the following problem. A bat and a ball cost £1.10. The bat costs £1 more than the ball. How much does the ball cost? Most people, at least for a few moments, decide incorrectly that the ball costs 10p. Kahneman and Tversky argue that the reason for this is that we use two systems for judgement and decision-making. One is intuitive and fast – the gut – and often provides the right answer, but it can lead to errors (for the ball in this example actually costs 5p). The second system for judgement and decision-making is a more deliberate set of thought processes: the head. While more likely to be correct, they are also more demanding on our cognitive resources, hence the bias towards intuitive guesswork – and potentially the wrong answer.

For several decades we have applied the equivalent of Economic Man to information operations, rather than genuinely seeking to understand psychology. If we wish to influence behaviour to determine more appropriate choices, then we have to change our approach. The book *Superfreakonomics*[12] states:

---

9   Taylor 2009.
10 Chatfield 2009.
11 Kahneman, Slovic and Tversky 1982.
12 Levitt and Dubner 2009.

People aren't "good" or "bad." People are people, and they respond to incentives. They can nearly always be manipulated – for good or ill – if only you find the right levers.

Influence is all about learning which levers to use and how to apply them. For 52 Brigade that meant investigating further concepts, mostly about choice. I found five concepts from behavioural economics directly relevant to behavioural conflict.

Prospect Theory

In the late 1970s Kahneman and Tversky developed *prospect theory* to explain how people behave when dealing with risk and uncertainty.[13] Of particular interest was what economists call our *discount rate* – we value owning something today more than a larger quantity of the same thing in the future. This theory assumes people are motivated more by losses than by gains, and devote more energy to avoid loss than to achieve gain. There are implications here for how we communicate with a population that has suffered several decades of conflict. The present becomes critical with the *discount rate* amplified by an understandable reluctance to consider *next week* when getting through *today* is the prism through which any messaging is viewed. An example of how prospect theory can be distorted in conflict is a tendency to over-promise, but subsequently under-deliver, development. Hopes are raised and subsequently dashed, causing individuals to mistrust longer-term development plans with the consequence that they seek to avoid further loss rather than buy in to overstated *gains*. Claims about improvements to power generation if the Kajaki Dam in Helmand is made operational mean little for most Afghans: the perceived benefits, or prospect, of a more efficient dam are so far away it cannot possibly be a factor that might alter their behaviour or cause them to limit insurgent activity around the dam. The lesson for influence is that it must be related to something tangible and immediately apparent, not fuzzy and indistinct, regardless of how strategically important a project such as the Kajaki Dam really is.

Anchoring

Kahneman's and Tversky's work demonstrated that individuals, when conflicted between *gut* and *head*, can be easily manipulated by *anchoring* their choice to a predetermined value. They demonstrated that people make estimates starting from an initial value which is adjusted to yield the final answer. It was this phenomenon that they called anchoring. It is best illustrated by quoting directly from their paper:

> In a demonstration of the anchoring effect, subjects were asked to estimate various quantities, stated in percentages (e.g. the percentage of African countries in the UN). For each question a starting value between 0 and 100 was determined by spinning a wheel of fortune in the subjects' presence. The subjects were instructed to indicate whether the given (arbitrary) starting value was too high or too low, and then to reach their estimate by moving upwards or downwards from that value. Different groups were given different starting values for each problem. These arbitrary values had a marked effect on the estimates. For example, the median estimates of

---

13   Tversky and Kahneman 1974.

the African countries in the UN were 25% and 45%, respectively, for groups which received 10% and 65% starting points.[14]

In other words, the arbitrarily chosen figure had a significant effect on decisions. This principle offers considerable utility in how to influence behaviour in conflict and may have profound implications for the way the military's actions can be shaped and influenced by an opponent. For example, a leaflet drop depicting images of the Taliban brutalising innocent civilians may *not* lead individuals to decide not to support the Taliban, but instead anchor their belief that supporting the Taliban is a better choice to avoid the outcome depicted on the leaflet.

The Wisdom of Crowds

This theory considers the importance of an individual's opinion in influencing a crowd, whose members are apt to emulate each other and conform, rather than think differently. Afghan society tends not to individual but to collective decision-making. Consider a roomful of people in Afghanistan, a shura, discussing how to reject the Taliban in their area. If they do it badly, the Taliban will return and kill them. How do we influence those individuals? How can we assist them make the right choice? Sometimes in an Afghan context it can be that one individual has so much charisma and power that it is not so much a collective decision as a polite way of endorsing his decision. In this case, the influence effort is subtly different; empowering individuals who have the right ideas but not always the requisite authority.

The Framing of Choices

Kahneman and Tversky also researched how choices can be framed, important for influence as it determines how messaging might be framed. For example, one group of subjects was told the US was preparing for an outbreak of a disease that would kill 600 people. Two alternative programmes to combat it are suggested – which should be chosen? Programme A, guaranteeing 200 people will be saved, or Programme B which offers a 1/3 probability that all 600 would be saved and a 2/3 probability that no one would be saved. A second group of subjects were given the same preamble but offered different choices: Programme C would see 400 people perish and Programme D a 1/3 probability that no one will die and a 2/3 probability that 600 people will die. Clearly the choice between A and B is exactly the same as the choices presented in C and D and yet the subjects provided different answers depending upon the manner in which their choices were framed.[15]

In Afghanistan we believe the Coalition has struggled to frame the choices we ask a war-torn nation to consider. The simplest example is the offer of democracy. Well understood in the West, it is less appealing in conflict-ridden countries, where the decision to vote is largely irrelevant compared with choices presented by the Taliban of life and death. In Afghanistan we have paid little attention to how choices might be framed to change individual and collective behaviour.

---

14   Tversky and Kahneman 1974.

15   Most subjects preferred to save one-third of the people for certain (Programme A), rather than taking a gamble to save everyone (Programme B). But change the framing and the choice changed, too: most subjects accepted a two-thirds risk of killing everyone (Programme D) rather than be certain that two-thirds of victims would die (Programme C). This preference reversal is clearly irrational because nothing about the costs and benefits of the two treatments changed, but people's choices did.

Many choices are too stark: poppy bad/wheat good; Taliban evil/ISAF good; and so on. The reality is that we have consistently failed to understand that what seems to us as irrational behaviour is entirely rational to the individual facing tough choices.

Libertarian Paternalism

This idea uses behavioural nudges to influence choices in positive ways, while still leaving individuals options. Cass Sunstein and Richard Thaler in their book *Nudge*,[16] write: 'In the past three decades, psychologists and behavioural economists have learnt that people's choices can be dramatically affected by subtle features of social situations.' Like the previous example, this idea considers the 'architecture of choice', altering the way choices are presented in order to 'nudge' people towards a beneficial action, without actually banning anything or creating incentives. In Afghanistan it may be possible to nudge the population of a village to resist Taliban influence, if we can find an appropriate architecture of choice. One early example of 'choice' architecture in Afghanistan was the National Solidarity Programme which in 2004 sought to nudge thousands of village communities into managing their own reconstruction process. The programme sought to decentralise decision-making and localise authority and responsibility. Block grants were allocated, provided three criteria were met: the village elected its leadership by secret ballot; held communal meetings to design its reconstruction plan; and posted its accounts in a public place. These were simple nudges, not explicit in determining specific outcomes, and were local in nature.

Understanding these types of concepts (prospect theory, anchoring, the wisdom of crowds, framing of choices and nudging) are absolutely seminal to how we might conduct influence operations in an era of hybrid conflict. They seek to influence behaviour within the context that exists, not the context we might wish for. Such ideas need to be set in the relevant social, cultural and economic environment; applying them through the prism of Western liberal democracy risks failure. For example, in Afghanistan, dealing with some of the economic problems in a country 181st out of 182 in the United Nations' Human Development Index also affects the success of the influence mission.

Economics

In applying influence effectively to behavioural conflict there is little point in seeking solely to fix security or lessen violence. Any effective political settlement requires governance (alongside its bedfellow rule of law), security and economic development, all consecutively not sequentially. In his book *The Bottom Billion*, Paul Collier outlines the four traps that prevent development for the billion bottom people in the world: conflict, natural resources, landlocked countries and bad governance. He argues the presence of one or more of these traps feature in every country caught in the bottom billion: Afghanistan features all four.[17]

Such considerations should form part of the pre-deployment educational process for both current and future operations. Many of 52 Brigade's soldiers had experience of Iraq and, whilst there were some areas of read-across, there could have been a real danger that the two would be conflated in thinking. If we accept Collier's argument, we may conclude that Iraq is not a good

---

16   Sunstein and Thaler 2009.
17   Collier 2008.

model for Afghanistan. Iraq, we might argue, is predisposed to succeed; Afghanistan is predisposed to fail. Yet with different choices, Afghanistan could choose to develop its infrastructure, feed its population and perhaps grow as an economy. Conventional wisdom suggests this is impossible while the insurgency continues, but you cannot succeed in a counter-insurgency campaign purely bottom up; a political settlement has to meet it from the top down at some point.

Making Influence Mainstream

It is not enough just to write about influence in military doctrine. Influence as a concept, in the way 52 Brigade sought to define it in Helmand, does not have a visible academic or doctrinal background. When we started thinking about influence operations during pre-deployment training, it became clear there was a significant lack of writing on the subject. There is much doctrine on information operations, psychological operations and similar concepts, but it is of little value at the tactical level: it did not tell soldiers how to execute influence. We needed tactical doctrine that explained how a company, battlegroup and brigade can influence a population. It is much more than simply passing a message. To stand any chance of enduring success it needs a thorough understanding of audiences. Influence differs from information operations in that it is more holistic in approach and has a higher purpose. Quite simply it is a way of thinking, and in an operational context it is multidimensional, necessitating second- and third-order consequence thinking. It must also recognise that conflict remains an extension of politics and that all military activity must contribute to the achievement of politically generated policy goals. It can be difficult to navigate these choppy waters given the consequences of getting it wrong. David Galula observed in counter-insurgency operations:

> [P]olitics becomes an active instrument of operation. And so intricate is the interplay between the political and the military actions that they cannot be tidily separated; on the contrary, every military move has to be weighed with regard to its political effects and vice versa.[18]

An influence strategy is therefore central to any political strategy which in turn provides the foundation for effective conduct of influence at tactical and operational levels without necessarily constantly controlling or directing that effort. In Iraq in 2007, for example, the higher influence strategy was designed to move various communities towards a political accommodation that would reduce communal violence. At a lower level it was about jobs, economic development and isolating the insurgent from the population. Generic messaging would just not work in this multidimensional layering of influence.[19]

One of the reasons why this was so problematic for 52 Brigade, and why this concept is relatively new, is that successful military careers are laid on hard power. As Norvell De Atkine notes: 'The death knell of a career is to be identified by the career makers and breakers as being out of the mainstream.'[20] Thus, our Armed Forces have no professional information operations practitioners, no media operators or professional psychological specialists. In their place, enthusiastic amateurs are seconded from across the military for two or three years, doing their best with minimal training

---

18   Galula 1964, 4–5.

19   This point is also made in Brigadier General H.R. McMaster's draft paper, *Centralization vs. Decentralization: Preparing For and Practising Mission Command in Counter-insurgency Operations.*

20   De Atkine 1999.

but unlikely to return to such duties again. Many of them are individual augmentees who often make their first appearance just a few weeks prior to deployment. No commander would accept his chief of staff appearing at this stage; he should not accept it for other critical staff officers either. While ideas of soft power are raised at staff colleges, what to do with these ideas is not. Hard power retains supremacy, reinforced by professional training courses throughout a soldier's career and by core texts such as the Principles of War. Yet today, winning kinetic battles is comparatively easy, winning the influence war, much more difficult.

Ivan Arreguin-Toft has shown that the outcome of conflict is not so much a function of the strong defeating the weak, but of he who uses the most strategically useful techniques of battle (soft, hard or asymmetric) that will prevail. He demonstrates that, since 1800, results of conflicts increasingly favour the actor willing to make conceptual jumps in thinking. This places considerable emphasis on willingness continually to refine, reorganise, adapt and transform.[21] This calls into question the basis of the educational process that underpins our training. For example, in a typical senior Army officer's career spanning 30 years, a general may spend around two years in staff colleges, on a variety of staff courses. Between these comparatively short periods of intellectual broadening lie long and extended periods of operations, support to operations, training, or in the Ministry of Defence fighting wars of budget attrition and programme procurement. In comparison to the Civil Service or commercial sector, two years is actually quite a long period of education. However, unlike industry, the Army's success is measured either by its lack of use (its deterrent value) or by its ability to respond quickly and successfully to a crisis that is different from before, in different parts of the world, and involving people with a myriad of different values, beliefs and cultures. There is no quick fix to preparing people for such challenges, but lifelong learning and education are key. However, it is not sufficient for people just to attend courses; they have to attend the right courses. And our staff colleges appear unable to adapt quickly enough to meet the needs of students. Courses are also expensive and, in a world increasingly driven by balance sheets, it is difficult to assign a monetary figure to their value. There is an increasing tendency to reduce officer education as a cost-saving measure.

Futurist Alvin Toffler said: 'The illiterate of the future are not those that cannot read or write. They are those that cannot learn, unlearn and relearn.' He speaks of the West's educational system being designed to meet an industrial discipline of a past age, unprepared for the future. Britain's Armed Forces are similarly predisposed; from the top of the Ministry of Defence to our staff colleges, structures are institutionally incapable of keeping pace with rapid change and the associated willingness to adapt quickly. As an example, in 2009 the British Army was placed on a campaign footing under Operation Entirety.[22] This is a quantum change in the way the Army is run but its implications receive almost no attention on staff courses. A second example is the absence of proper research within the Ministry of Defence. Research forms the basis of education and learning; education and learning the basis of training. Yet even at senior levels education is seen as a luxury and second to training. *Training* develops an individual's knowledge, skills and behaviour for particular jobs, but *education* develops an individual's intellectual capacity, knowledge and understanding; it equips them to come to reasoned decisions, judgements and conclusions, including in unpredictable and complex circumstances. The British Army rightly prides itself on the quality

---

21   Arreguin-Toft 2001.

22   Operation Entirety, issued by the then Commander in Chief UK Land Forces, General Sir David Richards, is the strategic direction to move the British Army to a campaign footing. The document states that the Army should: 'be resourced, structured and prepared – conceptually, morally and physically – for success in Afghanistan … through sustaining and improving Afghan campaign capability.'

of its training but careers are increasingly built on budgetary and management competence in place of the necessary education to conceptualise tomorrow's challenges.

Learning lessons is an important part of adaptation. The military places great stock in generating Lessons Identified (LIs) after each operation or exercise. A database is maintained at the Development Concepts and Doctrine Centre, Shrivenham, and lists all past LIs, including those from Iraq and Afghanistan. Yet they are classified, so their distribution is limited to those with necessary clearances and mechanisms to read the data. I do not argue for wholesale release of classified documents (although many are over-classified to prevent criticism becoming public) but we do need a better connection between LIs and military education so that LIs genuinely become lessons learnt. This does not currently happen in the area of influence. A casual search of the database suggests lessons are not learnt. Exercise Gibraltar Forum was conducted in 2002 and the LIs commented on 'the paucity of understanding of media operations'. Operation Kingower (Kosovo 1999) reported that 'the UK Information Operations capability was inadequate'. Operation Veritas (Afghanistan 2001) suggested that 'UK IO and PsyOps have been under-resourced for some time. Much of the thinking and experience dates from World War 2.' At the end of 2003 the first set of LIs from Iraq were compiled. Here we saw very similar commentary: 'the UK does not have a robust PsyOps capability' and 'this op demonstrated once again the paucity of media ops capability'. This would appear to be evidence of a more general malaise, a point endorsed by General Graeme Lamb at the Chilcot enquiry, when asked 'what lessons have been learned from Iraq?' He replied: 'a raft of lessons – few of them learnt, I sense'.[23] This points to the problems of innovating and facilitating change in a complex organisation, particularly where budgets have become a key driver and process often prevents innovative thought; but this is an explanation of, not an excuse for, inaction. This is entirely counter to Toft's research that shows winners are often those best able to make conceptual jumps in thinking (innovation) in complex environments. As Lieutenant General William Caldwell, Commander US Combined Arms Center US Army, observed in a recent article on the *Small Wars Journal* website:

> We need to educate soldiers ... and how their actions can have strategic implications. They need to know what the second and third order effects of their actions are. There are very few soldiers out there who would intentionally harm the mission ... when many of these incidents occur it is because they just don't know that it is going to have that kind of effect and cause that kind of damage.[24]

Or, as Rosen notes, the speed of change in the information age aggravates militaries' 'procedural conservatism'.[25] With so much evidence available that soft power is a force multiplier, I make the following suggestions.

Winning Tomorrow's Conflicts

In his book *The Age of the Unthinkable*, Joshua Cooper Ramo describes a world of inherent unpredictability and constant newness.[26] To Ramo it is a world where those we entrust with

---

23   Lamb 2009.
24   Caldwell 2008.
25   Rosen 1991.
26   Ramo 2009.

management of its problems constantly fail; indeed, their endeavours may actually achieve the opposite to that intended, *unless* they are prepared to adapt. We do not have to 'watch whilst history collides with our lives but can step forward and change history',[27] although, Ramo argues, to do so we must be prepared. There is one fundamental certainty confronting armed forces in any conflict: uncertainty. We must therefore address how we prepare our people for the kind of challenge that such uncertainty will bring. Changing the behaviour of individuals, groups, governments and societies is key to future success. When the Armed Forces engaged in industrial warfare, the attitude and behaviour of the enemy were largely placed at the periphery of a commander's thinking. But in behavioural conflict we need to confront very cerebral issues. For example, we may have to reassess notions of victory. What does victory in Afghanistan look like? I do not presume to have the answer but I believe that victory today, and in the future, will be very different from signature ceremonies on Lüneburg Heath in 1945 or Port Stanley in 1982. Indeed, victory may not even be immediately apparent. During 52 Brigade's deployment we chose to avoid using words such as *win* or *victory* as they are too absolute and antithetical to reconciliation. We settled instead on *succeed* or *success* as everyone can interpret their role in success. Also, if we accept from the outset that victory may prove illusory, then we may also have to question our objectives and what is, or more specifically what is not, achievable. In short we have to come to terms with an absence of absolutes.

Three areas of work need to be undertaken if we are to expect the UK's Armed Forces to succeed in the era of the information revolution. First, we need to broaden and expand the minds of all our people, from the strategic corporal to those who lead, requiring a wholesale broadening of military education. Secondly, we need to expand and professionalise certain key information age enablers – notably information, media and psychological operations practitioners and, of equal importance, their directing and command arrangements within the Ministry of Defence. Finally, an expansion of the defence research capability is vital if we are to cope meaningfully with future Rumsfeldian *unknown unknowns*.

Education

As already noted, the Ministry of Defence is deservedly a world-renowned training organisation, welcoming each year thousands of British and international students to its many courses. I do not denigrate their value, but education is the poor relation of training and is an easy cost-saving measure. If we are to prepare our people for the complexities of the future, we need life-long learning. There are many ways this can be achieved, at both macro and micro levels. For example, we should rehabilitate the strategic estimate process, effectively dismantled in 1994. Corporate appreciation of world events has been hindered by cuts in the Defence Intelligence Staff, reduction in defence attachés, and absence of deep specialist expertise. For example, during operations in Bosnia, Iraq and Afghanistan, we had to surge personnel through language training courses – a process that can take years. It is impossible to retain a corps of global linguists, but with proper research to determine likely conflict areas we can prepare at least a seed-corn cadre of linguists. This may mean linking such expertise to the attaché circuit, currently regarded as the preserve of older officers nearing retirement. For young officers the attaché circuit currently hinders career development; this is misguided and officers should be encouraged to become regional specialists.

---

27   Interview with Ramo, available at: http://www.hachettebookgroup.com/features/unthinkable/index. html [accessed: 7 February 2013].

The Defence Academy currently welcomes students from over 40 nations, but sends British officers in return to far fewer of them, as it is regarded an expensive luxury. This too is unhelpful; life-long relationships are built through such attachments. Officers returning from theatre should routinely be posted to the Defence Academy to mentor those on courses and to codify knowledge they have gained. In many training schools recent operational experience is keenly sought but this appears less the case in educational environments. Such a move would provide a bridge between operational adaptation and deeper institutional learning. Indeed, learning and acquisition of knowledge are paid scant attention. It is not helped by regulations that prevent officers from sharing ideas through modern media such as blogs and websites, or by Ministry of Defence computer networks that do not facilitate blog-type discussion. The US is making efforts to develop 'wiki-doctrine', envisaging web-based Army doctrine being updated directly by deployed units and formations, negating the necessity of time-consuming referral to higher command through tortuous staffing. It is not perfect but it does facilitate comparatively immediate exchanges by practitioners with appropriate operational experience.

I am envious of the freedom of senior US officers to engage with external and internal communities in their decision-making. Indeed, the inclusion of external organisations, particularly academic ones, is vital. I welcome the recent decision of the Ministry of Defence's strategy unit to post on King's College London *Kings of War* blog, inviting comments and views on future strategic threats. The quality, range and number of replies they received were indicative of the huge pool of talent that the Ministry can tap into. We also note that the US publishes many of its military students' thesis and staff papers on line, making them freely available to the general public and, more particularly, to each other for reference, comment and debate. The UK does not share Defence Research Papers, and key journals such as the *British Army Review* are not published on the internet.

In his 2009 lecture to the Royal United Services Institute the Chief of Defence Staff, Air Chief Marshal Sir Jock Stirrup, commented: 'we have lost an institutional capacity for and culture of strategic thought'.[28] Expanding education and learning, which in many instances does not need large-scale capital investment, but instead a shedding of process management and conventional wisdom, will help to regain our capacity and rebuild the culture for strategic thought.

Professionalisation

Influence, psychological operations and media operations should be professionalised under the banner of a strategic communication organisation – one that embraces the current Targeting and Information Operations and Directorate of Media and Communications. Intrinsic to restructuring should be recognition that in complex societies the Ministry may well not hold all answers and outside assistance needs to be sought. For example, despite 52 Brigade's research, the various ideas presented above still did not properly prepare the Brigade for operations, because the motivators and opinions of the population were not clearly and scientifically understood. Although countless surveys and opinion polls have been commissioned, these did not identify the real psychological drivers and influence levers for the diverse nature of Afghan society. Indeed, their findings were often counter-productive. Only in late 2009 has this seminal requirement been properly funded and undertaken by the US.

---

28 Stirrup 2009.

Contractors can in some ways meet some of the shortfall in professional military expertise, but their quality is variable, they do not communicate with each other, and they often provide conflicting advice. Professionalisation will facilitate proper understanding and scrutiny of contractor support.

There will inevitably be resistance to an information specialisation; but with some innovation it might be achieved at minimal cost. Military officers typically change their appointments every two to three years. At least once in every rank, and often more, they move away from their core specialisation for a broadening appointment. It should be possible to grow selected individuals on a twin-career ladder, where the broadening appointment is replaced by an information-related one.

Research

Only through research will the UK military be prepared for the future. At the macro level, the Ministry of Defence's in-house research capacity was almost eliminated by the privatisation of the Defence Evaluation and Research Agency to QinetiQ in 2001. This change occurred at the exact same time that the nature and complexity of the problems facing the UK military, and the need for equipment to meet those challenges, changed forever. At the micro level, I am concerned that the need for the Defence Academy has become to provide selection courses for promotion rather than embracing new concepts, innovating and researching. I note that UK staff courses are, at their core, *taught* courses, whilst US staff courses are significantly more research-based – indicated by the volume of highly original research published by US students; also by the number of US military officers with PhDs. The Defence budget at one time funded seven research chairs in UK universities; there are none today. Although the UK defence community nominally has access to a large number of King's College academics based at the Defence Academy, the Academy has no ability or remit to direct their research. In 2009, the Defence Academy's Advanced Research Group was dissolved as a cost-saving measure; in 2006 it was the only organisation across defence able to support 52 Brigade's operational design. Research, we believe, needs a champion and in the US there is just such a vehicle: the US Centre for Complex Operations at the National Defense University networks together with civilian and military educators, trainers and lessons-learned practitioners, dedicated to preparing for stability operations, counter-insurgency and irregular warfare. A similar capability is urgently required here in the UK. This is not to say all the answers lie in the US; the UK has its own rich tradition of innovation – the Political Warfare Executive and Special Operations Executive provide good historical examples. However, the US, with its vast budgets, seems increasingly willing to speculate and then invest in research. The nature of the special relationship should allow us to learn quickly rather than begin a long and costly, development process of our own.

Conclusion

This chapter accepts, at its heart, the Clausewitzian premise that conflict is a clash of wills. I have sought to advance the idea that alongside kinetic power there is potentially a more behaviourist approach which can affect the enemy's will and be as, or arguably more, effective than kinetic power in future conflict. The success of 52 Brigade in recapturing the town of Musa Qala – a key Taliban stronghold – indicates that this does not have to be at the expense of military effectiveness. We believe there to be multiple benefits to such an approach. Although we cannot prove causality (the absence of figures for enemy and civilian deaths prevents more granular analysis) there appears a strong correlation between operational design and both UK and wider Coalition casualty figures in Afghanistan. Intuitively this seems obvious. However, the absence of contemporary research, and the capacity to undertake it, means it cannot currently be proved. To do so there needs to be proper research and education; this does not currently exist, nor, if current trends prevail, will it do so. What is advocated in this chapter cannot be realised within the current structure of the Ministry of Defence, which has to adopt an adaptive capacity. It is self-evident that individual capabilities cannot be developed without corporate structures to support them. As the Commanding General of US Training and Doctrine, General Martin Dempsey, recently opined, military power, in the future, will be measured in terms of the 'ability to adapt'. I regard it as essential that the capacity to do so is now given serious attention by the Ministry of Defence if we are to meet CDS's idea of becoming 'nurturers' of strategic thinking rather than 'hunter gatherers'.[29]

---

29   Stirrup 2009.

Chapter 22
Campaigning: An Air Force Perspective

Iain McNicoll – 6 February 2008

When considering air campaigns from the last century, it is important to remember that powered flight has only been around for that long – in 2003, I reflected that I had been alive for half that period and flying for a third of it. With a focus on campaign planning, in particular the changes caused by improvements in global reach, C4ISTAR and precision attack, this chapter also covers air power's role in the context of other Service contributions and land–air interfaces, as well as the Comprehensive Approach.

It is always best (or at least well-worn) to start by deconstructing the title: is there such a thing as an Air Force perspective on campaigning? I hope to show that not only is *military* campaigning a joint activity, but it is also now (and perhaps always was) simply a part of a comprehensive approach, its importance varying by campaign and over time.

An Historical Context

Let us start with what more recent campaigns tell us about the air perspective, and the lessons from those campaigns – often not learned or put into practice. In my view the diversity of our recent campaigns is an important conclusion in itself: the need for a full spectrum of capabilities and the agility to respond to changed circumstances can be forgotten during a prolonged campaign of a single type.

When looking at *air* campaigns, the first question I wish to dispose of is whether air is decisive. I could start at any point from 1914, but I shall skip over the First World War and even mostly over the Second World War (although almost every lesson relevant to today might be found there, not least in the importance of integrated operations). But I cannot resist quoting the then General Wavell from a book published in 1941, compiled from the Lees Knowles Lectures delivered at Trinity College, Cambridge in 1939; the subject is generals and generalship and talking of the commander he said:

> It seems to me immaterial whether he is a soldier who has really studied the air or an airman who has really studied land forces. It is the combination of the two, never the action of one alone, that will bring success for a future war.[1]

That illustrates two points: first, the debate about whether airpower alone can win a campaign is a sterile one, and second, the need for joint action, which can of course also be applied to the maritime dimension.

It also helps me with a point I frequently make to my Army colleagues: that an airman can be a Joint Task Force Commander!

---

1   Wavell 1942.

There is a temptation to forget the Cold War, yet there are two important points about air power worth remembering. The first is that the West 'won' the Cold War for a number of interrelated reasons, but militarily we won the technological battle, mainly in the air, by driving the capability, and therefore cost, of weapon systems ever higher. Secondly, the asymmetry this caused has been pulled through to all subsequent conflicts – most noticeable in the prodigious effort made by the Soviet Union to develop SAMs to protect themselves from our air forces – and the consequent spiral development of Western (mainly US) efforts in EW and suppression. As an aside, the ever-increasing cost of military technology, combined with post-Cold War restructuring (or downsizing), now lies at the heart of our own difficulties with the current MOD financial planning round.

Returning to the great effort and expense put into air power during the Cold War, the key thinking was to use a technological edge to blunt an advance, but it was also to avoid a soldier's (and indeed a sailor's or marine's) worst nightmare: to operate without his own air forces controlling the skies above. We are in danger of forgetting this vital point in today's conflicts where the air threat is minimal, although I must point out that that threat is not absent. There are still plenty of shoulder-launched SAMs and there is an ever-present risk from unguided weapons, whether machine guns or rocket propelled grenades. The loss of an RAF Hercules in January 2005 was a sobering reminder, but you may not be aware that every week there are reports of various 'SAFIRE' incidents and the US, in particular, has lost a number of helicopters to surface fire in Iraq.

Turning to expeditionary conflicts, the Falklands, of course, both illustrates the need for a joint campaign and reinforces the importance of control of the air. It also demonstrates a point I shall return to – the nature of joint command and componency: that is, the relation between single environments and the joint commander.

I now move on to the first Gulf War in 1991. It is hard to believe, at the time of writing, that this was 17 years ago. The USAF has been at war continually for 17 years, a point recently made by the US Secretary of the Air Force Michael Wynne: some airmen are nearing the end of their 20-year engagement, having known nothing else. This war took air power into a new dimension – air supremacy. Indeed, there was over-provision of all coalition forces. The large and capable coalition air forces, starting on 17 January 1991, soon ranging across Iraq at will, completely destroyed the opposition, and the land campaign, starting on 24 February, was a consecutive, rather than coincident, affair, lasting only until 27 February.

In my view, this was not a triumph of air power: it seduced the non-military (especially politicians) and many military into thinking a new paradigm had been created: clinical high-tech, precision bombing at minimal risk to our own forces was '*the* future', rather than just part of the future.

Why is it that we always seem to do this? We take the most recent event as the new pattern – the 'new' way of warfare – as the template for all future conflicts. It was, of course, nothing of the sort, although it did contain some elements that persisted, such as the Cold War air campaign planning process: the 72-hour air-tasking order cycle – which was variously praised as a model of planning and execution (with 1,000 sorties or more per day) and criticised as an example of inflexibility. It is only now that forward planning and apportionment, necessary for preparation and coordination, and flexible employment able to react within minutes, have been reconciled. Furthermore, command and control (C2) arrangements from 1991 – both joint/component and multinational – have acted as a straightjacket, or at least have been misapplied, to this day.

The Balkans, especially Kosovo, illustrated the constraints of coalitions in the air and on the ground. The air campaign lasted from 24 March 1999 to 10 June 1999. The struggle was to get hundreds of aircraft into a small area, and to find enough targets for them. The widening of the air campaign to include selected Serbian industrial and political targets, combined, at last, with massing of NATO ground forces, finally applied the pressure that the earlier, well-publicised, lack of will for a ground campaign had eroded. It was a clear demonstration of the importance of a joint campaign, or at least the promise or threat of one.

I could continue with Afghanistan 2001, the Second Gulf War 2003, or the counter-insurgency campaigns in Iraq and Afghanistan, but I would prefer to treat these under my subsequent headings as they bring us to the present day.

Campaign Planning – Joint Campaigns

Air power is finally delivering on the promises made for many years, foreshadowed by the visionaries of the last century from Douhet and J.F.C. Fuller on strategic bombing, to Mitchell – with all his imagination about technological development and the broader use of air power. But there is more to come.

First, *global reach* is a reality, but the tyranny of distance can still lead to uncomfortably long reaction times: hence forward basing and Ground Close Air Support – the cab rank of today. In global reach I include air transport; the capability of the C17, for example, is quite remarkable. It can transport amazing quantities into theatre, even delivering some of the fuel which has long been the Achilles heel of expeditionary air operations. We look forward to our 5th and 6th C17, and to A400M and to FSTA – the Future Strategic Tanker Aircraft. All this represents a real change in emphasis in air power from the 'fast-jet mafia' to air transport, support helicopters and ISTAR.

Secondly, the *persistence* of air power has been limited in the past, but UAVs are beginning to change that – endurance is no longer dictated by the fragility of the human in the aircraft. Two weeks ago I visited the re-formed 39 Squadron at Creech Air Force Base in Nevada to present the Standard. The squadron is partnering with the USAF to fly both Predator As and our newest UAV, Reaper. The endurance of Reaper is well over 12 hours. Crews fly them over Iraq and Afghanistan operating in shifts from cabins in the Nevada desert, although of course the launch and recovery teams are in theatre. The link is by satellite and fibre optic cable – the operators are immersed in the battlespace and communicate with airspace and ground agencies, and then hand over to the oncoming shift and drive home to Las Vegas. The reader may wish to ponder on the Rules of Engagement (ROE) and decision-making problems this creates, not forgetting the human dimension.

Thirdly, *precision* is achieved by GPS or laser guidance, and also now by the tremendous accuracy of unguided weapons, forward firing or free fall.

Lastly, *ISTAR* is pervasive, from space, from manned aircraft, from UAVs; but our ability to process, exploit and disseminate is lagging. The US has 'Distributed Common Ground Stations', and much is beamed back to the US for analysis – reachback permits a smaller in-theatre footprint and therefore reduces risk and logistic support.

So, do we use these capabilities as well as we could in running our campaigns? Much, of course, is done well, but I argue we could do much better from tactical to operational levels.

At the lower end, artificial distinctions are made because of ownership and tasking inflexibility. For example, is Reaper an ISTAR or an attack asset? Of course it is both, but our tasking system does not allow for this, so the US tasks it as an attack asset and the UK currently tasks it as an ISR asset. Airmen have traditionally operated in 'stovepipes', such as air defenders and mud movers.[2] New equipment removes that distinction, but we have yet to remove it in our thinking and tasking.

---

2   'Mud movers' is RAF slang for those tasked with ground attack, in support of land forces.

At the operational level, it is worth having a quick look at doctrine; my background running Joint Doctrine and Concepts cannot be denied any longer!

Both we and the US have clear doctrine on running a Joint Task Force and its components. We exercise this well. In the UK we have a biennial exercise called Joint Venture. In 2006, I was the air component commander; the current Commander in Chief Air Command was the Joint Task Force Commander (JTFC); other Government departments and agencies were represented in a scenario designed to test the comprehensive approach. The major lessons were on the importance of integration at the component level; this was greatly facilitated by collocation. For example, air/maritime cooperation was achieved within minutes by Rear Admiral Neil Morisetti and me walking a hundred yards or so. The JTFC held daily component commanders' meetings; we were all on the same wavelength and could quickly adjust our component-level operational plans to take account of overriding strategic concerns.

I also had the privilege of taking part in a US Pacific Air Forces-run exercise for the USAF called Unified Engagement. Although a future wargame, it was similar to Joint Venture – we share a common doctrine with the US, and indeed with our NATO allies. Of course exercises are always much easier than operations and I do not suggest that this pure construct can be transplanted directly into the messiness of Iraq and Afghanistan.

But compare how these two theatres are organised. The two JTFCs are in Baghdad (General David Petraeus) and Kabul (General Dan MacNeill). The maritime component is in Bahrain and the air component is in al-Udeid, although the air component commander, Lieutenant General Gary North, is at CENTAF at Shaw Air Force Base in South Carolina. CENTCOM is the 'PJHQ' for Iraq, but NATO's Regional Command (North) at Brunssum is the operational level command for NATO's operations in Afghanistan. And NATO bureaucracy (and of course the nations') adds friction rather than removes it. Land componency is more blurred but is coincident with the JTF HQ.

So the obvious benefits of collocating the JTFC and all component commanders are lost, but I should mention that this set-up does allow for air assets to be switched between theatres and is consistent with the air power doctrine of centralised control and decentralised execution.

Naturally, personalities and effort can and do compensate to some degree, and so do Air Coordination Elements, such as the one in Kabul where we have Major General Kevin Kennedy and Air Commodore Sean Bell plus their staff. But I would argue that this C2 design is almost guaranteed to produce a land-centric and land-dominated campaign. When plans are produced, they tend to be land plans, with air power used as an afterthought in a reactive way. And we are doing it tremendously well. The average time from a land call for assistance in Regional Command (South), in Kandahar, to air power arriving is under ten minutes. This is stunning and we have partly become victims of our own success. Why plan a coordinated campaign when you can get yourself out of jail in under ten minutes?

Yet air power offers so much more.

We could do more to shape the battlespace. This does happen, perhaps most obviously in covert operations, where the pattern of life is observed through persistent ISTAR and fleeting opportunities are exploited with a mixture of helicopter-borne troops, attack helicopters, and kinetic effect from fast air or UAVs.

But it could become the norm for commanders to use air power presence and effect to dominate areas where land forces are stretched or absent, or to condition enemy behaviours by obvious presence or absence of air assets. The psychological effects of air power, when we dominate the air environment, are beginning to be apparent. I cite the example of the immediate impact of a low and fast Tornado on a nasty crowd threatening to swamp a patrol near Baghdad last year.

We could also ensure the availability of exactly the right asset at the right time, rather than exploit the inherent flexibility of air power. The planning cycles of air and land can be relatively easily aligned.

I do not wish to leave the reader with the impression we are doing badly or that we are not improving. Tremendous effort has been invested in improving air–land coordination. There are two specific programmes in the UK: Project Coningham-Keyes is a joint air and land initiative backed by the Chiefs of the General Staff and the Air Staff, and Project Tedder is an Air Command initiative to ensure that Air is really on a war footing and doing all it can. Successes from that have included the proper preparation of each deploying UK brigade in air–land training, and very rapid fitting of Sniper targeting pods to Harriers (the step up in quality from the old TIALD pods needs to be seen to be believed), whose images can be down-linked to ground forces. But again this is excellence mainly at tactical, not operational, level.

I should touch on two other aspects of air campaign planning and execution. The first is the perception that air is a blunt instrument and causes disproportionate destruction and casualties. Recognising that perceptions count for more than reality, and that single incidents colour the picture, I would still say the issue is more one of public relations than substance. President Karzai's statements in reaction to some incidents last year were made mainly for Afghan public consumption. Claims of civilian casualties are very hard to substantiate since many 'civilians' are actually unlawful combatants. However, the fact is that indirect fire from artillery and mortars has caused (as far as can be determined) more civilian casualties than air power.

This links to ROE and authorisation. For pre-planned targeting there is a clear method for gaining authorisation at the appropriate level (which might be the Prime Minister), but for incidents involving troops in contact (known as TICs), the right of self defence enables ground commanders and tactical air controllers to take decisions immediately, although still in line with clear guidelines on collateral damage. This entirely correct delegation of authority when our own troops are in danger needs constant attention to ensure short-term tactical gains do not endanger the strategic aim.

We could do better on rebuttal. I heard General Petraeus explain in a VTC to the UK's first 'Pinnacle Course' how he aimed to get on record first with the US version of events. So he would, for example, make a statement at 0400 that the Coalition action in Fallujah at 0300 had resulted from positive identification of the enemy engaged in using or preparing to use weapons against our forces, pre-empting the inevitable claim of 'civilians' at a wedding or some such story. We could do better in explaining the use of Coalition and UK air power in Afghanistan in this proactive fashion.

Comprehensive Approach

The comprehensive approach is much talked about but fraught with difficulty in implementation. However, it is self-evidently still the right thing.

The comprehensive approach relies on 'campaign authority' (not the UN mandate or some such legal authority, important though that is), but an authority in the eyes of various actors in the environment, born out of the perception of the legitimacy of what is being done and the perception of a common shared aim.

All military men understand that the use of force is a means to an end, which we hope does not involve the use of force. We understood, even before the doctrine was written (I would claim most eloquently in the 2004 edition of Peace Support Operations doctrine[3]) that a stable society depends on many things, notably sound governance, the rule of law, economic strength, education, healthcare and *lastly* – or as a last resort – the military.

Yet applying this is enormously difficult: because of cultural and historical reasons in the country concerned; because of the difficulty of 'donating' these things (to survive they must be home-grown); and because of the difficulty that Western nations have in providing expertise in these subjects to dangerous places. The Post-Conflict Reconstruction Unit (from the FCO, DfID and MOD) is a great idea, but it must be able to deploy far greater numbers of people.[4]

It is even more difficult when the operations engaged in are counter-insurgencies. The battlespace is inevitably confused and dangerous. In providing security, the challenge is to reconcile those who can be reconciled and to remove the irreconcilable. The application of kinetic effect is necessary but requires almost impossible judgements on when, where and how much.

We revert to the military dimension, sometimes inappropriately, because the military can be told to do things, and because security is the precondition for any chance of success. However, notwithstanding this, air has a far greater role in the comprehensive approach than is generally realised. Just taking the components I listed above, it can provide transport to support governance, surveillance to support the rule of law, assistance for well-run airports and air traffic systems to aid economic success. Iraq is heading in this direction, although Basra is still some way off gaining an International Civil Aviation Organization licence.

In the absence of civilian agencies, we should be better structured to take the strain in some of these areas – unless someone starts a transition, the comprehensive approach is stillborn.

I would like to conclude with the following key points. Notwithstanding the length of time we are likely to be engaged in counter-insurgency operations, history tells us that the next conflict will be different. We must adapt more for the current conflict, but not completely lose sight of the need to have a balanced force capable of dealing with the widest possible range of contingent operations. Failing to control the air runs the risk of total failure.

Notwithstanding that there are still limitations and definitely scope for improvement, air power is at last delivering its promise in reach, persistence and precise effect. We must therefore not be constrained in our thinking by the 'stovepipes' of roles such as attack, transport or reconnaissance.

Joint campaigns are essential – we should not just think of them as land campaigns with air as a bolt-on extra. This means we must seek to reduce the friction of physical dislocation and genuinely apply our doctrine of Joint Task Force Commander and integrated activity from each component. That integrated activity starts with planning together to maximise the strengths of each environment – and for air, this means not simply being rapid and highly effective emergency artillery.

Finally, the air campaign is part of the joint campaign, which is itself but one part of a comprehensive approach. In that approach, however, air has more to offer than is currently being used.

---

3   JWP 3-50 2004.
4   The Post-Conflict Reconstruction Unit was reformed as the Stabilisation Unit in 2007.

PART V
What Have We Learnt?

This section, unlike the others, is not bounded by geography or time. Instead it describes some of the wider influences and constraints at play on the generals whose chapters precede this, how the British Army has adapted to meet the challenges of war, and how it needs to continue to adapt even after withdrawal from Afghanistan post-2014.

Desmond Bowen, a senior civil servant in the Cabinet Office and Defence throughout this period, expounds on the political-military relationship in Chapter 23, pointing out some of the contradictions within that relationship. Such contradictions may, at least in part, account for some of the decisions made over Iraq and Afghanistan. Bowen also points out that, as an institution, the Ministry of Defence is too lenient and accepting of failure – despite all that has arguably gone wrong in Iraq and Afghanistan, no senior military officer or civil servant has yet been held accountable.

Colonel Alexander Alderson created and commanded the Afghanistan Counter-Insurgency Centre, based in Warminster. In Chapter 24, he explains some of the reasons why the British Army's relative lack of success in Iraq and, in the early years, in Afghanistan, including a lack of education in (and hence understanding of) counter-insurgency. He is critical of both military and political understanding of what insurgency means and how it should be dealt with. He further explains how we attempted to correct this through new doctrine and the creation of the Afghanistan Counter-Insurgency Centre; he emphasises the debt we owe the USA in both these endeavours.

Lieutenant General Sir Paul Newton was the first commander of the British Army's Force Development Command, charged with making the Army a learning organisation. Whereas Alexander Alderson, in the previous chapter, wrote on adaptation of our counter-insurgency skills *during* the current campaigns, Paul Newton is more concerned about the continuing relevance of UK Armed Forces *after* the British depart the operational cockpit of Helmand. In a wide-ranging Chapter 25, he analyses many of the institutional and cultural failings of UK Defence, including the deterioration in British Army staff training, and proposes significant enhancements to research, education, training and experimentation.

The final chapter, by Professor Sir Hew Strachan, draws together many of the main themes of the book. He considers a wide range of issues: doctrine, the strategic context, the UK–US relationship, working with indigenous forces, tour lengths, the role of the Permanent Joint Headquarters and theatre command, and the vocabulary of the 'Global War on Terror' and the 'long war' (both of which he finds unhelpful when it comes to articulating strategy, in particular for Iraq and Afghanistan). Strachan is particularly critical of the MOD's capacity for making strategy since the end of the Cold War. Perhaps, however, his greatest concern is reserved for the area of the education of the British Army and its senior officers, which has languished over the past 20 years, despite the success of the Higher Command and Staff Course, of which the majority of contributors to this book are graduates. At least some of the difficulties the UK has faced in Iraq and Afghanistan can be ascribed to inadequate officer education.

Chapter 23

The Political-Military Relationship on Operations

Desmond Bowen – 17 February 2010

I should start with a double bow in the direction of Clausewitz in order to acknowledge both the axiom that war is the continuation of policy by other means and the trinity which should exist between the people, the politicians and the military in war. We all accept that there is no military action which is not embedded in political purpose and we also know how difficult it is to sustain a military campaign without broad political and popular support. I should also say something about my own involvement in this business; I worked in the defence and security arena for most of my career as a civil servant, engaged mainly on policy in respect of overseas engagement and operations, disarmament and the wider management of Defence. I should also recognise that the title of this chapter refers to operations not war; that is significant in that it implies that there is a difference between a war of national survival and engagement in war-like activity. Included in the latter is a host of activities before and after the high-intensity phase of combat which are the stuff of most of the military operations in which we have been involved since the Falklands conflict.

It may also be helpful to set out for the sake of clarity how the machinery of Government works to bring the critical relationship between military and political leaders into being. First, the deciding voice is the political one: the Prime Minister and ministers are in charge. They are the decision-makers and the ones responsible for presenting and explaining the decisions made. But they need advice from the military and that is provided by the Chief of the Defence Staff. He is the Government's military adviser, and as the head of the Armed Forces is therefore responsible for implementing the political decisions made through the chain of command. There is also advice from civilian staff on the range of ancillary matters which are not military but bear on the issue: this ranges from the diplomatic to the financial to the pol-mil environment. It is worth noting that there is a subtle distinction between purely military advice and a defence view which factors in the wider pol-mil perspective. Separately, there is legal advice which is provided ultimately by the Government's legal authority, the Attorney General. The Cabinet Office has a coordinating role, in support of the Prime Minister and Cabinet, but it does not have a directing role. The constitutional settlement gives power to ministerial departments by allocating resources to them and making them accountable to Parliament, through their political head and their permanent Civil Service head, as Accounting Officer. Much of this is being exposed in an unedifying light by the Iraq Inquiry,[1] with each witness providing a defence of his or her own position or role in the machinery of Government, and thereby revealing the imperfect match of theory and life.

Defence is not the only domain of Government activity where policy making is dependent on the expert input and knowledge of others outside the political class. Education or health fall into such a category too. But there is a divide between the civil and the military domains which is not replicated elsewhere. The ethos of an organisation which is dedicated to delivering controlled

---

1   The Iraq Inquiry was established on 30 July 2009, under the chairmanship of Sir John Chilcot, 'to establish, as accurately as possible, what happened and to identify the lessons that can be learned'. Details are available at: http://www.iraqinquiry.org.uk/ [accessed: 31 May 2011].

violence on behalf of the state is organised for the inevitable consequences of such engagement, and while it draws its recruits from society and then trains, develops and sustains them apart from society, it is by definition different. And the understanding of what military force can achieve, what effect it can deliver, needs expert judgement, although that too can be imperfect. Above all, the intervention physically in the affairs of other sovereign nations and the uncontrolled dynamic that sets up, together with the potential loss of life (our own and locals), make this an undertaking which is different from the domestic actions of Government, indeed from the diplomatic and developmental interventions overseas which can also have serious consequences both for the delivering and receiving countries.

It would be remiss not to place all this in a broader context. The Government does not act on whim in the international arena. It has a policy baseline, not always well articulated and with all sorts of semantic confusion between policy and strategy (well documented by Professor Strachan).[2] Within that policy are priorities which derive from an assessment of the threats we face. The interesting thing about the recent efforts by Government to set out its security strategy is the much wider scope of the canvas on which the security picture is painted. In a seemingly contradictory way, one of the reasons is that the centre of gravity is the citizen not the state itself: it is the well-being of the individual and his ability to go about his normal business. The stated vision is to 'protect the UK and its interests in order to enable its people to go about their lives freely and with confidence'. So the banking crisis and global trading interdependence are as much factors to be taken into account as international terrorism, WMD proliferation or piracy. And the Armed Forces we have are geared to the country's policy aspirations – or at least that was the idea of the 1998 SDR which consecrated an expeditionary posture as the *raison d'être* of the British Armed Forces. It was this strategic decision-making that enabled the UK to embark with mixed success on Coalition/Alliance operations in Iraq and Afghanistan, because we had constituted our forces for just such exigencies, maybe without quite enough investment and with insufficient foresight on the nature of twenty-first-century insurgency.

Let us now look at some examples of the relationship in action and try to understand the issues that arise. It is helpful to start with a textbook example of harmony and concord. Operation Barras in 2001 was an undertaking to recover some soldiers taken captive and held hostage by a violent gang in Sierra Leone. There were attempts at negotiation but the prospect for recovering the soldiers without unacceptable concessions was diminishing with time. An operation was planned to attack the gang's camp and liberate the soldiers. The plan was put to ministers and approved, with some discussion no doubt of the likelihood of success and the risk to life on both sides. The plan was executed pretty much as intended, with the loss of one soldier's life on the UK side and some wounded. The Government, the Services and the nation basked in the military's reflected glory. The theory is demonstrated: expert advice is tendered, political control and decision-making are exercised; and the outcome delivered by the Armed Forces is excellent. But let us also consider the counterfactuals. What if the hostages had been removed at the eleventh hour to a redoubt deeper in the jungle? Or if the operation had been compromised? Or if heavy casualties had been sustained by the attacking force or the hostages? Well, none of those things happened. The result was that all could be satisfied. Success does not call for the counterfactuals to be answered. That arises when success is less than wholesale. Who demanded that a rescue be made exactly then? Were the risks properly understood? Was the plan fully explained so that the consequential effects were also examined? Were the legal aspects fully evaluated? Who was to blame and who was responsible? This latter point is important because the political and military approaches are divergent. Political

----

2   Strachan 2005.

accountability is clearly with the minister of the department concerned. The accountability of the military leadership is not always easy to identify when things go wrong, as they sometimes do. And examples such as the Iranian kidnapping of the Royal Navy/Marine 15[3] and the explosion of the Nimrod over Afghanistan[4] bear that out. We will return to this.

I would like to suggest that there are three key components of the relationship which give rise to problems: timeframe, strategic understanding and expectation, and culture. For the military commander time is important; there are issues about getting inside the enemy's decision loop, achieving surprise, maintaining momentum and the ability to sustain an operation. For the politician time is of a different order. First there is the question of what the public have been brought to believe about the speed at which success will be delivered; what in any case is the shape of success – military victory is a different thing from a durable strategic end state; then there is the matter of sustaining public support over time through loss of life and operational adversity; and above all the question arises of the timing of success or failure, or more likely uncertainty and stagnation, in relation to the big political cycles of elections, summits and the interaction of military affairs with the rest of politics. The military cries of strategic patience and maintenance of the aim do not count for much when the political cards are all falling the wrong way. If we take the example of the Kosovo campaign, or rather the bombing of Serbia, the military effect of assailing Serbia was expected by the military to need not much more than three days' worth of concerted operations. Close on 90 days later the desired effect was achieved. Whereas the military consider it normal that a plan will change after the first encounter with the enemy, the politician who has spelled out his expectations will regard it as close to criminally irresponsible and fear charges of incompetence. I would note in passing that Kosovo remains unfinished business. This malign mismatch works in the opposite direction too. Earlier in the Balkans it was clear, once the US had committed themselves on the ground, that they had a continuing and essential role to play, but that was not something that the President could commit to because Congress was not amenable and the electoral cycle did not support it. So the commitment was drip-fed to the military, which for planning purposes needed a longer time horizon. If we consider the conclusion of the UK's involvement in Iraq, there is no doubt that a variety of factors contributed to the decision that we should withdraw our combat forces. We had other priorities; we had done the job; the US was heading in the same direction out of Iraq, for example. But the overriding driver, I suggest, was a political concern to lance the boil of Iraq in good time before the election in 2010 in order to improve the chances of a better showing by the incumbent government. The US surge in Iraq in 2007 also had a political motivation to it, linked to the presidential election in November 2008. Political unpopularity is a powerful force in driving a political timetable. None of that is to say that the decision was a bad one, although there were worries that the desire to get out would be pursued so manically that we would do ourselves untold damage in the process – to our reputation as a military power, in the region with friends and foes, and above all with our salient political and military ally, the US. Consider also the Obama decision in 2009 on an increase of troop levels in Afghanistan followed by a decrease within 24 months.

The issue of timeframe and that of strategic understanding and expectation are closely connected. The latter case relates to how politicians interpret what they are being asked to make decisions about. Politicians are in the business of taking risks; they have a vision for a better life or world which can only be delivered by change and engagement, whether that is in education, health

---

3   Iranian military personnel seized 15 Royal Navy and Royal Marine personnel on 23 March 2007 in the North Arabian Gulf. They were held for 13 days.

4   Fourteen airmen died in the crash of a Nimrod aircraft over Afghanistan on 2 September 2006.

or the wider world. Their calculation of how the voters will react is a measure of their political acumen. Their ability to gauge political reactions both at home and abroad, and especially in a foreign country subject to outside intervention, is less certain. Of course domestic errors occur, such as over the poll tax. The old adage of nothing succeeds like success is surely applicable in overseas intervention. An example of the reverse is to be found in the deployment of British troops to Helmand province in Afghanistan in 2006. The then Secretary of State for Defence has been taken to task for suggesting that the UK expected to conduct their operations without firing a shot – I paraphrase. That is not what he said, as a close reading will reveal;[5] what he was trying to do was to distinguish between a mission conducted by the US which was focused on attacking al-Qaeda and a NATO mission which was geared to stabilisation and reconstruction: if there was fighting to be done it was counter-insurgency not counter-terrorism. In practice the distinction was lost both on the public and on the ground. The question arises whether there was a mutual understanding of what the UK was letting itself in for. The military saw the extension of the NATO mission to the whole of Afghanistan as mere military logic; and there was a role for the UK to play in giving a lead and taking on a tough job in Helmand. Ministers saw it as a risk, in terms of both what we might encounter and how robust our allies would be, even would they be present at all. There were also questions about cost, not least the knowledge that, once committed, extraction is very difficult. I will insert a sharp question here about how it came about that the UK became involved in two enduring medium-scale operations, above the level of the MOD's own planning assumptions which suggest that such overlap is tolerable for only about six months. Was it political pressure or military judgement? The complaints about under-resourcing derive at least in part from having to prioritise. It is fair to say that the intensity of the fighting, and the nature of the reception, were a surprise to Task Force Helmand. Despite precursor scoping and shaping missions, this was largely a battle with the Taleban, in support of the vestiges of an Afghan provincial administration. Now the military take this in their stride, adapt, produce a new plan and, inevitably, request more resources. At the political level this looks like a problem: the situation is not as advertised, the commitment is growing, the costs are rising and, above all, the human losses are increasing without any realistic perspective for success. The charge is one of political miscalculation; to the military this looks more like the age-old problem of not being able to see over the next hill.

There is a point to be made here about the nature of any military undertaking: is it discretionary in support of global peace and security, or is it necessary for the security of the country? If the former is the case then the willingness to continue the engagement may be limited; if the latter, there is little choice but to reinforce and bring allies with you. Making that distinction is an important step in the preparation for an operation. Success cannot be assumed, but retreating from a chosen course is tricky too. The non-discretionary nature of the Afghan operation is clear, in the interest of denying ungoverned space to al-Qaeda. But non-discretionary does not mean the same as total commitment. Criticism has been levelled at Whitehall for not being on a war footing during the Iraq 'phase 4' operations, contrasting the Second World War arrangements to mobilise the civilian effort. The fact is that this was not the Second World War; politicians did not give it that priority, as evidenced by the Prime Minister's statement of priorities after his third election victory in 2005, which were starkly domestic.

---

5 When announcing the British deployment to Helmand on 23 April 2006, John Reid, the then Secretary of State for Defence, stated 'We're in the south to help and protect the Afghan people to reconstruct their economy and democracy. We would be perfectly happy to leave in three years time without firing one shot.' Available at: http://www.channel4.com/news/articles/uk/factcheck%2Ba%2Bshot%2Bin%2Bafghanistan/32 66362.html [accessed: 31 May 2011].

The most obvious mismatch in strategic understanding and expectation occurs where the purely military objective shades into the comprehensive end state, which is ultimately determined by local politics. Why did the military not do more thinking about the aftermath of the invasion of Iraq? There are suggestions about catastrophic success denying sufficient time for planning; or experience showing that detailed planning served no purpose until taking ground truth on the spot; another comment is that the priority was WMD identification and elimination; and that the British practice was to get the UN to take on the task as soon as possible. Many, I am sure, should have asked more questions, myself included. What of the Chiefs of Staff in committing to the success of the operation? What success were they subscribing to? Or the FCO who were designated as the lead in planning the post-conflict phase? Much was no doubt expected of the Americans who had 'misunderestimated' the situation, to quote George W. Bush. Ensuring a shared understanding of the complexities of delivering the comprehensive approach to deliver stabilisation, or the subtle interplay of security and reconstruction, let alone the speed at which consent can evaporate, is a challenge. The blame has been liberally allocated by witnesses in the course of the Iraq Inquiry. The naked truth may be unpalatable, namely that we were not up to the job collectively, and as a nation, we were not prepared to allocate resources to do it properly. The substitution of the US for the UN was not a happy experiment.

Turning now to cultural differences, there is great political appreciation for the capabilities of the Armed Forces, their versatility and their can-do attitude. But that does not mean that politicians understand the military ethos. Let us take the example of the ARRC and its availability to be deployed as a corps headquarters. Consideration was given in 2004 to its deployment to Iraq, but instead it was committed to NATO in Afghanistan for 2006. Politically it may have looked quite attractive to be playing a major part in the command of operations in Iraq with the US. The primary motivation, however, was more the military desire to press into service a British capability of which they were proud and which they feared might be vulnerable to cutting if its utility was not demonstrated. There is also a certain braggadocio in the military's ownership of premium capabilities. I do not discount the benefit of assisting the US and sharing the burden. And I note the enthusiasm of successive commanders to take their headquarters to the field even when the political climate was latterly very much geared to reducing the UK's exposure. Military motives need careful scrutiny, lest the enthusiasm to do proper soldiering takes precedence over balanced judgement of the national interest. The Iraq Inquiry has taken an interest in why the UK decided to contribute a land division rather than to limit its liabilities to air and naval elements. Part of the answer has to be that the military wanted to be in on the invasion; a brigade was too small for influence or independence, and no land component meant complete marginalisation. It would be wrong to believe that the political demand was for that size of force, but if it was available that was a political plus.

Another unremarked but important difference is the reaction to casualties. The military regard that as an inevitable consequence of the business they are in. Not that they are cavalier about them or lack in risk minimisation. Politicians, on the other hand, see the impact on the public and the reaction to the undertaking embarked upon, particularly when it is already unpopular. At times, when there has been a glut of casualties, there has even been the risk of tactical incidents having strategic impact; fortunately, the strategic has trumped the tactical when decisions came to be made. Many will claim responsibility for deciding to acquire better-protected land vehicles, but my observation was that ministers were the most insistent about avoiding unnecessary death and injury with inadequately armoured trucks. Making do with available resources is a military characteristic which is admirable in some circumstances but when engaged in a campaign of indeterminate duration is unwise.

A final point on culture: for some time the military has been trying to get away from old ideas of military units of account – ships, battalions and planes – and deal in capabilities and concepts. A worthy aim, I believe, but completely unacceptable to the politicians (and the Treasury). Partly it is a method of control and partly it is a need to explain satisfactorily to the public what is being done in their name. An announcement that the UK is sending unspecified forces to shape the battlefield and squeeze the centre of gravity of the opponent just does not measure up.

Apart from cultural differences, there is the issue of experience. I think I am right in saying that Malcolm Rifkind was the first Defence Secretary since the Second World War not to have served in the forces.[6] This gave rise to some misgivings, but less so as his tenure unfolded. His predecessor, Tom King, had been an Army subaltern, but a long time before.[7] There is merit in the clear separation between the expert military adviser and the professional politician who takes the decision. There must be empathy but there should also be challenge and scrutiny, not mere assumption of mutual interest. The military can sometimes take advantage of the inequality of military knowledge and insist that there is only one proper military course to take; and they are not beyond threatening that they will expose the fact that military advice is turned down, if that course is not accepted. In reality there is never only one course of action. That may depend on how objectives are framed and what timescales are identified. It is also a question of what resources the nation is prepared to vouchsafe for a given end, and that is a political question. In the political arena over Afghanistan, words have been bandied about the need for extra troops and their denial by ministers. Some champion the right of generals to speak up publicly; I do not, and not least because every commander, at every level, has a different view apart from that of wanting more resources. None of this can be absolute. You don't need extra troops if others can do the job in the coalition. And defining the job is not up to the military, and especially so when the task is stabilisation, a new military task identified in 2009 as 'military assistance to stabilisation and development'. Above all, in constitutional terms, does the country want operations to be outside political control? I think not, and nor would Clausewitz.

Returning to military accountability, this issue has been given publicity by the Haddon-Cave report into the Nimrod disaster.[8] The report itself was occasioned by the absence of anyone in the MOD willing or able to stand up and accept responsibility. It is not clear to me that the right culprits were identified. And on the Royal Navy/Marine 15, notwithstanding a secret report shared with the House of Commons Defence Committee, the absence of a court martial, or senior naval or operational voice to take responsibility, was baffling, certainly to politicians. Voltaire's maxim about killing an admiral '*de temps en temps*' to encourage the others comes to mind. The UK approach also stands in stark contrast to the ruthless US mode of sacking those responsible for mismanagement or failure.

What is to be concluded from this complex relationship? That it is complex, for a start, and that the differences of perspective and experience are healthy. I conclude with two comments and a prescription. The comments are by way of dangers in the relationship. They are twofold: first, the confluence of interest; and second the conspiracy of optimism. On the first there is a desire by both parties to show themselves off to advantage, both at home and abroad. Playing on the big stage is very alluring when the plaudits come in. The UK may be a middle-size country, but it is on the UN Security Council, and is still one of the largest economies in the world. It believes

---

6   Malcolm Rifkind served as Secretary of State for Defence from 10 April 1992 to 5 July 1995.

7   Tom King served as Secretary of State for Defence from 24 July 1989 to 10 April 1992.

8   Charles Haddon-Cave conducted an independent review of the 2 September 2006 Nimrod accident over Afghanistan. See Haddon-Cave 2009.

in a rules-based international system, and wants to play a conspicuous part in that, shaping and promoting it. It has leadership ambitions. Ditto the military, which wants to be operating in the lead of a coalition or in close association with the US, its publicly acknowledged ally of choice. Small though they may be, they are not shrinking violets in their assessment of their abilities; nor of their willingness to tangle with the hard-edged and complicated end of the conflict spectrum. So both sides see it as being in their interest to play on the big stage. And that gives rise to risks, which is my second point. There is a tendency to acknowledge that there are risks but to discount them. Of course, if we heeded all the Jeremiahs we would sit at home and do nothing: just recall the catalogue of disasters that were paraded in 1990 in advance of the operation to liberate Kuwait from occupation by Iraq. Likewise, in 2003 there were real concerns about the use of chemical and biological weapons, and the management of the aftermath by the US. But past experience, and a sense of confidence about the efficacy of will, discounted known concerns and argued for optimism. The military did not disguise that there would be casualties and difficulties, but at no stage did the top leadership say that the job was not doable. Nor for that matter did anyone else, such as the FCO. And the enterprise was not being undertaken alone, rather the US were deploying their considerable resources and military capability.

Finally, I offer a prescription. Clarity is needed, above all in respect of the objectives of military activity and the risks involved. Where other international or national agencies are involved, from the UN to NGOs, the definition of their role and relationship are also vital, especially as they change. In modern operations the role of the military is rarely the decisive one in the ultimate success, although it is an essential component in enabling that success. It is said that the UK did not at the outset have objectives for Iraq: it did in broad terms, and in detail for the military campaign; but it is true to say that it took time to develop the objectives for the aftermath we found ourselves in, not least because the big part to be played was by the Iraqis, assuming their political responsibilities. My last point derives from this. It is essential to keep the strategic purpose and end state in view. Everything must be geared to that. Too often the energy in Whitehall goes into handling the day-to-day detail, whereas the effort should be concentrated on achieving the big objective. And unity at the top of the political and military command chain is vital to success.

Chapter 24

Too Busy to Learn: Personal Observations on British Campaigns in Iraq and Afghanistan

Alexander Alderson

Introduction

In June 2007, the *British Army Review* published a short article of mine in which I questioned whether the British Army really understood counter-insurgency (COIN).[1] I had seen a good deal of the British campaign in Iraq and, contrary to the mood at the time, which often verged on hubris, I challenged the view that the British Army knew what it was doing in such an unglamorous, difficult and highly complex form of conflict. My central argument was that the Army was struggling in Iraq because it had neglected COIN, forgotten its hard-fought lessons and failed to teach it at the Staff College. It was no longer part of the UK's institutionalised approach. We had to do better and doing better depended on knowing what we were talking about.

Even though British troops had been deployed in Afghanistan and Iraq for over four years, my article was the *Review*'s first to deal with COIN for some time. It prompted not one response and sadly reinforced in my mind Sir Michael Howard's observation that the army takes a surprising pride in 'complacent anti-intellectualism'.[2] In the years that followed, it took a major effort by a small group of activists, in itself a form of insurgency, to overcome this mindset and inject COIN, as General Sir Peter Wall later directed me, 'back into the lifeblood of the British Army'.[3]

From 2004 until I retired in summer 2012, I had a privileged insider view of both campaigns in Iraq and Afghanistan: I had ready access to both theatres of war and those who served there; and my personal involvement in the US Army's COIN renaissance from mid-2005 gave me a comparator against which I could judge developments in the UK – or the lack of them. I will take a chronological approach dealing largely with the army, first in Iraq and then Afghanistan. Many of my comments apply generally across the Services and into the government departments inexorably drawn into COIN. It covers UK and US efforts to redefine and overhaul COIN doctrine and training – I was closely involved with both – and my time working in Baghdad for General Petraeus in 2007–2008, where I saw the results of his reforms in action and the difficulties the UK faced in southern Iraq. The second half switches focus to Afghanistan and the role my small team of expert COIN practitioners played in reorienting the British Army onto COIN through doctrine and education.

My central argument is that in the absence of any formalised institutional understanding of the complexity and challenges which insurgency and COIN continue to present, and largely unaware of extant doctrine and the extensive COIN history and literature, the UK, like its US ally, had to

---

1   Alderson 2007: 16–21.
2   Michael Howard in von Clausewitz 1832: 38.
3   General Sir Peter Wall, then Commander-in-Chief, direction to the author, Land Warfare Centre, Warminster, 25 January 2010.

relearn COIN almost from scratch. The UK's starting point was far weaker than it should have been given its extensive involvement in such operations. This created an intellectual uncertainty which was reflected in both campaigns and exacerbated by long periods when almost constant re-interpretation took place by successive commanders. This was not because the political situation in Iraq or Afghanistan continued to change significantly after the campaigns started, rather a succession of tactical-level commanders were given the freedom to interpret what they saw and change course in ways that they saw fit. This was aggravated by the lack of any UK operational-level campaign plan to harmonise UK efforts in Iraq, or in Afghanistan until the UK's three-star officer in Afghanistan was dual-hatted in 2010 as both deputy ISAF commander and the UK's National Contingent Commander.

Historic Legacies and the Warfighting Ethos

From the British Army's first formal doctrine in 1909 which called for 'careful study of the … mode of fighting, habits and characteristics of the [irregular] enemy,'[4] to General Sir Frank Kitson's seminal work, *Low Intensity Operations*,[5] practitioners and theorists have emphasised the need to keep learning about small wars, low intensity warfare, COIN, irregular warfare, or whatever epithet contemporary thinking used. Its complexity is best studied and understood *before* embarking on it. Unfortunately, having to relearn old lessons has been a recurring theme in the last hundred years or so of British military history, certainly during Britain's end of empire security campaigns, the so-called heyday of 'classical' COIN. Contemporary references to Malaya, Kenya and Borneo ignore the fact that conventionally minded forces had to be retrained and often re-equipped to meet the very different demands of fighting insurgents. In Northern Ireland too, the need to learn and adapt became the driving force behind tactics and training.[6] The army which ended the campaign was trained and equipped very differently from when it first deployed.

Despite our institutional COIN heritage, for a crucial period in the late 1990s until late 2007, the study of low intensity warfare, counter-insurgency, irregular warfare, or whatever epithet current thinking used, was relegated to a position of almost complete institutional irrelevance. Attention concentrated almost exclusively on warfighting based on the compelling if incomplete argument that an army prepared for high intensity operations could 'step down' to operations short of war. Referring to a previous period of uncertainty, David French notes

> In the post-[First World] war era, when there was no one single obvious enemy to confront, it made sense to plan on a "worst-case assumption", for if the army was prepared to fight a "big" war, it could surely win a "small" one.[7]

Sixty years later, with the Cold War over and Bosnia starting to reshape views on the utility of conventional forces, the same logic was applied again. Amidst fears of further defence cuts, the warfighting ethos, suitably couched in joint service terms, became the central argument for strong, conventional forces. The logic was apparently simple. As Field Marshal Inge made clear in 1996, 'forces trained for high intensity combat can adapt to peace support operations but the reverse

---

4   British Army 1909: 127.
5   Kitson 1971.
6   See Iron 2008: 167–84.
7   French 2001: 13.

is not the case.'[8] Unfortunately, an important element had been left out: as we found in Malaya, Kenya and Northern Ireland, 'stepping down' from warfighting always needed doctrine, training and equipment *specific* to the new environment. This missing piece of institutionalised adaptation – theatre-specific doctrine, training and equipment – and the impact of its absence are central to what followed.

Iraq: Lurching into Insurgency

By early March 2004 I was a member of the Directing Staff at the Joint Services Command and Staff College (JSCSC) at Shrivenham. The war in Iraq had become a bitter asymmetric struggle between the US-led coalition and Saddam's regime loyalists and their al-Qaeda allies. The Coalition force, so successful in rapid, decisive, major combat operations to topple Saddam, proved to be too small and incorrectly postured for the complex challenges of post-conflict stabilisation.[9] Effective post-conflict nation-building was beyond both them and the Coalition Provisional Authority which was set up almost as an afterthought in April 2003. In the political and security vacuum of summer 2003, armed opposition groups emerged to challenge the Coalition and to secure their own position, establish their own authority and safeguard their own interests. Widespread looting across Iraq that summer demonstrated that the Coalition could not maintain order and the country started its slide into an intractable guerrilla war.

On Friday 5 March 2004, I was told to prepare a presentation on British COIN doctrine and our approach to it. My audience was to the US Army staff finishing its final training in Kuwait before moving to Baghdad to set up the four-star theatre HQ for General George Casey. My instructions were very clear: do not preach; do not hector; stick to the doctrine. I spent the weekend reading Army Field Manual (AFM) Vol. 1 Part 10 *Counter Insurgency Operations* (2001) and then writing the presentation. Dr Rod Thornton, a colleague at Shrivenham, prepared an historical analysis of COIN approaches (British, French and American) and joined me on the flight to Kuwait. We spent a day or so having our presentations vetted by a string of harried US Army colonels before we were allowed to present. Late on the Tuesday afternoon, we were ushered into a large auditorium and an audience of over two hundred colonels and general officers, all focused on the challenges ahead of them in Baghdad.

Within minutes of Thornton starting, the audience had turned hostile, interrupting him repeatedly and bombarding him with historically inaccurate or irrelevant questions. My lecture was met with complete silence, less for one interjection half way through by Lieutenant General Dave McKiernan, the Land Component Commander. 'Are you telling me we are facing an insurgency?' he asked. Given the degenerating security situation across Iraq at the time, I was somewhat surprised. I took him back to the definition of insurgency: 'the actions of a minority group within a state who are [sic] intent on forcing political change by means of a mixture of subversion propaganda and military pressure aiming to persuade or intimidate the broad mass of people to accept such a change.'[10] Insurgency, I concluded, was exactly what he faced. Banging the table, McKiernan declared he fundamentally disagreed with that and everything I had said. 'Damn it,' he shouted, 'we're warfighting!'

---

8   Inge 1996: 15.

9   HCDC 2004: Paragraph 387, 156.

10   British Army 2001: A-3.

What struck me from the whole experience was not that the US commanding general had challenged the suggestion that US forces faced an insurgency, but how relevant and well-written the British field manual was. The main outcome of my trip was not any notable refocusing of US efforts on insurgency and COIN – others would follow and meet with a similar reaction – but that I had actually read the Army's COIN doctrine. As I subsequently discovered, I was, and remain, in a minority.

Counter Insurgency Operations (2001) was written by Brigadier Gavin Bulloch, then the Army's principal doctrine writer. The 2001 edition refined the 1996 edition – also written by Bulloch – which had broken new ground by blending the Army's manoeuvrist doctrine with some long-understood fundamentals of COIN: the need for close civil–military cooperation; the need to uphold the rule of law; the importance of intelligence-led operations; an emphasis on minimum force; and the requirement for tactical adaptability and agility.[11] The 1996 edition also introduced a series of principles arranged in a logical sequence to provide 'a government with a general pattern on which to base and review its COIN strategy'.[12] The AFM clearly stated that it did not provide 'a general antidote to the problem of insurgency',[13] nor did it see COIN simply applying one form of military force against another. Instead it echoed General Sir Frank Kitson's view that once an insurgency had 'taken hold, politics and force, backed up by economic measures will have to be harnessed together for the purpose of restoring peaceful conditions'.[14] There is little to suggest that the UK's political, military and economic efforts were ever truly harnessed during our time in Iraq, and while the UK effort gradually improved in Afghanistan, as Sherrad Cowper-Coles and others have pointed out, it was often less than ideal.[15]

As luck would have it – for there is no evidence that any planning accurately predicted how the post-war security situation would unfold – the British were given responsibility for the four predominantly Shia provinces. They were spared the vicious backlash that American forces faced in Baghdad and the Sunni-dominated western province of al Anbar. Instead, British forces found a largely compliant Shia population which was glad to be free from the Ba'athist regime and quick to secure power and the resources that come with it. Herein lay the root of the problem that would grow as Iraqis re-established a new political hierarchy, both formal and, in keeping with Arab tradition, informal. The early months in Basra proved to be chaotic but, apart from terrorist attacks by former regime loyalists, the threats to political development and security were less clear. Charles Tripp is pointed in his criticism of this early period in Basra:

> The British had only a weak grasp of the personal histories, relationships, rivalries and status differences behind provincial networks. This was knowledge that came gradually, and by that stage people had already inserted themselves into positions of influence in local government. They used these posts to build up local fiefdoms, pursue feuds with rivals and initiate complex relationships with the emerging parties and leaders in Basra and Baghdad. In short, a distinctly Iraqi politics was

---

11   British Army 1995: i. See also Mockaitis 1990.

12   British Army 1995: B-3-2. The principles, developed by Brigadier Bulloch and Dr John Pimlott, a senior lecturer at the Royal Military Academy Sandhurst, were Political Primacy and Political Aim; Coordinated Government Machinery; Intelligence and Information; Separating the Insurgent from his Support; Neutralising the Insurgent; and Longer Term Post-Insurgency Planning. Ibid: B-3-1 to B-3-11.

13   Ibid.: B-2-1.

14   Kitson 1997: 283.

15   Cowper-Coles 2011.

developing which escaped the supervision, let alone control, of the allied forces in occupation of the country.[16]

By mid-2004, the UK only had 8000 troops in Iraq, concentrated in and around Basra. But what were they there to do? Peace support operations, nation building, or should the emergence of insurgent groups have redefined the campaign more appropriately as COIN? Regrettably, no one ever satisfactorily addressed Clausewitz's first of all strategic imperatives:

> The first, the supreme, the most far-reaching act of judgement that the statesman and commander have to make is to establish … the kind of war on which they are embarking, neither mistaking it, nor trying to turn it into, something that is alien to its nature.[17]

A campaign that started off as one of liberation by regime change, by force of circumstance following Iraq's total collapse, quickly developed into an occupation by any legal definition. The situation changed further in March 2004 when, as a former brigade commander described it, the campaign in the south 'lurched into insurgency'.[18] It was not like any insurgency we had faced before, being more akin to the brutal, widespread Algerian independence movement of 1954–1962 than the IRA, Mau Mau or Dhofari rebels. Although British and US forces quickly dealt with a major Shia uprising in early summer 2004, the UK maintained the line that its forces were not facing an insurgency, that things were different in the south and that stability operations were proceeding as planned.

With hindsight, the period of so-called stability and reconstruction in 2003 and early 2004 was a view only held by the Coalition. Without any meaningful Iraqi political authority and effective security, Shia political groups were quietly preparing to take control on their terms. Meanwhile, believing that stability was improving in the south, and faced with decreasing support at home, the UK continued to reduce its military footprint yet further. A full withdrawal was impossible, however attractive it might have been, because the UK's promise to stand shoulder to shoulder with the US meant it had to hold the south while something emerged from the political and security debacle which was fast developing in Baghdad.

Initial Iraqi compliance with, or ambivalence to, the Coalition was due to Iraqi uncertainty about how Iraq's new political process would work. Once Shia domination had been secured through elections in January 2005, those in power had little need of Coalition support and those left outside the process had no need to respect the law. Coalition forces found themselves the obstacle to Shia groups gaining or cementing power and therefore were now a justifiable target. They were now the problem not the solution, a position acknowledged controversially by General Sir Richard, now the Lord Dannatt in October 2006.[19] There was nothing new in this; British troops had found themselves in a similar position in the same part of Iraq in 1919 when the tribes rose up against British rule. In Aden too, in 1967, they found themselves in the middle of a violent, unwinnable security operation once the UK government declared its intention to withdraw completely. In Iraq in the mid-2000s, however, UK withdrawal was not an acceptable option. While the US remained decisively embroiled across the rest of Iraq, the UK had to hold on.

---

16 Tripp 2007.
17 von Clausewitz 1832: 88–9.
18 Brigade commander, interview with author, London, January 2007.
19 Sands 2006. See also Dannatt 2010: 328–9.

The critical point in the campaign came not with any political developments or military milestones but with the carefully calculated attack by al-Qaeda on the al-Askari Mosque in Samarra on 22 February 2006. The civil war which erupted changed the demographics of Baghdad as mixed areas were cleansed by Shia or Sunni terror groups, and the resultant levels of violence demonstrated that neither the US and its coalition partners, nor the still-developing ISF, could contain the sectarian violence. Worse still, it showed that the Iraqi government was incapable of acting and that some of its ministries were complicit in the bloodshed.

Attacks by Shia militia on British forces increased during 2006 and force reductions continued in line with the general policy of transition – handing over to ISF as they stood up to take responsibility for Iraqi security. As the several insurgencies gained momentum and violence escalated, the US tried to bolster Iraqi efforts to control the widespread violence which now blighted Baghdad. Large-scale security operations took place over summer 2006 but they were generally ineffective due partly to the limited capabilities of the ISF and partly to an operational concept focused on the insurgents rather than securing the Iraqi population. Crucially, they highlighted a marked difference in approach between the US and the UK. The UK continued to withdraw despite the worsening security situation; the US tried to fight it out even though security was worsening in Iraq and the Bush administration faced growing and considerable domestic criticism.

Nevertheless, in Basra, in a minor reversal more of approach than policy, two successive British generals at last characterised the campaign by the principal problem to be dealt with – insurgency – and not the condition to be sought, namely stability.[20] Throughout 2006 they used classic British COIN doctrine and their experience from Northern Ireland to shape the plan and the approach. The limited military, political and economic levers they had at their disposal were combined in a sustained, albeit limited, effort that demonstrated some British resolve and something of the capability of the Iraqi security forces. This was Operation Sinbad: unfortunately it only achieved temporary and localised security and development improvements in carefully targeted areas of Basra. The method resembled the classic Ink Spot approach, or Sir Robert Thompson's Clear-Hold-Winning-Won approach, but only in the logic not the scale of the operation. This did not happen until the Iraqis forced the Coalition to act in Basra in March 2008. Although Operation Charge of the Knights got off to a faltering start, once it was supported by Coalition forces the methodical Iraqi-led clearance operation soon wrested control of Basra from the militia and established sustainable *Iraqi* government control of the city.

Operation Sinbad ended in March 2007 with the change of British command in Basra.[21] The problem was now recast as criminality, not insurgency; 'Palermo rather than Beirut';[22] 'large scale gangsterism rather than all out war'.[23] The difference between Basra and Baghdad could not have been more marked. Sinbad had at least shown the US that there was some British resolve, and it had captured the imagination in Whitehall. By summer 2007, the US campaign had not only changed strategic direction from withdrawal to a troop surge, but it changed its approach, from

---

20   Major General John Cooper, commanding 1st (UK) Armoured Division, and then Major General Richard Shirreff, commanding 3rd (UK) Division. Lieutenant General Cooper was later Deputy Commander Multi-National Force Iraq 2008–2009, and Lieutenant, now General Sir Richard Shirreff commanded the Allied Rapid Reaction Corps and was later DSACEUR.

21   General Sir Peter Wall, interview with author, New York, 4 May 2007.

22   GOC Multi-National Division (South East), Address to Multi-National Force-Iraq Commanders' Conference, 17 February 2007.

23   GOC Multi-National Division (South East), Address to Multi-National Force-Iraq Commanders' Conference, 4 August 2007.

Security Sector Reform (SSR) and transition to local Iraqis, to population-centric COIN and an updated version of the same classic counterinsurgency doctrine reflected in Operation Sinbad.

From my perspective as one closely involved in drawing lessons from operations and developing doctrine, the Army's experience in Basra raised the question: was its doctrine still valid, or were circumstances so different that it was simply not applicable to post-conflict Iraq? Iraq posed a number of unique challenges for a US-led coalition unprepared for the responsibility of running the country after the collapse of Saddam's regime. It was not unreasonable to presuppose that without an effective Iraqi political system and in the face of increasingly violent and capable insurgencies, British doctrine, rooted in post-colonial campaigns, would be no longer relevant. Yet, despite the complicated Iraqi situation – political, security, diplomatic and economic – and despite initial confusion over the character of the campaign, a dishearteningly small group of practitioners found that British doctrine was both relevant and applicable. The problem was that it was not followed as a matter of course. From my perspective, this can be attributed to three factors: first, confusion over what sort of campaign it was – peace support, despite no peace to support, or COIN; secondly, policy which sought to limit and reduce the UK's physical presence in Iraq; and, thirdly, doctrine which did not provide the baseline of common understanding which was so evident in the initial ground invasion.

It is a startling fact that virtually none of the hundreds of commanders and principal staff officers who served in Iraq mentioned doctrine in their post-tour interviews.[24] Those that did confirmed that British COIN doctrine, in particular its principles and the method it laid out, remained valid. The issue, as it gradually became clear through 2005 and 2006, was that the doctrine was not understood and certainly not applied. The failure to apply COIN doctrine may be due in part to the mischaracterisation of the campaign, and the failure to adjust the approach as the insurgency intensified. However, it is much more to do with the failure to teach doctrine effectively to staff officers and commanders, as evidenced by the remedial education packages conducted in Iraq from 2006.

Doctrine is what is taught, and since 1997 COIN doctrine simply was not taught at JSCSC in a way which would instil even a basic understanding to soldiers, and not at all to the other two services. Tactics may have been amended as the campaign progressed and very sophisticated tactics developed, for example those for strike operations which were more closely related to Special Forces' tactics than generally associated with the Field Army. They were not, however, underpinned by the doctrine. It was left to senior commanders to inculcate a recognisable British approach to counter-insurgency, but very much dependent on individual interpretation.

2005–2008: The US COIN Renaissance and British Frustrations

Given the publicity which surrounded the publication of General Petraeus's US Army COIN manual in December 2006 and President George W Bush's surprising and counter-intuitive reversal of US strategy in Iraq – stay and fight not transition and withdraw – it would be easy to believe the story started with him. In fact, the US Army had started the project three years earlier when the absence of any relevant COIN doctrine was identified as troops were training for Baghdad. The Combined

---

24   In 2003, General Sir Timothy Granville-Chapman, the serving Commander-in-Chief, directed that all returning commanders and their principal staff were to be interviewed to record their personal experiences and observations on training for and conduct of the operation. From 2003 until 2012, Brigadier (Retired) Iain Johnstone conducted every interview. Sadly his outstanding work has gone largely neglected by the Ministry of Defence.

Arms Centre, Fort Leavenworth, was given six months to produce it and a new COIN Field Manual was published on 1 October 2004.[25] Given the urgency of the situation, an unendorsed interim version was authorised for distribution as quickly as possible to help establish the US Army's baseline of understanding. Despite the speed with which it was written, the new manual was well received, being intuitive and theoretically sound.[26]

Lieutenant Colonel Jan Horvath, a US Army Special Operations Force officer, was appointed to write it. Knowing of British COIN experience, the first thing he read was our extant doctrine.[27] The interim publication proved to be an important step, being the US's first COIN-related doctrine since 1965. It included new lessons from Iraq and Afghanistan and incorporated many of the traditional counterinsurgency strategies and tactics. Interim or not, it was a very sound piece of doctrine and it became the centrepiece of teaching at the US COIN Center for Excellence (CFE) at Taji, west of Baghdad. Every US brigade, battalion and company commander and all principal staff officers had to attend a Taji course before they deployed forward into their areas of operation. From December 2004, they were all taught COIN theory and a standard sequence of events to clear insurgents from an area, re-establish government control, maintain control of that area and to build confidence and capacity in the local area. This was the Clear-Hold-Build policy which was used to great effect in Baghdad between late 2006 and mid-2008. No similar training was instigated for UK forces until I set up the COIN Centre in 2009 to provide brigades preparing for Afghanistan with a common baseline of theory, doctrine, culture and history.

I became involved with the US project in 2005, co-chairing the US–UK working group on COIN doctrine and training, and I worked closely with Horvath as he developed the second edition.[28] By June 2006, the US project, by now under the direction of the then Lieutenant General Petraeus, had made considerable progress and the final draft was ready for general circulation. The new US doctrine – re-titled Field Manual 3-24 (FM 3-24) – was an ambitiously comprehensive and coherent publication which offered a clear approach to campaign design, planning and conduct of COIN operations. Despite some high profile criticism in the US media in summer 2006 – criticism which continues[29] – the project maintained its momentum and it provided its allies with well-founded benchmarks for any further reviews of doctrine.[30] These included a clear intellectual starting point which melded extant US and UK COIN doctrine with the classic COIN theories (particularly Robert Thompson and David Galula), and a clearly stated essential logic based on population-centric not insurgent-focused COIN.[31]

The British Army took the decision to revise *Counter Insurgency Operations* (2001) in June 2006. The task was given to the Land Warfare Centre (LWC) and was to be finished within twelve months.[32] The Army's decision challenged the new hierarchy of Joint and Single Service doctrine which resulted from the creation of the Development, Concepts and Doctrine Centre (DCDC, formerly the Joint Doctrine and Concepts Centre or JDCC) in April 2006. DCDC was now the

---

25   US Army 2004.

26   John Nagl, interview with author, Oxford, 15 October 2008. The idea of an interim manual was accepted into the doctrine writing process: 'Field Manuals Interim accelerates dissemination of urgently needed new doctrine to the field.' See US Army 2007: 18.

27   British Army 1995. Also British Army 1998.

28   US Army 2005.

29   Gentile 2009a.

30   See Hoffman 2007a: 71–87. For an evaluation of the doctrine from a tactical, operational and strategic perspective see Corum 2007: 127–42. For a highly critical view, see Peters 2007: 144.

31   Crane 2007. Also Nagl, interview, 15 October 2008.

32   ADCC 2006.

authority for the higher-level doctrine from which Army tactical doctrine should then flow. This would have worked had there been some Joint Service doctrine on which to base the Army's tactical doctrine. There was none, and DCDC declared it had no appetite to produce anything related to COIN. Instead, it would focus on stability operations doctrine because it would have broader long-term utility. While JWP 3-50 made mention of COIN, its general approach based on impartiality and consent was poorly constructed to cope with an aggressive insurgency. Its discussion of the use of force notably lacked any sense of conviction in its discussion of how to deal with violent and non-compliant adversaries.

The problem became one of primacy. Who had the lead? Was it DCDC as the higher authority, or was it the Army which owned the only extant COIN doctrine and whose people were feeling the perceived doctrine gap most keenly? DCDC's position was clear: the absence of any joint operational COIN doctrine precluded the Army from developing its own approach. Until such doctrine existed – and there were no plans for any – any Army COIN would be invalid since it would have been developed in isolation. DCDC's performance was baleful. Deference to hierarchy was one thing; meeting an operational need was another, and the Army pressed on determined to provide its soldiers with doctrine which reflected the challenges they now faced. Meanwhile, DCDC bundled disorder, insurgency, criminality and terrorism under the one heading of countering irregular activity (CIA). The final pamphlet was 23 pages long, which was a measure of how disinterested DCDC was in COIN. While British troops struggled in Basra, DCDC's mantra was that COIN was a tactic and therefore did not involve them. If only they had read or, even better, studied their history.

The Army's COIN project got under way in earnest in October 2006, mirroring the approach Horvath and Petraeus had followed. King's College London's Insurgency Research Group provided challenging and insightful contributions as the work developed. Despite a strong start, what transpired – consultation, analysis, development, discussion, debate, and finally disagreement – ended in failure and seriously undermined the Army's decades-old confidence that it could publish its own doctrine. Problems quickly developed in December 2007 when the final draft was circulated for ratification by the Army Doctrine and Concepts Committee. The overwhelming view was that the Army's revised AFM was fit for purpose. Unfortunately, DCDC disagreed and demanded more explicit reference to PSO and the work it had completed on the Comprehensive Approach and countering irregular activity, despite the fact that these were couched in terms not well attuned to COIN. The Army acceded and the final draft was handed to DCDC for amendment. This breached the principle of editorial primacy and the resultant manual ended up as an ugly, disjointed *mélange* of COIN and PSO. Not surprisingly, it was quickly and widely dismissed as unpublishable and the Army's project stalled. The result was that it was no closer to having relevant, up-to-date doctrine than it had been in June 2006.

By May 2007, there was growing concern that the UK was not moving forward with its development of COIN operations as quickly as the US. The senior British officer in Iraq and General Petraeus's deputy, Lieutenant General, later Sir Graeme Lamb, raised his concerns to PJHQ in May. As a result, the J7 Branch (responsible for joint training and doctrine) launched a review of current COIN doctrine and training and sought evidence from key personnel who had served in both operational theatres. Lamb had posed a simple question: had the UK fallen behind the US in COIN? There was a unanimous view from those consulted that we had. The US had made COIN the main effort once it recognised the character of the problem it faced. What was more, the US Army had shown great agility and determination in refocusing its forces, doctrine, training and approach so quickly.

In July 2007, General Lamb called me out to Baghdad to look at what the US had achieved under General Petraeus's leadership and to examine any gap between US and UK approaches. This was at the height of the so-called surge of five additional brigades which President Bush had authorised the previous December in his remarkable and successful reversal of US strategy.[33] The new doctrine had informed both the strategic decision to reinforce Baghdad and the operational design to secure the Iraqi capital. Its impact was evident everywhere I went across Baghdad and the surrounding hinterlands. There was now a much greater level of coherency in what the US was striving to achieve. FM 3-24 was the centrepiece and much talked about. I was struck too by the importance placed on doctrine by the US chain of command.

The heart of the problem was the need for a common understanding of doctrine, continuity[34] and best practice. The US had recognised this in 2004 and General Casey, the then Multinational Force Commander, set up the CFE at Taji in December 2005. It was exactly what its name suggested: a genuine centre of excellence working directly to the force commander. It enjoyed the same command relationship which had been so successfully employed before by the British: GOC Northern Ireland and the Northern Ireland Training and Advisory Team (NITAT) from 1972–2007; CinC Far East Land Forces and the Jungle Warfare School during the Malayan Emergency; and the Director of Operations and the East Africa Battle School in Kenya during the 1952–1954 Mau Mau uprising. But the CFE was far more than a training establishment. It was also at the forefront of COIN doctrine development and its application, with responsibility for identifying lessons from across Iraq, making amendments to tactics and then sharing best practice across the force. Its principal objective was to influence the US military mindset and culture to learn and adapt.

Every aspect of CFE's work was designed to improve how the US conducted COIN in Iraq, yet the UK paid little or no attention to what CFE was doing. This was due as much to ignorance of it as it was a misplaced view that Basra was somehow different and that the UK's pre-deployment training provided the same sort of training. But CFE was there to educate, not train tactics, and because of the UK's COIN reputation in the early 2000s, the US had very much wanted UK involvement almost from the start. As a result, there was an open invitation for a British instructor to work at Taji but it went unanswered and as a result British forces did not benefit from the wealth of experience and knowledge available at CFE. More importantly, the UK missed the opportunity to brief our allies on British-led operations in the south and to shape perceptions positively on what was going on there. Unfortunately, by 2007 much misunderstanding existed among US forces about what the UK was doing in Basra, and my impression was of an intellectual iron curtain between MND (SE) and the rest of the Force. David Kilcullen, for example, General Petraeus's Australian COIN advisor who presented to every CFE course, was able to tell US brigades that the UK was 'moon walking out of Iraq' (a reference to the illusion of a dancer being pulled backwards while attempting to walk forward) without any counter explanation from the UK.[35] By the time Richard Iron and I were invited to present to CFE courses in 2008, it was too late: the UK's reputation in Iraq had already been laid bare.

---

33   See Alderson 2012.

34   By 2005, US forces now deployed to Iraq for one year at a time. This was an undoubted challenge for those battalions operating in insurgent strongholds, but it did allow them to build up detailed intelligence pictures of their areas of responsibility and to develop a greater understanding and in some cases affinity with the Iraqi population they were there to help protect. UK policy remained unchanged: all units deployed for six months. In some cases, early on in the campaign, British commanders were cycled through Basra in order to give them operational experience, to the bewilderment of their Iraqi counterparts.

35   Kilcullen 2007c.

The CFE bridged the gap between the theoretical and operational application, and in my opinion it achieved important levels of consistency of approach and continuity among US forces. There was no UK direct equivalent which taught doctrine in the context of operational campaign design. In this sense, CFE benefited from the direct personal involvement of the most senior US military leaders at force, corps and divisional levels, all of whom presented their operational plans and views on the campaign to their incoming brigade command teams. The Operational Training and Advisory Group (OPTAG), based at Lydd in Kent and the direct successor to NITAT, was the closest the UK got to the COIN CFE. An internal army review of Operation Telic enthusiastically described OPTAG in 2006 as 'a war winner', yet it concentrated solely on life-saving TTPs and made no reference whatsoever to doctrine – generic or theatre-specific – or lessons from previous campaigns.[36] This was very different from NITAT, its predecessor, which taught and helped to develop doctrine and tactics on HQ Northern Ireland's behalf. In the 2000s, the UK's educational and training requirements were no longer set and owned by the HQ responsible for the theatre of operations. HQ Northern Ireland owned every aspect of the military campaign but PJHQ failed to take full responsibility for UK COIN training and education for Iraq. It ignored almost completely what the US was doing to close any gap in consistency and continuity of approach between those deployed in Iraq and those preparing for it. PJHQ was, in Richard Holmes's view, the 'dog which failed to bark'.[37]

Learning from Iraq: Creating the COIN Centre for Afghanistan

On 31 October 2008, in my first term as a Defence Fellow at Oxford, I submitted a proposal to Major General Andrew Kennett, then Director General Land Warfare (responsible for the Army's collective training and tactical doctrine) to establish the UK's own COIN centre. Richard Iron, Dan Marston[38] and I had talked at length about the doctrinal and educational challenges the British Army still faced. We knew the value of CFE and its sister COIN Center at Fort Leavenworth, Kansas, to getting the general approach right. It was equally clear to us that the British Army could not consolidate its lessons from Iraq as Defence was then configured. This was further complicated by PJHQ's inability to get beyond the demands of running two campaigns in order to develop and mandate a coherent approach to COIN training and education. The Army would have to go it alone and hope that the other services and partners across government would follow.

A small group of us who had served in Baghdad – Iron, Marston, Horvath, Mark O'Neill (an Australian Lieutenant Colonel with a keen interest in COIN and a faculty member at Taji) – recognised that the CFE at Taji, just like its imperial forebears, fulfilled three important functions, none of which were being carried out in the UK: developing and publishing COIN doctrine based on lessons new and old; teaching the new doctrine; and acting as a service advocate and an intellectual authority for all COIN-related matters in support of the theatre command. The UK needed a COIN Centre to carry out what we refined into four principal tasks: analysis, development, education and advocacy. The challenge was to get the idea of a COIN centre accepted.

Ironically for our purposes, the UK's painful lessons from Basra in 2007 and early 2008 were still smarting and they proved to be the catalyst we needed to initiate the reforms required.

---

36   British Army 2006: 21.

37   Professor Richard Holmes, email to author, 15 June 2009.

38   Dr Daniel Marston is an Oxford-educated American academic who had been the COIN instructor at RMA Sandhurst, and subsequently an instructor at CFE Taji. He was to prove an important factor in rekindling British interest in COIN in both Iraq and Afghanistan.

Operation Charge of the Knights had left a mark on many of those involved in Baghdad and Basra and they wanted those immediate lessons to be institutionalised. The question was 'how?' There was a rising but belated interest in what the US Army had done under Petraeus. His reforms had clearly worked; had we missed something? For those of us who had been so closely involved, the answer was obvious: we had. While it was too late for UK interests in Iraq, Afghanistan was now the main effort and was proving to be every bit as challenging. With the doctrine project now underway, the Army would need a more effective way of inculcating its doctrine and getting the foundation right through a dedicated centre.

My proposal was simple: the Army needed a focal point to analyse, develop and teach COIN, and act as its COIN advocate. Without it, I argued, our own and allied lessons, doctrinal development and operational experience could not be fused fully, integrated and exploited along with work from academia and other research institutions. Furthermore, the absence of a COIN centre was hindering work with other government departments, agencies and allies because they did not know to whom they should turn and they were frustrated by having to deal with a myriad of British organisations, all of whom claimed responsibility. Importantly, I argued, there was no obvious logic for, or operational effectiveness to be gained by, doing nothing.

The British Army was the only one of the principal allied COIN protagonists which did not have a COIN centre. The US Army and US Marine Corps had theirs at Fort Leavenworth (set up by Petraeus in 2006), the Canadian Forces had a Centre of Excellence for Peace Support Operations (PSO), and the Australian Army – at the insistence of its Chief of Army – was in the process of establishing a COIN and Irregular Warfare Centre. All three nations were working collaboratively, and all three organisations, and the armies they represent, were mystified why, given the obvious difficulties the UK had had in Basra, we had done nothing about it. To show how marginalised we had become, a US Army COIN Center presentation slide highlighted its Australian and Canadian counterparts 'front and centre' but the UK was listed below Germany, France, the Netherlands and NATO in a footnote at the bottom! Sadly, by 2008, the UK was not just the junior coalition partner to the US, but the junior intellectual partner as well.

By late 2008, it was clear to those involved that both the COIN doctrine and the COIN centre project needed top-level support if they were to succeed. A champion was needed to marginalise the gainsayers and, more importantly, to cut through the pedestrian bureaucracy which constrained personnel and funding issues. General Sir David Richards, the then Commander in Chief, later Chief of the General Staff and finally Chief of Defence, was to prove vital in what followed. Petraeus had had to sequence key events carefully: instigate a top-level review of the campaign in Iraq; sow the seed of doubt that withdrawal was the right strategy; propose the surge; publish the doctrine; replace Casey with Petraeus. On a smaller scale, the UK's COIN reform had to be sequenced correctly or someone in the chain of command between Richards and us would have derailed it through intransigence, hubris or 'not invented here'. Between October 2008 and March 2009, the COIN Centre idea was carefully briefed to key staff officers in MOD, HQ Land Forces and at PJHQ and their support gained. With little compelling evidence to counter the proposal, the main problem proved to be finding the money to pay for the COIN Centre staff. Richards broke the deadlock by stating in committee that it was 'disgraceful that the Army did not have a COIN centre' and issuing direction to find the money and the people.

The COIN Centre was established on 20 June 2009 and by December that year had a hand-picked team of top-grade lieutenant colonels and majors, all of whom had extensive experience from Iraq and Afghanistan. From then until I left in January 2012, we taught every brigade as it prepared for Afghanistan, we ran a series of high profile COIN conferences and workshops to inform and influence, and we published a myriad of doctrine notes to cover gaps as they emerged in AFM COIN. We worked closely with our US counterparts in Fort Leavenworth, had officers working in Kabul at the COIN Training Centre, and we kept an open dialogue with commanders and friends both on operations in Helmand and as they trained. The appetite to learn among our target audiences was high. The early brigades we worked with were a little uncertain about the value of what we had to offer. The cult of 'mission command' still prevailed and commanders enjoyed considerable freedom, just as they had in Iraq, to define the problem as they saw it. Fortunately, many of the commanding officers preparing for Helmand in 2009 had been company commanders in Basra. They were keen to learn from that experience and wanted our support. As a result, my team quickly found itself running study days across the Army. Demand was high. Somewhat counter-intuitively, despite the COIN Centre's successes, its staff was stripped out on my departure to concentrate on more mundane doctrinal tasks. One-star officers took the surprising view that the COIN Centre had served its purpose now that the UK effort in Afghanistan was to transfer responsibility to the Afghans. They could now turn their attention back to areas with which they were more comfortable, such as major combat operations. This was despite the fact that the UK operation had nearly two more years to run and that at least four more brigades would have to train for COIN operations.

Nevertheless, the COIN Centre's central event became the Operation Herrick Study week. It was the one recommendation from my visit to Taji in July 2007 which had survived. Mandated by PJHQ, every brigade preparing for Afghanistan had to run a study week focused on the campaign. Until the COIN Centre was established, the event ebbed and flowed according to successive brigades' whims, but we established a standard programme. Drawing on the many academic contacts I had made while at Oxford and using (and abusing) PJHQ's authority, we brought in the leading thinkers from around the world and operational commanders both recently returned and still serving in Afghanistan. Over five days we took every officer in the brigade and many of its senior NCOs through the geo-strategic situation in Afghanistan, its history and culture, the challenges of contemporary insurgency, British COIN doctrine and the campaign as it stood *that week*. As the reputation of the study week grew, so did the number of contributors who wanted to take part. Partners from across government and NGOs joined what became a crucial unifying event in the brigade's transition from a conventional to COIN focus. The final day was always the highlight and the British three-star deputy force commander could be relied upon to get back to give his views of the campaign to the brigade getting ready to deploy.

Summer 2009 proved to be a turning point in the British campaign in Helmand. Since the first deployment in 2006 which stirred up the hornets' nest, the operational rhythm had meant that successive brigades could rely on being able to conduct one major brigade-sized operation. It was the highlight of the tour and the brigade commander's trade test. Until summer 2009, these had been generally successful but had not been decisive. 19 Brigade's Operation Panther's Claw proved to be different and its high casualty rates were almost decisive for the UK effort in Southern Afghanistan. I sensed that the collective nerve wobbled as the media focused on the high number of casualties and concerns about the number of helicopters available to UK forces in Helmand. The work we were doing at the COIN Centre took on heightened importance with the new doctrine being a central theme in all our engagements with brigades and battalions. Demand for our study periods quickly outstripped supply and I was struck by how many seasoned mid-ranking officers wanted to know more about COIN, not just to satisfy their own professional curiosity but to help put their own experience in a broader context.

For most of autumn 2009, the Prime Minister and the MOD were besieged by media criticism of what was going on in Afghanistan. There appeared to be no answer to the acute problems we faced. In early November 2009, I attended an inter-departmental assessment on the Helmand campaign. It was a sobering experience. Not one of the campaign indicators showed anything other than a depressing downward trend. After all, General Sir Frank Kitson, arch British counter-insurgent, had insisted that 'officers must be prepared to pass their knowledge on when the need arises and to go on agitating for suitable action until all concerned are aware of what is required of them – *or more probably until they are sacked for being a nuisance*.'[39] I felt duty bound to speak up.

All the assessments showed that the British effort in Afghanistan was at its most vulnerable state since the move to Helmand in 2006. There were many contributing factors: the US strategic pause while President Obama considered his options, the unceasing negative comment from the domestic media on just about every aspect of the British campaign save the bravery and commitment of our forces, and the growing – and what I judged entirely correct – recognition that Task Force Helmand had overstretched itself beyond the point where it could hold the gains it made over in previous tours. Crucially, it could not secure the population.

The Prime Minister had made clear the strategic significance of the campaign in terms of the UK's national security, yet surprisingly no single British plan existed which linked ways and means to the objectives the Prime Minister so clearly articulated. In the absence of a plan that provided, synchronized, prioritized, coordinated and sustained all our ways and means, not just military, from top to bottom within the overall ISAF campaign, our strategic interests were hostage to the fortunes or misfortunes of Task Force Helmand. Our COIN doctrine said 'In COIN "success" may equate to handing over an internal security problem to the civil police, or simply not losing.' We might have been clear about the former – partnering with Afghan forces– but how could we avoid the latter?

To the best of my knowledge, no successful counter-insurgency – British or otherwise – has been concluded without an overall plan that interweaves all the considerable strengths and capabilities of the instruments at the Government's disposal. Those strengths were potentially far more powerful than anything the Taleban could offer the People of Afghanistan or could bring to bear. Although in 2012 the situation on the ground is much improved, our efforts in 2009 were still being applied piecemeal, and it was into the gaps that such an approach provided that the Taleban moved and still continues to exploit with frustrating success. Prompt, decisive action was needed. It was clear that we could not wait until after an election; indeed, if we did, the danger was the situation would have been lost and our national efforts wasted. Defeat would have taken us a generation at least to recover.

I recommended four things: a unified cross-government plan orchestrated by one cabinet minister (I now note the naivety of such a suggestion); a unified UK military chain of command from HQ ISAF down to the front line (later enacted but with too much power still resting in PJHQ for the UK three-star commander to be truly effective); a much more positive public information campaign based on small positive steps and a strong, credible, honest line, rather than one large media rabbit being pulled from the hat; and finally much greater support to the front line from professional expertise in non-military areas. All of this had to be part of an overall long-term campaign plan, and not something to be seen through the prism of a six-month operational tour. With Richards as CGS, the appointment of Lieutenant General Sir Nick Parker as the UK National Contingent commander in Kabul for a full year, and Operation Entirety put in place to unify the Army's efforts to support the campaign, the situation was clawed back during 2010 both in the UK and in Helmand. The arrival of 20,000 US Marines certainly helped, as did the narrowing of the UK's area of operation to concentrate solely on Central Helmand, and the development of much better, but by no means perfect, working relations with Afghan security forces.

---

39   Kitson 1981. Emphasis added.

Conclusions

This chapter offers a personal perspective on what happened between late summer 2003, when insurgency first emerged in Iraq, and mid-2012 as the campaign in Afghanistan entered the critical transitional phase between Coalition and Afghan control. This was a period of marked change, both in the priority the UK afforded to its contribution to the campaigns in Afghanistan and Iraq, and their respective fortunes. The progression was the same in both campaigns. An encouraging start was followed by confusion over the character of the problem which shaped the UK response. Both then experienced a period of steady decline which – despite the efforts and sacrifices of those deployed – took both campaigns to a point of near-failure. In Iraq that was in the period late-2007 to early-2008; in Afghanistan it was the summer 2009 when intense casualties in Helmand province brought the harsh reality of war into sharp focus to the British population and the then Labour government.

In both cases, as the British campaigns reached their lowest point, the UK's in-theatre and domestic political difficulties prompted sharp and largely successful changes in approach to redress the balance and to get the campaigns onto a more even footing. Periods of consolidation and adjustment then followed. In Iraq, a more stable situation in Basra allowed the UK operation to end quietly in June 2009, while in Afghanistan, at the time of writing, the UK is committed to the NATO plan of transitioning security responsibility to the Afghans and to end UK combat operations by 2014. From an Afghan perspective the signs are at least more promising than they were three years ago, a situation which might be more opaque to western eyes.

In both campaigns, continuity of approach was in short supply: in Iraq this eventually took us on a divergent path from that followed by our US allies to the point where the UK's military credibility was in question. By contrast, over the same period the US Army started with a poor institutional understanding of COIN and had no doctrine for it. Through strong, determined leadership, it quickly produced relevant doctrine, developed COIN training for Iraq and Afghanistan, redesigned the two campaigns to reflect doctrine, eventually changed US policy to match operational needs, and its senior leadership gripped COIN so that subordinates, to use the fashionable term, 'got it'.

All this had a marked impact on our relationship with the US Army. There are two aspects to this. First and somewhat ironically, the UK entered the Iraq war to win influence with the US – to fight shoulder to shoulder – and yet we ended up losing it through the desire to withdraw and a marked reluctance to face up to the true character of the conflict we faced. Secondly, the very kinetic approach we saw in Helmand between mid-2006 and mid-2010 was as much due to the necessity of a small force with too much ground to cover against an elusive, adaptive and resourceful adversary as it was due to commanders wanting to show the US that we were not afraid to fight. Perhaps if the UK had faced up to the challenge in Basra earlier, things in Helmand might have been different. Our US allies had expected us to face up to the challenge in the first place; instead, our equivocation in Iraq came as an unpleasant surprise. Professor Peter Mansoor is direct in his criticism: the UK failed in Basra because of a failure to understand Iraqi political dynamics, an arrogant unwillingness to learn and adapt, and a reluctance to commit blood and treasure to COIN.[40]

My contention is that the UK military and political bodies lacked a commonly understood view of what insurgency means and how it should be dealt with using the instruments of state as they exist, not as they were. For the military, this was largely because its doctrine, education and training had failed to keep sight of a rapidly changing strategic situation and the security challenges

---

40   Mansoor 2009: 11–14.

it would pose. Unfortunately the UK paid for its poor political and military understanding of the problem and the time it took to learn and adapt. It paid in blood, treasure, and support at home and in both theatres of operation. My sadness is that few, if any, of the complexities the UK faced or the remedies found were new or should have been a surprise. Richard Holmes, my doctoral supervisor, summed it up: as I put the finishing touches to my thesis he noted sadly, 'I am a little struck by the fact that a series of bright senior officers behaved just a little like Charles II, who never said a foolish thing nor ever did a wise one.'[41] Unlike their many subordinates – those we taught at the COIN Centre – perhaps they were too busy to learn.

---

41   Holmes, op cit.

Chapter 25

Adapt or Fail: The Challenge for the Armed Forces After Blair's Wars

Paul Newton

Un-Learning in Action: 'We can't just kill our way out of this'[1]

In 2007 I returned from a second Baghdad tour. Seen from there (if not from Basra) the Iraq campaign had taken a dramatically positive turn as a result of the US surge and the 'awakenings'. I had played a modest but unique role, an experience that left an indelible mark. Scholars argue about whether 'winning' is a relevant concept in today's unstructured conflicts:[2] I knew what 'losing' feels like, and I had seen that when 'more of the same' is patently unfit for purpose, innovative leaders can get a huge organisation, at pace, to 'unlearn' old, redundant, ideas. Leadership of this sort has a profound impact, particularly if firm top-down direction exploits rich bottom-up knowledge. Intelligent risk-taking based upon analysis and intuition; seizing the initiative to create unstoppable momentum – these were concepts I had been taught throughout my military career. Now for the first time (on such a grand scale) I was experiencing them and helping contribute to a quite remarkable change. Enthused by this, in my next job I was required to think about the changing character of warfare's implications. Then, in a fascinating new three-star post as the first Commander of the Force Development and Training Command (FDT), I tried to use our deductions to help the Army in a practical way. In all, this was a period of five years to think, build consensus and act; continuity is important in matters of change.

In FDT we started to help our Army make progress, not merely 'change'. Reform was accelerated by news of more cuts to the Service to help balance the MOD's books. My approach was to do force development, '*with, not to, the Army*'. Entrusted with a broad remit, I took force development to be all-encompassing; responding (reactive) and anticipating (proactive) with both stimuli working in combination to generate momentum. Warfare cannot be deconstructed neatly: so in transformational force development that encompasses every aspect of military capability, from relevant minor tactics to the confidence we have in the theories that shape how we fight and with what, organisational boundaries or time horizons are artificial. Nothing should be off limits, at least for exploration. This chapter argues that the Army is reaping a return on the investment in and chance it took with FDT. In exploring the concept of a 'learning organisation' with FDT as a case study, it challenges Defence as a whole, not just the British Army, to chart a similar course. FDT is not perfect, so there is no organisational template for a learning organisation here. It argues only that the MOD should seek the same, or better, effect. In now striving to implement a 'Whole Force Concept', the Services, Civil Service and new industry partners should collaborate in a campaign of systematic and systemic military modernisation: 'evolutionary' in that progress will

---

1 Commander MNF-I, Baghdad, May 2007. Author's notes.
2 For example, see Simpson 2012.

include adapting established ways; 'revolutionary' in signalling the need to abandon others – even cherished, totemic ones.

This chapter is about making things better. It focuses almost exclusively upon what is *not* working. I have been privileged to serve in Britain's Armed Forces: they are fine national institutions. I hope this contribution might help them be even more effective in future conflicts.

Scope

The problem and then the concepts are explained. Vignettes from all three Services and particularly from early FDT experience are used to bring the notion of and need for a learning organisation to life, illustrating how it can create opportunities and solve problems that are stark – once one looks for them.[3] I make no apology for the tactical examples: warfare in whatever form is a practical affair. The imperatives behind my case include: the changing character of conflict; recent British under-performance; and that in future conflicts the MOD is likely to be held more closely to account.[4] I argue for a more rigorous and critical ethos, not only for managing the budget or procurement (where long-overdue reforms are being addressed), but also for ensuring core military ideas are fit for purpose. In addressing this shortfall, Defence can create and exploit techniques in combination, achieving greater military return for scarce resource by 'gearing': such as linking training to structured research and command-led experimentation; and so tapping more deeply the well of talent that can be, but only if we choose to make it so, the UK's 'agile edge'.[5] This is what a learning organisation aims to do. It does it by turning theory and rhetoric into resourced action, as a command priority.

Relevance

The concept of a learning organisation derives from research in American business schools in the 1980s.[6] That alone might make practical officers and busy MOD officials stop reading. It sounds bookish at best, yet more facile process at worst: the stuff of a crowded second-class train compartment to Swindon for another Defence Away Day. Persevere a little longer: after all, the MOD has imported wholesale many of the techniques, terms and concepts from the business world. It even calls the strategic headquarters 'head office'. In FDT, I was feeling my way down a dimly lit path, trying to create a learning organisation that could concurrently help the Army to become one: the journey would have been easier, and I a more articulate advocate, with a little more theory to light my way.[7]

The UK's Chief of Defence Staff (CDS), General Richards, asserted recently,

---

3   I am grateful to Lieutenant Colonel Debi Lomax, a founder member of my FDT Initiatives Group, a natural and talented 'insurgent' for the Army and whose notes for my successor are a key reference.

4   Levene 2011: 13 '… weaknesses in … evidence-based analysis … allow advocacy to have greater weight in decision-making than it should.'

5   Jon Day, a senior MOD official, corrected a draft of the 2009 Paper, *The Future Character of Conflict* (FCOC 2009). It had said '*people **will** be UK's "agile edge"*'. Day observed this was a matter of choice and investment, not birthright.

6   Senge 1990.

7   I am grateful to many who helped me plot this erratic course, particularly in the US Army where TRADOC was the exemplar and General Marty Dempsey an inspiration.

... defence should respond to the new strategic, indeed economic, environment by ensuring *much more ruthlessly that our armed forces are appropriate and relevant* to the context in which they will operate ... many defence establishments have not yet fully adapted to the security realities of ... [a] dangerous new century.[8]

Richards's goal may be unachievable without adopting the command culture, structures and processes of a modern learning organisation as critics argue that recent progress is fragile.[9] However, a rigorous, sustained, networked campaign to audit old military ideas and seek, agree and adopt new ones could build upon those foundations. In FDT I likened our approach to an insurgency; to generate momentum it relied on decentralisation with disparate parts of the whole forging ahead to a general intent, sharing what worked across the network (in this case, an Army of over 100,000). Success in such a reform campaign, at a time when we are not waging an existential war, stands or falls on the priority senior leaders give it; the returns on their investment will be reaped in battles to come. As the agenda is primarily military, senior officers who complain they are marginalised have the chance to lead.[10] But senior leaders are consumed by present business; be that cuts of 20 per cent to the regular Army, or planning a dangerous extraction from Helmand, or protecting their fiefdoms.[11] All this is at a time of shrinking budgets and when credibility of military leadership is low in the wake of Blair's Wars.[12] A campaign as described here will not be about changing the wiring diagram, or even appointing a 'Director of Defence Learning'. It is more cultural than administrative, it will be hard work, and it will not be popular. It starts, as in Baghdad, with someone saying 'more of the same isn't good enough'.

Quis Custodiet Ipsos Custodes?[13]

My core contention is that Defence has learned, but it is not yet a *learning organisation*. The consequent risk is that the UK's Armed Forces fail CDS's test in the next conflict, whatever form that takes. Better managing that risk will entail a relentless audit of 'relevance'; command-led and as much a part of aligning responsibility, accountability and authority as coming in on budget. The present system assumes that the Services, and other interest groups in Defence, intrinsically know what is best in their area of business. Recent Defence reform has set the direction, but it assumes military interest groups within Defence can self-regulate under a thin joint umbrella.[14] Theory dares to challenge this, identifying systemic factors such as inertia, groupthink and self-interest, as will be illustrated.

Change in military matters is not evenly distributed across time, domains or geography: nor is it always blindingly obvious. Clusters of innovation produce major change, and where that change

---

8   Richards and Mills 2011: 6 (emphasis added).

9   King 2010.

10   Jackson 2006.

11   'Fiefdom' is not meant disparagingly: leaders protect their organisation. The Chiefs feel this acutely, whilst holding in trust 'important National institutions' (Levene 2011: 7).

12   Parris 2011.

13   Who will guard the guardians? The argument here is that even expert interest groups cannot be relied on to get things right.

14   Levene 2011: 7. If the Services are 'the rocks on which Defence is built', who is the independent structural engineer who systematically checks them?

is profound, it can be referred to as a Revolution in Military Affairs.[15] This tends to occur when technology and ideas combine and one set of core assumptions replace another – the classic 'horse and tank moment'. Gradual changes can be difficult to spot unless hunting for the signals. It can be argued that technology leads transformation and that so long as a military system stays close to the leading edge of technological progress ideas can follow: the concept of air-manoeuvre could not have led the invention of the helicopter. Yet who is to say when a military idea such as air-manoeuvre (or opposed amphibious operations to bracket all three Services in this opening salvo) has had its day? We do know that the West is losing the technological edge on which its preferred way of war and many long-established concepts are built. Globalisation gives wider, cheaper access to modern weapons and ideas flow instantly and constantly over the internet. For those who look, evidence that others have been thinking hard and making themselves more relevant and capable, relative to us, is clear,

> … adversaries are studying the American way of war and will develop methods to challenge our established and often predictable preoccupation with the science of warfare and speedy recourse to precision fire-power, materiel, and money as the answer.[16]

If this is not spur enough, consider the marked decline in political and public tolerance for error. The traditional British pattern of initial costly failure followed by prolonged adaptation as in the Boer War, both World Wars and, arguably, in the Iraq and Afghan campaigns, has had its day. In future conflict, the MOD and the Services – both singly and jointly – will be expected to get things right from the outset or be held to account.[17] Scholars may say this is unrealistic; war by nature is inherently unpredictable, but the political expectation (if not the intellectual elegance of the argument here) should sound a warning in MOD Main Building. The required changes are not esoteric; the benefits are tangible and they should be seen as building upon recent reform. By inculcating a learning culture in peacetime, the inevitable requirement to adjust once the character of the next conflict is revealed will be easier. Rather than a *wicked problem* (layers of increasing complexity with no single answer), a drive for relevance through adopting a learning organisation approach attacks *knotty puzzles*.[18] Puzzles can be solved using the right methods. However, as Clausewitz noted, in matters of war there are often simple solutions, but attaining them is made more difficult by war's inherent friction.[19] In this case the friction is partly self-imposed as a consequence of habit, competing priorities and institutional inertia. War is a duel not a drill, so over-reliance on familiar patterns and old habits contains the seed of future failure.

Torrents of Change

Many say there has been too much change. One academic notes:

> The breadth and depth of British military transformation is also remarkable given that militaries are famously slow to change. Indeed, all organizations are resistant to major change. It is simply not in their nature. Organizations run on routines and standard operating procedures, and depend

---

15   Freedman 2006: 599–600.
16   Richardson 2009.
17   Anderson 2012.
18   Grint 2008. See also Rittel and Webber 1973.
19   Mahnken 2007: 71–6.

on stability for functional integrity. Moreover, military organizations, as socially conservative and closed communities (not unlike religious orders), are especially disinclined to innovate.[20]

And a damning report on the loss of an RAF Nimrod over Afghanistan concluded:

> The scale, pace and variety of "change" which the MOD in general … underwent during the period 1998 to 2006 has been without precedent in recent times. Indeed, there existed a state of almost continual revolution, such that the MOD has almost become addicted to "change" and a "change culture". "Change" has been seen as a good thing *per se*.[21]

The 'show me where it's failing' school might say that gradual, incremental evolution is *exactly* what is now needed, pointing to the huge amount that has already been achieved.

There are also practical as well as cultural objections to more radical change. First, it requires a degree of consensus among key stakeholders that there is indeed a problem (surprising to those who assume that the military works by shouting orders). Second, even when a change is agreed, it requires new structures and processes implying some new resource – difficult in austere times. Third, even if a Service Chief (or equipment project leader) in isolation initiated a campaign of self-critical review, it would be potentially dangerous to openly admit failings during the endless battle for resources that defines the Department in austere times. Fourth, introspection – even under a professionally and intellectually justified quest for relevance – signals uncertainty, just when subordinates crave shelter from the storm of administrative change: after all, strategy is meant to provide certainty and continuity. It is counter-intuitive to hunt for signs of failure in what can seem – and must be presented externally – as a smoothly running organisation. One could point to the success of the Royal Navy and RAF in Whitehall battles and conclude it would be absurd to expect them to initiate changes to a decision-making game they demonstrably play well. Last, and perhaps most paradoxical in this brief illustrative list, is 'jointery'. The joint model is the success story of which UK Defence is most proud: woe betide the ambitious officer who is deemed 'un-joint' should he question, for example, whether it makes sense for a mid-ranking officer from one Service to teach command and staff skills to officers from the others, when the character of their fighting environments is so different. All the boundaries of jointery are patrolled and fiercely defended (though in a peculiarly British muted way), but they are agreed around an implicit assumption: that what is to be joined up and 'enabled' by jointery is already fundamentally militarily sound.

There has been much purposeful adaptation in the UK's Armed Forces over the past decade. On the fifth floor of the MOD is a huddle of cubicles; all that is left in London of the Army General Staff – a term and an opportunity discussed below. On purple (the corporate colour of jointery) partitions are pictures of British soldiers in the dust of Helmand overprinted with the slogan 'Transforming in Contact'. Battle with adaptive, resourceful adversaries, first in Iraq and now in Afghanistan, has acted as a powerful (though possibly transient) catalyst. Even the most fleeting, Camp Bastion-based, visitor to Afghanistan will be impressed by the sheer quantity and superb quality of the purpose-built equipment, much of it heavily armoured to protect against the ubiquitous IED or roadside bomb. These vehicles may even be driven by Royal Navy seamen, in an echo of the Anson Battalion (brought ashore from their Dreadnoughts to fight as soldiers at Gallipoli).[22] Overhead, the skies are patrolled by RAF Reaper drones, providing timely, precise, intimate close air support and

---

20   Farrell 2008: 777–807.
21   Haddon-Cave 2009: 491.
22   Carlyon 2002: 199, 307.

flown by 'aircrew' (not all of them jet pilots) thousands of miles away.[23] The Urgent Operational Requirement (UOR) system producing spirally developed equipment, and the adaptability of the UK's service men and women who have undertaken new roles and designed new tactics, have been supported by an excellent bespoke pre-deployment training system. These are not trivial achievements.

The British Army: Adaptation and Irrational Perseverance

So, adaptation, driven both by shrinking budgets and the imperative of combat, is a fact in an Army which is now, in effect, *demobilising* as well as *transforming* in contact.[24] The Army, especially, has learnt from hard, sometimes bitter, experience.[25] Since 1945 there has been only one year – 1968 – when a British soldier did not die on operations.[26] Surely an Army with such depth of constant operational experience does not need business jargon?

Learning from experience is essential, but it is not sufficient. Known as 'single-loop learning', experience can detect errors and keep the organisation on track, so long as the destination does not change. Kahneman notes that all organisations learn in the form of 'basic assessment'. Assessment is continuous, but bounded by and largely restricted to 'the main problems that an organism must solve to survive'.[27] Single-loop learning works best in organisations in which the dominant assumption is continuity, not the complexity and uncertainty described in the MOD's own assessment of the Future Character of Conflict (FCOC).[28] Single-loop learning has been likened to a thermostat that learns when it is too hot or too cold and turns the heat on or off. The thermostat receives information (the temperature of the room) and takes corrective action.[29] What if the thermostat is not receiving relevant information – as with a Service during protracted peace if it is not inclined to challenge itself for the reasons above, nor forced to learn, by rigorous external force development challenge? If this is the dominant approach to institutional adaptation, Kahneman says the organisation is taking 'the inside view' which can lead to 'searching for evidence from our own experience [leading to] irrational perseverance'.[30] Irrational perseverance is a risk in Armed Forces whose primary Principle of War is 'Selection and maintenance of the aim'.[31] An example of irrational perseverance and single-loop learning is the way 'police primacy', a key tenet of the Northern Ireland campaign, was grafted onto a very different campaign in southern Iraq, where there were fundamentally different social and security factors at play.[32, 33]

Although there has been a tsunami of change in Defence, at the strategic level most change has been financial and managerial, exemplified by the Levene Report. Generally positive of late, it has set structural and budgetary conditions that can be likened to re-aligning the 'means' in the classic

---

23   Hopkins 2011.

24   BBC 2012.

25   Little 2009, Vol. 154, No. 3.

26   RMA Sandhurst War Studies Department research findings: question from Commander FDT, 2011.

27   Kahneman 2011: 90.

28   FCOC 2009.

29   Argyris and Schon in Mintzberg et al. 1998: 209.

30   Kahneman 2011: 245–9.

31   JDP 0-01 2008: 2–6.

32   MOD 2006: 70. 'Lack of vetting of recruits' political affiliations emerges as a key issue in 2004/5 as local factional loyalties emerged.'

33   See also Stewart 2006: 224.

strategy formula of ends, ways and means.[34, 35] To date, though, the military drivers for radical adaptation, other than to meet efficiency targets, have been single-loop lessons or technological opportunity. Current operations have demanded fixes for identifiable problems, in relatively narrow, mainly land-centric operations: fielding protected mobility vehicles; filling an airborne surveillance and strike capability gap; or taking decisive action to address a low-level leadership deficit, albeit one that 'caused national humiliation'.[36] Having taken command of an operational brigade that was living off its reputation for, rather than a real proficiency in, the craft of counter-terrorism, leads me to suspect that when informal learning ends after the Army leaves Helmand, the primary driver for military adaptation, as well as the folk memory, will rapidly fade. What is to replace it? Some point to the 1968 statistic and assume another operation will turn up, maintaining impetus for (narrow) adaptation. But MOD policy says UK will in future be more circumspect about committing land forces.[37]

So balancing budgets and single-loop learning are important, but will not generate CDS's imaginative, sustained and 'ruthless' quest for military relevance. There is also evidence that, despite a finely tuned lessons machine, the Army was slow to read some important signs about modern warfare; it has not looked for, much less heeded, the 'weak signals'.[38] But which signals to heed? According to Colin Gray the future is inherently unknowable; he cites the fallibility of 'trends' with their implied linearity.[39] I too agree that 'gains in our ability to model (and predict) the world may be dwarfed by the increases in complexity – implying a greater role for the unpredicted'.[40] There are, however, trends to which a response is already overdue. For instance, FCOC assessed that future adversaries would contest all environments and domains, including the lower air space where even non-state actors would soon have access to Unmanned Aerial Vehicles (UAVs) that could be used in swarms to overwhelm conventional air defences.[41] In late 2012, Israel intercepted a Hezbollah UAV reportedly over a nuclear site, but a British military capability to deal with a similar threat is not a priority.[42] Sometimes the problem is not lack of signals or signposts in trends, but failure to act upon them.

Creeping Irrelevance: The Case of the British Army

Almost every piece of the British Army's core equipment – bought from the Defence vote for the wars we expected to fight – has been left at home in the conflicts we had to fight after the invasion of Iraq and in Afghanistan. Weeds grow between rows of greenish-red rusting vehicles, procured for a different type of conflict in an era when media intrusion and political risk appetite were

---

34   'Reaching a balanced budget represents an important milestone in the transformation of Defence which builds upon the recommendations of Lord Levene's review of the Department ... as we move forward with Defence Transformation.' Secretary of State for Defence, announcement to Parliament, quoted by BBC News, 14 May 2012.

35   See Yarger 2006: 5–6.

36   Harding 2008b.

37   SDSR 2010: 17.

38   A strand in trend analysis, 'weak signals' was a theme in General Dempsey's 2010 Kermit Roosevelt Lecture, see Dempsey 2010: 6–9.

39   Gray 2007: 37.

40   Taleb 2005: 136.

41   FCOC 2009: 32.

42   Reuters 2012.

themselves very different. Traditionally long procurement cycles are clearly a factor, but not the only one. Ideas about land warfare – the Army's core craft – lay unquestioned for years and, like its vehicle fleet, edged imperceptibly towards irrelevance. For much of the last decade, learning beyond the imperative for and narrow confines of stabilisation operations not only stalled – it went into reverse. The Intermediate Command and Staff Course (Land) – ICSC(L) – attended by all newly promoted majors had, by 2010, focused so firmly on irregular warfare, and on the 'buzz topics' of strategy, operational art and political science, that all field-based content had been dropped. Developing 'an eye for ground' or the practicalities of moving a combined arms force – core professional skills whatever the character of the land conflict – had gone; as had all classroom exercises in which at least some of the friction of executing a plan could be replicated. Other major gaps had opened; individually, they were hardly noticeable, but looking systemically, as FDT was charged to do, it became clear the Army had not been fully aware of accumulating risk. Those experiencing Afghan training learned such widely relevant skills as 'dynamic targeting'.[43] Those not bound for Afghanistan moved to the next career stage, as joint officers at the Advanced Command and Staff Course (ACSC), with accumulating gaps in professional expertise which will be carried forward for the rest of their service.[44] Through single-loop or informal learning (much as folk tales get passed down the generations), the craft of modern soldiering had largely been inculcated by intensive, narrow experience and bursts of pre-operational training.

A review of long-established military ideas, from the tactical to the military strategic, reveals a backlog of conceptual adaptation. 'Conceptual' does not mean abstract; soldiering is a practical endeavour, and ideas about it in all its forms need periodic testing. Despite policy that espouses evidence-based decision-making, much at grass roots level was being taken uncritically and for granted. I could begin with questionable operational and strategic notions, such as air-mobility and opposed amphibious landings, but instead, I will work from the bottom up. Until 2011, the Army had failed to update its core teaching; soldiers and officers were being taught things that were of diminishing relevance and not taught the things that are relevant.[45] The other point about these individually small examples is how a learning organisation (here, FDT) can use cases that resonate with the whole organism (here, the British Army) as a call to action. Directives that exploit tangible, evidence-based 'retail' examples can demonstrate ambition and strategic intent; and by holding a mirror up to the Army, even inspire 'wholesale' enquiry and change. The aim is rapid, broad, cumulative progress with ultimate strategic impact: in Baghdad, what Petraeus likened to starting a 'stampede' that would build 'irreversible momentum'.[46]

Seeing then Fixing: 'What Bad Looks Like'

Big organisations use routines to perform the multitude of daily tasks that occur whilst leaders attend to strategy and 'business'. Few senior officers (or retired ones) write about field craft. It is

43   Real-time fusion of different intelligence feeds enabling a commander to initiate (or not) a strike.

44   In an FDT audit of command and staff training discussed later, it emerged that ACSC assumed Army officers arrived expert in divisional operations and proficient in corps-level land warfare. Neither had been taught on any Army course for years, but the Army had not asked the Defence Academy to adjust the syllabus. The Academy is now completing a major review, as is the Army, under the 'ROCC2' project, initiated by FDT.

45   Hennessey 2009: 66: 'The things that matter, we seemed to learn without actually being taught them. The things we were taught, largely useless. I'd like to think we enjoyed our senior term because, a mere eight months into our training, we began to learn things that were relevant.'

46   MNF-I Campaign Review, October 2007. Author's notes.

important, but frankly mundane – it is a given. Yet for a soldier, of any rank, being skilled in the field is also an unstated point of pride, as much a totem and acid test in the profession of arms as making a clean incision is for a surgeon. Field craft is the body of core knowledge taught, at length and cost, to every officer and soldier, Royal Marine or member of the RAF Regiment. Along with such basics as skill-at-arms and fitness, it is the very essence of soldiering proficiency.[47] Yet, until 2011, pamphlets on which the thousands of corporals and the captains base their standard teaching had not been comprehensively updated since the 1950s. It was as if nothing new was worth recording or teaching about the field of battle. Countless man-training days over decades have not fully reflected the craft of modern soldiering.[48] To drive home the point about relevance, at my first briefing to an Army Conference I showed a picture of the lesson 'Why things are seen' taken from a 1950s pamphlet, then one from our latest edition: they were identical other than the uniforms (the modern one was also not so well photographed). Some military ideas endure: distinctive shape and shadow and shine will still get a soldier seen and killed. But our instructional manuals did not include 'new basics' such as 'ground sign awareness' (how disturbed earth may indicate the presence of an IED) or blending systematic technical surveillance and intuition to build a pattern of life to sense, record, retrieve and act upon the absence of the normal or the presence of the abnormal. In land operations amongst people these are basic indicators of professional relevance; as FCOC stated, 'final resolution of conflict will involve people and where they live'.[49] The solution in this case also shows how a learning organisation stimulates rapid progress. An officer at the Infantry Training Centre wrote saying he felt professionally embarrassed; forming a 'community of action' – experts from battle schools and across the Army – in under a year, and in addition to their busy jobs, they completely revised what is now taught to the British Army about the 'craft' of land warfare. More tellingly, this initiative led to emulation: a resourceful Royal Armoured Corps officer is producing a new field craft guide for mounted soldiering.

A second tactical example illustrates how a learning organisation hunts for signs of weakness or failure, even in places that look successful. In all modern land operations, using IT to record and exploit data (drawn from a blend of intuition, such as the atmosphere sensed during a patrol, and factual, such as political graffiti seen by the members of that patrol) is a professional basic skill right down at section and platoon level. It is not a mission-specific boutique skill that will go away as we brush the Helmand dust off our boots, nor is it the preserve of clerks or staff officers. Until FDT began sweeping changes to what and how the Army learns, fast, accurate management and exploitation of data was not taught at places like the Staff College, or Sandhurst. When first directing that officer cadets should arrive proficient in touch-typing, as well as fit, with a sharp haircut and carrying their own ironing board, I would not have got more quizzical looks had I proposed that they learn parade commands in Welsh.[50] In less than a year, data manipulation and numerous other 'new basics', alongside updated old ones, were introduced into a modernised RMAS syllabus, and proficiency in IT-enabled operational staff techniques formed a backbone of the ICSC(L) syllabus. RMAS and ICSC(L) were selected for special attention in the FDT campaign of learning because my theory of change was to focus on leader development: an overdue shake-up in these key nodes

---

47   'Skill at Arms' had also gradually eroded. Hits on targets during tactical exercises were not being checked: when spot checks were done, strike rates were as low as 10 per cent. An instructor noted 'Now they know we're checking the scores are improving'. The new 'Combat Capability Director' is charged with regaining British Army Skill at Arms.

48   Pamphlets provide the lesson plans from which to teach every recruit.

49   FCOC 2009: 3.

50   Sandhurst was also resistant to language training (not in Welsh) even as a recreational option. With the Commandant, FDT initiated a 'quiet revolution', of which more below.

would serve as exemplar and accelerant across my Command and into the whole Army. These are high-status establishments. Many of the Army's best captains and senior NCOs are selected to teach at RMAS, whilst excellent middle-ranking instructors teach at ICSC(L). Showing 'what good (and bad) looks like' at these establishments had a 'gearing' effect. A learning organisation finds ways to multiply the pace of progress. Rather than exhaustive, detailed plans or trying to change everywhere at once, an alternative approach is to find the pressure points … and press them very hard.

Preparing for the Right 'Field'

Codifying professional knowledge (what the military calls doctrine) helps define a learning organisation. Of course, knowledge evolves, especially when challenged by robust debate and tested in realistic training and operations: doctrine can both capture change and help to drive it. Yet, in the case of the Royal Armoured Corps, in 2010 the doctrine being practised in training by every tank soldier, from crewman to lieutenant colonel, was still optimised for open, rural combat. This was not mere idleness: it reflected one of the Army's core ideas about warfare and its image of itself. The result was that from first climbing onto a tank or reconnaissance vehicle, young tank troop leaders or drivers were taught to think about armoured warfare mainly in terms of a rural battlefield, of tactical bounds from ridge to ridge; their eye for terrain was not honed by learning about arcs of fire from street corner to market place, or to assess whether the culvert under the slum alleyway leading to it could bear their vehicle's weight.[51] By 2010 the Combined Arms Tactics Course (meant to be mandatory for all majors from the combat arms) was both the most expensive and least relevant of all the courses at the Land Warfare Centre. Students had great fun manoeuvring armoured groupings across the open plain, with no meaningful enemy and without the clutter of a modern battlefield to trouble them. Getting the formative ideas about warfare right is critically important. In 1944 Montgomery noticed a relevance gap but his belated corrective action caused tactical chaos. He discovered that those units which had spent years preparing for Operation Overlord in the UK, whilst he was busy in Africa and Italy, had been readying for the wrong battlefield. This is not a pseudo-intellectual military reference to an inability to think like manoeuvrists: they were quite simply trained to fight in the open; Normandy was littered with woods and villages, and held by a tactically adroit enemy who had worked out how to defend them.[52] On the eve of the invasion he directed a sudden change, but if anything it compounded the problem. 'The very structure and tactical conception behind British armoured divisions meant they were neither trained nor organised for the land battles they would have to fight in Normandy.'[53] An army that prepares for the wrong 'field' is setting itself up for future shock.

Much of the 'field' upon which the Army exercises would be familiar to the grandfathers of today's soldiers: the rolling, open prairies of Canada or Salisbury Plain, where the British Army

---

51   Having illustrated creeping irrelevance in the infantry with field craft, I single out the Royal Armoured Corps (RAC) for two reasons: first, the Army must better explain the key role for armour in modern conflict to counteract a slew of ill-informed 'relic of the Cold War' assertions; second, under a dynamic Director, the RAC responded, becoming an exemplar of how a learning organisation drives internal progress.

52   The Army produced a superb film series on Operation Goodwood in the 1970s. Using this as the exemplar, after a gap of some 40 years, FDT initiated a multimedia tactics project drawing upon Mission and Training Exploitation. The first teaching product is a re-creation, using actual footage and modern graphics, of Operation Moshtarak, an assault into Taliban-controlled territory.

53   Gooch 2006: 140.

still does most of its intensive training.[54] Champions of the Canada experience rightly point to some excellent training. Yet whilst the physical environment that defines land warfare is changing at great pace, Army organisations, core equipment, doctrine – and investment in realistic training – have not. The global urban population began to exceed the rural population in 2006 and is likely to grow from 6.9 billion in 2010 to 8.8 billion by 2040 with 65 per cent living in urban areas.[55] The gap between the Canada experience and the tactical proficiency needed to operate as a battlegroup or brigade amongst (or beneath) high-rise buildings, or fighting through a populous, sprawling shanty town, is stark. Starting the process on open terrain (the tactical equivalent of the drill square) makes sense. Indeed, if it is really lucky, the Army may in the future fight an adversary foolish enough to confront a western joint force on relatively open ground.[56] But unless combined arms manoeuvre – which must involve early integration of air and aviation – is taught in settings that replicate the most difficult and likely case, not only will training per se lack relevance, it will inculcate the wrong 'feel' for the craft of land warfare. 'Cities have always been centres of gravity, but now they are more magnetic than ever.'[57] The sort of training the Army enjoys by habit (and sunk investment) is in growing and stark contrast with both empirical trends in urbanisation, as well as a mass of historical experience that our Army tends to fight in close, cluttered terrain, not the open veldt.[58] All of this may seem very basic, but success in war depends upon getting the basics right. Of General DePuy, the founder of US Training and Doctrine Command (TRADOC) – on which FDT was modelled, it was said, 'His lifelong conviction was that if you get it right at the squad and platoon levels, the rest would fall into place.'[59] DePuy was also familiar with military ossification. Taking command of an infantry battalion in 1954 he recorded, 'It was just as if it was the day after WWII. Nothing had changed.'

There are practical solutions, once the nettle is fully grasped and old habit seen for what it is. In 2010 FDT discovered that the French Army had invested over 100 million euro in a purpose-built training town close to Calais. In December 2012 a British armoured infantry unit was due to conduct a field training experiment there as part of the FDT Agile Warrior programme. This, along with exploiting US facilities in Germany and a creative strategic training partnership with industry under the Whole Force Concept, could lead to relevant and affordable land force preparation that is fully integrated with air support. At the same time, it could add substance to the political rhetoric of the Anglo-French strategic partnership. Learning organisations hunt relevance, find novel but practical solutions and look constantly for 'gearing' opportunities.

Convenient Myth

If habit obstructs relevance, so too does its close cousin, myth. Ever-present in military affairs, myth can helpfully forge a common identity, such as with the selective telling (over many glasses of port) of glorious unit history. But when myth (or military wishful thinking) becomes the foundation for

---

54   The Army went to Canada when the British were ejected by Gaddafi from their Libya armoured training base, which they had used since capturing it in an armoured operation in 1943, reinforcing the sense of habit formed by history and preference.

55   *Global Strategic Trends* 2010: 163 and references throughout to urbanisation as a key trend.

56   Gray 2009.

57   Peters 1996.

58   Even in the Falkland Islands conflict, where all land fighting took place in the countryside, we were fortunate that the Argentinean army surrendered before we had to fight in the urban area of Port Stanley.

59   Cole 2008: 95.

key ideas about modern warfare, there is a high risk of not just surprise but catastrophic shock. There has been a powerful long-standing fixation in the British Army with massed armoured manoeuvre. With the exception of 100 hours during the First Gulf War, sweeping armoured manoeuvre has not been the Army's actual experience, or operational requirement, since the end of the desert campaigns of 1943. Yet doctrine of the Cold War period taught optimistically, 'Manoeuvre … enables a small force to engage a larger one with some chance of success instead of being forced into a battle of attrition that it could not sustain.'[60] At the height of the Soviet threat the Army rallied around a myth. It told itself that massed tanks could deal a 'counter-stroke' blow against a numerically superior Warsaw Pact enemy. The realities of terrain, equipment and physics entailed willing suspension of disbelief. Unlike the North African desert or Russian steppes, West Germany was even then cluttered and congested with buildings, streams, ditches and woods. Sweeping, striking armoured manoeuvres were possible only where the terrain was clear – like in Canada. Even had the Russians conveniently thrust into the Soltau training area, the British Corps' concept of operations made little military sense. The British were years away from fielding the equivalent of the 'Big Five' key systems on which similar US thinking relied.[61] British infantry were required to hold vital terrain to release our tanks to manoeuvre. Yet the infantry was equipped with a missile that could only defeat Soviet tanks from the side. This was like telling a lightweight boxer he can only hit his oncoming heavyweight opponent by punching sideways. A defence of the Rhine Army concept might be made on political grounds – it helped send a deterrent message, although deterrence requires credibility; presumably the Russians knew the size of a Milan missile warhead as it was published in the manufacturer's sales brochures. The Army embraced the manoeuvre myth for it gave a veneer of plausibility to an otherwise militarily meaningless proposition.

Is the Army Alone in This?

So given evidence that the Army has suffered from creeping irrelevance and the traps of group-think, what of the other Services? Both have been busy doing good work for the Nation, but how can we (and they) know that their own ideas about their fundamental craft are still sound? Who tests for relevance? The odds are that at least some of the ideas upon which so much is now built are unfit for purpose, as the Army found in 2004 when tested by an intensive form of insurgency that was more akin to Lebanon than Londonderry.[62] In 2009 the then CDS was questioned about military performance in Iraq and Afghanistan. He was quoted as saying that Defence had been 'smug' and 'complacent'.[63] The Review ordered by Parliament into the 'the broader issues' of the loss of an RAF Nimrod in Afghanistan in 2006 is sub-titled *A Failure of Leadership, Culture and Priorities*.[64]

---

60   *Design for Military Operations*, quoted in Jermy 2011: 184.

61   Tomes 2012. The Big Five were the Abrams and Bradley armoured vehicles, Apache and Black Hawk helicopters and Patriot air defence missile. All were linked by a new C2 network, and the force trained at a National Training Center against an adaptive, realistic adversary.

62   FDT studied tactics used in 2006–2007 against the Army in Basra; similarities with 2006 Israeli experience were striking but hardly surprising – if one looks for them – given Iran's proxy role in both conflicts.

63   Irvine 2009, quoting an interview in *The Economist*.

64   Haddon-Cave 2009.

Defence can take a cue from these pointers and much hard-won Army experience, especially if it recognises those failures as prompts to reflect beyond the immediate lessons of recent operations.[65] Acknowledging failure is a litmus test of a learning organisation. In these contentious conflicts, it has been the Army that has born the greatest load, suffering the greatest loss; yet not until Richards became Commander-in-Chief in 2007 was the Army put onto an operational campaign footing; Operation Entirety was his drive to add urgency within a Command that had not fully bent itself out of peacetime shape and habits.[66] As Chief of the General Staff (CGS) he then created FDT and, as CDS, Richards has overseen the formation of the Joint Forces Command (JFC). He has also initiated work by a small group that resulted in a position paper entitled 'How We Will Fight'; it introduces the idea of a Joint Expeditionary Force as the focus for post-Afghanistan UK hard power projection.[67] Champions are vital, and so too are spokesmen for change, but relying upon such champions emerging naturally, rather than adopting a system-wide learning approach as a matter of policy and due diligence, leaves open to chance that which should be embedded in strategic governance.

If the Army is not always quick to adapt and sometimes rallies around the wrong ideas, what is the record of the other Services? In the First Gulf War the RAF employed weapons expensively acquired in support of an operational airfield denial core idea. Developed over many peaceful years, these weapons and tactics were intended to beat the Soviets, yet an inferior Iraqi enemy pounded by massive Coalition bombardment forced the RAF in a matter of hours to abandon low-level bombing: determined aircrew gave it their all, but the big idea was fundamentally wrong. Similarly, the Royal Navy has not fought a fleet action since 1982. Then, air defence was a core capability around which the Cold War Navy was built, but it came up short when tested in battle, as shown by the destruction of HMS Sheffield and several other ships. Yet, off the Falklands, the Navy braved not modern Russian MIGs, but elderly Sky Hawks. So how, without the goad of the Provisional IRA, the Jaysh al-Mahdi or the Taliban swarming around isolated platoon bases, can we be confident that these Services have challenged deeply embedded attitudes and ideas about their own core business; where is their 'ruthless' quest for relevance? Andrew Gordon sums up well both the challenge and the opportunity facing the UK Defence establishment after 2014:

> After a century of peacetime sailoring it took a major war and perceived failure (or at least a massive disappointment) forcibly to complete the transformation of the British fleet back to a fully efficient fleet-fighting machine. That is a lesson we should not forget.[68]

The Single Loop Returns

Paradoxically, a clue that standard learning approaches have not served either Service well is the robust action taken following isolated cases of air and maritime failure. These were failures in tactical incidents, not the full test of a maritime or air-centric modern war. The Navy learnt fast,

---

65   Mansoor 2009: 14: 'The British failure in Basra was … due to … a failure by senior British civilian and military leaders to understand the political dynamics at play … compounded by arrogance that led to an unwillingness to learn and adapt'. Also, General Jack Keane US Army (retd) speaking of British performance in Iraq: 'We lost confidence in you', FDT Whither Warfare Conference, RMAS, May 2011, author's notes.

66   Dannatt 2009. As CGS he paid tribute to 'the immense efforts undertaken by Land Forces to place the Army onto a campaign footing … some 68 separate measures have been implemented'.

67   Richards 2012.

68   Gordon 2006: 169.

in a single-loop sense, after Iranians seized a boarding party. A swift review into core maritime skills and low-level leadership led to major changes in the way officers and sailors are trained; the solutions are designed to inculcate greater confidence in the use of force and restore robust junior leadership. In the case of the RAF, it was the loss of single Nimrod aircraft and the subsequent (external) investigation that led to the creation of a 300-strong Military Aviation Authority, and a shift in attitude to risk that has accelerated a process of 'juridification', which will have profound though as yet unexplored consequences for British military power.[69] Will these examples alone be sufficient to prompt a re-examination of culture or long-established military habits, or will it take further central direction?

Re-assess the Big Ideas

It is not that armies (or navies or air forces) always prepare to fight the last war. They are, though, selective in their use of evidence, adopting convenient or dominant habits that become enshrined in orthodoxy. Even once-good concepts can lose their currency and relevance. As Secretary Gates told the US Marine Corps:

> Looking ahead, I do think it is proper to ask whether large-scale amphibious landings along the lines of Inchon are feasible, when the proliferation of anti-access technologies, such as accurate cruise and ballistic missiles, will work to drive the starting point for amphibious operations farther and farther out to sea.[70]

Voluntary re-assessment of ideas that form a proud organisation's self-image (and may even be existential) is a dubious proposition: it brings to mind the phrase about votes, turkeys and Christmas. So some more centralised direction will be needed if a Defence-wide campaign of learning is going to question what Nagl calls 'the conventional wisdom of an organization about how to perform its tasks and missions'.[71] Responding to CDS's challenge cannot just be left to routine self-regulation. As Hew Strachan told the Army Conference in 2010, 'war changes things; without the First World War there would have been no catalyst at that time and place for the Bolshevik revolution'.[72] In war, change is imposed; in trying to achieve CDS's goal for war-like organisations, peace is the problem.

Towards a More Robust Learning Approach: Enter the Double Loop

It is time to look more closely at the notion of a learning organisation. After sketching some theory, FDT experience will be used as a prism. Then, taking the evidence as a signal, the British military establishment should take Defence Reform to the next stage, or run the risk of being in limbo; under firm management but suffering military conceptual drift. Armed Forces cannot rely on the daily challenge from market competitors, nor shareholders demanding dividends. Without the catalyst of combat in all its forms to test relevance across the spectrum of capability on which

---

69   Forster 2012.
70   Garmone 2010.
71   Nagl 2002: 21. Nagl was a member of the Social Sciences Faculty at West Point (the book is based upon his in-service PhD). There is no British equivalent.
72   Author's notes.

the UK spends over £30 billion annually, it cannot be sure what it is getting for the outlay. In a world where 'incentives are the cornerstone of modern life', military institutions lack incentives for profound internal challenge.[73] And that omission is likely to become politically, financially and morally indefensible.[74] Without testing ideas about warfare, adopting and communicating clearly and convincingly new ones, and discarding those that fail the relevance assessment, change will be dominated by other factors, including tribalism, the drive for efficiency, habit, politico-industrial lobbying and myth.[75]

In a learning organisation that is using double-loop stimuli, adaptation is said to occur when an error is detected and corrected in ways that involve the modification of the organisation's underlying norms and objectives. In simple terms, with double-loop learning, *nothing* is taken for granted and *nothing* is off limits, especially the big ideas that define the organisation's approach to its core task – in our case, fighting and winning the nation's wars. Double-loop learning is impossible without strong central direction, especially in situations where much is at stake, be that a totemic equipment programme or force structure. Whilst the emphasis in single-loop approaches is on making existing techniques more efficient, double-loop learning involves questioning fundamental assumptions and routines; hunting for signs of external and internal innovation, failure or redundancy; deciding, then acting upon them. Research indicates that normal reasoning processes employed by individuals in organisations inhibit challenge and the passage of information in ways that make double-loop learning difficult. The standard response in conservative organisations is likely to be 'show me where we are failing' rather than 'show me how we avoid future failure and do what we do even better'. Structure, processes and governance must work in ways that require the whole organisation actively and systematically to hunt for what is succeeding and share it; to abandon what is not working, and test for alternatives.

There are plenty of definitions of and models for a learning organisation. All agree that the disruption and effort can provide additional organisational adaptability in conditions of uncertainty and fierce competition – exactly the post-Cold War disorder set out in the MOD's own assessment of future conflict. The building blocks depend upon, 'three broad essential factors for organizational learning and adaptability: a supportive learning environment, concrete learning processes and practices, and leadership behavior that provides reinforcement'.[76] To put it another way, it has got to be led from the top, but mobilising (as in MNF-I and the US Embassy in Baghdad in 2007) the knowledge of those closest to experience; be a compulsory central element of the decision-making process, with mandatory elements (such as experimentation) that are open to scrutiny; and have the resourced capacity to ensure that new ideas or concepts are not only developed, but are implemented (of which more below). This chapter does not advocate a particular model: it flags up that the MOD does not have one.

In contrast, soon after arriving at Langley, David Petraeus created a new post, Chief of Corporate Learning. In selecting John Pereira, a senior officer with considerable experience and previously the Agency's Director for Support, Petraeus stated, 'I have found through hard experience that, for any organization, there is no substitute for continually learning, adapting, and improving. The smarter we are as an Agency, the more effective we are at our mission'. In remarks that could equally apply to the UK Armed Forces, Pereira said, 'We have a highly skilled, well trained, and deeply mission focused workforce in CIA, we owe them an environment that better links learning

---

73   Levitt and Dubner 2009.

74   Critics argue that MOD has already lost the 'ability to think, decide and plan strategically'. Cornish and Dorman, 2011: 343.

75   Communication – or advocacy – is a key driver of adaptation. See Agile Warrior Report 2011.

76   Garvin et al. 2008.

with performance, that challenges some of our old assumptions'. The CIA will work with partners in the Intelligence Community, academic institutions and established industry leaders (a 'Whole Force' approach) on implementing a learning strategy.[77] Whether a corporate learning director delivers the intended double-loop energy and output (better intelligence, in the case of the CIA) may depend in large measure on whether he has a place on the top board, and authorities to reach into other divisions to hunt and challenge. It is one to watch, and perhaps write up – in a concept.

One of the benefits of a more business-like culture in the MOD is sharper focus on outputs rather than inputs. An influential contributor to this field of research and originator of the term 'learning organisation' is the academic Peter Senge, who rose to prominence with the publication in 1990 of *The Fifth Discipline*.[78] He argues that competitive advantage flows from continuous learning, both individual and collective. Some leadership academics believe that the key is 'unlocking the human potential which always exists within every organisation'.[79] This sounds much like 'making people the agile edge', as we wrote in FCOC; a fine, though ephemeral, objective unless it is backed by purposeful action and investment. In practical terms, if the military is to adopt a learning organisation approach, then learning new ways of doing things and sharing them effectively is but one important aspect. The key point involves Defence adopting a continuous but disciplined process of *un-learning*, or abandoning, old ways of doing things that are now irrelevant, and then shifting the balance of investment accordingly. New ideas should be captured in doctrine if they are single-loop adjustments. If they are novel, in a learning organisation they are best expressed in 'concepts' that help focus decision-making.

Rehabilitating Concepts

Many papers on security and defence major on 'uncertainty' and 'complexity'. As a pre-emptive apology, the MOD's Future Character of Conflict (FCOC) quotes Michael Howard's oft-repeated warning:

> No matter how clearly one thinks, it is impossible to anticipate precisely the character of future conflict. The key is not to be so far off the mark that it becomes impossible to adjust once that character is revealed.[80]

His prescient reminder is misused to deride conceptual work that could, if it had a proper forum, challenge from military first principles some of the institutional positions, structures and programmes that have become totemic. It is also misused to justify the increasingly dubious status quo notion of maintaining 'balanced UK forces' when the evidence is that we cannot afford full-spectrum 'balance', and indeed are already unbalanced.[81] That some major new projects exist without an endorsed or tested concept says much about the MOD's decision-making culture. The

---

77   CIA 2012.
78   Senge 1990.
79   Hooper and Potter 2001: 27.
80   FCOC 2009: 2.
81   Capability gaps have already opened, such as that caused by the loss of the Nimrod MRA4. See Quintana 2012.

third leg on the stool of Fighting Power – the conceptual component – is very thin, which suits some interest groups well.[82]

Concepts should help manage a new risk or seize opportunity; they can suggest the 'ways' that should link 'ends' and 'means' in strategy. They should be evidence-based narratives about the choices Defence could make, laying out an argument for adopting new ideas or (though they are not generally used in this way) abandoning others. Responding to President Obama's 'pivot', the US military has recently published a Joint Operational Access Concept (JOAC). America's senior military leader writes in the introduction, 'JOAC development was supported by an experimental campaign including a multi-scenario war game, multiple Service-sponsored events, and other concept development venues … [it is] my vision for how joint forces will operate'.[83]

The MOD claims that '[c]oncepts are subjected to rigorous analysis, systematic evaluation and practical testing and experimentation to transform creative thought into credible, effective ways of operating for well-defined capability requirements.'[84] Yet the UK *High Level Operating Concept* (which was thoroughly researched and had some useful signposts) has sunk without trace.[85] Of more concern, the recent strategic decision to grow the part-time Reserves on the assumption that they could perform a wider range of roles in modern conflict was neither expressed in a concept nor was it tested by systematic experimentation involving industry and other stakeholders. It involves a profound change to Britain's military capability, but the UK's 'Whole Force Concept' is following the strategic decision, not informing it. Unlike management plans with savings targets and a codified system of reporting and accountability, in the overall MOD system concepts are unconnected to formal decision-making and have no coercive power. They are the softest of soft power tools. Once written they can be selectively quoted if deemed helpful and if not, put into a drawer and ignored. In the words of my DCDC successor, 'concepts are all revolutions and no torque'.[86] The 'weak signal' though is what DCDC has to do to get a concept endorsed. Successive drafts are passed gradually up the hierarchy en route to the MOD. At every stage, 'unhelpful' words are removed or the blessing of consensus will not be bestowed and the paper stalls. At DCDC, I finally put one draft concept out of its misery: it had begun life more than a decade earlier as a justification for an Army air assault brigade. Other interest groups had decided to block it (in many ways rightly – it was a flawed proposition) and so it had wandered the corridors of various committees for years, being neither endorsed nor axed. In a learning organisation, ideas must have an efficient route to the top.

Unlike in the USA, the MOD has no net assessment process, so horizons are 'scanned' at DCDC, but scanning is a passive activity unless it is linked to action. In the US, proposals for new capabilities have to be mapped to an agreed concept, tested by experimentation and then are used to 'guide force development'.[87] Rightly, there are other factors in US investment and policy decisions, but in the UK there is a marked aversion to tools that are meant to help find solutions: this is hardly indicative of an open, enquiring culture. It does not help that they are created away from the main stream of the MOD Main Building, where they tend to be regarded, at best, as mildly interesting if theoretical and, at worst, as conjecture getting in the way of concepts' stronger sibling, 'policy'.

---

82   JDP 0-01 2008. Chapter 4 defines fighting power as having three components: conceptual, physical and moral.

83   US DOD 2012.

84   MOD DCDC Web Site under 'Futures: concepts', available at https://www.gov.uk/development-concepts-and-doctrine-centre#futures-concepts [accessed on 13 December 2012].

85   HLOC 2007.

86   AVM Colley RAF. Conversation with the author.

87   US DOD 2009: iii.

The solution is not, as the MOD has recently done, to divide concepts by imposing an artificial time horizon; one that keeps the DCDC's 'conceptual force development' work focused on a future that never gets any closer, thus allowing the London policy community to work on more bounded 'strategic force development'. Conceptual development should link more closely with policy-making, and also with training, education and robust debate. To tap the potential of new military ideas, and revalidate old ones, requires not just well-written, brutally direct concepts, but their testing in rigorous, imaginative, command-led experimentation.[88]

Responsiveness and Discipline

To understand why this may be easier said than done, one must look at how the MOD 'does' strategy. The Department favours an organisational approach known as 'deliberate strategy'. This offers continuity: it focuses on control, rationality and consistency. It results, though, in policy derived from a limited range of sources, such as adjustments to previous policy due to reducing budgets, that may have little or even no military logic. Such a culture values stability 'almost to the exclusion of learning'.[89] Strategy in the MOD emerges from a set of management protocols and, less visibly, in deals amongst power blocks. This is not unique to the UK or even the MOD; Graham Allison in his seminal book *Essence of Decision* identifies such deals as normal organisational behaviour.[90] A decision to adopt an organisation-wide approach to active learning is not an idealistic or utopian notion; it would not threaten a rational preference for deliberate strategy. Rather, it would bring another set of factors (that entail greater transparency and military objectivity) into achieving consensus: it would add greater flexibility and tilt the balance rather more in favour of emergent rather than deliberate strategy-making.

A risk in creating a learning organisation is the degree of turmoil it might entail. Challenging everything, all the time, everywhere and by everyone, is anarchy. The primary agent of change should therefore sit at the heart of the command system, with formal responsibility, commensurate authority and be required to take a responsible role in the overall direction and accountability of the organisation. From that position, he is well placed to construct a more informal network, but he must be empowered to reach out widely, crossing horizontally into the vertical stovepipe chains of command that typify traditional military hierarchies.[91] This was the case with Commander FDT, who was at the same time responsible for 'leading and driving change' and was also a fully accountable member of the Army Board.[92]

The creation of FDT was a command-led response to a realisation that the Service had lost adaptive tempo, which can be defined as 'progress relative to the fast-evolving military problem'.

---

88   Progress was made during the 2010 Defence Review. Two DCDC seminar discussions chaired by the Vice Chief of Defence Staff tried to draw deductions from FCOC. In the final plenary most participants were tight-lipped when he asked 'In light of this, what would you give up?' Author's notes.

89   Mintzberg et al. 1998: 189.

90   Allison 1999.

91   In FDT this was enabled by the cooperation of the Adjutant General (on personnel matters) and the Commander of the Field Army (who also generously opened his organisation) in a way that should not be taken for granted.

92   An early case was the pre-2011 pattern of attendance at pre-Afghan collective training. FDT observed that significant manning churn due to peacetime personnel factors constantly disrupted the cohesion that builds well-trained teams. Recommendations from a *Stabilising the Training Audience* report were agreed: by 2012, operational capability was markedly enhanced.

FDT then started to construct and use practical levers that Defence more widely lacks, and which would be recognisable features of a learning organisation. Richards created FDT when, as CGS, he felt a profound unease that the Army had lost its ability to think and act accordingly, and that joint organisations meant to perform that role were not.[93] The new Command did not require great investment in staff or a smart new building. It does not even have a sign or a logo. It took existing organisations and functions and joined them with an ambitious mission under a new three-star commander. As that Commander, I considered force development not as a set of bounded staff processes, resulting in papers agreed by all and threatening none; but as the green light to start a family argument and thus generate constructive tension. Under this model, force development addresses what goes on in the whole force, all the time, present and future. FDT was heavily influenced by TRADOC, but had one distinct and controversial advantage; FDT is responsible for all education and training, individual and collective, whereas TRADOC's remit excludes collective training. Considering the pivotal role training plays in peace and in war, as described here, this gives FDT a powerful set of levers, especially when applied in synchronisation; linking training with experimentation, concepts, doctrine and through a system of hunting insights from operations derived from the new technique, 'mission exploitation' (MsnX).[94] With the right levers in place, it was relatively simple to make internal changes to structures (such as merging individual and collective training under a single two-star general) and processes (such as creating a new Army Force Development Committee which endorsed emerging ideas, including the logic of refocusing to take greater account of urbanisation). With a talented Chief of Staff and small finance team, genuine efficiencies were identified, which allowed re-investment in high-impact projects. Demonstrable, rapid progress was part of an influence operation designed to 'show what good looks like', such as providing Sandhurst with the money as well as the direction and support to modernise training. FDT proposals, be they to study a strategic training partnership with industry, or to rebalance the armoured/armoured infantry/light force mix (research-based experimental work that shaped the Army 2020 outcome), were presented early and often 'un-polished' to the Army Command Group. The Army's senior leadership – as a collective – had visibility before all the sharp edges had been smoothed by 'staffing'. A learning organisation may benefit from a 'constructive contrarian' on the Board, and what in FDT we called '80 per cent good-enough' process.

Starfish, Spider, or Both?

Sparked by a stimulating discussion at TRADOC and an early study on options for brigade command and control (C2), ideas about what 'control' now means shaped FDT's evolution and the contribution it started to make to Army force modernisation. Societal and technological changes are radically expanding the ways in which C2 can now take place. This is to do with IT, but is not about IT: it is about generating and exploiting knowledge and using it to adapt at pace. Decentralised

---

93   Storr 2012. Like Richards he is critical of the decision to pass what is often called '*the Army's brain*' to a joint organisation that later became DCDC.

94   'Exploitation' is a critical learning tool. Post-operational debriefs were being done and 'lessons' collected, but MsnX was designed to be 'the mother of all patrol de-briefs'. It now involves c.1000 members of the brigade most recently returned from Afghanistan, being 'squeezed' for knowledge over three months. A major event is held at RMAS (part of rebranding that venerable institution as an intellectual hub). What makes MsnX double-loop learning is that it connects 'the user' with the trainers, doctrine writers, psychologists, academics, equipment designers from industry, etc. It 'turbo-boosts' learning and adaptation. The technique was used to 'exploit' insights from Operation Olympics, and by 2011 was being applied to training (TrgX).

organisations ('starfish' – such as internet music pirates or franchised terrorist networks; so called because they can rapidly adapt, even re-growing new 'limbs' when attacked) are more agile though less efficient than traditional, hierarchical 'spider' ones (where the commander sits at the centre of an organisational web that responds consistently, but relatively slowly, when faced with unfamiliar challenge).[95] Both types of C2 work best if commanders are helped to control their organisation by a small, carefully selected and highly skilled cohort of staff officers. Our study showed that the Army had given up this edge as an unintended consequence of adopting a comprehensive (and largely joint) command and staff training system two decades earlier. FDT experimented with running the Command (some 16,000 strong) as a 'spifish'; a trial in creating a hybrid blend of centralised and decentralised approaches. For those seeking high tempo and willing to risk some loss of control, the early evidence is that this approach can add creativity as well as pace. An 'Enterprise Approach' taps latent talent in unexpected areas, by requiring disparate parts of the whole to work together in 'communities of action': be that to test a concept (such as 'what does the Whole Force Concept mean for the Army?'), or maybe hone new doctrine blended from insights from training and operations, but seen through the prism, perhaps, of an expert logistician.

Under the Enterprise Approach, the different parts of FDT were required to 'get out of lane', contributing their experience, energy and creativity to the task of designing a learning organisation, in order to help make the Army one. Some of the most productive parts of the Enterprise were in areas not normally regarded as 'leading edge'. The logistics schools were especially dynamic: their best practice in innovative teaching and in pioneering a 'new basic' of military contracting spread quickly. One of the hallmarks of a learning organisation is exploiting knowledge by moving it to where it is needed. The disadvantages of the spifish approach, as I applied it, included some genuine confusion and resistance (and a silly name). People used to following set patterns, some of whom guarded their part of the organisation closely, did not like the intrusion and disruption. It also resulted in some random activity. I am certainly not encouraging Defence to adopt the FDT model, merely to note the interesting work being done on non-traditional organisational methods that could serve well a wider learning campaign. The US Government is looking hard at such ideas.[96] The MOD should at the very least be exploring them; ideally launching its own project as a sequel to the Levene study, in what could be the first test for a new and mainstream concept.

A Learning Organisation in Action: Form and Function

If the argument does not resonate solely through intellectual force, it should do so on hard resource and accountability grounds.[97] How can Ministers know that they are getting value for money if the MOD has no system to ensure its military ideas are fit for purpose? It appointed a qualified accountant as Finance Director because it now takes balancing the books seriously. It has a three-star pilot running the Military Aviation Authority because it now takes air safety seriously. But who is to be made responsible (and empowered) to ensure Defence learns, and how will such a construct combine joint efforts and priorities with those of the recently re-empowered

---

95   Brafman and Beckstrom 2008. Brafman took part in US Army experimentation in 2010 at the invitation of General Dempsey.

96   Fuerth 2012. Thanks to Frank Hoffman, Honorary Fellow, Exeter SSI.

97   According to Lawton and Silim 2012, Defence faces cuts in real terms in 2015–2017 of a minimum of 3.8 per cent or £1.7 billion if cuts were spread evenly across Departments without protecting Health, International Development, etc.

single Services?[98] If this chapter makes a reasonable functional case for a more robust, open and intellectually challenging approach to testing, sharing and then turning ideas (about warfare, not just organisation, structure, process and financial management) into action, where should it seek (or be told to look) for possible models?

Two broad forms present themselves; either centralised control (the spider re-asserted) or a looser but still disciplined confederation (the starfish experiment). Both will clearly feature the new Joint Forces Command (JFC) which could be the enabler or, under the centralised model, catalyst to change behaviours, and with them military capabilities. Such a role is not fully covered by its present charter; by implication, testing for relevance and drawing the necessary conclusions are left to the Services and to the other major parts of the Defence establishment. The Levene Report was focused, as the title suggests, at 'structure and management'; it had little to say about how capabilities are to be assessed and tested beyond a positive role for JFC in joint warfare development and joint high-level training. Single Services are left to do their own environmental force development. This is a striking exception, given the growing culture of accountability in every other respect, from proving diversity of workforce to publishing expenditure on corporate hospitality. As argued, history and recent Army experience both indicate that it cannot just be left to the custodian of the capability to guarantee that it – or its replacement – is fit for future purpose. It will need a shift in top-level direction, some new arrangements for supervision, setting priorities and accountability, and changes to the way the officer corps allocates its time and effort.

One course of action would be to go further than Levene and explicitly make Commander JFC the Inspector of all force development. This would be unpopular with the single Services and other major players in Defence, for effective force development would have to encompass procurement and personnel, for example, as well as doing the work of the Services. An alternative would be to appoint him in a strong coordinating role, mandating the use of standard tools in each of the individual parts of Defence. Under this model, JFC would set additional standards, such as timetabling Service experimentation or doctrine reviews, and mandating the inclusion of the other parts of the joint community and outside experts. This is what FDT did, inviting all partners to play a role in Army force development, offering membership to the Royal Navy, RAF and Joint communities on the key internal Army committees. Under this looser model, JFC would convene and run an annual research programme that fed directly into major UK Defence war game experiments. These would be productive if 'players' included serving and retired senior officers, officials and Ministers, as was done during the Cold War.[99] Some of these mechanisms already exist in disparate form, such as the new FDT Agile Warrior research and experimentation programme. The JFC would ensure that each Service (and other parts of Defence, such as the intelligence staffs) focused on a set of threats and opportunities. A four-star JFC should be better able to ensure that the results (including new concepts) were directly geared to the higher management of Defence. The creation of the Armed Forces Committee allows the single Services to hold a constructive and evidence-based 'family argument' in private. There are numerous options; the point is that without going beyond Levene and constructing new authorities, structures and processes that draw upon a wider range of sources to generate a more rigorous range of options, the potential of the whole will not be maximised and progress left more to chance.

---

98 Levene has decentralised elements of capability development to the single Services.

99 This would not only draw upon senior judgement directly, it would address a UK deficit in personal preparation for crisis and consequence management. This was recommended by the US 9/11 Commission Report 2004.

US experience indicates that there are four conditions needed for successful military transformation, all of which imply a degree of organisational stability:[100] first, leaders who are actively engaged; second, a holistic approach to reform, with direct impact far beyond doctrine, encompassing personnel, equipment and training; third, the creation (or empowerment) of a specified organisational entity with the broad authority to craft, evaluate and execute reform (in the US Army this is TRADOC; in the British Army FDT although, as should be clear by now, there are still gaps above and to the flanks of FDT); and, fourth, an acknowledgement that adaptation is continuous (not a spasm every five years during Defence Reviews). FDT experience suggests that, of these four conditions, the most important is the direct engagement of senior leadership, thus demonstrating a 'ruthless' focus.

There are numerous ways in which we could improve force development and ensure continuing relevance for the UK's Armed Forces post-2014. I have selected four levers which together have the potential for the greatest positive impact to reap practical benefits: research, education, training and experimentation. This choice is based on the FDT agenda and experience which was wide-ranging though relatively immature. Individually, they have the potential to help guard against irrelevance, but, if used collectively as part of a modern force development campaign, their transformative power could be unlocked by a substantial but entirely feasible change in culture and MOD process.

Lever 1: Research

As a quasi-academic, I naturally start with the contribution research could make, if the MOD had not decimated its own research capacity. By research, I mean the capability and intent to investigate, establish new facts and reach new conclusions. The Defence Science and Technology Laboratory (DSTL) does research for the MOD, but at a distance from the mainstream military. With the demise of the Soviet Studies Branch at Sandhurst, successive cuts to the MOD's DCDC think tank and disbandment of the Advanced Research and Analysis Group in the Defence Academy, the UK now has no equivalent of the applied research organisations that are housed at US military intellectual hubs, such as the National Defense University or the War Colleges. There is nowhere producing equivalent applied research on a systematic, timely and responsive basis to meet the needs of an intelligent, enquiring military learning organisation.[101] Campaigns outside UK's immediate field of vision are not systematically analysed and turned into briefing papers for busy leaders, much less authoritative concepts.

A learning organisation is, in academic terms, 'research active', and that research is focused to suit the information needs of the end user, as intelligence collection informs the commander, whose obligation in turn is to set the research agenda by stating his personal critical information requirements.[102] The British Defence establishment has a poor record in this regard. As Williamson Murray reminds us,

> only the Germans studied the First World War ... with a degree of honesty that allowed them to carry forward those lessons into the next conflict. And because through that study they were able to understand more clearly the possibilities offered by future war, they won a series of devastating

---

100   Nielsen 2010.

101   See Biddle and Friedman 2008.

102   It is encouraging to see the Defence Academy co-sponsoring conferences. This is making good use of scarce resource, but is not a substitute for a funded, structured military research programme.

victories in the first years of World War II. In contrast, the British created the Kirke Committee only in 1932 ...[103]

To find evidence of the lessons of modern conflict we in the UK have requested copies of American publications, such as their work on the Second Lebanon War.[104] It is from American sources that evidence of rapid adaptation was gleaned, such as the fact that Hezbollah had defined novel Principles of War: this was then set out both in new UK doctrine and in the FCOC policy advice paper that advised, 'Adversaries, both state and non-state, are adapting fast to counter the west's preferred way of operating' or, as in the MOD's first doctrine on stabilisation, 'History shows that asymmetry is not new, but some of its modern manifestations are new to us.'[105] My introduction went on to argue, drawing primarily upon US evidence, that the pace of adaptation has 'made our assumptions, such as Rapid Decisive Effect, look dated if not obsolete'. Discovering the scale of Hezbollah's efforts to harden and conceal underground facilities, FDT had some solid evidence of the need to rethink the requirement for larger British infantry sections, modern training facilities, more robust logistics allocations and argue for more and better equipped assault engineers, to list a few practical deductions flowing from well-presented and timely research.

Recreating military research capacity in each Service is essential.[106] For the Army, retention of the highly successful Land Intelligence Fusion Centre (Afghanistan) (created on a temporary basis under Operation Entirety) would provide a ready-made tool for applied land warfare research. It could be based at Sandhurst, enhancing the existing civilian academic faculty, which presently has no formal research remit.[107] In generating a new applied intellectual capability (and sending a clear signal of intent for tiny investment) the Army could appoint some mid-career officers (bright mainstream majors or lieutenant colonels) to both teach as military professors and study for their PhD before going on to key command and staff posts; a straight copy of the proven West Point system that has produced a steady stream of soldier scholars who rise to lead the US Army.[108] For Defence, similar effect could be achieved by re-investment in DCDC. This would mean finding new resource, not taking it from force development staffs in the Services, which has been the pattern. The MOD's New Employment Model should bring well-qualified reservists into such roles; and through structured academic partnerships, the MOD could access and focus Research Council funds.

Research results in publication, so this will be a test of whether the MOD is capable of becoming a learning organisation. When universities focus ever more sharply on 'end user impact', the military sends talented officers to do higher degrees with scant thought given to exploiting their research. There is little or no culture of publication in the UK military, hence no equivalent of the vibrant debate that can be found online in the *Small Wars Journal* or, more strikingly, in the official US military press. In a candid exchange between John Nagl and (serving Army colonel) Gian Gentile carried in the National Defense University's Journal, Gentile criticises the Army leadership for 'dogma', allegedly driving through 'a set of flawed concepts upon which to re-model

---

103 Murray 2006: 79.

104 See Matthews 2008.

105 JDP 3-40 2009: xiii.

106 Each 'node' would be networked into a research community, including DSTL as a 'fusion hub' – DSTL is now engaging civilian partners by outsourcing more MOD research.

107 Several RMAS academics engaged enthusiastically with force development, such as providing the historical context for the first FDT senior officer staff ride Exercise Norman Warrior 2012.

108 See Cloud and Jaffe 2009.

the Army based upon short-term expediencies rather than long-term strategic goals'.[109] It would be unthinkable for such an article to make it through the MOD censor. Indeed, even this book has had chapters by serving officers withdrawn on orders of the MOD, including a chapter by the Vice Chief of Defence Staff on the difficulties of making strategy in the twenty-first century. Liberalising the MOD's rules on material that is challenging, critical, even perhaps embarrassing – but which does not risk National security – is overdue. Changes to structure and process will not deliver a learning organisation without a clear sign of confidence from the very top; the confidence to relax control of 'the message', which in the contemporary media environment drives such debate as there is into the realms of online speculation. FDT began to use the Army Knowledge Exchange web site as a spifish platform; a place where communities of action would develop and debate ideas, post draft doctrine for comment, or where, as a remote commander, I could engage with and occasionally respond directly to those who were willing to join the Enterprise. Defence has no such platform.

Levers 2 and 3: Education and Training

These next two powerful 'twin levers' are essential tools that can be better used. In Defence there is a flawed distinction made between professional education and training, one that elevates the general above the particular in the former case, and undervalues the importance and learning potential of the latter. It has become fashionable to say 'We should educate for uncertainty and train for certainty.'[110] Training and education are both about learning; 'Learning … is knowledge got by study.' The Oxford English Dictionary goes on to say, 'Training is a discipline and instruction directed to the development of powers … systematic instruction and exercise in some art, profession or occupation, with a view to proficiency in it.'[111] In a profession of arms, the core requirement is a thorough grounding in, and integration of, that body of knowledge; for example, not only discuss the laws of war, but integrate their practical application during the planning and conduct of a divisional attack with full air support, in an urban area. Unfortunately, over the past two decades the content of all Defence Academy command and staff courses, from major to brigadier, has converged on much the same over-theoretical ground; they focus on higher-level theory such as 'smart power' or the science of campaign planning (especially mastery of the ever more complicated decision-making tool, the 'estimate process'), and the higher management of Defence.

This drift away from and denigration of the practical though still intellectually challenging aspects of the profession have been accelerated by two factors: the joint nature of most command and staff training, and the introduction of an MA as an integral part of the year at Advanced Command and Staff Course (ACSC), which naturally shapes the syllabus. Joint warfare competence and relevance must be built upon foundations of environmental knowledge (not mere drills instilled in repetitive exercises). Does it make sense to wait until the age of 42 to acquire a degree which, by design, is meant to hone powers of analysis, independent thought and research? What is most striking is what has fallen out of the syllabus. By 2012, during the entire ACSC year, not one exercise required students to take their plan and 'fight it'. What was it that Moltke said about 'No plan survives contact …'? Modern technology allows students to both plan collaboratively and then test the plan in realistic simulated execution. Yet until 2011, when FDT both directed their use and funded their purchase, none of the Army's tactics courses for junior officers – nor the

---

109   Nagl 2009 and Gentile 2009b.
110   Former-Director UK Defence Academy 2010. Briefing attended by the author.
111   Quoted in the MOD's strategic leadership handbook.

Intermediate Course, ICSC(L) – had modern Command and Control tools; the joint Advanced Course still apparently sees no need for them.

Much of the problem at Shrivenham lies with the anomaly of Advanced Course instructors who are the same age as their students and, because it is joint, frequently have less relevant experience. It is difficult to teach without personal experience, so the syllabus of the Advanced Course has retreated into a theoretical shell, which can be taught by any intelligent instructor, regardless of experience. This largely explains the Course's emphasis on the formal estimate decision-making process, which can be taught and against which students can be marked and assessed using set criteria, rather than attempting to develop more relevant and intuitive decision-making skills in future senior commanders.[112]

Defenders of the status quo point to high student satisfaction ratings. An American Army student in 2009 said of ACSC, 'what's not to like?'; a fascinating year acquiring (another) MA and learning about a wide range of interesting topics, but he concluded 'I just don't think I've been at a Staff College.'[113] Politicians (and subordinates) look to the officer corps for broad knowledge and wisdom, but primarily for expert military advice and leadership. This is not to criticise the Defence Academy, which delivers well what the Service 'customers' say they require. FDT rapidly concluded that whilst the other Services were content with a generic, liberal education approach, the particular needs of experts in land warfare, which used to be addressed at the Army Staff College at Camberley (closed in 1997), were no longer being met.[114] The notable thing is that the Army had not noticed. Even after some FDT interventions, a British major now has only 10 days to learn about divisional operations; a French Army officer has 60.[115] The Services have much in common, but their professional development needs are different in important ways: a self-critical learning organisation might have spotted that rather earlier.

Meanwhile, in a strange throwback to 1960s social engineering, the British Army is the only one amongst its peers to adhere to a comprehensive system of military education. As an example, the ICSC(L) puts all majors into mixed-ability syndicates, and teaches them the same material, at the same pace, to the same standard. Said by defenders to be fairer, every major, be they from the SAS or the Dental Corps, is meant to be taught 'the basics'. The disadvantages were described by one frustrated member of the faculty who explained, 'General, it is like going for a run every day with the fattest bloke in the Company.'[116] The most important FDT initiative to date (endorsed by Army leaders in a new piece of 'process' – the Army Development Forum), is a full review of officer careers and education. Early changes under the 'ROCC2' project are already having a marked effect: an extended junior officers' tactics course and a new Captains' Warfare Course (CWC) will together partly fill the void left by abandoning the Army Junior Division.[117] The most significant strategic effect, though, is yet to come and will be achieved if the Army re-introduces a selective, unashamedly elite approach, by recreating a modern General Staff of the most talented majors.[118]

---

112   Storr 2002.

113   Reported to author by the then Editor of the British Army Review, Colonel (retd) John Wilson.

114   Based upon research for the ROCC2 project including extensive MsnX and TrgX.

115   FDT analysis for the ROCC2 Study.

116   Conversation with infantry member of the Directing Staff, at the (recently introduced under FDT direction) Normandy staff ride on brigade and divisional operations, 2011.

117   An admiral and an air marshal suggested to me that the Army should look at the Navy's Principal Warfare Officer course: the CWC is the result.

118   A US Army programme is a useful signpost, but early ROCC2 analysis indicated the need for a broader syllabus with perhaps a modular approach, matched to career fields as well as generic warfighting proficiency.

The aim would not be to divorce command and staff, nor turn back the clock to a Camberley golden era. This network of highly trained (and well educated – they should be required to acquire a relevant Master's degree by their early 30s) land environment experts would raise the quality and tempo of decision-making, and as a network help drive progress across the Army and add value to a joint community which is being short-changed.

Turning now specifically to training, the Army does a great deal of training and, historically, it has done rather a lot of it poorly. Not everyone is an expert trainer, in the same way that not every holiday video looks as if it was shot by Steven Spielberg. Designing and delivering imaginative, relevant training calls for experience, well-managed resources, and the creative skills of a film director; not all officers rotated through training appointments have these skills, although in all other respects they may be excellent commanders. A consequence of the Afghanistan campaign has been a superb pre-deployment training system. Rather than revert to old habits at the end of the campaign, even better training could be delivered more cheaply by a blend of civilian and military experts under a strategic training partnership.[119]

The Army tends to confuse 'ownership' of training with delivery. The chain of command must retain ownership of the output and set the purpose of training, not run its every detail. There are, however, key choices to be made about where, how and in what to train after Afghanistan. Training, especially that done in areas of vital national interest such as the Gulf, does not just prepare the force. It can – if it is demonstrably relevant and thus credible – send a powerful deterrent signal.

Whatever form the solution takes, the Army can build upon the work to better exploit expensive training by treating it not as National Service-era drill, but as 'collective learning'. The concept of Training Exploitation was an extension of Mission Exploitation; it involves widespread active debriefing, enabled by trained staff using cheap technology such as fixed and helmet-mounted cameras. This is fused with other data to build a picture (or 'narrative') of what happened and why. This can then be linked to online fieldcraft pamphlets, for example, bringing good and bad examples from real exercises into the classroom. By making training more adversarial (investing in an 'enemy' that is strong and cunning enough to occasionally win) and fusing modern simulation, data capture and structured After Action Review, the experience of an individual learning how to cook in the field, or a unit on a multi-million pound exercise in Kenya, can be made available in near real time, via the Army Knowledge Exchange website, to the whole Army, indeed, the joint community. The potential is limited mainly by old habits. For example, students in a Staff College syndicate room in England could receive orders issued by a brigade commander in Canada, make their own plan, issue their own orders, and have it fought to a conclusion by the exercising battlegroup on the other side of the Atlantic. Such techniques are being trialled in FDT and also codified in the first update to training doctrine since 1996 – but training is such a dynamic and exciting field that the doctrine had better be in 'wiki' format or it will rapidly fail its own relevance test.

Lever 4: Experimentation

When bright, experienced people are brought together, put under pressure and required to solve, not describe, difficult problems, the result can be new military knowledge. History shows a poor British Army record in this regard. It created an Experimental Brigade in 1927 which made good progress

---

119   Over £100 million per annum is spent on pre-Afghan live firing, without measuring fire effect (hits on target).

in the development of mechanised warfare, and was certainly 'exploited' by German observers. But faced with imperial over-stretch and in an age of austerity, the Experimental Mechanical Force was wound up (or down) at the end of the 1928 exercise season. Experimentation proceeded sporadically from then. It had not entered the Army's institutional DNA and until 2011 there was no meaningful experimentation programme.[120]

TRADOC of late has conducted an explicit 'campaign of learning' in which systematic, well-resourced experimentation culminates each year in a seminar war game, Exercise Unified Quest. US Army senior leaders and representatives from the other Services put aside time to test ideas and give command direction. Fortunately (for it has been a rich source) much of it and its results are open to close allies. Such confidence is another sign of a learning organisation. Similarly, when the US Joint community under General Mattis crafted a new Capstone Concept, they held a series of scenario-based war games to test and hone the main ideas. Participating in a Gulf scenario played over four days by senior officers, retired diplomats and members of Congress, it became clear that there were no neat solutions. Any Service bombast was stripped away by rigorous debate and demanding *kriegspiel*, during which the actions of an uncooperative Red Team put the Concept and us on our mettle. A dramatic example of the power of experimentation was the 2002 American Millennium Challenge exercise. Also set in the Gulf, a highly experienced retired general (and natural constructive contrarian) played the Red commander. The US Blue force was trialling a quasi-scientific concept called Effects-Based Operations.[121] In the space of one hour, Red's surprise tactics not only evaded the technological advantages on which American concepts were being based, they notionally sank 16 of Blue Force's ships. In a real war, 20,000 American service personnel would have been killed or wounded.[122] Until recently, there has been no equivalent forum in the British Army, and there is still nothing like it in UK Defence.

The nearest MOD equivalent is known as 'Joint Campaign Development Force Estimation', a process that follows established MOD policy to generate lists of units within a policy-capped manpower ceiling. Participants are mid-ranking officers; bounded by policy, the formulaic process becomes ever more self-reinforcing, for Service representatives are under remit to play a zero sum game. 'Success' is a list of forces where the Navy, Army and Air Force each secure a contribution supporting their MOD structural case. There is no adversary, and as the point is just to generate a list of forces, there is no battle. No one ever wins or loses. When these are the rules of the game, big organisations do what they need to do to survive. In contrast, this otherwise critical picture of American senior engagement in experimentation illustrates a learning organisation at work:

> When its high command plans for its future "needs", thanks to Chairman of the Joint Chiefs of Staff General Martin Dempsey, they repair (don't say "retreat") to a military base south of the capital where they argue out their future and war-game various possible crises while striding across a map of the world larger than a basketball court.[123]

In 2011 the Army Board endorsed an annual Army programme of research and experimentation under the title Agile Warrior. The first research cycle was to 'make sense of the implications of

---

120   Harris 2006: 198–201.
121   A version of the same 'science of war' planning fetish contributed to the Israeli defeat in 2006.
122   Gladwell 2005: 99–111. Thanks to Tim Robinson, ex-Commander 1 Mechanised Brigade, for drawing this book to my attention.
123   Engelhardt 2012.

hybrid warfare' by picking up the challenge laid down in FCOC two years earlier.[124] The approach, as with everything in those early years, was to move at speed, and risk a degree of incoherence. We began to engage with willing partners in universities and think tanks,[125] but experimentation works best if it engages the 'user', as well as critical friends in other Services and Government agencies (if future conflict will demand inter-agency solutions, then a further deduction is that an Army designed in isolation will not be fit for purpose).

The most ambitious early experiment was Exercise Urban Warrior in which both the Army's four-star Commander-in-Chief and the now top civil servant in the MOD played. Originally planned for Cyprus to introduce expeditionary realism, it was held for budget and policy reasons in Southampton. Combining the considerable talents and resources of two of the brightest brigadiers in the Army, the experiment pitted 1st (Mechanised) Brigade against a capable hybrid adversary in and around the City. Tactical vignettes were played out and the data recorded for later analysis. Atop high-rise apartment blocks, on sports grounds, in shopping streets and multi-storey car parks, a modern campaign was fought, without a shot being fired in anger. Outside West Quay shopping centre, MOD officials, Allied guests and local police officers debated whether to use kinetic strikes or social media to influence an insurgent group. NCOs from the Royal Tank Regiment looked at fields of fire down quiet suburban streets and grappled with problems of restricted gun elevation. Fusilier section commanders, recently returned from Helmand, and scientists from DSTL, calculated more realistic casualty, ammunition and water consumption rates when working out how to clear flats dominating a vital city junction. The insights from this and similar early FDT experiments proved timely in an MOD that now demands evidence not assertion, for within weeks the Army was told to redesign itself. General Carter and his Army 2020 Team had both some relevant military insights and a ready-made network of activists on which to draw.

Conclusion: We Can't Just Manage Our Way Out of This

Simply relying upon 'more of the same' but with better management will not guard against the gradual irrelevance that threatens UK's armed forces, even without continuing budgetary pressure.[126] Defence must be alert to the risk of reverting to comfortable old ways as unpopular counter-insurgency campaigns come to a close. Not all future operations will involve stabilisation. But finding a conveniently stupid near-peer enemy is unlikely, so Defence must recognise that capabilities such as target audience analysis and human intelligence collection – painfully built over recent years and with broad relevance in modern conflict – must not be abandoned in a post-Afghan mood swing back to 'proper' warfare.

Defence does not have to invent more FDTs. It does need to find additional ways to deal with institutional conservatism and rebuild lost credibility. New elements such as creating the potential for managed, deliberately disruptive change without falling victim to turmoil, and hunting for signs of irrelevance, concurrently from bottom up and top down, will help. Adopting and applying the concept of a learning organisation, not in place of good management, but to 'gear' it, would send a clear sign to concerned critics, that the Service and Civil Service establishment is addressing perceived under-performance, especially if presented as the next logical step in the Levene reform

---

124   'Hybrid warfare' is a divisive term but one used by FDT to challenge orthodoxy. See Hoffman 2007b.

125   For early examples, see Cornish and Grouille 2011, and Phillips 2011.

126   Blitz 2012: 'there are fears inside the MOD that the 2010 Strategic Defence and Security Review may need to be revised yet again.'

process. Greater delegation to Service Front Line Commands, when properly combined with a Joint Forces Command, offer military leaders new opportunities. Given that this is about relevant fighting power, these are opportunities the military should seize, not resist.

Integrating and networking the parts of the existing system, such as linking training with modest investment in research and more timely education, and in new tools such as a formal programme of experimentation, will, if placed under a governance system that includes the Joint Forces Commander, enhance and build better capability. No amount of learning can prevent surprise in warfare, but military leaders would then be more actively managing the risk of shock; responding to Howard's prompt about 'not being too far wrong'. Whether FDT is seen as a model to emulate or avoid, a sizable body of research and practice in industry over the past two decades,

> ... has revealed three broad factors that are essential for organizational learning and adaptability: a supportive learning environment, concrete learning processes and practices, and leadership behavior that provides reinforcement.[127]

If business school theory alone does not resonate, then the words of an historian of military adaptation (and failure) over the ages might: 'History indicates that the wisest course is to feel one's way along with careful study, radical experimentation, and freewheeling wargames.'[128] Leaders will be key to unlocking this wisdom, and the Joint Expeditionary Force, whilst still at a formative stage, could be an important vehicle for adaptation. Such changes as are sketched above will be hard, coming after so much turbulence. But as Haddon-Cave observed: 'Many of these lessons and truths may be unwelcome, uncomfortable and painful; but they are all the more important, and valuable, for being so. It is better that the hard lessons are learned now'.[129] The critical factor will be the confidence and vision of those at the top;

> A learning organisation rejects "if it ain't broke don't fix it". A learning organisation can learn at least as much from failure as success. Learning organisations fight the natural tendency to bury failure and forget about it as soon as possible.[130]

In this vein, Richards's successor as CGS, General Sir Peter Wall, reflected upon the first two years of FDT, remarking that it had 'made the Army Board comfortable with discomfort'.[131] That sounds like the test of a learning organisation. Who will now pick up the relevance challenge and create a post-Afghan 'stampede' of British military adaptation?

---

127   Garvin et al. 2008.
128   Boot 2006: 467.
129   Haddon-Cave 2009: 580.
130   Lampel 1998: 214.
131   Letter to author, January 2012.

Chapter 26

British Generals in Blair's Wars: Conclusion

Hew Strachan

If there is a single Western power, other than Britain, to which the contributors to this book refer, it is the United States of America. At one level that is totally unsurprising; at another it is. A book such as this, if published a century ago, in the years immediately preceding the First World War, would not have mentioned the United States. Instead it would have referred to two other powerful foreign influences on the British Army.

The first would have been that of Germany, cast as the global model for all armies after its stunning successes in the wars of unification in 1866 and 1870. Even as recently as the 1980s, the British Army on the Rhine, standing alongside the Bundeswehr ready to meet a Soviet attack along the inner German border, was inspired, as John Kiszely's chapter recalls, by German thinking on the operational level of war. Today that is a distant memory. The Germans are reluctant to define their mission in Afghanistan as anything more than peacekeeping, and their official refusal to use the word 'war' has become a metaphor for a wider reluctance to embrace a warrior ethos.[1]

The other influence on the British Army before 1914 was French. To be sure, the glory of Napoleon had been sullied by the defeat of 1870–71, but France was Britain's principal continental ally, and possessed a field army that on mobilisation would be more than ten times bigger than Britain's. Moreover, France was at least as great an intellectual influence as Germany. That may have been because more British officers could read French than German, but it also reflected the French discovery of doctrine as a tool for reform and regeneration after their defeat in the Franco-Prussian war. Forward-thinking British officers a hundred years ago urged their own newly formed general staff to use doctrine as a means to get an army which practised colonial warfare to raise its sights to what the big beasts might do in Europe.[2] British soldiers today may hold their French peers in higher esteem than they do the Germans, but the boot is still on the other foot. When France announced the end of conscription in 1996, it turned to Britain for a model of how a voluntarily enlisted professional army might behave. Even that noted critic of much that is British, President Jacques Chirac, had suggested that the French Army, which struggled to perform effectively in the first Gulf War in 1990–91, should emulate those who had been its enemies at Blenheim and Waterloo.[3]

So, when Tony Blair became Prime Minister in 1997, the British Army was one of the assets in the national armoury, and a key component in what the outgoing Conservative Foreign Secretary, Douglas Hurd, had described as Britain's capacity to punch above its weight. The question marks over the Army's performance in the first half of the twentieth century, beginning in January 1900 at Spion Kop in the second Boer War and extending forward to the summer of 1940 and the fall of France in the Second World War, had been replaced by a narrative of success, which ran in a seemingly continuous flow from El Alamein in 1942 to the first Gulf War in 1991, via Normandy,

---

1   Die Zeit editorial 2011.
2   Pope-Hennessy 1912.
3   Simpson 1999.

Malaya and the Falklands. There had been bumpy patches in many of the campaigns of colonial withdrawal, not least in the last, Aden, and the Northern Ireland conflict had started on the wrong foot, but these were glossed as the exceptions that proved the rule.

Much of this self-regard, although burnished by a selective reading of history, did rest on secure foundations. In particular, the legacy of Field Marshal Sir Nigel Bagnall, the Chief of the General Staff in 1985–88, had left the Army in probably better conceptual shape than it had ever been. When commanding in Germany, Bagnall had developed his thinking on the operational level of war and, when in Whitehall, he had instituted the Higher Command and Staff Course (HCSC) at the Staff College in Camberley. Relying on the principles of syndicate study, the HCSC had given those mid-ranking officers who had been identified as the Army's future stars an education in the best sense: it had got them to think about their profession. Most of the contributors to this volume, including John Kiszely, are its products. Paul Newton, in this book, questions whether Bagnall's concepts would have worked against a numerically superior enemy, fighting in semi-urbanised northern Germany, but they were never tested in the environment for which they were principally designed. When Tony Blair became Prime Minister in 1997, the pay-off for Bagnall's stress on the operational level was still the speedy Coalition victory over Iraq in 1991. Fears of a bloody and protracted war had proved groundless, and those at the heart of the success had either, like Rupert Smith, taught on the first HCSC or, like Patrick Cordingley, been a student. The outcome suggested that Bagnall's precepts were of enduring validity, particularly in their stress on manoeuvre (understood literally as mobility) and its outgrowth, 'manoeuvrism', which was more abstract and pointed to an ability to think faster and more flexibly than the enemy, and to operate at greater tempo as a result. An army possessed of these qualities, or so the argument ran, could use quality to offset lack of numbers.[4]

What was less clear to the incoming Labour Government was the strategic context within which this operational excellence would be used. The continentalism of the 1980s had favoured the Army (and a tank-heavy one at that), supported by the Royal Air Force. The defence review conducted by the Conservatives at the end of the Cold War, 'Options for Change', had been reluctant in 1991 to dismiss entirely the threat from Russia, and so did not administer too many shocks to the Army's assumptions. Continentalism lingered, and still does so in so far as much of the British Army remains quartered in Germany; full withdrawal is not due to be completed until 2020, and that is in turn dependent on the completion of sufficient updated accommodation against a background of sustained fiscal austerity. But by 1994 the Secretary of State for Defence, Malcolm Rifkind, was readier to acknowledge that Britain's membership of the United Nations Security Council might require it to have a more global reach than had found favour with the continentalists of a decade previously – Michael Carver, the Chief of the Defence Staff between 1973 and 1976, or John Nott, the defence minister between 1981 and 1983. So, to that extent, the Strategic Defence Review conducted by Tony Blair's Government in 1997–98 was pushing at an open door when it declared that its framework was to be driven not by the Treasury but by foreign policy objectives (although not until 2003 did the Foreign Office publish a white paper on British foreign policy, the first for over 20 years), and that its goal was to deliver an expeditionary capability. With threats within Europe confined to the Balkans, the geopolitical framework for British defence widened once again.

The expeditionary assumptions of the Strategic Defence Review swung the initiative more the Navy's way. Two aircraft carriers were to be ordered. The effect was to make inter-operability and 'jointery' the dominant themes of the review. The Army, having adapted to continentalism, and

---

4   Strachan 2010.

having realised the comparative advantage over the other two Services which it conferred, proved slow to shift. Army equipment, if it was to be inserted quickly, needed to be light to be air portable, but it would also be dependent on maritime support for sustainability. Intellectually, the HCSC, with its focus on the operational level, presumed a European strategic context, and one shaped by major conventional land warfare. In 1997 staff education, including HCSC, became joint, and a joint doctrine and concepts centre followed suit in 1999. But all senior appointments remained dependent on single-Service appointment boards and, as Army staff education was seemingly diluted by joint requirements, Army officers became increasingly wont to look back nostalgically to Camberley, rather than forward.

Success in the field continued to be the enemy of educated self-examination. The operation described in this book and conducted by the future Chief of the Defence Staff, David Richards, in Sierra Leone in 2000, and supported by HMS Illustrious, under the command of the future First Sea Lord, Mark Stanhope, became a model of the effectiveness of the new dispensation. Its strengths, that it was a British-led operation in what had been a British colony, could also have been its weaknesses, especially as it was conducted alongside United Nations forces who were reluctant to engage the rebels. But performance in the field, at the operational level, quashed the doubters at the strategic level. From the United States came admiration and congratulations: 'You guys have got a rapid reaction with a reach which nobody else has.'[5]

Britain's defence relationship with the United States in the 1990s had been a mixture of operational awe and strategic uncertainty. As the United States applied the technologies of precision guidance, using computers for intelligence collection and the global positioning system for targeting, its allies worried about keeping pace for fear of losing inter-operability. They reasoned that, although they might struggle in budgetary terms, they could at least track the Americans' conceptual development. And so 'the revolution in military affairs', 'network-centric warfare' and 'effects-based operations' all found their imitators in Britain, even if some of the terminology was adapted. The Americans presumed that their global primacy in military equipment not only would bring tactical success but also would convert into operational and even strategic outcomes. Superior speed, knowledge and precision would achieve simultaneous effects, and reduce the fog and friction of war.[6] What the British were less sure of was America's will to use these capabilities, or to use them wisely. The doctrine for the use of US military force enunciated by Colin Powell when he was chairman of the Joint Chiefs of Staff in 1992 had said that the United States should only go to war when it had clear political objectives and could commit overwhelming force to achieve decisive effects.[7]

If the memory which dictated this approach to strategy was derived from Vietnam, the context in which it was to be applied was the Balkans. In Bosnia, the British were far too influenced by their own experiences in Northern Ireland and sufficiently mindful of the complexities of ethnic and political division within south-eastern Europe to be ready to see the use of force in such stark terms, despite Serb atrocities. The 1995 Dayton peace accords left the two allies dissatisfied with each other and with themselves.[8] In 1999, both countries combined to good effect in Kosovo, but the friction between the Supreme Allied Commander Europe, the US General Wesley Clark, and the British commander of the Kosovo Force (KFOR), Lieutenant General Sir Mike Jackson, revealed a fundamental divide in how their two armies thought military force delivered results. The

---

5   Kampfner 2004, 72.
6   For a summary of what was achieved between 1991 and 2003, see Murray and Scales 2003, 241–51 and 259–77. On developments in US thought, see Kagan 2006.
7   Powell 1992.
8   Simms 2001, 335–6.

Americans, and particularly the United States Air Force, concluded that the Serbs had responded to the bombing of Belgrade; few in Britain did so.[9] For them, and for Jackson, as he makes clear in his chapter, the threat of ground troops, the intervention of the Russians and effective diplomacy were just as important.

Kosovo had three effects on Tony Blair. It confirmed in him Britain's obligation to act as the bridge between the United States and Europe; it persuaded him that humanitarian intervention was not only morally right but practically possible, a position he articulated in his Chicago speech delivered on 22 April 2009, in the middle of the crisis; and it convinced him that war not only had political utility but could also deliver effects in short order and with minimal casualties. From the Falklands to Kosovo, by way of the Gulf, the British experience of the last quarter of the twentieth century argued that war was effective, decisive and – paradoxically – really much safer than many other options.

In 2001 this was the mental context into which the news of the 9/11 attacks erupted. The response of the Labour Government was unequivocal. In London, Tony Blair joined the President of the United States, George W. Bush, in describing terrorism not as crime but as war, so breaking with the rubric followed by Britain in the Northern Ireland conflict. Legally, and possibly morally, Blair had put Britain in a different place: wars create obligations of those who wage them and gives rights to enemies that are different from those accorded criminals. In Brussels, George Robertson, the defence minister who had overseen the Strategic Defence Review and now Secretary General of NATO, persuaded the alliance to invoke Article 5 for the first time in its history – and so to treat the attack on the United States as an attack on its allies. Both Blair and Robertson were convinced of the need to keep the United States linked to Europe, and of Britain's role in achieving that.

The direct consequence of the 9/11 attacks was to subordinate British strategy, not just British operational thought, to America. Arguably, the United Kingdom had let its capacity for independent strategic thinking wither both during the Cold War and subsequently. Most deterrence theory after the Cuban missile crisis in 1962 was developed in the United States, in its think tanks and universities. Britain had only limited comparable capacity, and much of what existed was cut after 1990, as Andrew Mackay points out. The Ministry of Defence's scheme to establish defence lectureships in British universities ended after 1980, and the Armed Forces put the defence fellowships, which enabled mid-ranking officers with intellectual potential to pursue further study, into abeyance as the new century opened. The Joint Services Command and Staff College found its coherence undermined by the needs of the single Services, whose specific demands could easily result in agreement only on the lowest common denominator. The Royal College of Defence Studies, the college intended to address the strategic level, just as the Higher Command and Staff Course was designed to address the operational, was folded within the Defence Academy, an umbrella organisation created in 2002, and progressively lost status. With honourable exceptions (including both the Chief of the Defence Staff between 2006 and 2010, Jock Stirrup, and his Vice-Chief, Tim Granville-Chapman), most of the chiefs of staff who have served since 2001 have not been products of RCDS. Within Government, strategy lost its specific association with the use of war. The Ministry of Defence fused its functions as a department of state with the roles of a defence staff, and those who exercised command also became budget holders as power in the ministry derived from the control of money, not the wielding of military force. Given Blair's penchant for 'sofa government' and his reluctance to bring the issues surrounding the Iraq and Afghan wars to Cabinet, there was little pressure to disentangle strategy from policy, or to explore the relationships between means, ways and ends, with the sort of rigour required.

---

9   Keegan 1999.

This might not have mattered if the American strategy which Britain followed – or, rather, swallowed – had been subject to rigorous examination within the United States, but much of it had not been. The wars to which the 9/11 attacks gave rise were subsumed under two titles. The first, 'the global war on terror', failed to disaggregate one terrorist group from another or to prioritise one part of the world over another. It confronted the United States and its allies with a task too big even for its capacious means. And, crucially, it begged the question as to whether 'war' was the right instrument for dealing with the challenge. Needing to put the terrorist threat into a framework for which it had the tools, the Bush Administration adopted those of inter-state war, invading Afghanistan (which was a haven for terrorism) in 2001 and Iraq (which was not) in 2003. Although the 'global war on terror' was not formally rejected by the United States until Barack Obama was elected president, it had begun to fall out of favour by 2006. General John Abizaid at CENTCOM developed the idea of the 'long war', a conflict which conveniently embraced his arc of command, and so subsumed the wars in Iraq and Afghanistan within a wider but more amorphous struggle. By February 2006 the vocabulary of the 'long war' had migrated from Tampa to the Pentagon. The Quadrennial Defense Review of that year said, 'The struggle ... may well be fought in dozens of other countries simultaneously and for many years to come.' Ryan Henry of the Defense Department was no more successful when he attempted to put precision on the title of the 'long war':

> We in the Defense Department feel fairly confident that our forces will be called on to be engaged somewhere in the world in the next decade where they are currently not engaged but we have no idea whatsoever where that might be, when that might be or in what circumstances that they might be engaged.[10]

The following year, Abizaid's successor, Admiral William Fallon, tried to stop this imprecision. He rejected the idea of the 'long war' and told his command to focus on the war in hand, that in Iraq, but he was too late. As he did so the British Army was buying into the idea, and 'the long war', even if moderated in the 2010 Quadrennial Defense Review, remains central to American military thought. The argument that the struggle against terrorism will continue for the foreseeable future and that it may have to be carried to many different parts of the world is not at issue: such challenges require a coherent national policy. The question is whether a war that is not definable in terms of its enemy or its location can be called a war – or called one with sufficient rigour to be the basis for strategy.

Nor has strategy been much better directed when it has found a geographical focus. In terms of public statements, the war in Iraq was waged variously to eliminate weapons of mass destruction, to remove Saddam Hussein, to deliver humanitarian relief to persecuted minorities in Iraq and – as already mentioned – to deny the country's use to al-Qaeda. The war in Afghanistan began with the last of these motives, but is also being waged to bring good governance to the country, to uphold human rights and to destroy the poppy crop. Some of these objectives began as means to other ends, but became ends in themselves, and none of them has provided a clear and consistent focus for either war. Neither Bush nor Obama has defined an end state for the wars in Iraq or Afghanistan that has been able to provide the basis for strategy, which links their political ambitions to the character of the wars that they have undertaken and reflects the means that they are prepared to allocate to them. Without a clear and consistent lead on these points from Washington, the allies of the United States have also been unable to make strategy.

---

10 Tisdall and MacAskill 2006.

The result has proved disastrous for what passed for strategy in the United Kingdom, and especially for the Strategic Defence Review of 1998. Its leading principle, that of expeditionary warfare, a statement about means rather than ends, has fallen casualty to protracted warfare, in which semi-permanent structures like the Contingency Operating Base outside Basra or Camp Bastion in Helmand have been more redolent of garrisons and frontier forts than of raiding, speed and flexibility. The current conflicts have created 'urgent operational requirements', procurement programmes designed to meet the immediate needs of those in the field and whose costs are met by the Treasury, not the Ministry of Defence. The Army has been very largely re-equipped as a result, but the maintenance and subsequent operation of this unprogrammed equipment, once delivered, falls on the Ministry of Defence and so has created holes in its long-term budget.

Again, the Royal Navy's aircraft carrier programme is an illustration of the consequent confusion of priorities. Before the 2010 elections both parties were agreed that there was a pressing need for a defence review given that, since the last review in 1998, Britain had committed itself to two complex and protracted wars of medium size. In the event, what is remarkable, if little remarked upon, is how similar were the assumptions of the 2010 review to those of 1998. Reluctant to foreclose on any options, despite the impact of the economic crisis on top of the Ministry of Defence's structural deficit, the 2010 review retained the expeditionary ethos of the 1998 review in defiance of the events since 2001, and was driven by a long-term view that focused more on maritime-air capabilities than air-land.[11] On this reading, the pattern of war waged over the last decade by the British Armed Forces, and particularly by the British Army, cuts across the strategy which Britain, as an island power, with Western Europe secure, might naturally embrace. A tension has opened between the immediate operational necessity of the campaign in Afghanistan, recognising that waging war tends to require 'boots on the ground', and the tenets of putative British defence policy, which focuses on preventing war rather than conducting it. The 2010 Strategic Defence and Security Review skirted this issue, which only hard strategic thinking and determined prioritisation can resolve.

The failure to develop grand strategy, and to consider Britain's needs independently of the United States, has been seen as a failing on the part of politicians, and has meant that the disappointments and setbacks of the wars in Iraq and Afghanistan have been laid at the feet of the Labour Government in general, and of Tony Blair in particular, an argument developed to devastating effect in Jonathan Bailey's opening chapter. The implicit question is whether the buck stops here, or whether the Ministry of Defence and the Armed Forces confront charges to which they too must respond. If operational thinking is core business for senior officers, are they also not required to address the strategic implications of their advice? If they do not, are they in danger of guaranteeing the incoherence of strategy from the outset? Must they not confront unrealistic political ambitions with professional realism, given that this is how strategy is (or ought to be) made? And, if they have failed to do so, is that the fault of a Ministry of Defence structure which militates against such interventions through the fusion of military with civilian advice? Or have those in uniform used their claim to be apolitical as a cover for not contributing to the formulation of effective strategy?

Although at the time of writing the Chilcot enquiry into the Iraq War has yet to report, the press reaction to the public evidence sessions has focused, like the report of Lord Butler's committee in 2004, on the issues which surrounded Britain's decision to go to war in 2002–2003 more than on the conduct of the war itself. Moreover, public criticism of the campaigns themselves has tended to

---

11   See Liam Fox's speeches of 13 July 2010 to the Royal Institute for International Affairs and 20 July 2010 at Farnborough Air Show.

concentrate on issues for which it has held politicians, not civil servants or generals, responsible. Shortages of particular types of equipment, and especially of helicopters and sufficiently armoured vehicles, have been blamed on the Government and not on the procurement priorities set by the Services themselves within the Ministry of Defence's overall budget. The issue has been more the niggardliness of the Treasury in time of war, not the failure to concentrate the resources that have been made available on the main effort. As a corollary, the British Army's reputation is in the eyes of the British public surprisingly intact despite a decade of war in which decisive outcomes of the sort delivered in 1982, 1991 and 1999 have been conspicuously lacking.

Nonetheless, the Army has suffered at least some reputational damage, not least with its principal ally, the United States. In 2003–2004, the British press – and it must be said the British Army – was inclined to crow. The cultural fault line exposed by the clash between Wes Clark and Mike Jackson in Kosovo in 1999 became more evident as the war in Iraq moved from its initial phase of rapid manoeuvre, an operational triumph which prompted genuine British admiration for American brilliance, to so-called Phase 4 operations and 'post-conflict reconstruction'. Tim Cross describes the element of British responsibility for what was seen as overwhelmingly an American failing, and Andrew Graham and Andrew Stewart confront the consequences. American soldiers saw themselves as 'warriors' who did not do peace enforcement or counter-insurgency. Indeed, initially they did not even recognise the insurgency bubbling up around them, as Alex Alderson points out at the beginning of his chapter. By contrast, the British did, and they responded by taking off their helmets, donning berets and going out on foot patrols. The press in Britain conveniently ignored the fact that they were doing so in Basra, home to the more peaceful Shia rather than the Sunni. Nor could it understand why violence grew, rather than diminished, despite the British understanding of how to conduct counter-insurgency. Clashes in Basra were seen as the product of crime, not of insurgency, an extraordinary misreading given the British Army's experience in Northern Ireland, where terrorism and insurgency fed on the proceeds of crime, and as a result each penetrated the other. The Army was in danger of becoming the victim of its own narrative of success, stretching back to 1982 and even to 1942, and so of not recognising the realities of the situation unfolding in front of it.

It was a moment of hubris. At the end of 2005, the *Military Review*, published by the United States Army's Combined Arms Center, carried a critique of the Americans by a British officer, Brigadier Nigel Aylwin-Foster, who had served with US forces in Iraq in 2004. Two senior American officers, David Petraeus of the Army and Jim Mattis of the US Marine Corps, both of them determined to reform their Services, used the article to promote their cause, and by December 2006 had fathered a new manual on counter-insurgency, FM 3-24 in the Army's classification. No readiness to search souls or to promote self-criticism was as evident in the British Army at the same time. According to Barney White-Spunner, it was neither trained nor prepared for all three blocks of what General Krulak of the United States Marine Corps in 1997 had called 'three-block warfare', the capacity to fight different sorts of wars within three blocks of the same city. Indeed the Army had dismembered the agencies that might have done the job. Its own directorate of doctrine was abolished in 2005, its historical branch was charged with 'corporate memory' and had lost any input into doctrine if it had ever had any, and its capacity for timely lesson-learning from current operations had ossified. It may also not be without significance that the Defence Intelligence Staff had ceased to employ language specialists and so relied on others' translations of material.

Nor, as Desmond Bowen describes, was the British Army without fault in the process which resulted in 2006 in it defying defence planning assumptions and conducting two medium-level operations at the same time. At the end of the Cold War, fired by the Bagnall legacy, it was determined to retain its capacity to conduct operations at the corps level – in other words to be able to fight major conventional war. In 1992 it secured the command of NATO's Allied Command Europe Rapid Reaction Corps (ARRC), and in 2006 it seized the opportunity to deploy its prize, then commanded by David Richards, to Afghanistan. Chris Brown, the ARRC's chief of staff, outlines the operational intent in his chapter. Meanwhile, in Iraq, the British divisional commander, Richard Shirreff, was planning a counter-insurgency push in Basra, Operation Sinbad, which Justin Maciejewski describes in this book, but for which Shirreff did not have adequate numbers of troops and in which Whitehall seemed to have lost interest. On 19 September 2005 the Chief of Defence Staff, General Sir Mike Walker, told the Secretary of State for Defence, John Reid, that

> our ability to fulfill our plan in Afghanistan is not predicated on withdrawal of such capabilities from Iraq and, notwithstanding those qualifications, in the event that our conditions-based plan for progressive disengagement for withdrawal from southern Iraq is delayed, we shall still be able to deliver mandated force levels in Afghanistan.

Walker's calculations rested not just on an under-estimation of what would be required in Afghanistan, but also on a very different interpretation of the situation in Basra from that of Shirreff, who described it as 'full conventional war in built-up areas'. His predecessor, John Cooper, had only been able to spare 200 troops for patrols and offensive operations from the 3,000 under his command, because the balance was required to defend and sustain British bases. Shirreff looked to his American theatre command in Baghdad, rather than to London, to support his desire for success in Iraq.[12]

Unsurprisingly, General Sir Richard Dannatt, when he succeeded Mike Jackson as Chief of the General Staff in August 2006, was wont to describe the Army as running 'red hot'. His focus was on keeping the British Army in a state – in terms of both manpower and training – where it could survive in good order, irrespective of the strains imposed by the wars it was having to fight. On 12 October 2006 the *Daily Mail* published an interview with Dannatt, in which he saw the solution to the Army's problems as withdrawal from south-east Iraq by the end of 2007. This was not a decision yet reached by the Government. More seriously, it soon proved to be completely at odds with the policy adopted by the Bush Administration. The United States decided to 'surge' troops into Iraq in 2007. It could not be sure how things would turn out, given that the aims were defined by the ways and means: more 'boots on the ground' would create a security 'bubble', within which a political solution might emerge. Bill Rollo was on the inside of these events in Baghdad. The Americans struck lucky, not least because their actions chimed with shifts in opinion in Iraq itself. But the effect on US–UK military relations was bad. While US forces sought victory of a sort, the British Army seemed content to retreat.

That was not of course how some in the British Army – with some reason – saw its position. Dannatt was not alone in interpreting the Coalition forces in Iraq as part of the problem, their prolonged presence being seen increasingly as an occupation; American generals before 2007 were of the same view. But the real attraction for him and for the Labour Government was Afghanistan, which was still the 'good' war, its initiation not the response to a 'dodgy dossier' but to the fact that the country had given safe haven to al-Qaeda. The Afghans themselves seemed to welcome the opportunity which American intervention offered to throw off Taleban rule, and so British troops were moved into Helmand before they had completed their task in Iraq. The Army was paying for its 'can do' mentality, its reluctance to challenge political direction which contradicted strategic sense, and its institutional fear that if it were not used it would be cut.

---

12 Fairweather 2011: 262, 267, 385.

Between 2006 and 2008 it fought two campaigns without being able to resource either of them properly. Jonathan Shaw describes how in Iraq he found himself entering into a deal with the Jaysh al-Mahdi and abandoning Basra city for the Coalition Operating Base. When Maliki launched Operation Charge of the Knights ahead of time and the Iraqi Army ran into trouble, Richard Iron, who writes about the operation from the perspective of having advised the Iraqis, felt the frustration of having to seek American, rather than British, help for the Iraqis in Basra. The British, it seemed, were on the back foot. In Afghanistan, the first British brigade in Helmand, 16th Air Assault Brigade, found itself in some of the fiercest tactical engagements experienced by the British Army since the Korean War. In the process it lost the capacity to control the ground between their 'platoon houses', and so effectively forfeited the operational initiative. These were limited wars but they required masses of troops, and Britain did not have them.

A common feature of the chapters that describe this period of both wars is their regular reference to a RAND study of counter-insurgency which established an ideal ratio of 20–25 members of the security forces for every 1,000 of the population.[13] Indubitably there are other ways of fighting an insurgency, but they mostly trade numbers for time, and the RAND figures have now entered the dogma of the day. Significantly, Britain initially deployed 3,000 troops to Helmand and subsequently raised that figure to 7,000, then 10,000: nowhere near the RAND ideal. However, if an army takes the initiative it can concentrate numbers in time and space and so achieve sufficient local superiority to offset overall weakness. Logically enough, therefore, 3rd Commando Brigade, which succeeded 16th Air Assault Brigade, went raiding and so restored manoeuvre to the campaign. But in the process it lost the capacity to hold what it had cleared, as it lacked the troops to follow in behind their actions. They ended up 'mowing the grass' – repeating the same process again and again. So resources were undoubtedly a constraint, and one which meant that tactical successes were always in danger of being temporary and self-contained, incapable of conversion to operational – let alone strategic – outcomes.

But that was not the only explanation for the British Army's problems; it also reaped the whirlwind for its neglect of the thinking parts of war. Counter-insurgency is, as its title suggests, set within a strategic framework that is defensive: the aim is to prevent something from happening. Because they seek change, the insurgents have the initiative. Strategic defence can create requirements which vitiate the principles of success at the tactical and operational levels. The need to protect requires the defender to disperse his forces to guard against attack (and hence the defender's greater need for mass), but in the process he forfeits the capacity to concentrate strength and to manoeuvre. Of course, the defender can seize the initiative at the tactical level but, if that action is successful, he confronts a fresh challenge – how to convert what would be otherwise only a local success into a wider effect.

When Bagnall had confronted the problem of defending the inner German border in the 1980s he had dealt with the same need to integrate tactical and operational solutions with the strategic defence. It was precisely the potential incoherence between the levels of war that prompted him to give sustained attention to the operational level, the bridge between the tactical and the strategic. He forced the British Army on the Rhine to reject purely tactical responses to a possible Soviet attack by putting them into an operational context which would allow it to seize the initiative within a defensive strategy. Moreover, the quality of the work that resulted was due in no small part to the fact that, unlike the British Army of 2006, that of the 1980s understood its enemy. Bagnall served in an Army that sustained a Soviet Studies research centre at the Royal Military

---

13   Quinlivan 2003. The conclusions of the article were incorporated in FM 3-24, but have since been attacked: see Thiel 2011.

Academy Sandhurst. The Army's mistake after 1991 was to imagine that, in having cracked the paradox of how to wage a strategically defensive war with an operational offensive, it had found a panacea for all wars. It had not – and least of all not for counter-insurgency campaigns which are more regionally specific, much more permeated by religion, politics and culture than are so-called 'major wars', and which therefore demand a deep understanding of the enemy and the populations within which such campaigns are waged. The distinction between the last two is frequently unclear: as Barney White-Spunner observes, those on whose behalf British soldiers were fighting are those whom a previous generation would have called the enemy.

During the Cold War, the Army had had to 'double-hat' its forces, requiring those training to execute a corps counter-stroke in northern Germany also to conduct counter-insurgency operations in Northern Ireland. When the end of the Cold War removed the first pressure, successive Chiefs of the General Staff, up to and including Richard Dannatt, were determined to keep the capacity to wage 'major war' alive. That, and not counter-insurgency, remained the Army's benchmark. It also shaped its equipment needs. In this respect the Anglo-French agreement at St Malo in 1998 was as important as the Strategic Defence Review of the same year. Like the latter, the former rested on an expeditionary expectation, which required that ground forces be both air portable and capable of confronting main battle tanks once in theatre. The result, the Future Rapid Effects System (FRES), became the Army's main equipment programme. Designed around the idea of 'situational awareness', to offset the lack of armour determined by the need to ensure air mobility, the FRES programme became as much the focus of successive Chiefs of the General Staff as did its counterpart of 'conventional war'. The corollary of FRES was that the anti-IED needs of the wars in Iraq and Afghanistan were treated as secondary issues, solved by 'urgent operational requirements', rather than as the main effort in the development of armoured fighting vehicles.[14]

By 2008 the FRES programme seemed to be dying, although even in 2012 it was still not formally dead; but it took longer for the Army to reverse its intellectual assumptions. To be fair, the British Army's doctrine committee woke up to the need to revisit the subject at the same time as the Americans, in 2006, and ordered that its existing counter-insurgency manual, written in 2001, be revised in the light of recent experience. But 'jointery' meant that the Army was no longer master in its own house, and at the beginning of 2008 the Defence Concepts and Doctrine Centre cancelled the publication of the new text. A single Service found itself at odds with a joint agency, and nobody in the Ministry of Defence was ready to knock heads together. The Army responded by creating a dedicated Afghan COIN centre within the Land Warfare Centre at Warminster, which resumed the work, as described by Alex Alderson. Not until 2009, the year in which it completed its withdrawal from Iraq, did it publish a revised counter-insurgency doctrine, three years after the United States Army of which it had once been so critical.

Published doctrine is not the be all and end all of an army's intellectual engagement. Doctrine may exist, but that does not mean that it is read, and an army may have excellent doctrine but not be trained according to its precepts, or may have poor written doctrine and still be effective. The 2001 doctrine was perfectly adequate but it was ignored; at the beginning of the twenty-first century the British Army was more concerned to match itself against the 'revolution in military affairs' which then so concerned the United States, its principal ally and almost its only intellectual influence. In 2004, when called to conduct counter-insurgency warfare, it found itself unfamiliar with what by 2006 many would come to call 'high-intensity COIN'. Success in Northern Ireland, the benchmark which was meant to show British expertise in counter-insurgency, was in some respects a false friend. Those still in uniform at regimental level after 2003 who had served in

---

14   North 2009, especially 231–44.

Northern Ireland had done so at the tail end of the campaign and not in the 1970s or 1980s. They had experienced a more benign environment, and one in which the police had primacy and the Army had intelligence supremacy over its enemies. Neither of these assumptions applied in Iraq. Crucially, too, in Northern Ireland Britain had also been operating in its own sovereign territory and in its own name.

The latter points did not apply in Bosnia in the 1990s, but here too Britain was in a more forgiving environment than Basra or Helmand would be in 2006–2007. The operations of the 1990s had been characterised first as peace support operations and then as peace enforcement. The Army, influenced by another inspirational leader, Rupert Smith, realized, when he commanded the UN Protection Force in 1995, that the strict neutrality enjoined by the United Nations when keeping the peace could not protect those whom others were determined to kill. The new doctrine of peace enforcement, as opposed to peace keeping, acknowledged that the responsibility to protect might require the use of force on behalf of one side against the other. However, the right approach to the circumstances within Bosnia proved deleterious when applied unthinkingly later. It meant that counter-insurgency had become identified with peace keeping. Some units in Iraq seemed to think they were doing the latter and hence their surprise when the situation proved far more dangerous than they had expected. Both counter-insurgency and peace keeping elevate the principle of restraint, but they do so within different contexts. At the tactical level, the British Army by 2006–2007 was using proportionately as much firepower as in 'major war', and its soldiers were having to display as much courage in the face of the enemy as their predecessors in both world wars.[15] This was the environment which prompted the incoming Chief of the General Staff, General Sir David Richards, to conclude in 2008 that at the tactical level war against state and non-state actors might look very similar.[16]

In that case training for war has a generic quality that can indeed transfer from so-called conventional operations to counter-insurgency. The distinction between counter-insurgency, which is a form of war, and peace keeping, which is not, may be even more important than that between counter-insurgency and 'conventional war'. The US Army of 2003 suspected that an army which embraced 'hearts and minds' too warmly would confuse its strategic mission, that of 'being a force for good', with its operational task, and so would forget that it was in the business of using lethal force. Those fears were not baseless. The Americans had allies who seemed to regard their armed forces as gendarmeries or providers of international aid. To that extent those in Britain who preached 'hot war' as the gold standard had a point. However, there are still features of counter-insurgency which are distinct and even counter-intuitive to those trained to the conduct of high-end warfighting, and they require sensitivity to difference rather than to similarity. Among the first of these is how counter-insurgency forces generate mass.

Although reluctant to use the word 'limited war', a phrase particularly pregnant for Americans since its application in Vietnam is seen to have led to defeat, both the United States and the United Kingdom have been waging limited wars since 2001, even if they have been clothed with the rhetoric of major and even global war. They have not willed the means to wage them, and this has been a source of strategic incoherence. It has also been an operational problem. The formula of the US FM 3-24 demands that a counter-insurgency operation clears, holds and builds.[17] As the British found in Helmand, the holding and building stages are vital to campaign success but require manpower that they did not have. The mass in a war that is limited for Britain will come from

---

15   Fergusson 2008, especially 324.
16   Richards 2008.
17   Field Manual 3-24 2006, 5-51 to 5-67.

indigenous forces. Britain held its empire with an exiguous regular army by dint not only of the Indian Army but also of a host of locally raised formations and irregular levies. In the current wars, the equivalents are the Iraqi and Afghan armies and local militias, only more so because effective national forces are also attributes of the two states' sovereign status. The disbandment of the Iraqi Army by the Americans and the effective dissolution of the Soviet-trained Afghan Army have meant that one of the principal roles for the British Army in counter-insurgency today has been that of forming, training and mentoring indigenous forces. Two obstacles delayed development on this front. The first was an impatience, born of six-month tours, which concluded that it was better and quicker for the British to do a job themselves, so setting back the development of local self-reliance. The second was the reverse of the first, and is still a problem: the determination to see the creation of effective Iraqi and Afghan Security Forces as 'an exit strategy'. The creation of an army can only be a means to an end, and an exit in itself is not a coherent strategic objective. The phrase obscures the real strategic object of the exercise – which is success. That is what will lead to an 'exit'; the reason for wanting mass is the pursuit of victory.

The principle of fighting together, which underpins effective mentoring, is of course made more difficult by the possibility of those allies and partners pursuing different political agendas. This is another difference between counter-insurgency and 'conventional' warfare, and, at the operational level, is the key difference. Even the most senior operational commander in a major war, although of course he will be serving a political object by his decisions, rarely does so in such a direct sense that it affects his conduct of operations. For most of the time he can see war as a self-contained entity. This is not the case in counter-insurgency. Here, even decisions taken by junior NCOs can have strategic effect. The so-called 'strategic corporal' is so defined less because he or she is actively involved in the making of strategy and more because a wrong decision by him or her can have strategic consequences. The only British soldier convicted of war crimes since 2001, Donald Payne of the Queen's Lancashire Regiment, was a corporal at the time of the offence, not a commissioned officer. Neither he nor others in his battalion would have confronted a court martial if they had been made more aware of what had been learnt in Northern Ireland or if they had been better versed in the basic principles of the laws of armed conflict and international humanitarian law.

The oft-repeated proposition that in counter-insurgency only 20 per cent of the effects are military and 80 per cent political misses important realities. The first is that a campaign has its own tempo. By 2009, as the situation in Basra settled, Major General Andy Salmon could more readily apply the principles of human security which informed his approach than might have been possible during his predecessors' commands. Andrew Mackay, when commanding 52nd Brigade in Helmand between September 2007 and March 2008, took a similar view, preferring to win the support of the population rather than to seek battle.[18] But at other stages of the war, the counter-insurgents may have to use force in order to create the conditions for security. Knowing when to use what is born of experience, a resource on which by 2008 the Army could increasingly draw. As a result, to repeat a point made above but in a different context, at certain times and in certain places, for those engaged in battle with the enemy, the effort is 100 per cent military. Much of the fighting in Afghanistan since 2006, and not only in that year, was and is conducted at the tactical level with an intensity which can match that of the two world wars, and is characterized by terms drawn from the positional warfare of both those conflicts, with trenches, bunkers and no man's land, and with gains measured in yards not miles (or kilometres). The second point, evidenced throughout the wars in Iraq and Afghanistan, is that, even if the proportion that is political is true, much more than

---

18   Grey 2009.

20 per cent of the whole has to be delivered by the military. In other words, soldiers end up doing things that the norms of civil-military relations see as outside their constitutional competence.[19]

A coalition commander has to work with his allies and to adjust to the expectations of the host nation, as Andrew Graham, Bill Rollo, Jonathon Riley and others make abundantly clear. The success of David Petraeus as a commander in the operations in Iraq and Afghanistan related directly to his skills as a diplomat, his capacity to engage his allies and to make them feel valued, his contacts with the press at home, and his consequent capacity to get the ear of his own national political masters as well as those of the nation in which the war is being fought. Every British general who has fought in the wars of the last decade, and certainly all those who have contributed to this volume, recognise these as desirable – indeed essential – attributes, and ones which in part or in full they have had to exercise. If counter-insurgency wars are 'wars among the people', then they are also wars for influence. Moreover (and this aspect of Rupert Smith's now oft-quoted aphorism tends to be overlooked), the people are not just those in the theatre of operations but also those in the United Kingdom, since their opinions of the war can have as much effect as the events on the ground in the minds of national political leaders. When the Prime Minister, David Cameron, confirmed in November 2010 that British combat troops would be withdrawn from Afghanistan by the end of 2014, he explained his timeline not in relation to the conditions which he saw as likely to prevail in Afghanistan but in terms of what the British public would demand – and rightly in his view.[20]

Possibly a greater source of friction along the civil-military divide within Britain than the presumption of generals exercising direct political influence (even if that is what generates the headlines)[21] is the civil-military fault line within Government itself. In the Afghanistan theatre, the Armed Forces, the Foreign and Commonwealth Office and the Department for International Development have progressively formed better working relationships, particularly since about 2009. Confronted with real problems which need addressing in real time, they have responded with common sense. But there were two legacies to overcome, even in theatre. One was the failure to address the issues of governance in Iraq in 2003, before they had become critical and before the absence of British capability in this regard had already undermined the efforts of British arms.[22] The other was the perception created in the minds of the British Armed Forces by different operating philosophies in both of the other Government departments. The Foreign and Commonwealth Office had long since (for understandable reasons) downgraded the proconsular skills that the circumstances since 2003 have demanded, and had so hedged its personnel round with health and safety legislation that those in uniform were left with a sense of both frustration and superiority. Few, if any, of its consulate staff in Basra were Arabists, for whom the Foreign and Commonwealth Office had once been famed. The Department for International Development had been created to dispense aid, not to support British operations in a war zone, a point which in 2002–2003 Claire Short, as the responsible minister, was at pains to reiterate. At the time her views were a fair reflection of her department's interpretation of its international obligations.

Only gradually were these institutional mindsets brought into some sort of harmony. The Post-Conflict Reconstruction Unit, set up in late 2004, was designed to be an inter-departmental agency but was under-resourced and insufficiently supported by the parents which had given it birth. It was replaced in 2007 by the Stabilisation Unit, which operated under the auspices of the

---

19   For a discussion of this point at greater length, see Strachan 1997, 163–94.

20   David Cameron's briefing to the press at the NATO summit in Lisbon, 20 November 2010.

21   Most obviously in the case of Richard Dannatt after his interview with the *Daily Mail* in October 2006 and in the furore on his elevation to the peerage after his retirement from the Army.

22   On which see Synott 2008.

original triumvirate but with the addition of the Cabinet Office, and so proved better placed to prevent the determination and willingness to cooperate of those in theatre from falling prey to internecine warfare in Whitehall. But, as Nick Pounds makes clear, that cooperation still had to rest on collaboration not command and control. Each of the principal Government agencies had different philosophies for good reasons. In the rest of the world, in places where British troops were not at war, they were and are still fulfilling their core aims, whether it is the promotion of British business or the removal of poverty. In Iraq and Afghanistan, if these objectives had a role it could – at least in the eyes of the uniformed Services – only be as means to another end, that of success in theatre, not as ends in themselves. Those diplomats who forged careers in theatre, in the Provincial Reconstruction Teams, or even in the embassies, could sense that in the eyes of their peers they had become too military. Those who resisted the pressure to do so, or embraced it but then rejected it, might find themselves in a no man's land, embraced by neither side.[23]

As a result, the phrase 'comprehensive approach', which entered the vocabulary of British Government in 2006, tended to be viewed with suspicion by both the Foreign and Commonwealth Office and the Department for International Development. For them it was stamped 'made in the Ministry of Defence', and suggested that the latter, which enjoyed a much larger budget than either of them, was trying to take them over.[24] And in some senses they were right. In 2009 the Ministry of Defence's Defence Concepts and Doctrine Centre produced its own higher-level response to counter-insurgency campaigning, Joint Doctrine Publication 3-40, *Stabilisation Operations*. Like the Army's field manual on counter-insurgency of the same year, this was a publicly available document, freely downloadable from the internet, rather than classified as restricted, and as such an engine for wider public engagement. Its intended audience was as much the other Government departments which had to provide some of the effects in theatre, in terms of law, aid, development and governance, as it was the Armed Forces themselves. It was an aspirational document, seeking to unify civil and military effects in pursuit of campaign objectives. But it was also a document with an internal agenda, a recognition that the Army itself needed to do better. By the time of its publication, the Army was responding to the blows to its own self-esteem, had begun to learn from its errors, and was more open both to the lessons from its own recent experience and to fresh thinking from outside. The then director of DCDC, Major General Paul Newton, also oversaw a study on the future character of conflict, and in April 2010 went on promotion to head the Army's own response to the challenges of contemporary war, the newly created Force Development and Training Command. However, the biggest challenge, as both Andrew Mackay and Paul Newton argue in their chapters, is to ensure that such messages are also reflected in joint teaching, within the Defence Academy, as well as within joint doctrine.

JDP 3-40 showed how much by 2009 the Armed Forces' view, and particularly the Army's, of the operational level of war had changed since 2001. Its focus had moved from the relationship between operations and tactics, which had prevailed in Bagnall's day and which made sense when the strategic context was set by the Cold War, to the relationship between operations and strategy. It is a point made by all the contributors to this volume who have exercised three-star command in Iraq and Afghanistan: Andrew Graham, John McColl, John Kiszely, Bill Rollo, Jonathon Riley and Nick Parker. The framework for bringing together the different lines of operation – security, development, the rule of law and stabilisation – into a coherent whole is the business of campaign planning. This is the core competence required of generals and their staffs, and it is a skill which they

---

23   As possible examples of this, consider the positions and very differing perspectives of Stewart 2006, especially 425–34, and Cowper-Coles 2011.

24   Baumann 2008.

possess and which most of their civilian partners do not. Campaign planning, John McColl writes in his chapter, 'forces you to write down what you want to happen. It imparts intent coherently.'

So, although operational art may be a core professional responsibility, it has direct political effects. As McColl also observes, the role of the mission commander has moved from mission execution to mission interpretation and often mission definition. As a result, the biggest strain in the many relationships with which the British operational commander has to contend is that with his own immediate superiors in the Ministry of Defence.

In 1996 the Conservative Government established the Permanent Joint Headquarters (PJHQ) at Northwood, and appointed a three-star officer, the Chief of Joint Operations, to head it. In the expeditionary era which was formalised by their successors in office, Tony Blair's Labour Party, with the Strategic Defence Review in 1998, PJHQ was the ideal tool for the operational implementation of strategy. Relatively small-scale operations, requiring joint capabilities, sustained at a distance but for short periods, were best generated and maintained by just such a headquarters. But PJHQ has had difficulties adjusting to its role in larger-scale operations, such as Iraq and Afghanistan, which have dwarfed other commitments, in which Britain has been a junior partner, and which have become so protracted as to be the main effort of the British Armed Forces.

In these circumstances PJHQ has become the fifth wheel to the coach. A few miles away, the main building of the Ministry of Defence has remained not only a department of state but also a military headquarters. The latter is itself an awkward relationship, resulting in a convergence of civilian and financial needs with operational and military that is not necessarily to the advantage of either. The merging of civilian and military staffs seems to be sensible in terms of good practice in civil-military relations, but it can also result in 'group think' and in the subordination of military imperatives to the needs of Whitehall. Civil servants see their primary function as serving their ministers and saving them from embarrassment, not winning the war in hand. Internal debate and self-criticism struggle to find a voice in such an atmosphere, and external discussion is headed off by efforts to control the press and public communications.

The Chief of the Defence Staff is the principal military advisor to the government, but he has no specifically dedicated strategic staff to service his needs and he is physically removed from his operational headquarters. In 1984 Michael Heseltine, the Secretary of State for Defence, created a joint defence staff, simultaneously chaired by the Chief of the Defence Staff and the senior civil servant in the Ministry, the Permanent Under-Secretary. The effect was to emasculate the chiefs of staff as a strategic advisory body and to elevate financial management over professional military thought. The Chief of Defence Staff between 1982 and 1985, Dwin Bramall, argued that without an effective Chiefs of Staff Committee 'the CDS is little more than the head of a bureaucratic structure subject to political manipulation'. Bramall did his best to mitigate the worst consequences of the arrangements by fighting for an effective balance between the two sides of the house, but the 1994–1995 defence review destroyed the strategic planning function championed by Bramall, and brought in arrangements which further enhanced the authority of the senior civil servants.[25] The new performance management processes and structures functioned well enough in the context of 'normal' business in the 1990s, but failed when confronted with protracted and significant operations after 2003. This point was not addressed in June 2011 by Lord Levene's independent report into the structure and management of the Ministry of Defence, which focused on strategy as best business practice, not strategy in the sense in which a general staff would understand it. Indeed, it trumpeted the joint civil-military defence staff as a model for emulation abroad, despite the evidence of frustration then emanating from those in operational theatres. These

---

25   Jackson and Bramall 1992: 428–33, 445–8.

structural impediments to critical strategic thinking are more serious than other, sometimes more obvious, sources of frustration. From the top, ministers are wont to intervene in decisions that have operational and even tactical implications. There is a tendency to see this as new. It is not. Churchill did it, but he had a robust chiefs of staff organisation to check his wilder schemes.

One senior officer, speaking as part of the Changing Character of War Programme at Oxford under Chatham House rules, described how strategy is like flying a helicopter: it is inherently unstable and needs constant correction to ensure coherence between ends, ways and means. This is made the more difficult since ends, in a discretionary war, can be compromised. This may cause political embarrassment but not true strategic failure: Britain's political ambition for Iraq became more humble over time, and its ambition for Afghanistan is under constant review. Similarly, in a discretionary operation, the means the Government allocates can also be discretionary and will almost certainly be insufficient to achieve the ends. The ways are often seen as an alchemy that somehow can meet a rich man's ambition on a poor man's wages, such as, historically, using native levies or persuading other countries to pay the bill.

The instability of our speaker's strategic helicopter is exacerbated by at least three further factors. First is the coalition dimension, since Britain conducts very few campaigns on its own. Second is that its recent campaigns have been fought in countries that are sovereign states. The destabilising effect of these coalition and sovereignty dimensions on national strategy is significant, yet the degree to which Whitehall believes it has the power unilaterally to change (as opposed to influence) events which are more properly the preserve of the coalition chain of command or the sovereign state in whose country our operations are being conducted, is a constant source of surprise. The third ingredient of instability is UK departmental equity: the business of the comprehensive approach, which is showing real promise in Helmand, but is a long way from being institutionalised in Whitehall.

To be fair, there has been progress since the advent of the Coalition Government in May 2010. Its creation of a National Security Council provides an opportunity for joined-up debate of strategy at the highest level of Government. But, since strategy is inherently unstable and needs constant management and correction, the National Security Council's lack of a strategic staff or of a sufficiently resourced secretariat capable of such hands-on management is a serious weakness. In the Ministry of Defence, one little-noticed change has been the re-titling of the post of Deputy Chief of Defence Staff (Operations) to Deputy Chief of Defence Staff (Military Strategy and Operations): a belated recognition that the business of the ministry is very properly strategy, but still conflated, in title at least, with 'operations', which should be the preserve of PJHQ and the operational theatres. In 2012, following the recommendations of the Levene report, the Ministry of Defence established a new Joint Forces Command, headed by a four-star officer who sits on the Chiefs of Staff Committee, which has itself been given a greater role while its members have been encouraged to behave more collegially. The JFC is based at Northwood and subsumes the collocated Permanent Joint Headquarters. It has also taken responsibility for joint training and education, including the Defence Academy, the Development, Concepts and Doctrine Centre, and Defence Intelligence. Its creation is recognition of some of the structural problems inherent in Defence, but it does not address the fundamental strategic disconnects in Whitehall. The success of the new arrangements depends in large measure on the commitment of the Chief of Defence Staff to ensuring that the Chiefs of Staff Committee is made to work more effectively and more jointly than in the recent past, not least because under the terms of the Levene report the single Service staffs have been rusticated out of London.

British troops in theatre have normally done a six-month operational tour, a stint which, as Simon Wessely suggests, seems sensible in terms of mental health and fitness levels, but which has given Britain's conduct of campaigns a rhythm which follows its cycle of rotation more than the needs in theatre. Campaign continuity has been the casualty as each brigade or battlegroup commander has been anxious to make his mark within his tour, and so has paid less attention to the long-term direction of travel. Those with whom the British operate, notably the Americans, are in theatre for longer, and indigenous forces are, self-evidently, there continuously. The development of close working relationships as well as cultural understanding and awareness, both crucial to the conduct of counter-insurgency, have taken second place to the determination to rotate formed brigades. The latter results in troop levels in theatre which are not commensurate with the Army's overall size. Counter-insurgency campaigns, which tend to be protracted, evolve over time, and not all lines of operation can be pursued to the same effect at once: security may be the priority at one moment, the rule of law at the next and development thereafter. The campaign in Basra followed almost exactly this sort of phasing, and in Afghanistan different parts of the country can be at different places at the same time. Failing to recognise which point the campaign has reached, trying to do everything at once, rushing to finish a task before being rotated out of theatre, all vitiate the effective sequencing of actions.

So, if British operations in Iraq and Afghanistan have sought consistency, they have only been able – at least until recently – to find it through PJHQ. The effects were to squeeze the senior British officer in theatre, usually the deputy to the US force commander, out of the national decision-making cycle as the brigades in theatre spoke directly to PJHQ, and at the same time to render those troops more subservient to national imperatives than to the objectives of the alliance which they were meant to be supporting, and to which the British three-star general was also attached.

In 2009 steps were taken to resolve these tensions by appointing Lieutenant General Nick Parker to be Deputy Commander ISAF in Kabul for a one-year term. With Afghanistan as the Armed Forces' main effort and with DCOMISAF as both the senior British officer in theatre and a NATO commander, the post gave more coherence to the situation in theatre, but created a tension between the Chief of the Defence Staff, PJHQ and the national contingent commander. It also required a greater readiness on the part of the Ministry of Defence to trust its man on the spot.

Central here is the issue of the span of command. If campaigning now requires so many distinct lines of operation, its conduct has become much more complex and intellectually demanding. The move away from the 'conventional' norms of Cold War soldiering has displaced the corps as the principal operational unit and promoted the brigade. Today's brigades are typically described as modular, which means that they do not conform to any set configuration but have components bolted on according to tactical and operational need. Such flexibility is obviously desirable in theory, but in practice British brigades have reached strengths approaching what would have been divisions in past wars. In 2010 Major-General Nick Carter, appointed to head Regional Command South, was given a divisional headquarters to do so (and also exercised his command for a year). Counter-insurgency wars may be classified as small wars, but their complexity and their manpower demands mean that they are not just wars of section attacks and platoon patrols. The recognition of this within the higher command chain has begun to address the vices created for British counter-insurgency by the six-month tour cycle. But more responsible commanders possessed of campaign continuity present further challenges to the relationship between operational command and both PJHQ and the Ministry of Defence, and to the displacement effects between the operational level of war and its political results.

The current popular sympathy which the British Army commands with the wider British public generates both gratitude and wariness among senior officers: gratitude for the obvious signs of recognition, from the success of 'Help for Heroes' to David Cameron's determination to give the Armed Forces' Covenant the force of law, and wariness, because sympathy is not the same as understanding. If grief for those who are killed and seriously wounded generates a rejection of the use of armed force, then the Armed Forces are out of a job.

War does not of course exist to create employment for armies, but there are times when the debates which have been generated by two wars, which have been variously described as 'wars of choice' or discretionary wars, are in danger of describing the wars in Iraq and Afghanistan as unnecessary, which in turn makes the Army's determination to widen its commitment to the latter in 2006 look particularly suspect. It is worth recalling that, whatever the controversies surrounding the decision to invade Iraq, there was originally no such controversy in relation to the war in Afghanistan. NATO invoked Article 5 in support of the war. Both President Obama, who did not initiate the Afghan war but did inherit it, and Gordon Brown, who similarly was not Prime Minister (even if he was in Government) when Britain committed itself to Afghanistan, described the war as one of necessity in 2009, nearly eight years after its initiation. The trouble is that their publics no longer did: as Richard Haass, writing from an American perspective, has put it, 'wars of necessity have a way of becoming wars of choice'.[26]

In Britain in 2012, David Cameron and his Government continued to present the war in Afghanistan as a war of necessity, but increasingly reflected their public and the press in treating it as though it were a war of choice. For British generals this is worrying, as a war not deemed to be in the national interest can too easily transmogrify into a war fought in their interest. Their conduct of the Bosnian campaign had already been cast in this light.[27] Indubitably, both Iraq and, particularly, Afghanistan have served the interests of the Army over those of the other two Services, not least as economic pressures have borne down on the defence budget. Moreover, as Iain McNicoll argues, it is not necessarily clear that the Army's dominance has resulted in the most effective use of (in particular) expensive airborne capabilities. Land-centric campaign planning which includes air power as an afterthought, rather than as an integral element, is a practice which will not serve British defence well in a more contested aerial environment. The long shadow of Douglas Haig and popular perceptions of the First World War make senior officers sensitive to the accusation that they are donkeys leading lions.

On his return from Kabul, Sir Sherard Cowper-Coles, Britain's ambassador in Afghanistan between 2007 and 2010, was not sparing in the sort of public criticism of the Army calculated to feed generals' fears.[28] But there is a paradox in his attacks. His memoirs praise those British generals who exercised senior command in Afghanistan in 2010. 'Nick Parker's mischievous intelligence was a breath of fresh air. Not for him the boiler-plate clichés of counter-insurgency. He thought for himself, with an intellectual courage that didn't always endear him to the military machines back in Northwood and MOD Main Building.' Nick Carter was 'an outstandingly able officer', who in a presentation to the Foreign Secretary exhibited 'plenty of enthusiasm and understanding, but also realism'.[29]

Those with a sense for the regimental politics of the British Army may note that both officers are products of the Rifles, as is Justin Maciejewski, but the impression given by the generals who have contributed to this book, and indeed by the others who have spoken to the Campaigning and Generalship seminar series between 2006 and 2011, is similarly paradoxical. Regimental affiliations remain a source of pride, but they count for less than was once the case. The Army contains many more graduates than it had in the Cold War (and a surprisingly large number of those at the top of

---

26   Haass 2009, xxi–xxii.

27   Simms 2001, 221–2.

28   Borger 2011; Cowper-Coles's evidence to House of Commons Select Committee on Foreign Affairs, 2 March 2011.

29   Cowper-Coles 2011, 241–2 and 269.

today's Army are graduates of Oxford and Cambridge), but the Army's own educational capacities have passed through a period of turbulence, neglect and dissolution. 'Manoeuvrism', although cited less often these days, remains a fundamental presumption of British military capabilities, although it is one more obviously possessed by the insurgent. By contrast, the virtues of Western forces, manifested in abundant resources, lie in attrition, and are vested in firepower rather than mobility and flexibility. Paradoxical too is the exercise of command. Captured in these chapters is the point that command can be exercised in very different ways – through force of personality, like Graeme Lamb's, to cerebral engagement and diverse reading, as exemplified by Jonathan Shaw.

Paradox is a source of strength and diversity: it is essential to the proper understanding of how to conduct effective counterinsurgency operations, as both US FM 3-24 and Graeme Lamb's own typically pithy *Counter-insurgency: A Commander's Guidance*, issued in June 2009 when he was Commander of the Field Army, make clear. But what paradox forfeits is a sense of coherence, of how operational realities fit into and shape strategy, rather than become subordinated to policies that are incapable of fulfilment. The institutions which are currently charged with managing the relationship between politicians and the military and between the civil servants and the military (and these are not the same thing) are not fit for purpose. Put bluntly, PJHQ was never designed to make strategy, and the Ministry of Defence is not currently adapted for the task. If the machinery within Defence is not fit for the purpose of strategy, there is little prospect of the National Security Council, created in 2010, being able to harmonise strategy and policy.

Internally, the Army is only now developing a mechanism by which it can become an effective 'learning organisation', as described by Paul Newton. The lessons-learnt report from Iraq by Lieutenant General Chris Brown was only belatedly released thanks to a freedom of information request, and that by Brigadier Ben Barry is still not published: open debate and potential reform are therefore stifled at source for fear of reputational damage and political controversy. This book has itself fallen victim to such official paranoia, with six chapters written by still-serving officers withdrawn on the orders of the Ministry of Defence. These fears put at risk lives in theatre. Like many armies in the past, the British Army struggles to foster effective debate within a hierarchical command chain. Mission command is fine in principle, but in practice sits uneasily both with the ambitions of those in more senior positions and with the improved mechanisms for real-time national control. Change occurs continuously in theatre and is prompted from below rather than from above. Education and learning are about recognising change as well as stressing continuity, about framing the right questions rather than producing quick answers. The production of campaign planning, which may be the core discipline of the operational level of war, can become a short cut which forestalls sufficient analysis.

The answers to these conundrums do not lie in turning back: Bagnall produced the solution for his times and for geopolitical realities that no longer apply. So an Army-centric answer focused on Army strengths, while of value at the tactical level, will not address the complexity of modern conflict. It is also not sensible given the diminished resources available to all three Services and to defence collectively. Synergy, not separation, must be the path forward, via a strong and coherent defence staff, which is master of its own education and confident in its own strategic judgement.

Each counter-insurgency campaign is probably more different than is each 'conventional' campaign. The distinction is made solely to stress that different principles of war can apply in different circumstances: that concentration of force may be needed to win a battle but dispersal of effort is needed to sustain effective patrolling and contact with the population. Counter-insurgency can require, simultaneously, kinetic effects and 'hearts and minds', raiding and 'ink spots' of stability, and so the division between it and 'conventional' war-fighting is made in order to stress the conceptual difference, not to hide the many degrees of overlap. Judging those measures of difference and similarity is only possible in theatre. Iraq and Afghanistan may both be Muslim countries in central Asia, but that is just about where the similarities end. The use of comparable vocabulary in both theatres of war by Western forces, not least that a 'surge' is the means and 'exit' is the end, befuddles specific understanding of the individual theatres of operations.

Operational command is, above all, theatre command. At bottom that is the heart of Britain's problem: in its current wars it has not come to terms with this basic principle. The war in Iraq was run from Baghdad; that in Afghanistan is commanded from Kabul. The British have wanted to run both from London, and to treat their areas of operations, Basra or Helmand, as in some senses distinct from the theatre as a whole. Here is another lesson not learnt from Northern Ireland. There the operational centre of gravity of operations, the learning of tactical lessons, and the links between tactics and operations – and even upwards to policy and strategy – were, as Alistair Irwin makes clear, in the province itself. The cycle between tactical change and its operational reflection, aided by outstanding real-time intelligence and by campaign continuity in command structures, was short. Today, no British officer could confidently say where the centre of gravity in the exercise of British operational command lies. Without that clarity, generalship on campaign will remain an even harder task than it needs to be.

List of References

9/11 Commission Report. 2004. Available at: http://govinfo.library.unt.edu/911/report/911Report. pdf [accessed: 13 December 2012].

ADCC. 2006. Army Doctrine and Concepts Committee (ADCC). *Minutes of the 57th Meeting Army Doctrine and Concepts Committee*, held in the Bagnall Room, Upavon on Friday 16th June 2006. ADCC 2/304 dated 26 June 2006.

Agile Warrior Report 2011: Summary of Insights. Directorate of Force Development, distributed at Land Warfare Conference 2011.

Air Power Doctrine (AP 3000). 1991. London: Royal Air Force Staff.

Alderson, A. 2007. Counter-Insurgency: Learn and Adapt? Can We Do Better?, *The British Army Review*, Summer.

Alderson, A. 2013. Operation Iraqi Freedom (2003–2010), in *The Routledge Handbook of U.S. Diplomatic and Military History, 1865 to the Present*, edited by C. Frentzos and A. Thompson (forthcoming).

Allen, M. 2007. *Arabs*. London: Continuum Publishing Group.

Allison, G. 1999. *Essence of Decision: Explaining the Cuba Missile Crisis*, 2nd edition. London: Longman.

Anderson, S. 2012. Victory for families as dead soldiers' relatives told they can sue Government for negligence. *The Independent*, 19 October.

Army Doctrine Publication 1989. *Operations*. London: British Army General Staff.

Arreguin-Toft, I. 2001. *How the Weak Win Wars: A Theory of Asymmetric Conflict*. Cambridge, MA: Harvard University Press.

Baldwin, T. and Webster, P. 2006. London's bridge is falling down. *The Times*, London, 30 November.

Band, J. 2005. British High Command during and after the Falklands campaign, in *The Falklands Conflict Twenty Years On: Lessons for the Future*, edited by S. Badsey, R. Havers and M. Grove. London: Frank Cass.

Barker, A. 2008. Britain sees 'mission' to spread democracy. *The Financial Times*, London, 13 February.

Baumann, A.B. 2008. Clash of organisational cultures? The challenge of integrating civilian and military efforts in stabilisation operations. *Journal of the Royal United Services Institute*, 153(6), 70–73.

BBC. 2012. Army to Lose 17 Units Amid Job Cuts. *BBC Online*, 5 July. Available at: www.bbc. co.uk/news/uk-18716101 [accessed: 12 December 2012].

Bellamy, C. 1990. *The Evolution of Modern Land Warfare: Theory and Practice*. New York: Routledge.

Bennett, R. and Charter, D. 2006. We must rethink the war on terror. *The Times*, London, 2 August.

Biddle, S. and Friedman, J.A. 2008. *The 2006 Lebanon Campaign and the Future of Warfare: Implications for Army and Defense Policy*. Carlisle, PA: Strategic Studies Institute.

Blair, T. 1999. Doctrine of the International Community. Speech at the Economic Club, Chicago, 22 April. Available at: http://keeptonyblairforpm.wordpress.com/blair-speech-transcripts-from-1997-2007/#chicago [accessed: 16 June 2011].

Blitz, J. 2012. Armed Forces fear more manpower cuts. *Financial Times*, 8 December.

Boot, M. 2006. *War Made New*. London: Penguin.

Borger, J. 2011. Afghanistan war tactics are profoundly wrong, says former ambassador. *Guardian*, 25 May.

Brady, B. 2009. Cherie: Iraq was a close call – whatever Tony said. *The Independent*, London, 11 October.

Brafman, O. and Beckstrom, R. 2008. *The Starfish and the Spider: The Unstoppable Power of Leaderless Organisations*. London: Portfolio.

Braithwaite, R. 2006. Mr Blair, it is time to recognise your errors and just go. *The Financial Times*, London, 3 August.

British Army. 1909. *Field Service Regulations, Part I: Operations*. London.

British Army. 1995. *The Conduct of Counter Insurgency Operations*. London: Ministry of Defence.

British Army. 1998. *Army Field Manual Volume 1 Part 9 Counter Insurgency and Peace Support Operations Tactics*. London: Ministry of Defence, re-issued 2001.

British Army. 2001. *Army Field Manual Volume 1 Part 10 Counter-Insurgency Operations (Strategic and Operational Guidelines)*. London: Ministry of Defence.

British Army. 2006. *Stability Operations in Iraq (Op TELIC 2-5): An Analysis from a Land Perspective*. London: Ministry of Defence.

British Maritime Doctrine (BR 1806). 1995. London: Royal Navy Staff.

British Military Doctrine. 2001. London: MOD.

Brown, C. 2007. We were right to invade Iraq, defiant Mr Blair tells families. *The Independent*, London, 16 March, 8.

Brown, D. 2010a. Brown starved the Forces of cash before and after invasion, Hoon tells inquiry. *The Times*, London, 20 January, 18.

Brown, D. 2010b. MoD 'shambles' left troops vulnerable, former minister tells Iraq inquiry. *The Times*, London, 26 January, 11.

Brown, D. 2010c. War was right call, even if I didn't know much about it, admits Brown. *The Times*, London, 6 March, 1.

Browne, T., Hull, L., Horn, O., et al. 2007. Explanations for the increase in mental health problems in UK Reserve Forces who have served in Iraq. *British Journal of Psychiatry*, 190, 484–9.

Caldwell, W. 2008. Changing the organisational culture. *Small Wars Journal*, posted 3 February 2008. Available at: http://smallwarsjournal.com/blog/2008/02/changing-the-organizational-cu-1/ [accessed: 31 May 2011].

Carlin, B. 2006. War in Iraq could turn Muslims to terrorism says Reid. *The Daily Telegraph*, London, 21 November.

Carlyon, L.A. 2002. *Gallipoli*. London: Doubleday.

Chatfield, T. 2009. The bestselling persuaders. *Prospect*, November.

CIA. 2012. CIA announced New Position, Chief of Corporate Learning. *Central Intelligence Agency Press Release*, 5 January. Available at: https://www.cia.gov/news-information/press-releases-statements/2012-press-releasese-statements/cia-announces-new-position-chief-of-corporate-learning.html [accessed: 9 November 2012].

Clarke, A. (ed.). 1984. *The Defense Reform Debate*. Baltimore, MD: Johns Hopkins University Press.

Cloud, D. and Jaffe, G. 2009 *The Fourth Star*. New York: Random House.

Cohen, E. 2002. *Supreme Command*. New York: Simon & Schuster.

Cole, H.G. 2008. *General William E. DePuy: Preparing the Army for Modern War*. Lexington: University Press of Kentucky.

Collier, P. 2008. *The Bottom Billion: Why the Poorest Countries are Failing and What Can be Done About it*. Oxford: Oxford University Press.

Connable, B. and Libicki, M.C. 2010. *How Insurgencies End*. Rand Monograph MG-965.

Connaughton, R.M. 2001. Military intervention and peace-keeping: the reality. *Joint Force Quarterly Review*, 26 July.

Cornish, P. and Dorman, A. 2011. Dr Fox and the Philosopher's Stone: The Alchemy of National Defence in an Age of Austerity. *International Affairs*, 87(2).

Cornish, P. and Grouille, O. 2011. *Land Forces Fit for the 21st Century*. London: Chatham House. Available at: http://www.chathamhouse.org/sites/default/files/public/Research/Inter national%20Security/0711pp_grouille.pdf [accessed: 13 December 2012].

Corum, J.S. 2007. Rethinking U.S. Army Counter-Insurgency Doctrine. *Contemporary Security Policy*, 28(1).

Cowper-Coles, S. 2011. *Cables from Kabul: The Inside Story of the West's Afghanistan Campaign*. London: HarperCollins.

Crane, C.C. 2007. *The Production of FM 3-24*. Presentation to the Counterinsurgency and Peace Support Doctrine Conference, Institut Français des Relations Internationals, Paris, 5 June 2007.

Crick, M. 2009. Is historian the best judge of Iraq war history? *Michael Crick's Blog*, 15 June.

Daily Telegraph editorial. 2007. British Legion says ministers have failed the Forces. *The Daily Telegraph*, London, 14 September 2007, 14.

Dalrymple, T. 2007. Delusions of honesty. *City Journal*, New York.

Dandeker, C., Eversden-French, C., Greenberg, N., Hatch, S., Riley, P., van Staden, L. and Wessely, S. 2010. Laying down their rifles: The changing influences on retention of UK Volunteer reservists returning from Iraq: 2003–2006. *Armed Forces and Society*, 36, 264–89.

Dannatt, R. 2009. *Keynote Speech*, RUSI Land Warfare Conference, 23 June 2009. Available at: http://www.rusi.org/events/ref:E496B737B57852/info:public/infoID:E4A40D3C888784/ [accessed: 13 October 2012].

Dannatt, R. 2010. *Leading from the Front*. London: Random House, paperback edition 2011.

De Atkine, N.B. 1999. *Soldier Scholar or Cocktail Commando?* Available at: http://www.unc.edu/depts/diplomat/AD_Issues/amdipl_10/atkine.html [accessed: 31 May 2011].

de la Billière, P. 1992. *Storm Command*. London: HarperCollins.

Dempsey, M.E. 2010. A Campaign of Learning: Avoiding the Failure of Imagination. *RUSI Journal*, 155(3).

Die Zeit editorial. 2011. Fragile Erfolge am Hindukusch. *Die Zeit*, Hamburg, 27 January.

Donnelly, C.N. 1971. The Soviet concept of Desant. *RUSI Journal*, 116(3), 52–6.

Donnelly, C.N. and Vigor, P.H. 1975. The Soviet threat to Europe. *RUSI Journal*, 126(1), 72.

Economist editorial. 2000. Sierra Leone's agony. *The Economist*, 11 May.

Edwards, R. 2007. Morale of troops in Iraq hit by spin, says commander. *The Daily Telegraph*, London, 15 December.

Engelhardt, T. 2012. *Overwrought Empire: The Discrediting of US Military Power*. Available at: http://www.tomdispatch.com/post/175602/tomgram%3A_engelhardt,_disaster_on_autopilot/ [accessed: 13 December 2012].

Evans, M. 2007. Army chief predicts a 'generation of conflict'. *The Times*, London, 28 August, 1.

Fairweather, J. 2011. *A War of Choice: Honour, Hubris and Sacrifice: The British in Iraq*. London: Jonathan Cape.

Farrell, T. 2008. The Dynamics of British Military Transformation. *International Affairs*, 84(4).

FCOC 2009. *Global Strategic Trends Programme: Future Character of Conflict*. Shrivenham: DCDC.

Fear, N., Jones, M., Murphy, D., et al. 2010. What are the consequences of deployment to Iraq and Afghanistan on the mental health of the UK Armed forces? A cohort study. *Lancet*, 375, 1783–97.

Fergusson, J. 2008. *A Million Bullets: The Real Story of the British Army in Afghanistan*. London: Bantam Press.

Field Manual 100-5. 1976. *Active Defence*. US Army TRADOC.

Field Manual 3-24. 2006. *Counter-insurgency*. US Army TRADOC and Chicago, IL: University of Chicago Press.

Flecker, J.E. 1922. *Hassan: The Story of Hassan of Baghdad, and His Journey to Samarkand: A Play in Five Acts*. London: Heinemann, reprint 1937 edition.

Forster, A. 2012. British Judicial Engagement and the Juridification of the Armed Forces. *International Affairs*, 88(2), 283–300.

Freedman, L. 2006. *The Transformation of Strategic Affairs, Adelphi Paper 379*. London: IISS.

French, D. 2001. *Raising Churchill's Army*. Oxford: OUP.

Fuerth L.S. with Faber, E.M.H. 2012. *Anticipatory Governance Practical Upgrades: Equipping the Executive Branch to Cope with Increasing Speed and Complexity of Major Challenges*. Washington DC: NDU.

Fukuyama, Y.F. 1989. The end of history? *The National Interest*, 16(summer), 3–18.

Fuller, J.F.C. 1926. *The Foundations of the Science of War*. London: Hutchinson.

Galula, D. 1963. *Pacification in Algeria 1956–1958*, reprinted by RAND 2006.

Galula, D. 1964. *Counter-insurgency Warfare: Theory and Practice*. New York: Praeger, reprint 2006.

Garmone, J. 2010. Gates Orders Marine Corps Force Structure Review. *American Forces Press Service*, 12 August.

Garvin, D.A., Edmondson A.C. and Gino, F. 2008. *Is Yours a Learning Organization?* Cambridge, MA: Harvard Business Review.

Gentile, G.P. 2009a. A strategy of tactics: Population-centric COIN and the Army. *Parameters*, Autumn.

Gentile, G.P. 2009b. Let's Build an Army to Will *All* Wars. *Joint Force Quarterly*, 52(1), 27–33.

Gladwell, M. 2005. *Blink: The Power of Thinking Without Thinking*. London: Penguin.

Glantz, D. 1991. *Soviet Military Operational Art*. London: Frank Cass.

Gledhill, R. and Brown, D. 2009. Mr Blair 'would have gone to war without Iraqi WMD'. *The Times*, London, 12 December, 1.

Glenny, M. 1990. *The Rebirth of History: Eastern Europe in the Age of Democracy*. London: Penguin Books.

Global Strategic Trends Out to 2040, 4th Edition. 2010. Shrivenham: DCDC.

Gooch, J. (ed.). 1990. *Decisive Campaigns of the Second World War*. London: Frank Cass.

Gooch, J. 2006. History and the Nature of Strategy, in *The Past as Prologue*, edited by W. Murray and R.H. Sinnreich. Cambridge: Cambridge University Press.

Gordon, A. 2006 Military Transformation in Long Periods of Peace, in *The Past as Prologue*, edited by W. Murray and R.H. Sinnreich. Cambridge: Cambridge University Press.

Gray, C.S. 2007. *Another Bloody Century: Future Warfare*. London: Weidenfeld and Nicolson.

Gray, C.S. 2009. *Understanding Airpower: Bonfire of the Vanities*. Maxwell: US Air Force Research Institute.

Greenberg, N., Langston, V., Everitt, B., et al. 2010. A cluster randomized controlled trial to determine the efficacy of Trauma Risk Management (TRiM) in a military population. *Journal of Traumatic Stress*, 23(4), 430–6.

Grey, S. 2009. *Operation Snakebite: The Explosive True Story of an Afghan Desert Siege*. London: Viking.

Griffin, S. 2005. *Joint Operations: A Short History*. London: MOD.

Grint, K. 2008. Wicked Problems and Clumsy Solutions: The Role of Leadership. *Clinical Leader*, 1, 2 December.

Haass, R.N. 2009. *War of Necessity, War of Choice: A Memoir of Two Iraq Wars*. New York: Simon & Schuster, preface to the 2010 paperback edition.

Haddon-Cave, C. 2009. *The Nimrod Review*. London: HMSO.

Harding, T. 2008a. Troops killed 'by lack of basic equipment'. *The Daily Telegraph*, London, 16 February, 9.

Harding, T. 2008b. Iranian Hostage Royal Navy Captain Sacked. *The Daily Telegraph*, London, 28 July.

Harnden, T. 2010. Americans blame Britain for rise of Islamic extremism. *The Daily Telegraph*, London, 30 December.

Harris, J.P. 2002. The General Staff and the coming of war 1933–39, in *The British General Staff: Reform and Innovation c.1890–1939*, edited by D. French and B. Holden Reid. London: Frank Cass.

Harris, J.P. 2006. Obstacles to Innovation and Readiness, in *The Past as Prologue*, edited by W. Murray and R.H. Sinnreich. Cambridge: Cambridge University Press.

Haynes, D., Lloyd, A., Kiley, S. and Coghlan, T. 2010. The officers' mess. *The Times*, London, 9 June.

HCDC (House of Commons Defence Select Committee). 2004. *Lessons of Iraq*, Third Report of Session 2003–04, 1. London: The Stationery Office.

Helm, T. 2006. Blair admits Afghan error. *The Daily Telegraph*, London, 21 November, 2.

Hennessey, P. 2009. *The Junior Officers' Reading Club: Killing Time and Fighting Wars*. London: Penguin.

Higginson, J. 2009. Britain 'was not ready to invade Iraq'. *Metro*, London, 4 December, 12.

Hilder, J. 2008. Areas of Baghdad fall to militias as Iraqi Army falters in Basra. *The Times*, London, 27 March.

HLOC. 2007. *The UK High Level Operational Concept*. Shrivenham, DCDC.

Hoffman, F. 2007a. Neo-Classical Counterinsurgency? *Parameters*, Summer 2007.

Hoffman, F. 2007b. Conflict in the 21st Century: The Rise of Hybrid Wars. *Potomac Institute for Policy Studies*, December.

Hoge, C.W., Castro, C.A., Messer, S.C., et al. 2004. Combat duty in Iraq and Afghanistan, mental health problems, and barriers to care. *New England Journal of Medicine*, 351, 13–22.

Holden Reid, B. 1996. *Studies in British Military Thought: Debates with Fuller and Liddel Hart*. Lincoln, NE: University of Nebraska Press.

Holloway, A. 2009. How our pliant generals became Mr Blair's yes men. *The Daily Mail*, London, 8 December, 4.

Holmes, R. 2006. I'm angry that no one seems to know what our soldiers have to put up with in Iraq. *The Daily Telegraph*, London, 2 April.

Hooper, A. and Potter, J. 2001. *Intelligent Leadership: Creating a Passion for Change*. London: Random House.

Hopkins, N. 2011. RAF Tackles Taliban in Afghanistan – Using Joysticks in Las Vegas. *Guardian*, 5 July.

Hotopf, M., Hull, L., Fear, N., et al. 2006. The health of UK military personnel who deployed to the 2003 Iraq war: A cohort study. *Lancet*, 367, 1731–41.

Howard, M. 1974. Military science in an age of peace. *RUSI Journal*, 119(2), 6.

Hughes, C. 2009. British troops pull out of Iraq, *Daily Mirror*, 1 May.

Husseini, K. 2004. *The Kite Runner*. New York: Riverhead Books.

Inge, P. 1996. The roles and challenges of the British armed forces. *The RUSI Journal*, 141(1).

Iron, R. 2008. Britain's Longest War: Northern Ireland 1967–2007, in *Counterinsurgency in Modern Warfare*, edited by D. Marston and C. Malkasian. Oxford: Osprey.

Irvine, C. 2009. Armed Forces were 'smug' and 'complacent' about Afghanistan. *The Daily Telegraph*, 30 January.

ISAF. 2008. *ISAF Troops (Placemap)*. Available at: http://www.nato.int/isaf/docu/epub/pdf/ placemat.pdf [accessed: 12 May 2011].

ITN 2006. ITN News Archive, John Reid (Home Secretary) Speech on Anti-Terrorism Measures, 31 October. Available at: http://www.itnsource.com/shotlist/ITN/2006/10/31/R31100601/?v=1 [accessed: 26 February 2013].

Jackson, M. 2006. *The Richard Dimbleby Lecture*, London, 7 December 2006. Available at: http://www.bbc.co.uk/pressoffice/pressreleases/stories/2006/12_december/07/dimbleby.shtml [accessed: 12 December 2012].

Jackson, W.G.F. and Bramall, E.N.W. 1992. *The Chiefs: The Story of the United Kingdom Chiefs of Staff*. London: Brassey's.

JDN 4/05. 2006. *The Comprehensive Approach*. London: MOD.

JDP 0-01. 2008. *Joint Doctrine Publication 0-01, British Defence Doctrine*, 3rd edition. Shrivenham: DCDC.

JDP 3-40. 2009. *Security and Stabilisation: The Military Contribution*. Shrivenham: DCDC.

Jermy, S. 2011. *Strategy for Action*. London: Knightstone.

Johnson, D.D.P. 2004. *Overconfidence and War: The Havoc and Glory of Positive Illusions*. Cambridge, MA: Harvard University Press.

Johnston, P. 2006a. Adopt our values or stay away, Mr Blair tells migrants. *The Daily Telegraph*, London, 9 December, 1.

Johnston, P. 2006b. The 'what have we done?' moment when Labour faced its multicultural monster. *The Daily Telegraph*, London, 9 December.

Jomini, A.-H. 1838. *The Art of War*. Translated by G.H. Mendell and W.P. Craighill, 1862. Whitefish, MT: Kessinger Publishing, 2004 edition.

Jones, G. 2006. Iraq invasion a disaster, Mr Blair admits on Arab TV. *The Daily Telegraph*, London, 18 November, 1.

Jones, N., Roberts, P. and Greenberg, N. 2003. Peer-group risk assessment: A post-traumatic management strategy for hierarchical organizations. *Occupational Medicine*, 53, 469–75.

Jünger, E. 2004. *Storm of Steel*. London: Penguin Classics.

JWP 3-50. 2004. *Joint Warfare Publication 3-50; The Military Contribution to Peace Support Operations*, 2nd edition. Shrivenham: DCDC. Available at: http://pksoi.army.mil/doctrine_ concepts/documents/UK/jwp3_50.pdf [accessed: 11 May 2011].

Kagan, F.W. 2006. *Finding the Target: The Transformation of American Military Policy*. New York: Encounter Books.

Kahneman, D., Slovic, P. and Tversky, A. 1982. *Judgment Under Uncertainty: Heuristics and Biases*. Cambridge: Cambridge University Press.

Kahneman, D. 2011. *Thinking, Fast and Slow*. London: Penguin.

Kampfner, J. 2004. *Blair's Wars*. London: Free Press.

Keegan, J. 1999. Please, Mr Blair, never take such a risk again. *The Daily Telegraph*, 6 June.

Kemp, R. 2010. When the going got tough, Brown melted away. *The Times*, London, 6 March, 22.

Kilcullen, D.J. 2006. *Three Pillars of Counter Insurgency*. Remarks delivered at the US Government Counter-insurgency Conference, Washington DC, 28 September.

Kilcullen, D.J. 2007a. New paradigms for 21st century conflict. *Countering the Terrorist Mentality*, special edition, US Dept of State electronic journal, May.

Kilcullen, D. 2007b. *Counter-insurgency in Iraq: Theory and Practice*. Available at: http://usacac. army.mil/cac2/coin/repository/Dr_Kilcullen_COIN_Brief(Sep07).ppt [accessed: 7 February 2013].

Kilcullen, D. 2007c. *The Next Twenty Weeks*, presentation at COIN Center for Excellence, Taji, Iraq, June 2.

King, A. 2010. *Military Command in the Next Decade,* Annual Chatham House Defence Lecture, London, 23 September 2010.

Kingstone, H. 2007. Toppled in Baghdad, clueless in Whitehall. *Times Online*, 21 October.

Kirkup, J. 2009. Bob Ainsworth: Voters won't back extra spending on defence, Forces told. *The Daily Telegraph*, London, 15 September, 1.

Kirkup, J. 2010a. Treasury left MoD short of cash, inquiry hears. *The Daily Telegraph*, London, 9 March, 8.

Kirkup, J. 2010b. Brown admits defence spending error. *The Times*, London, 18 March, 4.

Kiszely, J.P. 1997. The British Army and approaches to warfare since 1945, in *Military Power: Land Warfare in Theory and Practice*, edited by B. Holden Reid. London: Frank Cass, Ch. 5.

Kitson, F. 1971. *Low Intensity Operations: Subversion, Insurgency, Peace-keeping*. London: Faber and Faber.

Kitson, F. 1981. *Practical Aspects of Counter Insurgency*, presented at the Kermit Roosevelt Lecture in May 1981 (Upavon: Tactical Doctrine Retrieval Cell, Annex A to DCinC 8109 dated 11 June 1981).

Kitson, F. 1997. *Bunch of Five*. London: Faber and Faber.

Lamb, C. 2008. Over and out. *The Sunday Times*, London, 20 July, 15.

Lamb, G. 2009. Oral evidence to the Iraq Inquiry on 9 December 2009. Available at: http://www. iraqinquiry.org.uk/media/41885/20091209pmlamb-final.pdf [accessed: 16 June 2011].

Lampel, J. 1998. Towards the Learning Organization, in *Strategy Safari*, edited by H. Mintzberg, B. Ahlstrand and J. Lampel. New York: The Free Press.

Langston, V., Greenberg, N. and Gould, M. 2007. Culture: What is its effect on stress in the Military? *Military Medicine*, 172, 931–5.

Lawson, D. 2010. Ooh, that Miliband, he'll scratch your eyes out. *The Sunday Times*, London, 3 January.

Lawton K. and Silim, A. 2012. *Tough Choices Ahead: Illustrating the Choices and Trade-offs in the Next Spending Review*. Institute for Public Policy Research. Available at: http://observgo. uquebec.ca/observgo/fichiers/57785_Pressures-and-priorities.pdf [accessed: 13 December 2012].

Leake, C. 2006. Army fury as chief in Afghanistan is told he won't get vital armour. *The Daily Mail*, London, 18 November.

Legault, A. 2000. NATO intervention in Kosovo: The legal context. *Canadian Military Journal*, Spring 2000.

Leonhard, R. 1991. *The Art of Maneuver*. Novato, CA: Presidio Press.

Levene, P.K. 2011. *Defence Reform: An Independent Report into the Structure and Management of the MOD*. London: MOD.

Levitt, S.D. and Dubner, S.J. 2009. *SuperFreakonomics: Global Cooling, Patriotic Prostitutes, and Why Suicide Bombers Should Buy Life Insurance*. New York: William Morrow.

Lind, W. 1985. *The Maneuver Warfare Handbook*. Boulder, CO: Westview Press.

Little, P. 2009. Lessons Unlearnt: A Former Officer's Perspective on the British Army at War. *RUSI Journal*, 154(3), 10–16.

Lloyd George, D. 1909. On the peers of the House of Lords, in a speech in Newcastle, 9 October 1909, printed in the *Manchester Guardian*, 11 October.

Luvaas, J. 1965. *The Education of an Army*. London: Cassell.

Macdonald, K. 2009. Intoxicated by power, Mr Blair tricked us into war. *The Times*, London, 14 December, 3.

Mader, M. 2004. *In Pursuit of Conceptual Excellence: The Evolution of British Military-Strategic Doctrine in the Post Cold-War Era 1989–2002*. New York: Peter Lang.

Mahan, A.T. 2003. *The Problem of Asia*. New Brunswick, NJ: Transaction.

Mahnken, T.G. 2007. Strategic Theory, in *Strategy in the Contemporary World*, edited by J. Baylis, J. Wirtz, and C. Gray. Oxford: Oxford University Press.

Mail editorial 2006. Government stunned by Army chief's Iraq blast. *The Daily Mail*, London, 13 October.

Mansoor, P.R. 2009. The British Army and the Lessons of the Iraq War. *The British Army Review*, 149.

Matthews, M.M. 2008. *We Were Caught Unprepared: The 2006 Hezbollah-Israeli War*. Long War Series Occasional Paper 26, Leavenworth: US Army Combined Arms Centre.

Meyer, C. 2005. *DC Confidential: The Controversial Memoirs of Britain's Ambassador to the US at the Time of 9/11 and the Run-up to the Iraq War*. London: Weidenfeld and Nicolson.

Mintzberg, H., Ahlstrand, B. and Lampel, J. 1998. *Strategy Safari*. New York: The Free Press.

Mockaitis, T.R. 1990. *British Counterinsurgency, 1919–1960*. London: Macmillan.

MOD. 2006. *Stability Operations in Iraq (OP TELIC 2-5)*. London: MOD.

Montgomery, B.L. 1942. *Some Brief Notes for Senior Officers on the Conduct of Battle*. Eighth Army.

Moon, Ban Ki. 2008. *The Situation in Afghanistan and its Implications for International Peace and Security*. Report of the Secretary-General. Available at: http://www.unama-afg.org/docs/_UN-Docs/_repots-SG/2008/08march06-SG-report-SC-situation-in-afghanistan.pdf [accessed: 11 May 2008].

Mulligan, K., Jones, N., Woodhead, C., et al. 2012. Mental health of UK military personnel while on deployment in Iraq: The Operational Mental Health Needs Evaluation (OMHNE). *British Journal of Psychology*, 197, 405–10.

Murray, W. 2006. Thoughts on Military History and the Profession of Arms, in *The Past as Prologue*, edited by W. Murray and R.H. Sinnreich. Cambridge: Cambridge University Press.

Murray, W. and Scales, R.H. Jr. 2003. *The Iraq War: A Military History*. Cambridge, MA: Harvard University Press.

Nagl, J.A. 2002. *Learning to Eat Soup with a Knife: Counter-insurgency Lessons from Malaya and Vietnam*. Westport, CT: Greenwood Press.

Nagl, J.A. 2008. Speech at the National Press Club, 23 July. Reported at: http://www.cnas.org/node/334 [accessed: 11 May 2011].

Nagl, J.A. 2009. Let's Win the Wars We're In. *Joint Force Quarterly*, 52(1), 20–26.

NATO. 2008. *NATO's Contribution to a Comprehensive Approach*. Available at: http://www.nato.int/docu/comm/2008/0804-bucharest/presskit.pdf [accessed: 11 May 2011].

Nielsen, S.C. 2010. *An Army Transformed: The US Army's Post-Vietnam Recovery and the Dynamics of Change in Military Organizations*. Letort Paper, Carlisle: US Army War College.

NATO Press Release. 2006. *Riga Summit Declaration Issued by the Heads of State and Government*. 29 November.

Naveh, S. 1997. *In Pursuit of Military Excellence: The Evolution of Operational Art*. London: Frank Cass.

Norman, M. 2007. Tony Blair's fatal craving for attention. *The Independent*, London, 23 February.

North, R. 2009. *Ministry of Defeat: The British War in Iraq 2003–2009*. London: Continuum Books.

Oliver, J. 2010. Now Hoon savages PM over Afghan war. *The Sunday Times*, London, 10 January, 1.

Orczy, E. 1903. *The Scarlet Pimpernel*. New York: Modern Library, reprinted 2002.

Owen, D. 2008. Inside Blair's brain. *The Sunday Times News Review*, London, 16 March.

Parris, M. 2003. Are we witnessing the madness of Tony Blair? *Times Online*, 29 March.

Parris, M. 2011. These buffoons don't deserve our salutes. They messed up in Iraq and Afghanistan … are our military leaders actually any good? *The Times*, 25 June.

Peters, R. 1996. Our Soldiers Their Cities. *Parameters*, Spring, 43–50.

Peters, R. 2007. Progress and Peril, New Counterinsurgency Manual Cheats on the History Exam. *Armed Forces Journal International*.

Phillips, M. 2011. *Exercise AGILE WARRIOR and the Future Development of UK Land Forces*. RUSI Occasional Paper, Available at: http://www.rusi.org/downloads/assets/agilewarrior.pdf [accessed: 13 December 2012].

Philp, C., Coghlan, T. and Jagger, S. 2009. Taleban-style laws for women put chances of NATO troop surge at risk. *The Times*, London, 3 April.

Pope-Hennessy, L.H.R. 1912. The place of doctrine in war. *Edinburgh Review*, 215(439), 1–30.

Powell, C. 1992. U.S. Forces: The way ahead. *Foreign Affairs*, winter.

Prins, G. 2002. *The Heart of War*. London: Routledge.

Prins, G. and Salisbury, R. 2008. Risk, threat and security: The case of the United Kingdom. *RUSI Journal*, London, February 2008.

Quinlivan, J.T. 1995. Force requirements in stability operations. *Parameters*, winter, 59–69.

Quinlivan, J.T. 2003. Burden of victory: The painful arithmetic of stability operations. *Rand Review*, 27(2).

Quintana, E. 2012. *Austere Air Power? British Air and Space Power in the Post-SDST Environment*. RUSI Workshop Report, distributed at the RAF Chief of Air Staff's 2012 Airpower Conference.

Radford, T. 2003. Blair mad? That's a barmy idea. Psychiatrist rejects magazine diagnosis of Blair as a psychopath. *Guardian*, London, 1 December.

Ramo, J. 2009. *The Age of the Unthinkable*. London: Little, Brown.

RAND. 2006. *Counter-insurgency in Afghanistan* (proof copy). Santa Monica, CA: RAND.

Reflections on Intervention: 35th Ditchley Foundation Lecture. 1998. Wilton Park, 26 June.

Reuters. 2012. Iran says Hezbollah drone sent into Israel proves its capabilities. *Reuters Online*, 14 October. Available at: http://www.reuters.com/article/2012/10/14/us-lebanon-israel-drone-iran-idUSBRE89D09N20121014 [accessed: 13 December 2012].

Richards, D. 2008. European armies: The challenge, in *Perspectives on International Security*, edited by T. Huxley and A. Nicoll. London: IISS Adelphi Paper 400-401, 53–62.

Richards, D. 2012. RUSI Annual 2012 Chief of Defence Staff Lecture, RUSI, London, 17 December. Available at: http://www.rusi.org/cdslectures/ [accessed: 19 December 2012].

Richards, D. and Mills, G. (eds). 2011. *Victory Amongst People: Lessons from Countering Insurgency and Stabilising Failed States*. London: RUSI.

Richardson, R. 2009. The Joint Narrative: Describing the Future Environment and Joint Operations. *Joint Force Quarterly*, 54, 81–6.

Rifkind, M. 2008. Our 100 dead in Afghanistan did not lay down their lives in vain. *The Daily Telegraph*, London, 10 June, 22.

Rittel, H. and Webber, M.M. 1973. Dilemmas in a General Theory of Planning, *Policy Sciences*, 4.

Romjue, J.L. 1984. *From Active Defense to AirLand Battle*. US Army TRADOC.

Rose, M. 1998. *Fighting for Peace*. London: The Harvill Press.

Rosen, S.P. 1991. *Winning the Next War: Innovation and the Modern Military*. Ithaca, NY: Cornell University Press.

Sands, S. 2006. Sir Richard Dannatt: A very honest General. Daily Mail, 12 October. Available at: www.dailymail.co.uk/news/article-410175/Sir-Richard-Dannatt--A-honest-General.html [accessed: 7 August 2012].

Savkin, V. 1972. *The Principles of Operational Art and Tactics*. Moscow. Translated and published by USAF in 1985, as part of the USAF's Soviet Military Thought series.

SDSR. 2010. *Securing Britain in an Age of Uncertainty: The Strategic Defence and Security Review*. London: HMSO. Available at: https://update.cabinetoffice.gov.uk/resource-library/strategic-defence-and-security-review-securing-britain-age-uncertainty [accessed: 13 December 2012].

Senge, P. 1990. *The Fifth Discipline: The Art and Practice of the Learning Organisation*. New York: Currency/Doubleday; 2nd revised edition. New York: Random House Business Books, 2006.

Shaw, G.B. 1934. The True Joy of Life, in *Seasons of Life: A Poetic Anthology*, compiled by N. Collins 2000. New York: Prometheus Books.

Shipman, T. 2009. The smoking gun. *The Daily Mail*, London, 30 November.

Sieghart, M.A. 2006. The two Tony Blairs: Superman and everyman. *Times Online*, 23 March.

Simms, B. 2001. *Unfinest Hour: Britain and the Destruction of Bosnia*. London: Penguin, revised edition, 2002.

Simpkin, R. 1985. *Race to the Swift: Thoughts on Twenty-First Century Warfare*. London: Brassey's.

Simpkin, R. 1987. *Deep Battle: The Brainchild of Marshal Tukhachevskii*. London: Brassey's.

Simpson, E. 2012. *War from the Ground Up: Twenty-First Century Combat as Politics*. London: Hurst.

Simpson, H.R. 1999. *The Paratroopers of the French Foreign Legion: Vietnam to Bosnia*. Oxford: Brassey's.

Sloboda, J. and Abbott, C. 2004. The 'Blair Doctrine' and after: Five years of humanitarian intervention. 21 April [Online: Open Democracy]. Available at: http://www.opendemocracy.net/globalization-institutions_government/article_1857.jsp [accessed: 31 May 2011].

Sloggett, D. 2007. Influence operations: A nexus of sociological, anthropological, psychological and cultural perspectives. Unpublished paper.

Smith, G. 2008. Talking to the Taliban. *The Globe and Mail*, Toronto. Available at: http://v1.theglobeandmail.com/talkingtothetaliban/ [accessed: 23 May 2011].

Smith, R. 2005. *The Utility of Force: The Art of War in the Modern World*. London: Allen Lane.

Spillius, A. and Farmer, B. 2009. President seeks to 'dismantle' al-Qaeda. *The Daily Telegraph*, London, 3 December, 4.

Steele, J. 2008. Guys, I'm afraid we haven't got a clue. *Guardian*, London, 21 January.

Stewart, R. 2006. *Occupational Hazards: My Time Governing in Iraq*, 2nd edition. London: Picador.

Stilwell, J. 1949. *The Stilwell Papers*; arranged and edited by White, T.H. London: Macdonald.

Stirrup, J. 2009. *Annual Chief of Defence Staff Lecture* at the Royal United Services Lecture, 3 December. Available at: http://www.rusi.org/events/past/ref:E4B184DB05C4E3/ [accessed: 31 May 2011].

Storr, J. 2002. The Commander as Expert, in *The Big Issue*, edited by D. Potts, SCSI Occasional. Upavon: SCSI, 95–111.

Storr, J. 2102. Letter in the *RUSI Journal*, 157(5), 4.

Strachan, H. 1997. *The Politics of the British Army*. Oxford: Oxford University Press.

Strachan, H. 2005. The lost meaning of strategy. *Survival*, 47(3), 33–54.

Strachan, H. 2010. Operational art in Britain, 1909–2009, in *The Evolution of Operational Art: From Napoleon to the Present*, edited by J.A. Olsen and M. van Creveld. Oxford: Oxford University Press.

SU. 2007a. *Helping Countries Recover from Violent Conflict*. PCRU Discussion Paper dated July.

SU. 2007b. *The UK Approach to Stabilisation: A Stabilisation Unit Guidance Note*, working draft dated 29 November.

Sunstein, C. and Thaler, R. 2009. *Nudge: Improving Decisions About Health, Wealth and Happiness*. London: Penguin.

Synott, H. 2008. *Bad Days in Basra: My Turbulent Times as Britain's Man in Southern Iraq*. London: I.B. Tauris.

Taleb, N.N. 2005. *The Black Swan: The Impact of the Highly Improbable*. London: Penguin.

Taylor, M. 2009. *Left Brain, Right Brain: Human Nature and Political Values*. Talk at RSA, London, 29 October.

Thiel, J. 2011. COIN manpower ratios: Debunking the 10 to 1 ratio and surges. *Small Wars Journal*, 15 January.

Tisdall, S. and MacAskill, E. 2006. America's long war. *Guardian*, London, 15 February.

Tkalec, M. 2000. Neocolonialism with a human face. *Berliner Zeitung*, 21 June.

Tom, D. and Barrons, R. 2006. *The Business General*. London: Vermilion.

Tomes, R.R. 2012. An Historical Review of US Defense Strategy from Vietnam to Operation Iraqi Freedom. *Defense and Security Analysis*, 28(4), 303–15.

Tripp, C. 2007. *A History of Iraq*, 3rd edition. Cambridge: Cambridge University Press.

Tuchman, B.W. 1984. *The March of Folly: From Troy to Vietnam*. New York: Alfred A Knopf.

Tversky, A. and Kahneman, D. 1974. Judgment under uncertainty: Heuristics and biases. *Science*, 185, 1124–30.

UK Glossary of Joint and Multinational Terms and Definitions (JWP 0-01.1). London: MOD.

United Nations, 1992. *Agenda for Peace*. 17 June.

US Army. 2004. *Field Manual–Interim No. 3-07.22 Counterinsurgency Operations*. Washington DC: Headquarters Department of the Army.

US Army. 2005. *Field Manual 3-07.22 Counterinsurgency Operations* (Draft). Washington DC: Headquarters Department of the Army.

US Army. 2007. *2007 Army Modernisation Plan*, Washington DC: Headquarters Department of the Army.

US DOD. 2009. *Capstone Concept for Joint Operations*, Version 3.0, 15 January 2009. Washington DC: US Department of Defense. Available at: http://www.jfcom.mil/newslink/storyarchive/2009/CCJO_2009.pdf [accessed: 13 December 2012].

US DOD. 2012. *Joint Operational Access Concept (JOAC)*, Version 1.0, 17 January 2012. Washington DC: US Department of Defense. Available at: http://www.defense.gov/pubs/pdfs/JOAC_Jan%202012_Signed.pdf [accessed: 12 December 2012].

von Clausewitz, C.P.G. 1832. *On War*, translated and edited by M. Howard and P. Paret, 1989. Princeton, NJ: Princeton University Press.

Wavell, A.P. 1942. *Generals and Generalship: The Lees Knowles Lectures*, delivered at Trinity College, Cambridge in 1939. London: Macmillan.

Webster, P. 2009. Sycophant Mr Blair tricked us into war. *The Times*, London, 14 December, 25.

Webster, P. 2010. We didn't think it through on Iraq, admits Blair aide. *The Times*, London, 17 March, 8.

Wessely, S. 2005. Risk, psychiatry and the military. *British Journal of Psychiatry*, 186 and 459–66.

Wessely, S. (ed.). 2006. The health of Gulf War veterans. *Philosophical Transactions of the Royal Society*, 361.

Wheatcroft, G. 2007. *Yo Blair*. London: Politico's.

Wilson, G. 2007. Brown wants a 'New Order' based on British values. *The Daily Telegraph*, London, 18 January.

Winton, H. 1988. *To Change an Army*. Lawrence, KS: University Press of Kansas.

World Bank. 2007. *Service Delivery and Governance at the Sub-national Level in Afghanistan*. New York: World Bank.

Wynne-Jones, J. 2009. Blair saw himself as a holy warrior, says his mentor. *The Sunday Telegraph*, London, 24 May.

Yarger, H.R. 2006. *Strategic Theory for the 21st Century: The Little Book on Big Strategy*. Carlisle: Strategic Studies Institute.

Zavis, A. 2007. As British draw down, violence in Basra is up. *Los Angeles Times*, 30 April.

Glossary

A400M	Transport aircraft, built by Airbus Industries; the Royal Air Force is due to receive 25 aircraft starting in 2011
Abizaid, John	General John Philip Abizaid, b. 1951, US Army officer; Commander of US Central Command 2003–2007
Abu Ghrayb	A suburb of Baghdad which houses the main Baghdad prison, used during the Saddam regime, the Coalition and by current the Iraqi Government
ACSC	Advanced Command and Staff Course, a joint course attended by selected officers at lieutenant colonel rank
Adams, Gerry	Irish politician, alleged to be a past commander in the Provisional Irish Republican Army, who played a leading role in the Northern Ireland peace process
ADZ	Afghan Development Zone
Aegis Group	Aegis Defence Services, a British private security company founded in 2002
AFRC	Armed Forces Revolutionary Council in Sierra Leone
Agile Warrior	British Army research and experimentation programme, conducted by Force Development and Training Command
Alikozai	A sub-tribe of the Pashtuns in Afghanistan
Allawi, Ayad	Ayad Allawi, b. 1945, Iraqi politician; interim prime minister 2004–2005
Al-Qaeda	International militant Islamist group founded by Osama bin Laden
Al-Rubaie	Mowaffak al-Rubaie, Iraqi National Security Adviser in 2008–2009
Al-Zarqawi	Abu Musab al-Zarqawi, 1966–2006, Leader of al-Qaeda in Iraq
ANA	Afghan National Army
Anbar Awakening	Common name of the Sons of Iraq programme which originated in the Anbar region of Iraq, in which Sunni militias and insurgent groups pledged allegiance to the Government of Iraq to fight against al-Qaeda in Iraq
Annan, Kofi	Secretary-General of the United Nations 1997–2006
ANP	Afghan National Police
ANSF	Afghan National Security Forces
APC	Armoured personnel carrier
Arba'een	Important Shia festival
Army 2020	The British plan for the restructuring of the army
ARRC	Allied Command Europe Rapid Reaction Corps
Ba'ath Party	Arab political party; the party of Saddam Hussein in Iraq
Badr	An Iraqi political party (previously known as the Badr Brigades)
Bagnall, Field Marshal	Field Marshal Sir Nigel Thomas Bagnall, 1927–2002; British Army officer

Baloch, Baluch	Ethnic group primarily found in Baluchistan in west Pakistan, south Afghanistan and east Iran
BAOR	British Army of the Rhine
Barakzai	A Pashtun tribe in Afghanistan and Pakistan
Barno	General David W. Barno, US commander of Combined Forces Command-Afghanistan 2003–2005
Bastion, Camp	The main UK–US base in Helmand Province
Belfast Agreement (Good Friday)	A political agreement signed in Belfast on Good Friday, 10 April 1998, that marked a significant step in the end of the Northern Ireland conflict
Bin Laden	Osama bin Laden, 1957–2011, the founder of al-Qaeda
Blackwater	US-based private military company and security consulting firm
Blair, Cherie	Cherie Blair (*née* Booth), QC, b. 1954, wife of Tony Blair
Blair, Tony	Anthony (Tony) Charles Lynton Blair, b. 1953, former British Labour Party politician and British Prime Minister 1997–2007
Blue Berets, Blue Helmets	Forces or individuals assigned to United Nations peacekeeping operations
Bonn talks	The negotiations in Bonn in 2001, Germany, resulting in the Bonn Agreement intended to recreate the State of Afghanistan after the toppling of the Taliban regime in 2001
Boutros-Ghali, Boutros	Secretary-General of the United Nations 1992–1996
Bremer, Paul	Lewis Paul Bremer III, b. 1941, US diplomat and the head of the Coalition Provisional Authority in Iraq 2003–2004
Brown, Gordon	James Gordon Brown, b. 1951, British Labour Party politician and British Prime Minister 2007–2010
B Specials	The Ulster Special Constabulary, a reserve police force in Northern Ireland, disbanded in May 1970
Bush, George W.	George Walker Bush, b. 1946, US politician and President 2001–2009
Butler, Lord	Frederick Edward Robin Butler, Baron Butler of Brockwell, b. 1938, British civil servant; chaired an inquiry in 2004 into the use of intelligence in the lead up to the 2003 invasion of Iraqi
C2	Command and control
C4ISTAR	Command, Control, Communications, Computers, Intelligence, Surveillance, Target Acquisition and Reconnaissance
C17	Boeing C-17 Globemaster III, strategic heavy lift transport aircraft
Campbell, Alastair	Alastair John Campbell, b. 1957, British journalist and political aide; Director of Communications and Strategy to Prime Minister tony Blair 1997–2003
Carter, Nick	Lieutenant General Nicholas Patrick Carter; British Army officer
Casey, George	George William Casey, Jr, b. 1948, US Army officer and commander Multi-National Force – Iraq 2004–2007
CCO	Centre for Complex Operations
CDF	Civil Defence Force in Sierra Leone
CDS	Chief of Defence Staff
CENTAF	US Central Command Air Forces

CENTCOM	US Central Command
CERP	Commander's Emergency Response Program
CFE	US Army Counter-Insurgency Center for Excellence at Taji, Iraq
CGS	Chief of the General Staff
Chamberlain, Neville	(Arthur) Neville Chamberlain, 1869–1940, British Prime Minister 1937–1940
Chatham House Rules	A principle of confidentiality in which participants at a meeting are free to use information received, but not divulge the identity of affiliation of the speaker
Chechen fighters	Rebels who fought against the Russian Federation for the independence of Chechnya during the First and Second Chechen Wars 1994–1996 and 1999–2009
Chernomyrdin, Viktor	Viktor Stepanovich Chernomyrdin, 1938–2010, Russian Prime Minister 1992–1998
Cheney, Dick	Richard Bruce 'Dick' Cheney, b. 1941, US Vice President 2001–2009
Chilcot Inquiry	The UK Government-sponsored inquiry into the UK's role in the Iraq War, under the chairmanship of Sir John Chilcot
Churchill, Winston	Sir Winston Leonard Spencer Churchill, 1874–1965, British Prime Minister 1940–1945 and 1951–1955
CIGS	Chief of the Imperial General Staff
CinC	Commander in Chief
CJTF-7	Combined Joint Task Force 7
Clark, Wesley 'Wes'	Wesley Kanne Clark, Sr, b. 1944, US Army officer and Supreme Allied Commander Europe 1997–2000
Clausewitz, Carl von	Carl Philipp Gottfried von Clausewitz 1780–1831, Prussian soldier and German military theorist
Clinton, Bill	William Jefferson Clinton III, b. 1946, US President 1993–2001
CN	Counter Narcotics
COB	Contingency Operating Base
COBR	Cabinet Office Briefing Room
COIN	Counter-insurgency
COM CENTCOM	Commander Central Command
COMISAF	Commander International Security and Assistance Force
COMKFOR	Commander Kosovo Force
Comprehensive Approach	The coordination and combination of both military and non-military activities in an operation
Conté, President	Lansana Conté, 1934–2008, President of Guinea 1984–2008
COS	Chief of Staff
Cordingley, Patrick	Major General Patrick Anthony John Cordingley, b. 1944; British Army officer; Commanded 7th Armoured Brigade in the First Gulf War 1991
CPA	Civilian Provisional Authority
Dannatt, Richard	General Sir Richard Dannatt, b. 1950; British Army officer; Chief of the General Staff
Dayton Agreement	The Dayton Peace Agreement, signed in Dayton, Ohio, on 14 December 1995, ending the Bosnian War
DCDC	UK Development, Concepts and Doctrine Centre

DCOM	Deputy Commander
de Gaulle	Charles André Joseph Marie de Gaulle, 1890–1970, French President 1959–1969
Deoband movement	An Islamic movement founded in India, in 1866
Desant capability	Originally a Russian term, used to mean the capability to deploy military force by air
DfID	Department for International Development
Dhofar, Dhofaris	A region in the south of the Sultanate of Oman, and its inhabitants, which gave its name to the war in that area 1962–1972
DOD	US Department of Defense
Douhet, Giulio	General Giulio *Douhet*, 1869–1930; Italian general and air-power theorist
DPA	Defence Planning Assumptions
DSACEUR	Deputy Supreme Allied Commander Europe
DSG	Defence Strategic Guidance
DSTL	UK Defence Science and Technology Laboratory
DTIO	Directorate of Targeting and Information Operations
Durrani	Pashtun tribal confederation in Afghanistan and Pakistan
ECOMOG	Armed monitoring group of the Economic Community of West African States
ECOWAS	Economic Community of West African States
EFP	Explosively Formed Projectile, an anti-armour IED
Eisenhower, Dwight	Dwight David Eisenhower, 1890–1969, US Army officer and President 1953–1961
Ellis, Jim	Admiral James O. Ellis, b. 1947; US Navy officer and Commander in Chief Allied Forces, Southern Europe 1998–2000
EOD	Explosive Ordnance Disposal
EU	European Union
EW	Electronic warfare
Executive Outcomes	South African-based private military company that operated in Sierra Leone 1995–97
FATA	Federally Administered Tribal Areas of Pakistan
FCO	UK Foreign and Commonwealth Office
FCOC	Future Character of Conflict Paper
FDT	British Army Force Development and Training Command
Feith, Doug	Douglas J. Feith, b. 1953, US politician and Under Secretary of Defense for Policy 2001–2005
Flanagan, Ronnie	Sir Ronald Flanagan, b. 1949; Chief Constable of the Royal Ulster Constabulary 1996–2001 and then of the Police Service of Northern Ireland 2001–02
FM 100-5 doctrine	*FM 100-5 Operations*, the US Army's keystone warfighting doctrine manual
Foot and mouth	An infectious animal disease that affected the UK's cattle population in an outbreak in 2001, requiring the deployment of UK military forces in support of the civil authority
FRE	Former Regime Elements in Iraq
FSTA	Future Strategic Tanker Aircraft
Fuller, J.F.C.	John Frederick Charles Fuller, 1878–1966, British Army officer and military theorist

FYROM	Former Yugoslav Republic of Macedonia
G8	The Group of Eight, consisting of Canada, France, Germany, Italy, Japan, Russia, the UK and the USA
Gaddafi, Muammar	Colonel Muammar Muhammed Abu Minyar al-Gaddafi, 1942–2011; ruler of Libya 1969–2011
Galula, David	David Galula, 1919–1967, French Army officer; expert in counter-insurgency, largely based on his experiences in Algeria
Garner, Jay	Lieutenant General Jay Montgomery Garner, b. 1938; US Army officer; Director of ORHA 2003
Gates, Secretary Robert	Robert Michael Gates, b. 1943, US civil servant; US Secretary of Defense 2006–2011
Ghilzai	A Pashtun tribal confederacy in Afghanistan and Pakistan
GIRoA, GOA	Government of the Islamic Republic of Afghanistan
GOC	General Officer Commanding
Good Friday Agreement	See Belfast Agreement
GPS	Global positioning system
Greenstock, Jeremy	Sir Jeremy Q. Greenstock, b. 1943; British diplomat and UK's Special Representative for Iraq 2003–2004
Green Zone	A secure zone in the centre of Baghdad that contains the main centres of government; also known as the International Zone
Guderian, Heinz	Heinz Wilhelm Guderian, 1888–1954, German general
Haig, Douglas	Field Marshal Douglas Haid, 1st Earl Haig of Bemersyde, 1861–1928; British Army officer; commanded the British Expeditionary Force 1915–1918
Hajj	The annual pilgrimage to Mecca, Saudi Arabia
Hamley, E.B.	Sir Edward Bruce Hamley, 1824–1993; British Army officer and military writer
Haqqani Network	An insurgent group in Afghanistan
Harmony Guidelines	A term used in the British military to specify a preferred interval between operational tours
Hazara	One of the ethnic groups of Afghanistan
HCSC	Higher Command and Staff Course
Hellfire	An air-to-ground missile system
Help for Heroes	A British charity launched in 1 October 2007 to support wounded British servicemen and servicewomen
Henderson, G.F.R.	George Francis Robert Henderson, 1854–1903, Army officer, historian and military writer
Hezb-i-Islami Gulbuddin, HiG	An insurgent group in Afghanistan
Hezbollah	A Shia militant group and political party in Lebanon
HMMWV	High Mobility Multipurpose Wheeled Vehicle (Humvee)
Holbrooke, Richard	Richard Charles Albert Holbrooke, 1941–2010, US diplomat
Holmes, Richard	Richard Holmes, 1946–2011, British soldier and military historian
IA	International Agencies

ICSC(L)	Intermediate Command and Staff Course (Land), the British Army's training course for majors
ICTY	The International Criminal Tribunal for the former Yugoslavia
IED	Improvised explosive device
IFOR	Implementation Force in Bosnia-Herzegovina
IGC	Iraqi Governing Council
IIA	Interim Iraq Authority
IIG	Iraqi Interim Government
Ink-spotting	A counter-insurgency technique in which small areas are secured first and gradually expanded
IO	Information operations
IPU	Iraq Planning Unit
IRA, PIRA	The Provisional Irish Republican Army, a Northern Ireland insurgent group
IRGC	Iranian Revolutionary Guards Corps
ISAF	International Security and Assistance Force
ISF	Iraqi Security Forces
ISR	Intelligence, Surveillance and Reconnaissance
ISTAR	Intelligence, Surveillance, Target Acquisition and Reconnaissance
J2	The military staff branch dealing with Intelligence
JAM, Jaysh al-Mahdi	A Shia militant group in Iraq, loyal to Moqtada al-Sadr
JDN	Joint discussion note or joint doctrine note
JFC	Joint Force Command or Joint Force Commander
JFCB	Allied Joint Force Command Brunssum
JFCOM	US Joint Forces Command
Jomini	Antoine-Henri, Baron Jomini, 1779–1869, Swiss-born general in the service of France and Russia; writer on the art of war
JTF	Joint task force
JTFC	Joint task force commander
Kabbah, President	Alhaji Ahmed Tejan Kabbah, b. 1934, President of Sierra Leone 1996–97 and 1998–2007
Kamajor	A traditional hunter of the Mende tribe in Sierra Leone
Karzai, Hamid	Hamid Karzai, b. 1957, President of Afghanistan
KFOR	Kosovo Force
KLA	Kosovo Liberation Army
Kuchis	Afghan Pashtun nomads
KVM	Kosovo Verification Mission
Lashkar-i-Taiba	An insurgent group in Afghanistan and Pakistan
Levene, Sir Peter; Levene Report	Peter Levene, Baron Levene of Portsoken, b. 1941; British businessman, banker and public servant; led the Defence Reform Group in 2010–2011 and authored the subsequent Levene Report

LIs	Lessons Identified
Liddell Hart, B.H.	Sir Basil Henry Liddell Hart, 1895–1970; British military thinker and historian
Line of operation	A term used in campaign planning to denote a particular theme, or grouping of activities, that together with other lines of operation should achieve the desired end-state; lines of operation are parallel simultaneous activities, rather than sequential phases
Loya jirga	Pashtun phrase meaning 'grand council' in Afghanistan where, traditionally, tribal elders meet together
LWC	British Army Land Warfare Centre
Mabey & Johnson	British engineering company which specialises in bridging, often used by military and aid organisations
Madrassa	Arabic for school; frequently used to describe Islamic religious school
Mahan, A.T.	Alfred Thayer Mahan, 1840–1914, US Navy officer; historian and naval strategist
Maliki, Nouri	Nouri Kamil Mohammed Hasan al-Malik (also known as Jawad al-Maliki or Abu Esraa), b. 1950; Prime Minister of Iraq from 2006
Manichean	From Manichaeism, one of the main Gnostic religions, originating in Sassanid Persia, with a doctrine focused on the difference between a good and spiritual world of light, and an evil, material world of darkness
Manifest Destiny	Nineteenth-century American belief that the United States was destined to expand across the North American continent
Marshall	George Catlett Marshall, 1880–1959, US Army officer
Mau Mau	An insurgent movement in Kenya, drawn mainly from the Kikuya tribe, responsible for the Mau Mau Revolt against British colonial rule 1952–1960
MEF	Marine Expeditionary Force
Meyer, Christopher	Sir Christopher John Rome Meyer, b. 1944; British diplomat and UK Ambassador to the USA 1997–2003
Meyer, Kurt	Kurt Meyer, 1910–61, Second World War German Army officer
Millennium Development Goals	Eight international development goals established following the Millennium Summit of the UN in 2000, agreed by all 193 member states
Milošević, Slobodan	Slobodan Milošević, 1941–2006, President of Serbia 1989–1997 and of the Federal Republic of Yugoslavia 1997–2000
Mission Command	The doctrine of military command that promotes decentralisation of command, freedom of action and initiative, within constraints
Mitchell, Billy	William Lendrum Mitchell, 1879–1936, US Army air force officer and air power theorist
MiTT	Military Transition Team, in Iraq
Momoh, President	Major General (Retired) Joseph Saidu Momoh, 1937–2003; President of Sierra Leone 1985–92
MNC(I), MNC-I	Multi-National Corps – Iraq
MND	Multi-National Division
MND(CS)	Multi-National Division (Centre South) in Iraq
MND(SE)	Multi-National Division (South-East) in Iraq
MNF	Multi-National Forces

MNF-I	Multi-National Forces Iraq
MNSTC-I	Multi-National Security Transition Command Iraq
MOD	UK Ministry of Defence
Mohammed al-Huwaidi	General Mohammed al-Huwaidi; Iraqi Army officer; Commander of 14th Division in Basra 2007–2008 and of Basra Operations Command from 2008
Mohan al-Furayji	General Mohan al-Furayji; Head of Iraqi Security Forces in Basra 2007–2008
Moltke the Elder	Helmuth von Moltke the Elder, 1800–1881, Prussian general
Monroe Doctrine	1823 policy of the USA instituted by President James Munroe declaring that European attempts to colonise lands in the Americas would be treated as acts of aggression by the USA
Montgomery, Bernard	Bernard Law Montgomery (Monty), first Viscount Montgomery of Alamein, 1887–1976; British Army officer
Moqtada al-Sadr	Sayyid Moqtada al-Sadr, b. 1973, radical Shia religious and political leader in Iraq
Moshtarak	Dari for 'together'
MSC	Major Subordinate Command
MTA	Military Technical Agreement
MUP	Serbian Ministry of Internal Affairs; often used to refer to the Serbian special police
National Solidarity Programme	A Government of Afghanistan initiative to rehabilitate and develop about 5,000 villages in Afghanistan
NATO	North Atlantic Treaty Organisation
NCC	National Contingent Commander or National Contingent Command
NCO	Non-commissioned officer
Negroponte, John	John Dimitri Negroponte, b. 1939, US diplomat and Ambassador to Iraq 2004–2005
NGO	Non-governmental organisation
NHS	UK National Health Service
NIO	Northern Ireland Office
NITAT	Northern Ireland Training and Advisory Team
NLA	Albanian National Liberation Army in Macedonia
NPRC	National Provisional Ruling Council in Sierra Leone
Obama, Barack	Barack Hussein Obama, b. 1961, US politician and President from 2009
OEF	Operation Enduring Freedom in Afghanistan
Omar, Mullah	Mullah Mohammed Omar, b. 1959, spiritual leader of the Taliban movement in parts of Afghanistan and Pakistan
OMLT	Operational Mentoring and Liaison Teams in Afghanistan
OMS	Office of the Martyr Sadr, the political wing of Jaysh al-Mahdi
Operation Banner	The British Army security operation in Northern Ireland 1969–2007
Operation Barras	An undertaking in 2001 to recover soldiers taken captive and held hostage in Sierra Leone
Operation Charge of the Knights	The Iraqi-led operation to clear Basra of the Jaysh al-Mahdi militia in March to May 2008

Operation Enduring Freedom [OEF]	The US counter-insurgency operation in Afghanistan since 2001
Operation Entirety	British Army's focus on the Afghanistan campaign as the main effort, from 2009
Operation Granby	The UK operation to liberate the Falkland Islands in 1982
Operation Goodwood	A 1944 British operation attempting to break out of the Normandy beachhead
Operation Herrick	The UK operation in Afghanistan following the initial defeat of the Taliban in late 2001
Operation Iraqi Freedom	The US operation for the invasion and counter-insurgency in Iraq
Operation Joint Guardian	The NATO operation in Kosovo which started in 1999
Operation Kingower	The name given to the British contribution to the NATO response to the 1999 Kosovo Crisis
Operation Medusa	A Canadian-led NATO and Afghan operation in 2006 in Kandahar Province
Operation Moshtarak	A joint UK, US and Afghan operation in 2010 to secure the town of Marja in Helmand Province
Operation Mountain Thrust	A major NATO and Afghan operation in 2006 against the Taliban insurgency in south Afghanistan, leading to NATO expansion in the country
Operation Motorman	The British Army operation in Northern Ireland in 1972 to clear the no-go areas in Belfast and Londonderry
Operation Olympics	The British security operation to protect the London 2012 Olympic Games
Operation Overlord	The Allied 1944 invasion of Normandy against Nazi Germany
Operation Panther's Claw	A 2009 British-led operation in Helmand Province; also known as Operation Panchai Palang
Operation Phoenix	A British operation in Basra in December 2006 that resulted in the capture of a Jaysh al-Mahdi rocket team; later the generic name given to all counter-rocket operations
Operation Salamanca	A British-planned operation for Basra in 2006, replaced by Operation Sinbad
Operation Sinbad	A British-led operation in Basra in late 2006, to attempt to clear the City of militias
Operation Snakebite	The British-led operation to capture Musa Kala, Afghanistan, in December 2007
Operation Telic	The UK operation for the invasion and counter-insurgency in Iraq
Operation Tolo	An Afghanistan-wide operation to promote development in 2009–2010
Operation Turtle	A NATO operation in Farah Province, Afghanistan, in 2006 to protect development projects
Operation Veritas	The UK operation against the Taliban Government of Afghanistan in 2001
Operation Zenith	The British name for the 2007 handover of British Army bases in Basra to Iraqi control
OPLAN	Operational plan
OPTAG	Operational Training and Advisory Group
OPWP	Office of Post-War Planning in Iraq
ORHA	Office for Reconstruction and Humanitarian Assistance in Iraq
OSCE	Organisation for Security and Cooperation in Europe
Owen, David	David Anthony Llewellyn Owen, Baron Owen, b. 1938, British politician and Foreign Secretary 1977–1979

PAG	Policy Action Group
Pashtun	A major tribal grouping in Afghanistan and Pakistan
Pashtunwali	A concept of living or philosophy for the Pashtun people; it is regarded as both an honour code and a non-written law for the people
Patton, George	George Smith *Patton*, 1885–1945, US Army officer
PCRU	Post Conflict Reconstruction Unit
Peshmerga	Kurdish armed fighters
Petraeus, David	David Howell Petraeus, b. 1952, US Army officer; Commander of Multi-National Force – Iraq 2007–2008; Commander International Security Assistance Force in Afghanistan 2010–2011; Director of the Central Intelligence Agency from 2011
PIC	Provincial Iraqi control
Pinnacle Course	Top level course for training the most senior military commanders
PJHQ	The UK's Permanent Joint Headquarters in Northwood, just outside London
Pol-mil	Political-military
Popalzai	A branch of the Durani Pashtun tribe
Powell, Colin	Colin Luther Powell, b. 1937, US Army officer and Secretary of State 2001–2005
Project Coningham-Keyes	A British military initiative to improve the coordination of air support to land and maritime forces, in the aftermath of the 2003 invasion of Iraq
PRT	Provincial Reconstruction Team
PSO	Peace Support Operations
PsyOps	Psychological Operations
PTSD	Post-traumatic stress disorder
Qods, Quds Force	The Quds Force is a section of the Iranian Revolutionary Guards Corps whose primary mission is to organise, train, equip and finance foreign Islamic revolutionary movements
R&R	Rest and recuperation
RAF	UK Royal Air Force
Ramadan	Islamic holy month
Rambouillet talks	Peace talks between the North Atlantic Treaty Organisation, the Federal Republic of Yugoslavia and a delegation of ethnic Albanian Kosovars in 1999
RC	Regional Commands
RCDS	Royal College of Defence Studies, the most senior British defence educational establishment, designed for those of one-star rank
Reid, John	John Reid, Baron Reid of Cardowan, b. 1947, British politician; Secretary of State for Defence 2005–2006 and Home Secretary 2006–2007
RMAS	Royal Military Academy Sandhurst, the British Army's officer training establishment
Robertson, George	George Islay MacNeill Robertson, b. 1946, Baron Robertson of Port Ellen; Secretary General of the North Atlantic Treaty Organisation 1999–2004
Rock drill	A form of rehearsal for a military operation
ROE	Rules of Engagement
RPG	Rocket propelled grenade
RSLAF	Republic of Sierra Leone Armed Forces

RUF	Revolutionary United Front in Sierra Leone
Rugova, Ibrahim	Ibrahim Rugova, 1944–2006, Albanian politician; first President of Kosovo 2002–2006
Rumsfeld, Donald	Donald Henry Rumsfeld, b. 1932, US politician; Secretary of Defense 2001–2006
RUSI	Royal United Services Institute
SACEUR	Supreme Allied Commander Europe
Saddam Hussein	Saddam Hussein Abd al-Majid al-Tikriti, 1937–2003, Iraqi President 1979–2003
Saddamists	Followers of Saddam Hussein
Sadrists	Followers of Moqtada al-Sadr
SAFIRE	Surface-to-air fire
Salafist	An Islamic movement, associated with violent jihad
SALT II	The second Strategic Arms Limitation Treaty signed between the Soviet Union and the USA in 1979
SAM	Surface-to-air-missile
SAMS	School for Advanced Military Studies, Fort Leavenworth, Kansas, USA
Sanchez, Ricardo	Lieutenant General Ricardo Sanchez, b. 1953; US Army officer and commander in Iraq 2003–2004
Sandhurst	The UK's officer training school at the Royal Military Academy, Sandhurst
Schlieffen (von Schlieffen)	Alfred von Schlieffen, Count Schlieffen, 1833–1913; German field marshal
Schwarzkopf, General	Norman H. Schwarzkopf, 1934–2012, US Army officer; Commander of Coalition Forces in Persian Gulf War 1991
SCIRI	Islamic Supreme Council of Iraq, an Iraqi political party
SDR	Strategic Defence Review
SDRs	Special Drawing Rights
SFOR	Stabilisation Force in Bosnia-Herzegovina
SHAPE	Supreme Headquarters Allied Powers Europe
Sharia law	The code of conduct or religious law of Islam
Shatt al-Arab	The river that is formed by the confluence of the Euphrates and Tigris at al-Qurnah, north of Basra, flowing through Basra and into the North Arabian Gulf; at its southern end it forms the border between Iraq and Iran
Shia	A denomination of Islam, second in size to Sunni Islam, but a majority in Iraq
SHIRBRIG	The UN's Standby High-Readiness Brigade
Short, Clare	Clare Short, b. 1946, British politician; Secretary of State for International Development 1997–2003
Shura	'Consultation' in Arabic; a mechanism for consultative local government in Afghanistan
Simpkin, Richard	Brigadier Richard Evelyn Simpkin, 1921–1986; British Army officer and military theorist
Sinn Fein	Irish republican political party; in Northern Ireland often associated with the Provisional Irish Republican Army
SLA	Sierra Leone Army

Slim, Bill	William Joseph Slim, first Viscount Slim, 1891–1970; British Army officer
SLPP	Sierra Leone People's Party
Smith, Rupert	General Sir Rupert Smith, b. 1943; British Army officer
SOAS	School of Oriental and African Studies, University of London
Sons of Iraq programme	See Anbar Awakening
SOP	Standard operating procedure
Spearhead Battlegroup	The British Army's highest readiness force, based on a battalion-sized group
SRSG	Special Representative of the United Nations Secretary-General
Stilwell, Joseph	Joseph Warren Stilwell, 1883–1946, American general
Straw, Jack	John Whitaker 'Jack' Straw, b. 1946, British politician; Foreign Secretary 2001–2006
Stryker battalion	US Army battalion equipped with the Stryker light armoured vehicle
SU	Stabilisation Unit
Sunni	The largest denomination of Islam
Svechin, Aleksandr	Alexander Andreyevich Svechin, 1878–1938, Russian and Soviet military leader; historian and theorist
SWET operations	Sewage, water, electricity, trash
Tadjik, Tajik	An ethnic group of Persian origin found in Afghanistan, Tajikstan and Uzbekistan
Taliban, Taleban	A group of Islamist militias operating in Afghanistan and Pakistan
Taylor, Charles	Charles McArthur Ghankay Taylor, b. 1948, former warlord and President of Liberia 1997–2003
Templer	Sir Gerald Walter Robert Templer, 1898–1979; British commander in Malaya
Territorial Army	The part-time volunteer force of the British Army
Thaçi, Hashim	Hashim Thaçi (or Thaqi), b. 1968, Kosovo politician and former leader of the Kosovo Liberation Army
Thompson, Sir Robert	Sir Robert Thompson, 1916–1992; British counter-insurgency expert who authored the influential book *Defeating Communist Insurgency: Experiences from Malaya and Vietnam* in 1966
TIALD pods	Thermal Imaging Airborne Laser Designator pod, for laser-guided bombs
TIC	Troops in Combat
Tito, Marshal	Josip Broz Tito, 1892–1980, Yugoslav President 1953–1980
TRADOC	US Army Training and Doctrine Command
Triandafillov	Vladimir Kiriakovitch Triandafillov, 1894–1931, Soviet military commander
TRiM	Trauma Risk Management
TTP	Tactics, Techniques and Procedures
Tukhachevskii	Mikhail Nikolayevich Tukhachevskii, 1893–1937, Soviet marshal
UAV	Unmanned aerial vehicle
ULIMO	United Liberation Movement for Democracy in Liberia
UN	United Nations
UNAMSIL	United Nations Mission in Sierra Leone
UNHCR	The Office of the UN High Commissioner for Refugees

UNMIK	UN international civil presence set up in Kosovo under UNSCR 1244
UNPROFOR	United Nations Protection Force in Bosnia-Herzegovina
UNSCR	*United Nations Security Council Resolution*
UOR	Urgent Operational Requirement
USAID	United States Agency for International Development
USMC	United States Marine Corps
Uzbeks	A Turkic ethnic group found across Central Asia including Afghanistan
VJ	Vojska Jugoslavije, the Serb Army
VTC	Video Tele Conference
Wahhabi	A branch of Sunni Islam associated with Salafism
Warsaw Pact	Warsaw Treaty Organization (1955–1991), a defence treaty established by Albania, Bulgaria, the Czech Republic, the German Democratic Republic, Hungary, Poland, Romania and the Soviet Union
Westmoreland	William Childs Westmoreland, 1914–2005, Commanding General Military Assistance Command Vietnam 1964–1968
West Side Boys	A guerrilla group in Sierra Leone, formed from the rump of the Armed Forces Revolutionary Command
WMD	Weapons of Mass Destruction
Wolfowitz, Paul	Paul Dundes Wolfowitz, b. 1943, US diplomat and Deputy Secretary of Defense 2001–2005
Yeltsin, Boris	Boris Nikolayevich Yeltsin, 1931–2007, Russian President 1991–1999

Index

Bold page numbers indicate figures.

9/11 attacks, consequences of 330–31
52 Brigade
   in Afghanistan 250–52
   shaping command thinking 252–4

accountability, military 278
Afghanistan
   civilian casualties 245–6
   corruption 230, 242–3
   the country 229–30, 237
   criminal groups and the Taliban 239
   Development Zones 220
   force presence as set by nations 231
   Hajj, transport of pilgrims to 111
   Helmand 2007–2008, behavioural conflict
      52 Brigade 250–52
      Afghans as pragmatists 250
      anchoring 254–5
      discount rate 254
      economics 256–7
      education 258–9, 260–61
      framing of choices 255–6
      influence, importance of 249
      influence operations defined 252
      Lessons Identified (LIs) 259
      libertarian paternalism 256
      mainstream, influence as 257–9
      MOD lack of understanding of challenge
         251
      National Solidarity Programme 256
      perceptions 249–50
      professionalisation of communications
         261–2
      prospect theory 254
      research, need for 262
      shaping command thinking 252–4
      tomorrow's conflicts 259–60
      victory, reassessing notions of 260
      Whitehall messages as irrelevant 251–2
      wisdom of crowds 255
   Helmand Province 223
   insurgency 230–31, 237–8, 237–9

ISAF forces
   Afghan Army development 241–2
   extent of 240–41
   Musa Qaleh, capture of 241
ISAF regional command structure 2011 215
motives for 331, 344
narco/insurgent activity as intertwined 243–4
nation-building in, problems with 94–6
NATO presence, reasons for 246–7
North Atlantic Treaty Organisation (NATO)
   2006 217–21
Obama Doctrine 19
Operation Eagle's Summit 245
Operation Medusa 220–21
opium production 243–4
Pakistan as haven for insurgents 239–40
police reform 242
Policy Action Group (PAG) 220
political situation 230
Provincial Reconstruction Teams (PRTs) 231–2,
   244–5
rationalisation of motives 18, 19
resourcing of campaign 21–2
Southern
   comprehensive approach 225–7, 233–4
   counter-insurgency 228–9, 233–4
   impediments to comprehensive approach
      229–32
   stabilisation 227–8
state weakness as main problem 242
strategic communications 245–6
Taliban 237–8
UK COIN Centre 291–3
as way out of Basra 162
Age of the Unthinkable, The (Ramo) 259–60
Ahmeti, Ali 91, 94
air campaigns
   air-land coordination 269
   authorisation 269
   Balkans 266–7
   blunt instrument, perception of as 269
   Cold War 266

comprehensive approach 269–70
as decisive 265
global reach 267
Gulf War 266
historical context 265–7
inflexibility in ownership and tasking 267
joint 267–9
persistence 267
precision 267
al-Fartusi, Ahmed 178–9
al-Furayji, Mohan 187, 188, 193
al-Huwaidi, Mohammed 194
al-Maliki, Nouri 166–7, 188, 193–4
al-Sadr, Moqtada 86, 198
al-Safi, Safa 166
Albanians
in Kosovo
meaning of Kosovo for 41
revenge attacks by 49
in Macedonia 91
alcohol misuse 206, 210–11
*Alignment Between the Security Forces and Civil
Government* (Northern Ireland Office) 31
anchoring 254–5
Annan, Kofi 58
Arreguin-Toft, Ivan 258
Ashdown, Paddy 7

Baghdad
2004
coalition, benefits and challenges of 103–4
command and control, importance of 107
deputy commanders 105
'enemy forces' 100–101
foreign Islamic extremists 100–101
former regime, elements from 100
friendly forces 101–2
Governing Council 101
influences on activities in Iraq 99
Interim Government 101
logistics 106
missions 102–3
money as command resource 106
omens in March-April 97–8
private security companies 105–6
Shia Extremists 100
stabilisation, move towards 101–2
Sunni Arab Rejectionists 100
transitional government 104–5
2005
leadership in the 21st century 134–5
Bagnall, Nigel 124, 328, 335–6

Bailey, Jonathan 49
Balkans
air campaigns in 266–7
UK/US relationship 329–30
Basra
2007, generalship during 175–9
Afghanistan as way out of 162
commitment thresholds 158
decisive action needed 161–2
Operation Charge of the Knights
ceasefire 191–2
changes during 198–9
consolidation of control 194–6
counter-insurgency plan following 194
forensics laboratory as legacy 195
Iran border as problem 195–6
Jaysh al-Mahdi 187–8, 190, 191, 196, 197–8
legal position of Iraqi Army 195
main security forces attack 191
malign Iranian influence 198
Marsh Arabs and Iran border 196
Military Transition Teams (MiTTs) 190
Operation Jebel an-Naar 196
planning 188–9
police force, reorganisation of 195
prelude to 187–9
withdrawal from Basra, reasons for 197–8
Operation Salamanca
planning 162–8
revision of 167
Operation Sinbad
assessment of 172–3
execution of 168–71
handover of bases 171–2
planning 162–8
publicity 169
purpose 163
reconstruction under 169
resources 163–5
Special Groups attacks 169–71
Province and City 155
reconciliation with Fartusi 178–9
seen as distraction 158–9
US/UK purpose 158
weakness of Iraqi army 165
battlefield, preparation for the right 306–7
Battlemind 211n11
behavioural conflict
52 Brigade 250–52
Afghans as pragmatists 250
anchoring 254–5
discount rate 254

economics 256–7
education 258–9, 260–61
framing of choices 255–6
influence, importance of 249
influence operations defined 252
Lessons Identified (LIs) 259
libertarian paternalism 256
mainstream, influence as 257–9
MOD lack of understanding of challenge 251
National Solidarity Programme 256
perceptions 249–50
professionalisation of communications 261–2
prospect theory 254
research, need for 262
shaping command thinking 252–4
tomorrow's conflicts 259–60
victory, reassessing notions of 260
Whitehall messages as irrelevant 251–2
wisdom of crowds 255
Blair, Cherie 8
Blair, Tony
    decision-making and personality of 7–9
    early thoughts on removal of oppressive regimes
        11–12
    humanitarian interventionism, move towards
        11–14
    on Islam 18
    multiculturalism in Britain 16–17
    rationalisation of motives 17–20
Blakeney, Percy 147
Bosnia, operational level thinking in 127
Bottom Billion, The (Collier) 256
Boutros-Ghali, Boutros 10
Braithwaite, Rodric 8
Bramll, Dwin 341
Bremer, Paul 77, 159
British Army
    9/11 attacks, consequences of 330–31
    Afghanistan, problems in 335
    counter-insurgency, changes towards 340–41
    counter-insurgency, problems with 335–8
    foreign influences on 327
    Iraq, problems in 334
    jointery 328–9
    neglect of thinking 335–42
    RAND ideal against counter-insurgency 335
    relationship with the United States 329–32
    responsibility for failure 332–3
    rotation of forces, consequences of 342–3
    Sierra Leone 2000 58–60
    span of command 343
    strategic context 328

subordination of strategy to US 330–32
    in the twentieth century 327–8
    valuing 116–17
Brodie, Bernard 119
Brown, Gordon 15, 24–5
budget on defence
    1990–2010 7
    resourcing campaigns 20–25
Bush, George W. 13
Butler, Richard 188

Caldwell, William 259
campaign management, issues with modern 149–50
Campbell, Alaistair 75
casualties, reactions to, political-military 277
Çeku, Agim 50, 51, 52
centralised/decentralised hybrid command 315–16
character of generals 144–5, 146–7
Chief of the Defence Staff 341–2
choices, framing of 255–6
Christian beliefs of Blair and decisions made 9
civil-military fault line within government 339–420
civil presence, development of in Kosovo 50–51
civilian casualties in Afghanistan 245–6
Clark, Wes 43, 47–8, 51
Clausewitz, Carl von 5, 28, 113, 147–8, 150, 285
Clegg, Nick 14
coalitions
    benefits and challenges of 103–4
    complexity of command and control 131
    political context 182–3
    reasons for countries to participate in 182
Cohen, Elliot 113, 114
Cold War 266
collective learning 322
Collier, Paul 256
command and control, importance of 107
commanders, place for on battlefield 37
communication
    of generals 145
    in multi-national command 88
    political-military 112–14
    professionalisation of 261–2
    strategic, in Afghanistan 245–6
    technology as threat and temptation 114
competence of generals 145
complexities of modern campaigning
    delivery 110–11
    junior partner warfare 116
    manoeuvrist approach and mission control 114–15
    media 115
    national, international and political context 109

other actors 111–12
    personality, importance of 110
    political-military relationships 112–14
    relationships, forging 110
    theatre context 110–11
    uncertainty 110
comprehensive approach
    air campaigns 269–70
    counter-insurgency 233–4
    impediments to in Afghanistan 229–32
    Southern Afghanistan 225–7
    as viewed with suspicion 340
concentration of force 112
Connaughton, Richard 58
constraints on independence in Northern Ireland
    35–6
context, national, international and political 109
continentalism 328
corruption in Afghanistan 230, 242–3
counter-insurgency
    Army Field Manual on 283–4
    British plan, lack of 293–4
    education in, lack of 281–2, 287
    historic legacies 282
    Iraq 283–7
    irrelevant, seen as 282
    MOD response to 340–41
    Operation Herrick Study week 293
    Operation Sinbad 286–7
    problems with 335–8
    recommendations 294
    relearning old lessons 282
    Southern Afghanistan 228–9
    UK COIN Centre 291–3
    UK frustrations with doctrine development
        288–9
    US renaissance in 287–8, 290–91
    warfighting ethos as dominant over 282–3
counter-terrorism, command-style for 34–5
Cross, Tim 24–5
crowds, wisdom of 255
cultural differences in political-military
    relationships 277–8
cultural empathy, Southern Iraq 2003–2004 87–8

data, managing and exploiting 305
De Atkine, Norvell 257
De Mello, Sergio 50, 51, 77
decision-making and Blair's personality 7–9
decompression 207–8
Defence Planning Assumptions (DPAs) 6
defence policy

assumptions and planning 5–7
    ethics and values 6–7
    Strategic Defence Review (SDR) 5–6
Defence Strategic Guidance (DSG) 6
deputy commanders 105
discount rate 254
double-loop learning 310–12

economics 256–7
education of officers 258–9, 260–61
    Higher Command and Staff Course (HCSC)
        124–5, 328
    see also learning organisations
elections, Iraqi opinions on 82–3
embedded support 62
Enterprise Approach 316
epidemiology, reasons for using 202–4, **203**
error tolerance, decline in 300
ethics in defence policy 6–7
Everard, James 161, 162, 165
experience, learning from 302–3, 309–10
experimentation in development 322–4

failure, responsibility for 332–3
Falklands Conflict, operational level thinking 126
al-Fartusi, Ahmed 178–9
field craft 304–5
52 Brigade
    in Afghanistan 250–52
    shaping command thinking 252–4
Flynn, George 193
Force Development and Training Command (FDT)
    297
    reasons for creation of 314–15
    relevance 298–9
foreign influences on the British Army 327
forensics laboratory as legacy in Iraq 195
framing of choices 255–6
France 327
French, David 282
Fuller, J.F.C. 119–21
al-Furayji, Mohan 187, 188, 193

Galula, David 257
Gapes, Mike 19
Garner, Jay 70, 71–2, 74, 76–7
generals and generalship
    Basra 2007 175–9
    campaign management, issues with modern
        149–50
    character 144–5, 146–7
    communication 145

competence 145
complex operations, requirements of 151
Iraq 2006 150–53
Iraq 2008
    ends 181–3
    integration of resources 183
    means, requirement for 184–5
    national agreement on objectives 183
    political context for coalitions 182–3
    politics and media, management of 183
    reasons for participation in coalitions 182
    relationship between ends and means 184
modern, requirements of 180
necessary attributes of 339
role of as not understood 148–9
selection of 145
Stilwell on 144
terrorists 147
war and peace as the world of 14–65
willpower 146
worthy life, living a 143–4
Germany 327
Goldsmith, Lord 14
Gordon, Andrew 309
government
    policy baseline for 274
    radical shake-up needed 77
Gulf War 126, 266
Gulf War syndrome 201–2

Harper, Stephen 19
Healey, Dennis 116
Helmand 2007–2008, behavioural conflict
    52 Brigade 250–52
    Afghans as pragmatists 250
    anchoring 254–5
    discount rate 254
    economics 256–7
    education 258–9, 260–61
    framing of choices 255–6
    influence, importance of 249
    influence operations defined 252
    Lessons Identified (LIs) 259
    libertarian paternalism 256
    mainstream, influence as 257–9
    MOD lack of understanding of challenge 251
    National Solidarity Programme 256
    perceptions 249–50
    professionalisation of communications 261–2
    prospect theory 254
    research, need for 262

    shaping command thinking 252–4
    tomorrow's conflicts 259–60
    victory, reassessing notions of 260
    Whitehall messages as irrelevant 251–2
    wisdom of crowds 255
Helmand Province **223**
Henderson, G.F.R. 119
heuristics 253
Higher Command and Staff Course (HCSC) 124–5, 328
Holbrooke, Richard 42
Holloway, Adam 21–2
Holmes, Richard 148
Homo Economicus 252–3
Hoon, Geoff 24
Howard, Michael 130
human rights, primacy of over the state 9–10
humanitarian interventionism, doctrine of 9–15
Hutton, John 21
al-Huwaidi, Mohammed 194

independence of action in Northern Ireland, constraints on 35–6
influence operations
    52 Brigade 250–52
    Afghans as pragmatists 250
    anchoring 254–5
    defined 252
    economics 256–7
    education of officers 260–61
    framing of choices 255–6
    importance of 249
    Lessons Identified (LIs) 259
    libertarian paternalism 256
    mainstream, influence as 257–9
    MOD lack of understanding of challenge 251
    perceptions 249–50
    prospect theory 254
    shaping command thinking 252–4
    tomorrow's conflicts 259–60
    Whitehall messages as irrelevant 251–2
    wisdom of crowds 255
information technology, managing and exploiting 305
infrastructure
    Kosovo 49, 52–3
    reconstruction in Iraq 2003 75–6
    Sierra Leone 2000 57
    Southern Iraq, state of on arrival 79–80
insignia of KLA 51
insurgency in Afghanistan 230–31, 237–9, 243–4
    see also counter-insurgency

International Commission on Intervention and State
    Sovereignty 12
intervention, reasons for 90
Iran
    Iraq border as problem 195–6
    as malign influence in Iraq 198
    as threat to Iraq 152
Iraq
    Baghdad 2004
        coalition, benefits and challenges of 103–4
        command and control, importance of 107
        deputy commanders 105
        doctrine 106
        'enemy forces' 100–101
        foreign Islamic extremists 100–101
        former regime, elements from 100
        friendly forces 101–2
        Governing Council 101
        influences on activities in Iraq 99
        Interim Government 101
        logistics 106
        missions 102–3
        money as command resource 106
        omens in March-April 97–8
        private security companies 105–6
        Shia Extremists 100
        stabilisation ,move towards 101–2
        Sunni Arab Rejectionists 100
        transitional government 104–5
    Baghdad 2005 and leadership in the 21st
        century 134–5
    Basra
        2007, generalship during 175–9
        commitment thresholds 158
        decisive action needed 161–2
        Province and City 155
        seen as distraction 158–9
        US/UK purpose 158
    as Blair's and MOD war 158
    counter-insurgency 283–7
    ethnic and sectarian divisions 67
    future for 152–3
    generals and generalship 2006 150–53
    generals and generalship 2008
        ends 181–3
        integration of resources 183
        means, requirement for 184–5
        national agreement on objectives 183
        political context for coalitions 182–3
        politics and media, management of 183
        reasons for participation in coalitions 182
        relationship between ends and means 184

Iranian-backed militias in 160–61
Iraqi Army 135
legality of intervention 14
militia infiltration of 165–6
motives for 331
multinational divisions, deployment of 141
Operation Charge of the Knights
    ceasefire 191–2
    changes during 198–9
    Coalition's Corps headquarters 190–91
    consolidation of control 194–6
    counter-insurgency plan following 194
    execution of 189–94
    forensics laboratory as legacy 195
    Iran border as problem 195–6
    Jaysh al-Mahdi 187–8, 189, 190, 191, 196,
        197–8
    legal position of Iraqi Army 195
    main security forces attack 191
    malign Iranian influence 198
    Marsh Arabs and Iran border 196
    Military Transition Teams (MiTTs) 190
    Operation Jebel an-Naar 196
    planning 188–9
    police force, reorganisation of 195
    prelude to 187–9
    withdrawal from Basra, reasons for
        197–8
Operation Phoenix 170
Operation Salamanca
    planning 162–8
    revision of 167
Operation Sinbad
    assessment of 172–3
    constraints 157–8
    counter-insurgency 286–7
    execution of 168–71
    handover of Basra bases 171–2
    planning 162–8
    publicity 169
    purpose 158, 163
    reconstruction under 169
    resources 163–5
    Special Groups attacks 169–71
    strategic context 157–62
operational level thinking 127–9
police, absence of mentors for 165–6
psychological impact of
    alcohol misuse 210–11
    Battlemind 211n11
    decompression 207–8
    early service leavers 211

epidemiological methods, reasons for using
202–4, 203
future 211–12
reasons for studying 201–2
research methods 204–5
reservists 206–7
stigma of asking for help 207, 211
in theatre 207
Trauma Risk Management (TRiM) 208
US/UK comparison 209–10, 210
rationalisation of motives 19
reconciliation with Fartusi 178–9
reconstruction 2003
arming, degree of 74
authority, lack of 76–7
chaotic start 75
concerns raised 73, 75
contacts in Washington 70–71
errors of judgement 77
exiled Iraqis, role of 73
gaps in the team 71–2
infrastructure 75–6
military/civilian tension 75
Office for Reconstruction and Humanitarian
Assistance (ORHA) 73
Office of Post-War Planning 70, 71–2
planning for, lack of 69–70, 72
political direction, lack of 71–2
skills sets needed 74
support, lack from UK 76–7
uncertainty on eve of war 75
Washington politics 73
reduction of forces 160
removal of bourgeoisie from positions 159–60
resourcing of campaign 20–21
security forces, British approach to developing
160
security forces, lack of British advisers 165
security forces development as low priority 159
southern, gulf with rest of Iraq 159
Southern Iraq 2003–2004
civil authority and control as aim 86
communication between partners 88
conditions placed on US by UK 79
cultural empathy 87–8
differences between provinces 82
different agendas 83
funding issues 81
infrastructure, state of on arrival 79–80
initial situation and directions 80–81
Japanese presence 84
local governance problems 81

media, dealing with 83
nations represented in the division 83
persuasion of local people not to fight 85
police, training of local 86
restraint of soldiers 87
security, need for 86
threats faced 84–5
voting in elections, opinions on 82–3
welcome, initial feeling of 81
threats to, real, realization of 151–2
time compression 152
weakness of Iraqi army in Southern 165
Islam, Blair on 18

Japan, Southern Iraq 2003–2004, presence in 84
Jaysh al-Mahdi 86, 187–8, 189, 190, 191, 196, 197–8
Jeffrey, Bill 25
Jomini, Baron 119
Judgment Under Uncertainty: Heuristics and Biases
(Kahneman and Tversky) 253
Jünger, Ernst 146
junior partner warfare 116, 126
justice systems in Kosovo 50–51

Kabbah, Ahmed Tejan 56, 62
Kahneman, Daniel 253, 254–5, 302
Kemp, Richard 24
Kilcullen, David 229, 290
Kosovo Force 1999
airfield, order to secure 46–7
bombing strikes 43, 44
civil presence, development of 50–51
demilitarisation of KLA 50
infrastructure issues 49, 52–3
insignia of KLA 51
KLA negotiations 49–50
Kosovo Liberation Army 41–2
Kosovo Verification Mission (KVM) 42
legitimacy 52
meaning of Kosovo for Serbs and Albanians 41
Military Technical Agreement, negotiations for
45–6
mission of 42
as NATO operation 52
Operation Joint Guardian 48–9
options for forced entry 43–4
order to block airport runway 48
planning 42–3
police and justice systems 50–51
refugee crisis 43, 49
revenge attacks by Albanians 49
Russian KFOR contingent 46–8

Russian pressure on Serbs 44–5
Serbs, negotiations with 45–6
transformation of KLA 51–2, 52

law as inhibition in Northern Ireland 36
leadership in the 21st century
    Baghdad 2005 134–5
    changes in 131
    collective approach 137
    Iraqi Army 135
    leader development 305–6
    Northern Ireland 135–6
    persistence 137
    pragmatism 137
    Sierra Leone 132–4
learning organisations
    adaptation 301–2
    army compared to other services 308–9
    battlefield, preparation for the right 306–7
    benefits of 324–5
    building blocks of 311
    centralised/decentralised hybrid command
        315–16
    change, degree of achieved 301–2
    collective learning 322
    comprehensive system, disadvantages of 321–2
    concepts, development and rehabilitation of
        312–14
    decline in error tolerance 300
    defence as 297
    denigration of the practical 320
    double-loop learning 310–12
    education and training 320–22
    Enterprise Approach 316
    experience, learning from 302–3, 309–10
    experience of instructors 321
    experimentation 322–4
    field craft 304–5
    Force Development and Training Command
        (FDT) 297
        reasons for creation of 314–15
    IT, managing and exploiting 305
    leader development 305–6
    liberalising MOD rules on access to information
        319–20
    mass armoured manoeuvres, fixation on
        307–8
    myth and modern warfare 307–8
    needs of different services 321
    originator of term 312
    re-assessment of big ideas 310
    relevance 298–9

    research, contribution to force development
        318–20
    responsibility for 316–17
    risk in not being 299–300
    single-loop learning 302–3, 309–10
    skills lost/not taught 304
    spifish approach 316
    strategy, MOD's approach to 314
    turmoil through creating 314
    unlearning old ideas 297, 312
Lessard, Marc 234
Lessons Identified (LIs) 259
libertarian paternalism 256
Liddell Hart, B.H. 120–21
logistics, Baghdad 2004 106
Lomé Agreement 57
long war 331
Lorimer, John 22

Macdonald, Ken 20
Macedonia 91–4
Mackay, Andrew 14
Mahan, A.T. 10
al-Maliki, Nouri 166–7, 188, 193–4
manoeuvrist approach and mission control 114–15,
    121–2, 124–5
Marsh Arabs and Iran border 196
mass armoured manoeuvres, fixation on 307–8
media
    complexities of modern campaigning 115
    management of 183
    Southern Iraq 2003–2004 83
mental health of personnel
    alcohol misuse 206, 210–11
    Battlemind 211n11
    decompression 207–8
    early service leavers 211
    epidemiological methods, reasons for using
        202–4, 203
    future 211–12
    PTSD, degree of identified 205
    reasons for studying 201–2
    research methods 204–5
    reservists 206–7
    stigma of asking for help 207, 211
    in theatre 207
    Trauma Risk Management (TRiM) 208
    US/UK comparison 209–10, 210
Meyer, Kurt 145
military
    enemies no longer nations 77–8
    radical shake-up needed 77

military-political relationships 112–14
Ministry of Defence, role of 341
modern campaigning, complexities of
    delivery 110–11
    junior partner warfare 116
    manoeuvrist approach and mission control
        114–15
    media 115
    multinationality, political/military compromise
        115
    national, international and political context 109
    other actors 111–12
    personality, importance of 110
    political-military relationships 112–14
    relationships, forging 110
    theatre context 110–11
    uncertainty 110
money as command resource, Baghdad 2004 106
moral imperatives, development of thinking on 78
multi-national command
    multinational divisions in Iraq 141
    political/military compromise 115
    Southern Iraq 2003–2004
        civil authority and control as aim 86
        communication between partners 88
        conditions placed on US by UK 79
        cultural empathy 87–8
        demands from national headquarters 80
        differences between provinces 82
        different agendas 83
        funding issues 81
        initial situation and directions 80–81
        Japanese presence 84
        local governance problems 81
        media, dealing with 83
        nations represented in the division 83
        persuasion of local people not to fight 85
        police, training of local 86
        restraint of soldiers 87
        security, need for 86
        threats faced 84–5
        voting in elections, opinions on 82–3
        welcome, initial feeling of 81
multiculturalism in Britain 16–17
Multinational Stand-by High Readiness Brigade for
    United Nations Operations (SHIRBRIG) 58
Murray, W. 318–19
myth and modern warfare 307–8

Nagl, John 106
nation-building
    Afghanistan 94–6

automatic reversion to the Army for 90
    failure of, reasons for 95–6
    intervention, reasons for 96
    Macedonia 91–4
    organisation/equipment for 90, 96
    reasons for intervention 90
    success of, reasons for 94
    three-block war 89
    understanding of countries 89–90
National Security Council 342
National Solidarity Programme, Afghanistan 256
new world order, vision of 15–16
non-concurrence 135
North Atlantic Treaty Organisation (NATO)
    Afghanistan 2006 217–21
    comprehensive approach 225–7
    crossroads 2006 217
    Provincial Reconstruction Teams (PRTs) 231–2
    reasons for presence in Afghanistan 246–7
Northern Ireland
    clarity of purpose, need for 31–2
    constant change as problem 29–30
    constraints on independence 35–6
    counter-terrorism, command-style for 34–5
    end result 34
    first troop deployment 28
    housing building programme 31–2
    impediments to planning 29–32
    imprecision of mission 29
    lack of 27–9, 33
    law as inhibition 36
    leadership in the 21st century 135–6
    maintenance of housing and the IRA 31–2
    NI as part of 20th century UK 30–31
    operational level 125–6
    place for commanders on battlefield 37
    police and campaign planning 32
    politicians, role of 36
    road transport 30
    South Armagh 30
    strategic goals, lack of 29
    tension between police and Army 35–6
    typical day for GOC 36–8
    undercover operations 36
    unity of command, need for 31–2
    watchtowers 30–31, 37–8
Nudge (Sunstein and Thaler) 256

Obama, Barack 19
Office for Reconstruction and Humanitarian
    Assistance (ORHA) 73
Office of Post-War Planning 70, 71–2

Operation Barras 274–5
Operation Charge of the Knights 172–3
    ceasefire 191–2
    changes during 198–9
    Coalition's Corps headquarters 190–91
    consolidation of control 194–6
    counter-insurgency plan following 194
    execution of 189–94
    forensics laboratory as legacy 195
    Iran border as problem 195–6
    Jaysh al-Mahdi 187–8, 189, 190, 191, 196,
        197–8
    legal position of Iraqi Army 195
    main security forces attack 191
    malign Iranian influence 198
    Marsh Arabs and Iran border 196
    Military Transition Teams (MiTTs) 190
    Operation Jebel an-Naar 196
    planning 188–9
    police force, reorganisation of 195
    prelude to 187–9
    withdrawal from Basra, reasons for 197–8
Operation Eagle's Summit 245
Operation Essential Harvest 91–4
Operation Herrick Study week 293
Operation Jebel an-Naar 196
Operation Joint Guardian 48–9
Operation Medusa 220–21
Operation Phoenix 170
Operation Salamanca
    planning 162–8
    resources 163–5
    revision of 167
    two-strand operation 166
Operation Sinbad
    assessment of 172–3
    constraints 157–8
    counter-insurgency 286–7
    execution of 168–71
    handover of Basra bases 171–2
    planning 162–8
    publicity 169
    purpose 158, 163
    reconstruction under 169
    resources 163–5
    Special Groups attacks 169–71
    strategic context 157–62
Operation Telic *see* Iraq
operational level thinking
    absence of, reasons for 120–23
    Bagnall, role played by 124
    Bosnia 127

collective approach 137
command 129
commander's role 135
complexity of 125
consequences of absence of 130
critical to contemporary operations 136–7
defined 119
Falklands Conflict 126
Gulf War 126
in history 119–20
impact on major operations 125–9
institutionalisation in British Army 125
Iraq 127–9
leadership
    Baghdad 2005 134–5
    Northern Ireland 135–6
    Sierra Leone 132–4
military science, progress through 130
Northern Ireland 125–6
persistence 137
and political context 129–30
pragmatism 137
preparation for appointment 129–30
raised awareness of 123–4
Simpkin, influence of 124
Soviet Studies Research Centre, influence of
    123–4
Vietnam war, debate following 123
Owen, David 7, 8

Page, Jacko 233
Pakistan as haven for insurgents 239–40
paternalism, libertarian 256
perceptions 249–50
Permanent Joint Headquarters (PJHQ) 341
personality of Blair, political decision-making and
    7–9
Petraeus, David 189, 311, 339
Pipes, Daniel 17
planning
    Iraq 2003, reconstruction planning, lack of 69,
        72
    Northern Ireland
        clarity of purpose, need for 31–2
        constant change as problem 29–30
        constraints on independence 35–6
        counter-terrorism, command-style for 34–5
        end result 34
        housing building programme 31–2
        impediments to planning 29–32
        imprecision of mission 29
        lack of 27–9, 33

law as inhibition 36
maintenance of housing and the IRA 31–2
as part of 20th century UK 30–31
place for commanders on battlefield 37
police and campaign planning 32
politicians, role of 36
road transport 30
South Armagh 30
strategic goals, lack of 29
tension between police and Army 35–6
typical day for GOC 36–8
undercover operations 36
unity of command, need for 31–2
watchtowers 30–31, 37–8
Operation Sinbad 162–8
political-military communication 114
tools, use of for 62
police
Afghanistan, reform of in 242
and campaign planning in Northern Ireland 32
Kosovo 50–51
Macedonia 93
reorganisation of Iraqi 195
Southern Iraq 2003–2004, training of local 86
tension with Army in Northern Ireland 35–6
Policy Action Group (PAG) 220
policy baseline for government 274
political context
for coalitions 182–3
decision-making and Blair's personality 7–9
defence policy 5–7
ethics and values 6–7
home front as front line 16–17
humanitarian interventionism, new doctrine of 9–15
and modern campaigning 109
new world order, vision of 15–16
and operational level thinking 129–30
resourcing of campaigns 20–25
political-military relationships 112–14
accountability, military 278
advice, military 273
ARRC deployment as headquarters 277
casualties, reactions to 277
civil-military divide 273–4
clarity of objectives 279
cultural differences 277–8
dangers in 278–8
deciding voice as political 273
discretionary/non-discretionary undertakings 276
example of harmony and concord 274–5
experience of decision-makers 278

Helmand Province 2006 276
Operation Barras 274–5
policy baseline for government 274
showing off, desire for 278–9
strategic understanding and expectations 275–7
politicians in Northern Ireland, role of 36
post-traumatic stress disorder (PTSD)
action against the MOD 202
degree due to Iraq operations 205
see also psychological impact of Iraq operations
Powell, Jonathan 24
pragmatists, Afghans as 250
private security companies, Baghdad 2004 105–6
professionalisation of communications 261–2
prospect theory 254
Provincial Reconstruction Teams (PRTs) 231–2, 244–5
psychological impact of Iraq operations
alcohol misuse 206, 210–11
Battlemind 211n11
decompression 207–8
early service leavers 211
epidemiological methods, reasons for using 202–4, 203
future 211–12
PTSD, degree of identified 205
reasons for studying 201–2
research methods 204–5
reservists 206–7
stigma of asking for help 207, 211
in theatre 207
Trauma Risk Management (TRiM) 208
US/UK comparison 209–10, 210

Race to the Swift: Thoughts on Warfare in the Twenty-First Century (Simpkin) 124
Ramo, Joshua Cooper 259–60
rationalisation of motives 17–20
reconstruction
Afghanistan 94–6
automatic reversion to the Army for 90
failure of, reasons for 95–6
intervention, reasons for 96
Iraq 2003
arming, degree of 74
authority, lack of 76–7
chaotic start 75
concerns raised 73, 75
contacts in Washington 70–71
errors of judgement 77
exiled Iraqis, role of 73
gaps in the team 71–2

infrastructure 75–6
military/civilian tension 75
Office of Post-War Planning 70, 71–2
planning for, lack of 69–70, 72
political direction, lack of 71–2
skills sets needed 74
support, lack from UK 76–7
uncertainty on eve of war 75
Washington politics 73
Macedonia 91–4
organisation/equipment for 90, 96
reasons for intervention 90
success of, reasons for 94
three-block war 89
understanding of countries 89–90
refugee crisis in Kosovo 43, 49
Reid, John 31
research
contribution to force development 318–20
need for 262
reservists 206–7
resources
integration of 183
Operation Sinbad 163–5
political context 20–25
responsibility, devolution of 62
Revolutionary United Front (RUF) 55, 56, 58, 59, 60
Richards, David 218, 220, 233, 309
Rifkind, Malcolm 18
rotation of forces, consequences of 342–3
Rumsfeld, Donald 70
Russia
KFOR contingent 46–8
pressure on Serbs in Kosovo 44–5
Rwandan crisis 58

al-Sadr, Moqtada 86, 198
al-Safi, Safa 166
Sankoh, Foday 55, 59
Senge, Peter 213
Serbs
meaning of Kosovo for 41
negotiations with over Kosovo 45–6
Shaw, George Bernard 143, 153
Shia Extremists 100
Shirreff, Richard 161–2, 162, 163–4
Sierra Leone 2000
action, not enough of 61
British intervention 58–60
civil war prior to 55–7
continuance of process 60
infrastructure 57

leadership in the 21st century 132–4
lessons learned from 60–63
Lomé Agreement 57
Revolutionary United Front (RUF) 55, 56, 58, 59, 60
UK/US relationship 329
UN Mission in (UNAMSIL) 57–8, 59, 60
single-loop learning 302–3, 309–10
Sloggett, Dave 251
South Armagh 30
Southern Iraq 2003–2004
civil authority and control as aim 86
communication between partners 88
conditions placed on US by UK 79
cultural empathy 87–8
differences between provinces 82
different agendas 83
funding issues 81
infrastructure, state of on arrival 79–80
initial situation and directions 80–81
Japanese presence 84
media, dealing with 83
nations represented in the division 83
persuasion of local people not to fight 85
police, training of local 86
restraint of soldiers 87
security, need for 86
threats faced 84–5
voting in elections, opinions on 82–3
welcome, initial feeling of 81
Soviet Studies Research Centre 123–4
span of command 343
spifish approach 316
stabilisation defined 227–8
Stabilisation Operations (Joint Doctrine Publication 3-40) 340–41
Stilwell, Joe 144
Stirrup, Jock 139
Storm of Steel, The (Jünger) 146
Strasser, Valentine 56
Strategic Defence Review (SDR) 5–6
strategy
goals in Northern Ireland 29
as inherently unstable 342
Sunni Arab Rejectionists 100
Sunstein, Cass 256
Superfreakonomics (Levitt and Dubner) 253–4
Supreme Command (Cohen) 113
Svechin, Aleksandr 119, 136–7

Taliban 237–8
Taylor, Charles 55, 60

Taylor, Mathew 253
Tebbit, Kevin 24
technology as threat and temptation 114
terrorism, counter-, command-style for 34–5
terrorists 147
Thaler, Richard 256
three-block war 89
Toffler, Alvin 258
Tootal, Stuart 18
training *see* education of officers; learning
    organisations
transitional government, Baghdad 2004 104–5
Trauma Risk Management (TRiM) 208
Tripp, Charles 284
Tversky, Amos 253, 254–5

UN Mission in Sierra Leone (UNAMSIL) 57–8,
    59, 60
uncertainty in modern campaigning 110

undercover operations in Northern Ireland 36
United States
    Army, qualities of 116
    relationship with British forces 329–32
unlearning old ideas 297

values in defence policy 6–7
victory, reassessing notions of 260
voting in elections, Iraqi opinions on 82–3

Walker, Mike 334
war on terror 331
watchtowers in Northern Ireland 30–31, 37–8
weapons collection in Macedonia 92–3
wisdom of crowds 255
Wolfowitz, Paul 13
worthy life, living a 143–4

Zavarin, Viktor 48